Sixth Edition

LEGAL TERMINOLOGY

Gordon W. Brown, J.D.
Member of the Massachusetts and Federal Bars
Professor Emeritus, North Shore Community College, Danvers, Massachusetts

Kent D. Kauffman, J.D.
Member of the Indiana Bar
Assistant Professor of Business Law,
Indiana-Purdue University—Fort Wayne, Fort Wayne, Indiana

Boston   Columbus   Indianapolis   New York   San Francisco   Upper Saddle River
Amsterdam   Cape Town   Dubai   London   Madrid   Milan   Munich   Paris   Montreal   Toronto
Delhi   Mexico City   São Paulo   Sydney   Hong Kong   Seoul   Singapore   Taipei   Tokyo

Editorial Director: Vernon R. Anthony
Executive Editor: Gary Bauer
Editorial Project Manager: Linda Cupp
Editorial Assistant: Tanika Henderson
Director of Marketing: David Gesell
Marketing Manager: Stacey Martinez
Senior Marketing Assistant: Les Roberts
Production Manager: Susan Hannahs
Senior Art Director: Jayne Conte
Cover Designer: Suzanne Behnke
Cover Art: Shutterstock
Full-Service Project Management: Niraj Bhatt/Aptara®, Inc.
Composition: Aptara®, Inc.
Text and Cover Printer/Bindery: Courier/Kendallville
Text Font: Times LT Std Roman

Photo Credits: All photos by Thinkstock® and Part Opener 7 on pg 299 is from iStockphoto.

Credits and acknowledgments borrowed from other sources and reproduced, with permission, in this textbook appear on the appropriate page within the text.

Many of the designations by manufacturers and sellers to distinguish their products are claimed as trademarks. Where those designations appear in this book, and the publisher was aware of a trademark claim, the designations have been printed in initial caps or all caps.

Library of Congress Cataloging-in-Publication Data

Brown, Gordon W.
   Legal terminology / Gordon W. Brown, Kent D. Kauffman.—6th ed.
     p. cm.
   ISBN-13: 978-0-13-273876-7
   ISBN-10: 0-13-273876-7
  1. Law—United States—Terminology. I. Kauffman, Kent D. II. Title.
   KF156.B725 2013
   349.7301'4—dc23

                           2011032855

10 9 8 7 6 5 4 3 2 1

PEARSON

ISBN 10:   0-13-273876-7
ISBN 13: 978-0-13-273876-7

For the 30 years that I taught full time at North Shore Community College, practiced law part time, and wrote textbooks such as this, I have many people to thank. Among them are talented people in the fields of education, publishing, and law. The ones who bore the burden of my efforts, however, are my wife, Jane, for her never-ending support and encouragement, and my children, Steven, Matthew, Deborah, Jennifer, Timothy, and David. They grew to be outstanding people even without my being with them during many of their growing-up activities because of my strong work ethic. It is to these wonderful family members that this book is dedicated with many thanks and much love.

GORDON W. BROWN

This is dedicated to my wife, Karen, whose radiance and resilience have renewed me every day, and without whose contributions I would never have been privileged to have my name on this book's cover.

KENT D. KAUFFMAN

CONTENTS

PREFACE

Legal Terminology, Sixth Edition is designed to develop your understanding of legal terms in concert with their usage in the legal field. Emphasis is placed on learning terms in context through the study of law itself and on using legal terminology in many different ways, rather than relying on rote memorization of terms. The short easy-to-understand chapters are written in a lively manner to hold your attention and engage your interest in the law.

KEY FEATURES OF LEGAL TERMINOLOGY, SIXTH EDITION

- **"Ante Interrogatory"** begins each chapter with a question intended to whet your appetite by testing you on the meaning of a legal term or concept before you study the chapter. This is followed by a chapter outline and a list of the key legal terms in the chapter with their phonetic pronunciations.
- **"Word Wise"** educates you on remembering the meanings of words by understanding Latin roots, prefixes, and suffixes. Everyday words that include some of the same elements as legal terms are used as reinforcing examples. Reviewing how words are constructed helps you to have a deeper understanding of why words mean what they do.
- **"Web Wise"** helps you to understand what to look for in a website in order to evaluate its credibility, type of website, and credentials of the creator of the website. This feature also recommends various websites for further study on topics.
- **"Sharpening Your Latin Skills"** is included in some chapters to help you practice defining relevant Latin legal terminology, which is still used today in the legal profession. A separate glossary of Latin terms and phrases is at the end of the book.
- **"Reviewing What You Learned"** poses questions about the subject matter in each chapter to test your comprehension of concepts and terms.
- **"Understanding Legal Concepts"** allows you to check your understanding of legal knowledge by focusing on an italicized word in a sentence, deciding whether the sentence is true or false, and then changing the italicized word to make it a true statement.
- **"Checking Terminology"** allows you to confirm your knowledge through completing an assignment by selecting a correct, concise definition for each term from a list of options.
- **"Using Legal Language"** is a project in paragraph format in which you fill in blanks with legal terms used in the chapter to practice understanding the terms in a story.
- **"Puzzle Over What You Learned"** is a crossword puzzle of legal terms from each chapter presented as a fun challenge to test your memory.
- **"Glossary of Legal Terms"** is a comprehensive, alphabetized glossary of terms at the end of the text that provides the same phonetic pronunciations and definitions given in each chapter.

NEW FEATURES IN THE SIXTH EDITION

- **"Terms in Action"** Text boxes have been added to each chapter to illustrate how terms are used in real-life situations. Some are current, quirky stories including celebrities Bill Murray, Brittney Spears, Allen Iverson, Mike Tyson, and Steve Jobs. Others are interesting historical cases involving luminaries such as King Henry VIII and Walt Disney, with surprise endings that will help you to remember the terms. Each chapter has two of these features.
- **New legal ethics chapter** in Part One highlights competence and truthfulness, the unauthorized practice of law, the duty of supervision, confidentiality, conflicts of interest, legal fees, advertising and solicitation, and attorney discipline.

- **New constitutional law chapter** introduces terms used in the structure of the U.S. Constitution, the branches of government, checks and balances, and amendments.
- **Recent updates in bankruptcy law** include current inflation-adjusted exemptions numbers and an expanded explanation of means testing.
- **Expanded alternative dispute resolution** section offers examples and explanations.
- **Same-sex marriage** and **right-to-die laws** have been addressed in detail, including a review of relevant Supreme Court case law.
- **More than 125 new terms** have been added, including *legal ethics, express powers, judicial review, pocket veto, federal district courts, arbitrator's award, caucus, counterclaim, statute of limitations, e-discovery, safe harbor provision, money laundering, threat of force, imminent danger, vicarious liability, compensatory damages, duty of care, click-wrap agreement, e-contract, contractual capacity, fraud in the execution, dummy corporation, homestead exemption laws, articles of incorporation,* and *means testing.*

STUDENT SUPPLEMENTS

Companion Website: http://www.pearsonhighered.com/brown
Use this book-specific website to check your mastery of terminology.

- Learning Objectives
- Chapter Summary
- Flashcards for Legal Terms
- Quizzes

New! Legal Terminology, Sixth Edition Printed Flashcards
This student supplement can be packaged with this textbook or purchased separately at www.mypearsonstore.com. (ISBN: 0-13-288138-1)

Legal Terminology, Sixth Edition Ebook
Access to the ebook version of the textbook can be purchased online at www.coursesmart.com. (ISBN: 0-13-286578-5)

INSTRUCTOR SUPPLEMENTS

- The **Online Instructor's Manual** provides answers to Reviewing What You Learned, Understanding Legal Concepts, Checking Terminology, Unraveling Legalese, Using Legal Language, and Puzzling Over What You Learned. A complete **Test Item File** is also included.
- **MyTest:** This computerized test-generation system gives you maximum flexibility in preparing tests. It can create custom tests and print scrambled versions of a test at one time, as well as build tests randomly by chapter, level of difficulty, or question type. The software also allows online testing and record-keeping, and the ability to add problems to the database.
- **PowerPoint Lecture Presentation:** Lecture presentation screens for each chapter are available online.
- Ready-made **WebCT** and **Blackboard** online courses are available and include access to **Pearson's MySearchLab**, a premium online research tool.

The Instructor's Resource Guide, Test Generator, and PPT Package can be downloaded from our Instructor's Resource Center. To access supplementary materials online, instructors must have an instructor access code. Go to www.pearsonhighered.com/irc to register for the code. Within 48 hours of registering, you will receive a confirming e-mail with your instructor access code. Once you have received your code, locate your text in the online catalog and click on the Instructor Resources button on the left side of the catalog product page. Select a supplement and a log-in page will appear. Once you have logged in, you can access instructor material for all Pearson textbooks.

ACKNOWLEDGMENTS

Special thanks to the following reviewers who provided excellent technical and practical suggestions for improvement and readability for the new edition:

Brian Craig, *Globe University/Minnesota School of Business*

Cathy Underwood, *Pulaski Technical College*

We would also like to express our gratitude to the reviewers of the previous edition:

Pam Cummings, Minnesota State Community and Technical College; Leslie Ratliff, Griffin Technical College; Paula Witt, Houston Community College; Linda Cupick, Daytona Beach Community College; Jody L. Cooper, Blackhawk Technical College; and Claudine Dulaney, International Institute of the Americas.

We would also like to thank the following survey respondents who helped us to refine the coverage of the textbook:

Joseph Kline, *South Plains College*

Barry Puett, *State College of Florida, Manatee-Sarasota*

Linda Wenn, *Central Community College*

Susan Balman, *Butler Community College*

Jerrold Fleisher, *Suny Rockland Community College*

Cathy Carruthers, *Lewis & Clark Community College*

Glenda Hanson, *Renton Technical College*

Teresa Harbacheck, *College of Western Idaho*

Gwendolyn Pope, *J. F. Drake State Technical College*

Sabrina Swann, *Central Georgia Technical College*

Diana Yohe, *Bristol Community College*

William Yenna, *Kingsborough Community College*

Jody Cooper, *Blackhawk Technical College*

Joyce Zweedyk, *Kalamazoo Valley Community College*

Bob Loomis, *Spokane Community College*

Larena Grieshaber, *Independence Community College*

Karin Kelley, *Bates Technical College*

Sharolyn Sayers, *Milwaukee Area Technical College*

Kim Phifer-Starks, *Mississippi Gulf Coast Community College*

Thea Hosselrode, *Allegany College of Maryland*

Georganne Copeland, *Centralia College*

Marilyn Wudarcki, *North Idaho College*

Betty Lambert, *Des Moines Area Community College*

Sonya Rambo, *West Kentucky Community & Technical College*

Toni Clough, *Umpqua Community College*

Gloria Bailey, *Atlantic Technical Center*

Crystal Sullivan, *Umpqua Community College*

Elizabeth Snodgrass, *Mountain Empire Community College*

Crystal Price, *Alvin Community College*

Douglas Rogers, *Jefferson State Community College*

Carolyn Sharpe, *Cleveland Community College*

Mary Balmages, *Cerritos College*

Amy Wilson, *Zane State College*

Lori Asante, *Cincinnati State Technical and Community College*

Maxine Boggy, *Atlantic Technical Center*

Marissa Wawrzyniak, *Brevard Community College*

Our hope is that this book will provide to instructors a clear roadmap for navigating the courses for which this book is used, and to the students a treasure chest of terms and principles that will assist you throughout your legal courses and into your careers.

Gordon W. Brown

Kent D. Kauffman

ABOUT THE AUTHORS

Gordon W. Brown is a Professor Emeritus of North Shore Community College, Danvers, Massachusetts, where he taught for 30 years. He also taught for two years at Pepperell High School, Pepperell, Massachusetts, and for six years at Endicott College in Beverly, Massachusetts.

In addition to writing the first five editions of this book, Professor Brown is the author of the first three editions of *Administration of Wills, Trusts, and Estates* published by Delmar Cengage Learning. Over a 30-year period, he co-authored eight editions of *Understanding Business & Personal Law* and seven editions of *Business Law with UCC Applications*, published by McGraw-Hill.

In 1998, Professor Brown was awarded the Outstanding Educator Award from his alma mater, Salem State University. He received his law degree from Suffolk University and practiced law part time while teaching full time. He is a retired member of the Massachusetts and federal Bars.

Kent D. Kauffman, J.D., is Assistant Professor of Business Law at Indiana University-Purdue University, Fort Wayne, in Fort Wayne, Indiana. He is licensed to practice law in Indiana and is certified as a mediator in Indiana. He is a summa cum laude graduate of Temple University and a graduate of The Dickinson School of Law of the Pennsylvania State University.

For 15 years, Professor Kauffman was the Chair of the Paralegal Studies Department at Ivy Tech Community College in Fort Wayne, Indiana. He is the author of other books, including *Legal Ethics*, in its third edition and published by Delmar Cengage Learning. He is a multiple recipient of Who's Who in American Education® and Who's Who in American Law®. Professor Kauffman is the recipient of various teaching awards, including Best Professor by Delta Sigma Pi, the business school fraternity at Indiana University-Purdue University.

Terms Used in Practice and Procedure

Whether you work as a court reporter, an office technician, a paralegal, or a business executive, knowledge of the procedures involved in taking a case to court is important. Indeed, people outside of the legal field also have an interest in court procedure, stemming either from their own personal experiences or from reading about trials and watching them in movies and on television. After differentiating between the federal and state court systems, Chapter 1 examines the subject of selecting the court, including the matters of jurisdiction and venue. This chapter also explores alternative dispute resolutions available for those who wish to settle disputes outside of court. Chapter 2 explains criminal trial procedure, beginning with the arrest, preliminary hearing, indictment, and arraignment, followed by sentencing and defendants' rights. Chapter 3 discusses civil trial procedure including court selection, pleadings, service of process, and attachments. Chapter 4 explains defensive pleadings including the demurrer, five commonly used motions, the defendant's answer, the counterclaim, the cross-claim, and the cross-complaint. Methods of discovery, including bills of particular, interrogatories, and depositions, are examined in Chapter 5. The process of impaneling the jury, including the examination and challenging of jurors, is explained in Chapter 6, and the steps in a trial are outlined in Chapter 7. Finally, Chapter 8 discusses how legal ethics rules affect the professional behavior of lawyers and their nonlawyer employees.

1

Court Systems and Jurisdiction

ANTE INTERROGATORY

(literally means "the before question" and is a sneak preview of the chapter)

The power of a court to review a lower court's decision is called (A) original jurisdiction, (B) in rem jurisdiction, (C) exclusive jurisdiction, or (D) appellate jurisdiction.

CHAPTER OUTLINE

Federal Courts
U.S. District Courts
U.S. Courts of Appeals
U.S. Supreme Court

State Courts
State Trial Courts
State Intermediate Appellate Courts
State Supreme Courts

Jurisdiction and Venue
In Rem Action
Quasi in Rem Action
In Personam Action
Venue

Alternative Dispute Resolution
Negotiation
Mediation
Arbitration
Mini-trial

KEY TERMS

admiralty *(AD·mer·ul·tee)*

alternative dispute resolution *(al·TERN·a·tiv dis·PYOOT res·o·LOO·shun)*

appeal *(a·PEEL)*

appellate courts *(a·PEL·et)*

appellate jurisdiction *(a·PEL·et joo·res·DIK·shen)*

arbitration *(ar·be·TRAY·shun)*

arbitrator *(AR·be·tray·tor)*

arbitrator's award *(ARE-bih-tray-terz uh-WARD)*

binding arbitration *(BINE·ding ar·be·TRAY·shun)*

caucus *(kaw-kuss)*

cert. den. (certiorari denied) *(ser·sho·RARE·ee dee·NIDE)*

change of venue *(VEN·yoo)*

circuits *(SER·kits)*

code *(KOHD)*

compulsory arbitration *(kom·PUL·so·ree ar·be·TRAY·shun)*

conciliation *(kon·sil·ee·AY·shun)*

conciliator *(kon·SIL·ee·ay·tor)*

concurrent jurisdiction *(kon·KER·ent joo·res·DIK·shen)*

court *(KORT)*

courts of appeal *(a·PEEL)*

diversity of citizenship *(dy·VER·sit·ee ov SIT·e·sen·ship)*

exclusive jurisdiction *(eks·KLOO·siv joo·res·DIK·shen)*

federal district courts *(FED·er·al DIS·trikt KORTS)*

federal question *(FED·er·ul KWES·chen)*

forum non conveniens *(FOR·em non kon·VEEN·yenz)*

in personam action *(in per·SOH·nem AK·shun)*

in personam jurisdiction *(per·SOH·nem joo·res·DIK·shen)*

in rem action *(in rem AK·shun)*

jurisdiction *(joo·res·DIK·shen)*

justice *(JUSS·tis)*

local action *(LO·kal AK·shun)*

long-arm statutes *(STAT·shoots)*

mandatory arbitration *(MAN·da·tor·ee ar·be·TRAY·shun)*

maritime *(MER·i·tym)*

mediation *(mee·dee·AY·shun)*

mediator *(MEE·dee·ay·tor)*

mini-trial *(tryl)*

negotiation *(neh·go·shee·A·shun)*

nonbinding arbitration *(non·BINE·ding ar·be·TRAY·shun)*

original jurisdiction *(o·RIJ·i·nel joo·res·DIK·shen)*

plenary jurisdiction *(PLEN·e·ree joo·res·DIK·shen)*

quasi in rem action *(KWAY·zi in rem AK·shun)*

res *(reyz)*

statute *(STAT·shoot)*

transitory action *(TRAN·zi·tore·ee AK·shun)*

venue *(VEN·yoo)*

writ of certiorari *(ser·sho·RARE·ee)*

 court is a body of government organized to administer justice. There are two court systems in the United States—the federal court system and the state court systems.

FEDERAL COURTS

The federal court system, established by Article III of the U.S. Constitution, includes the U.S. district courts, the U.S. courts of appeals, and the U.S. Supreme Court. Those courts hear cases that raise a **federal question**—a matter that involves the U.S. Constitution, acts of Congress, or treason. Federal courts also decide cases that involve **diversity of citizenship**—a term used to describe cases between persons from different states, between citizens of the United States and a foreign government, and between citizens of the United States and citizens of a foreign country. Diversity cases must exceed the sum of $75,000. In addition, federal courts hear bankruptcy cases, patent and copyright cases, and **admiralty** or **maritime** cases—those pertaining to the sea.

U.S. District Courts

U.S. district courts hear most federal cases when they originally go to court; that is, before there is an appeal. Each state and territory and the District of Columbia has at least one U.S. district court within its boundary. These courts are also called **federal district courts**.

1

> ### Sources of Law
>
> There are five principal sources of law in the United States:
>
> 1. Federal and state constitutions
> 2. English common law
> 3. Federal and state **statutes** (laws passed by a legislature)
> 4. Court decisions (when made by appellate courts, they are also called "common law," but not "English common law")
> 5. Administrative regulations
>
> The federal government and many state governments consolidate their statutes, administrative regulations, and other laws into a systematic collection called a **code** The United States Code and the California Civil Code are examples.

U.S. Courts of Appeals

U.S. courts of appeals decide cases that have been appealed from federal district courts. The United States is divided into 13 judicial districts called **circuits**. Each circuit has several U.S. district courts, but only one U.S. court of appeals. A group of three judges decides most cases that are appealed to this court.

> ### Word Wise
> *Different Meanings for "Court"*
>
> The court officer announced, "The court is now in session!" Used in this way, the term "court" means a body, including judge and jury, organized to administer justice. Lawyers are officers of the court.
>
> "May it please the court" is a sentence often used by lawyers when addressing a judge. The term "court" as used here means "judge."
>
> "I'll see you in court," the attorney said to her fellow attorney. Here, the term "court" probably refers to the courthouse building.

U.S. Supreme Court

The U.S. Supreme Court is the highest court in the land. It hears appeals from both the U.S. courts of appeals and the highest state courts when federal questions are involved. Coming from the Latin word *supremus* (the last), the term *supreme* means "superior to all other things."

In the U.S. Supreme Court, appeals are heard when four out of the nine **justices** (the title given to the highest appellate court judges) believe that the case is important enough to be heard. When it agrees to hear a case on appeal, the U.S. Supreme Court issues a **writ of certiorari** an order from a higher court to a lower court to deliver its records to the higher court for review. When the Court decides not to hear an appeal, as it does with most cases, the Court denies issuing the writ of certiorari by writing the abbreviation "**cert. den.**" on the court record.

> ### TERMS IN ACTION
>
> The **U.S. Supreme Court** has nine **justices**, who have their job for life. As of 2011, each justice earns $213,900 per year, but the Chief Justice earns $223,500. Originally, the Supreme Court had six justices. Because the Constitution doesn't state how many justices the Supreme Court should comprise, the number is determined by Congress. The first Congress chose six (one chief justice and five associate justices) as part of the Judiciary Act of 1789, which also established three **circuit courts** and 13 **district courts**. One of the Supreme Court's early

cases, *Chisholm v. Georgia*, concluded in 1793 that the individual states were within its **jurisdiction** and could be sued in a federal court. From 1789 until 1869, Congress increased the size of the Court to seven justices, then nine, and even ten. But in the Judiciary Act of 1869, Congress set the number of justices at nine, where it has remained.

Source: judiciary.senate.gov; supremecourt.gov

STATE COURTS

Each state in the United States has its own court structure that is separate from the executive and legislative branches of state government. Like the federal courts, state courts are divided into three broad categories—trial courts, intermediate appellate courts, and supreme courts.

State Trial Courts

State trial courts have general authority to hear cases involving activity that occurred in a particular state. Called **superior courts**, **circuit courts**, or **courts of common pleas**, they are typically arranged so that there is one in each county. Major civil and criminal cases, both jury and non-jury, are tried in these county courts.

In addition, somewhat lesser courts with limited jurisdiction (authority), including district, or municipal, courts; juvenile courts; traffic courts; housing courts; and land courts, are located throughout each county. Each county also has special courts that handle such matters as adoption, divorce, and the settlement of estates.

State Intermediate Appellate Courts

Following a court's decision, either party may file an **appeal**—that is, a request to a higher court to review the decision of the lower court that tried the case. Courts that review the decisions of lower courts are called **courts of appeal** or **appellate courts**. Many states have intermediate appellate courts where appeals must be taken and heard by a three-judge panel before deemed being eligible to go to the state's supreme court.

State Supreme Court

Each state has a court of last resort—a state supreme court. Parties aggrieved by lower state court decisions may appeal to their state's supreme court, whose decision is usually final. Appeals from this court may be made to the U.S. Supreme Court only when a federal or U.S. constitutional question is raised.

JURISDICTION AND VENUE

Jurisdiction is the power or authority that a court has to hear a particular case. Such power is given to the court either by the federal or state constitution or by a federal or state statute. If, by chance, a court without jurisdiction should hear a particular case and make a decision, the decision would be meaningless and void.

Some courts have **original jurisdiction** over certain cases, meaning that they have the power to hear the case originally—when it first goes to court. Other courts have **appellate jurisdiction**, which means that they have the power to hear a case when it is appealed—that is, when an aggrieved party is petitioning an appellate court to review the decision of a lower court. When only one court has the power to hear a particular case, to the exclusion of all other courts, the court is said to have **exclusive jurisdiction**. When two or more courts have the power to hear a case, they have **concurrent jurisdiction**. A court with concurrent jurisdiction has the right, under a doctrine called **forum non conveniens**, to refuse to hear a case if it believes that justice would be better served if the trial were held in a different court. Some courts have exclusive original

> **Word Wise**
> *To Speak*
>
> "Dic," "dict," and "dit," whether used as prefixes or suffixes, mean "to say" or "to speak," as in these words:
>
> > verdict *(VER·dikt)*
> > jurisdiction *(joo·res·DIK·shen)*
> > edict *(E·dikt)*
> > indictment *(in·DITE·ment)*
> > dictation *(dik·TAY·shun)*
> > dictator *(DIK·tay·ter)*
> > contradict *(kon·tra·DIKT)*

jurisdiction or exclusive appellate jurisdiction over particular cases. Similarly, some courts have concurrent original jurisdiction or concurrent appellate jurisdiction over certain cases.

When considering the question of jurisdiction, one of the first points that must be determined is whether the case is an in rem, quasi in rem, or in personam action.

In Rem Action

An **in rem action** is a lawsuit that is directed against property rather than against a particular person. The action usually concerns title to real property and, if so, is called a **local action**. It seeks to settle some questions about the property, and the court's decision affects everyone in the world, not merely the parties in the case. For a court to have jurisdiction over an action in rem, the property (called the **res**) must be located in the state (and, usually, in the county) where the court sits. In addition, some kind of notice must be given to people who may have an interest in the proceeding.

Quasi in Rem Action

If a defendant owns real property in one state and lives in another, the court where the real property is located has jurisdiction over the property only, but not over the person. If suit is brought in that court and the out-of-state defendant does not appear, the plaintiff's recovery will be limited to an amount up to the value of the property in question located in that state. Such a lawsuit is called a **quasi in rem action**. In such a case, the court has jurisdiction over the defendant's property, but not over the defendant's person; therefore, the most the defendant can lose is the out-of-state real property. Usually, when this type of jurisdiction prevails, the dispute that the court is asked to settle has nothing to do with title to the property.

In Personam Action

In an **in personam action** (personal action), the plaintiff must select a court that has jurisdiction over not only the subject matter, but also over the parties involved in the case. **In personam jurisdiction** (personal jurisdiction) means jurisdiction over the person. A court automatically has personal jurisdiction over the plaintiff because the plaintiff has submitted to the court's jurisdiction by filing a complaint in that court. In contrast, a court has jurisdiction over a defendant only if the defendant lives in the jurisdiction, has a business in the jurisdiction, or engages in legally significant behaviors, such as driving in the jurisdiction. An exception is that state courts will obtain personam jurisdiction over anyone who is served by process while inside the state's boundaries. Service of process is explained in Chapter 2.

Some so-called **long-arm statutes** allow one state court to reach out (with its long arm) to obtain personal jurisdiction over a person in another state if that person does much business in the state where the court is located. The term **plenary jurisdiction** refers to the situation in which a court has complete jurisdiction over the plaintiff, the defendant, and the subject matter of a lawsuit.

An action that does not concern land is called a **transitory action** and may be brought in more than one place as long as the court in which it is heard has proper jurisdiction.

Venue

The place where the trial is held is called the **venue**. Each state has established rules of venue for the purpose of providing convenient places for trials. Such rules state exactly where particular actions may be brought. If the plaintiff's attorney begins an action in a court of improper venue, the defendant's attorney may have the case transferred or dismissed by filing a motion for that purpose or by raising that issue in the defendant's answer (a document discussed in Chapter 18). If the defendant's attorney does not raise the question of improper venue, the court may hear the case as long as it has jurisdiction. The difference between venue and jurisdiction is that jurisdiction relates to the power of the court to hear a case, whereas venue relates to the geographic location where the action should be tried.

Sometimes, for the sake of justice, one of the parties will ask the court to change the place of the trial. The court, in some cases, has the power to order a change of venue. A **change of venue** is the removal of a suit begun in one county or district and the replacement of it to another county or district for trial. Pretrial publicity is often a reason for a defendant to seek a **change in venue**. In those instances, the defendant will argue in a pretrial motion that, because of negative media coverage, the defendant will be unable to be tried by an impartial jury unless the trial is moved elsewhere.

TERMS IN ACTION

On Christmas Eve, 2002, Scott Peterson murdered his wife, Laci, who was eight months pregnant with a boy whom the couple was going to name Connor. Laci's body was moved from their home in Modesto, California, and dumped into the Pacific Ocean. Connor's body was discovered in the San Francisco Bay in April 2003, and Scott Peterson was then arrested. By that time, the country was fixated on the story of this notorious sociopath and his many lies, including the secret relationship he had been having with a single mother named Amber Frey, who realized after it was too late that the man she was in love with was living a double life. Weeks before the double-murder trial was to begin, Scott Peterson's famous defense lawyer, Mark Geragos, made a motion for a change of venue, arguing that the overwhelming publicity about the case prevented Peterson from receiving a fair trial in Modesto. The judge agreed, and the trial was moved to Redwood City, California, about 90 miles west of Modesto. Still, Scott Peterson was convicted of murder, and in 2005 he was sentenced to death.

Source: Trutv.com

ALTERNATIVE DISPUTE RESOLUTION

In civil cases, rather than take their disputes to court, some people prefer to use quicker, less complicated, and less expensive methods to resolve disputes. The distinct and alternative processes for settling legal disputes by means other than litigation are known collectively as **alternative dispute resolution (ADR)**. The various forms of alternative dispute resolution include negotiation, mediation, arbitration, and mini-trials.

Negotiation

Negotiation is a two-party process by which each side, without the help of a neutral third party, attempts to conclude its dispute by bargaining with the other until one side agrees to the other side's offer of settlement. One doesn't have to be represented by an attorney in a negotiation; but, often, those involved in legal disputes that are being negotiated do have legal representation. Negotiated settlements are evidenced by a written agreement, which frequently requires the terms of the negotiated settlement to remain private.

Mediation

Mediation sometimes called **conciliation** is an informal process in which a neutral third person, called a **mediator** (or **conciliator**) listens to both sides and makes suggestions for reaching a solution. The mediator tries to persuade the parties to compromise and settle their differences. Often, the mediation takes place in stages; both sides meet together with the mediator and then break into private sessions called caucuses. In a **caucus**, the mediator uses his or her listening skills and the ability to ask probing questions in an attempt to learn what the interests are behind each side's demands. From that point on, the mediator seeks small gains from each side and works to try to bring the disputing parties together so that a mutually acceptable agreement (the settlement) can be reached. Although the mediator is not empowered to make the parties settle, the mediator has authority over the mediation process.

Arbitration

In contrast, **arbitration** is a method of settling disputes in which a neutral third party, called an **arbitrator** makes a decision after hearing the arguments on both sides. Arbitration takes place when parties contractually agree to resolve their dispute according to a predetermined arbitration process. Although arbitration is quicker and cheaper than a trial, parties can still agree to engage in a limited form of discovery and gather evidence in preparation for the arbitration hearing. At the hearing, documents can be submitted to the arbitrator or arbitration panel and witnesses can be called to testify. If the parties agree in advance to **binding arbitration**, the decision of the arbitrator or arbitration panel will be final and must be followed. The arbitrator's decision must be in writing and is commonly known as the **arbitrator's award**, regardless of which side the arbitrator rules in favor of. One of the serious consequences of binding arbitration is that the right to appeal a binding arbitration decision is nearly impossible to secure.

    If, instead, the parties agree to **nonbinding arbitration** the arbitrator's decision is simply a recommendation and need not be complied with. Arbitration that is required by agreement or by law is called **compulsory** or **mandatory arbitration**.

Mini-trial

An increasingly popular method of settling disputes is an informal trial, sometimes referred to as a **mini-trial** run by a private organization established for the purpose of settling disputes out of court. Retired judges and lawyers are often used to hear the disputes, and the parties agree to be bound by the decision.

Reviewing What You Learned

After studying the chapter, write the answers to each of the following questions:

1. What types of cases are heard by federal courts?

   _____

   _____

   _____

   _____

2. Under what circumstances may an appeal be made from a state supreme court to the U.S. Supreme Court? _____

   _____

   _____

   _____

3. What types of cases do U.S. courts of appeals decide?

_____

_____

_____

_____

_____

4. For a court to have jurisdiction over an in rem action, where must the property be located?

_____

_____

_____

_____

5. If a defendant owns real property in one state and lives in another, which court has jurisdiction in an in rem action?

_____

_____

_____

_____

6. In a situation such as that described in question 5, if suit is brought against the defendant in the state where the property is located and the out-of-state defendant does not appear, to what will the plaintiff's recovery be limited? _____

_____

_____

_____

_____

7. To bring a lawsuit against a person and hold that person personally liable, what kind of action must be brought? _____

_____

_____

_____

_____

_____

8. If the plaintiff's attorney begins an action in a court of improper venue, what may the defendant's attorney do? _____

_____

_____

_____

_____

_____

9. What is the difference between jurisdiction and venue?

_____

_____

_____

_____

10. What is the difference between mediation and arbitration?

_____

_____

_____

_____

11. Explain what negotiation is and how it is settled.

_____

_____

_____

_____

12. How is mediation done and what is a caucus?

_____

_____

_____

13. Explain what binding arbitration is.

_____

_____

_____

_____

Understanding Legal Concepts

Indicate whether each statement is true or false. Then, change the italicized word or phrase of each false statement to make it true.

ANSWERS

_____ 1. Cases heard by the U.S. courts of appeals are decided by *three* judges.

_____ 2. The U.S. Supreme Court hears appeals when *five* out of the nine justices believe that the case is important enough to be heard.

_____ 3. If, by chance, a court should hear a particular case and make a decision without having *jurisdiction,* the decision would be meaningless.

_____ 4. Some courts have *exclusive original jurisdiction* or exclusive appellate jurisdiction over particular cases.

_____ 5. Courts *never* have concurrent original jurisdiction over certain cases.

_____ 6. An action in rem is a lawsuit that is directed against *a particular person.*

_____ 7. For a court to have jurisdiction over an *in rem action,* the property must be located in the state (and, usually, in the county) where the court lies.

_____ 8. If a defendant owns real property in one state and lives in another, the court with jurisdiction where the real property is located has jurisdiction over the *person* and not the *property.*

_____ 9. When parties *negotiate,* there is no neutral third party involved.

_____ 10. When parties agree in advance to binding arbitration, the decision of the arbitrator *must be followed.*

Checking Terminology (Part A)

From the list of legal terms that follows, select the one that matches each definition.

ANSWERS

a. Admiralty
b. appellate courts
c. appellate jurisdiction
d. arbitrator's award
e. caucus
f. cert.den.
g. circuits
h. concurrent jurisdiction
i. court
j. courts of appeal
k. diversity of citizenship
l. exclusive jurisdiction
m. federal question
n. federal district courts
o. formus non conveniens
p. in personam action
q. in rem action
r. justice
s. local action
t. maritine
u. negotiation
v. original jurisdiction
w. plenary jurisdiction
x. quasi in rem action
y. transitory action
z. writ of certiorari

_____ 1. The power of two or more courts to hear a particular case.

_____ 2. The power to hear a case when it first goes to court.

_____ 3. A lawsuit that is directed against property rather than against a particular person.

_____ 4. The right of a court to refuse to hear a case if it believes that justice would be better served if the trial were held in a different court.

_____ 5. A lawsuit that can occur in only one place.

_____ 6. Courts that hear most federal cases when they originally go to court, before there is an appeal.

_____ 7. A lawsuit in which the court has jurisdiction over the defendant's property, but not over the defendant's person.

_____ 8. A lawsuit that may be brought in more than one place as long as the court in which it is heard has proper jurisdiction.

_____ 9. A matter that involves the U.S. Constitution, acts of Congress, or treason.

_____ 10. Pertaining to the sea. (Select two answers.)

_____ 11. Name given to the division of U.S. district courts.

_____ 12. Title given to an appellate court judge.

_____ 13. An order from a higher court to a lower court to deliver its records to the higher court for review.

_____ 14. A phrase used in connection with the jurisdiction of the federal courts.

_____ 15. The power of one court only to hear a particular case, to the exclusion of all other courts.

_____ 16. A lawsuit in which the court has jurisdiction over the person.

_____ 17. The power to hear a case when it is appealed.

_____ 18. Courts that review the decision of lower courts. (Select two answers.)

_____ 19. Final, written decision in binding arbitration.

_____ 20. Private session with a mediator.

_____ 21. Complete jurisdiction.

Checking Terminology (Part B)

From the list of legal terms that follows, select the one that matches each definition.

ANSWERS

a. alternative dispute resolution
b. appeal
c. arbitration
d. arbitrator
e. binding arbitration
f. change of venue
g. code
h. compulsory arbitration
i. conciliation
j. conciliator
k. in personam jurisdiction
l. jurisdiction
m. long-arm statutes
n. mandatory arbitration
o. mediation
p. mediator
q. mini-trial
r. negotiation
s. nonbinding arbitration
t. res
u. statute
v. venue

_____ 1. Arbitration that is required by agreement or by law. (Select two answers.)
_____ 2. Arbitration in which the decision of the arbitrator will prevail and must be followed.
_____ 3. An informal process in which a neutral third party listens to both sides and makes suggestions for reaching a solution. (Select two answers.)
_____ 4. The removal of a suit begun in one county or district and replacement of it to another county or district for trial.
_____ 5. The power or authority that a court has to hear a case.
_____ 6. The property; the thing.
_____ 7. Statutes that allow one state to exercise personal jurisdiction over a person in another state.
_____ 8. An informal trial run by a private organization established for the purpose of settling disputes out of court.
_____ 9. A term that means to settle disputes by a method other than litigation.
_____ 10. A method of settling disputes by which a neutral third party makes a decision after hearing the arguments on both sides.
_____ 11. A neutral third person in an arbitration who listens to both sides and makes a decision with regard to the dispute.
_____ 12. Arbitration in which the arbitrator's decision is simply a recommendation and need not be complied with.
_____ 13. A systematic collection of statutes, administrative regulations, and other laws.
_____ 14. The place where a trial is held.
_____ 15. A request to a higher court to review the decision of a lower court.
_____ 16. A law passed by a legislature.
_____ 17. A neutral third person in a conciliation session who listens to both sides and who makes suggestions for reaching a solution. (Select two answers.)
_____ 18. Two-party process of bargaining until one side agrees to an offer of settlement from the other side.
_____ 19. Jurisdiction over the person.

Using Legal Language

Read the following story and fill in the blank lines with legal terms taken from the list of terms at the beginning of this chapter:

To settle a dispute by means other than litigation over who owned the lot next to her, Susan tried to get Conrad to participate in a(n) _____ resolution. Conrad wanted to use _____, because he didn't want anyone else involved. Susan wanted to use _____ (also called _____ _____)—an informal process in which a neutral third person listens to both sides and makes suggestions for reaching a solution. This case was not one involving a defendant who owned land in one state and lived in another; therefore, it was not a(n) _____ action. The _____ for the trial was Salem because the disputed land was located there, and the court in that city had _____ over the case.

Because the case involved title to land, the trial had to be held in the county where the _____ was located, and because the suit was directed against property, it was a(n) _____ action, not a(n) _____ action. The suit was a(n) _____ action rather than a(n) _____ action, because it could be brought only in one place. In addition, because the Salem court was the only one that had the power to hear the case, it had __ _____ rather than _____ _____. Owing to the fact that the case was being tried for the first time, the court had _____ _____, not _____.

PUZZLING OVER WHAT YOU LEARNED

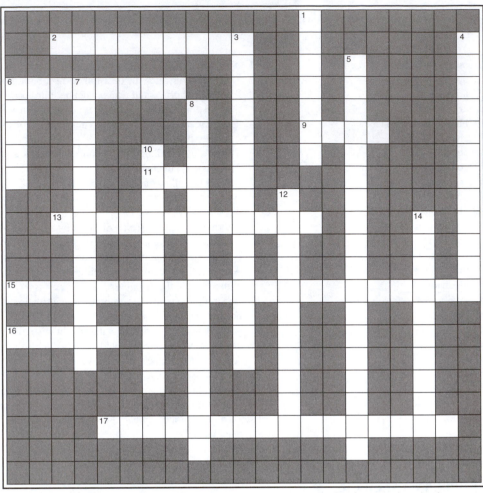

Caveat: Do not allow squares for spaces between words and punctuation (apostrophes, hyphens, etc.) when filling in crossword.

Across

2. An informal trial run by a private organization established for the purpose of settling disputes out of court.
6. Name given to the division of U.S. courts.
9. A systematic collection of statutes, administrative regulations, and other laws.
11. The property; the thing.
13. An informal process in which a neutral third person listens to both sides and makes suggestions for reaching a resolution.
15. The power to hear a case when it is appealed.
16. The place where a trial is held.
17. An order from a higher court to a lower court to deliver its records to the higher court for review.

Down

1. Title given to an appellate court judge.
3. Statutes that allow one state to reach out and obtain personal jurisdiction over a person in another state.
4. The power or authority that a court has to hear a case.
5. Arbitration in which the decision of the arbitrator will prevail and must be followed.
6. A body of government organized to administer justice.
7. The removal of a suit begun in one county or district to another county or district for trial.
8. A lawsuit in which the court has jurisdiction over the defendant's property, but not over the defendant's person.
10. A method of settling disputes in which a neutral third party makes a decision after hearing the arguments on both sides.
12. A neutral third person in a conciliation session who listens to both sides and makes suggestions for reaching a solution.
14. A neutral third person in an arbitration session who listens to both sides and makes a decision with regard to the dispute.

2

Criminal Trial Procedure

ANTE INTERROGATORY

*A formal written charge of a crime made by a grand jury is called
(A) an arraignment, (B) a criminal complaint, (C) a citation,
(D) an indictment.*

CHAPTER OUTLINE

Arrest

Preliminary Hearing

Indictment

Arraignment

Reasonable Doubt

Sentencing

Defendants' Rights

Trial Separation

KEY TERMS

action *(AK·shun)*

arraignment *(a·RAIN·ment)*

arrest *(a·REST)*

arrest warrant *(a·REST WAR·ent)*

bail

beyond a reasonable doubt *(REE·zen·e·bel)*

bifurcated trial *(BY·fer·kay·ted tryl)*

citation *(sy·TAY·shun)*

commutation of sentence *(kom·yoo·TAY·shun
ov SEN·tense)*

concurrent sentences *(kon·KER·ent
SEN·ten·sez)*

consecutive sentences *(kon·SEK·yoo·tiv
SEN·ten·sez)*

convict *(KON·vict)*

crime *(krym)*

criminal complaint *(KRIM·in·el
kom·PLAYNT)*

cumulative sentences *(KYOOM·yoo·la·tiv
SEN·ten·sez)*

defendant *(de·FEN·dent)*

extradition *(ex·trah·DIH·shun)*

fact finder *(fakt FINE·der)*

grand jury *(JOOR·ee)*

guilty *(GILL·tee)*

inadmissible *(in·ad·MISS·i·bel)*

indictment *(in·DITE·ment)*

information *(in·for·MA·shun)*

intent *(in·TENT)*

malefactor *(mal·e·FAK·ter)*

mandatory sentence *(MAN·da·tor·ee
SEN·tense)*

minimum sentence *(MIN·i·mum SEN·tense)*

Miranda warnings *(mer·AN·da)*

nolo contendere *(NO·lo kon·TEN·de·ray)*

pardon *(PAR·den)*

parole *(pa·ROLE)*

parole board

parole commission *(ke·MISH·en)*

parolee *(pa·role·EE)*

personal recognizance *(PER·son·al re·KOG·ni·zense)*

plaintiff *(PLAIN·tif)*

plea bargaining *(plee BAR·gen·ing)*

preliminary hearing *(pre·LIM·i·ner·ee HEER·ing)*

probable cause *(PROB·a·bel kawz)*

probable cause hearing *(PROB·a·bel kawz HEER·ing)*

prosecute *(PROS·e·kyoot)*

prosecution *(pros·e·KYOO·shun)*

reasonable doubt *(REE·zen·e·bel dowt)*

rules of criminal procedure *(KRIM·i·nel pro·SEED·jer)*

seizure *(SEE·zhur)*

sentence *(SEN·tense)*

severance of actions *(SEV·er·ense ov AK·shuns)*

suspended sentence *(sus·PEN·ded SEN·tense)*

victim's impact statement *(VIK·tems IM·pakt)*

The process of taking a criminal case to court is governed by rules that have been adopted by federal and state governments. The federal **rules of criminal procedure** govern criminal actions brought in federal courts. These rules are available on the Internet. Individual states have also adopted rules of procedure that must be followed when bringing criminal actions in those states.

A **crime** is an offense against the public at large. It is a wrong against all of society, not merely against the individual victim. For that reason, the **plaintiff**—that is, the one who **prosecutes** (brings the action)—in a criminal case is always the federal, state, or local government, which has the burden of proving its case. The one against whom the action is brought is known as the **defendant**. A person found guilty of a crime is known as a **malefactor** or **convict**.

ARREST

A criminal **action** (lawsuit or court proceeding), known as a **prosecution**, begins with the issuance of an **arrest warrant**, which is a written order of the court commanding law enforcement officers to arrest a person and bring him or her before the court. To **arrest** means to deprive a person of his or her liberty. Suspects can be arrested without a warrant when there is **probable cause**—that is, reasonable grounds for belief that an offense has been committed. Police searches of an arrested person or his or her property must be based on a valid search warrant or permissible exception such as a search of a person immediately after the arrest. All **seizures** of evidence of criminality must be based on a valid search warrant or on a permissible exception. For example, if police arrest a person and search that person's clothing for the safety of the police, and in so doing find a weapon, the police may seize that weapon without a warrant.

A process known as **extradition** permits the return of fugitives to the state where they are accused of having committed a crime. Extradition is ordered by the governor of the state to which they have fled.

Miranda Warnings*

When arrested, via a procedure called the Miranda warning, suspects must be told, before being questioned, that they have the following constitutional rights:

1. They have the right to remain silent.
2. Any statements made by them may be used against them to gain conviction.
3. They have the right to consult with a lawyer and to have a lawyer present during questioning.
4. A lawyer will be provided without cost for indigent defendants.

Any statements made by the accused that were obtained in violation of this rule are **inadmissible** (cannot be received) as evidence in court.

Miranda v. Arizona, 384 U.S. 436 (1966).

For minor offenses such as traffic violations, a citation is issued instead of an arrest warrant. A **citation** is a written order by a judge (or by a police officer) commanding a person to appear in court for a particular purpose.

PRELIMINARY HEARING

After the arrest, a **criminal complaint** (a written statement of the essential facts making up the offense charged) is drafted by the arresting authorities. Next, the suspect is brought before the court for a **preliminary hearing**, also called a **probable cause hearing**, which is a hearing before a judge to determine whether there is sufficient evidence to believe that the person has committed a crime. If the court finds probable cause, the defendant is either kept in jail, or released on **bail** (money or property left with the court to ensure that the person will return to stand trial) or on **personal recognizance** (a personal obligation to return to stand trial).

INDICTMENT

In misdemeanor cases, a date is set for a trial. In felony cases, formal charges must be brought either by an **indictment** (a formal written charge of a crime made by a grand jury) or, if waived in some states, by **information** (a formal written charge of a crime made by a public official rather than by a grand jury). A **grand jury** is a jury consisting of between 5 and 23 persons at the state level, and 23 people in the federal system, who listen to evidence presented by the prosecutor and decide whether or not the evidence is sufficient to charge someone with the commission of a crime.

ARRAIGNMENT

Following the indictment or information, the person charged with the crime must face **arraignment**, which is the act of calling a prisoner before the court to answer the indictment or information. The charge is read to the person, and he or she is asked to plead "**guilty**" (a plea of admission to having committed the crime), "**not guilty,**" or, when permitted, "**nolo contendere**" (a plea in which the defendant neither admits nor denies the charges). If the person pleads guilty or nolo contendere, he or she is sentenced by the court. Sometimes, the prosecution and defense will work out a mutually satisfactory disposition of the case through a process known as **plea bargaining**. In a plea bargain, the defendant often will plead guilty to a lesser offense in exchange for a lighter sentence. Any such arrangement must be approved by the court. A date is set for a trial when a person pleads not guilty.

REASONABLE DOUBT

To convict someone of a crime, the prosecution must prove its case to the fact finder beyond a reasonable doubt. **Beyond a reasonable doubt** means that the **fact finder** (the jury, or the judge in a nonjury trial) is fully persuaded that the accused has committed the crime with the required criminal **intent**, which is the necessary mental state that precedes the criminal act. Beyond a reasonable doubt does not require absolute certainty, but if there is a **reasonable doubt**—that is, a real doubt based on reason and common sense—the accused must be acquitted.

TERMS IN ACTION

During the ninth season of the television show "American Idol," one of the immediately-to-be-dismissed contestants sang a song with the often-repeated lyrics, "pants on the ground." For a police officer in Minnesota, the command "Put your hands in the air" led to pants-on-the-ground (almost) and the discovery of incriminating evidence. St. Paul police officer Kara Breci was patrolling a high-crime area in November 2008, when she spotted a car in a White

(Continued)

Castle restaurant parking lot with two men in the car and a third man, with no food, getting into the back seat. Believing that she was watching a drug deal in action, she and her partner approached the car, and after one quick question one of the occupants confessed to having "weed." The police ordered them to exit the car. One of the men, Frank Irving Wiggins, had low-slung pants that dropped when he got out of the car and put his hands in the air. Officer Breci immediately grabbed the pants' waistband to pull them up, and in so doing she found a handgun. Convicted **beyond a reasonable doubt** of illegal weapons possession, Wiggins appealed on the ground that the search of his pants was unconstitutional because the officer had no **search warrant**. But the Minnesota Court of Appeals upheld the conviction, concluding that Officer Breci's hiking of Wiggins's pants didn't constitute a **search** at all, but was reasonably done to protect her safety and also to prevent Wiggins from any unnecessary embarrassment.

Source: abajournal.com; *State v. Wiggins*, 788 N.W.2d 509 (Minn. App. 2010)

Web Wise

- For overviews of criminal and civil procedure, go to the Legal Information Institute (LII) at **www.law.cornell.edu**. Click on Wex legal dictionary/encyclopedia under the "Learn more" box; then type "civil procedure" or "criminal procedure" in the search box.
- In addition to the website just mentioned, the federal procedural rules can be found at **www.findlaw.com**. At that site, type "Federal Resources" in the search box. Then type "Rules of Civil Procedure" or "Rules of Criminal Procedure" in the box to search again.
- Find out about *Internet jurisdiction* by going to **www.findlaw.com** and keying in "internet jurisdiction" in the search box.

SENTENCING

When the defendant is found guilty in a criminal case, the judgment of the court imposing punishment is called a **sentence**. At the time of sentencing, most states allow victims to make impact statements. A **victim's impact statement** is a statement to the court, at the time of sentencing, relating the impact that the crime had on the victim or on the victim's family. Depending on state law, impact statements are made before or after sentencing and are often preserved for use at a later time by a **parole board** or **parole commission** (a group of people authorized to grant parole). **Parole** is a conditional release from prison, allowing the **parolee** (person placed on parole) to serve the remainder of a sentence outside of prison under specific terms.

When two or more sentences are imposed on a defendant, to be served one after the other, they are called **consecutive** or **cumulative sentences**. If they are to be served at the same time, they are called **concurrent sentences**. A **suspended sentence** is one given formally, but not actually served. Suspended sentences are sometimes given to first-time defendants and tied to certain conditions, such as completing community service, entering (and completing) a substance abuse program, or simply staying out of trouble. A **mandatory sentence** is a fixed sentence that must be imposed, with no room for discretion. A **minimum sentence** refers to the shortest amount of time that a prisoner must serve before being released or placed on parole.

The President of the United States in federal cases, and state governors in state cases, have the power to change sentences, making them less severe. Such a change is known as a **commutation of sentence**. A **pardon**, on the other hand, is a setting aside of punishment altogether by a government official, without the exoneration of guilt.

TERMS IN ACTION

Perhaps you never wondered what was the longest single prison **sentence** ever given. In case you did, you can stop. In 1981, a jury in Alabama sentenced triple-murderer Dwaye Kyzer to two **consecutive life sentences** and 10,000 years. Kyzer was convicted in 1976 of murdering his wife, mother-in-law, and a college student, and was sentenced to death. But his death sentence was overturned, and Kyzer was resentenced. At that hearing, the prosecuting attorney who originally won the conviction and death penalty asked for (and got) two consecutive life sentences and an additional 10,000 years. Even the *Guinness Book of World Records* deemed it the longest prison sentence. In light of his crime and sentence, it is amazing that Kyzer is eligible for **parole** in Alabama, but was denied parole by the Alabama **parole board** in 2010, when he was 69.

Source: tuscaloosanews.com; associatedcontent.com

DEFENDANTS' RIGHTS

In addition to certain rights that they are informed of when arrested (see the **Miranda Warnings** box in Chapter 1), defendants in criminal cases have the following rights:

1. The right to be free from any unreasonable search and seizure. (U.S. Constitution, Fourth Amendment)
2. The right to a speedy trial. (U.S. Constitution, Sixth Amendment)
3. The right to plead not guilty. (inherent in the U.S. Constitution, the Bill of Rights)
4. The right to be represented by an attorney. (U.S. Constitution, Sixth Amendment)
5. The right to a court-appointed attorney if the defendant cannot afford one. (*Gideon v. Wainwright*, 372 U.S. 335 (1963))
6. The right to summon witnesses and require their attendance. (U.S. Constitution, Sixth Amendment)
7. The right to confront and cross-examine witnesses. (U.S. Constitution, Sixth Amendment)
8. The right to be presumed innocent until proven guilty, by a judge or jury, beyond a reasonable doubt. (*Taylor v. Kentucky*, 436 U.S. 478 (1978))

TRIAL SEPARATION

Sometimes, trials are divided into separate parts. A **bifurcated trial** is a trial divided into two parts, providing separate evidence presentations and fact-findings for different issues in the same lawsuit. For example, in criminal cases, one portion may be held to determine the guilt or innocence of the defendant, followed by a separate hearing, if necessary, to determine sanity or punishment. In non-criminal personal-injury cases, separate hearings sometimes are held on the questions of liability and damages.

A different kind of trial separation, called **severance of actions**, occurs when a court separates lawsuits or prosecutions involving multiple parties into separate, independent cases resulting in separate final judgments.

Reviewing What You Learned

After studying the chapter, write the answers to each of the following questions:

1. Who brings the action in a criminal case?

2. When does a criminal action begin?

3. What happens to the defendant if the court finds probable cause that he or she committed a crime?

_____

_____

_____

4. How many people serve on a grand jury and what is the jury's function?

_____

_____

_____

5. How does an indictment differ from an arraignment?

_____

_____

_____

6. What must occur if the judge or jury finds that there is a reasonable doubt that the defendant committed the crime?

_____

_____

_____

7. When arrested, what must a suspect be told before being questioned?

_____

_____

_____

8. For what reason do you believe that victims' impact statements are often preserved for later use by a parole board?

_____

_____

_____

9. How does a commutation of a sentence differ from a pardon?

_____

_____

_____

10. What is the difference between a bifurcated trial and a severance of action?

_____

_____

_____

Understanding Legal Concepts

Indicate whether each statement is true or false. Then, change the italicized word or phrase of each false statement to make it true.

ANSWERS

_____ **1.** A crime is an offense against *the individual victim alone*. It *is not* a wrong against all of society.

_____ **2.** The one who brings an action in a criminal case is *usually* the federal, state, or local government.

_____ **3.** A grand jury is a jury consisting of *not more than* 23 people.

_____ **4.** An indictment is a formal written charge of a crime made by a *grand jury*.

_____ **5.** Nolo contendere is a plea in which the *plaintiff* neither admits nor denies the charges.

_____ **6.** To convict someone of a crime, the prosecution must prove *beyond a reasonable doubt* that the defendant committed the crime.

_____ **7.** A *pardon* is a conditional release from prison allowing the person to serve the remainder of a sentence outside of prison under specific terms.

_____ **8.** A *suspended* sentence is a sentence given formally, but not actually served.

_____ **9.** Two or more sentences imposed on a defendant to be served at the same time are *consecutive* sentences.

_____ **10.** A *severance of action* is a trial that is divided into two parts, providing separate hearings for different issues in the same lawsuit.

Checking Terminology (Part A)

From the list of legal terms that follows, select the one that matches each definition.

ANSWERS

a. action
b. arraignment
c. arrest
d. arrest warrant

_____ **1.** A written order by a judge or police officer commanding a person to appear in court for a particular purpose.

_____ **2.** An offense against the public at large.

_____ **3.** A person against whom a legal action is brought.

e. bail
f. beyond a reasonable doubt
g. bifurcated trial
h. citation
i. commutation of sentence
j. concurrent sentences
k. consecutive sentences
l. Convict
m. crime
n. criminal complaint
o. cumulative sentences
p. defendant
q. extradition
r. fact finder
s. grand jury
t. guilty
u. inadmissible
v. indictment
w. information
x. Intent

_____ **4.** A lawsuit or court proceeding.

_____ **5.** A written order of the court commanding law enforcement officers to arrest a person and to bring him or her before the court.

_____ **6.** The act of calling a prisoner before the court to answer an indictment or information.

_____ **7.** A written statement of the essential facts making up an offense charged in a criminal action.

_____ **8.** Money or property left with the court to ensure that a person will return to stand trial.

_____ **9.** The return of fugitives to the state where they are accused of having committed the crime.

_____ **10.** A formal, written charge of a crime, made by a grand jury.

_____ **11.** The fact finder who is fully persuaded that the accused has committed a crime.

_____ **12.** The jury in a jury trial or the judge in a non-jury trial.

_____ **13.** A trial that is divided into two parts, providing separate hearings for different issues in the same lawsuit.

_____ **14.** Two or more sentences imposed on a defendant to be served one after the other. (Select two answers.)

_____ **15.** The necessary mental state that precedes the criminal act.

_____ **16.** A formal written charge of a crime made by a public official rather than by a grand jury.

_____ **17.** Two or more sentences imposed on a defendant to be served at the same time.

_____ **18.** The changing of a sentence to one that is less severe.

_____ **19.** A person found guilty of a crime.

_____ **20.** To deprive a person of his or her liberty.

Checking Terminology (Part B)

From the list of legal terms that follows, select the one that matches each definition.

ANSWERS

a. mandatory sentence
b. minimum sentence
c. Miranda warnings
d. nolo contendere
e. pardon
f. parole
g. parole board
h. parole commission
i. parolee
j. personal recognizance
k. plea bargaining
l. preliminary hearing
m. probable cause
n. probable cause hearing
o. prosecute
p. prosecution
q. reasonable doubt
r. rendition
s. rules of criminal procedure
t. seizure
u. sentence
v. severance of actions
w. suspended sentence
x. victims' impact statements

_____ **1.** The judgment of the court imposing punishment when the defendant is found guilty in a criminal case.

_____ **2.** A person placed on parole.

_____ **3.** Reasonable grounds for belief that an offense has been committed.

_____ **4.** A person found guilty of a crime.

_____ **5.** The party by whom criminal proceedings are started or conducted; the state.

_____ **6.** A plea in which the defendant neither admits nor denies the charges.

_____ **7.** A hearing before a judge to determine whether there is sufficient evidence to believe that the person has committed a crime. (Select two answers.)

_____ **8.** A fixed sentence that must be imposed, with no room for discretion.

_____ **9.** A personal obligation by a person to return to stand trial.

_____ **10.** The shortest amount of time that a prisoner must serve before being released or placed on parole.

_____ **11.** A group of people authorized to grant parole. (Select two answers.)

_____ **12.** A setting aside of punishment altogether, by a government official.

_____ **13.** A statement to the court, at the time of sentencing, relative to the impact that the crime had on the victim or on the victim's family.

_____ **14.** A sentence that is given formally, but not actually served.

_____ **15.** A conditional release from prison allowing the person to serve the remainder of a sentence outside of prison under specific terms.

_____ **16.** Regulations that govern the proceedings in criminal cases.

_____ **17.** The working out of a mutually satisfactory disposition of a case by the prosecution and by the defense.

_____ **18.** The separation of lawsuits or prosecutions involving multiple parties into separate, independent cases, resulting in separate final judgments.

_____ **19.** The taking property on the basis of producing a search warrant.

_____ **20.** To proceed against a person criminally.

_____ **21.** Doubt based on reason.

Using Legal Language

Read the following story and fill in the blank lines with legal terms taken from the list of terms at the beginning of this chapter:

Alphonse, high on drugs and carrying a handgun, broke into Krista's apartment one evening, unaware that Krista and her dog Lilly were present. Lilly lunged at the surprised Alphonse, causing him to shoot himself in the foot. Krista disarmed the bleeding Alphonse and called 911. When the police arrived, Alphonse was placed under _____; that is, deprived of his liberty. He was also told about his rights, called _____. The next morning, Alphonse went before the court for a(n) _____ hearing, which is also called a(n) _____ hearing. The judge set a high _____ to ensure Alphonse's return to stand trial. The district attorney presented the case to a(n) _____ jury, which issued a(n) _____ —a formal written charge of a crime. This was followed by a court appearance called a(n) _____ at which Alphonse pleaded _____, denying that he had committed the crime. The trial that followed was governed by regulations known as _____. The state brought the action, that is, _____, against Alphonse, who was the _____. To find Alphonse guilty, the jury, that is, the _____, was required to find beyond _____ that Alphonse committed the crime. At the time of sentencing, Krista was able to give a(n) _____ pointing out the effect the crime had on her life. Alphonse was given a(n) _____ sentence—one that is fixed, with no room for discretion.

PUZZLING OVER WHAT YOU LEARNED

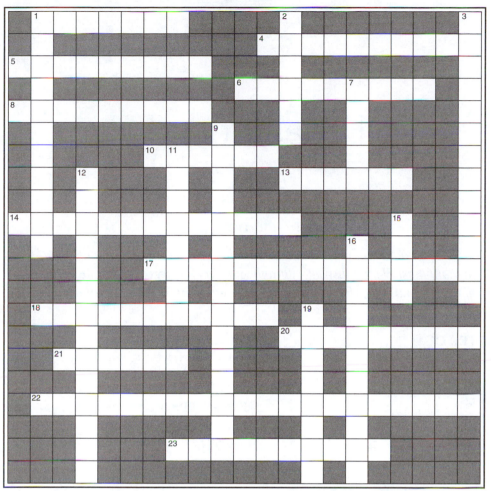

Caveat: Do not allow squares for spaces between words and punctuation (apostrophes, hyphens, etc.) when filling in crossword.

Across

1. A person placed on parole.
4. The jury in a jury trial or the judge in a nonjury trial.
5. A jury consisting of not more than 23 people who listen to evidence and decide whether or not to charge someone with the commission of a crime.
6. To proceed against a person criminally.
8. A person who brings legal action against another.
10. A lawsuit or court proceeding.
13. To deprive a person of his or her liberty.
14. A written order of the court commanding law enforcement officers to arrest a person and bring him or her before the court.
17. The constitutional right given to people when they are arrested to be told before being questioned of certain rights.
18. The act of calling a prisoner before the court to answer an indictment or information.
20. A person against whom legal action is brought.
21. A setting aside of punishment altogether by a government official.
22. Two or more sentences imposed on a defendant to be served one after the other.
23. A person found guilty of a crime.

Down

1. A group of people authorized to grant parole.
2. A conditional release from prison allowing the person to serve the remainder of a sentence outside of a prison under specific terms.
3. Reasonable grounds for belief that an offense has been committed.
7. A wrong against society.
9. A trial that is divided into two parts, providing separate hearings for different issues in the same lawsuit.
11. A written order by a judge or police officer commanding a person to appear in court for a particular purpose.
12. The working out of a mutually satisfactory disposition of a case by the prosecution and the defense.
15. Money or property left with the court to assure that a person will return to stand trial.
16. The party by whom criminal proceedings are started or conducted; the state.
19. The judgment of the court imposing punishment when the defendant is found guilty in a criminal case.

Civil Trial Procedure

ANTE INTERROGATORY

*A formal notice to the defendant that a lawsuit has begun and that the
defendant must file an answer within the number of days set by state law is a
(A) complaint, (B) declaration, (C) summons, (D) verification.*

CHAPTER OUTLINE

Beginning a Civil Action

Selecting the Court

Pleadings

Service of Process
    The Answer
    Default Judgment

Attachments
    Ex Parte Hearing
    Writ of Attachment
    Trustee Process and Garnishment

Burden of Proof

Enforcing the Judgment

Summary Proceedings

KEY TERMS

ad damnum *(ahd DAHM·num)*

affiant *(a·FY·ent)*

affidavit *(a·fi·DAY·vit)*

allege *(a·LEJ)*

allegation *(al·e·GAY·shun)*

answer *(an·ser)*

attachment *(a·TACH·ment)*

aver *(a·VER)*

averments *(a·VER·ments)*

cause of action *(AK·shun)*

civil action *(SIV·el AK·shun)*

class action *(klas AK·shun)*

complaint *(kom·PLAYNT)*

constructive service *(kon·STRUK·tiv
    SER·viss)*

counterclaim *(KOWN·ter klame)*

declaration *(dek·la·RAY·shun)*

default judgment *(de·FAWLT JUJ·ment)*

defendant *(dee·FEN·dent)*

deponent *(de·PONE·ent)*

docket *(DOK·et)*

docket number *(DOK·et NUM·ber)*

Doe defendants *(de·FEN·dents)*

encumbrance *(en·KUM·brens)*

ex parte *(eks PAR·tay)*

garnishee *(gar·nish·EE)*

garnishment *(GAR·nish·ment)*

gravamen *(GRAH·va·men)*

justiciable *(jus·TISH·e·bel)*

legal issues *(LEE·gul ISH·oos)*

lien *(leen)*

lis pendens *(lis PEN denz)*

litigant *(LIT·i·gant)*

litigation *(lit·i·GAY·shun)*

personal service *(PER·son·al SER·viss)*

petition *(pe·TI·shun)*

plaintiff *(PLANE·tiff)*

pleadings *(PLEED·ings)*

preponderance of evidence *(pre·PON·der·ens ov EVI·dens)*

process *(PROSS·ess)*

process server *(PROSS·ess SERV·er)*

ripeness doctrine *(RIPE·ness DOK·trin)*

rules of civil procedure *(SIV·el pro·SEED·jer)*

service of process *(SER·viss ov PROCESS·ess)*

standing to sue *(STAND·ing to SOO)*

statute of limitations *(STA·chewt ov lim·ih·TAY·shuns)*

substituted service *(SUB·sti·tew·ted SER·viss)*

summary proceeding *(SUM·e·ree pro·SEED·ing)*

summons *(SUM·ens)*

trial docket *(tryl DOK·et)*

trial list *(tryl list)*

trustee *(trus·TEE)*

trustee process *(trus·TEE PROSS·ess)*

verification *(ver·i·fi·KAY·shun)*

writ

writ of attachment *(a·TACH·ment)*

writ of execution *(ek·se·kyoo·shen)*

writ of garnishment *(GAR·nish·ment)*

A **civil action**—that is, a lawsuit other than a criminal one—comes about when two or more people become involved in a dispute that they are unable to settle by themselves. One of them seeks to have a third party, the court, settle the dispute for them. To do this, a court action known as **litigation** (a suit at law) must be brought. The parties to a lawsuit are called **litigants**. The person who brings the suit is called the **plaintiff**. The person against whom the suit is brought is called the **defendant**. A **class action** is a lawsuit brought, with the court's permission, by one or more persons on behalf of a very large group of people who have the same interest in the matter.

Under the **ripeness doctrine**, a court will not hear a case unless there is an actual, present controversy for the court to decide. Judges will not decide cases that are hypothetical or speculative. To be brought to court, potential cases must be **justiciable**—appropriate for court assessment.

The federal **rules of civil procedure** govern civil cases brought in federal courts. These rules can be found on the Internet. Individual states also have adopted rules of civil procedure that apply to cases brought in their state courts.

BEGINNING A CIVIL ACTION

To begin a civil lawsuit, the plaintiff usually makes an appointment with an attorney and tells the attorney the facts of the dispute as he or she understands them. The attorney, after listening to the client's version of the facts, determines the **legal issues** (questions of law) that are involved in the case. The attorney then tells the client about the law as it applies to the legal issues and gives the client an opinion as to how successful a lawsuit might be. The client, with the advice of the attorney, then decides whether or not to bring the lawsuit.

An important consideration is whether the client has standing to sue. **Standing to sue** means that a party has a tangible, legally protected interest at stake in a lawsuit. For example, you could not bring suit against someone who breached your friend's contract, because you were not a party to that contract. You would not have "standing."

Another critical consideration for the attorney is whether the applicable **statute of limitations** bars the lawsuit from being filed. Statutes of limitation set a time limit for how long plaintiffs can wait, after the plaintiff is aware of the action (or reasonably should be aware), to file a lawsuit. Time limits vary according to the kind of suit being filed, but in most jurisdictions the statute of limitations for personal injury is two years.

If the client decides to bring suit, the attorney usually writes a letter to the defendant, saying that he or she represents the plaintiff and has been authorized to bring suit against the defendant. In the letter, the attorney often makes an attempt to settle the case out of court and gives the defendant a few days to answer the letter. If no settlement can be reached, the plaintiff's attorney will begin the lawsuit.

1

SELECTING THE COURT

The attorney's first task in bringing suit is to select the court in which to bring the action. In choosing a court, the attorney must determine which court has jurisdiction over both the person who is being sued and the subject matter of the case, as discussed in Chapter 1.

PLEADINGS

Civil suits are begun and defended at the outset by the use of papers known as pleadings. **Pleadings** are the written statements of claims and defenses used by the parties in the lawsuit. Pleadings serve the purpose of giving notice to all parties of the claims and defenses in the suit; in addition, pleadings narrow the issues for trial so that both parties and the court know the legal issues that must be decided.

To begin a civil suit, the plaintiff's attorney files a complaint with the clerk of the court, which is the plaintiff's first pleading. A **complaint** (called a **declaration** at common law) is a formal document containing a short and plain statement of the claim, indicating that the plaintiff is entitled to relief and containing a demand for the relief sought. The complaint sets forth the plaintiff's **cause of action**, which is the ground on which the suit is maintained. The essential basis, or gist, of the complaint is known as the **gravamen** of the lawsuit. The complaint contains **allegations** (also called **averments**), which are claims that the party making the complaint expects to prove. To **allege**, or to **aver**, means to make an allegation; to assert positively. The clause in the complaint stating the damages claimed by the plaintiff is called the **ad damnum**. In some states, a complaint must be accompanied by a verification signed by the plaintiff. A **verification** is a written statement made by the plaintiff, under oath, confirming the correctness, truth, or authenticity of a pleading. In some states, especially in courts of equity (see Chapter 7), civil suits are begun by the filing of a **petition**—a written application for a court order.

The lawsuit begins when the complaint or petition is filed with the court. The plaintiff's attorney either mails (registered or certified) or hand-delivers the complaint to the court, with the proper filing fee. The clerk of court keeps a record, called a **docket**, of cases that are filed and assigns a **docket number** to each case. The term **trial docket** or **trial list** refers to the calendar of cases that are ready for trial.

Due to the advance of technology, pleadings and other papers may be filed or served electronically, according to Rule 5 of the Federal Rules of Civil Procedure, provided that the local federal courts allow for electronic filing and that other parties consent to electronic service. States have similar allowances. Indiana Trial Rule 5(F)(2) allows for the electronic filing of pleadings. And to protect the privacy of litigants, Rule 5.2 of the Federal Rules of Civil Procedure requires that certain personal information (Social Security number or date of birth) be presented in a way that does not entirely disclose the information. For example, the last four numbers of a person's Social Security number only may be listed.

Once the complaint is filed with the court, the defendant is notified of the suit by a method known as process. **Process** is defined as the means of compelling the defendant in an action to appear in court.

Word Wise
Truth

The root "ver-" used in the term "verification" is from the Latin word for "truth," *veritas*. Other words with the same root are:

Word	Meaning
verdict [*ver* (truth) + *dict* (to say)]	Decision of the jury (see Chapter 20)
verify [*ver* (truth) + *facere* (to make)]	To prove to be true

Even that most familiar word, "very," which means "truly" or "really," comes from the root "ver-."

SERVICE OF PROCESS

A summons is used to notify the defendant of the lawsuit. A **summons** is a formal notice to the defendant that a lawsuit has begun and that the defendant either must file an answer within the number of days set by state law or lose the case by default. **Service of process** is the delivering of summonses or other legal documents to the people who are required to receive them. A summons is obtained from the court, filled out, and given, along with a copy of the complaint, to a **process server** (a person who carries out service of process). The process server delivers copies of the summons and the complaint to the defendant and then fills in the back of the summons indicating when and how service was made. The summons is then returned to the court.

The process server may serve process by delivering a copy of the summons and complaint to the defendant personally, which is known as **personal service**. Service that is not personal service is called **constructive service** when the summons and complaint are left at the defendant's last and usual place of abode and **substituted service** when they are delivered to the defendant's agent, mailed, or published in a newspaper. If the defendant is a corporation, process may be served on an officer of the corporation, on a registered agent of the corporation, or on the person in charge of the corporation's principal place of business. When the defendant's whereabouts are unknown, process may be served by publication in a newspaper. In some states, service may be made by mail. And as stated earlier, the Federal Rules of Civil Procedure authorize electronic service, provided that there is written consent by the party to be served.

When names of defendants are unknown, summonses and complaints refer to people as **Doe defendants**, such as First Doe, Second Doe, John Doe, and Jane Doe.

TERMS IN ACTION

In the 2008 movie "Pineapple Express," Seth Rogan's character plays a **process server** who uses creative methods to get divorce papers or **civil complaints** served on defendants, including impersonating a doctor and serving a **summons** on a surgeon during an operation. That may not be too far from reality for those who sometimes have to use deception to find defendants, some of whom don't want to be found. Process servers might have to dodge menacing dogs while trying to find hiding homeowners who don't want to receive **service of process** on foreclosure actions, and they risk personal injury if they are attacked by angered recipients of subpoenas or legal documents. California and Washington State allow process servers to temporarily trespass in order to do their job. Whereas **substitute service** is allowed in all jurisdictions, nothing beats being able to say, "You've been served." Even Mark Zuckerberg, the billionaire who created Facebook, heard those words when a process server got past security at a fancy ski resort in Idaho, where Zuckerberg was having lunch in 2010. One process server in Seattle was so unpopular for his menacing tactics that the *Seattle Times* wrote an article about him in 2010, recounting how he once pitched a tent outside a target's house and camped there until the guy came home. Service of process can even be deadly. In 2008, a process server in Colorado was murdered after personally serving an irate husband at the divorcing couple's home.

Source: seattletimes.com; businessinsider.com; thedenverchannel.com

---

The Answer

Upon receiving the summons, the defendant has a time limit to file an **answer**, which is the defendant's pleading. An answer is a written response to the plaintiff's complaint, filed with the court where the complaint was filed. An answer denies or admits the specific allegations in the complaint, or it may claim a lack of knowledge about the truthfulness of the complaint's allegations. A defendant's answer may also include a **counterclaim**—a suit filed against the plaintiff—which would then require the plaintiff's written response.

Default Judgment

When a defendant fails to file an answer or other pleading in response to a summons and complaint, he or she may lose the case by default. A **default judgment** is a court decision entered against a party who has failed to plead or defend a lawsuit.

Differences Between Criminal and Civil Actions		
	Criminal Action	**Civil Action**
1. **Who brings the action?**	The government	The injured party
2. **What is the plaintiff's burden of proof?**	Prove guilt beyond a reasonable doubt	Prove preponderance of evidence
3. **What can be the result for a losing defendant?**	Prison, fine, or both; death; restitution	Pay money (damages) to the winning party; do or refrain from doing a particular act

ATTACHMENTS

At times, plaintiffs need the assurance that if they obtain a judgment against the defendant (that is, win the lawsuit), money will be available from the defendant to pay the amount of the judgment. This assurance is accomplished by attaching the defendant's property at the beginning of the action. An **attachment** is the act of taking a person's property and bringing it into the custody of the law so that it may be applied toward the defendant's debt if the plaintiff wins the suit.

The method of obtaining an attachment varies somewhat from state to state. Under a typical state law, the plaintiff's attorney files a motion for attachment with the court at the same time the complaint is filed. The plaintiff's attorney must also file an affidavit signed by the plaintiff, stating facts that would warrant a judgment for the plaintiff. An **affidavit** is a written statement sworn to under oath, before a notary public, as being true to the affiant's own knowledge, information, and belief. An **affiant** (also called a **deponent**) is a person who signs an affidavit. The motion, affidavit, summons, and complaint, together with a notice of hearing, are sent to the process server, who serves them on the defendant. A hearing is then held by the court to determine whether or not to allow the attachment. The court may allow the attachment if it finds that a reasonable likelihood exists that the plaintiff will recover a judgment against the defendant for the amount of the attachment over and above any insurance coverage that the defendant has.

Ex Parte Hearing

Sometimes, the plaintiff's attorney wishes to attach the defendant's property, but does not want to notify the defendant in advance that an attachment is going to occur. In such cases, the plaintiff's attorney attends an ex parte session of the court. **Ex parte** means that the hearing is attended by one party only. The plaintiff's attorney asks the court to allow the attachment without notifying the defendant beforehand. The court may allow the attachment without notifying the defendant if it finds (1) that the defendant is not within its jurisdiction (but the defendant's property is, thereby giving it quasi in rem jurisdiction), or (2) that a danger exists that the defendant will conceal the property, sell it, or remove it from the state, or (3) that a danger exists that the defendant will damage or destroy the property.

Writ of Attachment

A **writ** is a written order of a court, returnable to the same, commanding the performance or nonperformance of an act. If the court allows an attachment, the judge signs a paper called a **writ of attachment**. This written order is to the sheriff, commanding the sheriff to attach the real or personal property of the defendant, up to an amount approved by the court.

When real property is attached, the writ of attachment or a notice of **lis pendens** (pending suit) is recorded at the registry of deeds in the county where the property is located. This procedure has the effect of putting a lien on the property until the lawsuit is completed. A **lien** (also called an **encumbrance**) is a claim that one person or entity has against the property of another. The claim attaches to the property until the lawsuit is completed. If the plaintiff obtains a judgment against the defendant, an officer of the court, such as a sheriff, can sell the property under the court's direction and obtain the money to satisfy the judgment.

If personal property is attached, the court officer may take possession of it, or in some circumstances place a keeper over it, or sell it immediately as in the case of perishable property. With variations from state to state, certain items are exempt from attachment, such as necessary wearing apparel, furniture and books up to a particular value, tools necessary to carry on a trade, and materials and stock up to a specified value. Other technical restrictions on the attachment of personal property exist.

Trustee Process and Garnishment

Sometimes, it is necessary to attach property of the defendant that is being held by another person. This is most commonly done to attach money that the defendant has in a bank account or wages or other money that has been earned by the defendant, but not yet paid.

The procedure for attaching the defendant's property that is in the hands of a third person is called **trustee process** in some states and **garnishment** in others. To begin trustee process, the plaintiff's attorney obtains a trustee process summons, or a **writ of garnishment** from the court, fills it out, and files it with the court, together with the complaint, a motion for approval of attachment on trustee process, and a supporting affidavit. The defendant is notified (unless the attachment is on an ex parte basis), and a hearing is held by the court to determine whether the trustee process attachment should be allowed. If it is allowed, the summons is sent to the process server, who serves it on the **trustee** or **garnishee** (the one holding the defendant's property). The summons orders the trustee to file, within a prescribed number of days after service, a disclosure under oath of the goods, effects, or credits, if any, of the defendant that are in the possession of the trustee at the time of service. In some states, trustee process cannot be used in actions for malicious prosecution, slander, libel, assault and battery, and specific recovery of goods. Certain other actions are also exempt from trustee process. With some exceptions, the plaintiff must file a bond with the court before trustee process can be used. The bond is for the purpose of paying the defendant's court costs and damages in the event that the attachment was wrongfully brought by the plaintiff.

▌ TERMS IN ACTION

Although O.J. Simpson is currently incarcerated for a 2008 Las Vegas robbery conviction, he succeeded in winning his first criminal trial, known as "the trial of the century." Charged with the double murder of his ex-wife Nicole Brown Simpson and her friend Ron Goldman, Simpson was found not guilty after a nine-month-long nationally televised trial. But in 1997, Simpson was found liable in the civil wrongful-death case, filed after the criminal case, and the jury awarded the Brown and Goldman families $33.5 million. After failing to pay the damages, the plaintiffs began the process of **attachment**. Although Simpson's NFL pension was deemed to be exempt from **garnishment**, eventually much of his nonexempt property was sold at auction to help pay his judgment. Simpson's most famous personal property, his 1968 Heisman trophy, sold for $230,000. A grand piano at Simpson's home wasn't sold at auction, however, because a judge agreed with Simpson's lawyers that it was a gift made by Simpson and Nicole in 1984 to Simpson's mother, but was kept at his Brentwood mansion. In 1999, the State of California filed a tax **lien** against Simpson for well over $1,000,000.

Source: accountingtoday.com; people.com; web.archive.org

1

BURDEN OF PROOF

Recall that in criminal cases, the prosecution must *prove beyond a reasonable doubt* that the defendant committed the crime. In civil cases, the burden of proof is different. To win a civil case, the plaintiff must prove the case by a **preponderance of evidence**—evidence of the greatest weight. This degree of proof requires the judge or jury to believe that the evidence more likely or not favors the plaintiff.

ENFORCING THE JUDGMENT

If the losing party is ordered to pay money to the winning party and does not do so, the winning party must ask the court for a **writ of execution**. This process is used to enforce a judgment for the payment of money. The writ orders the sheriff to enforce the judgment.

SUMMARY PROCEEDINGS

Lengthy and complicated trials are expensive for the parties and the governmental agencies administering them. Whenever possible, it is beneficial to hold a trial quickly, in a simple manner. A **summary proceeding** is the name given to a short and simple trial. Proceedings held in small-claims courts are examples of summary proceedings.

Reviewing What You Learned

After studying the chapter, write the answers to each of the following questions:

1. How does the plaintiff's attorney begin a civil suit?

_____

_____

_____

2. What two purposes do pleadings serve?

_____

_____

_____

3. How is the defendant notified that a lawsuit has been brought against him or her?

_____

_____

_____

4. Describe three ways that process may be served on the defendant.

_____

_____

_____

_____

5. In what ways may process be served if the defendant is a corporation?

_____

_____

_____

_____

_____

6. How can plaintiffs be assured that money will be available from defendants if the plaintiffs win a lawsuit?

_____

_____

_____

_____

_____

7. Under a typical state law, what two documents must the plaintiff's attorney file with the court to obtain an attachment?

_____

_____

_____

_____

8. How is the defendant notified of the plaintiff's motion for attachment?

_____

_____

_____

9. The court may allow an attachment if it finds what?

_____

_____

_____

10. On what three occasions may the court allow an attachment without notifying the defendant beforehand?

_____

_____

_____

_____

11. What is done with the writ of attachment or notice of lis pendens when real property is attached?

_____

_____

_____

_____

_____

12. What is a statute of limitations, and why is it important?

_____

_____

_____

_____

_____

Understanding Legal Concepts

Indicate whether each statement is true or false. Then, change the italicized word or phrase of each false statement to make it true.

ANSWERS

_____ **1.** To begin a lawsuit, the plaintiff's attorney files a *summons* with the clerk of the court.

_____ **2.** *Pleadings* help to narrow the issues for trial so that both parties and the court know what legal issues must be decided.

_____ **3.** A *complaint* is a formal notice to the defendant that a lawsuit has begun and that the defendant either must file an answer within the number of days set by state law or lose the case by default.

_____ **4.** To obtain an attachment, under a typical state law, the plaintiff's attorney files a motion for attachment with the court *at the same time that* the complaint is filed.

_____ **5.** An affiant is also known as a *deponent*.

_____ **6.** An ex parte session of the court is attended by *both parties* to the suit.

_____ **7.** A *writ of attachment* is a written order to the sheriff to attach the property of the defendant.

_____ **8.** When real property is attached, the writ of attachment is recorded at the *city or town hall* where the property is located.

_____ **9.** The procedure for attaching the defendant's property that is in the hands of a third person is called *a writ of encumbrance* in some states.

_____ **10.** A trustee process *summons* orders the trustee to file, within a prescribed number of days, a disclosure under oath of the goods, effects, or credits of the defendant that are in the possession of the trustee.

Checking Terminology (Part A)

From the list of legal terms that follows, select the one that matches each definition.

ANSWERS

a. affiant
b. affidavit
c. allegation
d. allege
e. answer
f. attachment
g. aver
h. cause of action

_____ **1.** A record of cases that are filed with the court.

_____ **2.** A formal document containing a short and plain statement of the claim, indicating that the plaintiff is entitled to relief and containing a demand for the relief sought. (Select two answers.)

_____ **3.** The act of taking a person's property and bringing it into the custody of the law so that it may be applied toward the defendant's debt if the plaintiff wins the case.

_____ **4.** A person who signs an affidavit. (Select two answers.)

_____ **5.** On one side only.

i. civil action
j. class action
k. complaint
l. constructive service
m. counterclaim
n. declaration
o. default judgment
p. defendant
q. deponent
r. docket
s. docket number
t. Doe defendants
u. encumbrance
v. ex parte
w. garnishment
x. gravamen
y. justiciable
z. legal issues
aa. lien
bb. lis pendens
cc. litigant

____ 6. A claim that one person or entity has against the property of another. (Select two answers.)
____ 7. A procedure for attaching the defendant's property that is in the hands of a third person.
____ 8. The ground on which a suit is maintained.
____ 9. A number assigned to each case by the clerk of court.
____ 10. A written statement sworn to under oath, before a notary public, as being true to the affiant's own knowledge, information, and belief.
____ 11. A type of service in which the summons and complaint are left at the defendant's last and usual place of abode.
____ 12. References to defendants whose names are unknown.
____ 13. The defendant's pleading in written response to the plaintiff's complaint.
____ 14. A court decision entered against a party who has failed to plead or defend a lawsuit.
____ 15. The essential basis or gist of a complaint filed in a lawsuit.
____ 16. Appropriate for court assessment.
____ 17. Questions of law to be decided by the court in a lawsuit.
____ 18. A pending suit.
____ 19. Claims that the party making it expects to prove. (Select two answers.)
____ 20. To make an allegation; to assert positively. (Select two answers.)
____ 21. A defendant's suit filed against the plaintiff.
____ 22. A person against whom a lawsuit is brought.

Checking Terminology (Part B)

From the list of legal terms that follows, select the one that matches each definition.

ANSWERS

a. litigation
b. personal service
c. petition
d. plaintiff
e. pleadings
f. preponderance of evidence
g. process
h. process server
i. ripeness doctrine
j. rules of civil procedure
k. service of process
l. standing to sue
m. statute of limitations
n. substituted service
o. summary proceeding
p. summons
q. trial docket
r. trial list
s. trustee
t. trustee process
u. verification
v. writ
w. writ of attachment
x. writ of execution

____ 1. A written application for a court order.
____ 2. A party that has a tangible, legally protected interest at stake in a lawsuit.
____ 3. Parties to a lawsuit.
____ 4. Evidence of the greater weight.
____ 5. Regulations that govern the proceedings in civil cases.
____ 6. A suit at law.
____ 7. The principle under which the court will not hear a case unless there is an actual, present controversy for the court to decide.
____ 8. A short and simple trial.
____ 9. A written order to the sheriff, commanding the sheriff to enforce a judgment of the court.
____ 10. The written statements of claims and defenses used by the parties in the lawsuit.
____ 11. A formal notice to the defendant that a lawsuit has begun and that the defendant either must file an answer within the number of days set by state law or lose the case by default.
____ 12. The calendar of cases that are ready for trial. (Select two answers.)
____ 13. A written order to the sheriff commanding the sheriff to attach the real or personal property of the defendant.
____ 14. A person who holds legal title to property in trust for another.
____ 15. A written statement made under oath, confirming the correctness, truth, or authenticity of a pleading.
____ 16. The means of compelling the defendant in an action to appear in court.
____ 17. The delivering of summonses or other legal documents to the people who are required to receive them.
____ 18. Set time limit for how long plaintiffs can wait to file a lawsuit.
____ 19. The delivery of a copy of the summons and complaint to the defendant personally.
____ 20. A written order of a court, returnable to the same, commanding the performance or non-performance of an act.
____ 21. A type of service in which the summons and complaint are delivered to the defendant's agent, mailed, or published in a newspaper.
____ 22. A person who carries out service of process.
____ 23. One who brings a lawsuit.

Using Legal Language

Read the following story and fill in the blank lines with legal terms taken from the list of terms at the beginning of this chapter:

After checking to see whether the client's case wasn't too old, but was still within _____ _____, the attorney began the lawsuit by filing the _____, which is the plaintiff's first _____, with the clerk of the court, who assigned a(n) _____ to the case to identify it. The attorney then had the _____ serve copies of the _____ and complaint on the defendant, who was called a(n) _____ because of an unknown name. Because of the fact that _____—that is, the means for compelling the defendant to appear in court—occurred by leaving the papers at the defendant's last and usual place of abode, it was not _____ service; instead, it was called _____. The attorney also filed a motion for a(n) _____

at a(n) _____ session of the court to place a(n) _____, which is also called a(n) _____ on the defendant's real property, without the defendant being notified beforehand. Along with the motion, the attorney was required to file a(n) _____, which was signed under oath by the client, who was called the _____ or _____. The attachment was allowed by the court, and the _____ was recorded at the Registry of Deeds. Because this did not involve the attachment of property in the hands of a third party, _____, which is also called _____, was not used. When the case was ready for trial, it was placed on the _____, which is sometimes referred to as the _____.

PUZZLING OVER WHAT YOU LEARNED

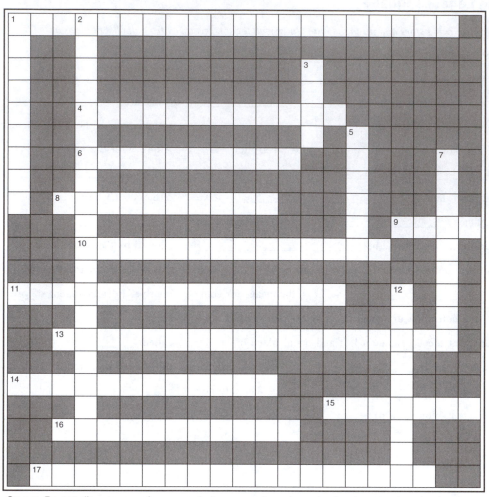

Caveat: Do not allow squares for spaces between words and punctuation (apostrophes, hyphens, etc.) when filling in crossword.

Across

1. Service in which papers are left at defendant's last and usual place of abode.
4. Calendar of cases that are ready for trial.
6. Another name for trial docket.
8. Act of bringing a person's property into the custody of the law.
9. Written order of the court commanding the performance of an act.
10. Defendants whose names are unknown.
11. Ground on which a suit is maintained.
13. Written order to a sheriff commanding the attachment of property.
14. Written statement under oath confirming the correctness of a pleading.
15. Person who signs an affidavit.
16. The common law name for a complaint.
17. The delivering of summonses or other legal documents.

Down

1. Formal document containing short statement of the plaintiff's claim.
2. Service in which summons and complaints are delivered to an agent or mailed.
3. Claim that one has against the property of another.
5. Record of cases that are filed with the clerk of court.
7. Written statement sworn to under oath.
12. Written statements of claims and defenses used in a lawsuit.

4

Defensive Pleadings in Civil Trials

ANTE INTERROGATORY

*A statement or claim that the party making it expects to prove
is a(n) (A) affirmative defense, (B) allegation, (C) demurrer,
and (D) cross-complaint.*

CHAPTER OUTLINE

Demurrer

Motions
    Motion to Dismiss
    Motion for a More Definite Statement
    Motion to Strike
    Motion for Judgment on the Pleadings

    Motion for Summary Judgment

Defendant's Answer
    Affirmative Defenses

Counterclaim

Cross-Claim

Cross-Complaint

KEY TERMS

affirmative defense *(a·FERM·a·tiv de·FENSE)*

answer *(AN·ser)*

confession and avoidance *(kon·FESH·en and a·VOY·dense)*

counterclaim *(KOWN·ter·klame)*

cross-claim *(kross klame)*

cross-complaint *(kross kom·PLAYNT)*

default judgment *(de·FAWLT JUJ·ment)*

demurrer *(de·MER·er)*

dismissal *(dis·MISS·el)*

dismissal without prejudice *(PREJ·e·diss)*

dismissal with prejudice

misnomer *(mis·NO·mer)*

motion *(MOH·shun)*

motion for a more definite statement *(DEF·e·net STATE·ment)*

motion for judgment on the pleadings *(JUJ·ment on the PLEED·ings)*

motion for recusal *(re·KYOO·zel)*

motion for summary judgment *(MOH·shun for SUM·er·ee JUJ·ment)*

motion to dismiss *(dis·MISS)*

motion to strike

nonsuit *(NON·soot)*

overrule *(o·ver·ROOL)*

recuse *(re·KYOOZ)*

reply *(re·PLY)*

summary judgment *(SUM·er·ee JUJ·ment)*

sustain *(sus·TANE)*

After a civil action has begun and the summons and complaint have been served on the defendant, it is necessary for the defendant to file one or more defensive pleadings within a certain number of days from the date of service of the summons. The number of days within which this filing must be done varies from state to state. In Massachusetts, a defensive pleading must be filed within 20 days; in California, 30 days. If a defensive pleading is not filed within the mandated period, the defendant will lose the case by default unless an exception is made by the court.

DEMURRER

A defensive pleading used at common law and infrequently used in a few states is the demurrer. A **demurrer** is a pleading available to the defendant to attack the plaintiff's complaint by raising a point of law, such as the failure of the complaint to state a cause of action on which relief can be granted. In effect, a demurrer points out that even if the plaintiff's allegations are true, no cause of action exists. Some grounds for using a demurrer follow:

1. The complaint does not state facts sufficient to constitute a cause of action.
2. The court has no jurisdiction over the subject matter of the case.
3. The plaintiff has no legal capacity to sue.
4. Another action is pending between the same parties for the same cause.
5. A defect, or misjoinder of the parties, in the suit exists.

If the court **sustains** (supports) the demurrer, the case will end by a nonsuit unless the court allows the plaintiff to amend the complaint. A **nonsuit** is the termination of an action that did not adjudicate issues on the merits. If the demurrer is **overruled** (annulled, made void, or not sustained), the defendant is given a certain number of days to file an answer (to be discussed later).

The federal courts and many states have done away with the demurrer, replacing it with one or more of the motions that will be discussed subsequently.

MOTIONS

A **motion** is a written or oral request made to a court for certain action to be taken. For example, when an attorney believes that the sitting judge is biased or prejudiced against a client, the attorney might make a **motion for recusal**. This is a request that the judge **recuse** (disqualify) himself or herself from the case because of the unfairness.

Motions are made for many different reasons and can be made by either party to a suit. Some of the important defensive motions follow:

1. motion to dismiss
2. motion for a more definite statement
3. motion to strike
4. motion for judgment on the pleadings
5. motion for summary judgment

Motion to Dismiss

In some cases, the plaintiff will do something that will give the defendant grounds to have the case dismissed. When this happens, the defendant may make a **motion to dismiss** the case. **Dismissal** is an order disposing of an action without trial of the issues. The motion must be made within a prescribed number of days after the defendant receives service of process.

After a motion to dismiss is filed with the court and sent to the opposing (plaintiff's) attorney, the attorney for the defendant marks up the motion to be heard by the court during one of its motion sessions. At this session, the attorneys for the parties argue their viewpoints as to the merits of the motion. The clients usually do not attend the motion session. The judge then makes a decision to either allow or deny the motion. If the motion to dismiss is allowed by an order for **dismissal without prejudice**, the plaintiff is allowed to correct the error and bring another action on the same claim. In contrast, if the order is a **dismissal with prejudice**, the plaintiff is barred from bringing another action on the same claim. If the motion to dismiss is denied, the defendant is given a certain number of days to file an answer.

The defendant may make a motion to dismiss for any of the following reasons:

1. lack of jurisdiction over the subject matter of the case
2. lack of jurisdiction over the defendant personally
3. improper venue
4. insufficiency of process (such as a defective summons)
5. insufficiency of service of process (as when service of process is made on someone not authorized to accept service)
6. failure to state a claim on which relief can be granted
7. failure to join a necessary party
8. **misnomer** (mistake in the name) of a party
9. pendency of a prior action in a court of the same state

Motion for a More Definite Statement

If a pleading is so vague that the other party cannot properly respond to it, a **motion for a more definite statement** may be made. If the motion is allowed, the other party must file the more definite statement within a prescribed number of days (usually, 10). The one who brought the motion then has 10 more days to answer the more definite statement. If the motion is denied, the answer must be filed within 10 days after notice of the court's denial.

Motion to Strike

A **motion to strike** may be used by either party to have stricken from any pleading any insufficient defense or any redundant, immaterial, impertinent, or scandalous matter.

Motion for Judgment on the Pleadings

A **motion for judgment on the pleadings** may be made by either the defendant or the plaintiff. It must be made only after both the plaintiff's complaint and the defendant's answer have been filed. The plaintiff might make the motion on the ground that the defendant's answer does not set forth a legally sufficient defense. The defendant might make the motion on the ground that the plaintiff's complaint does not state a claim on which relief can be granted.

TERMS IN ACTION

In 2009, a federal judge in Florida responded to a lawyer's **motion for dismissal** by denying it and writing in his order that the motion was "riddled with unprofessional grammatical and typographical errors that nearly render the entire motion incomprehensible." Reading the motion with a red pen in hand, U.S. District Judge Gregory Presnell marked it as if it had been turned in for a grade. Included in the lawyer's motion were typographical errors, apostrophe errors, spacing errors, and the use of wrong words (e.g., "attended to" instead of "intended to"). The judge made a copy of the motion with his corrections on it, attached it to his **order denying the motion without prejudice**, and ordered the lawyer to show a copy of the sloppy motion to his client.

Source: abovethelaw.com

Motion for Summary Judgment

A **motion for summary judgment** may be made when all of the papers filed in a case show that there is no genuine issue of material fact and that the party making the motion will win the case as a matter of law. A **summary judgment** is an immediate decision by the court, without a trial, based on the papers filed by the parties.

Defendant's Answer

Unless the case is dismissed by the allowance of a motion to dismiss, the defendant must file a written **answer** within a prescribed number of days after service of process, and in many jurisdictions the time limit is 20 days. The defendant's answer must state in short and plain terms the defenses he or she wishes to assert. In addition, each of the claims made by the plaintiff must be admitted or denied. If the defendant is without knowledge or information sufficient to form a belief as to the truth of an allegation, he or she may so state, which has the effect of a denial. If an allegation is partly true and partly false, the defendant may admit part and deny part of the allegation. If the defendant fails to deny an allegation made in the plaintiff's complaint, it is automatically admitted.

Failure to file an answer will cause a **default judgment** to be entered. This judgment is entered on failure of a party to appear or plead at the proper time.

TERMS IN ACTION

A blind lawyer in Philadelphia who sued an escort for overbilling him on his credit card faced a **counterclaim** by the escort, who claimed that the lawyer inappropriately touched her; but both claims were **dismissed**. In 2008, attorney John F. Peoples filed a federal lawsuit against Ginger Dayle, alleging that she overbilled him $11,000 for what he later stated in a deposition were prostitution services at her apartment. Because Peoples is blind, Ms. Dayle entered the dollar amounts for him on the credit card charge receipts she gave him, which he signed. He also sued the credit card company used for the transactions, accusing them of breach of contract for not removing the overcharges. Upon being sued, the credit card company filed an **answer** and a **motion for summary judgment**. It claimed that, because illegal contracts are void and because prostitution is illegal in Pennsylvania, it couldn't be liable for breach of contract relating to those charges. Ms. Dayle filed an **answer** denying overbilling Peoples, and she filed a counterclaim. She alleged that she was teaching a personal exercise class to Peoples and that he sexually harassed her during one of their 25 sessions. The federal district judge agreed with the credit card company and granted it the order of **dismissal**. He then **dismissed without prejudice** Ms. Dayle's counterclaim so that she could file it in state court, because having dismissed the entire case, he lacked jurisdiction over her suit. Mr. Peoples then appealed the decision to the 3rd Circuit Court of Appeals, where he lost. He then sought the U.S. Supreme Court's review on the matter, but in 2011 it refused to take the case.

Source: abajournal.com; *Peoples v. Discover Financial Services*, 209 WL 3030217 (unpublished)

Affirmative Defenses

Many times, the defendant will have done the act for which he or she is being sued, but will have some other reason that will stop the plaintiff from winning the case, which is called an **affirmative defense** (a **confession and avoidance** under the common law). The defendant admits the plaintiff's allegation, but introduces something new that constitutes a defense to it. When an affirmative defense is used in federal and in many state courts, it must be stated in the defendant's answer. If it is omitted from the answer, that particular defense is lost and cannot be used later.

The affirmative defenses are as follows:

accord and satisfaction	injury by fellow servant
arbitration and award	laches
assumption of risk	license
contributory negligence	payment
discharge in bankruptcy	release
duress	res judicata
estoppel	statute of frauds
failure of consideration	statute of limitations
fraud	waiver
illegality	

COUNTERCLAIM

If the defendant (after receiving the summons and complaint) wishes to bring a suit against the plaintiff, he or she will file a counterclaim. A **counterclaim** is a claim that the defendant has against the plaintiff. It is made a part of the defendant's answer. The counterclaim is *compulsory* if the defendant wishes to bring a claim that arises out of the same transaction or occurrence as that of the plaintiff's suit, the venue is correct, and the court has jurisdiction. If the defendant's counterclaim is not related to the event that caused the original suit, the counterclaim is *permissive*. For example, a neighbor could sue another for negligence, but the second neighbor could file a counterclaim for breach of contract, over an unpaid lawnmower. The plaintiff is required to file a reply to the defendant's counterclaim within a prescribed number of days after receiving the counterclaim. The **reply** is the legal name given to the answer to the counterclaim.

> **Word Wise**
> *Compound Words*
>
> In addition to words made up of prefixes, suffixes, and roots, English has many words made by compounding—that is, joining two or more words already in usage to create a new word with a new meaning. The term "counterclaim," introduced in this chapter, is such a word. Almost any combination of the parts of speech may be used to create a compound word. The following methods are the most common: noun with adjective (heartsick, airtight); adjective with noun (blackberry, hothouse); preposition with noun (overhead, downfall); verb with adverb (dugout, kickoff).

CROSS-CLAIM

Sometimes, a suit will be brought against two defendants, and one of those defendants will wish to bring a claim against the other defendant. A claim brought by one defendant against another defendant in the same suit is called a **cross-claim**. The subject matter of the cross-claim must arise out of the same transaction or occurrence as that of the original suit. A cross-claim must be answered within a prescribed number of days after it is received.

CROSS-COMPLAINT

The State of California uses a pleading known as a **cross-complaint** in place of a counterclaim and a cross-claim. The California cross-complaint may be used to file a claim by a defendant against (1) another defendant, (2) a third party, and (3) the plaintiff in the same action.

Reviewing What You Learned

After studying the chapter, write the answers to each of the following questions:

1. What must the defendant do after he or she has been served with a summons and a complaint? What will happen if this is not done?

_____

_____

_____

_____

2. What is one ground for using a demurrer?

_____

_____

_____

3. Who usually attends the hearing for the demurrer to be heard by the court?

_____

_____

_____

4. Name four important defensive motions.

_____

_____

_____

_____

5. Who attends a motion session? What happens at such a session?

_____

_____

_____

_____

6. What must the defendant do if the motion to dismiss is denied?

_____

_____

_____

_____

_____

7. List three grounds for a motion to dismiss.

_____

_____

_____

_____

8. What may the opposing party do if a pleading is so vague that the party cannot respond to it?

_____

_____

_____

_____

_____

9. What may the opposing party do if a pleading contains an insufficient defense or any redundant, immaterial, impertinent, or scandalous matter?

_____

_____

_____

_____

10. On what ground might a plaintiff make a motion for judgment on the pleadings? On what ground might a defendant make such a motion?

_____

_____

_____

11. What must the defendant's answer state?

_____

_____

_____

12. What will be the result if the defendant fails to deny any allegation made in the plaintiff's complaint?

_____

_____

_____

13. What will be the result if an affirmative defense is omitted from the defendant's answer?

_____

_____

_____

14. List three affirmative defenses.

_____

_____

_____

_____

15. What may the defendant do if he or she wishes to bring a suit against the plaintiff? In what way is this related to the defendant's answer?

_____

_____

_____

_____

16. How must the plaintiff respond to a defendant's counterclaim?

_____

_____

_____

_____

_____

_____

17. Who are the parties to a cross-claim? Out of what must the subject matter of a cross-claim arise?

_____

_____

_____

_____

_____

_____

Understanding Legal Concepts

Indicate whether each statement is true or false. Then, change the italicized word or phrase of each false statement to make it true.

ANSWERS

_____ **1.** After an action has begun, it is necessary for the defendant to file one or more defensive pleadings within _20 days_ from the date of service of the summons in California.

_____ **2.** If the court _sustains_ a demurrer, the defendant is given a certain number of days to file an answer.

_____ **3.** A motion to dismiss _may be_ allowed for failure to state a claim for which relief can be granted.

_____ **4.** A motion to dismiss may be allowed for _misnomer_ of a party.

_____ **5.** A motion for judgment on the pleadings may be made by _the defendant only_.

_____ **6.** The plaintiff might make a motion for judgment on the pleadings on the ground that the _defendant's answer_ does not set forth a legally sufficient defense.

_____ **7.** Unless the case is dismissed by the allowance of a motion to dismiss, the defendant must file a _written_ answer within a prescribed number of days after service of process.

_____ **8.** If the defendant fails to deny an allegation made in the plaintiff's complaint, the allegation is _automatically admitted_.

_____ **9.** When an affirmative defense is used, the defendant _denies_ the plaintiff's allegation.

_____ **10.** A _cross-claim_ is a claim that the defendant brings against the plaintiff.

Checking Terminology

From the list of legal terms that follows, select the one that matches each definition.

ANSWERS

a. affirmative defense
b. answer
c. confession and avoidance
d. counterclaim
e. cross-claim
f. cross-complaint
g. default judgment
h. demurrer
i. dismissal
j. dismissal without prejudice
k. dismissal with prejudice
l. freedom of assembly
m. freedom of speech
n. freedom of the press
o. free exercise clause
p. misnomer
q. motion
r. motion for a more definite statement
s. motion for judgment on the pleadings
t. motion for summary judgment
u. motion for recusal
v. motion to dismiss
w. motion to strike
x. nonsuit
y. overrule
z. recuse
aa. reply
bb. summary judgment
cc. sustain

_____ 1. A clause in the U.S. Constitution that guarantees to all persons the right to peaceably associate and assemble with others.
_____ 2. Mistake in name.
_____ 3. A dismissal in which the plaintiff is allowed to correct the error and to bring another action on the same claim.
_____ 4. A claim that the defendant has against the plaintiff.
_____ 5. To support.
_____ 6. A motion made by the defendant, asking the court to dismiss the case.
_____ 7. An order disposing of an action, without trial of the issues.
_____ 8. A claim brought by one defendant against another defendant in the same suit.
_____ 9. The termination of an action that did not adjudicate issues on the merits.
_____ 10. A defense that admits the plaintiff's allegations, but introduces another factor that avoids liability. (Select two answers.)
_____ 11. A motion asking the court to order the other party to remove from a pleading any insufficient defense or any redundant, immaterial, impertinent, or scandalous matter.
_____ 12. A motion by a party, when a pleading is vague, asking the court to order the other party to make a more definite statement.
_____ 13. A pleading used in California by a defendant to file a claim against another defendant, a third party, and the plaintiff in the same action.
_____ 14. A clause in the U.S. Constitution that guarantees to all persons the right to publish and circulate their ideas without governmental interference.
_____ 15. The main pleading filed by the defendant in a lawsuit in response to the plaintiff's complaint.
_____ 16. To annul, make void, or refuse to sustain.
_____ 17. A dismissal in which the plaintiff is barred from bringing another action on the same claim.
_____ 18. The plaintiff's answer to the defendant's counterclaim.
_____ 19. A motion by either party for a judgment, in that party's favor, based solely on information contained in the pleadings.
_____ 20. A clause in the U.S. Constitution that guarantees to all persons the right to freely practice their religion.
_____ 21. disqualify.
_____ 22. A judgment entered on failure of a party to appear or plead at the proper time.
_____ 23. A written or oral request made to a court for certain action to be taken.
_____ 24. A request that a judge disqualify himself or herself from a case because of bias or prejudice.

Sharpening Your Latin Skills

In the space provided, write the definition of each of the following legal terms, referring to the glossary when necessary:

ad damnum _____

ex parte _____

in personam _____

in rem _____

lis pendens _____

nolo contendere _____

quasi in rem _____

Using Legal Language

Read the following story and fill in the blank lines with legal terms taken from the list of terms at the beginning of this chapter:

After reading the allegations in the plaintiff's complaint and determining that they were not vague, the attorney for the defendant decided not to file a motion _____. Similarly, because the complaint contained nothing that was redundant, immaterial, impertinent, or scandalous, the attorney for the defendant did not file a(n) _____. The attorney did, however, file a motion _____ on the ground of _____ (mistake in name) of a party. A(n) _____ is an order disposing of an action without trial of the issues. When the defendant's motion was disallowed by the court, the defendant's attorney filed a(n) _____ within the prescribed time, which contained the _____ defense (called a(n) _____ under the common law) of the statute of frauds. Neither party filed a(n) _____, which may be filed only after the plaintiff's complaint and defendant's answer have been filed and which replaces the older _____. The defendant's attorney also filed a(n) _____ to bring a claim against the plaintiff, which arose out of the same transaction. In answer to this claim, the plaintiff filed a(n) _____. Because the case did not have two defendants, no _____ was filed.

1

PUZZLING OVER WHAT YOU LEARNED

Caveat: Do not allow squares for spaces between words and punctuation (apostrophes, hyphens, etc.) when filling in crossword.

Across

2. A judgment entered on failure of a party to appear or plead at the proper time.
4. A pleading used by the defendant to attack the plaintiff's complaint by raising a point of law.
11. A motion made by the defendant asking the court to dismiss the case.
12. A request that a judge be disqualified from a case because of bias or prejudice.
15. A clause in the U.S. Constitution that guarantees to all persons the right to peaceably associate and assemble with others.
17. Disqualify.
18. To annul, make void, or refuse to sustain.
19. A claim that the defendant has against the plaintiff.

Down

1. The main pleading filed by the defendant in a lawsuit in response to the plaintiff's complaint.
3. A clause in the U.S. Constitution that guarantees to all persons the right to publish and circulate their ideas without government interference.
5. Mistake in name.
6. A pleading used in California by a defendant to file a claim against another defendant, a third party, and the plaintiff in the same action.
7. A clause in the U.S. Constitution that guarantees to all persons the right to speak, both orally and in writing.
8. A claim brought by one defendant against another defendant in the same suit.
9. An immediate decision by the court without going to trial based on the papers filed by the parties.
10. A motion asking the court to order the other party to remove from a pleading any insufficient defense or any redundant, immaterial, impertinent, or scandalous matter.
13. An order disposing of an action without trial of the issues.
14. The termination of an action that did not adjudicate issues on the merits.
16. The plaintiff's answer to the defendant's counterclaim.

Methods of Discovery

ANTE INTERROGATORY

An agreement between the parties to an action regulating any matter relative to the proceedings is a(n) (A) deposition, (B) interrogatory, (C) subpoena, (D) stipulation.

CHAPTER OUTLINE

Bill of Particulars

Interrogatories

Depositions

    Depositions on Oral Examination

    Depositions of Witnesses on Written
      Questions

    Use of Depositions in Court Proceedings

Production of Documents and Things

e-Discovery

Permission to Enter on Land

Physical and Mental Examination

Requests for Admission

KEY TERMS

bill of particulars *(par·TIK·yoo·lars)*

cross questions *(kross KWES·chens)*

demand for bill of particulars *(de·MAND for bill ov par·TIK·yoo·lars)*

deponent *(de·PONE·ent)*

deposition *(dep·e·ZISH·en)*

deposition on oral examination *(eg·zam·in·AY·shun)*

deposition on written questions *(KWES·chens)*

discovery *(dis·KUV·e·ree)*

discovery sanction *(dis·KOV·er·ee SANK·shun)*

e-discovery *(ee·dis·KOV·er·ee)*

electronically stored information (ESI) *(ee·lek·TRON·i·cal·ee stored in·for MAY·shun)*

impeach *(im·PEECH)*

interrogatories *(in·te·RAW·ga·tore·rees)*

metadata *(met·a da·ta)*

motion for order compelling discovery *(com·PEL·ing dis·KUV·e·ree)*

notary public *(NO·te·ree PUB·lik)*

party to a suit *(PAR·tee)*

perjury *(PER·jer·ee)*

recross questions *(RE·kross KWES·chens)*

redirect questions *(re·de·REKT KWES·chens)*

safe harbor provision *(safe HAR·bore pro·VI·zshun)*

stipulate *(STIP·yoo·late)*

stipulation *(stip·yoo·LA·shun)*

subpoena *(suh·PEEN·a)*

subpoena ad testificandum *(suh·PEEN·a ad tes·te·fe·KAN·dem)*

subpoena duces tecum *(suh·PEEN·a DOO·sess TEK·um)*

verbatim *(ver·BATE·im)*

I n the past, it was considered good legal practice for one party to a lawsuit to give the other party as little information as possible about the case before the trial. Today, the opposite is true. Attorneys will often enter into agreements, called stipulations, about different aspects of the case. They may, for example, **stipulate** (agree) to extend the time for pleading, waive objections, admit certain facts, or continue the case to a later date. A **stipulation** is an agreement between the parties to an action regulating any matter relative to the proceedings.

Several methods, called methods of **discovery**, have been established that allow each party to obtain information from the other party and from witnesses about the case before going to trial. In this way, the real issues in the case are exposed early, and much less time is wasted. The most common methods of discovery follow:

1. Bill of particulars
2. Interrogatories
3. Depositions
4. Production of documents and things
5. Permission to enter on land
6. Physical and mental examinations
7. Requests for admission

BILL OF PARTICULARS

In some states, including California, the plaintiff is not required to set forth in the complaint the details of the amount due on a contract for the sale of goods. All that is required by the plaintiff is to set forth the total amount owed. If the defendant files a pleading, called a **demand for bill of particulars**, within a prescribed period (10 days after service of process in California), the plaintiff must deliver to the defendant details of the amount owed in the form of a bill of particulars. A **bill of particulars** is a written statement of the particulars of a complaint, showing the details of the amount owed. In California, the bill of particulars must include a verification if the complaint contains a verification.

INTERROGATORIES

After an action has begun, any **party to a suit** (any plaintiff and any defendant) may ask written questions of any other party to the suit. The written questions are called **interrogatories**. They may be served on any defendant, along with the summons and complaint or at a later time. They may be served on the plaintiff at any time after the action has begun. If not sent along with the summons and complaint, interrogatories are usually served by a copy being mailed to the opposing attorney, and the original copy is filed with the court. Rule 33 of the Federal Rules of Civil Procedure limits the number of interrogatories that may be served on a party to 25. Other states have similar limitations. In Massachusetts, up to 30 interrogatories may be served. Florida also limits interrogatories to 30, unless the court approves a motion for more, on the basis of good cause.

Interrogatories must be answered in writing, and signed by the client answering them under the penalties of **perjury**—that is, the giving of false testimony under oath. Each interrogatory must be answered separately and fully unless it is objected to, in which event the reasons for objection must be stated. The party interrogated has 30 or 45 days, depending on the jurisdiction, to file the answers to the interrogatories with the court and to mail a copy of the answers to the interrogating party. In California, interrogatories and answers to interrogatories are not filed with the court unless the court orders them to be filed.

Rules governing the failure of a party to answer interrogatories vary from state to state. For example, California law provides for the interrogating party to file a motion to compel interrogatories when necessary. Massachusetts law provides that if the party interrogated fails to file the answers within 45 days, the interrogating party may file an application for a request for final judgment (against the defendant) or a request for a dismissal (against the plaintiff), whichever is appropriate. The clerk of court will then notify all parties that a final judgment or a dismissal will be entered unless the answers are filed within 30 days. If 30 days elapse without an answer to the interrogatories being filed, the interrogator may reapply for a final judgment or a dismissal, and it will be allowed by the court if the answers are not, by then, on file.

DEPOSITIONS

An important method of discovery before the trial occurs is the **deposition**, which is the testimony of a witness given under oath, but not in open court. Unlike interrogatories, which may be served only on another party, depositions may be taken of any "person," according to Rules 30 and 31 of the Federal Rules of Civil Procedure. The witness who gives the testimony is known as a **deponent** (one who gives testimony under oath). Two principal types of depositions are (1) depositions on oral examination and (2) depositions of witnesses on written questions.

Depositions on Oral Examination

After an action begins, any party may take the testimony of any person, including a party, by **deposition on oral examination**. In this deposition, lawyers orally examine and cross-examine a witness. With a few exceptions, permission of the court is not required for this deposition. Witnesses may be compelled to attend by **subpoena**, sometimes called a **subpoena ad testificandum** (an order commanding a person to appear and testify in a legal action).

A party desiring to take the deposition must give a prescribed number of days' written notice to every other party to the action. The notice must state the time and place for taking the deposition and the name and address of each person to be examined. A **subpoena duces tecum** is an order commanding a person to appear and bring certain papers or other materials that are pertinent to the legal action. Accountants and record keepers are often subpoenaed this way. If a subpoena duces tecum is to be served on the person to be examined, the materials to be produced must be listed on the notice.

Depositions are taken before a person authorized to administer oaths, such as a **notary public**. Lawyers for each side examine and cross-examine the witnesses. The testimony is taken down by a stenographer, unless the court authorizes some other method of recording it. Usually, the stenographer is also a notary public and performs both functions of administering the oath and taking down the testimony. Instead of participating in the oral examination, parties may, if they wish, submit written questions to be answered by the witness under oath. The questions and answers are taken down **verbatim** (word for word) by the stenographer.

After the testimony is transcribed it is either read or shown to the witness whose testimony it is. Any changes that the witness desires to make are written on the deposition by the officer who administered the oath, with reasons given by the witness for the changes. The deposition is signed by the witness, or a reason is noted for the witness's failure to sign. It is then hand-delivered to the court or mailed to the court by registered or certified mail. Some states no longer require a deposition to be filed with the court.

Depositions of Witnesses on Written Questions

After an action begins, any party may take the testimony of any person, including a party, by **deposition on written questions**. In this type of deposition, lawyers examine and cross-examine a witness who has received in advance written questions to be answered. Witnesses may be compelled to attend, by subpoena. A party desiring to take such a deposition must serve the written questions on all parties to the action, together with the name and address of the person who is to answer them and the name and address of the officer before whom the deposition is to be taken. In some states, after the questions are served, a party may serve **cross questions** (questions asked by a deponent in response to questions asked at a deposition) on any other party. The party receiving the cross questions may serve **redirect questions** (further questions in response to cross questions) on all other parties. In addition, after being served with redirect questions, a party may serve **recross questions** (further questions asked in response to redirect questions) on all other parties.

The depositions of witnesses on written questions are handled by the stenographer and filed with the court in the same manner that depositions on oral examinations are handled, as explained earlier.

Use of Depositions in Court Proceedings

When the case goes to court, the depositions may be used to contradict or **impeach** (call in to question or cast doubt on) any contrary testimony of a witness. The deposition may also be used at the trial if the witness is dead; the witness is at a distance greater than 100 miles from the place of the trial; the witness is unable to testify because of age, sickness, infirmity, or imprisonment; or if other exceptional circumstances make it desirable that the deposition be used.

TERMS IN ACTION

In 1961, Marie Robertson gave a $35-million-dollar gift to Princeton University, which was set up as a foundation meant to support the Woodrow Wilson School of Public and International Affairs. In 2002, Mrs. Robertson's son and daughter sued Princeton, alleging mismanagement and fraud, and seeking to obtain control over the funds, which by then had grown to over $500 million. The lawsuit was the most expensive in Princeton's history, largely due to the extensive **discovery** in the case. By 2004, the plaintiffs had deposed close to 40 witnesses and were scheduled to depose 20 more. Thousands of **document examinations** took place in preparation of the depositions, some of which lasted many hours. One **deposition**, of a former Princeton administrator who graduated from Princeton in 1940, took over six days. The lawsuit eventually settled in 2008. Princeton retained control over the foundation, but part of the settlement included Princeton's paying to the plaintiffs over $40 million in legal costs incurred during the six-year litigation.

Source: dailyprincetonian.com; nj.com

PRODUCTION OF DOCUMENTS AND THINGS

Any party may serve on any other party a request for permission to inspect and copy documents (including writings, drawings, graphs, charts, photographs, and other data compilations) or to inspect and copy, test, or sample any tangible things.

The party on whom the request is made must serve a written response, within a prescribed number of days after the service of the request, stating that the request will be permitted or that it is objected to, with reasons given for any objection. If an objection occurs, the party submitting the request may make a **motion for order compelling discovery**. After a hearing, the court may allow or disallow the motion.

E-DISCOVERY

Parties may also obtain discovery of electronic communications or other information stored electronically rather than on paper. This form of discovery, known as **e-discovery**, has grown dramatically as more and more data are exclusively created and stored electronically, such as e-mail, text messages, or other forms of social media like Facebook.com. This type of information is often referred to as ESI (**electronically stored information**).

In 2006, the Federal Rules of Civil Procedure were amended to reflect the growth of e-discovery. The changes included a definition of ESI and the acknowledgment that ESI is discoverable. When documents are created on a computer, another form of data is created "underneath" the document. This information is about the creation of the document or file, and is called **metadata**. For example, as this textbook was being written on word processing software, information on the documents was being invisibly stored, including the dates the files were accessed, whose computers were being used, and the various changes made to the files before they were saved as final drafts. Metadata are akin to an electronic fingerprint, and they are discoverable.

Costs are a new concern for e-discovery. Traditionally, a party pays the costs of responding to the other side's discovery requests, which is expensive in and of itself. But the costs of finding and retrieving all the thousands—and sometimes, millions—of electronic data can be exorbitant. Therefore, Rule 26 of the Federal Rules of Civil Procedure now allows a party who is asked to produce ESI to shift the costs of production to the requesting party, where the ESI being sought is not readily accessible. And Rule 37(f) was amended to create a **safe harbor provision**, which protects a party from **discovery sanctions** (court-ordered penalties for failing to produce evidence) when a party cannot produce ESI because it was lost due to the routine good-faith operations of an electronic information system.

Web Wise

In the advent of e-discovery rules' becoming more common, websites and web log (blogs) have been created to inform the legal community about recent changes to e-discovery rules, or to provide cases dealing with e-discovery controversies. Following are a few websites and blogs that focus on e-discovery:

www.ediscoverylaw.com

www.discoveryresources.org

www.ediscoverynavigator.com

TERMS IN ACTION

It can be confusing to know whether **electronic communications** are subject to **e-discovery** or instead are protected by a privilege. A California appellate court ruled in 2011 that an e-mail sent by a client to his lawyer was not protected by the attorney–client privilege, and was discoverable, because the client sent the e-mail from his work e-mail account. In that case, the court found that the employee had no reasonable expectation of privacy in such an e-mail. But, in 2010, the New Jersey Supreme Court reached a nearly opposite conclusion in a similar case. In both cases, the plaintiffs were suing their employers and both employees had sent e-mails to their personal attorneys. One difference between the two cases was that in the California case, the employee sent the personal e-mail through his work e-mail account, whereas in the New Jersey case, the employee sent her e-mail by way of her work computer, but through her personal password-protected G-mail account, an e-mail service available on Google.com.

Source: wired.com; *Stengart v. Loving Care Agency, Inc.*, 990 A.2nd 651 (2010)

Word Wise
Time Prefixes

Prefix	Meaning	Examples
re-	again	reapply, rediscover, reorganization, rebuttal, recross questions, redirect questions, republish
post-	after	postpone, postgraduate, postmortem
pre-	before	preadolescence, prearrange, predecease, premarital, premeditated, prenuptial

PERMISSION TO ENTER ON LAND

Any party may serve on any other party a request to permit entry on land or other property in the possession or control of the party on whom the request is served. The entry may be for the purpose of inspecting, measuring, surveying, photographing, testing, or sampling the property. The party to whom the request is made must respond in the manner described in the section titled "Production of Documents and Things."

PHYSICAL AND MENTAL EXAMINATIONS

When the mental or physical condition of a party is in controversy, the court in which the action is pending may order the party to submit to a physical or mental examination. The order may be made only on motion for good cause and after notice is given to the person to be examined.

REQUESTS FOR ADMISSION

A party may serve on any other party a written request for admission of the truth of any matter that is relevant to the case. The request may relate to statements, opinions of fact or law, or the genuineness of documents.

The party to whom the request is directed must file a written answer within a prescribed number of days after service of the request. The answer must state, under the penalties of perjury, (1) a denial of the matter; (2) a reason that the answering party cannot truthfully admit or deny the matter; or (3) an objection, with reasons, to the request. If such an answer is not filed, the matter is considered by the court to be admitted.

Reviewing What You Learned

After studying the chapter, write the answers to each of the following questions:

1. How do methods of discovery used in the past compare with those of today?

   _____

   _____

   _____

   _____

2. List the seven most common methods of discovery.

   _____

   _____

   _____

3. To whom may interrogatories be asked?

   _____

   _____

   _____

4. Who signs the answers to the interrogatories?

   _____

   _____

   _____

5. What are the differences between a deposition and an interrogatory?

   _____

   _____

   _____

6. Depositions are taken before whom? The testimony is taken down by whom?

   _____

   _____

   _____

7. What occurs after the testimony of a deposition is transcribed?

   _____

   _____

   _____

8. Describe the back-and-forth questioning procedure that occurs when a deposition on written questions occurs.

   _____

   _____

   _____

9. Under what circumstances may depositions be used in court?

_____

_____

_____

_____

10. How must a party who is requested to produce documents respond to such request?

_____

_____

_____

11. For what purposes may a person request permission to enter on land of another?

_____

_____

_____

_____

12. Under what circumstances may the court order a party to submit to a physical or mental examination?

_____

_____

_____

_____

13. How must a party who is requested to admit a particular matter respond?

_____

_____

_____

_____

_____

14. What types of information or data are part of the e-discovery world?

_____

_____

_____

_____

15. How have the discovery rules changed to accommodate e-discovery?

_____

_____

_____

_____

_____

16. What are metadata and who creates them?

_____

_____

_____

_____

Understanding Legal Concepts

Indicate whether each statement is true or false. Then, change the italicized word or phrase of each false statement to make it true.

ANSWERS

_____ 1. Attorneys *never* enter into agreements about different aspects of a case.

_____ 2. After an action has begun, any *party to a suit* may ask written questions of any other party to a suit.

_____ 3. Interrogatories must be answered in writing and signed by the *attorney* answering them, under the penalties of perjury.

_____ 4. A deposition is the testimony of a witness given under oath *in open court.*

_____ 5. For a subpoena duces tecum properly to be served on a person to be examined, the materials to be produced *must be* listed on the notice.

_____ 6. When depositions are taken, lawyers for each side *examine and cross-examine* the witnesses.

_____ 7. A deposition of a witness *must not be* used at a trial if the witness is dead.

_____ 8. Any party may serve on *any other party* a request to permit entry on the other's land.

_____ 9. The court may order a party to submit to a physical, *but not* a mental, examination.

_____ 10. If a party to whom a request for admission is directed fails to answer, the matter is considered by the court to be *admitted.*

Checking Terminology

From the list of legal terms that follows, select the one that matches each definition.

ANSWERS

a. bill of particulars
b. cross questions
c. demand for bill of particulars
d. deponent
e. deposition
f. deposition on oral examination
g. deposition on written questions
h. discovery
i. discovery sanction
j. e-discovery
k. electronically stored information (ESI)
l. impeach
m. interrogatories
n. metadata
o. motion for order compelling discovery
p. notary public
q. party to a suit
r. perjury
s. recross questions
t. redirect questions
u. safe harbor provision
v. stipulate
w. stipulation
x. subpoena
y. subpoena ad testificandum
z. subpoena duces tecum
aa. verbatim

_____ 1. A person or organization participating or having a direct interest in a legal proceeding.
_____ 2. Methods that allow each party to obtain information from the other party and from witnesses about a case before going to court.
_____ 3. A form of discovery, in a civil action, in which parties are given a series of written questions to be answered under oath.
_____ 4. The testimony of a witness given under oath, but not in open court, and later reduced to writing.
_____ 5. An order commanding a person to appear and testify in a legal action. (Select two answers.)
_____ 6. An order commanding a person to appear and bring certain papers or other materials that are pertinent to a legal action.
_____ 7. A person authorized to administer oaths, attest to and certify documents, take acknowledgments, and perform other official acts.
_____ 8. The giving of false testimony under oath.
_____ 9. One who gives testimony under oath.
_____ 10. An agreement between the parties to an action regulating any matter relative to the proceedings.
_____ 11. Call into question.
_____ 12. Questions asked by a deponent in response to questions asked at a deposition.
_____ 13. Further questions asked by a deponent in response to redirect questions.
_____ 14. A deposition in which lawyers examine and cross-examine a witness who has received, in advance, written questions to be answered.
_____ 15. A written statement of the particulars of a complaint, showing the details of the amount owed.
_____ 16. Protection of a party from discovery sanctions when a party cannot produce ESI because it was lost due to routine operations.
_____ 17. Court-ordered penalties for failing to produce evidence.
_____ 18. A motion asking the court to order the other party to produce certain writings, photographs, or other requested items.
_____ 19. Discovery of electronic communication stored electronically rather than on paper.
_____ 20. **To** agree.
_____ 21. Word for word.
_____ 22. Electronic fingerprints, which are information about the creation of an electronic document or file.

Using Legal Language

Read the following story and fill in the blank lines with legal terms taken from the list of terms at the beginning of this chapter:

Before going to trial, attorney Mary Grey entered into an agreement, called a(n) _____, with the opposing attorney, admitting certain facts. She also used certain methods of _____ to obtain information from the other party and from witnesses about the case. She sent 30 questions, called _____, to be answered under oath by Conrad Allen, the defendant, who was a(n) _____ to the suit. She also sent a(n) _____, rather than a plain _____, to Leroy Henning, a witness, commanding him to bring with him certain payroll records of the defendant to a(n) _____, which is the testimony of a witness given under oath, but not in open court. Because written questions were submitted in advance to Leroy, the _____, this was known as a(n) _____. After receiving the questions, Leroy sent _____ to be answered by the plaintiff. The plaintiff, in turn, responded with further questions, called _____ to be answered by Leroy. The testimony was taken before a(n) _____, who was authorized to administer oaths, and written down _____ —that is, word for word—by a stenographer. When the case goes to court, the questions and answers may be used to _____ —that is, call into question— Leroy's testimony. If Leroy gives false testimony, it is known as _____

1

PUZZLING OVER WHAT YOU LEARNED

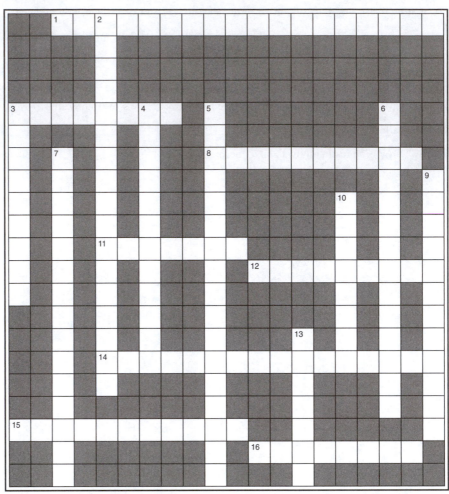

Caveat: Do **not** allow squares for spaces between words and punctuation (apostrophes, hyphens, etc.) when filling in crossword.

Across

1. An order commanding a person to appear and bring certain papers or other materials that are pertinent to a legal action.
3. An order commanding a person to appear and testify in a legal action.
8. The testimony of a witness, given under oath but not in open court, and later reduced to writing.
11. Call in to question.
12. Methods that allow each party to obtain information from the other party and from witnesses about a case before going to court.
14. Further questions asked by a deponent in response to redirect questions.
15. An agreement between the parties to an action regulating any matter relative to the proceedings.
16. Word for word.

Down

2. A written statement of the particulars of a complaint showing the details of the amount owed.
3. Agree.
4. A person authorized to administer oaths, attest to and certify documents, take acknowledgments, and perform other official acts.
5. Further questions asked by an examiner at a deposition in response to cross questions.
6. Questions asked by a deponent in response to questions asked at a deposition.
7. A form of discovery in a civil action in which parties are given a series of written questions to be answered under oath.
9. A person or organization participating or having a direct interest in a legal proceeding.
10. One who gives testimony under oath.
13. The giving of false testimony under oath.

Pretrial Hearing
and Jury Trial

ANTE INTERROGATORY

The examination of jurors by the court to see that they stand indifferent and have no biases against any of the parties is referred to as the (A) venire, (B) voir dire, (C) array, or (D) venue.

CHAPTER OUTLINE

Pretrial Hearing

Right to Jury Trial
    Selecting the Venire

Impaneling the Jury

Examination and Challenge of Jurors

KEY TERMS

alderpeople *(AL·der·pee·pel)*

alternate jurors *(AL·ter·net JOOR·ors)*

array *(a·RAY)*

bench trial *(tryl)*

capital criminal case *(KAP·i·tel KRIM·i·nel kase)*

challenge *(CHAL·enj)*

challenge for cause *(CHAL·enj for kaws)*

challenge to the array *(CHAL·enj to the a·RAY)*

foreperson *(FORE·per·son)*

impaneled *(im·PAN·eld)*

indifferent *(in·DIF·rent)*

jurors *(JOOR·ors)*

jury *(JOOR·ee)*

jury panel *(JOOR·ee PAN·el)*

jury pool *(JOOR·ee pool)*

jury waived trial *(JOOR·ee waved tryl)*

master *(MAS·ter)*

motion in limine *(MOH·shun in LIM·e·nee)*

motion to quash the array *(MOH·shun to kwash the a·RAY)*

one day–one trial jury system *(JOOR·ee SYS·tem)*

peremptory challenges *(per·EMP·ter·ee CHAL·en·jes)*

petit jury *(PET·ee JOOR·ee)*

pretrial (or pre-trial) hearing *(PRE·tryl HEER·ing)*

selectpeople *(sel·EKT·pee·pel)*

talesmen *(TAILZ·men)*

taleswomen *(tailz·WO·men)*

venire *(ven·EYE·ree)*

voir dire *(vwar deer)*

writ of venire facias *(ven·EYE·ree FAY·shes)*

PRETRIAL HEARING

Before a trial is held in the superior court, a **pretrial hearing** usually occurs. This hearing is for the purpose of speeding up the trial. Only the attorneys for each side are required to attend the hearing, but many attorneys like to bring their clients to have them available for questions that may arise. The attorneys appear before the judge to consider the possibility of doing any of the following:

1. simplify the issues
2. amend the pleadings
3. obtain admissions of fact
4. limit the number of expert witnesses
5. refer the case to a master[1]
6. settle the case
7. agree on damages
8. discuss other matters that may aid in the disposition of the action

Attorneys may make a variety of motions to the court during the pretrial hearing stage. A **motion in limine** is a pretrial motion asking the court to prohibit the introduction of prejudicial evidence by the other party. A report of the pretrial hearing becomes a part of the record of the case and may be read to the jury at the trial.

RIGHT TO JURY TRIAL

The right to a trial by jury in all criminal cases, and in civil cases involving more than $20, is found in Article III and the Sixth and Seventh Amendments of the U.S. Constitution. Under the Rules of Civil Procedure, any party may make a demand for a jury trial on the other party no later than 10 days after the service of the last pleading. If a jury trial is not requested, a trial without a jury, called a **jury waived trial** or **bench trial**, will usually be held.

A **jury** (from the Latin *jurare,* meaning "to swear") is a group of people, called **jurors**, selected according to law and sworn to determine the facts in a case. The ordinary jury of 12 people used for the trial of a civil or criminal action is known as a **petit jury** to distinguish it from a grand jury, which issues indictments. The system of selecting the jury varies from state to state. One system is described here.

Selecting the Venire

The **jury pool**, or large group of people from which juries are selected, is called the **jury panel** or the **venire**. Sometimes, it is referred to as the **array**. The selection of the venire has changed in recent years. Many jurisdictions have done away with the traditional method and replaced it with the "one day–one trial" system. Both methods are described here.

TRADITIONAL METHOD.   Under the traditional method of selecting jurors, each city and town is required to prepare a list each year of everyone of good moral character who is eligible to serve on a jury. Each name on the list is placed on a separate ballot and kept in a ballot box by the city or town clerk. Before each sitting of the court (a sitting lasts one month), the clerk of court sends a **writ of venire facias** to each city and town within the court's jurisdiction. This writ orders the city or town to provide a designated number of jurors for the next sitting of the court. Jurors' names are then drawn from the ballot box by the mayor and alderpeople of a city and by the selectpeople of a town. **Alderpeople** are men and women elected to serve as members of the legislative body of a city. **Selectpeople** are men and women elected to serve as the chief administrative authority of a town. Jurors whose names are drawn by the cities and towns are summoned to appear before the court for jury duty for a month.

---

[1]A **master** is a lawyer appointed by the court to hear testimony in the case and to report back to the court his or her findings or conclusions.

Under this traditional method of selecting the venire, members of the clergy, lawyers, practicing physicians and surgeons, nurses, public school teachers, and certain other people are exempt from jury duty. Persons 70 years of age or older and parents who are responsible for the daily care of a child under the age of 15 may elect to be exempt from jury duty if they so choose. The judge may exempt others from jury duty if it is best for the public interest or if such duty will impose an undue hardship on the person selected. In addition, no person who would be embarrassed by hearing the testimony or by discussing the case in the jury room is required to serve as a juror on sexually related cases.

ONE DAY–ONE TRIAL METHOD.   Another method of jury selection is coming into wider use. Called the **one day–one trial jury system**, it is designed to provide the courts with juries consisting of fair cross sections of the community and to reduce the burden of jury duty on certain classes of citizens.

The system varies from state to state. Under the Massachusetts system, a new group of jurors appears in the jury pool (venire) each day. Jurors who are not selected for a trial on that day are excused from further duty and cannot be called again for three years. Jurors who are selected for a trial serve only for that trial and no longer.

Under this system, there are no exemptions from jury duty. Generally, every citizen 18 years old or older who can speak and understand the English language and is physically fit must serve. Citizens 70 years old or older may choose not to serve. To be eligible to serve, persons must have been a resident or inhabitant for six months or more in the county in which they are summoned. Jurors are selected randomly by computer from an annual census list provided by the cities and towns. Each juror, when summoned, is entitled to one postponement of up to one year from the date summoned. This postponement allows a juror to choose a more convenient date if the assigned date is not suitable. Each juror, when summoned, may request a transfer of courthouse location if the juror encounters a hardship in reporting to the assigned location.

Word Wise
"People" Rather than "Men"

The use of "man" or "men" as a generic term was found to be obsolete in 1971 by both the National Council for Teachers of English and the *Oxford English Dictionary.* Use of the term "people" in this chapter, such as *alderpeople* and *selectpeople,* reflects this shift.

Alternatives to the generic terms "man" and "men" include person, people, human being(s), civilization, society, individual(s), somebody, someone, anyone, all of us, everyone, humankind, humanity, the public, citizen(s), worker(s), member(s) and women and men.

Under this particular state's system, jurors must be compensated by their employers for the first three days of jury duty at their normal rate of pay and by the county after that at a rate of $50 per day.

IMPANELING THE JURY

On the day the jurors are summoned to court, the clerk of court places each juror's name on a ballot and puts it in a ballot box. When a case is ready for trial, the members of the venire are brought into open court. Twelve of their names are picked out of the ballot box, and those chosen take seats in the jury box. In some states, if the case is expected to be lengthy, 14 or 16 jurors are **impaneled** (enrolled) to hear the case instead of 12, but before deliberations begin, the jury is reduced (by lot) to 12 members who decide the case. Those who are removed are retained as **alternate jurors** (additional jurors impaneled in case of sickness or removal of any of the 12 who are deliberating). In some states, including California, alternate jurors are chosen separately from regular jurors at the beginning of the trial and designated as such. The plaintiff and defendant may stipulate that the jury shall consist of any number less than 12 if they wish to do so.

In some states, the judge chooses one of the members of the jury to be the **foreperson** (the presiding member of a jury who speaks for the group). In other states, the foreperson is elected by members of the jury.

If at least seven jurors have been chosen for a case, but not enough jurors are left on the venire to make up a complete jury, the judge has the power to send the sheriff out onto the street to obtain bystanders or people from the county at large to serve on the jury. Jurors who are chosen this way are called **talesmen** and **taleswomen**.

TERMS IN ACTION

In 1991, one of Senator Ted Kennedy's nephews, William Kennedy Smith, was accused of raping a woman late in the evening of Good Friday on the beach at the Kennedy family estate in Palm Beach, Florida. William Kennedy Smith is the son of Jean Kennedy Smith and is a medical doctor. According to the prosecution, William, Senator Kennedy, and the Senator's son Patrick went to a Palm Beach nightclub. There, William met Patricia Bowman, who went back with the men to the Kennedy estate. William claimed that the sex was consensual and not rape, and the trial was broadcast on national television. The defense team, led by renowned lawyer Roy Black (whose clients include West Palm Beach resident and radio talk show host Rush Limbaugh), used jury consultants before and during **voir dire** to help pick the six-member **jury**. Choosing the jury of four women and two men took almost four weeks. The defense succeeded in its **motion in limine** to exclude from the trial the testimony of three women whom the prosecution planned on calling to testify that William had sexually assaulted them also. After a 10-day trial, the jury **deliberated** for 77 minutes and returned a "not guilty" verdict on December 11, 1991. One of the **jurors**, Lisa Heller, later began dating Roy Black, and they were married in 1994.

Source: ABA Journal; washingtonpost.com; people.com; trutv.com

---

EXAMINATION AND CHALLENGE OF JURORS

Members of the jury must stand indifferent—that is, they must have a neutral, or unbiased, opinion before the trial begins. To establish such indifference, the jurors are examined under oath. This examination is called the **voir dire**, an expression meaning "to speak the truth." In law in the Anglo–Norman language, however, it means "an oath to say what is true." During voir dire, the court attempts to determine whether any of the jurors

1. are related to either party or either attorney;
2. have any interest in the case;
3. have expressed or formed an opinion about it;
4. are aware of any bias or prejudice that they may have in the case; or
5. know of any reason that they do not stand indifferent.

Any juror who does not stand indifferent is replaced (by lot) by another juror from the venire.

An attorney from either side may **challenge** (call or put into question) any member of the jury and ask the court to have him or her removed from the jury. A **challenge to the array**, sometimes called a **motion to quash the array**, is a challenge to the entire jury because of some irregularity in the selection of the jury. If allowed by the court, the entire jury must step down and a new jury is selected. **Challenges for cause** are challenges to individual jurors when it is believed that a juror does not stand **indifferent**—that is, impartial, unbiased, and disinterested. No limit exists to the number of challenges for cause that may be made. **Peremptory challenges** are challenges for which no reason need be given. State law varies as to the number of peremptory challenges allowed. In a **capital criminal case** (one in which the death penalty may be inflicted) in Massachusetts, each side is entitled to as many peremptory challenges as there are jurors. In a noncapital criminal case and in a civil case, each side is entitled to four peremptory challenges, and an additional one if 14 jurors are selected, or two additional challenges if 16 jurors are selected.

In 1986, the U.S. Supreme Court held, in *Batson v. Kentucky*, that peremptory challenges based on race are unconstitutional. Today, lawyers who argue that a peremptory challenge was granted for unlawfully discriminatory reasons are said to make a "Batson challenge."

TERMS IN ACTION

In 1986, the U.S. Supreme Court ruled, in *Batson v. Kentucky*, 476 U.S. 79, that it was unconstitutional to use **peremptory challenges** on four black members of the **jury venire**, because attempting to eliminate the possibility of having any black jurors in order to get an all-white jury was a form of racial discrimination. And in 2008, the Court confirmed that doctrine in *Snyder v. Louisiana*, 552 U.S. 472. In that case, the prosecuting attorney in a death penalty case against a black defendant used a peremptory challenge on a black member of the venire, arguing in part that the juror appeared nervous and had too busy a schedule to serve. But the Supreme Court concluded that the trial judge erred in granting the peremptory challenge, because other white jurors weren't subject to the same nervousness analysis nor removed because of similar busy schedules.

Source: oyez.org

Web Wise

Since *anyone* can publish *anything* on the Web, here are **5 W's** to ask whenever you consider the information you find there:

   Who created the site?
      Does the author have suitable credentials?
      Is the "author" an organization or association?
   What type of site is it?
      .edu = educational
      .com = commercial
      .org = organization
      .gov = government
      .net = network/utilities
      .mil = military
   When was the site created or updated?
      Is the site being maintained, or has it been abandoned?
   Where can you find more information?
      Are sources documented with footnotes or links?
   Why was this site created?
      To sell, entice?
      To inform, give facts and data?
      To persuade?
      To advocate a point of view?

Reviewing What You Learned

After studying the chapter, write the answers to each of the following questions:

1. Who may demand a jury trial?

   _____

   _____

   _____

   _____

   _____

2. What is the purpose of a pretrial hearing?

   _____

   _____

   _____

   _____

   _____

3. Under the traditional method of selecting a jury, who is exempt from jury duty? How long do jurors serve?

   _____

   _____

   _____

   _____

   _____

4. Under the one day–one trial system of jury selection, who is exempt from jury duty? How long do jurors serve?

   _____

   _____

   _____

   _____

5. Describe the method that is used to impanel a jury in a particular trial.

   _____

   _____

   _____

   _____

6. Under what circumstances may more than 12 jurors hear a case? How many jurors ultimately decide such a case?

   _____

   _____

   _____

   _____

   _____

7. In what two ways may jury forepersons be selected?

   _____

   _____

   _____

   _____

8. Under what circumstances may the judge send the sheriff out into the street to obtain jurors?

   _____

   _____

   _____

   _____

9. List two of the five points that would cause a juror not to stand indifferent.

   _____

   _____

   _____

   _____

   _____

   _____

10. How many challenges for cause may be made?

   _____

   _____

   _____

   _____

   _____

11. In Massachusetts, how many peremptory challenges may be made in a capital criminal case? How many in a noncapital criminal case or a civil case?

   _____

   _____

   _____

   _____

   _____

Understanding Legal Concepts

Indicate whether each statement is true or false. Then, change the italicized word or phrase of each false statement to make it true.

ANSWERS

_____ 1. The ordinary jury of 12 people used for the trial of a civil or criminal action is known as a *petit* jury.

_____ 2. A pretrial hearing is held for the purpose of *delaying* the trial as much as possible.

_____ 3. When a writ of venire facias is sent to a city, the mayor and alderpeople *personally choose* the names of people for jury duty.

_____ 4. Under the traditional method of selecting the venire, *members of the clergy and lawyers* are exempt from jury duty.

_____ 5. Under the one day–one trial system of jury selection, practicing physicians and surgeons, nurses, and public school teachers *are exempt* from jury duty.

_____ 6. Under the U.S. Constitution, peremptory challenges *may* be based on race.

_____ 7. When a case is ready for trial, the names of 12 members of the venire are *picked out of a ballot box* to serve on the jury.

_____ 8. If at least seven jurors have been chosen for a case, but not enough jurors are left on the venire to make up a complete jury, the judge *may* send the sheriff out onto the street and obtain bystanders to serve on the jury.

_____ 9. Members of the jury *must* stand indifferent.

_____ 10. When jurors are challenged, a limit exists to the number of *challenges for cause* that may be made.

Checking Terminology

From the list of legal terms that follows, select the one that matches each definition:

a. alderpeople
b. alternate jurors
c. array
d. bench trial
e. capital criminal case
f. challenge
g. challenge for cause
h. challenge to the array
i. foreperson
j. impaneled
k. indifferent
l. jurors
m. jury
n. jury panel
o. jury pool
p. jury waived trial
q. master
r. motion in limine
s. motion to quash the array
t. one day–one trial jury system
u. peremptory challenge
v. petit jury
w. pretrial hearing
x. selectpeople
y. talesmen and taleswomen
z. venire
aa. voir dire
bb. writ of venire facias

ANSWERS

_____ 1. A case in which the death penalty may be inflicted.

_____ 2. The presiding member of a jury who speaks for the group.

_____ 3. Members of a jury.

_____ 4. A challenge of a juror for which no reason need be given.

_____ 5. A challenge to the entire jury because of some irregularity in the selection of the jury. (Select two answers.)

_____ 6. Bystanders or people from the county at large chosen by the court to act as jurors when there are not enough people left on the venire.

_____ 7. The large group of people from which a jury is selected for a trial. (Select four answers.)

_____ 8. A system designed to provide the courts with juries consisting of fair cross sections of the community and to reduce the burden of jury duty on certain classes of citizens.

_____ 9. listed as members of the jury.

_____ 10. People elected to serve as members of the legislative body of a city.

_____ 11. A written order to cities and towns to provide a designated number of jurors for the next sitting of the court.

_____ 12. A challenge of a juror made when it is believed that the juror does not stand indifferent.

_____ 13. Impartial, unbiased, and disinterested.

_____ 14. The ordinary jury of 6 or 12 people used for the trial of a civil or criminal action.

_____ 15. Additional jurors impaneled in case of sickness or removal of any of the regular jurors who are deliberating.

_____ 16. To speak the truth. The examination of jurors by the court to see that they stand indifferent.

_____ 17. A trial without a jury. (Select two answers.)

_____ 18. A group of people selected according to law and sworn to determine the facts in a case.

_____ 19. A lawyer appointed by the court to hear testimony in a case and report back to the court his or her findings or conclusions.

_____ 20. A pretrial motion asking the court to prohibit the introduction of prejudicial evidence by the other party.

Using Legal Language

Read the following story and fill in the blank lines with legal terms taken from the list of terms at the beginning of this chapter:

The plaintiff's attorney, Mary Grey, attended a(n) _____ before the judge, prior to the trial, in an attempt to speed up the trial. Mary wanted a jury trial instead of referring the case to a(n) _____ —that is, a lawyer appointed by the court to hear testimony. In addition, she did not want a(n) _____ _____ or a(n) _____ _____, which is a trial without a jury. The clerk of court sent a(n) _____ to each city and town within the court's jurisdiction to obtain jurors for the next sitting of the court. When the trial began, jurors were selected by lot from the _____ (the jury pool), and after the _____ was held to be sure that they

stood _____, 14 jurors were _____ to hear the case. The number included two _____ who would be used in case of sickness or removal of any of the regular jurors. No _____ for cause existed, but several _____ did, which required no reason to be given. The lawyers did not wish to stipulate to a lesser number of jurors, and no need to obtain _____ existed—that is, bystanders or people from the county at large selected to serve on the jury. This trial was not a(n) _____, because it did not involve the death penalty. A woman was chosen to be the _____, who would speak for the group.

PUZZLING OVER WHAT YOU LEARNED

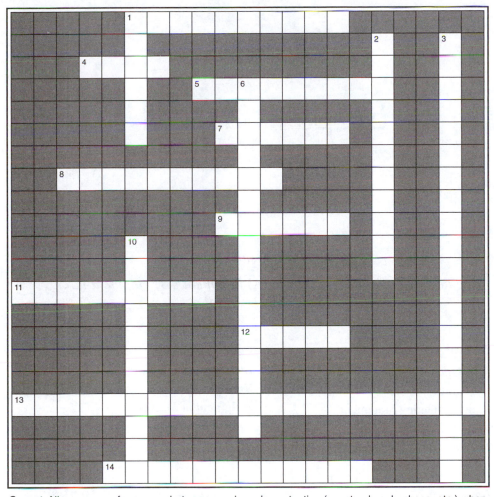

Caveat: Allow squares for spaces between words and punctuation (apostrophes, hyphens, etc.) when filling in crossword.

Across

1. Large group of people from which a jury is selected for a trial.
4. Group of people sworn to determine the facts in a case.
5. Listed as members of the jury.
7. Jury pool.
8. Ordinary jury of twelve people used for a trial.
9. Lawyer appointed by the court to hear testimony and report findings to the court.
11. Examination of jurors by the court to see that they stand indifferent.
12. Another name for venire.
13. Written order to cities and towns to provide jurors for the next court sitting.
14. People elected to serve as chief administrative authority of a town.

Down

1. Members of a jury.
2. Impartial, unbiased, and disinterested.
3. Challenges of jurors when it is believed they do not stand indifferent.
6. A hearing before the judge prior to a trial.
10. People elected to serve as members of the legislative body of a city.

Steps in a Trial

ANTE INTERROGATORY

The decision of a jury is called a (A) judgment, (B) judgment n.o.v.,
(C) decree, (D) verdict.

Chapter Outline

Plaintiff's Opening Statement
Plaintiff's Case in Chief
Defendant's Opening Statement
Defendant's Case in Chief
Requests for Instructions to Jury

Final Arguments
Instructions to Jury
Verdict
Judgment or Decree
Appeal

Key Terms

adjudicating *(a·JOO·di·kay·ting)*
adjudication *(a·joo·di·KAY·shun)*
admissible evidence *(ad·MISS·e·bel*
  EV·i·dens)
affirm *(a·FERM)*
appeal *(a·PEEL)*
appeal bond
appellant *(a·PEL·ent)*
appellee *(a·pel·EE)*
case in chief *(Cheef)*
circumstantial evidence *(ser·kum·STAN·shel*
  EV·i·dens)
closing argument *(AR·gyoo·ment)*
consent decree *(kon·SENT de·KREE)*
court of equity *(EK·wi·tee)*
cross-examination *(kross·eg·zam·in·AY·shun)*
decree *(de·KREE)*

defendant in error *(de·FEN·dent in ERR·er)*
deliberate *(dee·LIB·e·rate)*
direct evidence *(de·REKT EV·i·dens)*
direct examination *(de·REKT*
  eg·zam·in·AY·shun)
DNA
DNA sample
documentary evidence *(dok·u·MENT·ta·ree*
  EV·i·dens)
equity *(EK·wi·tee)*
exhibit *(eg·ZIB·it)*
hung jury *(JOOR·ee)*
injunction *(in·JUNK·shun)*
judgment *(JUJ·ment)*
judgment notwithstanding the verdict
  (VER·dikt)
judgment n.o.v. (or jnov)
judgment on the merits *(MER·its)*

judgment on the pleadings *(PLEED·ings)*

jury charge *(JOOR·ee charj)*

leading questions *(LEE·ding)*

mistrial *(MIS·tryl)*

motion for a directed verdict *(de·REK·ted VER·dikt)*

non obstante verdicto *(non ob·STAN·tee ver·DIK·toh)*

opening statement *(O·pen·ing STATE·ment)*

polling the jury *(POLE·ing)*

preliminary injunction *(pre·LIM·i·ner·ee in·JUNK·shun)*

prima facie case *(PRY·mah FAY·shee)*

questions of fact *(KWES·chens)*

questions of law

real evidence *(reel EV·i·dens)*

rebuttal *(re·BUT·el)*

relevant evidence *(REL·e·vent EV·i·dens)*

remand *(re·MAND)*

respondent *(re·SPON·dent)*

reverse *(re·VERSE)*

ripe for judgment *(JUJ·ment)*

sequester *(see·KWEST·er)*

set aside *(a·SIDE)*

summation *(sum·AY·shun)*

testimonial evidence *(tes·ti·MOH·nee·el EV·i·dens)*

vacate *(VA·kate)*

verdict *(VER·dikt)*

verdict contrary to law *(KON·trare·ee)*

> ### Steps in a Jury Trial
>
> 1. Plaintiff's opening statement
> 2. Plaintiff's case in chief
> 3. Defendant's opening statement
> 4. Defendant's case in chief
> 5. Requests for instructions to the jury
> 6. Final arguments (summation)
> 7. Instructions to the jury (jury charge)
> 8. Jury's verdict
> 9. Court's judgment or decree
> 10. Appeal
> 11. Execution, in civil cases
> 12. Sentencing, in criminal cases

PLAINTIFF'S OPENING STATEMENT

After the jury is impaneled, the plaintiff's attorney makes an **opening statement**. The attorney outlines the case by telling the jury (the judge, in a nonjury trial) what the evidence will prove. The opening statement must set forth a **prima facie case**—that is, the statement must be legally sufficient as proof of the case unless it is rebutted by contrary evidence.

PLAINTIFF'S CASE IN CHIEF

Next, the plaintiff's attorney puts in the **case in chief**—that is, he or she introduces evidence to prove the allegations that were made in the pleadings and in the opening statement. Evidence that is pertinent and proper to be considered in reaching a decision, according to specific rules, is known as **admissible evidence**. Evidence tending to prove or disprove an alleged fact is termed as **relevant evidence**. Evidence is classified as testimonial, documentary, or real. **Testimonial evidence** consists of oral testimony of witnesses made under oath in open court. **Documentary evidence** consists of such evidence as written contracts, business records, correspondence, wills, and deeds. **Real evidence** consists of actual objects that have a bearing on the case, such as an item of clothing, a weapon found at the scene of the crime, a photograph, a chart, a model, fingerprints, or **DNA** (deoxyribonucleic acid)—the double strand of molecules that carries a cell's unique genetic code. A **DNA sample** is biological evidence of any nature that is utilized to conduct DNA analysis. Tangible items that are introduced as evidence are referred to as **exhibits**.

When a witness testifies as to something that he or she observed, such as "I saw that man shoot the gun," it is called **direct evidence** because the testimony directly relates to the fact in issue. (Did that man shoot the gun?) When the testimony relates to some fact other than the fact in issue, such as "I heard the sound of a gun being fired and then saw that man run past me," it is called **circumstantial evidence**.

To begin this phase of the trial, the plaintiff's attorney calls his or her first witness to the witness stand. The examination of one's own witness is called **direct examination**. The attorney must ask questions in such a way as to draw the information from the witness, in the witness's own words, without asking **leading questions** (questions that suggest to the witness the desired answer). When the plaintiff's attorney has no further questions, the witness may be questioned by the opposing attorney on **cross-examination**. Leading questions are allowed on cross-examination. The plaintiff's attorney may conduct a redirect examination on issues brought up in the cross-examination, which may be followed by a re-cross-examination by the defendant's attorney.

Word Wise
Around

The Latin root "circum" used in the term "circumstantial evidence" means "around." The distance around a circle is its circumference. Besides the concrete image and implied action, "circum" can also indicate the *idea* of "around." *Circumstantial evidence* relies on proving facts indirectly; it "goes around" evidence from which other facts are to be inferred.

After all of the plaintiff's witnesses are examined in this way and all other evidence that the plaintiff has is introduced, the plaintiff's attorney rests the case. At this point, the defendant's attorney may make a **motion for a directed verdict**—that is, ask the court to find in favor of the defendant without giving the case to the jury. The motion will be allowed if the court finds that the evidence is insufficient as a matter of law to support a verdict in the plaintiff's favor.

DEFENDANT'S OPENING STATEMENT

After the plaintiff's attorney rests the case, the defendant's attorney makes an opening statement. He or she outlines the defendant's side of the case and tells the jury of the evidence that will be introduced to rebut or to contradict the plaintiff's evidence.

DEFENDANT'S CASE IN CHIEF

The defendant's attorney must introduce the evidence that is necessary to support the defensive claims that were made in the defendant's answer and in the opening statement. As before, one cannot ask leading questions of one's own witnesses.

After all of the defendant's witnesses have been examined and cross-examined, the defendant's attorney rests the case. At this point, the plaintiff's attorney may come in **rebuttal**—that is, introduce evidence that will destroy the effect of the evidence introduced by the other side. Either party may make a motion for a directed verdict at this time.

REQUESTS FOR INSTRUCTIONS TO JURY

At the close of the evidence, the attorneys may file written requests that the judge instruct the jury on the law as set forth in the requests. The judge must inform the attorneys of his or her decision on the requests before the attorneys give their final arguments to the jury.

FINAL ARGUMENTS

Each attorney is given 30 minutes (unless reduced or extended by the court beforehand) to argue his or her side of the case to the jury, or to the judge in a nonjury trial. In this **closing argument** or **summation** the attorneys summarize the evidence that has been introduced in their favor.

TERMS IN ACTION

Juror misbehavior can sometimes result in a declaration of a **mistrial**, or a **reversal** in an **appeal**, requiring a new trial. Recently, jurors have been caught using their Blackberries, iPhones, and Twitter accounts during trials. In a 2009 civil case from Arkansas, a juror tweeted eight times during the trial, including sending one tweet that read, "I just gave away TWELVE MILLION DOLLARS of someone else's money!" The trial judge, however, denied the defense's motion for a new trial. Sometimes, jurors don't misbehave, but they get sick. In 2007, former University of Notre Dame football coach Charlie Weiss sued two doctors and Massachusetts General Hospital for medical malpractice. During trial one day, a juror passed out in the jury box. The two doctors immediately left the defendants' table and went to the aid of the juror, who was taken to the hospital. Weiss's attorney then sought and received a mistrial, arguing that the remaining jurors could have been tainted by seeing the defendants offering volunteer medical assistance.

Source: abajournalnews.com; law.com; boston.com

INSTRUCTIONS TO JURY

Jurors are not expected to know the law. For this reason, the jury must be told what the law is in that particular case. After the closing arguments, the judge tells the jury the law that must be applied. This is called the **jury charge**. When it **deliberates**—considers the case slowly and carefully—the jury must apply that law to the facts in making its decision. In highly publicized cases, jurors are sometimes **sequestered**—that is, isolated, or set apart, from society in a hotel during the deliberation period to prevent them from being exposed to outside influences.

VERDICT

The decision of the jury is called the **verdict**. In a criminal case, the jury must agree unanimously in order to reach a verdict. If it cannot do so, a **mistrial** (an invalid trial of no consequence) is called, and a new trial may be held. In a civil case, five-sixths of the members of the jury must reach agreement to arrive at a verdict unless the plaintiff and the defendant agree that a different majority of the jurors will be taken as the verdict. It is called **polling the jury** when individual jurors are asked whether they agree with the verdict given by the jury foreperson. A deadlocked jury is often referred to as a **hung jury**.

Web Wise

- For an overview of evidence, go to the Legal Information Institute (LII) at ***www.law.cornell. edu***. When there, click on Wex legal dictionary/encyclopedia in the Learn More box. Then in the search box type "evidence." In addition to the Federal Rules of Evidence, you will find federal and state cases on the subject.
- Look for practice and procedure information for your state by going to ***www.findlaw.com***. When there, type "jurisdiction" in the search box, then click the name of your state.

JUDGMENT OR DECREE

Following the jury's verdict, the court issues a **judgment**, also called an **adjudication**, which is the decision of a court of law. The judgment is the act of the trial court finally **adjudicating** (determining) the rights and liabilities of the parties. This determination is the court's decision in the case. A case is said to be **ripe for judgment** when it reaches the stage when everything has been completed except the court's decision. A **judgment on the merits** is a court decision based on the evidence and facts introduced. In contrast, a **judgment on the pleadings** will be rendered without hearing evidence if the court determines that it is clear from the pleadings that one party is entitled to win the case as a matter of law. Similarly, if the judge believes that the jury's verdict is incorrect as a matter of law (a **verdict contrary to law**), he or she may issue a **judgment notwithstanding the verdict** also called a **judgment n.o.v.** (from the Latin **non obstante verdicto**), which is a judgment in favor of one party notwithstanding a verdict in favor of the other party.

The decision of a court of equity is called a **decree**. **Equity** means that which is just and fair. A **court of equity** is a court that administers justice according to the system of equity. It is able to grant relief to people when no adequate remedy is otherwise available. To illustrate, a court of law can usually do nothing more than award money to an injured party. In contrast, a court of equity can issue an **injunction**—that is, order someone to do or refrain from doing a particular act. Sometimes, a court of equity will issue a **preliminary injunction** before hearing the merits of a case in order to prevent injustice. A **consent decree** is a decree that is entered by consent of the parties, usually without an admission of guilt or wrongdoing. This type of decree cannot be appealed because the parties have agreed to it.

TERMS IN ACTION

A British nanny named Louise Woodward, living in Massachusetts, was convicted in 1997 of second-degree murder for the killing of an eight-month-old baby boy under her care. The evidence presented was that Woodward, hired to be the boy's au pair by his parents (both of whom were doctors), was careless and irresponsible and that she killed the infant in what is commonly called "shaken baby syndrome." But after her conviction, her defense attorneys—who included Barry Scheck, one of O.J. Simpson's attorneys from his 1994 double-murder trial—made a motion to the trial judge, asking that he set aside the conviction because it was a **verdict contrary to law.** The trial judge granted that motion and, in a rare instance of judicial discretion, replaced the second-degree murder conviction with an involuntary manslaughter conviction, which was **upheld** when the prosecution **appealed**. Ms. Woodward was released from jail and moved back to Britain.

Source: nytimes.com

APPEAL

If a party is not satisfied with the final judgment or legal ruling of a trial court, the party may ask a higher court to reverse the decision. That request is made in an **appeal**, which is directed to an appellate court. Appellate courts resolve questions (or issues) of law, unlike trial courts, which resolve questions of fact. A party bringing an appeal is called an **appellant**. A party against whom an appeal is brought is called an **appellee** a **respondent** or a **defendant in error**. Only questions of law may be raised on appeal. **Questions of law** are questions relating to the application or interpretation of law. Such questions are not decided by a jury. **Questions of fact**—that is, questions about the activities that took place between the parties that caused them to go to court—are for the jury to decide and cannot be appealed unless the jury is plainly wrong as a matter of law. To be heard by an appellate court, an appeal must be filed within a prescribed period—typically, 30 days from the entry of judgment.

When an appellate court takes a case and agrees with the lower court's decision, it will **affirm**—that is, approve—the decision. In contrast, when an appellate court disagrees with a lower court decision, it will **reverse** or **set aside** (make void) the decision, or it will **vacate** (annul) the judgment and **remand** (send back) the case to the lower court for further proceedings. An **appeal bond** is often required as security to guarantee the cost of an appeal, especially in civil cases.

Reviewing What You Learned

After studying the chapter, write the answers to each of the following questions:

1. List the steps in the order that they occur in a jury trial.

2. What is one requirement of an opening statement?

3. Differentiate among testimonial evidence, documentary evidence, and real evidence.

4. Give an example for each of testimony that is (a) direct evidence and (b) circumstantial evidence.

5. Under what circumstances are leading questions allowed and not allowed?

6. Under what circumstances may a motion for a directed verdict be allowed?

7. Under what circumstances may the plaintiff's attorney introduce rebuttal evidence?

8. What is the difference between questions of law and questions of fact, and which may be raised on appeal?

9. To reach a verdict, how must the jury agree, in a criminal case?

10. What is the difference between a judgment and a writ of execution?

Understanding Legal Concepts

Indicate whether each statement is true or false. Then, change the italicized word or phrase of each false statement to make it true.

1

ANSWERS

_____ 1. In the *opening statement,* the attorney outlines the case by telling the jury what the evidence will prove.

_____ 2. When a witness testifies as to something he or she observed, such as "I saw that man shoot the gun," it is called *circumstantial* evidence.

_____ 3. Leading questions are allowed on *direct* examination.

_____ 4. After the plaintiff's attorney rests the case, the defendant's attorney *makes an opening statement.*

_____ 5. When final arguments are made, the plaintiff's attorney argues *first.*

_____ 6. A jury never decides questions of *fact.*

_____ 7. In a criminal case, the jury must agree unanimously to reach a *verdict.*

_____ 8. Following the jury's verdict, the court issues a *judgment.*

_____ 9. The decision of a court of equity is called a *decree.*

_____ 10. Only questions of *fact* may be raised on appeal.

Checking Terminology (Part A)

From the list of legal terms that follows, select the one that matches each definition.

ANSWERS

a. adjudicating
b. adjudication
c. admissible evidence
d. affirm
e. appeal
f. appeal bond
g. appellant
h. appellee
i. case in chief
j. circumstantial evidence
k. consent decree
l. court of equity
m. cross-examination
n. decree
o. defendant in error
p. deliberate
q. direct evidence
r. direct examination
s. DNA
t. DNA sample
u. documentary evidence
v. equity
w. exhibit
x. hung jury
y. injunction
z. judgment
aa. judgment notwithstanding the verdict
bb. judgment n.o.v.
cc. judgment on the merits
dd. judgment on the pleadings
ee. respondent

_____ 1. The examination of one's own witness.

_____ 2. A bond often required as security to guarantee the cost of an appeal, especially in civil cases.

_____ 3. Approve.

_____ 4. A deadlocked jury; one that cannot agree.

_____ 5. A tangible item that is introduced in evidence.

_____ 6. Determining finally by a court.

_____ 7. Evidence that directly relates to the fact in issue.

_____ 8. A party bringing an appeal.

_____ 9. A court decision based on the evidence and facts introduced.

_____ 10. A party against whom an appeal is brought. (Select three answers.)

_____ 11. A judgment rendered in favor of one party notwithstanding a verdict in favor of the other party. (Select two answers.)

_____ 12. A court that administers justice according to the system of equity.

_____ 13. A judgment rendered without hearing evidence if the court determines that it is clear from the pleadings that one party is entitled to win the case.

_____ 14. That which is just and fair.

_____ 15. Evidence that is pertinent and proper to be considered in reaching a decision, according to specific rules.

_____ 16. The decision of a court of equity.

_____ 17. Evidence that relates to some fact other than the fact in issue; indirect evidence.

_____ 18. The decision of a court of law.

_____ 19. Evidence consisting of such documents as written contracts, business records, correspondence, wills, and deeds.

_____ 20. A court judgment.

_____ 21. The examination of an opposing witness.

_____ 22. A request to a higher court to review the decision of a lower court.

_____ 23. The introduction of evidence to prove the allegations that were made in the pleadings and in the opening statement.

_____ 24. An order of a court of equity to do or refrain from doing a particular act.

_____ 25. The double strand of molecules that carries a cell's unique genetic code.

_____ 26. Biological evidence of any nature that is utilized to conduct DNA analysis.

_____ 27. A decree that is entered by consent of the parties.

_____ 28. To consider slowly and carefully.

Checking Terminology (Part B)

From the list of legal terms that follows, select the one that matches each definition.

ANSWERS

a. closing argument
b. jury charge
c. leading questions
d. mistrial
e. motion for a directed verdict
f. non obstante verdicto
g. opening statement
h. polling the jury
i. preliminary injunction
j. prima facie case
k. questions of fact
l. questions of law
m. real evidence
n. rebuttal
o. relevant evidence
p. remand
q. reverse
r. ripe for judgment
s. sequester
t. set aside
u. summation
v. testimonial evidence
w. vacate
x. verdict
y. verdict contrary to law

_____ 1. Send back.
_____ 2. In a jury trial, a motion asking the court to find in favor of the moving party as a matter of law, without having the case go to the jury.
_____ 3. Questions about the activities which took place between the parties that caused them to go to court.
_____ 4. Final statements by the attorneys, summarizing the evidence that has been introduced. (Select two answers.)
_____ 5. The decision of a jury.
_____ 6. Actual objects that have a bearing on the case, such as an item of clothing, a weapon found at the scene of a crime, a photograph, a chart, or a model.
_____ 7. Notwithstanding a verdict.
_____ 8. Annul.
_____ 9. Instructions to a jury on matters of law.
_____ 10. Evidence tending to prove or disprove an alleged fact.
_____ 11. An attorney's outline, related to the jury, of anticipated proof.
_____ 12. Legally sufficient for proof unless rebutted or contradicted by other evidence.
_____ 13. A procedure in which individual jurors are asked whether they agree with the verdict given by the jury foreperson.
_____ 14. Questions that suggest to the witness the desired answer.
_____ 15. Oral testimony of witnesses made under oath in open court.
_____ 16. Questions relating to the application or interpretation of law.
_____ 17. An invalid trial of no consequence.
_____ 18. Make void. (Select two answers.)
_____ 19. The introduction of evidence that will destroy the effect of the evidence introduced by the other side.
_____ 20. An injunction issued by a court before hearing the merits of a case.
_____ 21. A verdict that is incorrect as a matter of law.
_____ 22. The stage of a trial when everything has been completed except the court's decision.
_____ 23. To isolate or set apart from society.

Sharpening Your Latin Skills

In the space provided, write the definition of each of the following legal terms, referring to the glossary when necessary.

certiorari _____

non obstante verdicto _____

prima facie _____

subpoena _____

subpoena ad testificandum _____

subpoena duces tecum _____

venire _____

venire facias _____

Using Legal Language

Read the following story and fill in the blank lines with legal terms taken from the list of terms at the beginning of this chapter.

The plaintiff's attorney, Mary Grey, was required to set forth a(n) _____ in her opening statement before the jury. Her evidence consisted of a photograph, which was _____; payroll records, which were _____; and oral statements of a witness, which were _____.

On the stand, Mary's witness, Leroy Henning, said, "I am the payroll clerk, and these payroll records are true and correct." This was _____ evidence, not _____, and because she was examining her own witness, Mary's examination was called _____. Mary could not ask _____, which suggest to the witness the desired answer. The opposing attorney could do so, however, on _____. At the close of Mary's case, the opposing attorney made a(n) _____, asking the court to find in favor of his client. This request was de-nied, and the case went to the jury, whose decision is called a(n) _____. Following this decision, the court issued its _____, which is some-times called a(n) _____ in a court of equity. Mary's client won the case, and the opposing attorney de-cided not to _____ to a higher court because only _____ may be raised at that time. Had he done so, his client would have been called the _____ and would have had to put up a(n) _____ as security.

PUZZLING OVER WHAT YOU LEARNED

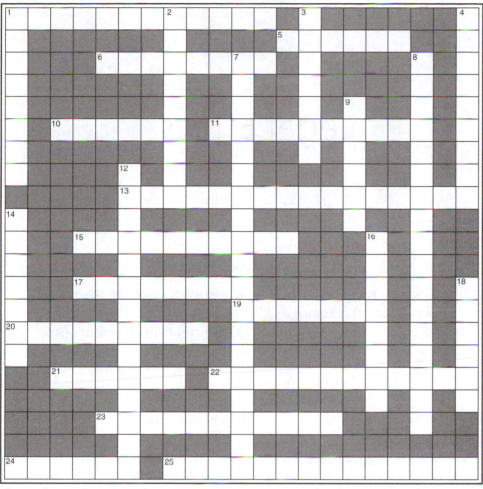

Caveat: Do not allow squares for spaces between words and punctuation (apostrophes, hyphens, etc.) when filling in crossword.

Across

1. Actual objects that have a bearing on the case, such as an item of clothing or a weapon found at the scene of the crime.
5. Decision of a court of equity.
6. Make void; reverse.
10. Approve.
11. Instructions to a jury on matters of law.
13. An attorney's outline to the jury of anticipated proof.
15. To consider slowly and carefully.
17. A deadlocked jury; one that cannot agree.
19. A tangible item that is introduced in evidence.
20. Closing argument.
21. A request to a higher court to review the decision of a lower court.
22. A court judgment.
23. A judgment rendered in favor of one party notwithstanding a verdict in favor of the other party.
24. That which is just and fair.
25. Evidence that directly relates to the fact in issue.

Down

1. The introduction of evidence that will destroy the effect of the evidence introduced by the other side.
2. Biological evidence of any nature that is utilized to conduct DNA analysis.
3. The decision of a jury.
4. A party bringing an appeal.
7. Evidence consisting of documents.
8. The examination of one's own witness.
9. Annul.
12. A procedure in which individual jurors are asked whether they agree with the verdict given by the jury foreperson.
14. Make void; set aside.
16. An invalid trial of no consequence.
18. Send back.

Legal Ethics

ANTE INTERROGATORY

*A lawyer's requirement to keep secret what he or she learns
about the client is known as (A) the attorney–client privilege,
(B) a frivolous claim, (C) the duty of lawyer–client confidentiality,
(D) the duty of competence.*

CHAPTER OUTLINE

Competence and Truthfulness

**The Unauthorized Practice of Law and the
 Duty of Supervision**

Confidentiality

Conflicts of Interest

Legal Fees

Advertising and Solicitation

Attorney Discipline

KEY TERMS

American Bar Association (ABA)
 (uh·MARE·i·can bar uh·SO·she·A·shun)

attorney–client privilege *(uh·TURN·ee
 KLY·ent PRI·vi·lej)*

bar exam

Cannons of Professional Ethics *(CAN·ons
 of pro·FEH·shun·al E·thicks)*

comments *(KOM·ents)*

competent *(KOM·peh·tent)*

confidential communication *(kon·fi·DEN·shal
 kom·yewn·i·KAY·shun)*

conflict of interest *(KON·flict of IN·ter·est)*

contingency fee *(kon·TIN·jen·cee fee)*

costs *(KOSTS)*

diligence *(DIL·uh·jents)*

disbarment *(dis·BAR·ment)*

disciplinary commission *(dis·i·plin·AIR·ee
 kom·i·shun)*

duty of confidentiality *(DEW·tee of
 kon·fi·den·she·AL·i·tee)*

ex parte communication *(ex PAR·tay
 kom·YOU·ni·kay·shun)*

flat fee

frivolous suits *(FRIV·uh·luss sutes)*

grievance *(GREE·vance)*

guidelines *(guyd·lines)*

hourly billing *(OUW·er·lee BIL·ing)*

informed consent *(in·FORMED kon·SENT)*

legal assistant *(LEE·gl uh·SIS·tant)*

legal ethics *(LEE·gl e·thicks)*

legal fees *(LEE·gl FEES)*

license suspension *(LYE·senz suh·SPEN·shun)*

Model Code of Professional Responsibility *(MAH·dl kode of pro·FEH·shun·al ree·SPON·si·bil·i·tee)*

Model Rules of Professional Conduct *(MAH·dl ROOLS of pro·Feh·shun·al KON·dukt)*

nonbillables *(non·BIL·uh·bls)*

paralegal *(pare·uh·LEE·gl)*

private reprimand *(PRYE·vit REH·pri·mand)*

public reprimand *(PUH·blik REH·pri·mand)*

Rules *(roolz)*

soliciting *(so·LIH·sih·ting)*

Legal Ethics was originally a tradition of do's and don't's informally applied in the legal profession. In 1887, Alabama became the first jurisdiction to adopt rules of legal ethics, and in 1908 the **American Bar Association (ABA)**, the largest voluntary bar association in America, created its first set of ethics rules, called the **Canons of Professional Ethics**. The ABA adopted the **Model Code of Professional Responsibility** in 1969, and then replaced it in 1983 with the **Model Rules of Professional Conduct**, which were updated in 2003. The ABA Model Rules are formatted with mandatory **Rules**, followed by explanatory **Comments** designed to help the reader understand the focus of the rules.

Lawyers are licensed in the jurisdiction where they have passed the **bar exam**, which is usually a multi-day exam on that jurisdiction's common law, statutory law, and regulatory law. Applicants for law licensure must also pass a national ethics exam. Lawyer conduct is regulated by the highest appellate court in a state, which adopts or creates a set of legal ethics rules and then investigates accusations of lawyer misconduct. Forty-nine states and the District of Columbia have adopted the ABA Model Rules as the operative lawyer conduct rules. California still uses its own set of legal ethics rules. Most states have also adopted **guidelines** for the use, by lawyers, of paralegals or legal assistants. These guidelines are directed to lawyers and address how to ethically use their employees in the support of clients' needs. The two largest paralegal and legal assistant organizations are the National Federation of Paralegal Associations (NFPA) and the National Association of Legal Assistants (NALA); both organizations have their own sets of ethics rules that apply to their members.

COMPETENCE AND TRUTHFULNESS

Lawyers have a mandatory duty to provide **competent** representation, in Model Rule 1.1, which means that a lawyer may not take on a case or engage in litigation in which the area of the law or intricacy of the procedure involved is beyond the lawyer's knowledge base or skill. **Diligence** is an important component of competence, and Model Rule 1.3 requires the lawyer to act with reasonable diligence and promptness. Competence and diligence also involve keeping the client reasonably informed about the status of his or her matter, and responding to client requests for information.

Despite what the public may think about the general character of lawyers, truthfulness toward clients, the court, and even third parties is required by various ABA Model Rules. Part of being dishonest includes failing to disclose one's status as an attorney or paralegal, and engaging in **ex parte communication**. "Ex parte" literally means "by or for one party," but in the context of dishonest communication it refers to a lawyer involved in a case who communicates with the judge while the other party's lawyer is unaware of the communication. Lawyers are also prohibited from bringing **frivolous suits** or frivolous appeals. Something is "frivolous" if it is meant to harass someone, or if there is no basis in law or fact for bringing the claim or appeal.

> ### ▮ TERMS IN ACTION
>
> Abraham Lincoln was a lawyer at the time that he wrote "Notes for a Law Lecture," which was found by his secretaries after his assassination in 1865. Although it isn't known that Lincoln ever presented it as a speech, "Notes on a Law Lecture" is thought to be from 1850. A little over 700 words long, this straight-as-an-arrow sermonette provides unique insight into Lincoln's view of what it meant to be a successful attorney. Lincoln got right to the point: "The leading rule for the lawyer, as for the man of every other calling, is **diligence**. Leave nothing for tomorrow which can be done today. Never let your correspondence fall behind. Whatever piece of business you have in hand, before stopping, do all the labor pertaining to it which can then be done." And realizing back then what many lawyers seem hesitant today to recommend, Lincoln wrote, "Discourage litigation. Persuade your neighbors to compromise whenever you can. Point out to them how the nominal winner is often a real loser—in **fees, expenses**, and waste of time. . . .There will still be business enough. Never stir up litigation. A worse man can scarcely be found than one who does this." Discussing his view on legal fees, Lincoln wrote, "The matter of fees is important, far beyond the mere question of bread and butter involved. An exorbitant fee should never be claimed." Lincoln's final paragraph is the most often cited portion and discusses his view on the need for honest lawyers. Part of that paragraph includes the following caution: "Let no young man choosing the law for a calling for a moment yield to the popular belief—resolve to be **honest** at all events; and if in your own judgment you cannot be an honest lawyer, resolve to be honest without being a lawyer."
>
> Source: *Notes for a Law Lecture, Abraham Lincoln*

THE UNAUTHORIZED PRACTICE OF LAW AND THE DUTY OF SUPERVISION

ABA Model Rule 5.1 prohibits a lawyer from assisting a nonlawyer in the unauthorized practice of law. ABA Model Rule 5.3 governs a lawyer's supervision of his or her nonlawyer employees. Because paralegals and legal assistants are not licensed members of the bar, lawyers (as their employers) are held responsible for the ethical misconduct of their employees and for failing to adequately supervise them. Included in the requirement of supervision is ensuring that **paralegals** and **legal assistants** do not commit the unauthorized practice of law, which includes giving legal advice. Paralegals are those nonlawyer employees trained or educated to engage in substantive legal work under the supervision of their employing attorneys. Legal assistants are often synonymous with "paralegals," although some lawyers consider a legal assistant to be someone less trained or educated than a paralegal. Even when paralegals are allowed to engage in substantive legal work, they are not allowed to engage in the practice of law.

CONFIDENTIALITY

ABA Model Rule 1.6 requires a lawyer to protect his or her client information. This duty applies to statements made to the lawyer, documents given to the lawyer, as well as any other information the lawyer learns about the client, whatever its source. The **duty of confidentiality** applies to the lawyer's employees, as well. Prospective clients are protected by Model Rule 1.18, which prohibits lawyers from using information that they learn from those whose cases they do not take. Exceptions to the duty of confidentiality include implied authorizations, which are necessary to meet the client's needs; disclosures that are intended to prevent the client from committing a serious or dangerous crime; or disclosures that a lawyer needs to make in order to defend against a charge made by the client against the lawyer.

The **attorney–client privilege** is related to the duty of confidentiality, but its concept comes from evidence law. It protects a lawyer from having to testify against his or her client, even when issued a subpoena. However, for the attorney–client privilege to apply, the attorney has to be asked to divulge a **confidential communication** (a conversation or writing that expresses personal or private information) that the client had with his or her attorney. For example, the client's location is a fact and not a confidential communication, and is generally not protected by the attorney–client privilege.

CONFLICTS OF INTEREST

Lawyers and their employers are expected to avoid **conflicts of interest**. A conflict of interest is a situation in which the lawyer is torn between loyalty between two or more clients or loyalty between the client and the lawyer. For example, a lawyer's loyalty would be at issue if the lawyer, who is representing a wife in a divorce, would be asked by the husband to represent him against the wife in a negligence lawsuit alleging that the husband slipped and fell in a restaurant owned by the wife. Model Rules 1.7–1.13 concern conflicts of interest, and those rules prohibit a lawyer from representing two clients against each other or one client against a former client, or from being involved romantically with a current client (unless the personal relationship predates the professional relationship).

One important conflict of interest rule prohibits a lawyer or paralegal from changing jobs and working at a law firm that has a client involved in a case against a party that was a former client at the lawyer's or paralegal's law firm. With most of the conflicts of interest rules, exceptions are made when the client whose interests are to be protected gives **informed consent** (acknowledged awareness of the likely consequences for taking a course of action) and waives the conflict of interest problem. Waiver is the voluntary relinquishment of a known privilege, or right.

LEGAL FEES

Lawyers are required to charge reasonable **legal fees** and **costs**. Reasonableness is discussed in Model Rule 1.5 and includes the lawyer's experience, the difficulty of the case, and the chance that the lawyer will be prevented from taking other similar cases, due to the conflict of interest rules. Unlike legal fees (which are the charges for the lawyer's time or efforts), costs are the expenses associated with a legal matter, such as filing fees.

Lawyers who engage in **hourly billing** may not charge two different clients for the same amount of time. Lawyers are allowed to bill separately for the use of their paralegals, provided that the client is aware and approves. Certain law firm costs, such as overhead expenses (rent, paperclips, utilities), are considered **nonbillables**, and the act of charging them is unreasonable. Some lawyers charge a **flat fee** for their work and don't bill for the hours involved. A flat fee is a sum-certain cost of the lawyer's services and is not based on the lawyer's hourly rate times the lawyer's billable hours.

When a lawyer charges a **contingency fee**, that fee agreement must be in writing and signed by the client. Contingency fees are commonly charged for personal injury cases and other tort cases, and if the plaintiff wins, the contingency fee is calculated as a percentage of the plaintiff's awarded damages. Under Model Rule 1.5, contingency fees are not allowed to be charged in criminal cases and divorce cases. Model Rule 5.4 prohibits lawyers from sharing a percentage of their legal fees with their paralegals and legal assistants.

ADVERTISING AND SOLICITATION

ABA Model Rule 7.1 prohibits all lawyer communication about the lawyer's services from being misleading, whereas Model Rule 7.2 allows lawyers to advertise their services in print, on radio and television, and on the Internet. The ABA leaves to individual jurisdictions the decision to govern what may and may not be presented in an advertisement, and most jurisdictions do not allow lawyers to include their past successes in their advertisements. Some jurisdictions prohibit lawyers from using actors in their commercials.

Model Rule 7.3 prohibits a lawyer and his or her employees from **soliciting** a prospective client through live contact (including online contact), unless the prospective client is also a lawyer, or is a family member or close friend of the lawyer. When written solicitations (such as a letter sent by a lawyer to an accident victim, intended to ask that person to become the lawyer's client) are sent to prospective clients, lawyers are required to put "Advertising Material," on the envelope and solicitation documents.

ATTORNEY DISCIPLINE

The ABA does not regulate lawyers; the highest court in a given jurisdiction does. If a client believes that he or she has been subject to the lawyer's misconduct, the client can file a written accusation against the lawyer, called a **grievance**. The grievance is filed with that jurisdiction's **disciplinary commission**, which is empowered by its jurisdiction's supreme court to investigate the grievance and decide whether or not to bring ethics charges against the attorney. If a lawyer is found to have violated his or her jurisdiction's rules of professional conduct, a disciplinary sanction is given. Such sanctions range from a **private reprimand** (where the lawyer's name is not included with the official censure), to a **public reprimand**, to a short **license suspension** (involving the lawyer's automatically being allowed to practice law at the suspension's conclusion), to a longer suspension (under which the lawyer must apply for reinstatement to the practice of law at the suspension's conclusion), to even **disbarment**, which is permanent loss of a law license.

▌TERMS IN ACTION

F. Lee Bailey was, for over 40 years, one of America's most famous lawyers. He was a criminal defense lawyer who had some of the most infamous clients in recent memory. He successfully won the U.S. Supreme Court appeal and then the retrial of Dr. Sam Sheppard, who was convicted in 1954 of murdering his wife. Dr. Sheppard's story was thought to be the inspiration for *The Fugitive*, a 1960s television series and a 1993 film. Bailey represented the notorious "Boston Strangler" in the 1960s and represented Patty Hearst, who was kidnapped by terrorists in the 1970s and later arrested for having robbed a bank with them. He argued in her case that she was brainwashed, a tactic that didn't work. Bailey got into a bit of an ethics scrape as a result of that case when a federal court ruled that he violated the **conflicts of interest** rules because, when he still represented her, he wrongfully acquired the rights to use Ms. Hearst's dramatic story in his own published account of the case. And many Americans know him through his role on O. J. Simpson's "Dream Team," the name for the group of lawyers who succeeding in winning Simpson a not-guilty verdict in 1995 after O. J. was charged with murdering his ex-wife, Nicole Brown-Simpson, and Ron Goldman. But in 2001, F. Lee Bailey was **disbarred** from the practice of law in Florida, where he was licensed. His disbarment stemmed from his representation of a drug kingpin, Claude Duboc. As a result of Duboc's guilty plea, Bailey was given the task to sell Duboc's assets and turn the proceeds over to the federal government. In the course of doing so, Bailey kept millions of dollars as his **legal fee**, in violation of a court order; he was **untruthful** about his actions; and he engaged in **ex parte communication** with the federal judge in charge of the case. There were other instances of misconduct as well, and the Florida Supreme Court concluded that each count of misconduct was worthy of disbarment. Because Bailey was also licensed in Massachusetts, he was disbarred there in 2005.

Sources: *Florida Bar v. Bailey*, 803 So.2d 683 (Fla. 2001); *Legal Ethics*, 2d Ed., Kent Kauffman

Reviewing What You Learned

After studying the chapter, write the answers to each of the following questions:

1. List the current set of rules that the American Bar Association uses for legal ethics.

_____

_____

_____

2. What do lawyers need to pass before they can practice law? Explain what it is.

_____

_____

_____

3. What are two mandatory duties lawyers have, according to Model Rules 1.1 and 1.3?

_____

_____

_____

_____

4. What does truthfulness include, according to the ABA Model Rules?

_____

_____

_____

_____

5. Explain how a lawyer is responsible for his paralegal's conduct.

_____

_____

_____

6. What are the exceptions to the duty of confidentiality?

_____

_____

_____

_____

7. What is the purpose of the attorney–client privilege?

_____

_____

_____

_____

8. What is the difference between a flat fee and a contingency fee?

_____

_____

_____

9. What are the guidelines for advertising and soliciting?

_____

_____

_____

10. List and explain the disciplinary sanctions that may be given to a lawyer.

_____

_____

_____

_____

Understanding Legal Concepts

Indicate whether each statement is true or false. Then change the italicized word or phrase of each false statement to make it true.

ANSWERS

_____ **1.** The *American Bar Association* regulates lawyer conduct.

_____ **2.** Most states have adopted *guidelines* for the lawyer's use of paralegals.

_____ **3.** A *frivolous suit* has no basis in law for bringing a claim or appeal.

_____ **4.** Paralegals are not allowed to engage in *substantive legal work.*

_____ **5.** Overhead expenses may be charged in *hourly billing.*

_____ **6.** *Flat fees* are commonly charged for personal injury and other tort.

_____ **7.** A client can file a written accusation against a lawyer, called a *reprimand.*

_____ **8.** Lawyers are required to put the words "advertising material" on *written solicitations.*

_____ **9.** *Private reprimand* is permanent loss of a law license.

Checking Terminology

From the list of legal terms that follows, select the one that matches each definition.

ANSWERS

a. attorney–client privilege
b. bar exam
c. Canons of Professional Ethics
d. comments
e. competent
f. confidential communication
g. conflict of interest
h. contingency fee
i. diligence
j. disbarment
k. disciplinary commission
l. duty of confidentiality
m. ex parte communication
n. flat fee
o. frivolous suit
p. grievance
q. informed consent
r. legal assistant
s. legal ethics
t. legal fees
u. license suspension
v. Model Code of Professional Responsibility
w. Model Rules of Professional Conduct
x. nonbillables
y. paralegal
z. private reprimand
aa. public reprimand
bb. Rules
cc. soliciting

____ 1. Torn between loyalties to two or more clients.
____ 2. Originally, a list of do's and don't's for lawyers,
____ 3. Permanent loss of a law license.
____ 4. Lawyer's name is not on official censure.
____ 5. Protection from having to testify against one's clients.
____ 6. Not allowed to practice law for a short period.
____ 7. Sum-certain cost of lawyer's services; not per hour.
____ 8. Test on law and ethics for lawyer licensure.
____ 9. Act of seeking a specific client.
____ 10. Staying on top of a case with promptness.
____ 11. Charges for the lawyer's time or efforts.
____ 12. Within a lawyer's knowledge base and skill.
____ 13. Knowledge of the likely consequences.
____ 14. Help for the reader to understand the focus of Rules.
____ 15. First set of ethics rules by ABA.
____ 16. Law firm costs that cannot be charged to clients.
____ 17. Mandatory format in the ABA Model Rules.
____ 18. Protecting client information.
____ 19. Nonlawyer trained to do substantive legal work.
____ 20. Ethics rules adopted in 1969 by the ABA.
____ 21. Meant to harass someone or having no basis in law.
____ 22. Payment in a percentage of plaintiff's damages.
____ 23. Nonlawyer trained less than a paralegal.
____ 24. Lawyer's name on official censure.
____ 25. Investigates grievances; brings ethics charges.
____ 26. Ethics rules adopted by ABA in 2003.
____ 27. Written accusation against a lawyer.
____ 28. Private client information shared with a lawyer.
____ 29. Unethical lawyer communication with a judge.

PUZZLING OVER WHAT YOU LEARNED

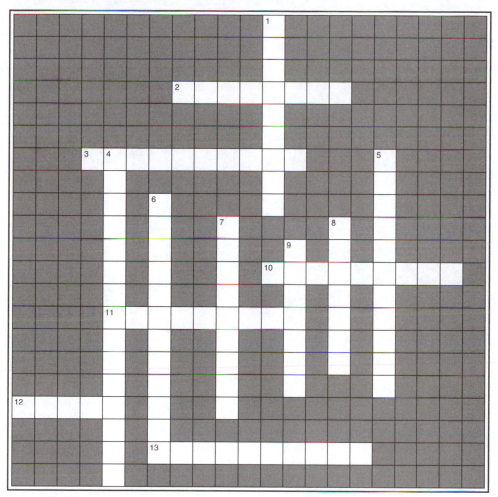

Caveat: Do not allow squares for spaces between words and punctuation (apostrophes, hyphens, etc.) when filling in crossword.

Across

2. Help reader understand the focus of rules
3. Permanent loss of a law license
10. Nonlawyer trained to do substantive legal work
11. Staying on top of a case with promptness
12. Mandatory format in the ABA Model Rules
13. Act of seeking a specific client

Down

1. Written accusation against a lawyer
4. Knowledge of the likely consequences
5. List of do's and don'ts for lawyers
6. Law firm costs that cannot be charged to clients
7. Within a lawyer's knowledge base and skill
8. Sum-certain cost of lawyer's services not per hour
9. Test on law and ethics for lawyer's licensure

Terms Used in Constitutional and Criminal Law

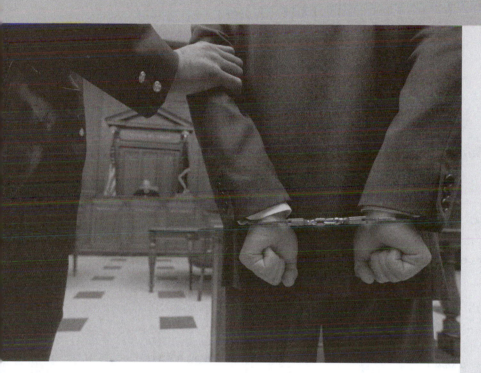

2

In our society, criminal law not only dominates the news, but also penetrates deeply into our culture by way of TV thrillers, violent movies, and suspense-filled mystery stories. And yet, the criminal law is bound by the limits set in the U.S. Constitution, so Part Two opens with an overview of the Constitution and a summary of its key parts. Then, Part Two discusses many of the crimes that we have heard about or have been exposed to since childhood. After defining a crime and explaining its components, Chapter 10 highlights the three broad classes of crimes and describes accomplices and criminal defenses. Chapter 11 explains the elements of crimes and discusses crimes against property, including larceny, embezzlement, bribery, extortion, coercion, receipt of stolen goods, and forgery. Chapter 12 explores crimes against the person, such as robbery, mayhem, assault, battery, and rape, in addition to crimes against human habitation—that is, burglary and arson. The subject of homicide is explained in Chapter 13. Crimes against morality, including adultery, fornication, bigamy, polygamy, incest, sodomy, miscegenation, abortion, pornography, and drug abuse are examined in Chapter 14.

Constitutional Law

ANTE INTERROGATORY

The first 10 amendments in the U.S. Constitution are known as the (A) Supremacy Clause, (B) judicial review doctrine, (C) Articles of Confederation, (D) Bill of Rights.

CHAPTER OUTLINE

The Constitution's Structure

The Branches of Government

Checks and Balances

Amendments

KEY TERMS

amendments *(uh.MEND.mentz)*

Articles of Confederation *(ARE·tih·clz ov kon·FED·er·a·shun)*

articles *(ARE·tih·clz)*

bicameral *(bye·KAM·er·al)*

Bill of Rights *(bil ov rites)*

cabinet *(KAB·ih·net)*

checks and balances *(chex and BAL·en·says)*

clause *(klawz)*

elastic powers *(ee·LASS·tick pow·erz)*

executive branch *(ex·ECK·kew·tiv branch)*

express powers *(ex·PRESS pow·erz)*

federalism *(FED·er·al·izm)*

House of Representatives *(howse ov rep·ree·ZEN·tah·tivz)*

judicial branch *(jew·DIH·sheel branch)*

judicial review *(jew·DIH·sheel ree·VEE·U)*

legislative branch *(lej·uh·SLAY·tiv branch)*

pocket veto *(PAH·ket VEE·tow)*

Senate *(SEN·it)*

separation of powers *(she·per·A·shun ov POW·ers)*

Supremacy Clause *(sue·PREM·a·see klawz)*

treaties *(TREE·teez)*

U.S. Constitution *(you ess kon·stih·TWO·shun)*

U.S. Supreme Court *(you ess sue·PREEM)*

veto *(VEE·tow)*

The **U.S. Constitution** is the first governing document in world history that creates representative democracy, expressly limits the powers of government, and grants specific rights to the people. But it was not the first foundational governing document in American history. The **Articles of Confederation** loosely governed the colonies, and then the states, from 1777, until the Constitution was ratified in 1789. The Articles of Confederation lacked some elements that were put into the Constitution, including an executive branch, a judicial branch, a national army, and the power to tax.

THE CONSTITUTION'S STRUCTURE

At the Constitutional Convention in 1787, the framers decided to create a federal constitution that would provide for direct and indirect representation, and would have **separation of powers** by giving independent authority to each of the three branches of government. Those branches of government are the **legislative branch**, **executive branch**, and **judicial branch**. The constitution consists of seven **articles**, which are the separate, original parts of the constitution, and 27 **amendments**, which modify or invalidate earlier parts of the constitution. The constitution's structure provides for **federalism**, which allows state governments to retain their individual governing powers, even though the federal government is given broad powers.

THE BRANCHES OF GOVERNMENT

Article I of the constitution is directed to the establishment of the federal Congress. The federal legislature is **bicameral**, which means that there are two chambers, or houses of representation. The **House of Representatives** has 435 members. Members of the House of Representatives serve two-year terms, and the number of representatives in the House is based on each state's population. The **Senate** has 100 senators who serve six-year terms. Each state gets two senators. Article I gives the power to make laws to the Congress. Either chamber of Congress may begin a legislative bill, with the exception that taxing legislation must start in the House of Representatives. Congress's **express powers** are the specifically stated powers of Congress and are found in Article I, Section 8. Included in those powers are the power to declare war and the power to regulate interstate commerce. Congress also has the power to make all laws necessary and proper to carry out its express powers, sometimes called its **elastic powers**.

Article II creates the executive branch, which is headed by the U.S. President. The president's responsibilities include carrying out the laws passed by the Congress, directing all federal military forces, and appointing all federal judges. The president also appoints the heads of the executive departments of the government, called the **cabinet**. The cabinet includes the Department of State, the Department of Defense, and the Department of the Treasury. The president also makes **treaties**, which are legally enforceable agreements with foreign governments.

Article III of the constitution creates the **U.S. Supreme Court**. Its jurisdiction is primarily appellate, but it also is given original jurisdiction over certain legal matters, such as the case that would arise if a state were to sue another state. Beyond being the highest court in the federal judicial system, the Supreme Court is the highest and most powerful court in the country because Article VI of the constitution has a **clause**) (a distinct part of a constitutional Section known as the **Supremacy Clause**, which makes federal law preeminent when federal and state law conflict. And due to the doctrine of **judicial review**, the Supreme Court has the power to declare acts of Congress and acts of the executive branch unconstitutional.

CHECKS AND BALANCES

In order to prevent one branch of government from becoming too dominant, the constitution creates a system of **checks and balances**, which allows each branch to counteract the powers of the other branches. For instance, the president can **veto** a bill rather than signing it into law. Veto is Latin for "I forbid," and if the president strikes down a piece of legislation through a veto, or refuses to sign it (called a **pocket veto**), the Congress can override the veto with a two-thirds majority vote. The Senate can refuse to vote for the president's judicial or cabinet appointees. And the Supreme Court can declare federal legislation unconstitutional.

2

TERMS IN ACTION

The **veto** power is one of the presidential powers that demonstrates the **separation of powers** and the **checks and balances** inherent in the Constitution. Whether the president uses a traditional veto, directly striking down the legislation, or refuses to sign a bill, called a pocket veto, Congress can exercise its checks and balances power by **overriding** the veto, provided both houses again vote for passage of the bill by a two-thirds majority. In the history of the U.S. Constitution, there have been 2,563 vetoes and only 110 instances of vetoes being overridden. George Washington issued two vetoes, and both were overridden, whereas James Adams and Thomas Jefferson never vetoed any legislation. But Franklin Roosevelt (who was president from 1932 until his death in1945) issued a total of 645 vetoes. Of these, 372 were regular vetoes and 263 were pocket vetoes. Only 9 were overridden.

Source: senate.gov

AMENDMENTS

In order to make changes to the constitution, as later generations would desire, Article V of the U.S. Constitution provides for a process to amend the constitution. A total of 27 amendments have been passed, although the first 10 amendments, known as the **Bill of Rights**, were passed simultaneously in 1791. The Bill of Rights provides specific freedoms to Americans, such as the First Amendment's guarantee of freedom of religion, freedom of speech, and freedom of press clauses. The Bill of Rights also puts certain restrictions on the federal government, such as the Fourth Amendment's prohibition on warrantless searches, or the Eighth Amendment's prohibition on cruel and unusual punishment. Later amendments have made slavery illegal, granted equal protection to former slaves, granted women the right to vote, and reduced the voting age to 18.

TERMS IN ACTION

Does the freedom of speech guarantee in the **Bill of Rights** include all speech? No. Not only are some categories of speech unprotected by the Constitution (pornography, for instance), but also, other categories of speech are illegal (extortion, for example). In 2011, the U.S. Supreme Court dealt with the question of whether the First Amendment protected the ranting of a small religious sect whose members are infamous for going to the funerals of soldiers and picketing with signs that say hateful things to the surviving family members. From Topeka, Kansas, family members belonging to what is known as the Westboro Baptist Church have gone to over 600 funerals of those who died serving the country in Afghanistan and Iraq. Carrying pickets that say things like, "God Hates Fags" and "Thank God for Dead Soldiers," the group also yells at the grieving family members, if given the chance. The family of Matthew Snyder, a marine who died in Iraq in 2006, were subject to the picketing at their son's funeral and sued the tiny fringe group. The case reached the Supreme Court, who decided in an eight-to-one vote in March 2011 that the hateful speech was protected "public speech." Chief Justice John Roberts wrote in the majority decision that, despite the noxiousness of what was being said, the content was protected because the protestors were expressing their view that America was being divinely punished for its tolerance of homosexuality. That qualified the statements as commentary on a public matter. Justice Samuel Alito was the lone dissenter, and he wrote that the First Amendment doesn't protect people from brutalizing others.

Source: *Snyder v. Phelps, 562* U.S. (2011); washingtonpost.com

Constitution Wise

First Amendment Rights

establishment clause	Prohibits the government from establishing a state religion.
freedom of speech	Guarantees to all persons the right to speak, both orally and in writing.
freedom of the press	Guarantees to all persons the right to publish and circulate their ideas without government interference.
freedom of assembly	Guarantees to all persons the right to peaceably associate and assemble with others.
free exercise clause	Guarantees to all persons the right to freely practice their religion.

Protection for Criminal Defendants

right to trial by jury	Gives criminal defendants the right to a speedy and public jury trial (Sixth Amendment).
right to confront witnesses	Gives criminal defendants the right to confront witnesses against them (Sixth Amendment).
self-incriminating protection	Gives criminal defendants the right to refuse to testify against themselves (Fifth Amendment).
cruel and unusual punishment	Protects criminal defendants from being subject to excessive bail and cruel and unusual punishment (Eighth Amendment).
double jeopardy protection	Protects criminal defendants from being tried twice for the same offense (Fifth Amendment).

Meaningful Clauses

commerce clause	Gives Congress the power to regulate commerce with foreign nations and among the different states (Art. IV, § 1).
Supremacy Clause	Makes the U.S. Constitution and federal laws the supreme law of the land (Art. VI, § 1).
full faith and credit clause	Requires each state to recognize the laws and court decisions of every other state (Art. IV, § 1).
privileges and immunities clause	Requires states to give out-of-state citizens the same rights as they give their own citizens Art. IV, § 2; Fourteenth Amendement).
equal protection clause	Requires that similarly situated persons receive similar treatment under the law (Fourteenth Amendment).
due process clause	Provides that no person shall be deprived of life, liberty, or property without fairness and justice (due process of law) (Fifth Amendment; Fourteenth Amendment).

2

Reviewing What You Learned

After studying the chapter, write the answers to each of the following questions:

1. What are the differences between the U.S. Constitution and the Articles of Confederation?

   _____

   _____

   _____

   _____

   _____

2. How was the federal government given separation of powers by the constitution?

   _____

   _____

   _____

   _____

3. What are the differences between articles and amendments?

   _____

   _____

   _____

   _____

4. What is federalism?

   _____

   _____

   _____

   _____

5. What does *bicameral* mean?

   _____

   _____

   _____

   _____

6. How many members of the House of Representatives are there, and what term length do they serve?

   _____

   _____

   _____

   _____

7. How many members of the Senate are there, and what term length do they serve ?

   _____

   _____

   _____

   _____

8. What are some powers in Article I of the U.S. Constitution that Congress has the power to exercise?

   _____

   _____

   _____

   _____

   _____

9. What do the executive branch powers include in Article II of the U.S. Constitution?

   _____

   _____

   _____

   _____

10. Describe some of the powers of the U.S. Supreme Court listed in Article III of the constitution.

    _____

    _____

    _____

    _____

11. What does the Supremacy Clause say?

    _____

    _____

    _____

    _____

12. What does *the doctrine of judicial review* express?

    _____

    _____

    _____

    _____

13. What are checks and balances and how does each branch of government exercise them?

_____

_____

_____

_____

14. What does the Bill of Rights do? What are some of the purposes of amendments?

_____

_____

_____

_____

Understanding Legal Concepts

Indicate whether each statement is true or false. Then, change the italicized work or phrase of each false statement to make it true.

ANSWERS

_____ **1.** The _U.S. Constitution_ was the first foundational governing document in American history.

_____ **2.** Our federal constitution provides _national_ representation.

_____ **3.** _Articles_ modify or invalidate earlier parts of the constitution.

_____ **4.** _Federalism_ allows state governments to retain their individual governing powers, even though the federal government is given broad powers.

_____ **5.** The number of representatives in the _Senate_ is based on each state's population.

_____ **6.** Congress's _elastic powers_ are the specifically stated powers of Congress and are found in Article 1, section 8.

_____ **7.** The _executive branch_ is headed by the U.S. President.

_____ **8.** The jurisdiction of the _U.S. Supreme Court_ is primarily appellate, but it also is given original jurisdiction over certain legal matters.

_____ **9.** Latin for _treaties_ is "I forbid."

_____ **10.** The _pocket veto_ puts certain restrictions on the federal government.

Checking Terminology

From the list of legal terms that follows, select the one that matches each definition.

a. amendments
b. Articles of Confederation
c. articles
d. bicameral
e. Bill of Rights
f. cabinet
g. checks and balances
h. clause
i. elastic powers
j. executive branch
k. express powers
l. federalism
m. House of Representatives
n. judicial branch
o. judicial review
p. legislative branch
q. pocket veto
r. Senate
s. separation of powers
t. Supremacy Clause
u. treaties
v. U.S. Constitution
w. U.S. Supreme Court
x. veto

ANSWERS

_____ 1. The first governing document in world history that created representative democracy.

_____ 2. Allows state governments to retain their individual governing powers; federal government is given broad powers.

_____ 3. Branch of government that makes laws.

_____ 4. Legally enforceable agreements with foreign countries.

_____ 5. Specifically stated powers of Congress.

_____ 6. To modify parts of the Constitution.

_____ 7. Highest court in the United States.

_____ 8. U.S. Supreme Court.

_____ 9. Based on each state's population.

_____ 10. Power to make laws in order to carry out express powers.

_____ 11. Smaller house of representation.

_____ 12. Loosely governed colonies and states until 1789.

_____ 13. The president's official refusal to sign a bill.

_____ 14. Independent authority to each branch of government.

_____ 15. Seven separate, original parts of the Constitution.

_____ 16. Makes federal law preeminent when federal and state law conflict.

_____ 17. Supreme Court's power to declare acts of Congress and the executive branch unconstitutional.

_____ 18. U.S. President

_____ 19. The act of the president's striking down a piece of legislation.

_____ 20. The two chambers of Congress.

_____ 21. A distinct part of a constitution section.

_____ 22. Allows each branch of government to counteract powers in another branch.

_____ 23. Heads of executive departments of government.

_____ 24. First 10 amendments to the U.S. Constitution.

PUZZLING OVER WHAT YOU LEARNED

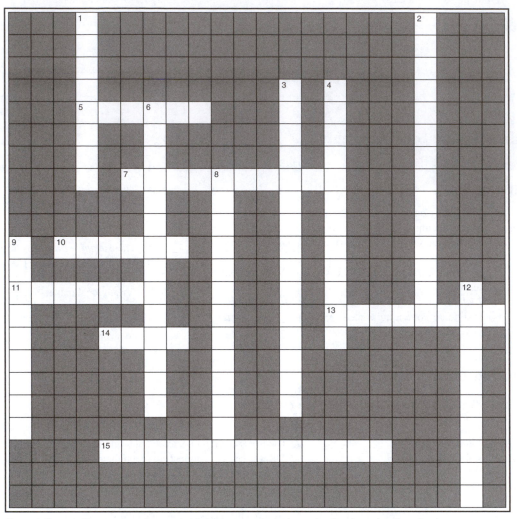

Caveat: Do not allow squares for spaces between words and punctuation (apostrophes, hyphens, etc.) when filling in crossword.

Across

5. A district part of a Constitutional Section
7. President refusing to sign a piece of legislation
10. 100 members
11. Heads of executive departments of government
13. Legally enforceable agreements with foreign governments
14. President striking down a piece of legislation
15. Specifically stated powers of Congress

Down

1. Original parts of the constitution
2. Highest court in federal judicial system
3. Federal law is preeminent when federal and state law conflict
4. First ten amendments
6. The governing document of the United States
8. The power to make laws to carry out express powers
9. Two chambers of representation
12. States have individual powers, federal government has broad powers

Crimes, Accomplices, and Defenses

ANTE INTERROGATORY

Being tried twice for the same offense is (A) entrapment, (B) petit treason, (C) double jeopardy, (D) ex post facto.

KEY TERMS

accessory after the fact *(ak·SESS·o·ree)*

accessory before the fact

accomplice *(a·COM·pliss)*

actus reus *(AHK·tus REE·us)*

aiding and abetting *(a·BET·ing)*

alibi *(AL·i·by)*

common law *(KOM·on)*

conspiracy *(kon·SPIR·a·see)*

constructively *(kon·STRUC·tiv·lee)*

cybercrime *(SY·ber·krym)*

cyberlaw *(SY·ber·law)*

defense *(de·FENSE)*

double jeopardy *(DUB·el JEP·er·dee)*

entrapment *(en·TRAP·ment)*

exclusionary rule *(eks·KLOO·shun·a·ree)*

ex post facto *(eks post FAK·to)*

felony *(FEL·en·ee)*

fruit of the poisonous tree doctrine *(DOK·trin)*

good faith exception to the exclusionary rule *(ex·SEP·shun)*

high treason *(hy TREE·zun)*

hot pursuit doctrine *(pur·SOOT DOK·trin)*

illegal profiling *(ill·EE·gul PRO·fyl·ing)*

incarceration *(in·kar·ser·AY·shun)*

intoxication *(in·tox·i·KAY·shun)*

insanity *(in·SAN·i·tee)*

mala in se *(MAL·ah in seh)*

mala prohibita *(MAL·ah pro·HIB·i·ta)*

mens rea *(menz RAY·ah)*

misdemeanor *(mis·de·MEEN·er)*

penal laws *(PEE·nel)*

petit treason *(PET·ee TREE·zun)*

plain view doctrine *(DOK·trin)*

principal in the first degree *(PRIN·se·pel)*

principal in the second degree *(de·GREE)*

prosecutor *(PRAW·se·kew·tor)*

search warrant *(WAR·ent)*

self-defense *(de·FENSE)*

stop and frisk rule

treason *(TREE·zun)*

A crime consists of either the voluntary commission or the voluntary omission of an act (known as **actus reus**), punishable by a fine, imprisonment, or both. No act is criminal unless it is both prohibited and penalized by the law of the place where it is committed. In addition, to protect the innocent, the English common law required the act to be committed with a particular state of mind known as **mens rea**, which means criminal intent. Laws that impose a penalty or punishment for a wrong against society are called **penal laws**. The U.S. Constitution prohibits Congress or any state from passing a law that is **ex post facto** (after the fact)—that is, one that holds a person criminally responsible for an act that was not a crime at the time of its commission. Similarly, the Fifth Amendment of the U.S. Constitution prevents people from being tried twice for the same offense, which is known as **double jeopardy**. For example, if a man is charged with burglary and the jury's verdict is not guilty, the **prosecutor** (the person, representing the jurisdiction where alleged crimes occur, who brings charges against those whom the police have arrested) cannot re-file the charges, viewing the first trial as a practice round. However, if the jury cannot reach a verdict, the judge can declare a "hung jury," which ends the trial. In this situation, the prosecutor would not violate the double jeopardy provision by seeking to retry the defendant.

Web Wise

- For an overview of criminal law and a link to your state criminal code, go to **www.law.cornell.edu/topics/criminal.html**.
- Read about computer crime by going to **www.cybercrime.gov**.
- The website of the U.S. Department of Justice is located at **www.usdoj.gov**.

CRIMES MALA IN SE AND MALA PROHIBITA

Crimes are divided into two classes: those that are wrong in and of themselves, such as murder, rape, and robbery; and those that are not in themselves wrong, but are criminal simply because they are prohibited by statute. The former are called crimes **mala in se** (wrongs in themselves) and require a wrongful or unlawful intent on the part of the perpetrator. The latter are called crimes **mala prohibita** (prohibited wrongs) and require no wrongful intent on the part of the perpetrator. All that is necessary is the doing of the act regardless of the intent of the actor. Under the **common law**—that is, the law used in England and the American Colonies before the American Revolution—all crimes were mala in se.

To illustrate a crime mala prohibita, a 1906 state statute made it a crime to transport intoxicating liquor within the state without a license. A truck driver in the employ of a common carrier (which was bound to accept all packages offered to it for transportation and which had no right to compel a shipper to disclose the package's contents) was convicted of violating the statute when he transported an unmarked sugar barrel filled with liquor. Nothing about the appearance of the barrel caused suspicion as to its contents, and the truck driver was ignorant of the fact that it contained intoxicating liquor. The appellate court upheld the conviction, saying that the only fact to be determined is whether the defendant did the act. The court held that knowledge of the wrongdoing or wrongful intent was immaterial in the case of a crime mala prohibita. The court said that the legislature has the power to prohibit certain acts regardless of moral purity or ignorance.

PRINCIPAL CRIMINAL CATEGORIES

Crimes are divided into three principal groups: treason, felonies, and misdemeanors.

Treason

Treason was divided into **high treason** (acts against the king) and **petit treason** (acts against one's master or lord) under the common law of England. Such a division was never followed in this country, however. Instead, **treason** is defined in the U.S. Constitution as levying war against the United States or giving aid and comfort to the nation's enemies. The charge of treason has been brought only a few dozen times in U.S. history. The first treason charge since the end of World War II was brought in 2006 against a California man who allegedly appeared in propaganda videos for Al Queda during the war on terrorism.

Felonies and Misdemeanors

A **felony** is a major crime, although its exact definition differs from state to state. It is defined in some states as "punishment by hard labor" and in others as "an infamous crime" or a crime subject to "infamous punishment." A **misdemeanor** conversely, is a less serious crime than a felony. Many states distinguish between a felony and a misdemeanor by the length of **incarceration** (confinement) involved in the sentence. For example, in Massachusetts, "A crime punishable by death or imprisonment in the state prison is a felony. All other crimes are misdemeanors." In that state, the minimum sentence in a state prison is two-and-one-half years. Many states have classified felonies and misdemeanors according to punishment by using a lettering or numbering system. A "class A felony," for example, would have a different punishment from a "class B felony." Murder, rape, armed robbery, and assault with a deadly weapon are examples of felonies. Misdemeanors call for a lighter penalty, such as a fine or jail sentence in a place other than a state prison. Disturbing the peace, simple assault, and petty larceny are examples of misdemeanors.

ACCOMPLICES

The crime of conspiracy takes place when two or more people agree to commit an unlawful act. **Conspiracy** is the getting together of two or more people to accomplish some criminal or unlawful act. The crime of conspiracy exists even when the crime or unlawful act that was agreed upon is never carried out. In some states, proof of an agreement between the parties to commit a criminal or unlawful act is all that is necessary to convict the parties of conspiracy. In many states, however, to obtain a conviction it is necessary to prove, in addition, that the parties took some action toward the commission of the crime or unlawful act. Anyone who takes part with another in the commission of a crime is called an **accomplice**.

Principal in the First Degree

A **principal in the first degree** is a person who actually commits a felony either by his or her own hand or through an innocent agent. A principal in the first degree is the one who pulls the trigger or strikes the blow. One who intentionally places poison in a glass, for example, would be considered a principal in the first degree even though the glass containing the poison was delivered to the victim by an innocent third person.

Principal in the Second Degree

A **principal in the second degree** is one who did not commit the act, but who was actually or constructively present, aiding and abetting another in the commission of a felony. **Aiding and abetting** means participating in the crime by giving assistance or encouragement. One who is positioned outside as a lookout, for example, while his or her companions are inside committing burglary would be considered **constructively** present—that is, made present by legal interpretation. In a Nevada case, a lookout stationed miles away sent a smoke signal to fellow robbers, signaling that a stagecoach was coming. The court found the lookout guilty as a principal in the second degree, holding that the lookout was constructively present even though he was miles away from the scene of the crime.

At common law, and in most states today, a principal in the second degree is subject to the same punishment as that given to a principal in the first degree.

Accessory before the Fact

An **accessory before the fact** is one who procures, counsels, or commands another to commit a felony, but who is not present when the felony is committed. Mere knowledge that a crime is going to be committed by another person is not enough to become an accessory before the fact to the crime that is subsequently committed by the other person, however. It must be shown that the accessory before the fact was active in inducing or bringing about the felony.

An accessory before the fact will be responsible for the natural and probable consequences that ensue from the crime that he or she induced, but not for a crime of a substantially different nature. Thus, if one person procures another to beat someone up and the beating results in death, the one who arranged for the beating would be an accessory before the fact to the killing because death is a natural and probable consequence of beating someone up.

Conversely, in the situation in which one person hires a man to beat up a woman and he rapes her instead, the procurer would not be an accessory before the fact to the rape, because it is a crime of a substantially different nature than that which was ordered by the procurer. Some states would view a person who hires another to commit a crime as a principal in the first degree rather than an accessory before the fact, because hiring a "hit man" makes one equally as guilty of the crime as if the hiring party had committed it.

Some states still follow the common law rule that an accessory before the fact cannot be tried in court until a principal is first convicted. Many states' criminal codes, however, now state that an accessory before the fact may be tried without regard to the principal and may be found guilty even though the principal is acquitted.

Word Wise
"Mal-" . . . "Mala"

"Mal(e)" is a prefix or word part used in many legal terms to mean bad, wrong, or fraudulent.

malconduct	malefaction	Malefactor
malice	malicious	Malfeasance

"Mala" is the plural form of the Latin word "malum," which also means bad, evil, or wrongful.

"Mala" appears in many legal phrases, including

mala fides	bad faith
mala in se	wrongs in themselves
mala praxis	malpractice
mala prohibita	prohibited wrongs or offenses

Accessory after the Fact

An **accessory after the fact** is one who receives, relieves, comforts, or assists another, with knowledge that the other person has committed a felony. To be convicted of being an accessory after the fact, a felony must have been committed by another person, and the accessory after the fact must intend that that person avoid or escape detention, arrest, trial, or punishment.

At common law, a wife could not be guilty as an accessory after the fact under the theory that she was under her husband's control and the assumption that he was the principal. Modern statutes have extended that exception, although for a different reason, to include close relatives as well. The reason is that it would be natural for spouses and close relatives to protect their loved ones who were in trouble with the law. Rhode Island and Massachusetts, for example, do not allow a criminal's spouse, parent, grandparent, child, grandchild, brother, or sister to be convicted of being an accessory after the fact to the criminal. For example, if a mother harbors her son from the police, after knowing he has committed a felony, she would not be charged as an accessory after the fact. However, under a different fact pattern, she could be guilty as a conspirator with him.

CRIMINAL DEFENSES

Evidence offered by a defendant to defeat a criminal charge or civil lawsuit is known as a **defense**. Some common criminal defenses are alibi, entrapment, insanity, and self-defense. **Alibi** is a defense that places the defendant in a different place than the crime scene, so that it would have been impossible to commit the crime. **Entrapment** may be used as a defense when a police officer induces a person to commit a crime that the person would not have committed otherwise, and would not be predisposed to commit as demonstrated by the person's lack of criminal history. **Insanity** is a defense available to mentally ill defendants who can prove that they did not know the difference between right and wrong or did not appreciate the criminality of their conduct. **Self-defense** is a justification for the use of force in resisting an unlawful, imminent attack. Those claiming self-defense may use no more force than is reasonably necessary to stop the attack. Most states require someone claiming self-defense to retreat—if reasonably possible—except when that person is in his or her own home. One defense that rarely ever works, assuming it is allowed in a jurisdiction, is the defense of **intoxication**. This defense is based on the idea that someone might be unable to form the mens rea to commit a crime if he or she is so intoxicated (which would include being under the influence of drugs, as well). Involuntary intoxication can be a defense, but in most jurisdictions there is no defense allowed to those who voluntarily take drugs or drink alcohol before committing crimes.

TERMS IN ACTION

Woody Will Smith was charged in 2009 with the **felony** of all felonies: murdering his wife Amanda Hornsby-Smith by strangling her with an extension cord. The physical evidence against him was overwhelming and conclusive that he killed his wife. But Smith claimed in his defense that he was **insane** at the time he killed his wife, due to caffeine **intoxication**. According to his defense lawyer, Smith suspected that his wife was going to leave him weeks earlier and that, as a result of his anxiety and sleeplessness, he began drinking energy drinks and ingesting diet pills, one after another. This condition, the lawyer claimed, rendered Smith unable to form the intent (**mens rea**) to kill. The jury was unmoved by that defense. It found Smith guilty of murder in 2010 and sentenced him to life in prison.

Source: cbsnews.com; nydailynews.com

The U.S. Constitution provides broad protection for criminal defendants. For example, under the Fourth Amendment, a **search warrant** (a written order of the court authorizing law enforcement officers to search and seize certain property) must, generally, be obtained before officers may enter private property without permission. A search warrant is not needed to seize items that are in plain view of a lawfully positioned police officer, under the **plain view doctrine**. Likewise, a search warrant is not needed, under the **hot pursuit doctrine** when police pursue a fleeing suspect into a private area. Similarly, under the **stop and frisk rule** a police officer who believes that a person is acting suspiciously and could be armed may stop and frisk the suspect

2

for weapons, without a search warrant. The same is true when police lawfully arrest someone. Police officers are also allowed to stop and search a motor vehicle and to order all passengers out of the vehicle, but only when they have probable cause to do so.

Illegal profiling may also be used as a defense. **Illegal profiling** is a law enforcement action, such as a detention or arrest, based solely on race, religion, national origin, ethnicity, gender, or sexual orientation of the person being charged, rather than on that person's behavior or on information identifying the person as having engaged in criminal activity.

Under the **exclusionary rule** (a doctrine created by the U.S. Supreme Court) evidence obtained by an unconstitutional search or seizure cannot be used at the trial of a defendant. Similarly, under the **fruit of the poisonous tree doctrine** evidence derived from an illegal search is inadmissible. Thus, law enforcement officers could not use as evidence illegal weapons found in a building that they had unlawfully searched while looking for illicit drugs. The **good faith exception to the exclusionary rule** makes admissible evidence discovered by unlawful search by officers acting in a good faith, but in the mistaken belief that the search was valid.

CYBERLAW

Cyberlaw, the area of law that involves computers and their related problems, is a term that has recently come into common usage. **Cybercrimes**—criminal activity associated with a computer network—include such crimes as Spamming, hacking, computer fraud, identity theft, stalking, blackmail, and cyber-terrorism. For instance, what once was thought of as being only drug trafficking can now include operating an illegal, online pharmacy. The first federal legislation to respond to the increase of computer crime was the 1986 Computer Fraud and Abuse Act, which predated the Internet (at least what we think of as the World Wide Web). So many criminal acts are committed through the use of computers and the Internet that the Computer Fraud and Abuse Act has been amended at least six times, including through the Patriot Act, passed after 9/11.

Web Wise

The United States Department of Justice has a website dedicated to inform the public about computer crimes, including legal resources and news releases on the latest arrests of those accused of cybercrimes. The website can be found at **http://www.cybercrime.gov**.

TERMS IN ACTION

Cybercrimes, such as hacking and online identity theft, are most often committed for financial gain. Every now and then, though, a cybercrime is committed for no other reason than spite. Allan Eric Carlson was a long-suffering Philadelphia Phillies fan who had had enough of the team he hated to love—the baseball team with the most losses in Major League Baseball history. Rather than writing a letter to the editor of a Philadelphia newspaper, around 2001, he sent thousands of Spam emails expressing his disgust. But he didn't send them from his own e-mail account. According to the Department of Justice, Carlson hacked into computers around the country, hijacking the return e-mail addresses of Philadelphia sports writers, ESPN, Fox Sports, as well as Phillies employees, and had those e-mail accounts launch his e-mail tirades. Those e-mails were then bounced back to the original victims of the hacking. Carlson was arrested in 2003 and was eventually convicted of 79 counts of identity theft and computer fraud. In 2005, Carlson was sentenced to four years in prison. In 2008, the Phillies won the World Series, and the next year they played in it again. Carlson maintains his own web log, and calls himself a "political prisoner of the United States government."

Sources: usdoj.gov; justice.gov; allancarlson.blogspot.com

Reviewing What You Learned

After studying the chapter, write the answers to each of the following questions:

1. Who brings the action in a criminal case? _____
   _____
   _____
   _____

2. What is an ex post facto law? _____
   _____
   _____
   _____

3. How does a crime that is mala in se differ from a crime that is mala prohibita? _____
   _____
   _____
   _____

4. List the three classifications of crimes. _____
   _____
   _____
   _____

5. What is the difference between a felony and a misdemeanor?
   _____
   _____
   _____

6. What is the difference between a principal in the first degree and a principal in the second degree? _____
   _____
   _____
   _____

7. How does the punishment of a principal in the first degree compare with that of a principal in the second degree?
   _____
   _____
   _____
   _____

8. What is the difference between an accessory before the fact and an accessory after the fact? _____
   _____
   _____
   _____

9. Is the punishment for an accessory before the fact the same as that for a principal to a crime? _____
   _____
   _____
   _____

10. Under Rhode Island law and Massachusetts law, who cannot be held liable as an accessory after the fact? _____
    _____
    _____
    _____

2

Understanding Legal Concepts

Indicate whether each statement is true or false. Then, change the italicized word or phrase of each false statement to make it true.

ANSWERS

_____ 1. A crime is an offense against *the individual victim alone*. It *is not* a wrong against all of society.

_____ 2. A felony is a *less* serious crime than a misdemeanor.

_____ 3. A crime that is wrong in and of itself is called a crime *mala in se*.

_____ 4. *Petit treason* is a crime that is defined in the U.S. Constitution.

_____ 5. No act is criminal unless it is both *prohibited and penalized* by the law of the jurisdiction in which it is committed.

_____ 6. One who intentionally places poison in a glass is a *principal in the first degree* even though the glass containing the poison is delivered to the victim by an innocent third person.

_____ 7. A *principal in the second degree* is one who procures, counsels, or commands another to commit a felony, but who is not present when the felony is committed.

_____ 8. Mere knowledge that a specific crime is going to be committed by another person *is enough* for someone to become an accessory before the fact.

_____ 9. At common law, a wife *could not* be held as an accessory after the fact to a crime committed by her husband, under the theory that she was under the husband's coercion.

_____ 10. In general, an *accessory before the fact* is subject to the same punishment as that given to a principal.

Checking Terminology

From the list of legal terms that follows, select the one that matches each definition.

ANSWERS

a. accessory after the fact
b. accessory before the fact
c. accomplice
d. actus reus
e. aiding and abetting
f. alibi
g. common law
h. conspiracy
i. constructively
j. cybercrime
k. cyberlaw
l. defense
m. double jeopardy
n. entrapment
o. exclusionary rule
p. ex post facto
q. felony
r. fruit of the poisonous tree doctrine
s. good faith exception to the exclusionary rule
t. high treason
u. hot pursuit doctrine
v. illegal profiling
w. incarceration
x. insanity
y. intoxication
z. mala in se
aa. mala prohibita
bb. mens rea
cc. misdemeanor

_____ 1. Evidence discovered unlawfully by officers acting in good faith, but under the mistaken belief that a search that was valid, can be used at the trial of a defendant.

_____ 2. Under the influence of alcohol or drugs—a defense that rarely works.

_____ 3. A minor crime; not a felony.

_____ 4. Wrong in and of itself.

_____ 5. Evidence offered by a defendant to defeat a criminal charge or civil lawsuit.

_____ 6. One who actually commits a felony.

_____ 7. A major crime, punishable by imprisonment in a state prison.

_____ 8. One who procures, counsels, or commands another to commit a felony, but who is not present when the felony is committed.

_____ 9. Tried twice for the same offense.

_____ 10. After the fact.

_____ 11. One who did not commit the act, but who was present, aiding and abetting another in the commission of a felony.

_____ 12. A defense available to mentally ill defendants who can prove that they did not know the difference between right and wrong or did not appreciate the criminality of their conduct.

_____ 13. Prohibited wrong.

_____ 14. The statutory and case law used in England and in the American Colonies before the American Revolution.

_____ 15. A written order of the court authorizing law enforcement officers to search and seize certain property.

_____ 16. One who receives, relieves, comforts, or assists another, with knowledge that the other has committed a felony.

_____ 17. An excuse for the use of force in resisting attack.

_____ 18. Acts against the king (under the English common law).

_____ 19. A defense that may be used when a police officer induces a person to commit a crime that the person would not have otherwise committed.

_____ 20. Participating in a crime by giving assistance or encouragement.

_____ 21. A search warrant is not needed to seize items that are in plain view of a lawfully positioned police officer.

dd. penal laws	
ee. petit treason	
ff. plain view doctrine	
gg. principal in the first degree	
hh. principal in the second degree	
ii. prosecutor	
jj. search warrant	
kk. self-defense	
ll. stop and frisk rule treason	

_____ 22. A defense that places the defendant in a different place than the crime scene so that it would have been impossible for the defendant to have committed the crime.

_____ 23. Acts against one's master or lord (under the English common law).

_____ 24. The getting together of two or more people to plan and accomplish some criminal or unlawful act.

_____ 25. Anyone who takes part with another in the commission of a crime.

_____ 26. Laws that impose a penalty or punishment for a wrong against society.

_____ 27. The person who brings charges against those whom the police have arrested for crimes.

_____ 28. A search warrant that is not needed when police pursue a fleeing suspect into a private area.

_____ 29. A rule that allows police officers who believe a person is acting suspiciously and could be armed to stop and frisk the suspect without a search warrant.

_____ 30. Made so by legal interpretation.

_____ 31. Evidence generated or derived from an illegal search or seizure that cannot be used at the trial of a defendant.

_____ 32. Evidence obtained by an unconstitutional search or seizure that cannot be used at the trial of a defendant.

_____ 33. Levying war against the United States or giving aid and comfort to its enemies.

_____ 34. A law enforcement action, such as a detention or arrest, based solely on the race, religion, national origin, ethnicity, gender, or sexual orientation of the person charged.

_____ 35. Criminal intent.

_____ 36. A voluntary act.

Using Legal Language

Read the following story and fill in the blank lines with legal terms taken from the list of terms at the beginning of this chapter:

Abigail hired two _____, Bonnie and Clyde, to rob a bank. She waited at home while the others carried out the act, which was a(n) _____, because it was an offense against the public at large. Bonnie, with a state of mind known as _____, went into the bank and committed the robbery, while Clyde, who was _____ and _____, waited outside in the get-away car. Abigail would be classified as a(n) _____, Bonnie a(n) _____, and Clyde a(n) _____ to robbery, which is a(n) _____ rather than a(n) _____. It is also a crime that is mala _____ because it is wrong in and of itself. After the commission of the crime, Bonnie and Clyde drove to the home of their sister, Dinah, who took them in, knowing that they had robbed the bank. Dinah was found not guilty of being a(n) _____, because she is a close relative. She could not be tried—that is, _____—

a second time for the same offense because it would put her in _____, which is against the U.S. Constitution. When Abigail, Bonnie, and Clyde agreed to commit the robbery and took action to carry it out, they committed the crime of _____. Once they were convicted, they were called _____. They had no _____—that is, evidence to defeat the criminal charges against them—and they had no _____ that placed them in a different place than the crime scene. Had Bonnie and Clyde been born generations later, they wouldn't have needed to physically go to a bank to access its assets. Instead, they could have _____ into the bank's computer mainframe and transferred the bank's electronically listed deposits into their own accounts. Or, they could have sent thousands of _____ to unsuspecting Internet users, attempting to commit _____, which would allow Bonnie and Clyde to use other people's identities.

PUZZLING OVER WHAT YOU LEARNED

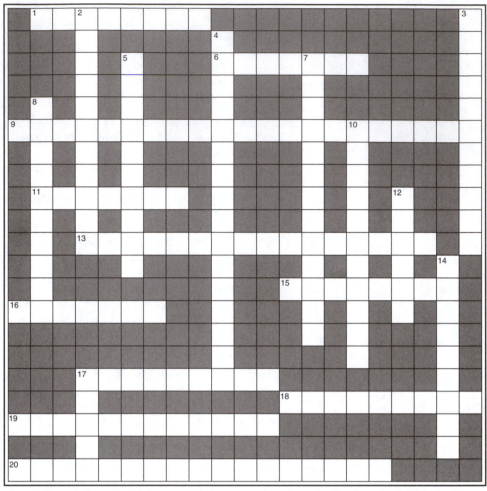

Caveat: Do not allow squares for spaces between words and punctuation (apostrophes, hyphens, etc.) when filling in crossword.

Across

1. A defense available to mentally ill defendants.
6. The levying of war against the United States or giving aid and comfort to its enemies.
9. One who receives, relieves, comforts, or assists another with knowledge that the other has committed a felony.
11. Criminal intent.
13. Evidence obtained by an unconstitutional search or seizure that cannot be used at the trial of a defendant.
15. Wrong in and of itself.
16. Evidence offered by a defendant to defeat a criminal charge or civil lawsuit.
17. A voluntary act.
18. The case law used in England and the American colonies before the American Revolution.
19. Acts against one's master or lord.
20. Participating in a crime by giving assistance or encouragement.

Down

2. An excuse of the use of force in resisting attack.
3. After the fact.
4. A rule that allows police officers who believe a person is acting suspiciously and could be armed to stop and frisk that person for weapons without a search warrant.
5. The getting together of two or more people to accomplish some criminal or unlawful act.
7. A written order of the court authorizing law enforcement officers to search and seize certain property.
8. Anyone who takes part with another in the commission of a crime.
10. Acts against the king (under the English common law).
12. A major crime, punishable by imprisonment in a state prison.
14. Laws that impose a penalty or punishment for a wrong against society.
17. A defense that places the defendant in a different place than the crime scene so that it would have been impossible to commit the crime.

CHAPTER 11

Crimes Against Property

ANTE INTERROGATORY

The wrongful taking and carrying away of personal property of another with the intent to steal is (A) trespassing, (B) larceny, (C) asportation, (D) extortion.

CHAPTER OUTLINE

Elements of Crimes

Larceny
Wrongful Taking
Carrying Away
Personal Property
Property of Another
Intent to Steal
Degrees of Larceny

Embezzlement

Larceny by False Pretenses

Bribery, Extortion, and Coercion
RICO

Receipt of Stolen Goods

Forgery

KEY TERMS

animus furandi *(AN·i·mus fer·AN·day)*

asportation *(as·por·TA·shun)*

attempted larceny *(a ·TEMPT· ed LAR ·sen·ee)*

bailee *(bay·LEE)*

bribery *(BRY·be·ree)*

chattels *(CHAT·els)*

chose in action *(shohz in AK·shun)*

circumstantial evidence *(ser·kum·STAN·shel EV·i·dens)*

coercion *(ko·ER·shen)*

computer fraud *(frawd)*

constructive possession *(kon·STRUK·tiv po·SESH·en)*

criminal fraud *(KRIM·i·nel frawd)*

custody *(KUS·te·dee)*

efficacy *(EF·i·ka·see)*

embezzlement *(em·BEZ·ul·ment)*

extortion *(eks·TOR·shun)*

forgery *(FOR·jer·ee)*

fraud in esse contractus *(ESS·ay kon·TRAKT·es)*

grand larceny *(LAR·sen·ee)*

larceny *(LAR·sen·ee)*

larceny by false pretenses *(PRE·ten·sez)*

mail fraud *(frawd)*

money laundering *(MUN·ee LAWN·der·ing)*

negotiable instrument *(ne·GO·she·a·bul IN·stru·ment)*

personal property *(PER·son·al PROP·er·tee)*
petit larceny *(PET·ee LAR·sen·ee)*
petty larceny *(PET·ee LAR·sen·ee)*
possession *(po·SESH·en)*
prosecution *(pros·e·KYOO·shun)*
racketeering *(rak·a·TEER·ing)*
real property *(PROP·er·tee)*

receiving stolen goods *(re·SEEV·ing STOH·len)*
RICO *(REE·coh)*
uttering *(UT·er·ing)*
white collar crime *(wite·KALL·er kryme)*
wire fraud *(frawd)*

ELEMENTS OF CRIMES

To be criminal, in addition to having to be committed voluntarily with wrongful intent, acts must have exact definitions. This is so that there can be no question about what is against the law. At common law, exact definitions came about by assigning specific elements to each crime. No person could be convicted of a crime unless each element of the crime was proved beyond a reasonable doubt. Most states still define crimes in this manner. This chapter discusses the elements of some of the most commonly committed crimes against property.

LARCENY

The common law definition of **larceny** is "the wrongful taking and carrying away of personal property of another with the intent to steal." Broken down into its elements, the crime consists of the following:

1. a wrongful taking
2. a carrying away
3. personal property
4. of another
5. with intent to steal

Wrongful Taking

A wrongful taking means a trespass to someone else's possession of personal property. More precisely, it is the exercise of dominion and control over the personal property in the possession of another, without the right to do so.

Carrying Away

In addition to the wrongful taking, a carrying away must occur, which is called an **asportation** in legal terminology. This act involves a removal of the property from the place it formerly occupied.

To illustrate, in a case in which a thief attempted to steal a fur coat from a store dummy, but was unable to do so because the coat was attached to the dummy by a chain, the court held that no larceny occurred, because the coat was not carried away. Instead, this would have been the crime of **attempted larceny** (an attempt to commit larceny, falling short of its commission), but this offense was not placed in the original charge. The defendant was protected by the right to freedom from double jeopardy. In another case, a thief opened a cash register and picked up some bills, but dropped them back into the register drawer when he was discovered by the owner. In holding that a carrying away occurred, the court said, "If he had actually taken the money into his hand, and lifted it from the place where the owner had placed it, so as to entirely sever it from the spot where it was so placed, with the intention of stealing it, he would be guilty of larceny, though he may have dropped it into the place it was lying, upon being discovered, and had never had it out of the drawer."

Personal Property

The subject matter of larceny must be **personal property** (also called goods or **chattels**), which is defined as "everything that is the subject of ownership not coming under the category of real estate." A **negotiable instrument** (a written, unconditional order or promise to pay money, which can be transferred by the original receiver to others), such as a check, draft, or promissory note, was not the subject of larceny at common law, as it was not personal property. Such an instrument is called a **chose in action**, which is evidence of a right to property, but not the property itself. For example, a check is evidence of the right to the amount of money for which the check is written, but it is not the money itself. Statutes have been enacted by most states making it a crime to commit larceny of choses in action.

The item stolen must be capable of being owned to be the subject of larceny. Older cases held that it was not larceny to steal a dead body, as a dead body could have no owner; however, it was larceny to steal the casket containing the body as well as the clothing on the body, as these things were owned by the personal representatives of the decedent's estate. Wild animals having no owner could not be the subject of larceny for the same reason, even though they were taken from another's land.

Real property (land or anything permanently affixed thereto) is not the subject of larceny unless made so by statute. Thus, such things as growing trees, fences, doors or other fixtures, seaweed, and minerals or stone not yet mined or quarried are not the subject of common law larceny. The cutting down and carrying away of a standing tree would not be larceny; however, the carrying away of wood already cut would be larceny. Statutes have been passed by some states making it larceny to steal many things not included in common law larceny.

Property of Another

The general rule is that a person cannot commit larceny of his or her own property, with the exception of stealing his or her own property from a **bailee** (one to whom it has been rightfully entrusted). The property must be taken from the possession of another. The law, however, distinguishes between possession and custody. **Custody** is the care and keeping of anything; **possession** is the detention and control of anything. A person is said to have constructive possession of property when it is held in custody for that person by another. **Constructive possession** is possession not actual, but assumed to exist. For example, a supermarket cashier has custody of the money in the cash register. The store itself (or the store owner) has possession of it. Anyone stealing it from the cashier commits larceny from the possession of the owner, which is true even if the cashier is the thief.

Intent to Steal

An essential element of larceny is called **animus furandi** an intent to steal. This term means "the intent to deprive the owner of the property permanently." Thus, at common law, the borrowing of a neighbor's horse without consent, but with the intent to return it later in the day, was not considered to be larceny. (It was, if anything, a trespass to personal property.) Some more recent cases, although still requiring intent to steal, define larceny as "appropriating the goods to a use inconsistent with the owner's rights," thus avoiding the problem mentioned earlier.

The intent to steal must exist at the time of the taking. A person who takes another's goods with permission or with the intent to return them, and later changes his or her mind and decides to steal them, is guilty of embezzlement rather than common law larceny. Embezzlement is discussed later.

Degrees of Larceny

By statute, larceny is divided into two degrees, **petit larceny** (usually spelled **petty larceny**) and **grand larceny**. The former is usually a misdemeanor; the latter is a felony. Although the states differ in their distinctions between the two, one common distinction makes it a misdemeanor to steal property with a value of $250 or less (petty larceny) and a felony to steal property with a value exceeding $250 (grand larceny).

2

> **Word Wise**
> *"Animus" [Latin for mind; intention]*
>
> | Examples | Meaning |
> | --- | --- |
> | **animus cancellandi** | intent to cancel or destroy (as applied to wills) |
> | **animus capiendi** | intent to capture or take |
> | **animus defamandi** | intent to defame |
> | **animus derelinquendi** | intent to abandon or relinquish |
> | **animus lucrandi** | intent to make a gain or profit (become lucrative) |
> | **animus recuperandi** | intent to recover or recuperate |
> | **animus signandi** | intent to sign an instrument (such as a will) |
> | **animus testandi** | intent to make a will (testament) |

EMBEZZLEMENT

Embezzlement, which is essentially a breach of trust, consists of the same elements as larceny except that instead of "wrongful taking," a "rightful taking" occurs. The crime did not exist at common law, but was created by statute to fill the gap in the law of larceny when someone, such as an employee or bailee, was entrusted with property of another and appropriated it to his or her own use, or when property was stolen before it came into the possession of the owner.

To illustrate, if a customer pays a supermarket cashier money for groceries and the cashier puts the money directly into his or her pocket rather than into the cash register, it is embezzlement because the money did not come into the possession of the supermarket before it was stolen. It would have been larceny, however, if the cashier had first placed the money into the cash register and then stolen it later, as it would have come into the constructive possession of the store before it was stolen.

LARCENY BY FALSE PRETENSES

Larceny by false pretenses also called **criminal fraud** is another crime created by statute to fill a gap in common law larceny. In general, it is the act of knowingly and deliberately obtaining the property of another by false pretenses with intent to defraud. The elements of this crime are quite similar to the elements of the tort of deceit, which is discussed in a later chapter.

Some states have consolidated larceny, embezzlement, and larceny by false pretenses into one statute so that the need no longer exists for the **prosecution** (the state bringing the action) to distinguish among them. The defendant is merely charged with violating that particular chapter and section of the statute, which includes all three common law crimes.

> ## TERMS IN ACTION
>
> Garth Flaherty lived near Washington State University, and living near a large university is a good place to live if, like Flaherty, you're interested in stealing women's undergarments. Throughout the apartment complexes in Pullman, Washington, many women reported their underwear and bras having been stolen from their laundry rooms. In 2007, the 24-year-old Flaherty was spotted leaving a laundry room with women's underwear, and the police tracked him down at his apartment. Inside, they found 1,613 pairs of women's underwear, bras, and other garments, which the police said weighed over 93 pounds and filled five garbage bags. Charged with 12 counts of second-degree **burglary** and one count of first-degree **larceny**, Flaherty pleaded guilty in 2008 and was sentenced to 45 days in jail.
>
> Source: msnbc.msn.com

BRIBERY, EXTORTION, AND COERCION

It is illegal to give money or other items to public officials to sway their official activity. The giving or receiving of a reward to influence any official act is called **bribery** and is against the law. It is also illegal for public officials to demand payment from others for doing official acts. This type of action is known as **extortion** and is defined as "the corrupt demanding or receiving by a person in office of a fee for services that should be performed gratuitously." **Coercion** also a crime, means "compelling someone to do something by threat or force."

RICO

A federal statute referred to as **RICO** (an acronym for the Racketeer Influenced and Corrupt Organizations Act) is designed to stop organized criminal activity from invading legitimate businesses. Under RICO, it is illegal to conduct a legitimate business with funds obtained from a pattern of racketeering activity. **Racketeering** (activities of organized criminals who extort money from legitimate businesses) includes many kinds of criminal activity such as arson, robbery, bribery, extortion, and **money laundering**. "Money laundering" is a metaphor used to describe how money acquired through criminal activities is "washed" so that it can look like it was earned legitimately. That is usually done by putting the "dirty" money through a business, which treats it like regular income so that the cash appears clean. Also included in the definition of racketeering are of the crimes of **mail fraud wire fraud** and **computer fraud** (the offense of using mail, wire, or computers to obtain money, property, or services, by false pretenses). Those types of crimes are part of the category of crimes commonly called **white-collar crimes**. "White-collar crime" is a term first coined by a sociologist in 1939 to refer to crimes committed by those with high status and respect, but whose crimes are committed in the course of their employment.

TERMS IN ACTION

The **Racketeer Influenced Corrupt Organizations Act (RICO)** laws were designed to combat organized crime, particularly by the mafia. One of the more famous RICO cases brought against the mafia was also one of longest criminal trials in American history, known as the "Pizza Connection Trial." Following an FBI investigation into the link between Sicilian and New York mobsters and the use of pizza restaurants as outlets for **money laundering** from heroin smuggling and distribution, the U.S. Department of Justice prosecuted 24 alleged crime family members. The Pizza Connection trial began in Manhattan in October 1985 and ended in March 1987. Eighteen defendants were convicted. One of the key federal prosecutors was future New York City Mayor (and 2008 presidential candidate) Rudy Giuliani, and one of the key witnesses was Joseph Pistone, the first FBI agent to go undercover in the New York mafia, and who was played by Johnny Depp in the 1997 movie, titled after Pistone's undercover identity, *Donnie Brasco*.

Source: history.com; americanmafia.com; nytimes.com

RECEIPT OF STOLEN GOODS

It is a crime to buy, receive, or aid in the concealment of stolen or embezzled property, knowing it to have been stolen. This is the crime of **receiving stolen goods**. To constitute the crime, the receiver must have knowledge that the goods of which he or she is taking possession were stolen, and the receiver must have felonious intent.

One of the major issues in determining the guilt or innocence of people accused of the crime is whether or not they actually knew that the goods were stolen. If they either knew or believed that the property was stolen at the time it came into their possession or if at any time while it was in their possession they ascertained that it was stolen property and undertook to deprive

2

the owner of the rightful use of it, they may be convicted of the crime. If they did not know that the goods were stolen, they cannot be found guilty. **Circumstantial evidence** is relevant here. As opposed to eyewitness testimony, circumstantial evidence is of an indirect nature and requires someone to draw an inference about a fact. For example, the evidence that the defendant paid an unreasonably low purchase price for goods is often used to prove that he or she had knowledge that the goods were stolen.

Web Wise
Need to find out what an acronym like RICO stands for?

Web Address	Definition
http://www.ucc.ie/cgi-bin/acronym	The **Acronym Database** allows you to find out what an acronym means; you may also search for a word to see what acronyms it is used in.
www.wikipedia.org	Type in "RICO" to read about it.

FORGERY

Forgery is defined as "the fraudulent making or altering of a writing whereby the rights of another might be prejudiced." The subject matter of forgery must be a writing or a document that has some legal **efficacy** (effectiveness), such as a deed, mortgage, will, promissory note, check, receipt, or other writing. The forgery of a person's signature to a will that is invalid because of an improper number of witnesses would not be a forgery, because the will had no legal efficacy because of insufficient witnesses.

People can commit forgery by signing their own name if they fraudulently hold themselves out to be someone else of that same name, sign another's name with intent to defraud, or write something in a document above another's existing signature. It has also been held to be forgery to obtain someone's genuine signature by **fraud in esse contractus**—that is, fraud as to the essential nature of the contract—as when a person signs a promissory note, thinking he or she is signing a receipt or other instrument.

Fraudulent intent is necessary to commit forgery. Thus, if someone is authorized to sign another's name, or reasonably believes that he or she has that authority, it would not be the crime of forgery to sign the other's name.

Uttering a forged negotiable instrument, such as a check or promissory note, is also a crime. **Uttering** means offering a forged negotiable instrument to another person, knowing it to be forged and intending to defraud.

Reviewing What You Learned

After studying the chapter, write the answers to each of the following questions:

1. List the five elements of common law larceny. _____

2. Describe a wrongful taking. _____

3. What is a carrying away? _____

_____

_____

_____

_____

4. Of what must the subject matter of larceny consist? _____

_____

_____

_____

5. Describe and give an example of a chose in action. _____

_____

_____

_____

_____

6. Why did the court hold that it was not larceny to steal a dead body? _____

_____

_____

_____

_____

7. When is real property the subject of larceny? _____

_____

_____

_____

8. Under what circumstances is it considered larceny to steal one's own property? _____

_____

_____

_____

9. Describe the difference between possession and custody.

_____

_____

_____

_____

10. Define "intent to steal." _____

_____

_____

_____

11. At common law, is borrowing with intent to return considered to be larceny? Why or why not? _____

_____

_____

_____

12. Under what circumstances must the intent to steal exist for the action to constitute larceny? _____

_____

_____

_____

13. Name the two degrees of larceny. _____

_____

_____

_____

_____

14. What is the amount that divides the two degrees of larceny, by statute in some states? _____

_____

_____

_____

15. In comparing the crimes of larceny and embezzlement, what is the one element that differs? _____

_____

_____

_____

2

16. What have some states done, by statute, to larceny, embezzlement, and larceny by false pretenses so that no need exists to distinguish among them? _____

_____

_____

_____

_____

17. In what way does bribery differ from extortion? _____

_____

_____

_____

_____

Understanding Legal Concepts

Indicate whether each statement is true or false. Then, change the italicized word or phrase of each false statement to make it true.

ANSWERS

_____ 1. In addition to a wrongful taking, a carrying away must occur to constitute *larceny*.

_____ 2. The subject matter of larceny must be *personal property*.

_____ 3. Older cases held that it *was* larceny to steal a dead body.

_____ 4. The cutting down and carrying away of a standing tree *was* larceny, at common law.

_____ 5. One cannot commit larceny of *ones own* property except from a bailee.

_____ 6. To constitute larceny, the property must be taken from another's *custody*.

_____ 7. An essential element of *larceny* is an intent to steal.

_____ 8. Petty larceny is usually a *misdemeanor* and grand larceny is a *felony*.

_____ 9. Embezzlement includes a *wrongful* taking.

_____ 10. The crime of bribery is *the same as* the crime of extortion.

Checking Terminology

From the list of legal terms that follows, select the one that matches each definition:

ANSWERS

a. animus furandi
b. asportation
c. attempted larceny
d. bailee
e. bribery
f. chattels
g. chose in action
h. circumstantial evidence
i. coercion
j. computer fraud
k. constructive possession
l. criminal fraud
m. custody
n. efficacy
o. embezzlement
p. extortion
q. forgery
r. fraud in esse contractus
s. grand larceny
t. larceny
u. larceny by false pretenses
v. mail fraud
w. money laundering

_____ 1. Using the computer to obtain money, property, or services by false pretenses.

_____ 2. Using mail to obtain money, property, or services by false pretenses.

_____ 3. The care and keeping of anything.

_____ 4. A federal statute designed to stop organized criminal activity from invading legitimate businesses.

_____ 5. One to whom personal property is given under a bailment contract.

_____ 6. Activities of organized criminals who extort money from legitimate businesses.

_____ 7. Everything that is the subject of ownership not coming under the category of real estate. (Select two answers.)

_____ 8. The corrupt demanding or receiving by a person in office of a fee for services that should be performed gratuitously.

_____ 9. Possession not actual, but assumed to exist.

_____ 10. The party by whom criminal proceedings are started or conducted; the state.

_____ 11. A written, unconditional promise to pay money, which can be transferred by the original receiver to others.

_____ 12. Effectiveness.

_____ 13. Compelling someone to do something by threat or force.

_____ 14. Using the wires to obtain money, property, or services, by false pretenses.

_____ 15. At common law, the wrongful taking and carrying away of personal property of another with the intent to steal.

_____ 16. The giving or receiving of a reward to influence any official act.

_____ 17. The detention and control of anything.

_____ 18. Crimes of racketeering, mail fraud, wire fraud, and computer fraud.

x. negotiable instrument
y. personal property
z. petit larceny
aa. possession
bb. prosecution
cc. racketeering
dd. real property
ee. receiving stolen goods
ff. RICO
gg. uttering white collar crime
hh. wire fraud

____ 19. Knowingly and deliberately obtaining the property of another by false pretenses, with intent to defraud. (Select two answers.)
____ 20. Making money look like it was earned legitimately.
____ 21. The fraudulent misappropriation of property by a person to whom it has been entrusted.
____ 22. The ground and anything permanently attached to it, including land, buildings, and growing trees, and the airspace above the ground.
____ 23. Evidence of a right to property, but not the property itself.
____ 24. Larceny that is a misdemeanor rather than a felony.
____ 25. An attempt to commit larceny, but falling short of its commission.
____ 26. Evidence of an indirect nature.
____ 27. Offering a forged negotiable instrument to another person, knowing it to be forged and intending to defraud.
____ 28. The fraudulent making or altering of a writing whereby the rights of another might be prejudiced.
____ 29. The carrying away of goods.
____ 30. Larceny that is a felony.
____ 31. An intent to steal.

Using Legal Language

Read the following story and fill in the blank lines with legal terms taken from the list of terms at the beginning of this chapter:

A blind woman named Alice bought some items of stolen furniture from a corrupt salesperson. She could not be convicted of _____ because she did not know that the goods were stolen and no _____ was uncovered, such as the payment of a low price, to prove that she had such knowledge. The corrupt salesperson committed _____ when he told Alice that she was signing a receipt when she was actually signing a check made out to the crook. Even though Alice signed her own name, it was a(n) _____, and the check certainly had some legal _____. The corrupt salesperson committed the crime of _____, when he tried to cash the check at a local bank. Oddly, it was probably the crime of _____ when the bank employee took the check, because she had been entrusted with it, and the judge said that the check that was taken was actually a(n) _____ rather than an item of _____. When an automobile was stolen from the bank's parking lot, however, the attorney for the _____ claimed that it was the crime of _____, which is divided into two degrees: _____ and _____ _____. The attorney claimed that the thief had the intent to steal, known as _____, and that a(n) _____ existed—that is, a carrying away of goods, which is called _____. Because the owner of the car had control of it, he had _____ rather than _____ of the car, and he was not a(n) _____. In addition, because the owner's possession was actual rather than assumed, this case did not involve _____. No fraud occurred; therefore, the crime was not _____, which is also called _____. Because this crime had nothing to do with land, _____ was not involved. The crime of _____ occurred, however, when the thief paid the prosecuting attorney $1,000 to drop the case. It would have been _____ if the thief had compelled someone to do something by threat or force.

PUZZLING OVER WHAT YOU LEARNED

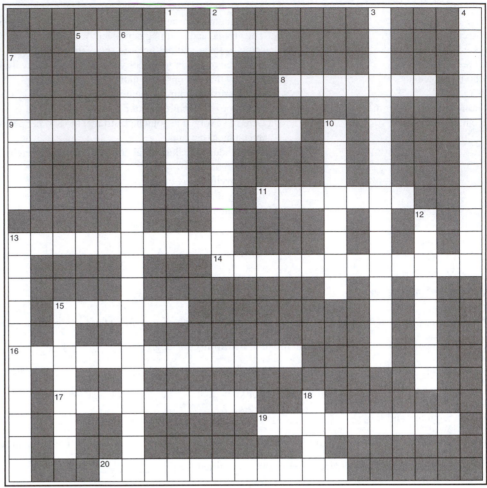

Caveat: Do not allow squares for spaces between words and punctuation (apostrophes, hyphens, etc.) when filling in crossword.

Across

5. Using the wires to obtain money, property, or services by false pretenses.
8. The fraudulent making or altering of a writing.
9. Evidence of a right to property but not the property itself.
11. The care and keeping of anything.
13. The detention and control of anything.
14. Larceny that is a felony.
15. One to whom personal property is given under a bailment contract.
16. Knowingly and deliberately obtaining the property of another by false pretenses with intent to defraud.
17. The corrupt demanding or receiving by a person in office of a fee for services that should be performed gratuitously.
19. Using mail to obtain money, property, or services by false pretenses.
20. The carrying away of goods.

Down

1. Effectiveness.
2. Activities of organized criminals who extort money from legitimate businesses.
3. An attempt to commit larceny, falling short of its commission.
4. Larceny that is a misdemeanor rather than a felony.
6. The buying, receiving, or aiding in the concealment of stolen or embezzled property, knowing it to have been stolen.
7. The wrongful taking and carrying away of personal property of another with the intent to steal.
10. Anything that is the subject of ownership other than real property.
12. Compelling someone to do something by threat or force.
13. A criminal action. The party by whom criminal proceedings are started or conducted; the state.
15. The giving or receiving of a reward to influence any official act.
18. Racketeer Influenced and Corrupt Organizations Act.

Crimes Against the Person and Human Habitation

2

ANTE INTERROGATORY

One of the elements of common law arson is (A) in the nighttime,
(B) a breaking, (C) with malice, (D) personal property

KEY TERMS

aggravated assault *(AG·ra·va·ted a·SALT)*
arson *(AR·sen)*
assault *(a·SALT)*
attempted arson *(a·TEMT·ed)*
battery *(BAT·er·ee)*
breaking *(BRAKE·ing)*
burglary *(BUR·gler·ee)*
carnal knowledge *(KAR·nel NOL·ej)*
convicted *(kon·VICT·ed)*
curtilage *(KUR·til·ej)*
cyber-bullying *(SI·ber BULL·ee·ing)*
cyber-harrassment *(SI·ber har·ASS·ment)*
cyber-stalking *(STAWK·ing)*

dangerous weapon *(DAYN·jer·ess WEP·en)*
deadly weapon *(DED·lee WEP·en)*
domestic violence *(do·MES·tik VY·o·lense)*
dwelling house *(DWEL·ing)*
lesser included offense *(o·FENSE)*
maim *(maym)*
mayhem *(MAY·hem)*
nighttime
rape
rape shield laws *(sheeld)*
restraining order *(re·STRANE·ing)*
robbery *(ROB·e·ree)*
sexual assault *(SEKS·yoo·el a·SALT)*
stalking *(STAW·king)*

statutory arson *(STAT·shoo·tore·ee AR·sen)*

statutory burglary *(STAT·shoo·tore·ee*
 BUR·gler·ee)

statutory rape *(STAT·shoo·tore·ee)*

summarily *(sum·EHR·i·lee)*

threat of force *(thret ov fors)*

unlawful sexual intercourse *(un·LAW·ful*
 SEKS·yoo·el IN·ter·kors)

Crimes against the person were considered to be more serious than crimes against property at common law and were subject to a harsher punishment. And in modern criminal codes, crimes against persons are classified more seriously than those against property. This is because crimes against the person involve face-to-face confrontation, increasing the chance for violence against the victim.

ROBBERY

Robbery is defined as the wrongful taking and carrying away of the personal property of another from the other's person or personal custody, and against the other's will by force and violence, or by threat of force. The essence of the crime is the exertion of force (or threat) against another to steal personal property from that person. The elements of robbery consist of the following:

1. wrongful taking
2. carrying away
3. personal property of another
4. from the person or personal custody
5. against the other's will by the use of force or threat of force

---

Web Wise

- Log onto the Internet Law Library at **www.lawguru.com** for links to the text of the U.S. Constitution, state constitutions, and other legal subjects.
- Look up U.S. Supreme Court opinions from 1893 to the present by going to **www.findlaw. com**. At that site, you can look for cases by specific year, citation, the name of a party, or specific words used in the opinion.
- Look up robbery (and other crime) statistics throughout the world at **www.nationmaster. com**, and use the website's search bar. America is not the leading country in crimes of robbery, by the way.

Because all of the elements of larceny are included in the crime of robbery, larceny is a lesser included offense of robbery. A **lesser included offense** is a crime that contains some, but not all, elements of a greater offense, making it impossible to commit the greater offense without also committing the lesser offense. One can be convicted of either the greater or the lesser offense, but not both. The first three elements of robbery are discussed in Chapter 11 under the heading "Larceny." Understand, though, that while larceny and robbery share some elements, robbery is more serious than larceny because it involves a personal confrontation with the victim. The last two elements of robbery are discussed here.

Taking from the Person or Personal Custody

One of the principal differences between larceny and robbery is that in robbery a taking "from the person" occurs, whereas in larceny it does not. To constitute robbery, the taking must be from the person or in the presence of the one in possession of the goods at the time of the robbery.

In a case in which a man held a woman at gunpoint in his room and ordered her to telephone her maid to deliver the woman's jewels to his room, the court, in holding the crime to be robbery, said: "A thing is in the presence of a person, in respect to robbery, which is so within his reach, inspection, observation, or control, that he could, if not overcome by violence or prevented by fear, retain his possession of it."

When the owner is kept in one room of the house and is forced to tell where his or her property may be found in another room, and the assailant goes there and takes the property, it has been held that such a taking is a robbery.

Taking against the Other's Will

The taking must be against the will of the person in possession of the goods. If the person from whom the goods are stolen is unaware of the crime's occurrence, as when a pocket is picked, the crime is larceny rather than robbery. In one case, a drunken man knocked over a woman whose purse was separated from her possession when she fell to the ground. He picked up her purse and ran away. The man was convicted of robbery, but got a new trial on appeal, arguing that he didn't form the intent to take her purse until after he accidentally knocked her down. The appellate court agreed, finding that "if" the man could convince a new jury that he didn't intend to knock her over so that he could take her purse, then the charge should be larceny, not robbery.

Force and Violence

Some force or violence must be used against the possessor of the goods to constitute robbery. The degree of force is immaterial so long as it is sufficient to obtain the victim's property against his or her will. The court, for example, held that the dispensing of a drug to a person so as to make him unconscious in order to steal his property was enough force to constitute robbery.

An intimidation, or a putting in fear, commonly called a **threat of force**, is equivalent to force and will replace the force requirement. Thus, even though no actual force is used, if victims are put in fear, as when threatened by a superior force or by the threat of harm to their persons or property, the element of force and violence will be satisfied.

Penalty for Robbery

In general, the penalty for robbery is greater than that for larceny. For example, in Massachusetts, the punishment for robbery (whether armed or unarmed) is "imprisonment in the state prison for life or for any term of years." In contrast, one form of larceny, shoplifting, is punished by "a fine of not more than one thousand dollars or by imprisonment in the house of correction for not more than two and one-half years, or by both such fine and imprisonment."

MAYHEM

At common law, **mayhem** was violently depriving others of the use of such members as may render them less able in fighting, either to defend themselves or to annoy their adversary. Examples of mayhem were cutting off a person's hand, foot, or finger and putting out an eye. It was not mayhem to cut off another's nose or ear or to disfigure a person in a way that did not interfere with the ability to fight. Interestingly, it was mayhem to knock out a person's front tooth, but it was not mayhem to knock out a back tooth, because such a tooth was not needed to bite someone while fighting. Mayhem was a misdemeanor at common law, except for castration, which was a felony.

In modern times, mayhem has become a felony in most states and includes many types of disfiguration. It is commonly called **maim**, which means to cripple or mutilate in any way. To illustrate, Nevada's mayhem statute reads, in part, as follows:

> Mayhem consists of unlawfully depriving a human being of a member of his body, or disfiguring or rendering it useless. If a person cuts out or disables the tongue, puts out an eye, slits the nose, ear or lip, or disables any limb or member of another, or voluntarily, or of purpose, puts out an eye, that person is guilty of mayhem which is a category B felony and shall be punished by imprisonment in the state prison for a minimum term of not less than 2 years and a maximum term of not more than 10 years, and may be further punished by a fine of not more than $10,000.

ASSAULT AND BATTERY DISTINGUISHED

An **assault** is an attempt to commit a battery; a **battery** is the actual contact or touching of another without permission or privilege. Thus, the shooting of a gun at another is the assault; the bullet striking the person is the battery. An assault can and often does occur without a battery, but battery necessarily includes an assault. In the tort law, however, battery is an unlawful touching, and assault is putting someone in fear of an unlawful touching. For example, kissing a stranger on the lips who is sleeping while riding a train is battery, while lunging at a waitress standing behind the counter of a diner is an assault—regardless of whether or not the waitress is actually touched.

Battery

A battery is the physical contact with another person, without that person's permission, in an angry, revengeful, rude, insolent, or reckless manner. It may also be defined as "the unlawful application of force on another person." The intentional pushing or hitting of someone or grabbing someone's purse or wallet would be a battery. An accidental bumping of another in a crowded room, however, would not be a battery because the crime requires a general criminal intent or reckless behavior on the part of the perpetrator. Battery is classified various in ways in many jurisdictions, including aggravated battery, domestic battery, sexual battery, and even battery by bodily waste.

Assault

An assault is an attempt, real or apparent, to commit a battery. Some overt act, such as the movement of an arm or pointing of a gun toward the victim, is required to accomplish the crime. Mere threats or words alone are not enough to commit the offense. A criminal assault may occur even though a battery is impossible, as when an unloaded gun is aimed at another, or even if the victim is unaware of the offense and is not put in fear.

The Texas code has merged the separate crime of battery into the state's definition of assault and included threatening to assault someone as part of that crime.

Simple assault and battery is generally a misdemeanor. **Aggravated assault**, which is an assault committed with the intention of committing some additional crime, is a felony by statute in most states. Examples of aggravated assault are assault with intent to murder, assault with a **dangerous** or **deadly weapon** (an item that is, from the way it is used, capable of causing death or serious bodily injury), assault with intent to commit unarmed robbery, and assault with intent to commit a felony.

To illustrate, in October 2000, Boston Bruins hockey player Marty McSorley was found guilty by a Canadian court of *assault with a weapon* when he hit Vancouver Canucks player Donald Brashear in the head with a hockey stick, with three seconds left in the game. Brashear was knocked unconscious and suffered a concussion and memory lapse. McSorley was sentenced to 18-months probation.

RAPE

At common law, **rape** was defined as the unlawful, forcible carnal knowledge by a man of a woman, against her will, or without her consent. The essential elements of the crime follow:

1. carnal knowledge
2. force by the man
3. nonconsent by the woman

Carnal knowledge meant the slightest penetration of the sexual organ of the woman by the sexual organ of the man. The force by the man had to be such that it would overcome physical resistance by the woman, and the woman had to resist "to the uttermost" to prove that force occurred and that she did not consent to the act. The punishment for the crime was death.

It was impossible, under the common law, for a woman to commit the crime of rape, because the definition required carnal knowledge "by a man of a woman." A woman could be **convicted** (found guilty) of rape, however, as a principal in the second degree or as an accessory to the crime if she aided another in its commission. Similarly, a husband could not be convicted of raping his wife; however, he could be found guilty as a principal in the second degree by assisting another to do the act. The rape of a spouse is now a crime in many states.

Many states today have changed the definition of rape to include unnatural sexual acts on men as well as women and to include the threat of bodily harm as well as actual force on the victim. The following is an example of a modern rape statute:

Whoever has sexual intercourse or unnatural sexual intercourse with a person, and who compels such person to submit by force and against his will or compels such person to submit by threat of bodily injury, shall be punished by imprisonment in the state prison for not more than twenty years; and whoever commits a second or subsequent such offense shall be punished by imprisonment in the state prison for life or for any term of years.

Word Wise
Prefix "Carn-" (Latin for "flesh")

Term	Meaning
carnal	Fleshly; of or pertaining to the flesh or body (adjective)
carnage	Destruction of life; slaughter of many people as in battle (noun)
carnaged	Covered with carnage or slaughtered bodies (adjective)
carnalism	The practice of what is carnal; sensualism (noun)
carnalist	A person who pursues sensual, especially sexual, pleasure (noun)
carnality	State of being flesh; fleshiness (noun)
carnalize	To make carnal or rob of spirituality; to sensualize (verb)
carnally	Corporeally; bodily (adverb)
carnalness	Carnal quality or state; sensuality (noun)
carnivorous	Flesh-eating (adjective)

The same statute provides for a punishment of up to life imprisonment in cases in which the rape results in serious bodily injury or is committed by more than one person. **Rape shield laws** have been passed to help prevent rape victims from being re-victimized, by prohibiting a defendant from using the victim's sexual history as evidence against her own testimony, with limited exceptions. In addition, some states require people charged with rape to be tested for AIDS.

Sexual assault is much broader than rape, sometimes defined as any unwanted sexual contact.

Statutory Rape

Statutory rape referred to as **unlawful sexual intercourse**, is sexual intercourse with a child under the age set by the particular state statute, regardless of whether the child consented or not. It is often referred to as *child abuse*. At common law, a child under the age of 10 was considered incapable of consenting, and sexual intercourse with a child under that age was deemed rape even if the child could be considered to have consented. Present-day statutory rape statutes vary from state to state and have increased the age to 12, 16, and even 18 years in some states. Thus, sexual intercourse with a person under that particular age is rape even if the child consented to or encouraged the act.

2

TERMS IN ACTION

Rape is a crime that traditionally involved the use of force or threat of force against the victim. But some states, including Tennessee and California, have added **sex by deception** (or by fraud) as conduct that also constitutes **sexual assault**. In a strange case from Tennessee, a man dubbed "The Fantasy Man" by the press was convicted of rape by fraud. Robert Mitchell, III, of Nashville, called hundreds of women late at night, talking in a hushed voice, pretending to be their boyfriends or fiancés. Although most women hung up on him, eight of them believed that he was their boyfriend, and they followed his requests to unlock their doors and put on blindfolds, or meet him in black-as-night hotel rooms. One victim had blindfolded sex with him twice a week for two months, mistakenly thinking he was her significant other. Mitchell was eventually caught when the blindfold of one of his victims slipped off her eyes during one of their encounters. He was **convicted** of rape by fraud and of attempted rape by fraud, and sentenced to 15 years in prison.

Source: Nashvillescene.com; *State v. Mitchell*, 1999 WL 559930

DOMESTIC VIOLENCE AND STALKING

In recent years, states have enacted laws attempting to decrease the amount of **domestic violence** (the abuse of a closely related person such as a present or former spouse or cohabitant). Among other things, states have made it easier for victims to obtain restraining orders against their attackers. A **restraining order** is an order forbidding a person from doing a particular act. A temporary restraining order is often given **summarily** (quickly), followed by a hearing, which may or may not result in a permanent restraining order. In California, police officers must give domestic violence victims a "Victims of Domestic Violence" card, notifying them of their rights and of the availability of counseling centers and 24-hour counseling service telephone numbers. Many states in recent years have made it a crime, called **stalking** to follow someone around, threatening him or her with violence. **Stalking** is the willful, malicious, and repeated following, harassing, and threatening of another person, intending to place the person in fear of death or serious bodily injury.

Because the Internet has made stalking or harassing someone even easier, jurisdictions have passed laws against **cyber-stalking** and **cyber-bullying**. Some states interchangeably use the terms **cyber-harassment** and cyber-bullying. Cyber-harassment is using the Internet to repeatedly interfere with someone's life; cyber-bullying is using the Internet to malign or threaten someone; and cyber-stalking is using the Internet to put another person in fear for their—or their loved ones'—safety or life.

Web Wise

• The National Council of State Legislatures has a website that includes a webpage listing all the cyber-bullying and related crimes throughout the country. Log onto **www.ncsl.org** and look under the "Issues & Research" tab.

CRIMES AGAINST HABITATION

The crimes of burglary and arson were considered to be crimes against habitation under the common law. For this reason, their definitions include, among other elements, "a dwelling house."

Burglary

Burglary under common law, is defined as the breaking and entering of a house (dwelling house) of another, in the nighttime, with intent to commit a felony. All of the following elements of the crime must be proved by the state to convict someone of the crime of common law burglary:

1. a breaking
2. an entering
3. a dwelling house of another
4. in the nighttime
5. with the intent to commit a felony

BREAKING. A **breaking** is the forced entry of the dwelling house, that which is the security against intrusion. It can consist of such an activity as opening a door or window (whether locked or unlocked), opening a screen, opening a shutter or blind, digging under a sill, or even climbing down a chimney. At common law, it was held not to be a breaking when a window was left partly open and a burglar raised it further to enter. Modern decisions, however, have held such an act to be a breaking.

ENTERING. To constitute a burglary, an entry must occur of some part of the body or of some instrument by which the felony is sought to be accomplished. The entry may consist of an arm, leg, head, or the slightest part of the body such as a finger or foot. An interesting case arose when a person bored a hole with an auger up through the floor of a grain storage area that was part of a dwelling house, causing the grain to spill out of the hole into a sack placed below it. The court held that an entry occurred when the auger entered the storage area.

DWELLING HOUSE OF ANOTHER. A **dwelling house** is a house in which the occupier and his or her family usually reside and includes all outbuildings within the curtilage, such as a garage or other outbuilding. **Curtilage** means the enclosed space of ground and buildings immediately surrounding a dwelling house, sometimes enclosed by a fence or wall. The requirement that the dwelling house be of another refers to occupancy rather than ownership. A landlord, for example, may be guilty of burglary for entering a house owned by him or her, but rightfully occupied by tenants, if the other elements of burglary are present.

NIGHTTIME. In ancient times, **nighttime** was defined as that period between sunset and sunrise during which the face of a person could not be discerned by the light of day (not including moonlight). In modern times, the word "nighttime" has been defined more precisely. For example, one state statute reads as follows:

> If a crime is alleged to have been committed in the nighttime, nighttime shall be deemed the time between one hour after sunset on one day and one hour before sunrise on the next day; and the time of sunset and sunrise shall be ascertained according to mean time in the place where the crime was committed.

INTENT TO COMMIT A FELONY. Under the common law definition of burglary, the breaking and entering must be done with the intent to commit a felony within the house. If the person breaking in intended merely to commit a misdemeanor, the crime would not be common law burglary. In an interesting case that occurred in the 1860s, a group of men, in the nighttime, broke into and entered a dwelling house of a person with the intent to cut off his ear. The men were found not guilty of burglary, because the cutting off of an ear was not a felony at the time. It was merely a misdemeanor because one did not need an ear to protect oneself. Today, in most states, the crime would be a felony.

STATUTORY BURGLARY. Many states have enacted statutes making it a criminal offense to do certain acts similar to, but not included in, the common law crime of burglary. Such crimes are sometimes referred to as **statutory burglary**. They include breaking and entering a building other than a dwelling house, and breaking and entering with the intent to commit a misdemeanor. And the nighttime requirement is often eliminated.

TERMS IN ACTION

Jeane Thomas, of Boynton Beach, Florida, decided to take matters into her own hands after her house had been **burglarized** once in 2008. So, she set up a surveillance camera in her home and put it on a live-feed over the Internet, allowing her to monitor the sanctity of her home from nearly anywhere. Thanks to her technological skills, in April 2009, she was able to watch on her Fort Lauderdale office computer (live and in color, with sound) two men committing burglary at her home. The two burglars entered her house by way of the doggie door, and as she and her two dogs—who were in the house, lounging on her couch at the time—watched the **breaking and entering**, she called 911. The police arrived in time to catch the burglars. A total of four defendants were charged with **statutory burglary**. Not only was Ms. Thomas's five-minute video of the crime in action the best evidence the police could have hoped for, it also was posted on YouTube, naturally.

Source: Thesmokinggun.com

Arson

The common law definition of **arson**, which is still followed in many states, is "the willful and malicious burning of the dwelling house of another." Broken down into its elements, the common law crime consists of the following elements:

1. a burning
2. of a dwelling house
3. of another
4. with malice

The mere scorching or blackening of the wood of a dwelling house is not enough to constitute arson. Some portion of the house must actually have been on fire, so that the wood or other building material is charred, to constitute the crime of arson. If someone attempts to commit the crime of arson, but falls short of its commission, the crime of **attempted arson** is committed. This crime is also a punishable offense. In some states, such as Indiana, damaging by fire is sufficient to constitute the burning requirement.

Because the common law crime of arson was directed toward the protection of people rather than property, the burning of a building other than a dwelling house was not considered to be arson.

The dwelling house must have been occupied by someone other than the perpetrator of the crime, and the fire must have been set intentionally and not through negligence or by accident.

Statutory arson. Although most states have retained the common law definition of arson and still follow it, they have added, by statute, other forms of arson such as the burning of a building other than a dwelling house and the burning of one's own house to collect insurance. This act is referred to as **statutory arson** in contrast to common law arson.

Reviewing What You Learned

After studying the chapter, write the answers to each of the following questions:

1. List the elements of robbery. _____

_____

_____

_____

2. The first three elements of robbery are the same as those for what other crime? _____

_____

_____

3. What is one of the principal differences between larceny and robbery? _____

_____

_____

4. In addition to the use of force, what else could constitute robbery, instead of larceny? _____

_____

_____

5. What is the difference between assault and battery? _____

_____

_____

6. What is the difference between simple assault and battery and aggravated assault? _____

_____

_____

7. List the three essential elements of rape at common law. _____

_____

_____

_____

8. Explain how a woman in earlier times or a husband could be guilty of rape. _____

_____

_____

9. In what ways have many states changed the common law definition of rape? _____

_____

_____

_____

10. How does statutory rape (unlawful sexual intercourse) differ from ordinary rape? _____

_____

_____
_____

11. List the elements of common law burglary. _____

_____

_____

12. Describe the present law with respect to a breaking when a burglar enters a partially open window. _____

_____

_____

13. Would it be burglary if you entered an open garage during the afternoon to avoid a hailstorm and then stole an expensive tool that you noticed while standing in the garage? _____

_____

_____

14. What is statutory burglary, and why does a need for the term exist? _____

_____

_____

15. List the four elements of common law arson. _____

_____

_____

_____

16. Describe the amount of burning that must occur to constitute arson. _____

_____

_____

_____

_____

17. Describe statutory arson. _____

_____

_____

_____

_____

2

Understanding Legal Concepts

Indicate whether each statement is true or false. Then, change the italicized word or phrase of each false statement to make it true.

ANSWERS

_____ 1. At common law, crimes against the person were *not as serious as* crimes against property.

_____ 2. One of the principal differences between larceny and robbery is that in *robbery* a taking "from the person" occurs, whereas in *larceny* it does not.

_____ 3. A *battery* is an attempt to commit an *assault*.

_____ 4. The accidental bumping of another in a crowded room *is* a battery.

_____ 5. If the person from whom goods are stolen is unaware of the crime's occurrence, the crime is *larceny* rather than *robbery*.

_____ 6. Many states today have changed the definition of rape to include *unnatural sexual acts* on men as well as women.

_____ 7. Sexual intercourse with a child under the age set by state statute *is* rape even though the child consented to or encouraged the act.

_____ 8. Opening an *unlocked* door or window is considered a breaking.

_____ 9. A landlord *may be* guilty of burglary for entering a house owned by him or her, but rightfully occupied by a tenant, if the other elements of burglary are present.

_____ 10. Cyber-bullying *is not* considered a crime, although it is a tort.

Checking Terminology

From the list of legal terms that follows, select the one that matches each definition.

ANSWERS

a. aggravated assault
b. arson
c. assault
d. attempted arson
e. battery
f. breaking
g. burglary
h. carnal knowledge
i. convicted
j. curtilage
k. cyber-bullying
l. cyber-harassment
m. cyber-stalking
n. dangerous weapon
o. deadly weapon
p. domestic violence
q. dwelling house
r. lesser included offense
s. maim
t. mayhem
u. nighttime
v. rape
w. rape shield laws
x. restraining order
y. robbery
z. stalking
aa. statutory arson
bb. statutory burglary
cc. statutory rape
dd. summarily
ee. threat of force
ff. unlawful sexual intercourse

_____ 1. Using the Internet to put someone in fear for their own or their loved ones' safety or lives.

_____ 2. The willful, malicious, and repeated following, harassing, and threatening of another person, intending to place the person in fear of death or serious bodily injury.

_____ 3. An item that is, from the way it is used, capable of causing death or serious bodily injury. (Select two answers.)

_____ 4. Laws passed to help prevent rape victims from being victimized.

_____ 5. At common law, violently depriving others of the use of such members as may render them less able in fighting.

_____ 6. An intimidation or putting in fear; equivalent to force.

_____ 7. Using the Internet to malign or threaten someone.

_____ 8. The unprivileged touching, not permitted, of another person; the unlawful application of force on another person.

_____ 9. An assault committed with the intention of committing some additional crime.

_____ 10. An order forbidding a person to perform a particular act.

_____ 11. The abuse of a closely related person such as a present or former spouse or cohabitant.

_____ 12. The wrongful taking and carrying away of the personal property of another from the other's person or personal custody, against his or her will, by force and violence.

_____ 13. At common law, the unlawful, forcible carnal knowledge by a man of a woman against her will or without her consent.

_____ 14. Sexual intercourse; the slightest penetration of the sexual organ of the woman by the sexual organ of the man.

_____ 15. A crime that contains some, but not all, elements of a greater offense, making it impossible to commit the greater offense without also committing the lesser offense.

_____ 16. Sexual intercourse with a child under the age set by state statute regardless of whether the child consented or not. (Select two answers.)

_____ 17. Use of force against someone to steal personal property from that person.

_____ 18. The willful and malicious burning of the dwelling house of another.

_____ 19. An attempt to commit the crime of arson, but falling short of its commission.

_____ 20. The burning of a building other than a dwelling house, or the burning of one's own house to collect insurance.

_____ 21. At common law, the breaking and entering of a dwelling house of another, in the nighttime, with intent to commit a felony.

_____ 22. The putting aside of the dwelling house that is relied on as security against intrusion.

_____ 23. A house in which the occupier and family usually reside, including all outbuildings within the curtilage.

_____ 24. The enclosed space of ground and buildings immediately surrounding a dwelling house.

_____ 25. Burglary that does not contain all of the elements of common law burglary.

_____ 26. Found guilty of a crime.

_____ 27. An attempt to commit a battery.

_____ 28. Quickly.

_____ 29. Using the Internet to repeatedly interfere with someone's life.

_____ 30. To cripple or mutilate in any way.

Using Legal Language

Read the following story and fill in the blank lines with legal terms taken from the list of terms at the beginning of this chapter:

The suspect was charged with _____ when he sexually attacked a young woman late at night as she entered her house. Since the young woman was an adult, it was not the crime of _____, which is called _____ in California. The suspect was not _____ of the crime, because the state could not prove the element of _____. The state was able to prove, however, a(n) _____ and a(n) _____ because the suspect had lunged at the young woman with a knife, which struck her hand. A knife is considered to be a(n) _____ or a(n) _____. The suspect was found guilty of _____ and also _____, which was called _____ at common law, because the knife had cut off the tip of the young woman's finger. The entire incident was not considered to be _____ because it was not the exertion of force against another person in order to steal from that person. Also, it was not _____ because the suspect had not repeatedly followed and harassed the young woman. In addition, after _____ into the woman's garage, which was part of the _____ because it was within the _____, the suspect deliberately set fire to a pile of rubbish. The fire scorched some molding before it went out. Because the wood did not char, the suspect could be convicted of _____ but not _____ along with the crime of _____. Had this building been a factory, the crimes might have been _____ and _____.

PUZZLING OVER WHAT YOU LEARNED

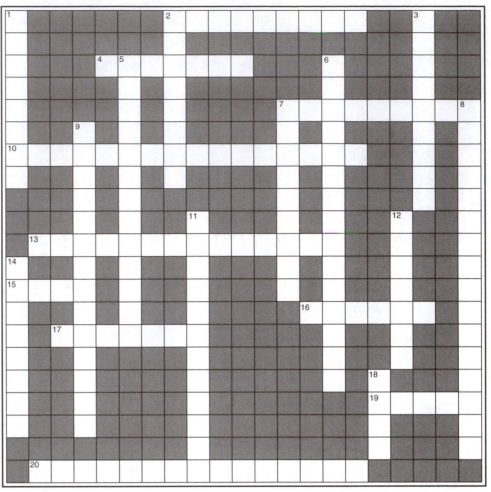

Caveat: Do not allow squares for spaces between words and punctuation (apostrophes, hyphens, etc.) when filling in crossword.

Across

2. Quickly.
4. The intentional creation of a reasonable apprehension of an imminent battery. An attempt to commit a battery.
7. Found guilty of a crime.
10. An order forbidding a person from doing a particular act.
13. Laws passed to help prevent rape victims from being victimized.
15. The unlawful, forcible carnal knowledge by a man of a woman, against her will, or without her consent.
16. Violently depriving others of the use of such members as may render them less able in fighting.
17. Intentional contact with another person without that person's permission and without justification.
19. The willful and malicious burning of a dwelling house of another.
20. Sexual intercourse.

Down

1. The breaking and entering of a dwelling house of another, in the nighttime, with intent to commit a felony.
2. The willful, malicious, and repeated following, harassing, and threatening of another person, intending to place the person in fear of death or serious bodily injury.
3. The time between one hour after sunset on one day and one hour before sunrise on the next day.
5. Any unwanted sexual contact.
6. An item that is, from the way it is used, capable of causing death or serious bodily injury.
7. The enclosed space of ground and buildings immediately surrounding a dwelling house.
8. The abuse of a closely related person, such as a present or former spouse or cohabitant.
9. An attempt to commit the crime of arson, falling short of its commission.
11. An item that is, from the way it is used, capable of causing death or serious bodily injury.
12. The wrongful taking and carrying away of personal property of another from the other person or personal custody against his or her will with force and violence.
14. The putting aside of the dwelling house that is relied on as security against intrusion.
18. To cripple or mutilate in any way.

Homicide

ANTE INTERROGATORY

The killing of a human being by another human being is the definition of (A) euthanasia, (B) homicide, (C) manslaughter, (D) murder.

CHAPTER OUTLINE

Justifiable Homicide
    Self-Defense
    Exclusions under Common Law
Proximate Cause

Felonious Homicide
    Murder
    Suicide
    Degrees of Murder
    Manslaughter

KEY TERMS

capital crime *(KAP·i·tel)*
castle doctrine *(KAS·el DOK·trin)*
corpus delicti *(KOR·pus de·LIK·tie)*
euthanasia *(yooth·e·NAY·zha)*
excusable homicide *(eks·KYOO·se·bel HOM·i·side)*
felon *(FEL·en)*
felonious homicide *(fe·LONE·ee·us HOM·i·side*
felony murder *(FEL·en·ee MER·der)*
feticide *(FET·e·side)*
first-degree murder *(de·GREE MER·der)*
fratricide *(FRAT·re·side)*
genocide *(JEN·o·side)*
homicide *(HOM·i·side)*
imminent danger
infanticide *(in·FANT·e·side)*
involuntary manslaughter *(in·VOL·en·ter·ee MAN·slaw·ter)*
justifiable homicide *(jus·ti·FY·a·bel HOM·i·side)*

malice aforethought *(MAL·iss)*
manslaughter *(MAN·slaw·ter)*
matricide *(MAT·ri·side)*
murder *(MER·der)*
patricide *(PAT·ri·side)*
premeditated malice aforethought *(pre·MED·i·tay·ted MAL·iss a·FORE·thawt)*
proximate cause *(PROK·si·met)*
right-to-die laws
second-degree murder *(SEK·end-de·GREE MER·der)*
self-defense *(de·FENSE)*
sororicide *(so·ROR·i·side)*
suicide *(SOO·i·side)*
uxoricide *(ux·OR·i·side)*
viable *(VI·a·bel)*
voluntary manslaughter *(VOL·en·ter·ee MAN·slaw·ter)*
year-and-a-day rule

2

Homicide is the killing of a human being by another human being. The term comes from the Latin *homo* (man) and *cidere* (to kill). Other terms with the same suffix include the following:

feticide: killing a fetus in the womb—abortion

fratricide: killing one's brother

genocide: killing a racial or political group

infanticide: killing an infant soon after birth

matricide: killing one's mother

patricide: killing one's father

sororicide: killing one's sister

suicide: killing oneself

uxoricide: killing one's wife

mariticide: killing one's husband

JUSTIFIABLE HOMICIDE

Justifiable homicide (which is also known as **excusable homicide** in some jurisdictions) is the taking of human life when a justification exists. A justification defense involves a defendant's arguing that he or she is responsible, but not wrong. It includes the legal execution of murderers, the killing of others during battle, the killing of a dangerous felony suspect by a police officer to prevent bystanders from being harmed or killed, and the killing of another in self-defense.

Self-Defense

Self-defense is justification for the use of force in resisting attack, especially for killing an assailant. Before it can be used as a justification for homicide, the one claiming self-defense must establish that he or she was in **imminent danger** (that the unlawful attack was just about to happen) so that the only possible way to escape death or bodily injury was to kill the assailant. In addition, except when in one's own house (and in some southern and western states), one must retreat if possible before killing an assailant. When in one's own house, one need not retreat before using deadly force when being attacked. Frequently referred to as the **castle doctrine**, the rule is based on the common law principle that one's home is one's castle.

TERMS IN ACTION

Can someone kill in **self-defense**, and yet be wrong in believing that an unlawful deadly attack is imminent? Yes. Self-defense requires a **reasonable belief**, but not necessarily a correct belief. In the middle of the night on October 2, 2009, in Winter Springs, Florida, John Tabutt awoke to the sound of someone in his house. So, he got out of his bed, grabbed his handgun, and then shot at the intruder standing in his hallway, whose form he could barely make out in the darkness. His aim was correct, but his belief was wrong, because Tabutt shot and killed his fiancée, Nancy Dinsmore. They were supposed to be married the next day. A grand jury was convened, and in July 2010 it announced that it would not indict Tabutt for murder. Tabutt had claimed from the beginning that he thought that his fiancé was in bed with him at the time he got out of bed, and that—at the time he fired—he believed that an intruder was in his home. Although he was not in **imminent danger** when he fired his gun, Tabutt was the beneficiary of Florida's **castle doctrine**, which grants greater freedom to engage in deadly force self-defense in one's home. And the grand jury believed that he was sincere about his mistaken belief.

Sources: foxnews.com; truecrimereport.com

Exclusions under the Common Law

At common law, the killing of an unborn child in its mother's womb was not homicide because to be such, the child must have had a circulation independent of its mother—that is, it must have breathed and thus have supplied oxygen to its own lungs. Such an act, however, could amount to criminal abortion. Modern decisions in many states have changed this rule, making it homicide to kill an unborn child in its mother's womb when the child is **viable**—that is, having the appearance of being able to live outside the womb.

At common law, the death of the victim must have occurred within a year and a day after the blow occurred for the defendant to be convicted of a homicide. This rule, known as the **year-and-a-day rule** is still followed in some states. Many other states, including Indiana, Massachusetts, New Jersey, New York, Ohio, Oregon, and Pennsylvania, have abolished the year-and-a-day rule because modern medical techniques allow injured people to be kept alive for long periods. California has increased the time under the rule to three years and one day, but it still allows a prosecutor to charge someone with murder even if the victim lived longer than three years and a day, by overcoming the presumption that the victim died of natural causes.

PROXIMATE CAUSE

To win a conviction of homicide, the prosecution must show that the defendant's act was the **proximate cause**—that is, the dominant cause of death. It need not, however, be the sole cause of death. For example, a defendant who inflicted a gunshot wound on another was found guilty of the homicide even though the victim was negligently treated by a physician and died from lockjaw. In addition, the **corpus delicti** (the body on which a crime has been committed) must be accounted for to convict someone of homicide. Proof of death must exist. The term "corpus delicti" also refers to all of the elements that must be proved in a particular crime. As discussed in Chapter 12, for example, the corpus delicti of robbery consists of five elements: (1) wrongful taking, (2) carrying away, (3) personal property of another, (4) from the person or personal custody, and (5) against the other's will with force and violence.

TERMS IN ACTION

The **year-and-a-day rule** is a centuries-old rule that controls the doctrine of causation in murder cases. But many states have abandoned it in favor of allowing the jury to decide whether the defendant's conduct was the **proximate cause** of the victim's death, regardless of the time between the attack and death. In 2009, Walter Hutchinson was convicted in New Hampshire of **first-degree murder** for strangling his girlfriend, Kimberly Ernest, whom he suspected of cheating on him. Had New Hampshire followed the year-and-a-day rule, Hutchinson could not have been convicted, because he strangled her in 1991, leaving her in a vegetative state. She died in 2005. At the time of his murder conviction, Hutchinson was due to have been released from prison, having been convicted of attempted murder 18 years earlier. He lost the legal argument—before his murder trial—that he was the victim of double jeopardy, and then he lost the trial. This time, he was sentenced to life behind bars.

Sources: unionleader.com; wmur.com

FELONIOUS HOMICIDE

Felonious homicide is homicide done with the intent to commit a felony. It is a **capital crime** in some states—that is, one that is punishable by death. It is divided into two kinds: murder and manslaughter. A person who commits a felony is called a **felon**.

Murder

Murder is defined as "the unlawful killing of a human being by another with **malice afore-thought**." Malice aforethought is evil intent, which was historically referred to as "depraved state of mind." It is the state of mind that is reckless of law and of the legal rights of others which prompts one to take the life of another without just cause or provocation. When malice is present, the person is motivated by cruelty, hostility, or revenge.

Suicide

Suicide was held to be murder at common law, and the punishment was the forfeiture of the deceased's goods to the state and burial under the highway leading into town so that, henceforth, every person, wagon, and animal going in and out of town would run over the body. Suicide is not punished in the United States and generally is not considered a crime because of the fact that the perpetrator cannot be punished. In some states, anyone who counsels another to commit suicide and who is present when the act is committed would be considered a principal in the second degree to the crime of murder. In 1997, The U.S. Supreme Court decided in *Washington v. Glucksberg* that states may ban doctor-assisted suicides, and most states have done so. The Florida law, for example, states the following:

> Every person deliberately assisting another in the commission of self-murder shall be guilty of manslaughter, a felony of the second degree . . . . (Florida Statutes §782.08)

As of this writing, Oregon and Washington are the only states that have enacted physician-hastened-suicide laws. Called the Death with Dignity Act, this type of statute allows doctors to prescribe lethal doses of medication to terminally ill people who have six months (or less) left to live. In 2006, the U.S. Supreme Court impliedly upheld Oregon's Death with Dignity Act, in *Gonzales v. Oregon*, by striking a regulation by the U.S. Attorney General that prohibited doctors from prescribing such dosages.

    Euthanasia, which is not the same as assisted suicide, is the act of painlessly putting to death someone suffering from an incurable disease, as an act of mercy, and it is illegal in the United States. However, **right-to-die laws**, which allow dying people to refuse extraordinary treatment to prolong life, are very popular. Right-to-die laws are discussed in Chapter 22.

Degrees of Murder

No degrees of murder existed at common law; however, by statute in many states, the crime has been divided into two and, sometimes, three degrees. Under early statutes, the punishment for murder in the first degree was death, and the punishment for murder in the second degree was life imprisonment. Today, punishment for the crime varies from state to state.

FIRST-DEGREE MURDER. With some variations from state to state, **first-degree murder** is defined as murder committed in any of the following ways:

1. with deliberately premeditated malice aforethought,
2. with extreme atrocity or cruelty, or
3. while in the commission or attempted commission of a felony, which is sometimes referred to as a **felony murder**

    Deliberately **premeditated malice aforethought** means thinking over, deliberating on, or weighing in the mind beforehand. Examples of murder committed with extreme atrocity or cruelty are those committed with repeated violent blows, sexual attacks, or repeated stabbing. Examples of felony murders are those committed in connection with rape, robbery, kidnapping, and, sometimes, arson and burglary.

SECOND-DEGREE MURDER. In some states, murder that is not found to be in the first degree is charged as **murder in the second degree**. Other states differentiate between the two degrees depending on whether the malice was express or implied, the latter being second-degree murder. Still others base the difference on whether or not deliberation or premeditation occurred.

Manslaughter

Manslaughter is the unlawful killing of one human being by another without malice afore-thought. The major difference between murder and manslaughter is that malice is essential in all degrees of murder, whereas it is not present in manslaughter. Manslaughter is either voluntary or involuntary.

VOLUNTARY MANSLAUGHTER. **Voluntary manslaughter** occurs when an intention to kill exists, but through the violence of sudden passion (which concerns emotional outbursts, not necessarily sexual feelings), occasioned by some great provocation. The provocation must be such that a reasonable person might naturally be induced to commit the act. For example, suppose that a wife comes home unexpectedly and finds her husband in the act of adultery with her best friend. She becomes enraged and, in a fit of irresistible passion, kills the husband or the best friend. When voluntary manslaughter occurs, an intent to kill exists, but it is done in the heat of passion, without malice. But Indiana's voluntary manslaughter definition is nearly identical to the state's definition of murder, except that the manslaughter statute includes the "sudden heat" aspect. Later, the statute explains the difference between the two crimes by saying, "The existence of sudden heat is a mitigating factor that reduces what otherwise would be murder under section 1(1) of this chapter to voluntary manslaughter."

INVOLUNTARY MANSLAUGHTER. **Involuntary manslaughter** is the unintentional killing of another while in the commission of an unlawful act, not amounting to a felony or in the commission of a wanton or reckless act. For example, the accidental killing of a pedestrian while driving at a high speed along a thickly settled, residential street could be involuntary manslaughter.

Word Wise
"Manslaughter"—A Sexist Term

Should we continue to use the term "manslaughter" even though it is sexist? *The Dictionary of Bias-Free Usage: A Guide to Nondiscriminatory Language* (1991) recommends continuing to use the word until a nonsexist term is created to replace it. The language associated with English and American law, courts, and government is largely male oriented because men, in the past, dominated the field. Women, for example, were not allowed to vote until 1920 in this country and did not often hold policymaking positions. When the Founding Fathers wrote that "all men are created equal" in the Declaration of Independence, they meant men specifically, not generically—and even more precisely, white, male, property owners. In government, terms such as "city fathers," "favorite-son candidate," and "gentlemen's agreement" remain in common usage. Can you suggest a nonsexist term that might realistically replace the word "manslaughter"? Would it be "humanslaughter" or "personslaughter?"

Reviewing What You Learned

After studying the chapter, write the answers to each of the following questions:

1. What is the difference between justifiable homicide and felonious homicide?

   _____

   _____

   _____

   _____

2. What must appear before self-defense can be used as a justification for homicide?

   _____

   _____

   _____

2

3. What must be shown to win a conviction of homicide?

_____

_____

_____

_____

4. At common law, what was the punishment for suicide?

_____

_____

_____

_____

5. In some states, what happens to one who counsels another to commit suicide and is present when the act is committed?

_____

_____

_____

_____

6. At common law, what were the degrees of murder?

_____

_____

_____

_____

7. Under early statutes, what was the punishment for murder in the first degree and murder in the second degree?

_____

_____

_____

_____

8. Generally, first-degree murder is murder committed in what three ways?

_____

_____

_____

_____

9. What is second-degree murder?

_____

_____

_____

_____

10. What is the difference between murder and manslaughter?

_____

_____

_____

_____

11. Under what circumstances does voluntary manslaughter occur?

_____

_____

_____

_____

12. Under what circumstances does involuntary manslaughter occur?

_____

_____

_____

_____

Understanding Legal Concepts

Indicate whether each statement is true or false. Then, change the italicized word or phrase of each false statement to make it true.

ANSWERS

_____ 1. Legal execution is an example of _felonious_ homicide.

_____ 2. Except when a person is in his or her own home, he or she _must_ retreat, if possible, before killing an assailant in self-defense.

_____ 3. At common law, the killing of an unborn child in its mother's womb _was not_ homicide.

_____ 4. The corpus delicti _must be_ accounted for to convict someone of homicide.

_____ 5. _Malice_ is defined as the unlawful killing of a human being by another.

_____ 6. _Three_ degrees of murder existed at common law.

_____ 7. Deliberately _premeditated malice aforethought_ means thinking over, deliberating on, or weighing in the mind beforehand.

_____ 8. The major difference between murder and manslaughter is that malice is essential in all degrees of _murder_, whereas it is not present in _manslaughter_.

_____ **9.** _Involuntary manslaughter_ includes an intent to kill, but it is done in the heat of passion, without malice.

_____ **10.** The accidental killing of a pedestrian while violating the speed limit is an example of _voluntary manslaughter._

Checking Terminology

From the list of legal terms that follows, select the one that matches each definition.

ANSWERS

a. capital crime
b. castle doctrine
c. corpus delicti
d. euthanasia
e. excusable homicide
f. felon
g. felonious homicide
h. felony murder
i. feticide
j. first-degree murder
k. fratricide
l. genocide
m. homicide
n. imminent danger
o. infanticide
p. involuntary manslaughter
q. justifiable homicide
r. malice aforethought
s. matricide
t. manslaughter
u. murder
v. patricide
w. premediated malice aforethought
x. proximate cause
y. right-to-die laws
z. second-degree murder
aa. self-defense
bb. sororicide
cc. suicide
dd. uxoricide
ee. viable
ff. voluntary manslaughter
gg. year-and-a-day rule

_____ 1. The killing of a human being by a human being.
_____ 2. The taking of a human life when a valid excuse exists. (Select two answers.)
_____ 3. Homicide done with the intent to commit a felony.
_____ 4. A body on which a crime has been committed.
_____ 5. The unlawful killing of a human being by another with malice aforethought.
_____ 6. Evil intent; that state of mind that is reckless of law and of the legal rights of others.
_____ 7. A person who commits a felony.
_____ 8. Murder committed with deliberately premeditated malice aforethought, with extreme atrocity or cruelty, or while in the commission of a crime punishable by life in prison.
_____ 9. The situation in which an unlawful attack is just about to happen.
_____ 10. The unlawful killing of one human being by another without malice aforethought.
_____ 11. The unlawful killing of another without malice when an intention to kill exists, but provoked by the violence of sudden passion.
_____ 12. The unintentional killing of another while in the commission of an unlawful act or while in the commission of a reckless act.
_____ 13. A valid excuse for the use of force in resisting attack, especially for killing an assailant.
_____ 14. The dominant cause that produces an injury or death.
_____ 15. The act of painlessly putting to death someone suffering from an incurable disease, as an act of mercy.
_____ 16. Killing oneself.
_____ 17. Thinking over, deliberating on, or weighing in the mind beforehand.
_____ 18. Laws that allow dying people to refuse extraordinary treatment that would prolong life.
_____ 19. Killing a fetus in a womb—abortion.
_____ 20. Killing one's brother.
_____ 21. Killing a racial or political group.
_____ 22. Killing an infant soon after birth.
_____ 23. Killing one's mother.
_____ 24. Killing one's father.
_____ 25. Killing one's sister.
_____ 26. Killing one's wife.
_____ 27. death must have occurred within a year and a day after the blow occurred for a defendant to be convicted of homicide.
_____ 28. Murder committed while in the commission or attempted commission of a felony.
_____ 29. Having the appearance of being able to live.
_____ 30. A crime that is punishable by death.
_____ 31. when being attacked in one's house, a person need not retreat before using deadly force against the assailant.
_____ 32. Murder that is not found to be in the first degree.

Using Legal Language

Read the following story and fill in the blank lines with legal terms taken from the list of terms at the beginning of this chapter:

A gruesome killing was discovered when the maid found the _____, on the floor, riddled with bullet holes.

The victim was not an infant or a father or a mother; therefore, the

crime could not have been _____, _____, or _____. It turned out that the butler shot his wife, making the crime

_____. The shooting was held to be the _____, or dominant cause that produced the death. This case was not one in which the killer had a valid excuse for the use of force in resisting attack; therefore, he could not claim _____. When the killer was executed by the state, it was a type of _____ known as _____ or _____ rather than _____, of which the killer was guilty. The _____ had been convicted of _____, which is _____

committed with deliberately premeditated _____ aforethought. Although it found malice, the jury decided against _____, because premeditation had occurred. _____ is the unlawful killing of one human being by another without malice aforethought. Because of the malice in this case, the killing was neither _____ nor _____. It was, however, a(n) _____, because it is punishable by death in that state.

PUZZLING OVER WHAT YOU LEARNED

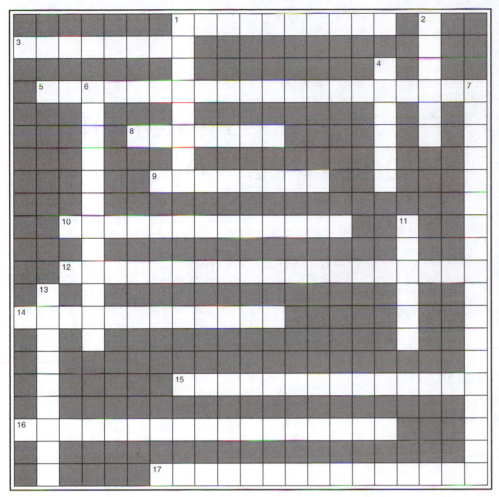

Caveat: Allow squares for spaces between words and punctuation (apostrophes, hyphens, etc.) when filling in crossword.

Across

1. Killing one's brother.
3. The killing of a human being by a human being.
5. The taking of a human life when an excuse exists.
8. Self-destruction.
9. Killing a racial or political group.
10. Murder committed while in the commission of a felony.
12. Death must occur within year and day for a person to be guilty of homicide.
14. Unlawful killing of human being by another without malice.
15. The body on which a crime has been committed.
16. Laws that allow dying people to refuse extraordinary treatment.
17. The dominant cause that produces an injury or death.

Down

1. Killing a fetus in the womb—abortion.
2. Evil intent.
4. Having the appearance of being able to live.
6. An excuse for the use of force in resisting attack.
7. The taking of a human life when an excuse exists.
11. Unlawful killing of a human being by another with malice aforethought.
13. Killing one's mother.

Crimes Against Morality and Drug Abuse

ANTE INTERROGATORY

With some variations, most states prohibit marriage between people who are related by (A) fornication, (B) affinity, (C) consanguinity, (D) miscegenation.

KEY TERMS

abortion *(a·BOR·shun)*

adultery *(a·DUL·ter·ee)*

affinity *(a·FIN·i·tee)*

bestiality *(bee·stee·AL·i·tee)*

bigamy *(BIG·a·mee)*

consanguinity *(kon·san·GWIN·i·tee)*

controlled substance *(kon·TROLED SUB·stanse)*

copulation *(kop·yoo·LA·shun)*

drugs

drug trafficking *(TRAF·ik·ing)*

fornication *(for·ni·KA·shun)*

impediment *(im·PED·i·ment)*

incest *(IN·sest)*

miscegenation *(mis·sej·e·NA·shun)*

obscenity *(ob·SEN·i·tee)*

ordinance *(OR·di·nense)*

polygamy *(po·LIG·a·mee)*

pornography *(por·NAW·graf·ee)*

preponderance of evidence *(pre·PON·der·ense ov EV·i·dens)*

pro-choice *(pro-choys)*

pro-life *(pro-life)*

prurient interest *(PROO·ree·ent IN·trest)*

reasonable doubt *(REE·zen·e·bel dowt)*

sodomy *(SOD·e·mee)*

ADULTERY AND FORNICATION

Adultery is voluntary sexual intercourse by a married person with someone other than his or her spouse or by an unmarried person with a married person. In addition to being a ground for divorce, it is a crime in many states. The statute of one state reads as follows:

> A married person who has sexual intercourse with a person not his spouse, or an unmarried person who has sexual intercourse with a married person shall be guilty of adultery and shall be punished by imprisonment in the state prison for not more than three years, or in jail for not more than two years, or by a fine of not more than $500.

To convict someone of the crime of adultery, the prosecution must prove beyond a reasonable doubt that the illegal act occurred. In contrast, to obtain a divorce on the ground of adultery, it is merely necessary to prove by a preponderance of evidence that the illegal act occurred. Preponderance of evidence is evidence of the greatest weight, indicating that it is more likely than not that the act occurred. The subject of adultery is discussed further in Chapter 38.

TERMS IN ACTION

Suzanne Corona, of Batavia, New York, was charged with **adultery** in June 2010. Surprisingly, New York is a state that still has in its penal code (Section 255.17) such a crime. Unsurprisingly, adultery is a charge that is rarely brought in New York. According to the news accounts, a distraught woman first spotted Mrs. Corona and Justin Amend on top of a picnic table in the park, and when the police arrived they viewed what they believed was a public act of sexual intercourse. So, Corona and Amend were charged with public lewdness. But because one of the officers knew that Corona was married, he charged her with adultery, making her the 13th New Yorker to be so charged since 1972. There must no longer be a **fornication** law in New York, because Amend, who was single, was not charged with that, but he did get 30 days in jail for the lewdness charge. The adultery charge was dropped as part of a plea bargain on the public lewdness count, for which Mrs. Corona was given probation. But she went to jail in 2011 for violating her probation, after she was arrested for shoplifting.

Sources: nydailynews.com; abcnews.go.com; thedailynewsonline.com

---

Fornication, which is sexual intercourse between two unmarried persons, is also a crime in some states. The Massachusetts statute reads as follows:

> Whoever commits fornication shall be punished by imprisonment for not more than three months or by a fine of not more than thirty dollars.

As of 2007, Florida, Michigan, Mississippi, North Carolina, Virginia, and West Virginia have laws prohibiting an unmarried man and woman from living together as if they were married. The Florida statute (§798.02) reads as follows:

> If any man and woman, not being married to each other, lewdly and lasciviously associate and cohabit together, or if any man or woman, married or unmarried, engages in open and gross lewdness and lascivious behavior, they shall be guilty of a misdemeanor of the second degree.

Many states have done away with laws that made adultery and fornication crimes. Many other states have kept the laws on their books, but seldom enforce them. Because of the outcome of a Supreme Court case, *Lawrence v. Texas*, discussed later in the chapter, it is doubtful whether laws prohibiting adultery or fornication are constitutional.

BIGAMY AND POLYGAMY

Bigamy is the state of a man who has two wives, or of a woman who has two husbands, living at the same time. **Polygamy** is the state of having several wives or husbands at the same time. All states in the United States consider bigamy and polygamy to be criminal offenses. In addition, a marriage contracted while either party thereto has a wife or husband is void and of no legal effect unless the previous marriage has been terminated by annulment, divorce, or death of that spouse. In some states, if one of the parties entered the marriage in good faith without knowledge of the **impediment**—that is, the hindrance to the making of a contract (the fact that the other spouse is married)—the second marriage will become valid upon the death or divorce of the former spouse if the parties continue to live together in good faith on the part of one of them.

Word Wise
Numbers

Word Element	Meaning	Examples
uni-	one	unilateral, universe
bi-, di-, du-	two	bilateral, dichotomy, duet
tri-	three	trifurcate, tricycle
quadr-, quart-	four	quadrangle, quartet
quint-, penta-	five	quintuplets, pentagon
ses-, sext-, hexa-	six	sestet, sextet, hexagon
sept-	seven	septet
oct-	eight	octagon, octet
non-, nov-	nine	nonagon, novena
deca-	ten	decathlon, decade

INCEST AND SODOMY

Incest is sexual intercourse between people who are related by **consanguinity** (blood) or affinity in such a way that they cannot legally marry. **Affinity** is the relationship that one spouse has to the blood relatives of the other.

At common law, people could not marry the following relatives:

Consanguinity	**Affinity**
mother or father	stepmother or stepfather
grandmother or grandfather	step-grandmother or step-grandfather
daughter or son	stepdaughter or stepson
granddaughter or grandson	step-granddaughter or step-grandson
unt or uncle	mother-in-law or father-in-law
sister or brother	grandmother-in-law or grandfather-in-law
niece or nephew	daughter-in-law or son-in-law
	granddaughter-in-law or grandson-in-law

Today, many states no longer prohibit marriages between people who are related by affinity. With some variations, most states still prohibit marriages between people who are related by consanguinity.

Sodomy was formerly referred to in many state statutes as the "abominable and detestable crime against nature." Although that is a nonspecific description, the crime of sodomy has been interpreted by the courts as referring to oral intercourse, anal penetration, and **bestiality**, the later being carnal **copulation** (sexual intercourse) by a man or woman with an animal. In 2003, the U.S. Supreme Court case of *Lawrence* v. *Texas* (539 U.S. 558) held anti-sodomy laws to be unconstitutional. The Court said that the parties' right to liberty under the due process clause gives them the full right to engage in private conduct without government intervention. But the court's majority opinion limited itself to non-commercial, heterosexual and homosexual sodomy, and so it does not affect the constitutionality of laws against bestiality or those against prostitution.

MISCEGENATION AND ABORTION LAWS

At one time, many states prohibited marriage between people of different races, which was called **miscegenation**. Such marriages were often held to be illegal and void, and the parties thereto were punished. The U.S. Supreme Court has held miscegenation statutes to be against the law. They violate the equal protection clause and the due process clause of the Fourteenth Amendment of the U.S. Constitution.

The question of whether to legally allow a pregnant woman to have an **abortion** (the act of preventing a live birth by terminating a pregnancy) is an extremely emotional issue. Many people are **pro-life**—they believe that abortions should not be allowed except in the case of rape or incest and when necessary to save the life of the mother. They believe that an abortion takes the life of a human being and is no different from killing someone who is alive. Others are **pro-choice**—they believe that a pregnant woman should have the choice of having an abortion or not, without interference from the government.

In 1973, in *Roe* v. *Wade* (413 U.S. 113), the U.S. Supreme Court held that laws prohibiting abortion were unconstitutional. The Court said that during the first three months of pregnancy, a woman can have an abortion; the decision is up to her, without interference by the state. States are allowed to pass laws to protect the mother's health during the second three months of pregnancy by making rules as to who can perform abortions and where they can be performed. State laws may prohibit abortions during the last three months of pregnancy, the Court said, with exceptions to protect the life or health of the mother.

In 1989, the U.S. Supreme Court held, in *Webster* v. *Reproductive Health Services* (492 U.S. 490) that states may ban public employees from performing abortions in public hospitals other than to save the life of the mother and that states may pass laws requiring doctors to determine through various tests whether a fetus at least 20 weeks old is viable. In the 1991 case *Rust* v. *Sullivan* (500 U.S. 173), the U.S. Supreme Court upheld laws which prohibit agencies that receive federal or state funding from giving information on or performing abortions. In 1992, in the case *Planned Parenthood* v. *Casey* (505 U.S. 833), the U.S. Supreme Court reaffirmed its essential holdings in the *Roe* v. *Wade* case. In addition, the Court upheld laws that require minors seeking an abortion to obtain a parent's or guardian's consent, but struck down laws that require wives to notify husbands of an intended abortion.

In 2003, in *Scheidler* v. *National Organization for Women* (537 U.S. 393), the U.S. Supreme Court held that federal racketeering laws, such as RICO laws, could not be used as the foundation for criminal charges against pro-life protesters who rally outside abortion clinics. Four years later, in 2007, the same court held in *Gonzales* v. *Carhart* (550 U.S. 124) that the Partial Birth Abortion Ban Act passed by Congress in 2003 is constitutional. It does not violate a woman's right to have an abortion even though it contains no exception to allow an abortion if needed to preserve a woman's life. Partial birth abortion procedures, now illegal, involved partially removing the fetus intact from a woman's uterus and cutting or crushing its skull.

PORNOGRAPHY AND OBSCENITY

Pornography in general, refers to material or conduct that shows or describes some kind of sexual activity and is designed to make people become sexually aroused. The term that is more commonly used by courts and legislatures to describe pornography is **obscenity**, although one could make the technical, legal distinction that pornography is that which is intended to sexually arouse and is subject to regulation, whereas obscenity is a subset of pornography and is that which is patently offensive and subject to criminalization.

The First and Fourteenth Amendments to the U.S. Constitution, which give to all Americans the right of free speech and free expression, do not protect obscenity. Each individual state may, under a U.S. Supreme Court decision, enact laws regulating obscenity. In 1970, the Court issued a decision, in *Miller* v. *California* (413 U.S. 15), that established a three-part test to determine whether material is obscene, and all three parts of the test must be present for material to be deemed obscene. The three-part test follows:

1. An average person, applying modern community standards, would find that the work, taken as a whole, appeals to prurient interests. **Prurient interest** means "a shameful or morbid interest in sex." Local, rather than national, standards may be used as a guide.
2. The matter must show or describe sexual conduct in a way that is openly offensive. The sexual conduct that is not allowed to be shown or described must also be clearly defined by state law. This guideline exists so that people will know exactly what the state considers to be obscene.
3. The work, taken as a whole, has no serious literary, artistic, political, or scientific value.

In 1975, the U.S. Supreme Court issued a decision in an obscenity case that is worthy of a summary: A drive-in theater showed a movie in which people were nude. The theater was located in such a position that the screen could be seen from two public streets and a nearby church parking lot. A local **ordinance** (law passed by a city council) made it unlawful for a drive-in theater to show films containing nudity when the screen was visible from a public street or public place. The theater was charged by the city with violating the ordinance. The U.S. Supreme Court held that the city ordinance was unconstitutional because it was too broad. As written, the ordinance prevented drive-in theaters from showing movies containing any nudity at all, however innocent or educational. The court said, "clearly, all nudity cannot be deemed obscene even as to minors." (*Erznoznik* v. *City of Jacksonville*, 422 U.S. 205)

DRUG ABUSE

The abuse of **drugs** (chemical substances that have an effect on the body or mind) has been a major national concern since the 1930s. Both federal and state laws deal with drug abuse.

Federal Drug Abuse Laws

The Federal Controlled Substances Act, passed in 1970, places strict controls on drugs. Under the act, five schedules have been established. Drugs are placed on one of five schedules, depending on their medical use, potential for abuse, and potential for dependence. A drug that is included on any of the five schedules is called a **controlled substance**. Drugs that are placed on Schedule I, such as heroin, are strictly controlled. They have little or no medical use, are usually addictive, and have a high potential for abuse. Drugs that are placed on Schedule V, such as codeine cough medicine, are not as strictly controlled.

Penalties for violating federal drug abuse laws are found in the United States Sentencing Guidelines. They range from imprisonment for one year and a $1,000 fine, to imprisonment for life. Penalties also include the forfeiture of personal property (such as motor vehicles, boats, and aircraft) and real property used to facilitate the possession of a controlled substance.

The law has a provision for allowing minor punishment without giving the offender a criminal record if an offender is in possession of only a small amount of drugs. In such cases, the government has the option of imposing a civil fine of up to $10,000 rather than a criminal penalty. In determining the amount of the fine, the offender's income and assets are considered. For a first offense for which the offender has paid all fines, can pass a drug test, and has not been convicted of a crime after three years since the conviction, the proceedings can be dismissed. When this occurs, the drug offender can lawfully say that he or she had never been prosecuted, either criminally or civilly, for a drug offense. This law may not be used if (1) the drug offender has been previously convicted of a federal or state drug offense; or (2) the offender has been fined twice under this special program.

The federal act imposes penalties on persons for illegal **drug trafficking**. This activity is the unauthorized manufacture or distribution of any controlled substance, or the possession of such a substance with the intention of manufacturing or distributing it illegally. The penalty for being convicted of a first offense of drug trafficking of a Schedule I or II drug is not less than 5 years or more than 40 years in prison. The penalty increases to not less than 10 years or more than life in prison for a second offense. The penalty increases even more for the trafficking of very great quantities of illegal drugs.

The Drug Enforcement Administration (DEA) enforces the federal drug laws. It also strives to cut off the sources of supply of illegal drugs before they reach people who might use them.

State Drug Abuse Laws

Many states have adopted the Uniform Controlled Substances Act and have made it part of their state law. The uniform law is similar to the Federal Controlled Substances Act. It contains the same five Schedules that are found in the federal act and provides a procedure for adding, removing, and transferring drugs from one Schedule to another. It also contains controls that are similar to those found in the federal act. It does not, however, establish penalties for violation of the law. Instead, the act leaves it up to each state to set its own penalties.

TERMS IN ACTION

Marijuana is the most famous and most popular of the **controlled substances**. It is classified as a Schedule I drug, according to the Federal Controlled Substances Act of 1970, which has five categories, or Schedules, of drugs. Schedule I is the most serious of the five categories. Marijuana comes from female Cannabis plants and has been used for centuries. In America, marijuana was a legal substance until the early twentieth century, when states began criminalizing it. In 1913, California became the first state to criminalize marijuana, and many states followed suit. The federal government first began regulating marijuana with the passage of the Marijuana Tax Act of 1937. Marijuana usage or **trafficking** may be thought to be no big deal, but in New York City in 2010, over 50,000 people were arrested for marijuana, making it the cause of 15 percent of all NYC arrests that year. In the last four decades, though, some states have attempted to decriminalize marijuana, including California, which passed a law in 2010 decriminalizing possession of up to one ounce of marijuana. But federal law still controls.

Sources: justice.gov; drugpolicy.org; drugabuse.gov

Reviewing What You Learned

After studying the chapter, write the answers to each of the following questions:

1. What is the difference between fornication and adultery?

   _____

   _____

   _____

2. What is the status of a marriage contracted while either party has a spouse still living?

   _____

   _____

   _____

3. Under what circumstance will a bigamous marriage become valid in some states?

   _____

   _____

   _____

4. Name five relationships by consanguinity in which one cannot legally marry.

   _____

   _____

   _____

5. Name three relationships by affinity in which one could not legally marry at common law.

   _____

   _____

   _____

6. What is the difference between being related by consanguinity and being related by affinity?

   _____

   _____

   _____

7. Explain the present legal status of miscegenation statutes.

   _____

   _____

   _____

8. Under what circumstances is abortion legal?

   _____

   _____

   _____

9. Describe the three-part test that must be used to determine whether or not material is obscene.

   _____

   _____

   _____

10. The Federal Controlled Substances Act places drugs on different Schedules depending on what three considerations?

    _____

    _____

    _____

11. Give an example of a drug that is placed on Schedule I of the Federal Controlled Substances Act.

    _____

    _____

    _____

12. In what ways does the Uniform Controlled Substances Act deal with penalties for drug abuse?

    _____

    _____

    _____

Understanding Legal Concepts

Indicate whether each statement is true or false. Then, change the italicized word or phrase of each false statement to make it true.

ANSWERS

_____ 1. In addition to being a ground for divorce, adultery is a *crime* in many states.

_____ 2. Fornication *is not* a crime in *any* state.

_____ 3. All states in the United States consider bigamy, *but not polygamy*, to be criminal.

_____ 4. Incest and sodomy are *synonymous*.

_____ 5. With some variations, most states *still prohibit* marriage between people who are related by consanguinity.

_____ **6.** The U.S. Supreme Court has held miscegenation statutes to be *valid and legal*.

_____ **7.** During the first *six* months of pregnancy, a woman can have an abortion without interference by the state, under the 1973 Supreme Court decision.

_____ **8.** The First and Fourteenth Amendments to the U.S. Constitution *do not* protect obscenity.

_____ **9.** The penalties are *greater* for the illegal trafficking of drugs on Schedule I than they are for drugs on Schedule V, under the Federal Controlled Substances Act.

_____ **10.** The Uniform Controlled Substances Act *establishes* penalties for violation of the law.

Checking Terminology

From the list of legal terms that follows, select the one that matches each definition.

ANSWERS

a. abortion
b. adultery
c. affinity
d. bestiality
e. beyond a reasonable doubt
f. bigamy
g. consanguinity
h. controlled substance
i. copulation
j. drugs
k. drug trafficking
l. fornication
m. impediment
n. incest
o. miscegenation
p. obscenity
q. ordinance
r. polygamy
s. pornography
t. preponderance of evidence
u. pro-choice
v. pro-life
w. prurient interest
x. reasonable doubt
y. sodomy

_____ **1.** Voluntary sexual intercourse by a married person with someone other than his or her spouse or by an unmarried person with a married person.

_____ **2.** The state of a man who has two wives, or of a woman who has two husbands, living at the same time.

_____ **3.** Sexual intercourse by a man or woman with an animal.

_____ **4.** Disability or hindrance to the making of a contract.

_____ **5.** The act that state statutes often describe as an "abominable and detestable crime against nature."

_____ **6.** Doubt based on reason.

_____ **7.** Evidence of the greatest weight.

_____ **8.** The act of stopping a pregnancy.

_____ **9.** Material or conduct that shows or describes some kind of sexual activity and is designed to make people become sexually aroused. (Select two answers.)

_____ **10.** A law passed by a city council.

_____ **11.** The unauthorized manufacture or distribution of any controlled substance or the possession of such a substance with the intention of manufacturing or distributing it illegally.

_____ **12.** Sexual intercourse between two unmarried persons.

_____ **13.** The state of having several wives or husbands at the same time.

_____ **14.** Sexual intercourse between people who are related by consanguinity or affinity in such a way that they cannot legally marry.

_____ **15.** The relationship that one spouse has to blood relatives of the other.

_____ **16.** Marriage between people of different races.

_____ **17.** Chemical substances that have an effect on the body or mind.

_____ **18.** A shameful or morbid interest in sex.

_____ **19.** Favoring legislation that disallows abortion.

_____ **20.** A drug that is included in any of the five Schedules established by the Federal Controlled Substances Act.

_____ **21.** Sexual intercourse.

_____ **22.** Favoring legislation that allows abortion.

_____ **23.** Related by blood.

Sharpening Your Latin Skills

In the space provided, write the definition of each of the following legal terms, referring to the glossary when necessary:

actio criminalis _____

actus reus _____

animus furandi _____

corpus delicti _____

doli capax _____

ex post facto _____

mala in se _____

mala prohibita _____

mens rea _____

nolle prosequi _____

Using Legal Language

Read the following story and fill in the blank lines with legal terms taken from the list of terms at the beginning of this chapter:

Janice's husband, Rodney, who was white, became acquainted with some people who were taking _____, which is the name for illegal drugs. Because he did not manufacture or distribute the _____, he could not be convicted of _____ Rodney's friends often watched X-rated movies, which were allowed by a local _____—that is, a law passed by the city—but which were close to being _____, because, among other points, they appealed to _____, which means a shameful or morbid interest in sex. Without divorcing Janice, Rodney married another woman, thereby committing the crime of _____. Both of these marriages were later dissolved. Rodney then met Doris, an Asian woman, with whom he had sexual intercourse. This crime was one of _____ because they were not married to each other. Because neither of them was married to anyone else, it was not the crime of _____, and because they were not related by _____ or _____, it was not the crime of _____. When she became pregnant, Doris decided to carry the baby to term—that is, not have a(n) _____. The fact that the two were of different races did not prohibit them from getting married, because all _____ statutes are now illegal.

PUZZLING OVER WHAT YOU LEARNED

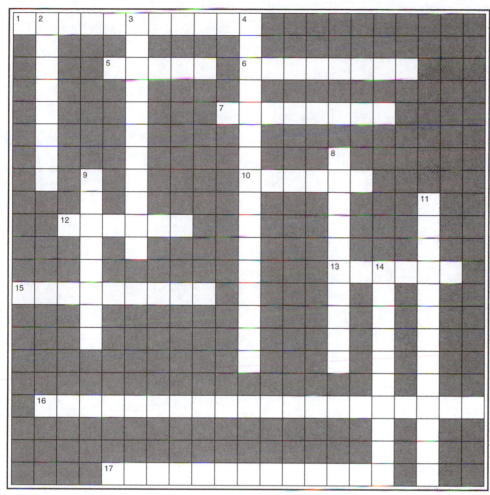

Caveat: Allow squares for spaces between words and punctuation (apostrophes, hyphens, etc.) when filling in crossword.

Across

1. The jury or the judge in a nonjury trial.
5. Chemical substances that have an effect on the body or mind.
6. Related by marriage.
7. The state of having several wives or husbands at the same time.
10. The state of a person with two spouses living at the same time.
12. Act often described as an "abominable and detestable crime against nature."
13. Sexual intercourse between people related by consanguinity.
15. Law passed by a city council.
16. A drug that is included in a schedule of the Federal Controlled Substances Act.
17. Marriage between people of different races.

Down

2. Sexual intercourse by a married person with someone other than a spouse.
3. Sexual intercourse between two unmarried persons.
4. Doubt based on reason.
8. Disability or hindrance to the making of a contract.
9. The act of stopping a pregnancy.
11. Related by blood.
14. Sexual intercourse.

Terms Used in Law of Torts

3

Some wrongful acts, although not in themselves criminal, may cause injuries to other people. To provide monetary relief to people who suffer losses from the wrongs of others, the law of torts has developed over the years. Chapter 15 defines the elements of a tort action and then discusses imputed liability, liability of minors, immunity from tort liability, and joint tortfeasors. Chapter 16 explains the intentional torts of assault and battery, infliction of emotional distress, deceit, defamation, malicious prosecution, trespass, and conversion. The most common tort—negligence—is saved for last, and its elements, degrees, and defenses are examined in Chapter 17.

Torts and Tortfeasors

ANTE INTERROGATORY

A tort is defined as (A) a breach of contract, (B) a wrong against the public at large, (C) a wrong against a town government, (D) a wrong against an individual.

CHAPTER OUTLINE

Elements of a Tort Action

Imputed Liability

Liability of Minors

Immunity from Tort Liability
Charitable Immunity
Sovereign Immunity

Joint Tortfeasors

KEY TERMS

agent *(AY·jent)*

cybertort *(SY·ber·tort)*

doctrine of charitable immunity *(DOK·trin ov CHAR·i·ta·bel im·YOO·ni·tee)*

doctrine of respondeat superior *(res·PON·dee·at soo·PEER·ee·or)*

doctrine of sovereign immunity *(SOV·er·in im·YOO·ni·tee)*

Good Samaritan statutes *(sem·EHR·i·ten STAT·shoot)*

immune *(im·YOON)*

imputed liability *(im·PEW·ted ly·a·BIL·i·tee)*

joint liability *(joynt ly·a·BIL·i·tee)*

joint tortfeasors *(tort·FEE·zors)*

master *(MAS·ter)*

principal *(PRIN·se·pel)*

right of contribution *(kon·tri·BYOO·shun)*

servant *(SER·vent)*

several liability *(SEV·er·el ly·a·BIL·i·tee)*

tort

tortfeasor *(tort·FEE·zor)*

vicarious liability *(vi·KARE·ee·us ly·a·BIL·i·tee)*

A **tort**, which means "wrong" in French (from the Latin *tortus,* meaning "twisted"), is a wrong against an individual (a private wrong), as opposed to a crime, which is a wrong against the public at large. A tort action is a civil suit brought by the injured party to recover money damages to compensate him or her for losses caused by the tortious act of the **tortfeasor** (the one who commits the tort). It differs from a criminal action, which is brought by the state to punish the defendant for the wrongdoing. In some situations, such as in the case of assault and battery, the wrong is both a tort and a crime. In such a case, the state can bring a criminal action against the defendant, and the injured party can bring a separate tort action against the defendant for the same occurrence. The term **cybertort** means a tort associated with a computer.

In comparing a tort with a breach of contract, a tort is a breach of duty imposed by law, whereas a breach of contract is a breach of duty imposed by agreement of the parties.

ELEMENTS OF A TORT ACTION

Although each tort has its own particular elements that must be alleged and proved by the plaintiff in order for the plaintiff to win a case, four basic elements are common to all torts. In general, the plaintiff must allege and prove all of the following:

1. the existence of a duty owed to the plaintiff by the defendant;
2. a violation of that duty;
3. a showing that the violation was the cause of the plaintiff's injuries; and
4. damages.

Several years ago, an intoxicated person tipped over while paddling a canoe on a lake. The proprietor of a boathouse watched from the shore while the person yelled for help and finally drowned. The proprietor was sued by the decedent's estate for negligence (a tort to be discussed later) for not attempting to rescue the drowning person. The court held in favor of the boathouse proprietor, saying that he owed no duty to go to the rescue of the person who was drowning.

The rule that people are not legally bound to help others who are in trouble has been modified somewhat in recent years. For example, the janitor of a building was held to be negligent when he failed to turn off the electricity to an elevator after he was told that a child had climbed through the opening in the elevator car's roof. The child was killed when the elevator was set in motion by an unsuspecting person. In that case, the court held that the janitor owed a duty to go to the aid of the child by shutting off the electricity (*Pridgen v. Boston Housing Authority*, 364 Mass. 696 (Mass. 1974)).

3

Word Wise
Homonyms

Homonyms are words that have the same pronunciation, but that differ in meaning. Here are some examples:

Word	Meaning	Examples
principle	Rule; precept	It would be contrary to my *principles* to vote for that person.
		There were no guiding *principles* to follow when we landed on the moon.
principal	Chief; main	The *principal* of the school was the *principal* objector to the plan to invest the *principal* at 3 percent.
counsel	Advice; deliberation; one who gives advice	I asked for *counsel* from my aunt's *counsel* before making my investments.
		The defendant consulted his *counsel* before answering the question.
council	An assembly	The city *council* discussed the matter at its last meeting.
		Council Bluffs, Iowa, commemorates the *council* that Lewis and Clark held with the Indians on the high bluffs.

Although in most cases people are not legally bound to help others, if they do so and are negligent, they will be liable for any injuries that they may cause. For this reason, people in the medical field would, in the past, sometimes refuse to assist injured people at accident scenes or in other emergencies. States have passed laws, known as Good Samaritan statutes, to alleviate this problem. **Good Samaritan statutes** provide that physicians, nurses, and certain other medical personnel will not be liable for negligent acts that occur when they voluntarily, without a fee, render emergency care or treatment outside of the ordinary course of their practice. For instance, Colorado's Good Samaritan Statute (C.R.S. §13-21-108) covers nonmedical personnel as well, and states as follows:

> Any person licensed as a physician and surgeon under the laws of the state of Colorado, or any other person, who in good faith renders emergency care or emergency assistance to a person not presently his patient without compensation at the place of an emergency or accident, including a health care institution as defined in section 13-64-202 (3), shall not be liable for any civil damages for acts or omissions made in good faith as a result of the rendering of such emergency care or emergency assistance during the emergency, unless the acts or omissions were grossly negligent or willful and wanton.

IMPUTED LIABILITY

Although all people are responsible for their own torts, in some situations one person may be held responsible for the torts that are committed by another person; this is known as **imputed liability**. Often, the term **vicarious liability** is used interchangeably with the term "imputed liability." Vicarious liability applies most frequently when an employee commits a tort while working for an employer. Under the **doctrine of respondeat superior masters** (employers) can be held responsible for the torts of their **servants** (employees) that are committed within the scope of employment. A tort committed within the scope of employment is a wrongful act committed by an employee that is nonetheless committed inside the zone of that person's employment authority. Similarly, **principals** (people who authorize others to act for them) can be held responsible for the torts committed by their **agents** (people authorized to act) while acting within the scope of the principals' authority. Similarly, a partner may be held liable for torts committed by another partner while acting in the ordinary course of the partnership.

▌ TERMS IN ACTION

Predicting when **imputed liability** or **vicarious liability** applies in employment situations can be difficult. Try a couple of examples. In the first scenario, a woman who was being transported to a hospital in Washington, D.C., was sexually assaulted in the ambulance by one of the ambulance employees. Six months later, another Washington, D.C., woman was sexually assaulted under the same circumstances, allegedly by the same man. And in Virginia, an employee—who five minutes earlier had left an employer-sponsored Christmas party where he had been drinking alcohol served by the employer—injured someone while driving drunk. In the first two cases, the District of Columbia, as the employer of the ambulance company, was sued under the doctrine of **Respondeat Superior**, as was the employer in the Virginia case. In the first ambulance case, the jury returned a verdict for the District of Columbia, because it was not aware of the possibility of such an act (which was not within **the scope of employment**), but the same jury awarded an $180,000 verdict for the second woman, because the District was on notice from the first allegation. In the Virginia case, the jury awarded the plaintiff $11 million in damages, but the trial judge reversed the verdict (which was upheld on appeal), concluding that the employee was not within the scope of employment at the time of the accident.

Sources: washingtonpost.com; *Sayles v. Piccadilly Cafeterias, Inc.*, 410 S.E.2d 632 (Va. 1991).

LIABILITY OF MINORS

Minor children (those under the age of 18) are just as liable for their torts as adults. In fact, in 2010, a Manhattan judge ruled that a 4-year-old girl could be sued in tort law for allegedly negligently riding her bike and hitting an 87-year-old woman, who broke her hip in the fall and died three months later. The estate of the woman sued the girl and her biking buddy (who was 5), with whom the girl was racing down the street, on her bike with training wheels, at the time she hit the woman. It is usually impossible to collect court judgments from minors, however, because in most cases they have no money. Under the common law, parents were not responsible for the torts of their minor child unless the act was committed in the parents' presence or while the minor was acting as the agent or servant of the parents. Some states have modified this rule by enacting statutes that make parents liable up to a limited amount of money for the willful torts committed by their minor children.

IMMUNITY FROM TORT LIABILITY

In the past, charitable and governmental institutions could not be sued, with some exceptions, for their wrongdoings.

Charitable Immunity

Until recently, charitable institutions such as hospitals and churches were **immune**—that is, exempt—from tort liability. They could not be sued in tort for the wrongdoings of their agents or employees that occurred in the course of the charitable activity. This regulation was known as the **doctrine of charitable immunity**. By 1969, most U.S. states had abolished the doctrine of charitable immunity. To illustrate, in 1969, the Massachusetts Supreme Judicial Court (the highest court in that state) declared that it would abolish the doctrine in the next case involving that issue unless the legislature acted on the matter. This decision caused the Massachusetts legislature to pass a statute in 1971 abolishing the doctrine of charitable immunity in cases arising from a charity's commercial activity and setting a limit of $20,000 on the amount that may be recovered from a charity for torts arising out of charitable activity.

Sovereign Immunity

The **doctrine of sovereign immunity**, which makes a governmental body immune from tort liability unless the government agrees to be held liable, stems from the old common law rule that "the king can do no wrong." For hundreds of years, under this doctrine, individuals could not sue the federal, state, or local government for its torts unless a statute allowed a suit for that particular wrong. This doctrine has also been modified by the U.S. Congress, and by statute in many states.

For example, the U.S. government has waived its sovereign immunity in order to allow civil suits for actions arising out of negligent acts of its agents. To bring such an action, strict rules under the Federal Tort Claims Act must be followed precisely.

Under the Massachusetts Tort Claims Act, public employers (state and local governmental agencies) are liable up to $100,000 for personal injury, property damage, or death, caused by the negligent or wrongful act or omission of any public employee while acting within the scope of employment. In addition, the public employee whose negligent or wrongful act or omission caused the claim cannot be sued if the act occurred while he or she was acting within the scope of employment and if it was not an intentional tort. Before suit may be brought under the act, a claim must be presented in writing, within two years after the cause of action arose, to the executive officer of the public employer involved. The public employer has six months in which to pay the claim, deny it, refer it to arbitration, or reach a settlement. Only then may the suit be brought against the public employer, and it must be brought within three years after the cause of action arose.

TERMS IN ACTION

The doctrine of **sovereign immunity** applies to a variety of government employees, including judges. The most infamous case of **judicial immunity** is *Stump v. Sparkman*, a 1978 U.S. Supreme Court case. In that case, an Indiana trial judge granted the request of a mother that her "somewhat retarded" 15-year-old daughter be sterilized. When the daughter went in for surgery, she was told that she was having her appendix taken out. Later, when she married and couldn't get pregnant, she then learned what had been done to her. She sued the judge for violating her civil rights and due process rights by granting a sterilization order, something over which he had no jurisdiction. Judge Sparkman got the case dismissed on the basis of sovereign immunity, but the 7th Circuit of Appeals reversed the decision. Then, the Supreme Court reversed, holding that the judge was absolutely immune from liability because he had been performing a function normally performed by a judge and acting in his official capacity when granting the wrongful sterilization order.

Source: *Stump v. Sparkman*, 435 U.S. 349 (1978)

JOINT TORTFEASORS

If more than one person participates in the commission of a tort, they are called **joint tortfeasors**. They may be held either jointly or severally liable for their wrongdoings. **Joint liability** means that all joint tortfeasors must be named as defendants in the lawsuit and, if found liable, together they owe the damages awarded to the plaintiff. **Several liability** means that the joint tortfeasors may be sued separately for the wrongdoing. Suppose that two drag-racing teens wreck into a home situated next to the highway, causing extensive property damage, and one of the teens joins the armed services the next day, leaving the jurisdiction. The plaintiffs sue the other teen, who is now the only one around. If that teen-driver is found liable, he or she owes the entire damages. By statute in some states, if one joint tortfeasor is required to pay more than his or her share to the injured party, he or she may sue the other joint tortfeasor for the excess. This regulation is known as the **right of contribution** between joint tortfeasors.

Reviewing What You Learned

After studying the chapter, write the answers to each of the following questions:

1. What is the difference between a tort and a crime? _____

   _____

   _____

   _____

   _____

2. Give an example of a wrong that is both a tort and a crime. ___

   _____

   _____

   _____

   _____

3. How does a tort differ from a breach of contract? _____

   _____

   _____

   _____

   _____

4. What four basic requirements must the plaintiff allege and prove in order to recover damages for a tort? _____

   _____

   _____

   _____

   _____

5. Describe and name the term for the situation in which one person may be held responsible for the torts that are committed by another person. _____

_____

_____

_____

6. What liability do minor children have for their torts? _____

_____

_____

_____

7. In what way are parents liable for torts committed by their children? _____

_____

_____

_____

8. Describe the statute enacted in 1971 by the Massachusetts legislature, dealing with the tort liability of a charitable organization.

_____

_____

_____

_____

9. Describe the main features of the Massachusetts Tort Claims Act. _____

_____

_____

_____

_____

10. What is the difference between joint liability and several liability?

_____

_____

_____

_____

Understanding Legal Concepts

Indicate whether each statement is true or false. Then, change the italicized word or phrase of each false statement to make it true.

ANSWERS

_____ **1.** A tort is a wrong against *society.*
_____ **2.** Under the doctrine of *respondeat superior,* a governmental body is immune from tort liability.
_____ **3.** In the past, charitable institutions and government bodies were immune from *tort* liability.
_____ **4.** "Master" is the legal name that means *employer.*
_____ **5.** *Several* liability means that all joint tortfeasors must be named as defendants in a lawsuit.
_____ **6.** Minor children are liable for their *torts* just the same as adults.

_____ **7.** In comparing a tort with a breach of contract, a tort is a breach of duty imposed by *the parties,* whereas a breach of contract is a breach of duty imposed by *law.*
_____ **8.** A *tort* is a criminal action brought by the state to punish the defendant for the wrongdoing.
_____ **9.** If one joint tortfeasor is required to pay more than his or her share to the injured party, he or she *may* sue the other joint tortfeasor for the excess.
_____ **10.** An *agent* is a person who is authorized to act on behalf of another and subject to the other's control.

Checking Terminology

From the list of legal terms that follows, select the one that matches each definition.

ANSWERS

a. agent
b. doctrine of charitable immunity
c. doctrine of respondeat superior
d. doctrine of sovereign immunity
e. Good Samaritan statutes
f. immune

_____ 1. A wrong against an individual.
_____ 2. One who commits a tort.
_____ 3. Vicarious responsibility for the torts committed by another person. (Select two answers.)
_____ 4. A legal doctrine under which a master is responsible for the torts of his or her servants, that are committed within the scope of employment.

g. imputed liability

h. joint liability

i. joint tortfeasors

j. master

k. principal

l. right of contribution

m. servant

n. several liability

o. tort

p. tortfeasor

q. Vicarious Liability

_____ 5. An employer.

_____ 6. An employee.

_____ 7. A person who authorizes an agent to act on his or her behalf and subject to his or her control.

_____ 8. A person authorized to act on behalf of another and subject to the other's control.

_____ 9. Exempt.

_____ 10. A legal doctrine under which charitable institutions are immune from tort liability.

_____ 11. A legal doctrine under which governmental bodies are immune from tort liability.

_____ 12. Two or more people who participate in the commission of a tort.

_____ 13. Liability under which all joint tortfeasors must be named as defendants in a lawsuit.

_____ 14. Liability under which joint tortfeasors may be sued separately in a lawsuit.

_____ 15. The right to share a loss among joint tortfeasors or other codefendants.

_____ 16. Laws providing that physicians, nurses, and certain other medical personnel will not be liable for negligent acts that occur when they voluntarily, without a fee, render emergency care or treatment outside of the ordinary course of their practice.

Using Legal Language

Read the following story and fill in the blank lines with legal terms taken from the list of terms at the beginning of this chapter:

Amy and Barry, while working for the Red Cross, committed a _____ when they violated a duty imposed on them by law. Because they committed the wrongful act together, they were joint _____, but because they could be sued separately, their liability was _____ rather than _____. Because the doctrine of _____ no longer applies, the Red Cross, which is the _____ of Amy and Barry, has _____ liability for the torts of its _____ under the doctrine of _____. If it turns out that Amy is required to pay more than Barry for the damages they caused, Amy has the right of _____ to recover the excess from Barry. This case is not one involving the doctrine of _____, because it does not involve a governmental body being _____ from tort liability, nor does it involve a(n) _____ or _____—that is, a person who authorizes another to act or one who is authorized to act.

PUZZLING OVER WHAT YOU LEARNED

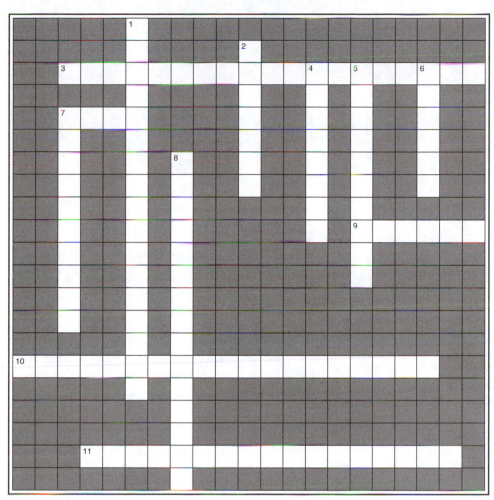

Caveat: Allow squares for spaces between words and punctuation (apostrophes, hyphens, etc.) when filling in crossword.

Across

3. Doctrine under which a master is responsible for the torts of his or her servants.
7. A wrong against an individual.
9. People authorized to act on behalf of others and subject to the others' control.
10. Doctrine under which charitable institutions are immune from tort liability.
11. Two or more people who participate in the commission of a tort.

Down

1. Vicarious responsibility for the torts committed by another person.
2. Employers.
4. Employees.
5. People who authorize agents to act on their behalf and subject to their control.
6. Exempt.
7. One who commits a tort.
8. Liability under which all joint tortfeasors must be named as defendants.

Intentional Torts

ANTE INTERROGATORY

A defamatory statement that is made by an online message or Internet communication is called (A) slander, (B) libel, (C) defamation, (D) invasion of privacy.

3

CHAPTER OUTLINE

Assault and Battery
False Imprisonment
Infliction of Emotional Distress
Deceit
Defamation
    Libel
    Slander

Privileges and Defenses
   to Defamation
Invasion of Privacy
Malicious Prosecution
Trespass
Conversion
Nuisance and Waste

KEY TERMS

acquitted *(a·KWIT·ed)*
actionable *(AK·shun·a·bel)*
assault *(a·SALT)*
battery *(BAT·er·ee)*
conversion *(kon·VER·shun)*
damages *(DAM·e·jez)*
deceit *(dee·SEET)*
defamation *(de·fa·MA·shun)*
false arrest *(a·REST)*
false imprisonment *(im·PRIS·on·ment)*
fraud *(frawd)*
intentional infliction of emotional distress (IIED) *(in·TEN·shun·al in FLICK·shun ov e·MO·shun·al dis·TRES)*
intentional torts *(in·TEN·shun·al)*
invasion of privacy *(in·VA·shun ov PRY·va·see)*
libel *(LY·bel)*

malicious prosecution *(ma·LISH·us pros·e·KYOO·shun)*
misrepresentation *(mis·rep·rez·en·TA·shun)*
nuisance *(NOO·sens)*
per se *(per say)*
private nuisance *(PRI·vet NOO·sens)*
public nuisance *(PUB·lik NOO·sens)*
right of privacy *(PRI·va·see)*
scienter *(si·EN·ter)*
slander *(SLAN·der)*
tortious *(TOR·shus)*
trespass *(TRES·pass)*
trespass de bonis asportatis *(de BO·nis as·por·TAH·tis)*
unintentional torts *(un·in·TEN·shun·al)*
waste
willful torts

Tortious (wrongful) acts may be committed either intentionally or unintentionally. Those that are committed intentionally—that is, deliberately rather than by accident or mistake—are known as **intentional or willful torts**. Conversely, those that are committed accidentally, such as negligence, are referred to as **unintentional torts**.

ASSAULT AND BATTERY

Assault and battery are examples of intentional torts that are also crimes. In such cases, the state can bring a criminal action; in addition, victims can bring a tort suit against the wrongdoer. **Battery** is defined as the intentional contact with another person without that person's permission and without justification. **Assault** is the intentional creation of a reasonable apprehension of an imminent battery. Pointing a gun at someone is an assault; the bullet striking the person is a battery.

Verbal threats alone, in most states, are not enough to constitute an assault. To convert a threat into an assault requires some act to indicate that the battery will ensue immediately. Although every battery includes an assault, an assault does not necessarily require a battery.

FALSE IMPRISONMENT

False imprisonment (also called **false arrest**) is the intentional confinement of a person without legal justification. It is a restraint on a person's liberty. The person who is confined need not be held within an enclosure of any kind or even touched by the other person. It is considered to be a confinement if a person apprehends that physical force will be used if he or she attempts to leave.

Many cases of false imprisonment arise out of situations in which suspected shoplifters are detained by store proprietors without reasonable grounds for doing so. The person who is detained may sue the store for damages arising from the false imprisonment.

Store owners, in some states, have the protection of statutes that allow the detention, for a reasonable length of time and in a reasonable manner, of a person suspected of shoplifting if reasonable grounds for such suspicion exist. Generally, it is reasonable to detain a person if goods that were not purchased are concealed in the clothing or among the belongings of a shopper.

INFLICTION OF EMOTIONAL DISTRESS

Under earlier law, except in the case of false imprisonment, one could not recover damages from another for the infliction of emotional distress unless the emotional suffering was accompanied by some outer physical injury such as a break in the skin or a broken bone.

This earlier law was changed by court decisions and state statutes. For example, in a 1976 case, the manager of a restaurant called a meeting of all waitresses and told them that some stealing was occurring and that the identity of the person responsible was unknown. He said that until the person responsible was discovered, he would begin firing all the present waitresses in alphabetic order. He then fired a waitress whose name began with the letter "A," having no evidence that she had been involved in the thefts. She became greatly upset and began to cry, sustaining emotional distress and mental anguish. The court allowed her to recover damages for her emotional suffering (*Agis v. Howard Johnson, Co.*, 355 N.E.2d 315 (Mass. 1976)).

The tort of **intentional infliction of emotional distress** (IIED) is defined as "emotional suffering caused by the infliction of extreme and outrageous intentional conduct by another." By contrast, there is an unintentional tort called "negligent infliction of emotional distress (NIED)." NIED occurs where a defendant commits an accidental act that is foreseeable to lead to the plaintiff's emotional distress, and where such distress occurs—even in the absence of physical injury. Because NIED allows for the recovery of damages even where there is no physical harm from the negligence, NIED has been criticized and limited in many states.

3

Word Wise
Suffixes

Many words in this chapter are a combination of the basic part of a word, called a root, and a suffix, which is a word element that follows the root. Some of the words use suffixes to form nouns; others form adjectives. Some suffixes form both nouns and adjectives.

Suffixes That Form Nouns

Suffix	Meaning	Examples
-ment	state, quality, act of	imprisonment, statement
-sion, -tion	act or state of	defamation, recognition

Suffixes That Form Adjectives

-able, -ible	capable of	actionable, visible
-al	like, relating to	emotional, intentional

Suffixes That Form Nouns or Adjectives

-ery, -ary,	relating to, connected with	robbery (noun)
-ory, -ry		customary (adjective)
-ful	full of	spoonful (noun)
		plentiful (adjective)

DECEIT

The tort of **deceit**, which is also known as **fraud** or *fraudulent misrepresentation,* comes about when one person, by false representation of material facts, induces another to act and thereby suffer a financial loss. To recover for this tort, the plaintiff must allege and prove all of the following five elements:

1. a misrepresentation of a material, existing fact;
2. made with knowledge of its falsity;
3. made with the intent that it be relied on;
4. that it was reasonably relied on; and
5. damages.

To be actionable, the **misrepresentation** (false or deceptive statement or act) must be of a material, existing fact. It is not actionable if it is an opinion or a promise of something to happen in the future.

The misrepresentation must be made with knowledge of its falsity. This act is known as the **scienter** requirement, which is from the Latin word meaning "knowingly." This element of deceit may be satisfied if the person who made the misrepresentation had actual knowledge of its falsity or made it recklessly without regard to its truth or falsity. In some states, it may also be satisfied if the person who made the misrepresentation actually had no knowledge of its falsity, but was susceptible of knowledge—that is, was in a position in which he or she was expected to know.

To illustrate the latter, in some states if a buyer asks a homeowner who is selling a house, "Does the house have termites?" and the homeowner does not know whether it does or not, but replies, "No, it does not have termites," the court will hold that the homeowner was susceptible of knowledge and therefore satisfied the knowledge requirement.

The person who makes the misrepresentation must intend that the other person rely on it. Suppose, for example, that A made false representations when he sold goods to B. B then sold the goods to C. C would have no right of action against A for the misrepresentations because A did not intend that C rely on them.

In addition, the person to whom the misrepresentation was made must reasonably rely on it. Suppose, for example, that a prospective buyer of a house says to the owner, "Does the house have termites?" and the owner replies, "No, it does not have termites." If the buyer, before buying, has the house inspected by a termite inspector who negligently fails to discover termites that are in the house, the buyer could not sue the seller for deceit, because the buyer did not rely on the seller's misrepresentation.

To recover for deceit, the injured party must prove that he or she suffered some **damage** (financial loss) as a result of the misrepresentation.

DEFAMATION

Defamation is the wrongful act of damaging another's character or reputation by the use of false statements. It is divided into two classes, libel and slander. **Libel** is defamation that is communicated by a writing, drawing, photograph, television program, Internet posting, or other means that is directed toward the sense of sight. **Slander** is defamation that is communicated by the spoken word. It is a communication that is directed toward the sense of hearing.

To be **actionable**—that is, to furnish legal ground for a lawsuit—both libel and slander must be communicated to a third person. Unless a third person hears or sees the defamatory material, no one can sue.

Libel

Because of its more permanent longer-lasting form and its ability to reach more people, libel is considered to be more serious than slander. It is actionable **per se**—that is, in and of itself. A suit can be brought in all instances of libel.

Slander

Slander, conversely, is not actionable per se. It is actionable only in the following situations:

1. when someone is falsely accused of committing a crime of moral turpitude (immorality);
2. when someone is falsely accused of having a contagious disease, such as leprosy, AIDS, or venereal disease;
3. when someone makes a false statement that injures a person in his or her business, profession, or trade; or
4. when the injured person can prove that he or she suffered special damages from the slanderous statements.

Slander that does not fall within one of the preceding four categories cannot be a reason to sue.

■ TERMS IN ACTION

Sunda Croonquist is a stand-up comedian who was sued by her mother-in-law in 2009 for **defamation**. Ms. Croonquist, who is half-black and half-Swedish and who was raised Catholic, didn't tell ordinary mother-in-law jokes; she told jokes focusing on her in-laws as Jews. And not just that, but the jokes made it seem that her in-laws were racists. One of her jokes, about the first time she went to her mother-in-law's house, went this way: "I walk in, I say, 'Thank you so much for having me here, Ruthie.' She says, 'The pleasure's all mine, have a seat. Then, she said to her husband in a loud voice, 'Harry, put my pocketbook away!'" Croonquist's stand-up act took aim at other members of her husband's family; she compared her sister-in-law's voice to a cat in heat. It was actually the sister-in-law who first sued her for **slander** and **libel** (because of Croonquist's website), but the mother-in-law joined the lawsuit in 2009, and it was moved to federal court in Los Angeles. In May, 2010, the case was dismissed. The judge ruled that Croonquist's statements weren't assertions of fact, but simply opinions, which aren't subject to defamation claims. Making the matter even more awkward for Thanksgiving dinners, Croonquist was represented by her husband's law firm.

Sources: nydailynews.com; abajournal.com

> **Web Wise**
>
> - To read current information about defamation, go to www.findlaw.com. At that site, view all the subjects under "Legal Topics." Look under the heading "Accidents and Injuries" for the topic "Defamation, Libel and Slander" and click on it to read more information.
> - For a summary of your state law on wiretapping and eavesdropping, log on to www. google.com. Type in the words "wiretapping and eavesdropping laws" and click "State-by-state summaries."

Privileges and Defenses to Defamation

The law gives privileges to certain people, making them immune from suit for slander and libel. Judges, lawyers, and witnesses, while they are participating in trials, and members of the legislature during its sessions, have an absolute privilege against defamation suits. They cannot be sued for libel or slander.

Newspapers have a qualified privilege when they report about public events and matters of public concern. Actual malice on the part of the newspaper must be proved for someone to recover damages from the newspaper in such cases. Public figures such as actors, actresses, and politicians must prove that the defamatory material was spoken or written with actual malice before they can recover damages against others for defamation.

Truth is an absolute defense against libel or slander.

INVASION OF PRIVACY

The **right of privacy** encompasses the right to be left alone, the right to be free from uncalled-for publicity, and the right to live without unreasonable interference by the public in private matters. A violation of the right of privacy is known as **invasion of privacy**. Using someone's photograph without permission for advertising purposes, wiretapping someone's house, and publishing someone's medical or financial condition are examples of invasion of privacy. As Internet use, text-messaging, and social media have become more prevalent, examples of online invasion of privacy have increased. In 2002, a special federal appeals court gave the U.S. Government permission to use secret wiretaps as a weapon against terrorism.

> ### TERMS IN ACTION
>
> One of the more disturbing trends in the issue of **invasion of privacy** is the use of secretly placed video equipment to spy on others. In Miami, Florida, Kenneth Ryals, a 60-year-old IRS agent placed an ad on Roommates.com, under the screen name "Buttercup," seeking to rent out one of the furnished bedrooms of his home. A 27-year-old woman responded and rented the room, which came with a TV and DVD player. While living in Ryals's home, the woman confronted Ryals about his inappropriate behavior, which took place near her room. Ryals then asked her to move out within a month. While cleaning her room in preparation for leaving, the woman noticed a small hole in the DVD/VCR player, which was pointed at her bed. She called the police, who found a mini-wireless camera implanted in the DVD player. Ryals admitted what he had done, but, somehow, the misdemeanor criminal charges against him were dropped. The former tenant did win her invasion of privacy civil suit, and in 2011 a jury awarded her $476,000 in damages.
>
> Sources: miamiherald.com; abajournal.com

MALICIOUS PROSECUTION

The right of action for the tort of **malicious prosecution** arises when one person has unsuccessfully brought criminal or civil charges against another, with malice and without probable cause. The one against whom the original charges were brought may bring a tort suit for malicious prosecution against the person who brought the original charges. To bring such a suit, all of the following must be proved:

1. Criminal or civil charges were brought against the plaintiff.
2. The plaintiff was **acquitted**—that is, discharged from accusation.
3. The defendant brought the charges maliciously and without probable cause.

TRESPASS

The intentional and unauthorized entry on the land of another is called **trespass**. Suit may be brought against a trespasser by the one who is in possession of the land whether or not he or she has suffered any damages from the trespass. It has been held to be a trespass to do any of the following: step on another's land without permission, hit a golf ball into another's airspace, and string a wire into another's airspace.

Trespass to personal property is a tort called **trespass de bonis asportatis** (trespass for goods carried away). To recover for this tort, it is necessary to prove that actual damages occurred as a result of the trespass. Trespass is an example of a wrongful action that is both a tort and a crime.

CONVERSION

Conversion is the wrongful exercise of dominion and control over the personal property in the possession of another. It is different from trespass in that it is using another's property as though it belonged to the wrongdoer, rather than interfering with the owner's possession as in trespass. Some examples of conversion are misdelivery of goods by a carrier, theft of goods, failure to return borrowed goods, and sale of goods belonging to another without authority.

NUISANCE AND WASTE

The tort of **nuisance** involves the use of one's property in a way that causes annoyance, inconvenience, or discomfort to another. The emission of smoke, offensive odors, and loud noises often generate nuisance lawsuits. Airlines are sometimes sued, for example, by people who live near airports, because of the loud noise, smoke, and odors of the planes taking off. The tort is called a **public nuisance** when the disturbance affects the community at large and a **private nuisance** when it disturbs one neighbor only.

Another tort, called **waste** is the abuse or destructive use of property that is in one's rightful possession. A tenant who damages the landlord's property, for example, commits the tort of waste.

Reviewing What You Learned

After studying the chapter, write the answers to each of the following questions:

1. What must occur to convert a verbal threat into an assault?

_____

_____

_____

_____

2. Out of what situations do many false imprisonment cases arise?

_____

_____

_____

_____

3. What five elements must the plaintiff allege and prove to recover for fraud or deceit? _____

_____

_____

_____

4. Give an example of a person not relying on a misrepresentation and thus not being able to recover for fraud or deceit.

_____

_____

_____

_____

5. What is the difference between libel and slander? _____

_____

_____

_____

6. To whom must libel and slander be communicated to be actionable? _____

_____

_____

_____

_____

7. Under what circumstances is libel actionable? _____

_____

_____

_____

8. Under what circumstances is slander actionable? _____

_____

_____

_____

9. What positions do people enjoy an absolute privilege against defamation suits? _____

_____

_____

10. What must be proved for someone to recover for libel from a newspaper when it reports about public events and matters of public concern? _____

_____

_____

_____

11. What three elements must be proved for one to recover for malicious prosecution? _____

_____

_____

_____

12. Give three examples of trespass to real property. _____

_____

_____

_____

13. Give three examples of conversion. _____

_____

_____

Understanding Legal Concepts

Indicate whether each statement is true or false. Then, change the italicized word or phrase of each false statement to make it true.

ANSWERS

_____ **1.** In the case of false imprisonment, the person confined *must be* held within an enclosure of some kind.

_____ **2.** Although every battery includes an assault, an *assault* does not necessarily require a battery.

_____ **3.** Verbal threats alone *are* enough to be an assault.

_____ **4.** To be actionable fraud, the misrepresentation *must be* an opinion or a promise of something to happen in the future.

_____ **5.** To recover for emotional suffering, the plaintiff must prove that the emotional suffering was caused by the *extreme and outrageous* intentional conduct of the defendant.

_____ **6.** To be actionable, *both* libel and slander must be communicated to a third person.

_____ **7.** *Libel* is defamation that is directed toward the sense of hearing.

_____ **8.** *Slander* is actionable per se.

_____ **9.** Hitting a golf ball into another's airspace is *not* a trespass.

_____ **10.** Failing to return borrowed goods is an example of *conversion*.

Checking Terminology

From the list of legal terms that follows, select the one that matches each definition.

ANSWERS

a. acquitted	_____ 1. The wrongful act of damaging another's character or reputation by the use of false statements.
b. actionable	
c. assault	_____ 2. Defamation that is communicated by a writing or by other means that is directed toward the sense of sight.
d. battery	
e. conversion	_____ 3. Defamation that is communicated by the spoken word.
f. damages	_____ 4. In and of itself; taken alone.
g. deceit	_____ 5. Prosecution begun in malice without probable cause.
h. defamation	_____ 6. The intentional and unauthorized entry on the land of another.
i. emotional distress	_____ 7. The wrongful exercise of dominion and control over the personal property in another's possession.
j. false arrest	
k. false imprisonment	_____ 8. Wrongful; implying or involving tort.
l. fraud	_____ 9. Torts that are committed intentionally. (Select two answers.)
m. intentional infliction of emotional distress	_____ 10. The intentional contact with another person without that person's permission and without justification.
n. intentional torts	_____ 11. The intentional creation of a reasonable apprehension of an imminent battery.
o. invasion of privacy	_____ 12. The intentional confinement of a person without legal justification (Select two answers.)
p. libel	_____ 13. A misrepresentation of a material, existing fact, knowingly made, that causes someone reasonably relying on it to suffer damages. (Select two answers.)
q. malicious prosecution	
r. misrepresentation	_____ 14. A false or deceptive statement or act.
s. nuisance	_____ 15. The monetary loss suffered by a party as a result of a wrong.
t. per se	_____ 16. Discharged from accusation.
u. private nuisance	_____ 17. Furnishing legal ground for a lawsuit.
v. public nuisance	_____ 18. Trespass for goods carried away.
w. right of privacy	_____ 19. Emotional suffering caused by the infliction of extreme and outrageous intentional conduct by another.
x. scienter	
y. slander	_____ 20. Knowingly.
z. tortious	_____ 21. Torts that are committed accidentally.
aa. trespass	_____ 22. A violation of the right of privacy.
bb. trespass de bonis asportatis	_____ 23. The use of one's property in a way that causes annoyance, inconvenience, or discomfort to another.
cc. unintentional torts	
dd. waste	_____ 24. A nuisance that affects the community at large.
ee. willful torts	_____ 25. The right to be left alone, the right to be free from uncalled-for publicity, and the right to live without unreasonable interference by the public in private matters.
	_____ 26. The abuse or destructive use of property that is in one's rightful possession.
	_____ 27. A nuisance that disturbs one neighbor only.
	_____ 28. Emotional suffering caused by the infliction of extreme and outrageous intentional conduct by another.

3

Using Legal Language

Read the following story and fill in the blank lines with legal terms taken from the list of terms at the beginning of this chapter:

While looking at cars in a used car lot, Henry recognized a car that had once belonged to his friend Sam. He knew that the car had been abused by Sam and was in poor condition. A salesperson, noticing Henry looking at the car, went up to Henry and said, "This car's a beauty! It belonged to a little old lady who took it out only on Sunday morning to drive to church." Angered by this _____ and knowing that the salesperson was committing _____, which is also known as _____, Henry picked up a hubcap that was on the ground and threw it at the salesperson, but missed. Legally, this action was _____ but not _____. In any case, it was a(n) _____ act. The salesperson, now enraged, grabbed an innocent passerby, thinking she was with Henry. He detained the passerby in his office for 10 minutes, thereby committing the tort of _____, which is also called _____. Later that day, Henry accidentally sold his next-door neighbor's lawn mower to a stranger at his yard sale. When his next-door neighbor,

Martha, learned of the _____, she called up her friend Mildred and told her that Henry was a no-good dirty rat. Although this statement was a form of _____, it was not actionable _____, because it was not one of the four situations for which suit may be brought. Later, Martha wrote a letter to the editor of the local newspaper, saying that Henry was a no-good dirty rat. The newspaper refused to print the letter because it did not want to be sued for _____, which is actionable _____. When Henry heard that Martha had written the letter to the newspaper, he went outside, picked up a huge pile of trash from his yard, and dumped it all over Martha's front lawn, thereby committing the tort of _____. He then swore out a criminal complaint against Martha for disturbing the peace. Martha was tried for the crime and found not guilty. She then sued Henry in tort for _____ _____.

PUZZLING OVER WHAT YOU LEARNED

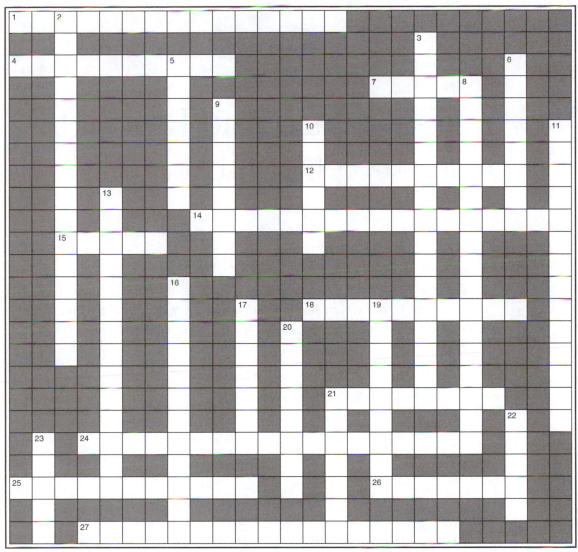

Caveat: Do **not** allow squares for spaces between words and punctuation (apostrophes, hyphens, etc.) when filling in crossword.

Across

1. A nuisance that disturbs one neighbor only.
4. Furnishing legal ground for a lawsuit.
7. The abuse or destructive use of property that is in one's rightful possession.
12. The wrongful exercise of dominion and control over the personal property of another.
14. The intentional confinement of a person without legal justification.
15. Defamation that is communicated by a writing.
18. The wrongful act of damaging another's character or reputation by the use of false statements.
21. Knowingly.
24. Torts that are committed accidentally.
25. Another name for false imprisonment.
26. The monetary loss suffered by a party as a result of a wrong.
27. A violation of the right of privacy.

Down

2. Torts that are committed intentionally.
3. A false or deceptive statement or act.
5. The intentional contact with another person without that person's permission and without justification.
6. The use of one's property in a way that causes annoyance to another.
8. Emotional suffering caused by the infliction of extreme and outrageous intentional conduct by another.
9. The intentional and unauthorized entry on the land of another.
10. Another name for fraud.
11. The right to be left alone.
13. A nuisance that affects the community at large.
16. Another name for intentional torts.
17. The intentional creation of a reasonable apprehension of an imminent battery.
19. Discharged from accusation.
20. Wrongful; implying or involving tort.
21. Defamation that is communicated by the spoken word.
22. In and of itself; taken alone.
23. A misrepresentation of a material, existing fact, knowingly made, that causes someone reasonably relying on it to suffer damages.

Negligence and Product Liability

ANTE INTERROGATORY

The doctrine that protects children who trespass is called the (A) attractive nuisance doctrine, (B) contributory negligence doctrine, (C) comparative negligence doctrine, (D) assumption of the risk doctrine.

CHAPTER OUTLINE

Elements of Negligence
Duty of Care
Breach of Duty (Negligent Act)
Damages
Causation

Defenses to Negligence
Contributory Negligence
Comparative Negligence
Assumption of the Risk
Discharge in Bankruptcy
Statutes of Limitations and Repose

Product Liability

KEY TERMS

absolute liability *(ab·so·LOOT ly·a·BIL·i·tee)*

assumption of the risk *(a·SUMP·shun)*

attractive nuisance doctrine *(a·TRAK·tiv NOO·sens DOK·trin)*

bare licensee *(ly·sen·SEE)*

business invitee *(BIZ·ness in·vy·TEE)*

causation *(kaw·ZAY·shun)*

comparative fault *(kom·PAR·uh·tiv FALT)*

comparative negligence *(kom·PAR·e·tiv NEG·li·jens)*

compensatory damages *(kom·PEN·sa·tor·ee DAM·e·jez)*

contributory negligence *(kon·TRIB·u·tor·ee NEG·li·jens)*

culpable negligence *(KUL·pa·bel NEG·li·jens)*

damages *(DAM·e·jez)*

dangerous instrumentalities *(DAYN·jer·ess in·stroo·men·TAL·i·tees)*

design defect

duty of care

fact finder *(fakt FINE·der)*

failure to warn

foreseeable *(fore·SEE·a·bel)*

general damages *(GEN·er·al DAM·a·jez)*

gratuitous guest *(gra·TOO·i·tes)*

gross negligence *(NEG·li·jens)*

humanitarian doctrine *(hew·man·i·TAR·ee·en DOK·trin)*

last clear chance doctrine *(DOK·trin)*

liability *(ly·a·BIL·i·tee)*

malpractice *(mal·PRAK·tiss)*

manufacturing defect

negligence *(NEG·li·jens)*

ordinary negligence *(OR·di·ner·ee NEG·li·jens)*

pain and suffering *(SUF·er·ing)*

privity of contract *(PRIV·i·tee ov KON·trakt)*

product liability *(PROD·ukt ly·a·BIL·i·tee)*

proximate cause *(PROK·si·met kaws)*

prudent *(PROO·dent)*

reasonable care *(REE·zen·e·bel)*

res ipsa loquitur *(reyz IP·sa LO·kwe·ter)*

special damages *(SPE·shal DAM·a·jez)*

statute of limitations *(STAT·shoot ov lim·i·TA·shuns)*

statute of repose *(STAT·shoot ov re·POSE)*

strict liability *(strikt ly·a·BIL·i·tee)*

supervening cause *(su·per·VEEN·ing)*

willful, wanton, and reckless conduct *(WIL·ful WON·ten and REK·les KON·dukt)*

wrongful death action *(RONG·ful deth AK·shun)*

wrongful death statutes *(RONG·ful deth STAT·shoots)*

Negligence occurs when one person suffers a loss because of the carelessness of another person. It is an unintentional tort and is the subject matter of more lawsuits than any other tort. **Negligence** is defined as "the failure to use the amount of care and skill that a reasonably prudent person would have used under the same circumstances and conditions."

ELEMENTS OF NEGLIGENCE

To recover for negligence, the injured party must prove all of the following:

1. Duty of care;
2. Breach of duty (negligent act);
3. Damages; and
4. Causation.

Duty of Care

In order to be liable to another for a harmful action (or inaction), the person who commits the harm must first owe a duty of care to the injured party. Although difficult to define, a duty of care is a legal obligation of carefulness or prudence owed to those who are likely (or foreseeably likely) to be injured by one's conduct. For instance, a parent owes a duty of care to his or her child, not to someone else's child, generally. But duties change according to the circumstances. So, if that parent's child has a friend visit, then the parent has now voluntarily undertaken a duty of care to the other child. A duty of care is generally created through relationships (parent to child), through statute (drivers of cars to others on the road or in their paths), or through contract (lifeguards employed to keep watch over swimmers).

Until recently, the law recognized different *degrees of care* owed to different people. The duty of care owed to a **business invitee** (one invited on the premises for a business or commercial purpose) was to refrain from **ordinary negligence** (the want of ordinary care). The duty of care owed to a **gratuitous guest** (one invited on the premises for nonbusiness purposes) was to refrain from gross negligence. **Gross negligence** is extreme negligence. Under this older law, a gratuitous guest could not recover for damages caused by a host's ordinary negligence. The duty of care owed to a trespasser and a **bare licensee** (a person allowed on another's premises by operation of law, such as a firefighter or police officer) was to refrain from **willful, wanton, and reckless conduct**. This conduct, also called **culpable negligence** is the intentional commission of an act that a reasonable person knows would cause injury to another. It is more serious than gross negligence.

Many states have eliminated the different degrees of negligence. Instead, they hold that property owners owe a duty to use **reasonable care** toward everyone who is rightfully on their premises. This degree of care is one that a reasonable person would have used under the circumstances then known. Because a trespasser is not rightfully on the premises, the duty of care owed to such a person is to refrain from willful, wanton, and reckless conduct.

One exception to the latter rule is the **attractive nuisance doctrine**, which protects children who are enticed to trespass on another's property because of an attraction that exists there, such as a swimming pool in a backyard. In states that follow the doctrine, property owners owe a duty to refrain from ordinary negligence, rather than simply from willful, wanton, and reckless conduct, toward children who are attracted to the premises by a condition that normally attracts children, even though the children are trespassers.

Breach of Duty (Negligent Act)

Whether or not an act is negligent and, therefore, breaches the duty of care owed to the plaintiff is normally a question of fact (rather than a question of law) to be decided by the fact finder. The **fact finder** (or trier of fact) is the jury in a jury trial or the judge in a nonjury trial. The fact finder must ask the question, "Did the defendant do (or fail to do) that which a reasonably **prudent** (cautious) person would have done under the same circumstances and conditions?" If the defendant is a child, the fact finder must ask, "Did the defendant exercise the degree of care that a reasonably prudent child of the same age, intelligence, and experience would have exercised under the same circumstances and conditions?" If the defendant is a physician, the fact finder must ask, "Did the defendant exercise the degree of care and skill of the average qualified physician, considering the advances in the medical profession?" Negligence of a physician, attorney, or other professional is commonly referred to as **malpractice**.

DOCTRINE OF RES IPSA LOQUITUR.   To recover for negligence, evidence must be introduced by the plaintiff to prove the negligent act of the defendant. Sometimes, the plaintiff has no evidence to prove that a negligent act was committed by the defendant; however, the plaintiff can prove that he or she was injured by an act that normally does not occur unless someone is negligent, such as in a rear-end automobile collision. The doctrine of **res ipsa loquitur**, which means "the thing speaks for itself," can sometimes be used by the plaintiff when he or she cannot prove an actual negligent act of the defendant. Under this doctrine, the mere fact that an act occurred can be used by the jury (or by the judge in a nonjury trial) to infer that the defendant was negligent. When the doctrine is used, the case can go to the jury if it is probable (not just possible) that a negligent act of the defendant caused the plaintiff's injury.

ABSOLUTE LIABILITY.   People who handle **dangerous instrumentalities** such as explosives or wild animals are liable, regardless of fault, for injuries to others caused by the dangerous item. Such liability regardless of fault is known as **absolute** or **strict liability**.

Word Wise
Res Ipsa Loquitur ("the thing speaks for itself")

The "ipsa" in *res ipsa loquitur* is a form of the Latin term *ipse* meaning "myself, himself, herself, or itself." Here are some other uses of the term:

> *ipse dixit* = he himself said it (something asserted, but not proved).
>
> *ipso facto* = by the fact (or act) itself (by the mere effect or nature of an act or fact).
>
> *ipso jure* = by the law itself (by the mere operation of the law).

Damages

To recover for negligence, the plaintiff must prove **damages**—that is, some actual loss. Even though a negligent act may be committed by the defendant, no recovery by the plaintiff can occur unless he or she suffers damages. Various kinds of damages are discussed in Chapter 18.

The amount of **compensatory damages**, sometimes called actual damages, that the plaintiff can recover is the amount of money that will place the plaintiff in the same position that he or she was in immediately before the negligent act occurred. **Special damages** are measurable amounts of losses and include the cost of hospital and medical treatment, and any loss of wages. **General damages** is money meant to compensate the plaintiff for **pain and suffering** (physical discomfort and emotional trauma) that she or he endured.

When someone dies as a result of another's negligence, the suit that is brought is called a **wrongful death action**. This suit is brought by the decedent's personal representative against the negligent party for the benefit of the decedent's heirs. Such suits are governed by **wrongful death statutes** found in each state.

Causation

To recover for negligence, the plaintiff must prove **causation**—that is, that the negligent act of the defendant was the direct and **proximate cause** (the dominant, or moving, cause) of the plaintiff's injuries. In determining proximate cause, the court asks whether the harm that resulted from the conduct was **foreseeable** (known in advance; anticipated) when it took place. Proximate cause is about that which is probable, rather than that which is possible (because anything is possible). So, the more likely or probable an outcome, the more foreseeable it is. In a case in which an intoxicated person was served liquor in a bar and on leaving the bar drove negligently into another car, killing someone, the court held that the bartender's act of serving a drink to the intoxicated person was the proximate cause of death. The court said that the bartender could have foreseen that the intoxicated person would be driving home and might cause death or injury to another.

Conversely, no recovery can be made if a break in the chain of causation exists. For example, when a car owner leaves the key in a car (which is a statutory violation in some states) and a thief steals the car and injures someone while driving negligently, the act of leaving the key in the car is not the direct and proximate cause of the injury. Rather, the negligent act of the thief was a **supervening cause**—that is, a new occurrence that becomes the proximate cause of the injury. The injured party cannot recover from the car owner.

DEFENSES TO NEGLIGENCE

The principal defenses to negligence actions are (1) contributory negligence, (2) comparative negligence, (3) assumption of the risk, (4) discharge in bankruptcy, and (5) running of the statute of limitations.

Contributory Negligence

Contributory negligence is negligence on the part of the plaintiff that contributed toward the injuries and was a proximate cause of them. Under the doctrine of contributory negligence, when the plaintiff sues the defendant for negligence, if the defendant can prove that the plaintiff was also negligent, no matter how slightly, the plaintiff can recover nothing. An exception exists under a rule known as the **last clear chance doctrine** in some states and as the **humanitarian doctrine** in others. Under this doctrine, a defendant who had the last clear chance to have avoided injuring the plaintiff is liable even though the plaintiff had also been responsible for contributory negligence.

Many states no longer follow the doctrine of contributory negligence, because of its unfairness to plaintiffs who were only slightly negligent. These states have adopted the doctrine of comparative negligence in its place.

Comparative Negligence

Under the doctrine of **comparative negligence** (called **comparative fault** in some jurisdictions), the negligence of all parties is compared, and the plaintiff's damages are reduced in proportion to his or her negligence. In determining by what amount the plaintiff's damages are to be diminished, the negligence of the plaintiff is compared with the total negligence of all persons against whom recovery is sought. The combined total of the plaintiff's negligence and all of the negligence of all defendants must equal 100 percent. For example, in a case in which the total damages are $100,000, if the jury finds that the plaintiff was 40 percent negligent and the defendant was 60 percent negligent, the plaintiff will recover $60,000. In the same case, if the jury finds that each party was 50 percent negligent, the plaintiff will recover $50,000. If the jury finds that the plaintiff was 51 percent negligent and the defendant was 49 percent negligent, the plaintiff will recover nothing.

TERMS IN ACTION

In 2003, a man riding the train home from his job in Chicago exited his passenger car at his stop and immediately fell to the ground. Because the train had overshot the platform, the man, who was riding in the first car, fell to the ground, severely injuring his knee, including tearing his anterior cruciate ligament (ACL) and his lateral meniscus cartilage. He sued the railroad for **negligence**, not only because the train conductor failed to stop the train at the platform correctly, but also because the train car doors opened, which isn't supposed to happen when the train overshoots the platform. At the trial in 2009, the judge gave a directed verdict to the man, but ordered the jury to determine how much of the man's own conduct contributed to his injuries. Although the railroad company failed to use **reasonable care** and was the **proximate cause** of the accident, the jury determined that the man was **comparatively negligent** for immediately exiting his train car when he knew the car wasn't at the platform and didn't ask for help. The jury calculated his comparative fault at 50 percent and reduced his **damages** from $250,000 to $125,000. Curiously, the man who was stung by the doctrine of comparative fault was an attorney.

Sources: passenlaw.com; *Richard C. Moenning v. Union Pacific Railroad, et al.* No. 1-08-0543 (unpublished, 2009).

Assumption of the Risk

In a suit for negligence, if the defendant can show that the plaintiff knew of the risk involved and took the chance of being injured, he or she may claim **assumption of the risk** as a defense. This defense has sometimes been used by baseball clubs when they are sued by spectators for being injured by baseballs hit into the stands.

Discharge in Bankruptcy

A lawsuit cannot be brought for a cause of action for negligence against a defendant if the defendant is discharged in bankruptcy and the plaintiff's claim is included among the defendant's debts.

Statutes of Limitations and Repose

Every cause of action has a time limit for bringing suit. A **statute of limitations** is a time limit, set by statute, within which a suit must be commenced after the cause of action accrues. A cause of action accrues when a suit may be brought for damages. In negligence cases, the statute of limitations begins to run either on the date of the injury or on the date that the injury is, or should have been, discovered. A **statute of repose** on the other hand, places an absolute time limit for bringing a cause of action regardless of when the cause of action accrues. The following is an example of a statute that contains both a statute of limitations and a statute of repose:

> An action of tort for damages arising out of any deficiency or neglect on the design, planning, construction, or general administration of an improvement to real property shall be commenced only within three years next after the cause of action accrues, provided, however, that in no event shall such actions be commenced more than six years after the substantial completion of the improvement and the taking of possession for occupancy by the owner.

The first part of the statute (a statute of limitations) contains a time limit of three years from the date of injury for bringing suit, which could be any number of years after the completion of the improvement. The second part (a statute of repose), however, places an absolute time limit for bringing a suit of six years following the completion and taking of possession by the owner.

PRODUCT LIABILITY

Liability (legal responsibility) of manufacturers, sellers, and lessors (those who lease products) to compensate people for injuries suffered because of defects in their products is a tort known as **product liability**. Under modern legal theory, people who are injured by defective products can bring suit against the manufacturers or sellers of the products whether or not the injured persons purchased the products. There is no requirement of **privity of contract** (relationship between contracting parties) to recover for injuries from defective goods. In addition, it is not necessary to prove a negligent act on the part of the manufacturer or seller. Product liability is based on alternative theories of liability. **Design defect** is the theory that the product was negligently designed or could have been designed more safely. **Manufacturing defect** is the theory that the product was negligently built or built with substandard materials. **Failure to warn** (also called inadequate warnings) is the theory that the product's dangers were inadequately labeled or communicated to the consumer or user.

Under a theory of **strict liability**, which was first applied in America by the California Supreme Court in 1963, manufacturers and sellers are liable without regard to fault. They can be held liable if it can be shown that the product was sold in a defective condition, that it was unreasonably dangerous to the user or consumer, and that the defective condition was the proximate cause of the injury or damage. The rationale of strict liability is that if neither the plaintiff nor the defendant is at fault, the defendant should pay the damages because it is a corporation and therefore is more able to absorb the costs of injury.

TERMS IN ACTION

George Allan Ward brought a **product liability** lawsuit against the maker of RMAMMER— from federal prison. What could baking soda have done that caused so much harm? According to Ward's complaint, ARM & HAMMER was the proximate cause of his 200-month prison sentence for having made and sold crack cocaine. Crack is relatively simple to make (once one has cocaine), and baking soda is one of its ingredients. Ward alleged that ARM & HAMMER, which had put five warnings on its baking soda boxes (including "do not administer to children under 5 years of age"), failed to provide adequate notice to him that using its product for illegal drug manufacturing is illegal and would be harmful to his freedom. Furthering his **failure to warn** theory, Ward stated in his complaint, "I feel as if I was forewarned by this company that I'd never used this product as I was charged with. . . ." Ward's case was dismissed in 2004. The U.S. District Judge said that a manufacturer of a product has no duty to warn of the potential consequences of its criminal misuse.

Sources: legalreader.com; overlawyered.com

Reviewing What You Learned

After studying the chapter, write the answers to each of the following questions:

1. Name the tort that is the subject matter of more lawsuits than any other tort._____

_____

_____

2. List three elements that an injured party must prove to recover for negligence._____

_____

_____

_____

3. Who is the fact finder in a jury trial? In a nonjury trial?_____

_____

_____

_____

4. What degree of care must be exercised by a child to avoid negligence?_____

_____

_____

_____

5. What degree of care must be exercised by a physician to avoid negligence?_____

_____

_____

_____

6. Until recently, what degree of care was owed to a business invitee? To a gratuitous guest? To a bare licensee?_____

_____

_____

_____

7. What degree of care is owed to the parties named in question 6, under modern law in many states?_____

_____

_____

8. What degree of care is owed to a trespasser?_____

_____

_____

_____

9. When may the doctrine of res ipsa loquitur be used to prove negligence?_____

_____

_____

_____

10. What is the difference between special damages and general damages?_____

_____

_____

_____

11. Damages include what three elements?_____

_____

_____

_____

12. What must the plaintiff prove relative to causation in order to recover for negligence?_____

_____

_____

_____

_____

13. List five defenses to negligence._____

_____

_____

_____

14. What is the difference between contributory negligence and comparative negligence?_____

_____

_____

_____

15. What defense is sometimes used by a baseball club when it is sued by a spectator for being injured by a ball that is hit into the stands?_____

_____

_____

_____

16. What is the difference between a statute of limitations and a statute of repose?_____

_____

_____

_____

17. List and explain three product liability theories._____

_____

_____

_____

_____

Understanding Legal Concepts

Indicate whether each statement is true or false. Then, change the italicized word or phrase of each false statement to make it true.

ANSWERS

_____ **1.** Whether or not an act is negligent is normally a question of *law.*

_____ **2.** For a *negligent* act to occur, a duty of care must be owed by the defendant to the plaintiff, and a breach of that duty must occur.

_____ **3.** In states that follow the attractive nuisance doctrine, property owners owe a duty to refrain from *gross negligence* toward children who are attracted to the premises by a condition that normally attracts children.

_____ **4.** When the doctrine of res ipsa loquitur is used, the case can go to the jury if it is *probable* that a negligent act of the defendant caused the plaintiff's injury.

_____ **5.** Even though a negligent act may be committed by the defendant, no recovery by the plaintiff can occur unless he or she *suffers damages.*

_____ **6.** When a thief steals a car with keys left in it and injures a pedestrian, the pedestrian *can* recover from the car owner for damages.

_____ **7.** Many states *no longer* follow the doctrine of contributory negligence, because of its unfairness to plaintiffs who were only slightly negligent.

_____ **8.** Contributory negligence is negligence on the part of the *defendant,* which contributed toward the injuries and was a proximate cause of them.

_____ **9.** In a case involving comparative negligence, if the jury finds that the plaintiff was 51 percent negligent and the defendant was 49 percent negligent, the plaintiff will recover *nothing.*

_____ **10.** *No* time limit exists for bringing suit for the tort of negligence.

_____ **11.** Money for the plaintiff to compensate for pain and suffering is called *special damages.*

_____ **12.** *Manufacturing defect* is the theory that a product was negligently designed.

Checking Terminology

From the list of legal terms that follows, select the one that matches each definition.

a. absolute liability
b. assumption of the risk
c. attractive nuisance doctrine
d. bare licensee
e. business invitee
f. causation
g. comparative fault
h. comparative negligence
i. compensatory damages
j. contributory negligence
k. culpable negligence
l. damages
m. dangerous instrumentalities
n. design defect
o. duty of care
p. fact finder
q. failure to warn
r. foreseeable

ANSWERS

_____ 1. Extreme negligence.

_____ 2. One invited on the premises for a business or commercial purpose.

_____ 3. The thing speaks for itself.

_____ 4. A time limit, set by statute, within which a suit must be commenced after the cause of action accrues.

_____ 5. The intentional commission of an act that a reasonable person knows would cause injury to another. (Select two answers.)

_____ 6. A relationship between contracting parties.

_____ 7. The failure to use that amount of care and skill that a reasonably prudent person would have used under the same circumstances and conditions.

_____ 8. A person allowed on another's premises by operation of law, such as a fire fighter or police officer.

_____ 9. A doctrine under which a defendant who had the last clear chance to have avoided injuring the plaintiff is liable even though the plaintiff had also been responsible for some contributory negligence. (Select two answers.)

_____ 10. A monetary loss suffered by a party as a result of a wrong.

_____ 11. The situation wherein the plaintiff assumes consequences of injury; the employee agrees that dangers of injury shall be at his or her own risk.

_____ 12. Professional misconduct; negligence of a professional.

s. general damages
t. gratuitous guest
u. gross negligence
v. humanitarian doctrine
w. last clear chance doctrine
x. liability
y. malpractice
z. manufacturing defect
aa. negligence
bb. ordinary negligence
cc. pain and suffering
dd. privity of contract
ee. product liability
ff. proximate cause
gg. prudent
hh. reasonable care
ii. res ipsa loquitur
jj. special damages
kk. statute of limitations
ll. statute of repose
mm. strict liability
nn. supervening cause
oo. willful, wanton, and reckless conduct
pp. wrongful death action
qq. wrongful death statutes

_____ 13. The degree of care that a reasonable person would have used under the circumstances then known.

_____ 14. Liability of manufacturers and sellers to compensate people for injuries suffered because of defects in their products.

_____ 15. The proportionate sharing between the plaintiff and the defendant of the legal responsibility for injuries, according to the relative negligence of the two. (Select two answers.)

_____ 16. A new occurrence that became the proximate cause of the injury.

_____ 17. One invited on the premises for nonbusiness purposes.

_____ 18. The jury in a jury trial or the judge in a nonjury trial.

_____ 19. Physical discomfort and emotional trauma.

_____ 20. Liability for an act that causes harm without regard to fault or negligence. (Select two answers.)

_____ 21. A suit brought by a decedent's personal representative for the benefit of the decedent's heirs, claiming that death was caused by the defendant's negligent act.

_____ 22. Cautious.

_____ 23. Hazardous items such as explosives and wild animals.

_____ 24. Legislative enactments that govern wrongful death actions.

_____ 25. Measurable amounts of losses including the cost of medical treatment and loss of wages.

_____ 26. A doctrine establishing property owners' duty to use ordinary care toward trespassing children who might reasonably be attracted to their property.

_____ 27. Negligence on the part of the plaintiff, which contributed toward the injuries and was a proximate cause of them.

_____ 28. An absolute time limit for bringing a cause of action regardless of when the cause of action accrues.

_____ 29. Money meant to compensate the plaintiff for pain and suffering he endured.

_____ 30. The theory that a product was negligently built.

_____ 31. The direct and proximate cause of someone's injuries.

_____ 32. Legal responsibility.

_____ 33. The amount of money that will place the plaintiff in the same position that he was in immediately before the negligent act occurred.

_____ 34. A legal obligation of carefulness owed to those who are likely to be injured by one's conduct.

_____ 35. A theory that the product was negligently designed or could have been designed more safely.

_____ 36. A theory that the product's dangers were inadequately labeled.

_____ 37. The dominant or moving cause.

_____ 38. Known in advance; anticipated.

_____ 39. The want of ordinary care.

Sharpening Your Latin Skills

In the space provided, write the definition of each of the following legal terms, referring to the glossary when necessary.

nul tort _____

per se _____

res _____

res ipsa loquitur _____

respondeat superior _____

scienter _____

Using Legal Language

Read the following story and fill in the blank lines with legal terms taken from the list of terms at the beginning of this chapter:

While shopping in a grocery store, Alison slipped on some fat that had accumulated in front of the meat counter. Alison was a(n) _____ (customer), and the _____ (carelessness) of the store employees, who were not _____ (cautious), caused the accident. Because the wrongful act was not extreme, the degree of wrong would probably be considered _____ rather than _____. The physician who treated Alison for her injuries was capable and not responsible for _____ _____, although the amount of the physician's bill became part of Alison's _____. When Alison arrived home, she noticed a police car in front of her house and saw a police officer inside. The officer, who was a(n) _____, told her that a neighborhood child had wandered without permission into Alison's pool area and had almost drowned. A friend of Alison, who was visiting at the time, had rescued the child from drowning. The legal status of the friend was that of a(n) _____. Because

the child was a trespasser, Alison's obligation to her would normally have been to refrain from _____ unless the _____ doctrine required her to use ordinary care. Should the case go to court, the jury, which is the _____, will have to determine whether the child was negligent if the state follows the doctrine of _____ or the percentage of negligence of each party if the state follows the doctrine of _____. Because it is not probable, but merely possible, that Alison was negligent, the plaintiff would not be able to use the doctrine of _____ to prove the case. Similarly, it is doubtful that Alison can use the defense of _____ or _____ if suit is brought promptly.

3

PUZZLING OVER WHAT YOU LEARNED

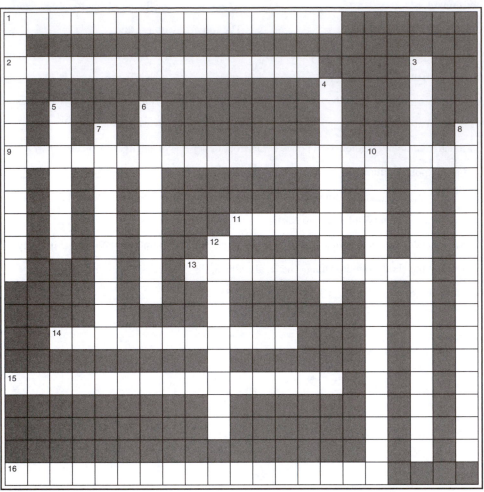

Caveat: Do **not** allow squares for spaces between words and punctuation (apostrophes, hyphens, etc.) when filling in crossword.

Across

1. One invited on the premises for a business or commercial purpose.
2. The degree of care that a reasonable person would have used under the circumstances then known.
9. The proportionate sharing between the plaintiff and the defendant of compensation for injuries, based on the relative negligence of the two.
11. Cautious
13. Professional misconduct; negligence of a professional.
14. Known in advance; anticipated.
15. Extreme negligence.
16. A relationship between contracting parties.

Down

1. A person allowed on another's premises by operation of law, such as a fire fighter or police officer.
3. The want of ordinary care.
4. The failure to use that amount of care and skill that a reasonably prudent person would have used under the same circumstances and conditions.
5. A monetary loss suffered by a party as a result of a wrong.
6. Legal responsibility.
7. The jury in a jury trial or the judge in a nonjury trial.
8. The thing speaks for itself.
10. One invited on the premises for nonbusiness purposes.
12. The direct and proximate cause of someone's injuries.

Terms Used in Law of Contracts

4

The law of contracts lies at the core of most personal and business transactions that we become involved with during our lifetime. A contract occurs whenever we buy or sell something, provide or receive services for a fee, employ someone or become employed, rent an apartment, attend college, and in many other contexts during our lives. Chapter 18 breaks down the subject of contracts into various classifications. Contract requirements, including consideration, writing essentials, defective agreements, and illegality, are examined in Chapter 19. After discussing the subjects of assignment and delegation of contracts, Chapter 20 surveys the various methods of ending contractual obligations.

18

Formation of Contracts

ANTE INTERROGATORY

*In most cases, contracts made by minors are (A) misdemeanors,
(B) void, (C) voidable, (D) illegal.*

CHAPTER OUTLINE

Contract Formation

Contract Classifications
  Express and Implied Contracts

Bilateral and Unilateral Contracts
Valid, Void, Voidable, and Unenforceable
Contracts
Executed and Executory Contracts

KEY TERMS

acceptance *(ak·SEP·tense)*

avoid *(a·VOID)*

bargain *(BAR·gen)*

bilateral contract *(by·LAT·er·el KON·trakt)*

capacity *(ka·PAS·e·tee)*

clickwrap agreement *(KLIK·rap uh-
  GREE-ment)*

condition precedent *(kon·DISH·en
  pree·SEE·dent)*

contract *(KON·trakt)*

contract implied in fact *(KON·trakt im·PLIDE)*

contract implied in law

counteroffer *(KOWN·ter·off·er)*

disaffirm *(dis·a·FERM)*

e-contract *(EE·KON·trakt)*

executed *(EK·se·kew·ted)*

executory *(eg·ZEK·yoo·tor·ee)*

express contract *(eks·PRESS KON·trakt)*

implied contract *(im·PLIDE KON·trakt)*

infant *(IN·fent)*

invitation to deal *(in·vi·TA·shun)*

invitation to negotiate *(ne·GO·shee·ate)*

majority *(ma·JAW·ri·tee)*

minor *(MY-ner)*

necessaries *(NE·se·ser·ees)*

nullity *(NUL·i·tee)*

offer *(OFF·er)*

offeree *(off·er·EE)*

offeror *(off·er·OR)*

quasi *(KWAY·zi)*

quasi contract *(KWAY·zi KON·trakt)*

ratify *(RAT·i·fy)*

rejection *(re·JEK·shun)*

restitution *(res·ti·TEW·shun)*

revocation *(rev·o·KA·shun)*

unenforceable contract *(un·en·FORS·e·bel
  KON·trakt)*

unilateral contract *(yoon·i·LAT·er·el
  KON·trakt)*

unjust enrichment *(un·JUST en·RICH·ment)*

valid *(VAL·id)*

void

voidable *(VOID·e·bel)*

4

CONTRACT FORMATION

In its simplest terms, a **contract** is any agreement that is enforceable in a court of law.

To reach an agreement, one party (called the **offeror**) makes an **offer** (a proposal) to another party (called the **offeree**) to enter into a legally enforceable (binding) agreement. If the offeree assents to the terms of the offer, an **acceptance** occurs and an agreement, sometimes called a **bargain** comes into existence. To illustrate, if one person says to another, "I'll sell you my car for $495" (the offer) and the other person replies, "I'll buy it" (the acceptance), a contract is formed the moment the words of acceptance are spoken. If instead, the other person replies, "No way!" that is a **rejection**—the refusal by the offeree of an offer. A rejection terminates the offer. When the other person responds with a different offer instead of accepting the one that was made, that is called a **counteroffer**. For instance, if instead of saying, "No way!" the offeree says, "I like your old car, but not that much. I'll give you $400 for it," that would be a counteroffer. Like a rejection, a counteroffer ends an offer. A **revocation** occurs when the offeror has a change of mind and takes back the offer before it is accepted by the offeree. Suppose that, before the offeree can say yes or no to the offer of the car for $495, the seller says, "Never mind. I don't feel like selling it today." That would be a revocation, which terminates the offer.

When an offer (or contract) contains a condition precedent, the parties are not obligated until the prerequisite is carried out. For example, if I agree to buy your car if you have the brakes fixed, I would have no obligation to buy it unless you have the repairs made. A **condition precedent** is an event that must first occur before an agreement (or deed or will) becomes effective.

TERMS IN ACTION

Does breaking off an engagement constitute a **breach of contract**? Few, if any, contracts questions are more personal than those relating to agreements to marry. Most jurisdictions stay out of romantic disputes, because those types of agreements are thought to not include the kind of **consideration** that courts want to measure. Likewise, no-fault divorces can be obtained without the party seeking the divorce having to prove a breach of any promise by the other spouse. But, in 2008, a Georgia six-man six-woman jury awarded a woman $150,000 because her fiancé called off their wedding. Evidently, RoseMary Shell (the **offeree**) agreed to marry Wayne Gibbs (the **offeror**) and then moved from Pensacola, Florida, to Gainesville, Georgia, where Gibbs lived. She left behind an $81,000-per-year job and found a job paying $34,000 annually. Three months later, Gibbs broke off the engagement. He had contemplated it even earlier, letting her know of his change of heart with a note in their bathroom. In his defense, Gibbs testified that he had made some of Shell's mortgage payments and paid off $30,000 of Shell's debts, but when he realized she had even more debt, he broke off the wedding. The trial judge instructed the jury that "breach of a promise to marry is a common law contract action. By the very nature of this action, there must be an actual promise to marry and **acceptance** of that promise before one can be held liable for a breach." The damages amount was based on Shell's old salary, bonuses, and benefits.

Sources: gainesvilletimes.com; today.msnbc.msn.com

Advertisements, including price tags, prices on merchandise, signs, and prices in catalogs are not usually treated as offers. Instead, such an advertisement is called an **invitation to negotiate** or an **invitation to deal**. Although it seems counterintuitive to think this way, the common law of contracts treats an advertisement—such as listing your car for $495 in a classified ad—as being your invitation to the reader to find you and then "offer" you $495 for your car. For this reason, a contract does not usually arise when a customer offers to buy a mismarked product unless the store accepts the customer's offer and agrees to sell the product at the mismarked price. Stores might honor the price for a mismarked product for the sake of customer relations, but that does not affect the underlying doctrine that, generally, advertisements are not offers.

CONTRACT CLASSIFICATIONS

Contracts may be classified in the following ways:

1. express and implied
2. bilateral and unilateral
3. valid, void, voidable, and unenforceable
4. executed and executory

Express and Implied Contracts

An **express contract** is one in which the terms of the contract are stated by the parties, either orally or in writing. An **implied contract** is one in which the terms of the contract are not stated by the parties, but their behavior shows them to be in a contract. For instance, if a business has for many months delivered parts that the receiving company uses to make a product and then resell, and the two parties have long since stopped exchanging terms (because the price hasn't gone up, let's say), the parties are in an implied contract.

Two types of implied contracts are a contract implied in fact and a contract implied in law. A **contract implied in fact** is a contract that arises from the conduct of the parties rather than from their express statements. For example, when you board a bus and pay the fare without saying anything to the driver, and the driver says nothing to you, no express contract exists because the terms were not stated; however, a contract implied in fact exists that the bus driver will take you to a destination along that bus's particular route.

Unjust enrichment occurs when one person retains money, property, or other benefit that in equity and justice belongs to another. Sometimes, to prevent unjust enrichment, the court will impose a contract on the parties when one actually does not exist or when an express contract cannot be enforced. This court-imposed obligation is called a **contract implied in law** or **quasi contract**. The term **quasi** means "as if" or "almost as it were," for example, if a cable TV customer gets premium channels for a year that the customer didn't order (or protest), but has paid only the standard rate for a year, the customer has been unjustly enriched and could be required to pay 12 months of premium-channel prices. A person who has been unjustly enriched at the expense of another is required to make **restitution**—that is, restore the other person to his or her original position prior to the loss.

Bilateral and Unilateral Contracts

The primary distinction between an unenforceable agreement and that which qualifies as a contract is that a contract involves an exchange between the parties, and at least one of the things being exchanged has to be a promise. Contracts are classified according to the number of promises made by the parties. A **bilateral contract** is a contract containing two promises, one made by each party to the contract. One party makes a promise in exchange for the other party's promise. For example, if someone says, "I'll sell you my laptop computer for $400," and the other party replies, "I'll buy it," a bilateral contract has been made, because both parties made and exchanged promises.

A **unilateral contract** is a contract containing only one promise in exchange for an act, often referred to as a performance. Suppose, for example, that a person offers a $100 reward for the return of a lost dog. The only way that the offer can be accepted is by the actual return of the lost dog to the offeror. When that happens, the offer is accepted.

In a bilateral contract, consideration (which is discussed in Chapter 19) is found in the promises of each party. In a unilateral contract, consideration is found in the promise of the offeror and the act of the offeree. Winning a prize for being first in a contest or race (think of the Indianapolis 500) is the result of a unilateral contract, because promising to win the contest or promising to try to win the contest has no bearing on the prize being given.

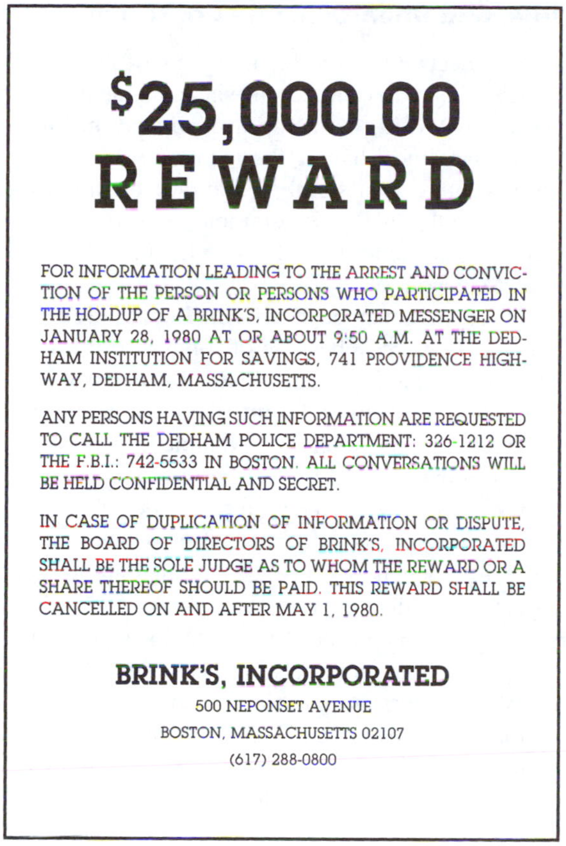

$25,000.00 REWARD

FOR INFORMATION LEADING TO THE ARREST AND CONVICTION OF THE PERSON OR PERSONS WHO PARTICIPATED IN THE HOLDUP OF A BRINK'S, INCORPORATED MESSENGER ON JANUARY 28, 1980 AT OR ABOUT 9:50 A.M. AT THE DEDHAM INSTITUTION FOR SAVINGS, 741 PROVIDENCE HIGHWAY, DEDHAM, MASSACHUSETTS.

ANY PERSONS HAVING SUCH INFORMATION ARE REQUESTED TO CALL THE DEDHAM POLICE DEPARTMENT: 326-1212 OR THE F.B.I.: 742-5533 IN BOSTON. ALL CONVERSATIONS WILL BE HELD CONFIDENTIAL AND SECRET.

IN CASE OF DUPLICATION OF INFORMATION OR DISPUTE, THE BOARD OF DIRECTORS OF BRINK'S, INCORPORATED SHALL BE THE SOLE JUDGE AS TO WHOM THE REWARD OR A SHARE THEREOF SHOULD BE PAID. THIS REWARD SHALL BE CANCELLED ON AND AFTER MAY 1, 1980.

BRINK'S, INCORPORATED
500 NEPONSET AVENUE
BOSTON, MASSACHUSETTS 02107
(617) 288-0800

FIGURE 18-1 A reward offer is an example of a unilateral contract, which comes into existence when the offer is accepted by the performance of an act.

4

TERMS IN ACTION

Karen Kershaw, of Akron, Ohio, couldn't afford to pay the remaining $600 for a truck she wanted to buy from Rick Remmy, a used car dealer. So, according to her lawsuit, Remmy presented to her—on Valentine's Day, 2000—a **contract** allowing her to pay for the truck by performing certain "favors" for him. The value of each payment was based on its type of favor. Although Kershaw denied agreeing to such a contract, she made two of these types of personal-services payments, and Remmy kept track of her remaining balance on the front of an envelope. She also helped to pay for the truck by giving him cigarettes, and she got a receipt for that. Eventually, Ms. Kershaw went to the police, who told her that she was committing prostitution. Since that is illegal, their alleged **bilateral contract** would be **void**. Yet, Ms. Kershaw filed a small claims court suit seeking $212. Both parties then agreed to resolve their dispute on the television show "The People's Court," whose judge was at that time Jerry Sheindlin, who is married to TV's "Judge Judy." Judge Jerry awarded Ms. Kershaw $125 (paid by the show's producers). When Remmy returned home from New York, where the show is taped, he was arrested—not for compelling prostitution, but for violating his probation (stemming from a 1998 car theft) by leaving the state. He was sentenced to nine months in jail.

Sources: thesmokinggun.com; nydailynews.com

Valid, Void, Voidable, and Unenforceable Contracts

A **valid** contract is one that meets all of the requirements of an enforceable agreement. In a sense, the term "valid contract" is redundant because an agreement that is unenforceable isn't a contract, so it couldn't be valid. A **void** contract, conversely, is a **nullity** and has no legal effect. For the same reason that an agreement having the required elements of enforceability doesn't need to be called a "valid" contract, but simply a contract, an alleged agreement that fails to qualify as a contract is considered void, but is commonly referred to as a void contract. For instance, an illegal contract, such as one for the sale of an item that is prohibited to be bought and sold (marijuana, for instance), is void.

A **voidable** contract is one that may be **disaffirmed** or **avoided** (repudiated; gotten out of) by one of the parties, if he or she wishes, because of some rule of law that excuses that party's performance. It is sometimes said that a voidable contract is one that is valid unless voided. For example, a contract entered into between an **infant** (the legal name for a **minor**) and an adult is voidable by the minor, but not by the adult. For example, if a 16-year-old buys a car from an adult, the minor may disaffirm the contract and return the car in exchange for the money paid (even if the seller spent the money). An exception to the doctrine that minors may disaffirm their contracts while they are still minors concerns contracts that minors make for necessaries. **Necessaries** are food, clothing, shelter, and medical care that are needed by the minor, but not being supplied by the parent or guardian.

Although minors are responsible for paying for the fair value of their necessaries, at their option they may disaffirm most other contracts on the ground that they lack **capacity** (legal competency) to contract. When minors reach **majority** (adulthood, which is 18 in most jurisdictions), they may **ratify**—that is, approve or confirm—earlier contracts made during their minority and thus be bound by them. Ratification can be made by continuing to make payments for an item purchased during infancy, or even by failing to disaffirm a contract within a reasonable time after reaching majority status.

An **unenforceable contract** is one that is valid, but cannot be enforced for some legal reason. An oral contract for the sale of real property is an example of an unenforceable contract, because a real estate contract is required to be in writing to be enforceable. But, where parties have already acted as if they were in an enforceable contract, courts will not undo their past contractual transactions, because unenforceability is about being able to avoid future contract performance.

Word Wise
Necessaries v. Necessities

The definition of "necessities" in standard dictionaries lists food, clothing, and shelter as specific items necessary to sustain life. In legal dictionaries, however, the term is given a broader meaning as well as a different spelling. For example, a "see necessaries" reference is listed under the term "necessities" in *Black's Law Dictionary.* This is because, in the legal use of the term, "necessaries" include not only what maintains life, but also what is required to preserve the standard of living to which an individual is accustomed. Thus, "necessaries" often relate to the standard established by the rank, position, and earning power of a buyer or those of his or her parent or spouse.

Executed and Executory Contracts

Contracts that are completely carried out (both sides' performance duties have been fully completed) are said to be **executed**. Those that have come into existence, but are not yet carried out are **executory**. For example, if one student agrees to sells her textbook to another student for $50, and the seller gives the book to the buying student, but the buyer has to wait until getting paid on Friday to pay for the text, the contract is valid, but is executory. When the buyer pays the seller $50, the contract is executed.

E-CONTRACTS

Because so many items are bought and sold on the Internet, including the licenses to use software, contracts entered into over such a medium have been termed **e-contracts**. There is no separate body of contract law that governs e-contracts, but the traditional contract doctrines have been applied to e-contracts. For instance, how do users know whether hitting the "Enter" bar on their laptop while viewing an item on eBay is the binding acceptance to a valid offer? Furthermore, what makes an offer on the Internet sufficient to be binding? In a 2007 federal case dealing with such an issue, a lawyer who paid to advertise on Google.com and was billed $100,000 over three years, sued Google. Google's contract with advertisers required the advertisers to pay Google every time someone using Google clicked on selected keywords leading to the advertiser's web-site. The advertising contract was, naturally, online and is known as a **"clickwrap" agreement**, because the offeree enters into the contract by clicking on a dialog box, which is on the screen. The lawyer claimed that Google's clickwrap contract was fraudulent because the terms weren't clearly identified. The court disagreed, in part, because Google provided the entire contract by way of a web page link, which then placed the entire agreement in a text box. Furthermore, the contract's clickwrap was preceded by a button with text that said, "Yes, I agree to the above terms and conditions," and that had to be clicked before the user could enter into the contract. The court ruled in favor of Google (*Feldman v. Google, Inc.*, 513 F.Supp.2d 229).

Reviewing What You Learned

After studying the chapter, write the answers to each of the following questions:

1. Explain how a contractual agreement is reached. _____
   _____
   _____
   _____

2. Why does a contract not usually arise when a customer offers to buy a mismarked product? _____
   _____
   _____
   _____

3. Give an example of a contract implied in fact. _____
   _____
   _____

4. For what reason does the court impose a contract on the parties when a quasi contract arises? _____
   _____
   _____

5. What is the difference between a bilateral contract and a unilateral contract? _____
   _____

_____
_____
_____

6. Give an example of a void contract, a voidable contract, and an unenforceable contract. _____
   _____
   _____
   _____
   _____

7. How does an executory contract differ from an executed contract? _____
   _____
   _____
   _____
   _____

8. Explain how a clickwrap agreement works. _____
   _____
   _____
   _____
   _____

4

Understanding Legal Concepts

Indicate whether each statement is true or false. Then, change the italicized word or phrase of each false statement to make it true.

ANSWERS

_____ 1. A *rejection* occurs when an offeror has a change of mind and calls back an offer before it is accepted.

_____ 2. Prices on merchandise and in catalogs are usually treated as *offers*.

_____ 3. Boarding a bus and putting money in the coin slot without saying anything to the driver is a *quasi contract*.

_____ 4. A *bilateral contract* results when someone says, "I'll sell you my stereo for $100," and the other party replies, "I'll buy it."

_____ 5. A *voidable* contract is one that is valid unless voided.

_____ 6. An oral contract for the sale of real property is an example of a contract that is *void*.

_____ 7. Infants *may* ratify contracts at any time during their minority.

_____ 8. When someone says, "I'll sell you my stereo for $100," and the other party replies, "I'll buy it," a contract comes into existence, and it is in its *executory* stage.

_____ 9. It is known as a *rejection* when the offeree declines an offer.

_____ 10. A *void* contract is said to be a nullity.

Checking Terminology

From the list of legal terms that follows, select the one that matches each definition.

ANSWERS

a. acceptance
b. avoid
c. bargain
d. bilateral contract
e. capacity
f. clickwrap agreement
g. condition precedent
h. contract
i. contract implied in fact
j. contract implied in law
k. counteroffer
l. disaffirm
m. e-contract
n. executed
o. executory
p. express contract
q. implied contract
r. infant
s. invitation to deal
t. invitation to negotiate
u. majority
v. minor
w. necessaries
x. nullity
y. offer
z. offeree
aa. offeror
bb. quasi
cc. quasi contract
dd. ratify
ee. rejection
ff. restitution
gg. revocation

_____ 1. Any agreement that is enforceable in a court of law.

_____ 2. A contract in which the terms are stated or expressed by the parties.

_____ 3. The refusal by an offeree of an offer.

_____ 4. A proposal made by an offeror.

_____ 5. A contract containing two promises, one made by each party.

_____ 6. A contract entered into over the Internet.

_____ 7. The assent to the terms of an offer.

_____ 8. Approve; confirm.

_____ 9. A contract in which an offeree enters into a contract by clicking on a dialog box on an Internet web site.

_____ 10. occurs when one person retains money, property, or other benefit that in equity and justice belongs to another.

_____ 11. Full age; adulthood.

_____ 12. Carried out or performed.

_____ 13. The legal name for a minor.

_____ 14. A contract that cannot be enforced for some legal reason.

_____ 15. To get out of a voidable contract; to repudiate. (Select two answers.)

_____ 16. Not good; having no legal effect.

_____ 17. The taking back of an offer by an offeror before it has been accepted by an offeree.

_____ 18. One who makes an offer.

_____ 19. Good; having legal effect.

_____ 20. Capable of being disaffirmed or voided.

_____ 21. A contract in which the terms are not stated or expressed by the parties.

_____ 22. A response to an offer in which the terms of the original offer are changed.

_____ 23. A contract that is imposed by the court to prevent unjust enrichment. (Select two answers.)

_____ 24. As if; almost as it were.

_____ 25. Under the age of majority; usually under 18.

_____ 26. Legal competency.

_____ 27. A contract containing one promise in exchange for an act.

_____ 28. That which is yet to be executed or performed.

_____ 29. One to whom an offer is made.

_____ 30. Agreement.

_____ 31. Restore an injured person to his or her original position prior to a loss.

hh. unenforceable contract
ii. unilateral contract
jj. unjust enrichment
kk. valid
ll. void
mm. voidable

____ 32. A request to an individual or the public to make an offer. (Select two answers.)

____ 33. A contract that arises from the conduct of the parties rather than from their express statements.

____ 34. Food, clothing, shelter, and medical care that are needed by an infant, but not supplied by a parent or guardian.

____ 35. Nothing; as though it had not occurred.

Using Legal Language

Read the following story and fill in the blank lines with legal terms taken from the list of terms at the beginning of this chapter.

Monica placed a sign on her car that read, "FOR SALE: $1,000." Seeing the sign, Alex approached Monica and said, "I'll give you $800 for it." Monica replied, "I'll take $900 for it." The sign was a(n) _____, or _____. Alex's statement was a(n) _____, and Monica's response was a(n) _____, which required a(n) _____ on the part of Alex to create a(n) _____. Alex did not answer immediately, causing Monica to change her mind about the $900 offer and to take it back. However, before she voiced her _____, Alex answered with a(n) _____ by saying, "I don't want it at that price." Alex left Monica and took a bus to visit his nephew. This action resulted in a(n) _____ between Alex and the bus company, because the terms of the contract were not stated. Because the contract arose from the conduct of the parties, it was a contract _____. When Alex got off the bus, he noticed that he was being followed by a small poodle that looked just like one that was advertised as being lost, in the newspaper he had just read. The advertisement offered a reward of $150 to anyone who returned the lost poodle to its owner. Alex went to the address given in the newspaper and returned the dog to its owner, thus creating a(n) _____. While there, he noticed a car for sale in front of the house and said to the dog owner, "I'll take that car instead of the $150 reward." Alex was the _____; the dog owner was the _____. The dog owner replied, "It's a deal." At this point, the contract was in its _____ stage, because it had not been carried out completely. When the dog owner turns the car over to Alex, the contract will be _____. In addition, because the terms of the contract were stated, this agreement was a(n) _____. It was not a contract _____ (which is also known as a(n) _____), because no unjust enrichment occurred. Because both parties made promises, it was a(n) _____. The contract met the requirements of law; therefore, it was _____. Alex said to his 14-year-old nephew, Otto, "I'll sell you my baseball glove for $15." Otto replied, "I'll buy it." This contract was _____ because of Otto's age. He was still a(n) _____ and could disaffirm all contracts except for _____ unless he _____ them after reaching _____. Otto then said to Alex, "I'll bet you $2,000 that the White Sox will win the pennant this year." Alex asked, "Where will you get the money if you lose?" "From a loan shark at 50 percent per annum interest," Otto answered. This loan would involve charging a greater amount of interest than is allowed by law. Such a contract is a(n) _____ and is absolutely _____. This type of agreement is *not* an example of a(n) _____ contract, which is a contract that is valid, but that cannot be enforced for some legal reason.

4

PUZZLING OVER WHAT YOU LEARNED

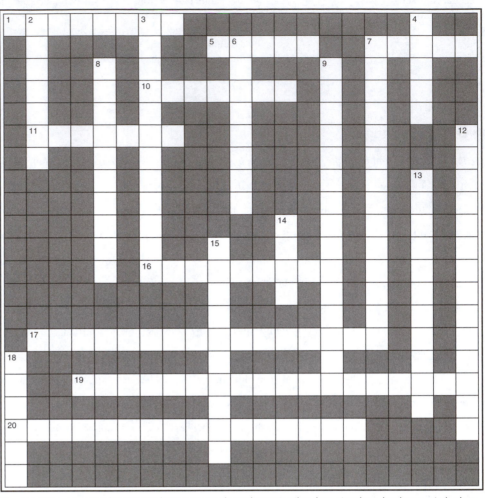

Caveat: Allow squares for spaces between words and punctuation (apostrophes, hyphens, etc.) when filling in crossword.

Across

1. Any agreement that is enforceable in a court of law.
5. To get out of a voidable contract.
7. As if; almost as it were.
10. Nothing; as though it had not occurred.
11. One to whom an offer is made.
16. The refusal by an offeree of an offer made by an offerer.
17. A contract in which the terms are stated or expressed by the parties.
19. A request to an individual or the public to make an offer.
20. A contract in which the terms are not stated or expressed by the parties.

Down

2. One who makes an offer.
3. A response to an offer in which the terms of the original offer are changed.
4. Good; having legal effect.
6. Capable of being disaffirmed or voided.
7. A contract imposed by law to prevent unjust enrichment.
8 The assent to the terms of an offer.
9. A contract that arises from the conduct of the parties.
12. Another name for a quasi contract.
13. Food, clothing, shelter, and medical care that are needed.
14. Not good; having no legal effect.
15. The taking back of an offer by an offeror before it has been accepted.
18. Approve; confirm.

Contract Requirements

ANTE INTERROGATORY

A binding promise by an offeror to hold an offer open, requiring consideration from the offeree to make it binding, is called a (an) (A) firm offer, (B) option contract, (C) promissory estoppel, (D) nundum pactum.

CHAPTER OUTLINE

Contractual Capacity

Consideration

Contracts Required to Be in Writing
　Statute of Frauds
　Requirements of a Writing
　Parol Evidence Rule

Defective Agreements
　Mistake
　Fraud
　Duress and Undue Influence
　Unconscionable Contracts

Legality

4

KEY TERMS

adhesion contract *(ad·HEE·shen KON·trakt)*

affirm *(a·FIRM)*

avoid *(a·VOID)*

bilateral mistake *(by·LAT·er·el mis·TAKE)*

boilerplate *(BOY·ler·plate)*

consideration *(kon·sid·er·AY·shun)*

contractual capacity *(kon·TRAK·chew·al ka·PAA·si·tee)*

duress *(der·ESS)*

e-signature *(EE-SIG·na·choor)*

exculpatory clause *(eks·KUL·pa·toh·ree)*

failure of consideration *(FAYL·yer ov kon·sid·er·AY·shun)*

firm offer *(OFF·er)*

forbearance *(for·BARE·ense)*

fraud *(frawd)*

fraud in the execution *(frawd in the ex·e·KEW·shun)*

fraud in the inducement *(in DEWSS·ment)*

in pari delicto *(in PAA·ree de·LIK·toh)*

lack of consideration *(kon·sid·er·AY·shun)*

locus *(LOH·kus)*

locus sigilli *(LOH·kus se·JIL·i)*

memorandum *(mem·o·RAN·dum)*

mutual mistake *(MYOO·choo·el mis·TAKE)*

nudum pactum *(NOO·dum PAK·tum)*

option contract *(OP·shen KON·trakt)*

parol evidence rule *(pa·ROLE EV·i·dens)*

promisee *(prom·i·SEE)*

promisor *(prom·i·SOHR)*
promissory estoppel *(PROM·i·sore·ee es·TOP·el)*
public policy *(PUB-lik POL-i-cee)*
quid pro quo *(quid pro quo)*
rescind *(ree·SIND)*
rescission *(ree·SIZH·en)*
seal

statute of frauds *(STAT·shoot ov frawds)*
unconscionable *(un·KON·shun·a·bel)*
undue influence *(UN·dew IN· flew·ens)*
unilateral mistake *(yoon·i·LAT·er·el mis·TAKE)*
usury *(YOO·zer·ee)*

CONTRACTUAL CAPACITY

As discussed in Chapter 18, minors make voidable contracts, because their age makes them legally incapable of making a fully binding contract. But age is not the only impediment to **contractual capacity**. One can lack the mental capacity to make a contract due to being too drunk (or otherwise under the influence of drugs) to realize that she or he is making a contract. A judicial declaration of insanity also makes one incapable of legally entering into a contract.

CONSIDERATION

The key ingredient that, when added to an unenforceable agreement, turns that agreement into a binding contract is **consideration**. Consideration is the exchange of benefits and promises by the parties to the agreement. It is the cement that binds the parties to the contract. The Latin phrase describing this concept is *quid pro quo*, meaning "this for that" or "one thing in return for another."

Contracts are, in a metaphoric sense, two-way streets, imposing both an obligation to perform (the duty) and a right to receive (the benefit). Consideration is both sides of that street. By contrast, a promise to make a gift to someone is unenforceable (a one-way street), because that promise isn't binding, since the other side hasn't promised something in return. So, if someone isn't bound to keep a promise, it's because the other side hasn't promised anything in return, and the agreement lacks consideration. The difference between "Please, take my coat" and "Please take my coat for $100" is more than a comma. The money in the second sentence represents the other half of the exchange, and consideration is all about an exchange.

Promising not to do something that one has a right to do is known as **forbearance**, and it can be consideration, just as promising to do something that one has a right to do can be consideration. For example, in exchange for a huge plate of chocolate chip cookies promised by a next-door neighbor, the other neighbor could promise not to use his charcoal grill to cook hamburgers for a particular week when the cookie-making neighbor has vegan family members visiting.

When one who made the promise (the **promisor**) is under no legal obligation to give the object to the one to whom the promise was made (the **promisee**), the agreement is a **nudum pactum**—that is, a barren promise with no consideration.

In a bilateral contract, consideration is found in the promises exchanged by each party. In a unilateral contract, it is found in the promise of one and in the act or performance of the other, and, therefore, it does not come about until the act is completed.

In the past, and today in some states, a **seal** on a contract furnished consideration when none existed. This mark, impression, the word "seal," or the letters "L.S." are placed on a written contract next to the party's signature. "L.S." stands for **locus sigilli**, which means the place of the seal.

Word Wise
One "Locus"; Several "Loci"

Most nouns in the English language form plurals by adding "s" to the singular. However, some nouns adapted from Latin, Greek, French, or Italian rely on the original language for the plural. Here are some examples:

Singular	Plural
locus	Loci
medium	media
datum	data
beau	beaux
memorandum	memoranda
criterion	criteria
phenomenon	phenomena
stimulus	stimuli
radius	radii
larva	larvae
crisis	crises
matrix	matrices

An **option contract** is a binding promise by an offeror to hold an offer open and requires consideration from the offeree to make it binding. For instance, someone who wants to buy a home, but does not immediately know whether financing can be arranged, might offer the seller a sum of money to take the home off the market to other prospective buyers for, let's say, 30 days, so that bank financing may be sought. If the seller accepts the money, an option contract has been created (for 30 days). An exception occurs when a merchant promises in writing to hold an offer open for the sale of goods. This promise by a merchant (someone, according to the Uniform Commercial Code, who is in the business of buying and selling goods) is known as a **firm offer** and requires no consideration to be binding.

In a lawsuit, the defense of **lack of consideration** refers to a barren promise containing no consideration in the agreement. In contrast, the defense of **failure of consideration** refers to a contract containing consideration that was not in fact given to the party being sued.

Under an equitable doctrine known as **promissory estoppel** no consideration is necessary when someone makes a promise that induces another's detrimental reliance on the promise and injustice can be avoided only by enforcing the promise. Suppose that a man works in a catering business and offers to buy the business when the owner retires. The owner says, "I tell you what, I'll sell it to you," but she then suggests that the employee get a degree in culinary arts first. So, the employee borrows money to go to culinary school, which takes a few years. Then, the owner mentions that caterers should understand business and says, "You'll need to have a business degree, too." So, the employee borrows more money to earn a business degree and spends more years studying. Then, the owner says that to be the owner of her catering business, the employee would have to move to the city where the business is located rather than live in the cheaper town 15 miles away. So, the employee moves to the city, increasing his housing costs by 30 percent. When the owner finally retires, she refuses to sell her business to her longsuffering employee. This would likely be a case for promissory estoppel. However, the damages would be the money lost by the employee in reliance on the promise; it wouldn't be the forced sale of the business to the employee or what the business is worth.

TERMS IN ACTION

Allen Iverson was one of the most gifted scorers in NBA history, averaging 26.7 points per season over a 13-year career, most of it spent with the Philadelphia 76ers. Iverson won a Rookie of the Year award in 1997 and a Most Valuable Player award in 2001. Iverson's nickname was "The Answer," and this name was the source of a breach of contract claim made by one of Iverson's close friends. Jamil Blackmon was a family friend who had a mentor-like relationship with Iverson when Iverson was still in high school. Before Iverson went to the University of Georgetown in 1994, Blackmon suggested that Iverson take for his nickname "The Answer"—as in, Iverson would be the answer to all of the NBA's woes. Iverson loved the idea and promised Blackmon 25 percent of all of the money that Iverson made from future merchandising of that nickname. Iverson repeated that promise as he began profiting from using "The Answer." The promises were repeated through 2001, but never honored, so Blackmon sued Iverson. But the trial judge dismissed the case in 2003, concluding that there was no **consideration** for the promise. As the court examined the allegations made in Blackmon's complaint, Iverson's promises to pay Blackmon came after Blackmon, in effect, gave him the nickname. There was no **exchange**, because promises made after one has already performed are insufficient to create a contract. It was **nudum pactum**. Blackmon then refiled his complaint, alleging **promissory estoppel**, but lost again. No evidence showed that Blackmon detrimentally and reasonably relied on Iverson's 1994 promise.

Source: *Blackmon v. Iverson*, 324 F.Supp.2d 602 (E.D. Pa. 2003), affirmed in an unpublished opinion, 317 Fed. Appx. 123 (3rd Cir. 3008)

CONTRACTS REQUIRED TO BE IN WRITING

Although it makes sense to put a contract in writing, the law requires only certain contracts to be in writing; others are fully enforceable even though they are oral.

Statute of Frauds

Under a rule of law known as the **statute of frauds** certain contracts must be in writing to be enforceable. With some variations from state to state, the following contracts must be in writing to be enforceable:

1. contracts that are not to be completed within a year
2. promises to answer for the debt or default of another
3. contracts for the sale of an interest in real property
4. contracts in which marriage is the consideration (such as prenuptial agreements)
5. promises by personal representatives of estates to pay debts of the estate personally
6. promises to leave something to someone in a will
7. with four exceptions, contracts for the sale of goods of $500 or more

Requirements of a Writing

The writing that is necessary to satisfy the statute of frauds is called a **memorandum**. It may consist of any writing (such as words on a piece of scrap paper, receipt, or check) so long as it meets the following requirements:

1. identifies the parties to the contract
2. states the terms of the contract
3. identifies the **locus** of land—that is, the exact parcel of land under contract
4. states the price
5. is signed by the person against whom enforcement is sought

If the parties agree, the federal law and many state laws allow contracts to be signed with an **e-signature** (electronic signature)—a method of signing an electronic message that identifies the sender and signifies his or her approval of the message's content.

TERMS IN ACTION

In the world of American contract law, very few cases are more famous than *Lucy v. Zehmer*. This 1954 case involves the **statute of frauds**, the unwitting sale of the family farm, and lots of whiskey. It seems that Mr. and Mrs. Zehmer owned a 471-acre farm in Virginia, a farm that Mr. Lucy wanted for quite some time. One time, Zehmer reneged on a promise to sell the farm to Lucy for $20,000, because his promise was oral and **real estate contracts** need to be in writing to be enforceable. On another occasion, Lucy came to the restaurant–gasoline station that Zehmer owned, armed with a bottle of whiskey, and began to drink with Zehmer. While talking about Zehmer's farm, Lucy said to Zehmer, "I bet you wouldn't take $50,000 for that place." Zehmer responded, "Yes, I would, too; you wouldn't give fifty." Lucy said that he would, and Zehmer wrote a basic contract on the back of a restaurant check. However, Lucy noticed that Zehmer wrote "I agree to sell," rather than "We," and the farm was owned by Zehmer and his wife. So, Zehmer ripped up the paper, wrote it again, and had Lucy's wife—who was actually working in the restaurant—sign the document with him and Lucy. You probably know where this is going. By the time Zehmer realized that he had sold his farm, he cried foul—that he never intended to do such a thing. But Virginia's statute of frauds had been met, and the Virginia Supreme Court failed to find any substance to Zehmer's claims of lacking **contractual capacity** to make a contract due to drunkenness, or his claim that he was just joking when making the contract.

Source: *Lucy v. Zehmer*, 84 S.E.2d 516 (Va. 1954)

4

Parol Evidence Rule

The law assumes that when a contract is reduced to writing, and signed, all of its terms are contained in the writing. Consequently, under a special rule of evidence known as the **parol evidence rule** oral evidence of prior or contemporaneous negotiations between the parties is not admissible in court to alter, vary, or contradict the terms of a written agreement. Because of this rule, it is important to include all terms that are orally agreed upon whenever a contract is reduced to writing. If one believes that he or she was lied to during negotiations because the contract doesn't reflect what was stated by the other party, the party making the accusation of lying will not be able to testify about what was supposed to be in the contract.

DEFECTIVE AGREEMENTS

Certain agreements are defective and are therefore not recognized as valid, binding contracts. The most common of these are agreements involving mutual mistake, fraud, duress, and undue influence. Unconscionable contracts may also be declared unenforceable by the courts.

Mistake

When both parties are mistaken about an important aspect of an agreement that they entered into, so that no meeting of the minds occurs, it is known as a **bilateral** or **mutual mistake** and the contract is voidable at the option of either party. In contrast, when only one of the parties makes a mistake, it is known as a **unilateral** (one-sided) **mistake** and the contract cannot be **avoided** (made void) by the parties, as a general rule.

Fraud

Fraud (which also exists in tort law, where occasionally it is called deceit) occurs when one party to the contract makes a misrepresentation of a material, existing fact that the other party to the contract relies on and thereby suffers damages. If the defrauded party was induced by fraud to enter into the contract, it is called **fraud in the inducement** and the contract is voidable at the option of the injured party. If, conversely, fraud as to the essential nature of the transaction occurred, such as telling a blind man that he is signing a receipt when it is really a check, it is called **fraud in the execution** (originally, "fraud in esse contractus and the contract is void. A defrauded party always has the right to **rescind** (cancel) the contract and to return any consideration received. Thus, **rescission** (cancellation) restores the parties to their original positions. A defrauded party may choose, instead, to keep the consideration and **affirm** (approve) the contract and bring suit for damages.

The elements that must be proved by the party claiming fraud are discussed in more detail in Chapter 16 in the section on fraud.

Duress and Undue Influence

Contracts that are entered into because of duress or undue influence may also be avoided by the injured party. **Duress** is the overcoming of a person's free will by the use of an unlawful threat or physical harm. **Undue influence** is the overcoming of a person's free will by misusing a position of trust and taking advantage of the other person who is relying on the trust relationship.

Unconscionable Contracts

Some contracts (or parts of them) are so harshly one-sided and unfair that they—as is the operative legal phrase—shock the conscience of the court. Such contracts are considered **unconscionable** by the courts and will not be enforced. This is because unconscionable contracts (in some cases called **adhesion contracts**) are drawn by one party to that party's lopsided benefit and must be accepted as is, on a take-it-or-leave-it basis if a contract is to result. Sometimes, **adhesion contracts** fall into this category. Adhesion contracts often contain **boilerplate**, which is standardized language commonly used in similar legal documents. Although no longer descriptive of its history, boilerplate is still alive and well, and is usually found at the end of contracts, with such heading titles as "Attorney's Fees," "Waiver," or "Limitations on Damages." Boilerplate is found in legal form books or stored on law-office computers for use in the drafting of legal documents. **Exculpatory clauses** (clauses that are used to escape legal responsibility) are generally used in boilerplate and are looked on with disfavor by courts. However, such clauses will usually be enforced if they do not offend public policy and if the bargaining power between the parties is equal.

LEGALITY

To be valid and enforceable, contracts must be about that which is legal to do or perform. Illegal contracts are void; they have no legal effect. **Usury** for example, which is the charging of a higher amount of interest than is allowed by consumer protection law, is illegal in every state. Gambling is illegal in many states, with exceptions such as state lotteries, horse and dog racing, and bingo. Sunday contracts are illegal in some states, with certain specific exceptions. Contracts in restraint of trade, such as agreements not to compete, are also illegal, along with other types of contracts that are opposed to public policy. **Public policy** is a doctrine that is often difficult to identify, but it is generally thought to be underlying, foundational principles that bind various peoples into a close-knit society. It represents those ideas that reflect the moral or cultural fabric of a jurisdiction. For instance, a contract prohibiting someone from marrying is thought to be against public policy.

Except when the parties are not **in pari delicto** (in equal fault), the court will not aid either party to an illegal contract. It will leave the parties where they placed themselves.

Reviewing What You Learned

After studying the chapter, write the answers to each of the following questions:

1. Give an example of a contract containing consideration.

   _____

   _____

   _____

   _____

2. Give an example of an agreement that does not contain consideration. _____

   _____

   _____

   _____

3. Where is consideration found in a bilateral contract? In a unilateral contract? _____

   _____

   _____

   _____

4. List seven kinds of contracts that must be in writing in order to be enforceable. _____

   _____

   _____

   _____

   _____

5. What are the requirements of a memorandum that will satisfy the statute of frauds? _____

   _____

   _____

   _____

6. Explain the meaning and significance of the parol evidence rule.

   _____

   _____

   _____

   _____

7. Describe the kind of contract that is voidable because of a mistake, and compare it with the kind of contract that is not voidable because of a mistake. _____

   _____

   _____

   _____

8. List the five elements of fraud. _____

   _____

   _____

   _____

   _____

9. Describe an unconscionable contract. _____

   _____

   _____

   _____

   _____

10. Describe three kinds of contracts that are illegal and void in many states. _____

    _____

    _____

    _____

    _____

Understanding Legal Concepts

Indicate whether each statement is true or false. Then, change the italicized word or phrase of each false statement to make it true.

ANSWERS

_____ 1. A binding contract *comes* into existence when one person says to another, "I'm going to give you my stereo as a gift," and the other replies, "Fine, I'll accept it."

_____ 2. In the past, and still today in some states, a seal on a contract *furnishes* consideration when none exists.

_____ 3. Under a rule of law known as the *statute of limitations*, certain contracts must be in writing to be enforceable.

_____ 4. Contracts for the sale of an interest in *real property* must be in writing to be enforceable.

_____ 5. With four exceptions, contracts for the sale of goods of *$600* or more must be in writing to be enforceable.

_____ 6. A memorandum *may* consist of words on a piece of scrap paper, receipt, or check.

_____ 7. The law assumes that when a contract is reduced to writing, *all* of its terms are contained in the writing.

_____ 8. When a mutual mistake occurs, a contract *cannot* be avoided by the parties.

_____ 9. When a person is induced by fraud to enter into a contract, it is called *fraud in the execution*, and the contract is void.

_____ 10. Illegal contracts are *void;* they have no legal effect.

Checking Terminology

From the list of legal terms that follows, select the one that matches each definition.

ANSWERS

a. adhesion contract
b. affirm
c. avoid
d. bilateral mistake
e. boilerplate
f. consideration
g. contractual capacity
h. deceit
i. duress
j. e-signature
k. exculpatory clause
l. failure of consideration
m. firm offer
n. forbearance
o. fraud
p. fraud in the execution
q. fraud in the inducement
r. in pari delicto
s. lack of consideration
t. locus
u. locus sigilli
v. memorandum
w. mutual mistake
x. nudum pactum
y. option contract
z. parol evidence rule
aa. promisee
bb. promisor
cc. promissory estoppel
dd. public policy
ee. quid pro quo
ff. rescind
gg. rescission
hh. seal
ii. statute of frauds
jj. unconscionable
kk. undue influence
ll. unilateral mistake
mm. usury

_____ 1. The giving up of a legal right.

_____ 2. Place; locality.

_____ 3. Cancellation.

_____ 4. In equal fault.

_____ 5. Standard language commonly used in documents of the same type.

_____ 6. The overcoming of a person's free will by misusing a position of trust and taking advantage of the other person who is relying on the trust relationship.

_____ 7. Underlying foundational principles which bind various peoples into a close-knit society.

_____ 8. oral evidence of prior or contemporaneous negotiations between the parties is not admissible in court to alter, vary, or contradict the terms of a written agreement.

_____ 9. Refraining from taking action.

_____ 10. The overcoming of a person's free will by the use of threat or physical harm.

_____ 11. A clause that is used in a contract to escape legal responsibility.

_____ 12. A contract that is drawn by one party to that party's benefit and must be accepted, as is, on a take-it-or-leave-it basis if a contract is to result.

_____ 13. A misrepresentation of a material, existing fact, knowingly made, that causes someone reasonably relying on it to suffer damages. (Select two answers.)

_____ 14. The writing that is necessary to satisfy the statute of frauds.

_____ 15. A mark, impression, the word "seal," or the letters "L.S." placed on a written contract next to the party's signature.

_____ 16. Approve.

_____ 17. So harshly one-sided and unfair that the court's conscience is shocked.

_____ 18. Fraud as to the essential nature of the transaction.

_____ 19. A defense available when the consideration provided for in an agreement is not in fact given to the party being sued.

_____ 20. A mistake made by only one party to a contract.

_____ 21. To annul, cancel, or make void.

_____ 22. One to whom a promise is made.

_____ 23. A defense available to a party being sued when no consideration is contained in the agreement that is sued on.

_____ 24. Cancel.

_____ 25. A binding promise to hold an offer open.

_____ 26. A doctrine under which no consideration is necessary when someone makes a promise that induces another's action or forbearance and injustice can be avoided only by enforcing the promise.

_____ 27. A merchant's written promise to hold an offer open for the sale of goods.

_____ 28. Capability of making a fully binding contract.

_____ 29. When both parties are mistaken about an important aspect of an agreement. (Select two answers.)

_____ 30. Certain contracts must be in writing to be enforceable.

_____ 31. Barren promise with no consideration.

_____ 32. An exchange of benefits and detriments by the parties to an agreement.

_____ 33. Fraud that induces another to enter into a contract.
_____ 34. The charging of a greater amount of interest than is allowed by law.
_____ 35. A method of signing an electronic message.
_____ 36. One thing in return for another
_____ 37. One who makes a promise.
_____ 38. Place of the seal.

Using Legal Language

Read the following story and fill in the blank lines with legal terms taken from the list of terms at the beginning of this chapter:

The smooth-talking salesperson promised a free cataract operation to an elderly woman who was almost blind. The salesperson was the _____ and the elderly woman was the _____; however, because the elderly woman promised nothing in exchange for the cataract operation, she suffered no _____. For this reason, no _____ occurred, and the agreement was a _____. Had the promise been in writing and put under _____ by the use of the letters "L.S." (which stand for _____), it would have been binding in some states. The salesperson also committed _____ or _____ when he lied to the elderly woman. He talked her into buying some worthless land with a shack on it by telling her that the _____ was beautiful, high ground; actually, it was swampland. The type of fraud was _____, because the salesperson's lie induced the woman to enter into the contract. Because the salesperson was not in a position of trust, the wrongful act was not _____ and it was not _____, because the woman's free will was not overcome by threats or physical harm. It was _____, however, when the sales-

person told the woman that she was signing a second copy of the contract when she was actually signing a check for $10,000. The writing that the woman signed met the requirements of a(n) _____ and, for that reason, was sufficient to satisfy the _____. Because it was drawn up by the seller to the seller's advantage and offered to the woman on a take-it-or-leave-it basis, the court might consider the contract to be a(n) _____. In addition, the court might consider the contract to be _____, because the woman agreed to buy a shack on an acre of worthless swampland for $250,000. Under the terms of the contract, she was to pay $100,000 in cash and sign a note for the balance at 50 percent per annum interest, which is _____. Although the _____ does not allow prior oral statements by the parties into evidence in court to alter the terms of a written agreement, an exception exists when fraud is committed. In addition, because both parties were mistaken as to the existence of the subject matter when they signed the contract (the shack on the property had burned down two days before the contract was signed), the contract was voidable. The mistake was a(n) _____, which is also known as a(n) _____, not a(n) _____.

4

PUZZLING OVER WHAT YOU LEARNED

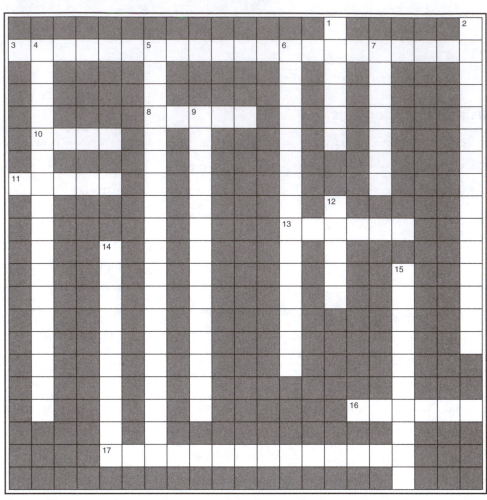

Caveat: Allow squares for spaces between words and punctuation (apostrophes, hyphens, etc.) when filling in crossword.

Across

3. A defense available when no consideration is contained in an agreement.
8. The charging of a greater amount of interest than is allowed by law.
10. A mark, impression, the word "seal," or the letters "L.S."
11. Place; locality.
13. The overcoming of a person's free will by the use of threat or physical harm.
16. Approve.
17. Another name for a bilateral mistake.

Down

1. Misrepresentation of a material, existing fact knowingly made.
2. Overcoming a person's free will by misusing a position of trust.
4. One-sided contract that must be accepted as is.
5. Fraud that induces another to enter into a contract.
6. In equal fault.
7. Annulled, canceled, or made void.
9. So harshly one-sided and unfair as to shock the court's conscience.
12. Another name for deceit.
14. The writing that is necessary to satisfy the statute of frauds.
15. A merchant's written promise to hold an offer open for the sale of goods.

Third Parties and Discharge of Contracts

ANTE INTERROGATORY

Damages that are agreed upon by the parties at the time of the execution of the contract in the event of a subsequent breach are called (A) consequential damages, (B) exemplary damages, (C) incidental damages, (D) liquidated damages.

CHAPTER OUTLINE

Third-Party Beneficiaries

Assignment and Delegation

Ending Contractual Obligations
  Performance
  Agreement

Impossibility
Operation of Law
Breach of Contract

4

KEY TERMS

accord and satisfaction *(a·KORD and sat·is·FAK·shun)*

anticipatory breach *(an·TISS·i·pa·tore·ee)*

assignee *(ass·en·EE)*

assignment *(a·SINE·ment)*

assignor *(ass·en·OR)*

bankruptcy *(BANK·rupt·see)*

breach of contract *(KON·trakt)*

compensatory damages *(kom·PEN·se·tor·ee DAM·e·jez)*

consequential damages *(kon·se·KWEN·shel DAM·e·jez)*

damages *(DAM·e·jez)*

delegation *(del·e·GA·shun)*

exemplary damages *(egs·ZEMP·le·ree DAM·e·jez)*

impossibility *(im·pos·i·BIL·i·tee)*

incidental beneficiary *(in·si·DEN·tel ben·e·FISH·ee·air·ee)*

incidental damages *(in·si·DEN·tel DAM·e·jez)*

intended beneficiary

legal tender *(LEE·gul TEN·der)*

liquidated damages *(LIK·wi·day·ted DAM·e·jez)*

mitigate *(MIT·i·gate)*

nominal damages *(NOM·i·nel DAM·e·jez)*

novation *(no·VAY·shun)*

performance *(per·FORM·ens)*

191

privity of contract *(PRIV·i·tee ov KON·trakt)*

punitive damages *(PYOON·i·tiv)*

specific performance *(spe·SIF·ic per·FORM·ens)*

statute of limitations *(STAT·shoot ov lim·i·TA·shuns)*

substantial performance *(sub·STAN·shel per·FORM·ens)*

tender of payment *(TEN·der)*

tender of performance *(per·FORM·ens)*

third-party beneficiary *(ben·e·FISH·ee·air·ee)*

time is of the essence *(ESS·ens)*

toll *(tohl)*

THIRD-PARTY BENEFICIARIES

A **third-party beneficiary** is someone who is not a party to a contract, but is benefited by a performance in the contract. But being benefited by a contract performance does not necessarily give that beneficiary rights under the contract, because **privity of contract**—the legal name for the relationship that exists between contracting parties—is generally required in order to acquire contract rights. In order to have rights to sue under a contract, the third-party beneficiary must be an **intended beneficiary**, which means that the contract was made with the purpose of benefiting the third party. The child whose birthday cake (with his name on it) is made by a bakery is a third-party beneficiary, but a child who eats a piece of cake at the birthday party is only an **incidental beneficiary** (one who is indirectly benefited by a contract).

ASSIGNMENT AND DELEGATION

Parties who enter into contracts receive rights and incur duties. (Remember, from Chapter 19, that consideration is like a two-way street.) For example, if I agree to sell you my car for $2,000 and you agree to buy it from me for that price, I receive the right to the money and incur the duty to give you the car. Your rights and duties are the opposite. With some exceptions and unless otherwise agreed, rights and duties can be transferred to other people.

The transfer of a right is called an **assignment**. The person who transfers the right is called the **assignor** and the person to whom the right is transferred is called the **assignee**. In the preceding example, if before receiving the $2,000 from you I assign my right to the money under the contract to a third person, you would have to pay the money to the third person upon learning of the assignment.

The transfer of a duty is known as a **delegation**. Duties to perform personal services cannot be delegated without the consent of the person for whom the duty is to be performed. For instance, an artist hired to paint someone's portrait cannot delegate the job to another painter without the customer's permission.

When two contracting parties agree that one of them will transfer both rights and duties to a third person, and the remaining party and the third person agree to deal solely with each other, privity of contract changes, and a novation occurs. A **novation** is an agreement whereby an original party to a contract is replaced by a new party, creating a completely new contract and ending the original one.

Web Wise

- Learn more about terms in contracts, including common boilerplate, by going to ***www.nolo.com*** and typing "boilerplate" into the search bar.
- To learn some of the fun, and sometimes curious, things that musicians and celebrities insist upon having when they travel, or perform at concerts or speaking engagements, go to ***www.thesmokinggun.com*** and then click on the "Backstage" tab. There you will find many contracts to examine, organized by style of music and other categories.

ENDING CONTRACTUAL OBLIGATIONS

The principal ways that contractual obligations end are as follows:

1. performance
2. agreement
3. impossibility
4. operation of law
5. breach of contract

Performance

Most contracts come to an end by **performance**—that is, the parties do as they agreed to do under the terms of the contract. At common law, the parties were required to do absolutely everything they agreed to do, without exception, to be in a position to bring suit against the other party for breach of contract. That was known as full performance. Under today's law, the doctrine of **substantial performance** allows a contracting party to sue the other party for breach even though slight omissions or deviations were made in his or her own performance of the contract.

The time for performance of a contract is sometimes important to the parties. If a time for performance is stated in a written contract, the court may allow additional time for its performance without recognizing a breach. If a time for performance is stated in the writing and the words **time is of the essence** (meaning that time is critical) are added, however, a breach of contract will occur at the end of the stated time if the contract has not been performed. If no time for performance is put in the contract, it must be performed within a **reasonable time**. This time, left to the discretion of the judge or jury, may be fairly allowed depending on the circumstances.

To be in a position to bring a suit against another for breach of contract, it is necessary for a party to make tender. **Tender of performance** means to offer to do that which one has agreed to do under the terms of the contract. **Tender of payment** means to offer to the other party the money owed under the contract. For the sale of goods under the Uniform Commercial Code, tender of payment may be made by any means or in any manner that is commonly used in the ordinary course of business. The seller may demand legal tender, but must give the buyer a reasonable time to obtain it. **Legal tender** is coin, paper, or other currency that is sufficient under law for the payment of debts.

Agreement

Sometimes, when there is a dispute, instead of completing the terms of a contract, the parties will agree to end the contract altogether. Other times, they will agree to perform in a different manner from that agreed upon originally. This latter arrangement is called an accord. When the agreed-upon performance is completed, a satisfaction occurs. Together, this arrangement is known as an **accord and satisfaction**.

Impossibility

Contracts that are impossible to perform, not merely difficult or costly to do so, may be discharged by a defense called **impossibility**. Legal reasons for this kind of discharge of performance include the following:

1. death of a person who was to perform personal services
2. destruction of the exact subject matter of the contract
3. subsequent illegality of that particular performance

Operation of Law

Sometimes, contracts will be discharged by operation of law. The filing of bankruptcy, for example, discharges the contractual obligations of the debtor. **Bankruptcy** (discussed in Chapter 40) is a legal process under the Federal Bankruptcy Act that aims to give debtors who are overwhelmed with debt a fresh start and to provide a fair way of distributing a debtor's assets among all creditors.

Contract rights are also discharged by the operation of **statutes of limitations**. These are laws that set forth time limits for bringing legal actions. For example, in the case of a breach of contract for the sale of goods, suit must be brought within four years from the date of the breach to be actionable. Other time limits vary from state to state for different causes of actions.

TERMS IN ACTION

When does being too sick to work become **impossibility of performance**? A case from Indiana sheds some light on the matter. Rose Acre Farms was an egg company that produced 250,000 dozen eggs per day and attempted to motivate its 300 employees through unique bonus programs. Employees had been paid car-payment bonuses for three years for buying new, white cars that advertised Rose Acre Farms and were always kept clean, or had been paid bonuses for wearing a silver feather at work. In all the bonus programs at Rose Acre Farms, employees forfeited the money if they ever missed work for any reason—illness included—or even if they were tardy for work by one minute. All employees who competed in these bonus programs were made aware of the exact requirements.

Mark Dove worked at Rose Acre Farms and participated in a bonus program to help construct a building in 12 weeks, for an extra $6,000. Because he was going to law school before the 12th week, he was allowed to compete for a $5,000 bonus for 10 weeks of work. But on Thursday of his 10th week, Dove got strep throat with a 104-degree temperature, and missed the remaining days of work. After being paid no bonus, Dove sued for breach of contract, claiming that he had **substantially performed**, as well as claiming that his illness qualified as impossibility of performance.

Dove lost on both counts. The Indiana Court of Appeals concluded that substantial performance didn't apply, because the bonus program was specifically and strictly based on full performance. Moreover, the court held that impossibility of performance didn't apply for the same reason that substantial performance didn't, and for a more important reason, as well: Impossibility is a defense raised by defendants, not a claim made by plaintiffs.

Source: *Dove v. Rose Acre Farms, Inc.*, 434 N.E.2d 931 (Ind. App. 1981)

Word Wise
Prefixes That Mean "Not"

Prefix	Examples
dis-	disbelief, disaffirm, dishonor
in-	indirect, intestate
im- (before p, b, m)	immature, impeach, impossibility
il- (before *l*)	illegal, illegitimate child
ir- (before *r*)	irregular, irreconcilable differences, irrevocable trust
non-	nonliving, nonsuit
un-	unscrupulous, unconscionable, undisclosed principal, unenforceable

---

Statutes of limitations are tolled—that is, they do not run—while a plaintiff is under a disability such as infancy or mental illness. Similarly, they do not run while a defendant is out of the state and not under the jurisdiction of the court. In the case of a lawsuit for money owed, partial payment of the debt has the effect of starting the full statutory period running all over again from the beginning. The word **toll** means to bar, defeat, or take away. Thus, to toll the statute of limitations means to show facts that would prevent a lawsuit from being dismissed due to its being filed too late.

Breach of Contract

A **breach of contract** occurs when one of the parties fails to carry out the terms of the contract. When the breaching party announces before the time for performance that he or she is not going to perform, it is known as an **anticipatory breach**. Some states allow suit to be brought at that moment; other states require the injured party to wait until the time for performance before bringing suit, to test the breaching party's ability to perform.

When a breach of contract occurs, the injured party may bring suit for **damages,** which is the money lost as a result of the breach. **Nominal damages**—that is, damages in name only—are sometimes recovered in the amount of $0.01 or $1 by a party who wins a lawsuit by proving that the defendant breached the contract, but suffers no actual monetary loss. **Compensatory damages** compensate the plaintiff for actual losses resulting from the breach. **Punitive** or **exemplary damages** such as those that are double or triple the amount of actual damages, are occasionally awarded to the plaintiff as a measure of punishment for the defendant's egregious acts related to breaching the contract. **Liquidated damages** are damages that are agreed upon (pre-determined) by the parties at the time of the execution of the contract in the event of a subsequent breach. **Incidental damages** may be awarded to the injured party to cover reasonable expenses that indirectly result from a breach of contract. **Consequential damages** are losses (such as lost profits) that flow not directly from the breach, but from the consequences of it. In order for a plaintiff to win consequential damages, the consequential losses must be a foreseeable (likely) result of the breach, and the parties must have considered those losses when making the contract.

Whenever a contract is breached, the injured party owes a duty to the breaching party to **mitigate** the damages—that is, keep them as low as possible. For example, if a tenant breaches a lease agreement by leaving the property six months early, the landlord has a duty to try and find a new tenant, in order to mitigate the damages. If the landlord did nothing for six months, the tenant would not owe six months of unpaid rent because of the doctrine of mitigation.

Sometimes, the court will order the breaching party to do that which he or she agreed to do under the terms of the contract. This order is known as **specific performance** and is used only when the subject matter of the contract is either unique or rare so that money damages are not an adequate remedy for the injured party. Because the court considers real property to be unique, it will often order a contract for the purchase or sale of real property to be specifically performed.

4

TERMS IN ACTION

The legal world was rocked in 1985 with the news that a jury had awarded over $10 billion in total **damages**. The lawsuit pitted two oil companies, Pennzoil against Texaco. In 1984, Pennzoil sought to purchase the Getty Oil Company, which had been founded by J. Paul Getty, a reclusive billionaire who was so cheap that he kept a payphone in his mansion. Gordon Getty, one of Getty's sons and the CEO of the Getty Oil Company, verbally agreed to the sale, and the picture of his handshake with Pennzoil executives ran in many newspapers. But Getty Oil had not officially agreed to the sale, and Texaco offered more money to Getty Oil than Pennzoil had. So, Getty Oil broke its deal with Pennzoil. Pennzoil sued Texaco for tortuous interference of a contract, rather than suing Getty Oil for **breach of contract**, because Texaco's offer to Getty included covering any breach of contract legal costs. Texaco argued at trial that Gordon Getty's informal intent to enter into a contract with Pennzoil wasn't sufficient to form a contract. But Pennzoil was represented by Houston's Joe Jamail, one of the best trial lawyers on the planet. The jury ruled in favor of Pennzoil and awarded it $3.53 billion in **compensatory damages** and $7 billion in **punitive damages**, making it then the biggest damages award ever. Eventually, the parties reached a deal in 1987, with Texaco agreeing to pay Pennzoil $3 billion. Joe Jamail's legal fee has never been confirmed, but is believed to be in the hundreds of millions of dollars. For quite some time, he has been a billionaire, himself.

Source: forbes.com; lawnix.com; *Economic Foundations of Law and Organization*

Reviewing What You Learned

After studying the chapter, write the answers to each of the following questions:

1. Explain the difference between an assignment and a delegation.

_____

_____

_____

_____

2. List the five ways that contractual obligations may come to an end. _____

_____

_____

_____

_____

3. If the time for performance is not mentioned in a contract, when must the contract be performed? _____

_____

_____

_____

_____

4. What is necessary for a person to be in a position to bring suit against another for breach of contract? _____

_____

_____

_____

_____

5. Explain the difference between accord and satisfaction.

_____

_____

_____

_____

6. List three legal reasons for discharging a contract for impossibility. _____

_____

_____

_____

_____

_____

7. Describe two situations that toll the statute of limitations.

_____

_____

_____

_____

8. How do nominal damages, punitive damages, liquidated damages, incidental damages, and consequential damages differ from one another? _____

_____

_____

_____

_____

9. Under what circumstances may the court order specific performance of a contract?

_____

_____

_____

_____

_____

Understanding Legal Concepts

Indicate whether each statement is true or false. Then, change the italicized word or phrase of each false statement to make it true.

ANSWERS

_____ 1. The transfer of a *duty* is known as an assignment.

_____ 2. With some exceptions and unless otherwise agreed, rights and duties *cannot* be transferred to other people.

_____ 3. Most contracts come to an end by *agreement*.

_____ 4. If a time for performance is stated in a written contract, the court *may* allow additional time for its performance.

_____ 5. If no time for performance is put in a contract, it must be performed within a *reasonable* time.

_____ **6.** When parties agree to perform in a different manner than originally agreed upon and the new performance is completed, it is called an accord and *completion.*

_____ **7.** The law of *bankruptcy* aims to give a fresh start to debtors who are overwhelmed with debt.

_____ **8.** In the case of a breach of contract for the sale of goods, suit must be brought within *six* years from the date of the breach, to be actionable.

_____ **9.** Whenever a contract is breached, the *breaching* party owes a duty to keep the damages as low as possible.

_____ **10.** *Specific performance* is used only when the subject matter of a contract is either unique or rare so that money damages are not an adequate remedy for the injured party.

Checking Terminology

From the list of legal terms that follows, select the one that matches each definition.

ANSWERS

a. accord and satisfaction
b. anticipatory breach
c. assignee
d. assignment
e. assignor
f. bankruptcy
g. breach of contract
h. compensatory damages
i. consequential damages
j. damages
k. delegation
l. exemplary damages
m. impossibility
n. incidental beneficiary
o. incidental damages
p. intended beneficiary
q. legal tender
r. liquidated damages
s. mitigate
t. nominal damages
u. novation
v. performance
w. privity of contract
x. punitive damages
y. specific performance
z. statute of limitations
aa. substantial performance
bb. tender of payment
cc. tender of performance
dd. third-party beneficiary
ee. time is of the essence
ff. toll

_____ 1. The transfer of a right from one person to another.
_____ 2. One who transfers a right by assignment.
_____ 3. One to whom a right is transferred by assignment.
_____ 4. The transfer of a duty by one person to another.
_____ 5. Coin, paper, or other currency that is sufficient under law for the payment of debts.
_____ 6. An agreement to perform in a different manner than originally called for and the completion of that agreed-upon performance.
_____ 7. A method of discharging a contract that is impossible to perform, not merely difficult or costly.
_____ 8. A legal process that aims to give a fresh start to debtors who are overwhelmed with debt and to provide a fair way of distributing a debtor's assets among all creditors.
_____ 9. The failure of a party to a contract to carry out the terms of the agreement.
_____ 10. The announcement, before the time for performance, by a party to a contract that he or she is not going to perform.
_____ 11. Compensation in money for loss or injury.
_____ 12. Damages as a measure of punishment for the defendant's wrongful acts (also called punitive damages).
_____ 13. Damages that are agreed upon by the parties at the time of the execution of a contract, in the event of a subsequent breach.
_____ 14. Reasonable expenses that indirectly result from a breach of contract.
_____ 15. Losses that flow not directly from a breach of contract, but from the consequences of it.
_____ 16. The relationship that exists between two or more contracting parties.
_____ 17. An agreement whereby an original party to a contract is replaced by a new party.
_____ 18. Discharging a contract by doing that which one agreed to do under the terms of the contract.
_____ 19. A doctrine allowing a contracting party to sue the other party for breach even though slight omissions or deviations were made in his or her own performance of the contract.
_____ 20. Time is critical.
_____ 21. A period, left to the discretion of the judge or jury, that may be fairly allowed depending on the circumstances.
_____ 22. To offer to do that which one has agreed to do under the terms of a contract.
_____ 23. To offer to the other party the money owed under a contract.
_____ 24. Law that sets forth time limits for bringing legal actions.
_____ 25. To bar, defeat, or take away.
_____ 26. One who is indirectly benefited by a contract.
_____ 27. Damages as a measure of punishment for the defendant's wrongful acts (also called *exemplary* damages).
_____ 28. The condition that exists when a contract is made with the purpose of benefiting the third party.
_____ 29. An order by the court ordering a breaching party to do that which he or she agreed to do under the terms of the contract.
_____ 30. Damages that compensate the plaintiff for actual losses resulting from the breach.
_____ 31. Someone for whose benefit a promise is made, but who is not a party to the contract.
_____ 32. Lessen; keep as low as possible.
_____ 33. Damages in Name Only.

4

Sharpening Your Latin Skills

In the space provided, write the definition of each of the following legal terms, referring to the glossary when necessary:

assumpsit _____

locus sigilli _____

ex contractu _____

non assumpsit _____

gratis _____

nudum pactum _____

in pari delicto _____

quasi _____

Using Legal Language

Read the following story and fill in the blank lines with legal terms taken from the list of terms at the beginning of this chapter:

Needing a car for a trip she was planning, Holly entered into a contract to buy a late-model Toyota from Enrique for $7,000. Time was of the _____ with regard to this contract, because Holly planned to leave on the trip the next day. Before she could carry out the contract, however, Holly's trip was canceled. She decided to transfer her right to the car to her friend Maxine. The transfer of a right is called a(n) _____ rather than a(n) _____, which is a transfer of a duty. Holly was the _____, and Maxine was the _____. Enrique agreed to deal solely with Maxine and to release Holly from all obligations under the contract, thus creating a(n) _____. Enrique and Maxine were in _____, which is the legal name for the relationship that existed between them. When the time for _____— that is, the carrying out of the contract—arrived, Enrique made _____ by offering to turn the car over to Maxine. She offered to pay him with Mexican pesos, which is not _____ in the United States. Enrique refused the _____ but then reached an agreement with Maxine to change the price for the car to $6,000 and to postpone the time for performance for a week. This agreement to change the performance is called a(n) _____.

When the agreed-upon performance is completed, it will be known as a(n) _____. The next day Maxine told Enrique that she had changed her mind and was not going to buy the car. Because this occurred before the time for performance had arrived, it is known as a(n) _____. Enrique would not be able to ask the court to order _____, because the subject matter of the contract was not unique. Similarly, because the parties had not agreed on damages at the time of the execution of the contract, no _____ existed. If Enrique suffered no actual monetary loss because of the _____ by Maxine, he would be able to recover only _____ from her in court, plus _____ to take care of any reasonable expenses resulting from the breach. Enrique owed a duty to Maxine to _____ the damages—that is, keep them as low as possible. This case was not one involving _____ or _____ such as double or triple the amount of actual damages. The _____ _____—that is, the time limit for bringing suit—had not run out.

PUZZLING OVER WHAT YOU LEARNED

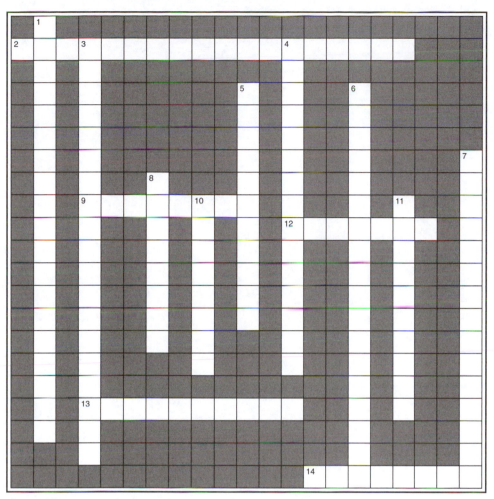

Caveat: Allow squares for spaces between words and punctuation (apostrophes, hyphens, etc.) when filling in crossword.

Across

2. The failure of a party to a contract to carry out its terms.
9. One who transfers a right by assignment.
12. Compensation in money for loss or injury.
13. The transfer of a right from one person to another.
14. One to whom a right is transferred by assignment.

Down

1. The relationship that exists between two or more contracting parties.
3. Announcement before time for performance of a breach of contract.
4. Damages in name only.
5. Discharging a contract by doing that which one agreed to do.
6. Damages agreed to at the time of the execution of a contract.
7. A time that may be fairly allowed depending on the circumstances.
8. Lessen; keep as low as possible.
10. An agreement whereby an original party to a contract is replaced.
11. The transfer of a duty by one person to another.

PART FIVE

Terms Used in Law of Personal Property and Agency

5

We are surrounded by personal property from the moment we are born to the moment we die. In fact, whether for good or bad, much of our lives is spent in the pursuit of more personal property of one kind or another. In addition, we are touched by the law of agency in many aspects of our lives, either by dealing with people who are principals, agents, employers, and employees, or by being involved in those roles ourselves. Chapter 21 discusses contracts for the sale of goods (a common type of personal property) and then gives an explanation of bailments. Chapter 22 covers the subject of intellectual property, including patents, copyrights, trademarks, and trade secrets. Chapter 23 begins by distinguishing among the different kinds of agency relationships and continues with an examination of the various kinds of agents, the authority of agents, and the subject of vicarious liability.

Personal Property and Bailments

ANTE INTERROGATORY

When you borrow a cup of sugar from a neighbor, with the intention of returning the sugar, it is known as a (A) bailment for the sole benefit of the bailor, (B) mutuum, (C) mutual benefit bailment, (D) bailment for the sole benefit of the bailee.

CHAPTER OUTLINE

Sale of Goods
    Electronic Commerce

Warranties
Auction Sales
Bailments

KEY TERMS

auction sale *(AWK·shen)*

auction with reserve *(ree·ZERV)*

auction without reserve

bailee *(bay·LEE)*

bailment *(BALE·ment)*

bailment for the sole benefit of the bailee
    (bay·LEE)

bailment for the sole benefit of the bailor
    (bay·LOR)

bailor *(bay·LOR)*

bidder *(BID·er)*

bill of sale

bulk transfer *(TRANS·fer)*

chattels *(CHAT·els)*

chose in action (singular) *(shohz in AK·shun)*

conforming goods *(kon·FORM·ing)*

contract to sell *(KON·trakt)*

cover *(KUV·er)*

cure *(kyoor)*

destination contract *(des·te·NAY·shun*
    KON·trakt)

donee *(doh·NEE)*

donor *(DOH··ner)*

e-commerce *(EE·KOM·ers)*

express warranty *(eks·PRESS WAR·en·tee)*

fixture *(FIKS·cher)*

f.o.b. the place of destination
    (des·te·NAY·shun)

f.o.b. the place of shipment *(SHIP·ment)*

full warranty *(WAR·en·tee)*

fungible goods *(FUN·ji·bel)*

future goods *(FEW·cher)*

goods

gratuitous bailment *(gra·TOO·i·tes*
    BAYL·ment)

identified goods *(eye·DENT·i·fyd)*

implied warranty *(im·PLIDE WAR·en·tee)*

5

intangible personal property *(in·TAN·je·bel PER·son·al PROP·er·tee)*

limited warranty *(LIM·i·ted WAR·en·tee)*

merchant *(MER·chent)*

mutual benefit bailment *(MYOO·choo·el BEN·e·fit BAYL·ment)*

mutuum *(MYOO·choo·um)*

nonconforming goods *(non·kon·FORM·ing)*

output contract *(OWT·put KON·trakt)*

personal property *(PER·son·el PROP·er·tee)*

personalty *(PER·sen·el·tee)*

puffing

requirements contract *(re·KWIRE·ments KON·trakt)*

risk of loss

sale

sale on approval *(a·PROOV·el)*

sale or return *(re·TURN)*

shipment contract *(SHIP·ment KON·trakt)*

tangible personal property *(TAN·je·bel PER·son·al PROP·er·tee)*

title *(TY·tel)*

tortious bailee *(TOR·shus bay·LEE)*

trade fixture *(FIKS·cher)*

Uniform Commercial Code *(YOON·i·form ke·MERSH·el kode)*

warranty of fitness for a particular purpose *(WAR·en·tee ov FIT·ness)*

warranty of merchantability *(WAR·en·tee ov mer·chent·a·BIL·e·tee)*

warranty of title *(WAR·en·tee ov TY·tel)*

Broadly speaking, **personal property**, also called **personalty** or **chattels**, is anything that is the subject of ownership other than real property (real estate). **Tangible personal property** is property that has substance and that can be touched, such as a flat screen television, an item of clothing, or an automobile. **Intangible personal property** conversely, is property that is not perceptible to the senses and cannot be touched, such as ownership interests in partnerships or corporations; patents, copyrights, and trademarks; and claims against others, both in tort and in contract. Such an intangible interest or claim, including a check or promissory note, is also called **chose in action** (singular; the plural is choses in action), which means evidence of the right to a property but not the property itself.

When personal property is physically attached to real property, it is known as a **fixture** and becomes part of the real property. A built-in dishwasher and a permanently installed lighting unit are examples of fixtures. In contrast, when a business tenant physically attaches personal property, such as machinery, that is necessary to carry on the trade or business to real property, it is called a **trade fixture**. It does not become part of the real property and may be removed by the business tenant upon termination of the tenancy.

SALE OF GOODS

The **Uniform Commercial Code (UCC)** is a set of model statutes governing various types of commercial activities, and it has been adopted in whole or in part in every state. When adopted by a jurisdiction, the UCC's legal rules replace the common law contract doctrines that have evolved over the centuries. A common commercial activity is a contract for the sale of goods, and the UCC's statutes on sales of goods (Article 2 of the UCC) apply everywhere (except in Louisiana) and concern all sales of goods, whether transacted by businesses or by persons. **Goods** may be defined as "personal property; anything that is movable." Your books, clothing, motor vehicles, computers, furniture, food, animals, and growing crops are all examples of goods—another name for tangible personal property. If the goods are not yet in existence (such as goods not yet manufactured) or under anyone's control (such as fish not yet caught), they are known as **future goods**. If they are the type of goods that are usually sold by weight or measure and are stored in bulk quantities, such as grain or oil, they are called **fungible goods**. These are defined as goods of which any unit is the same as any like unit.

If the goods that are delivered to the buyer are in accordance with the obligations under the contract, they are called **conforming goods**. In contrast, if the goods are not the same as those called for under the contract or are defective, they are called **nonconforming goods**. Sellers who deliver nonconforming goods are allowed to **cure** (correct) the defect if they do so within the contract period. If the defect is not cured, buyers have the right to **cover** the sale—that is, buy similar goods from someone else and bring suit for the difference between the agreed price and the cost of the purchase. **Identified goods** is the name given to specific goods that have been selected as the subject matter of a contract. Goods must be identified as those goods to which a contract refers before title to them can pass from a seller to a buyer.

A contract for *services* is not governed by the UCC because it is not a sale of goods. Such a contract is governed by the common law of contracts, discussed in Chapters 18–20. Some contracts, however, involve the sale of goods and services associated with the goods (in-home installation of a new appliance, for instance). According to the UCC, if the predominate factor in the contract is the sales of goods, then everything in the contract is governed by the UCC.

A **sale** is defined by the Uniform Commercial Code as "the passing of **title** (ownership) from the seller to the buyer for a price." Sometimes, a **bill of sale** a signed writing evidencing the transfer of personal property from one person to another, is given by the seller to the buyer. If title is to pass at a future time, the transaction is called a **contract to sell** rather than a sale. A **sale on approval** occurs when the goods are for the buyer's use (consumer goods) rather than for resale (commercial goods), and they may be returned even though they conform to the contract. Such goods remain the property of the seller until the buyer's approval is expressed or a reasonable time elapses. In contrast, a **sale or return** occurs when the goods are primarily for resale and may be returned even though they conform to the contract. In this latter instance, title passes to the buyer at the time of sale, but reverts to the seller if and when the goods are returned. The key distinction between a sale on approval and a sale or return is that the buyer bears the **risk of loss** (responsibility in case of damage or destruction) in a sale or return until the goods have been returned to the seller. A gift is not a sale, because the person receiving the gift (the **donee**) pays no price to the person making the gift (the **donor**).

Sometimes, businesses will dispose of their entire stock of merchandise and other supplies in one transaction. This disposal is called a **bulk transfer**, which is defined as "a transfer not in the ordinary course of business, but in bulk of a major part of the materials, supplies, merchandise, or other inventory of an enterprise." When a bulk transfer is made, all creditors of the transferor must be notified of the forthcoming transfer at least 10 days before the transfer occurs. This notice gives creditors time, if they wish, to attach the goods before the goods are transferred. In this way, creditors can have the goods sold under the supervision of the court and obtain the money owed to them.

Unique terms are used to describe certain contracts for goods. A contract to sell "all the goods a company manufactures" or "all the crops a farmer grows" is called an **output contract**. In contrast, a contract to buy "all the fuel needed for one year" is called a **requirements contract**. A contract under which the seller turns the goods over to a carrier for delivery to a buyer is termed a **shipment contract** and is often designated **f.o.b. the place of shipment** (such as Boston), meaning free onboard (no delivery charges) to the place of shipment. In a shipment contract, title to the goods and **risk of loss** pass to the buyer when the goods are turned over to a carrier. On the other hand, a contract that requires the seller to deliver goods to a destination is called a **destination contract** and is designated **f.o.b. the place of destination** (such as Chicago). In a destination contract, title and risk of loss pass to the buyer when the goods are tendered at their destination, and the shipper (e.g., in Boston) assumes ownership responsibility until then.

▌ TERMS IN ACTION

After noticing an advertisement for a mail order coin club, a New York man joined the club and ordered some coins valued at almost $600 (which was a lot of money in 1976). The coin company sent the coins by registered mail, which required someone to sign for the package. The postal service delivered the coins to the man's address, and someone signed for the package, but the man claimed that he never received them and refused to pay for the coins. The coin company sued for breach of contract, and the issue came down to whether the coins, which are **goods** and therefore covered by the **Uniform Commercial Code**, were sold as a **sale on approval** or a **sale or return**. The appellate court concluded that, because the buyer was a coin collector, but wasn't in the business of selling coins, he didn't qualify as a **merchant**. Therefore, the sale was a sale on approval, which makes a seller liable for the goods until they have been received and approved (accepted). Even though the coin company could prove that the package was signed for at the buyer's address, the buyer wasn't the one who signed for them, and since there was no proof that the buyer had the coins, he didn't have to pay for them.

Source: *First Coinvesters, Inc. v. Coppola*, 388 N.Y.S.2d 833 (N.Y. Dist. Ct. 1976)

Electronic Commerce

Shopping, paying bills, and doing business on the Internet have become a way of life for many people. The general term that describes this practice is **e-commerce** (electronic commerce)—the buying and selling of goods and services or the transfer of money over the Internet.

Web Wise

Learn more about e-commerce at the following sites:

- http://www.google.com and type "e-commerce"
- http://www.ilr.cornell.edu and type "e-commerce" in the Search bar
- http://e-comm.webopedia.com/

Warranties

Sellers of goods often guarantee their products by making promises or statements of fact about them. This guarantee is known as an **express warranty** and comes about when sellers, as part of a transaction, make statements of fact or promises about the goods, describe them, or show samples of them. On the other hand, statements made by sellers that are opinions and attempts to put their goods in the best light possible are not warranties, but are known as **puffing**. Under federal law, when a **full warranty** is given for consumer goods, the seller must repair or replace, without cost to the buyer, defective goods or else refund the purchase price. Any express warranty that does less must be labeled a **limited warranty**.

An **implied warranty** is one that is imposed by law rather than given voluntarily by the seller. Two kinds are (1) the warranty of merchantability, and (2) the warranty of fitness for a particular purpose.

The **warranty of merchantability** is made whenever merchants sell goods. It is not given by private parties. Merchants warrant, among other guarantees, that their goods are fit for the ordinary purpose for which they are to be used. A **merchant** is a person who sells goods of the kind sold in the ordinary course of business or who has knowledge or skills peculiar to those goods.

The **warranty of fitness for a particular purpose** is made when any buyer relies on a seller's skill and judgment in selecting the goods. When this happens, the seller impliedly warrants that the goods are fit for the purpose for which they are to be used.

Implied warranties may be excluded by the seller by indicating in a conspicuous fashion that they are excluded or by writing "as is" or "with all faults" on the sales slip. Exclusion of these warranties is not effective when express warranties are made for consumer goods.

Another warranty that is made by all sellers of goods, whether merchants or not, is called the **warranty of title**. This warrants that the title being conveyed is good, that the transfer is rightful, and that no unknown liens on the goods exist. Unlike other implied warranties, the warranty of title cannot be excluded by the seller.

5

TERMS IN ACTION

It can be difficult to know when a seller's positive statements about the quality of its goods become a **warranty**. In a case from Indiana, a farming corporation that made a substantial portion of its revenues from selling watermelons ordered about 40 pounds of watermelon seeds from a seed company. The seeds were "Prince Charles," a type of seed known for its resistance to disease. On the top of the cans in which the seeds were shipped was a label that described the seeds as "top quality seeds with high vitality, vigor and germination." But when the watermelons grew and became diseased, the buyer sued the seller for breach of express and implied warranties. In interpreting Indiana's version of the UCC's warranty requirements, the Indiana Supreme Court held that the phrase "top quality seeds" didn't qualify as a warranty, because it lacked a definite assertion of fact about the quality of the seeds. That statement was considered **puffing**. But the court concluded that the seller's claim that the seeds had "high vitality, vigor and germination" could qualify as an express warranty, as well as the **implied warranty of merchantability**, which is an implied warranty applying only to **merchants**.

Source: *Martin Rispens & Son v. Hall Farms, Inc.*, 621 N.E.2d 1078 (Ind. 1993), reversed on other grounds

Auction Sales

An **auction sale** is a sale of property to the highest **bidder** (offeror). In an **auction with reserve** the auctioneer may withdraw the goods without accepting the highest bid. In contrast, in an **auction without reserve** the auctioneer may not withdraw the goods after one bid has been placed. An auction is presumed to be *with reserve* unless otherwise stated by the auctioneer. Those who sell goods through online bidding sites, such as eBay, need to be clear in communicating the type of auctions in which they are engaged.

BAILMENTS

A **bailment** occurs whenever one person places personal property in the possession of another person without intending to transfer title to that person. For example, a bailment occurs when someone leaves a car with an auto repair shop to be fixed, loans a lawnmower to a neighbor, or takes care of a friend's goldfish for a week. The one who owns the goods and places them in the possession of another person is the **bailor**. The one who takes possession of the goods is the **bailee**. It is not a bailment when someone borrows something such as a cup of sugar and intends to return a similar amount of the same goods, because the exact item that was borrowed will not be returned. Instead of a bailment, that type of borrowing is known as a **mutuum**.

It is called a **mutual benefit bailment** when both the bailor and the bailee benefit from the transactions. For example, when someone leaves a watch with a jeweler to be repaired, the watch owner receives the benefit of having the watch repaired, and the jeweler receives the benefit of being paid for the service rendered. In this type of bailment, the bailee owes a duty to use ordinary care toward the property and would be responsible for ordinary negligence if the goods were lost or damaged.

A **gratuitous bailment** is one in which no consideration is given by one of the parties in exchange for the benefits bestowed by the other. It may be for the sole benefit of either the bailor or the bailee. For example, if someone stores his or her car in a friend's garage for safekeeping while away on a trip, it would be a **bailment for the sole benefit of the bailor**. In this type of bailment, the bailee owes a duty to exercise only slight care over the property and would be responsible only for gross negligence, because he or she is receiving no benefit. When someone loans a camera or other item to a friend, conversely, it is a **bailment for the sole benefit of the bailee**. Here, the bailee owes a duty to use great care with the property and would be responsible for even slight negligence in the event of loss or damage to the bailed property.

A **tortious bailee** is one who has intentional, wrongful possession of another's goods. For example, a person who takes another's goods without authority, or keeps another's goods after they should be returned, or uses another's goods for a purpose other than agreed upon is a tortious bailee.

Word Wise
More Words Ending in "or" and "ee"

assignor (ass·en·OR)	a person who transfers contract rights or property to another
assignee (ass·en·EE)	one to whom contract rights or property is transferred
bailor (bay·LOR)	one who transfers goods to another temporarily
bailee (bay·LEE)	one to whom goods are transferred temporarily
consignor (kon·sine·OR)	a party shipping goods under a bill of lading
consignee (kon·sine·EE)	a party to whom goods are shipped under a bill of lading
donor (doh·NOR)	one who makes a gift
donee (doh·NEE)	one to whom a gift is made

Reviewing What You Learned

After studying the chapter, write the answers to each of the following questions:

1. Name and give an example of each of the two kinds of personal property.

2. What is the difference between a fixture and a trade fixture?

3. What do "goods" include?

4. What is the name given to the type of goods that are usually sold by weight or measure and are stored in bulk quantities?

5. Why is a gift not a sale?

6. Under what circumstances do express warranties come about?

5

7. What is the difference between a full warranty and a limited warranty?

_____

_____

_____

8. Under what conditions is the warranty of merchantability made, and what does it include?

_____

_____

_____

9. Under what conditions is the warranty of fitness for a particular purpose made?

_____

_____

_____

10. How may implied warranties be excluded?

_____

_____

_____

11. What is the warranty of title, and who makes it?

_____

_____

12. Under what circumstances does a bailment occur?

_____

_____

_____

13. Why is it not a bailment when someone borrows a cup of sugar from a neighbor?

_____

_____

_____

14. Give an example of a mutual benefit bailment.

_____

_____

_____

15. Give an example of a bailment for the sole benefit of the bailor.

_____

_____

_____

16. Why does the bailee in a bailment for the sole benefit of the bailor owe a duty to use only slight care over the property?

_____

_____

_____

17. Give an example of a tortious bailee.

_____

_____

_____

Understanding Legal Concepts

Indicate whether each statement is true or false. Then, change the italicized word or phrase of each false statement to make it true.

ANSWERS

_____ 1. *Tangible* personal property is property that is not perceptible to the senses and cannot be touched.

_____ 2. Goods that are not yet in existence or under anyone's control are called *fungible* goods.

_____ 3. Under federal law, when a *limited* warranty is given for consumer goods, the seller must repair or replace, without cost to the buyer, defective goods or else refund the purchase price.

_____ 4. The warranty of *merchantability* is made whenever merchants sell goods.

_____ 5. Implied warranties *may be* excluded by writing "as is" on the sales slip.

_____ 6. The warranty of *title* cannot be excluded by the seller.

_____ 7. It is a *bailment* when someone borrows a cup of sugar from a neighbor.

_____ 8. In a mutual benefit bailment, the bailee owes a duty to use *slight* care toward the property.

_____ 9. In a bailment for the sole benefit of the bailee, the bailee owes a duty to use *great* care with the property.

_____ 10. A person who uses another's goods for a purpose other than agreed upon is a *tortious bailee*.

Checking Terminology (Part A)

From the list of legal terms that follows, select the one that matches each definition.

ANSWERS

a. auction sale
b. auction with reserve
c. auction without reserve
d. bailee
e. bailment
f. bailment for the sole benefit of the bailee
g. bailment for the sole benefit of the bailor
h. bailor
i. bidder
j. bill of sale
k. bulk transfer
l. chose in action
m. conforming goods
n. contract to sell
o. contract to sell
p. cover
q. cure
r. destination contract
s. donee
t. donor
u. e-commerce
v. express warranty
w. fixture
x. f.o.b. the place of destination
y. f.o.b. the place of shipment
z. full warranty
aa. fungible goods
bb. future goods
cc. goods

_____ 1. Offeror.
_____ 2. Correct.
_____ 3. A Contract under which title to goods is to pass at a future time.
_____ 4. Personal property that is physically attached to real property and becomes part of the real property.
_____ 5. An auction in which the auctioneer may withdraw the goods without accepting the highest bid.
_____ 6. Goods that are not yet in existence or under anyone's control.
_____ 7. Goods that are in accordance with the obligations under the contract.
_____ 8. Anything that is movable.
_____ 9. A gratuitous bailment benefiting only the bailor.
_____ 10. An auction in which the auctioneer must sell the goods to the highest bidder.
_____ 11. Free-on-board (no delivery charges) to the place of shipment (the shipper).
_____ 12. A contract that requires the seller to deliver goods to a destination.
_____ 13. A signed writing evidencing the transfer of personal property from one person to another.
_____ 14. The relationship that exists when possession (but not ownership) of personal property is transferred to another for a specific purpose.
_____ 15. A sale of property to the highest bidder.
_____ 16. Free on-board (no delivery charges) to the place of destination (the receiver).
_____ 17. A person who receives a gift.
_____ 18. The owner of personal property that has been temporarily transferred to a bailee under a contract of bailment.
_____ 19. An express warranty given for consumer goods under which the seller must repair or replace, without cost to the buyer, defective goods or else refund the purchase price.
_____ 20. Evidence of the right to property, but not the property itself.
_____ 21. A statement of fact or promise that goods have certain qualities.
_____ 22. The person to whom personal property is delivered under a contract of bailment.
_____ 23. A person who gives a gift.
_____ 24. Goods such as grain or oil, of which any unit is the same as any like unit.
_____ 25. A transfer not in the ordinary course of business, but in bulk, of a major part of the materials, supplies, merchandise, or other inventory of an enterprise.
_____ 26. The right of a buyer, after breach by a seller, to purchase similar goods from someone else.
_____ 27. A gratuitous bailment benefiting only the bailee.
_____ 28. The buying and selling of goods and services or the transfer of money over the internet.

Checking Terminology (Part B)

From the list of legal terms that follows, select the one that matches each definition.

ANSWERS

a. chattels
b. gratuitous bailment
c. identified goods
d. implied warranty
e. intangible personal property
f. limited warranty
g. merchant
h. mutual benefit bailment

_____ 1. Ownership.
_____ 2. A loan of goods, on the agreement that the borrower may consume them and will return to the lender an equivalent in kind and quantity.
_____ 3. A law in every state that governs different types of commercial transactions.
_____ 4. A bailment for the sole benefit of either the bailor or the bailee, in which no consideration is given by one of the parties in exchange for the benefits bestowed by the other.
_____ 5. Property that has substance and that can be touched.
_____ 6. A contract to sell "all the goods a company manufactures" or "all the crops a farmer grows."

i. mutuum
j. nonconforming goods
k. output contract
l. personal property
m. personalty
n. puffing
o. requirements contract
p. risk of loss
q. sale
r. sale on approval
s. sale or return
t. shipment contract
u. tangible personal property
v. title
w. tortious bailee
x. trade fixture
y. Uniform Commercial Code
z. warranty of fitness for a
   particular purpose
aa. warranty of merchantability
bb. Warranty of Title

_____ 7. An implied warranty, given by merchants in all sales unless excluded, that goods are fit for the ordinary purpose for which such goods are used.

_____ 8. An express warranty given for consumer goods that is less than a full warranty.

_____ 9. A sale of goods that are primarily for resale and may be returned even though they conform to the contract.

_____ 10. Anything that is the subject of ownership other than real property. (Select three answers.)

_____ 11. A guarantee that title is good, that the transfer is rightful, and that no unknown liens on the goods exist.

_____ 12. The passing of title from the seller to the buyer for a price.

_____ 13. A warranty that is imposed by law rather than given voluntarily.

_____ 14. An implied warranty, given when a buyer relies on any seller's skill and judgment in selecting goods, that the goods will be fit for a particular purpose.

_____ 15. Goods that are not the same as those called for under the contract.

_____ 16. A contract under which the seller turns the goods over to a carrier for delivery to a buyer.

_____ 17. Goods that have been selected as the subject matter of a contract.

_____ 18. A sale of goods that are for the buyer's use rather than for resale and that may be returned even though they conform to the contract.

_____ 19. A bailment in which both the bailor and the bailee receive some benefit.

_____ 20. Responsibility in case of damage or destruction.

_____ 21. Personal property, necessary to carry on a trade or business, that is physically attached to real property, but does not become part of the real property.

_____ 22. Property that is not perceptible to the senses and that cannot be touched.

_____ 23. A contract to buy "all the fuel (or other goods) needed for one year."

_____ 24. A person who sells goods of the kind sold in the ordinary course of business or who has knowledge or skills peculiar to those goods.

_____ 25. A person who is wrongfully in possession of another's personal property.

_____ 26. Statements made by a seller that are opinions and attempts to put their goods in the best light possible; not warranties.

Using Legal Language

Read the following story and fill in the blank lines with legal terms taken from the list of terms at the beginning of this chapter.

Roland went shopping for an outdoor gas grill to give to his friend Rita for her birthday. Broadly speaking, the grill would be called _____, _____, or _____, because it is the subject of ownership other than real property. Because it has substance and can be touched, it is _____. It is also called _____, because it is movable. The grill that Roland looked at had a 90-day guarantee, which is known as a(n) _____ in legal terminology. The guarantee was not a(n) _____, however, because any defective part would have to be shipped at the buyer's expense to the factory for repair or replacement. For that reason, the guarantee is known as a (n) _____. In addition, a(n) _____ would exist—

that is, a type of guarantee that is imposed by law. Called the _____, it guarantees that the goods are fit for the ordinary purpose for which they are to be used and is made when goods are sold by a(n) _____ —that is, one who sells goods of the kind sold in the ordinary course of business. This guarantee was not a(n) _____, because Roland did not rely on the seller's skill and judgment in selecting the grill. When Roland bought the grill, it was a(n) _____ because _____ (ownership) passed from the seller to the buyer for a price. Had title passed at a future time, it would have been called a(n) _____. Under its _____, the store guaranteed that title to the grill was good and that its transfer was rightful. When Roland gave the grill to Rita, he was the _____, and she was the _____. The next morning, Rita left the gas tank in the possession of a bottled-gas company to be filled and picked up later, creating a(n) _____. Rita was the _____; the bottled-gas company was the _____. Because both parties benefited from the transaction, it was a(n) _____. The gas that was put into the tank is known as _____,

because any unit is the same as any like unit. Rita paid for the gas by check, which is a(n) _____, or a type of _____. Rita's neighbor Ruth borrowed not only her grill, but also some hot dogs that Rita had in the freezer. The loan of the grill was a(n) _____, because no consideration was given, and the loan of the hot dogs was a(n) _____, because the identical ones would not be returned. Ruth moved away without returning Rita's grill, becoming a(n) _____.

PUZZLING OVER WHAT YOU LEARNED

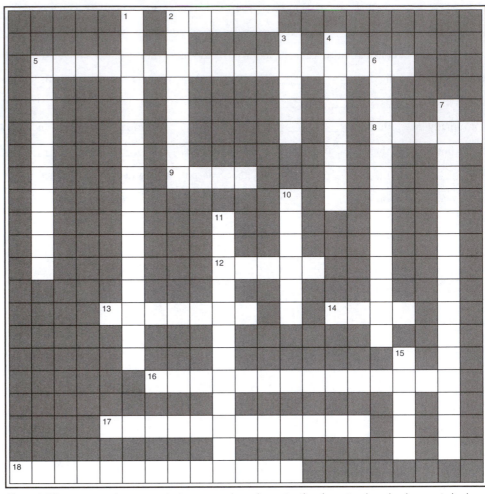

Caveat: Allow squares for spaces between words and punctuation (apostrophes, hyphens, etc.) when filling in crossword.

Across

2. The right of a buyer, after breach by a seller, to purchase similar goods from someone else.
5. Anything that is the subject of ownership other than real property.
8. A person who gives a gift.
9. The passing of title from the seller to the buyer for a price.
12. Ownership.
13. Personal property attached to real property.
14. Correct.
16. Goods such as grain or oil, of which any unit is the same as any like unit.
17. Written evidence of the transfer of personalty from one person to another.
18. A transfer in bulk of the majority of a merchant's inventory.

Down

1. Evidence of the right to property but not the property itself.
2. Anything that is the subject of ownership other than real property.
3. Anything that is movable.
4. Person who sells goods of the kind sold in the ordinary course of business.
5. Another name for personal property.
6. Personal property attached to real property necessary for business.
7. Contract under which title to goods is passed at a future time.
10. Owner of personal property that has been temporarily transferred to a bailee.
11. Goods that are not yet in existence or under anyone's control.
15. A person who receives a gift.

5

Intellectual Property

ANTE INTERROGATORY

The exclusive right given to an author, composer, artist, or photographer to exclusively publish and sell a work for the life of the author plus 70 years is called (A) a copyright, (B) a trademark, (C) a patent, (D) a trade secret.

CHAPTER OUTLINE

Patents

Copyrights

Trademarks

Trade Secrets

KEY TERMS

confidentiality agreement *(kon·fe·den·shee·AL·i·tee a·GREE·ment)*

copyright *(KOP·ee·rite)*

copyright infringement *(KOP·ee·rite in·FRINJ·ment)*

enjoin *(en·JOYN)*

fair-use doctrine *(DOK·trin)*

generic term *(jen·ER·ik)*

injunction *(in·JUNK·shun)*

intellectual property (IP) *(in·te·LEK·choo·el PROP·er·tee)*

nondisclosure agreement *(non·dis·KLOH·zher a·GREE·ment)*

patent *(PAT·ent)*

patent infringement *(PAT·ent in·FRINJ·ment)*

privileges and immunities clause *(PRIV·i·leg·es and im·YOON·i·teez)*

public domain *(PUB·lik doh·MAYN)*

servicemark *(SER·viss·mark)*

trademark *(TRADE·mark)*

trade secret *(SEE·kret)*

5

Intellectual property (IP) is a category of property that is the result of intellectual creativity. It is the creations of the mind, or can be thought of as an original work fixed in a tangible medium of expression. The term is a broad, encompassing term used to describe the fields of patents, copyrights, trademarks, and trade secrets. Examples of intellectual property are literary and artistic works, inventions, audio and video recordings, computer programs, and trade secrets (e.g., the 11 herbs and spices in Kentucky Fried Chicken). Owners of such property are given protection by the government to prevent their creative works from being taken and used, without authority, by others. In fact, the U.S.

Constitution gives authority to Congress to protect the creation of intellectual property, which is done by granting authors and inventors some form of a limited monopoly over their work. Intellectual property law is often abbreviated "IP law."

PATENTS

A **patent** is a grant by the U.S. Government of the exclusive right to make, use, and sell an invention for 20 years. For protection, inventors may have their inventions patented by the U.S. Patent and Trademark Office in Arlington, Virginia. But in order to qualify for patent status, the invention must be new, useful, and nonobvious to a person with ordinary skill in that particular field. A *utility patent* is granted for the invention of a new process or item of manufacture. In contrast, a *design patent* is given (for a 14-year period) on the way an item is fashioned; that is, the way it looks. For example, the curvy shape of the Coca-Cola bottle was granted a design patent in 1915. Utility and design patents can be obtained for the same invention. A *plant patent* is issued for asexually producing a new plant; that is, by other than the use of seeds—for example, by grafting. When the 20-year period expires, the invention loses its protection and becomes part of the **public domain**—that is, it is no longer protected for anyone claiming ownership. When an invention falls into the public domain, the invention may be made, used, or sold by anyone, including the original inventor.

■ TERMS IN ACTION

In order to qualify for **patent** protection, an invention must be deemed "useful." Evidently, that was the case for the invention of Albert Cohen, who received U.S. Patent No. 5,356,330 on October 18, 1994, for his device: a spring-loaded mechanical high-five device. Intended to satisfy the desires of people who watch sports at home alone, the "Hi-5" can be attached onto the wall, allowing the solo sports enthusiast to turn and slap an enthusiastic high-five after a home-run or touchdown, or whatever suits the fan's fancy. The device has a hand and forearm facing up, with the rest of the arm above the elbow at a 90-degree angle. Unfortunately, it does not pat you on the shoulder if your team loses.

Sources: findarticles.com; uspto.gov

5

A **patent infringement** is the unauthorized making, using, or selling of a patented invention during the term of the patent. Federal courts have the power to enjoin anyone from infringing on another's patent. **Enjoin** means to require a person to perform or to abstain from some act, and it is usually done by the court's issuance of an **injunction**, which is an order to do or refrain from doing a particular act.

COPYRIGHTS

A **copyright** is the exclusive right given to an author, composer, artist, or photographer to publish and sell a work for the life of the author plus 70 years. The things that may be copyrighted include the following: literary works; pantomime and choreographic works; pictorial, graphic, and sculptural works; motion pictures and other audiovisual works; and sound recordings. Computer programs fall under the category of literary works and may also be copyrighted.

In 1998, Congress enacted the Sonny Bono Act (named after a Congressman who was once the shorter half of Sonny and Cher, and who died in a skiing accident in 1998), which extended the life of a copyright from 50 to 70 years after the author's death. The act was held to be constitutional by the U.S. Supreme Court in 2003.

To register a copyright, it is necessary to fill out a government form and send it with the proper fee and two copies of the work to the U.S. Copyright Office in Washington, D.C. Although formerly required, it is now optional to put the symbol © or the word "copyright," followed by the date and the name of the owner, on the work. But copyright protection begins at the moment one's creative work is "fixed in a tangible medium," which is a fancy way of saying that one doesn't need to register a copyrighted work in order to own it, under copyright law. However, ideas aren't copyrightable. So, for example, there's no protection when an author tells a friend what his next great novel plot is; but, there is protection when the author writes the plot down on paper.

Copyrighted work may not be reproduced without permission of the copyright owner. The unauthorized use of copyrighted material is known as **copyright infringement**. Under the **fair-use doctrine**, however, the fair use (limited copying) of a copyrighted work for purposes such as criticism, comment, news reporting, teaching (including making multiple copies for classroom use), scholarship, or research is not a copyright infringement.

▋ TERMS IN ACTION

Fred Lawrence, of Racine Wisconsin, was like most grandpas: completely unaware of what his grandchildren do on his computer. So, when his 12-year-old grandson downloaded four movies onto Lawrence's computer, the Motion Picture Association of America (MPAA) came calling. In 2005, it sued Mr. Lawrence for **copyright infringement**, seeking over $600,000 in damages, an amount allowed by federal law. Electronic copyright infringement is blamed on the IP address, not necessarily the one who is illegally downloading the files. In the case at hand, Mr. Lawrence's grandson acknowledged downloading "The Grudge," "I Robot," "The Incredibles," and "The Forgotten," even though his family already owned three of those movies. The MPAA initially sought $4,000 from Lawrence, but when he refused to pay, it sued him. After a publicity ruckus, a settlement was reached, requiring the boy to publicly apologize and to speak at a school assembly about the risks of illegally downloading copyrighted materials.

Sources: msnbc.msn.com; p2pnet.net

TRADEMARKS

A **trademark** is any word, name, symbol, or device used by a business to identify goods and distinguish them from those manufactured or sold by others. A **servicemark** is the term used to describe trademark protection for services.

In addition to being established by usage under the common law, trademarks may be obtained from state governments by following state trademark laws. The most common type of trademark, however, is one obtained by registering with the U.S. Patent and Trademark Office. A federal trademark provides protection for 10 years and may be renewed for additional 10-year periods. Under the federal law, an application to register a trademark may be filed six months before the mark is used in commerce. The mark then becomes reserved and cannot be used by anyone else for six months. An additional six-month reservation period is allowed, and other extensions may be obtained by showing good cause. The trademark registration becomes effective when the mark is actually used in the ordinary course of trade.

Although not required by law, notice that a trademark is registered with the federal government may be given by using the symbol ® or by using the phrase "Registered in U.S. Patent

5

& Trademark Office" or "Reg. U.S. Pat. & Tm. Off." If the mark is not federally registered, the symbol ® may not be used. The symbol ™ or ^{SM} may be used, however, to give notice of the trademark or servicemark established by usage under the common law. No symbol has been established to designate state-registered trademarks.

Trademark protection qualifies for those marks that are distinctive, and it can be lost by non-use or by the mark's becoming a generic term used by a large segment of the public for a long period. A **generic term** is a term that relates to, or is characteristic of, a whole group. "Corn flakes," "nylon," "escalator," "bikini," "aspirin," and "yo-yo" are examples of former trademarks that were lost by becoming generic terms. To prevent products from losing their trademarks, businesses use the word "brand" after their product name. They also place advertisements in journals reminding people that their products are trademarked. For example, the Xerox Corporation advertised the following in a 1991 issue of the *ABA Journal*: "You can't Xerox a Xerox on a Xerox, but we don't mind if you copy a copy on a Xerox copier." And in March, 2010, Xerox Corporation placed an ad in the *Hollywood Reporter*, asking that the word, "Xerox" be used only as an adjective (a Xerox copy), not a noun ("a Xerox") or a verb ("Xerox this for me").

TRADE SECRETS

A **trade secret** is a plan, process, or device that is used in business and is known only to employees who need to know the secret to accomplish their work. Examples of trade secrets are customer lists, chemical formulas, food recipes, manufacturing processes, marketing techniques, and pricing methods. Unlike the aforementioned forms of intellectual property, trade secrets take their value from *not* being disclosed and from the trade secret holder's reasonable attempts to protect the secrecy of the information.

Businesses often protect trade secrets by having employees sign **nondisclosure** or **confidentiality agreements** consenting to refrain from disclosing trade secrets to others. Even without

---

Word Wise
The "Gen" in "Generic"

The root "gen-" may mean "birth, origin, or race" as in

> gene
>
> generation
>
> genesis

Or it may mean "type" as in

> gender
>
> generic
>
> genus

How the word is used in the context of a sentence will generally show whether "gen-" indicates "birth" or "type" in a particular word. Consider the use of "gen-" in the following terms found in the text:

> miscegenation
>
> general agent
>
> primogeniture
>
> genocide
>
> generic term

such an agreement, however, courts prohibit employees from disclosing their employer's trade secrets both while they are employed and after they leave the employment. When this employee duty is violated, courts will often enjoin the use of the trade secret by others to whom the secret has been given.

Reviewing What you Learned

After studying the chapter, write the answers to each of the following questions:

1. Name the fields that "intellectual property" describes.

2. What are the requirements for an invention to be patented?

3. Describe what happens to an invention when the protection period covered by a patent expires.

4. What may a court do when a patent infringement occurs?

5. Explain the procedure to copyright a work.

6. When is the copying of a copyrighted work not an infringement?

7. In what three ways may a trademark be obtained?

8. How may a trademark be reserved?

9. When does a trademark registration become effective?

10. For how long may the federal trademark protection period be renewed?

11. How may trademark protection be lost?

12. Give three examples of trade secrets.

13. How do businesses often protect their trade secrets?

14. In what other way are trade secrets protected?

5

Understanding Legal Concepts

Indicate whether each statement is true or false. Then, change the italicized word or phrase of each false statement to make it true.

ANSWERS

_____ 1. A patent owner has the exclusive right to make, use, and sell an invention for *50 years.*

_____ 2. *State* courts have the power to enjoin anyone from infringing on another's patent.

_____ 3. Copyright protection lasts for *the life of the author.*

_____ 4. It is now *optional* to put the symbol © or the word "copyright," followed by the date and the name of the owner, on a copyrighted work.

_____ 5. The fair use of copyrighted work for purposes of teaching, *including making multiple copies for classroom use,* is allowed.

_____ 6. *Trademark* is the term used to describe protection for services.

_____ 7. Trademark protection may be obtained from *state governments.*

_____ 8. The most common type of trademark is obtained by *usage under the common law.*

_____ 9. A registered trademark provides protection for *15 years.*

_____ 10. Trademark protection *can* be lost by the mark's becoming a generic term.

Checking Terminology

From the list of legal terms that follows, select the one that matches each definition.

ANSWERS

a. confidentiality agreement
b. copyright
c. copyright infringement
d. enjoin
e. fair-use doctrine
f. generic term
g. injunction
h. intellectual property
i. nondisclosure agreement
j. patent
k. patent infringement
l. privileges and immunities clause
m. public domain
n. servicemark
o. trademark
p. trade secret

_____ 1. To require a person to perform or to abstain from some act.

_____ 2. An order to do or refrain from doing a particular act.

_____ 3. A term used to describe trademark protection for services.

_____ 4. The unauthorized use of copyrighted material.

_____ 5. A grant by the U.S. government of the exclusive right to make, use, and sell an invention for 20 years.

_____ 6. A rule stating that the use of a copyrighted work for purposes such as criticism, comment, news reporting, teaching, scholarship, or research is not a copyright infringement.

_____ 7. Any word, name, symbol, or device used by a business to identify goods and distinguish them from those manufactured or sold by others.

_____ 8. An agreement to refrain from disclosing trade secrets to others. (Select two answers.)

_____ 9. An original work fixed in a tangible medium of expression.

_____ 10. Owned by the public.

_____ 11. A term that means relating to or characteristic of a whole group.

_____ 12. A secret plan, process, or device that is used in business and is known only to employees who need to know the secret to accomplish their work.

_____ 13. The unauthorized making, using, or selling of a patented invention during the term of the patent.

_____ 14. The exclusive right given to an author, composer, artist, or photographer to publish and sell a work for the life of the author plus 70 years.

_____ 15. A clause in the U.S. Constitution requiring similarly situated persons to receive similar treatment under the law.

Using Legal Language

Read the following story and fill in the blank lines with legal terms taken from the list of terms at the beginning of this chapter:

Millin, an inventor, obtained _____ on two products that she had invented, giving her the exclusive right to make, use, and sell them for 20 years. Since she had obtained one of them more than 20 years ago, it was now in the _____. The other type of _____ (original work fixed in a tangible medium of expression) was much newer and was copied by a competitor, causing Millin to bring a(n) _____ suit for the unauthorized making of the product. Millin won the case, and the court _____ the competitor by issuing a(n) _____ ordering it to refrain from making Millin's product. When Millin began to sell the product, she obtained a(n) _____ for it to identify it and to distinguish it from products made by others. She did not obtain a(n) _____, because the product was a good rather than a service. To prevent the product from becoming a(n) _____, Millin used the word "brand"

in all product advertisements. For further protection, Millin required all of her employees to sign _____, also called _____, agreeing to refrain from disclosing _____ to others. The product turned out to be so successful that she wrote a book about her success. A(n) _____ gave her the exclusive right to publish the book except for a limited amount of copying that could be done by others under a rule known as the _____.

PUZZLING OVER WHAT YOU LEARNED

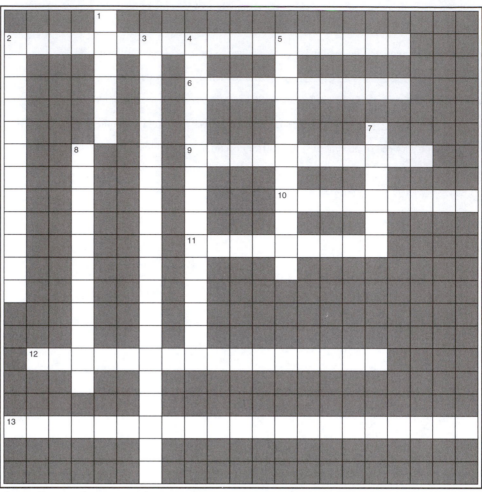

Caveat: Do **not** allow squares for spaces between words and punctuation (apostrophes, hyphens, etc.) when filling in crossword.

Across

2. The unauthorized making, using, or selling of a patented invention during the term of the patent.
6. An order to do or refrain from doing a particular act.
9. A term used to describe trademark protection for services.
10. Any word, name, symbol, or device used by a business to identify goods and distinguish them from those manufactured or sold by others.
11. The exclusive right given to an author, composer, artist, or photographer, to publish and sell exclusively a work for the life of the author plus 70 years.
12. A clause in the U.S. Constitution requiring that no person shall be deprived of life, liberty, or property without fairness and justice.
13. A clause in the U.S. Constitution requiring similarly situated persons to receive similar treatment under the law.

Down

1. To require a person to perform or to abstain from some act.
2. Owned by the public.
3. An original work fixed in a tangible medium of expression.
4. A rule stating that the use of a copyrighted work for purposes such as criticism, comment, news reporting, teaching, scholarship, or research is not a copyright infringement.
5. A term that means relating to or characteristic of a whole group.
7. A grant by the U.S. government of the exclusive right to make, use, and sell an invention for 20 years.
8. A plan, process, or device that is used in business and is known only to employees who need to know the secret to accomplish their work.

Law of Agency

ANTE INTERROGATORY

One who performs services under the direction and control of another is known as a(n) (A) agent, (B) servant, (C) independent contractor, (D) consignee.

CHAPTER OUTLINE

Relationships Distinguished

Kinds of Agents

Authority of Agents

Vicarious Liability

KEY TERMS

agency *(AY·jen·see)*

agency by estoppel *(AY·jen·see by es·TOP·el)*

agency by ratification *(AY·jen·see by rat·i·fi·KAY·shun)*

agent *(AY·jent)*

apparent authority *(a·PAR·ent aw·THAW·ri·tee)*

attorney-in-fact *(a·TERN·ee)*

consignee *(kon·sine·EE)*

consignment *(kon·SINE·ment)*

consignor *(kon·sine·OR)*

del credere agent *(del KREH·de·reh AY·jent)*

dummy corporation *(DUM·mee KOR·por·a·shun)*

employee *(em·PLOY·ee)*

employer *(em·PLOY·er)*

express authority *(eks·PRESS aw·THAW·ri·tee)*

factor *(FAK·ter)*

general agent *(JEN·e·rel AY·jent)*

implied authority *(im·PLIDE aw·THAW·ri·tee)*

impute *(im·PEWT)*

independent contractor *(in·de·PEN·dent KON·trak·ter)*

malfeasance *(mal·FEE·zense)*

master *(MAS·ter)*

misfeasance *(mis·FEE·zense)*

nonfeasance *(non·FEE·zense)*

power of attorney *(POW·er ov a·TERN·ee)*

principal *(PRIN·se·pel)*

respondeat superior *(res·PON·dee·at soo·PEER·ee·or)*

scope of employment *(skope ov em·PLOY·ment)*

servant *(SER·vent)*

special agent *(SPESH·el AY·jent)*

third party *(PAR·tee)*

undisclosed principal *(un·dis·KLOZED PRIN·se·pel)*

vicarious liability *(vy·KEHR·ee·us)*

5

It is common to have one person act on behalf of another in dealing with third parties. Very few businesspeople transact all business on their own behalf. For example, when salespeople sell goods and collect money, they are acting on behalf of the owner of the establishment; when corporate executives sign contracts, they are acting on behalf of the stockholders who own the business.

RELATIONSHIPS DISTINGUISHED

When discussing this subject matter, three types of relationships need to be distinguished: (1) principal–agent, (2) employer–employee, and (3) employer–independent contractor.

An **agency** relationship exists when one person, called an **agent**, is authorized to act on behalf of, and under the control of, another person, called a **principal**. The person with whom the agent deals is known as the **third party**. When a principal authorizes an agent to enter into a contract on the principal's behalf, the resulting contract is between the principal and the third party. The authorized agent is not a party to the contract and cannot be sued for its breach. Only when an agent acts without authority or fails to disclose the existence of the agency relationship can the agent be held liable on the contract by the third party.

When the third party deals with an agent and is not aware of the agency relationship, the principal is called an **undisclosed principal**. In such a case, privity of contract exists between the third party and the agent, and the agent can be held liable on the resulting contract. In the event of a suit for breach of contract, the third party may elect to hold liable either the principal or the agent. Occasionally, a principal will conceal its identity even beyond being an undisclosed principal, and have the agent act on behalf of a **dummy corporation**, which is a lawful corporation created to take title to assets while safeguarding the owner corporation's identity and liability.

TERMS IN ACTION

Suppose that you're Walt Disney, you want to create a much larger theme park than Disneyland, and you want it in central Florida, but you want to pay as little for the land as possible. You realize that if your plans are known, the price of land would skyrocket. How would you buy the land? If you were as shrewd as Walt Disney, you would use secret **agents** and **dummy corporations** to buy small tracts of land in the Orlando area, which is exactly what Mr. Disney did in 1964 and 1965. Dubbed "Project X," the plan involved sending buyers to the farmlands around Orlando, who purchased small plots from sellers who did not know that there was an **undisclosed principal** behind the buyers. One of the dummy corporations was named "M. T. Lott Real Estate Investments." (Think about that name for a second). Eventually, title to the land was turned over to the Disney Corporation.

By October 1965, word began to spread throughout Orlando that something was going on—27,000 acres had changed hands in a matter of months—and after the *Orlando Sentinel* made its guess, land prices increased around 1000 percent. By the time the buying spree ended, Disney owned 43 square miles, about twice the size of Manhattan. One of the agents who worked on behalf of Disney (the **principal**), was an Orlando real estate broker named Nelson Boice, who passed away in 2009.

Sources: *Economics: Private and Public Choice*; ehow.com; lifthill.com

---

An employment relationship exists when one person, called an **employee** (formerly known as a **servant**), performs services under the direction and control of another, called an **employer** (formerly known as a **master**). Employees may also be agents if they have been authorized to enter into contracts with third parties on behalf of their employers.

Independent contractors differ from employees in that they perform services for others, but are not under the others' control. People who have independent contractors perform work for them do not withhold taxes from their pay and are not responsible for their wrongdoings. For example, a lawyer is an independent contractor to her or his client (who hires a lawyer for a desired outcome), whereas the lawyer's paralegal or legal assistant is the lawyer's employee (because the lawyer has management authority over the paralegal's or legal assistant's "process" and work outcomes). But a lawyer who works for a corporation's in-house legal department is no longer an independent contractor, but is an employee, just like any paralegals or legal assistants who also work at the company.

KINDS OF AGENTS

A **general agent** is one who is authorized to conduct all of a principal's activity in connection with a particular business. A person hired to manage a business would be an example of a general agent. A **special agent**, conversely, is one who is authorized to carry out a single transaction or to perform a specified act. For example, a person authorized to sell a house for someone who is away on a trip would be a special agent.

Sometimes, goods are sold on **consignment**—that is, they are left by a bailor (**consignor**) with a bailee (**consignee**) who tries to sell them. Title to the goods does not pass between these parties, and the goods may be returned if not sold. The bailee to whom the goods are consigned for sale is a type of agent called a **factor**. If the factor sells consigned goods on credit and guarantees to the consignor that the buyer will pay for them, the factor is known as a **del credere agent**.

AUTHORITY OF AGENTS

Agents are often given their authority expressly, which may be done either orally or in writing. **Express authority** is authority that is given explicitly. Sometimes, agents are appointed formally by a written instrument known as a **power of attorney**, which authorizes an agent to act for a principal. When a power of attorney is used, the agent is referred to as an **attorney-in-fact**.

In addition to the express authority given them, agents have a certain amount of **implied authority**. This is the type of authority that the agent customarily and reasonably needs in order to perform incidental functions that enable the agent to accomplish the overall purpose of the agency. For instance, a bus driver who is hired to drive tourists around the Grand Canyon has the implied authority to fuel up the bus when the tank gets low.

Apparent authority comes about when a principal, through some act, makes it appear that an agent has authority when none exists. This type of authority is also known as **agency by estoppel** because the principal will be stopped from denying that an agency relationship existed if he or she attempts to do so.

Word Wise
Negative Prefixes—A Further Clarification

Prefix	Meaning	Examples
mis-	incorrect; improper	misspell
		misfeasance
		misdemeanor
		mistrial
		misrepresentation
mal-	bad; evil	malice
		malfeasance
		malpractice
non-	not	nonentity
		nonfeasance
		nonmarital child
		nonconforming use

5

When an agent acts on behalf of a principal without authority to do so, but the principal later approves of the act, it is known as an **agency by ratification**.

Sometimes, agents fail to act when they are supposed to, or they act improperly. Three terms are used to describe such situations. **Misfeasance** is the improper doing of an act, **malfeasance** is the doing of an act that ought not to be done at all, and **nonfeasance** is the failure to do an act that ought to have been done.

VICARIOUS LIABILITY

Principals and employers are responsible under a rule known as the doctrine of **respondeat superior** (let the superior respond) for the torts of their agents and employees that are committed within the scope of authority (in the case of agents) and within the **scope of employment** (in the case of employees). Principals and employers are said to have **vicarious liability**, which means that the wrongdoings of their agents and employees are **imputed** (charged) to them. Employer–employee liability was once referred to as the master–servant rule. The scope of employment is that legal zone in which employees operate—acknowledged to be broader than the employee's stated job description or task, which is why the employee's wrongful conduct makes the employer vicariously liable. Injured parties may recover damages from the employee who committed the tort (the agent) and from the employer (the principal), because of vicarious liability. Usually, plaintiffs will recover from the employer, because that person or business is in a better financial position to pay the damages. Some refer to this as the employer having the "deep pockets."

▌ TERMS IN ACTION

While it is true that, under the doctrine of **respondeat superior**, employers are vicariously liable for the torts of their employees, it is not always easy to determine under what circumstances an employee's misconduct is still within **the scope of employment**. In what one would hope is a rare occurrence, an employee at a Bronx bar, called the Pot Belly Pub, poked a patron in the eye with a knife, blinding the man in that eye. The injured patron sued the bar for vicarious liability and the employee for negligence. Even more strange than the story so far is how the injury occurred. The employee in question was talking with the patron about the increase of muggings in the area, and during their discussion the employee got out his pocket knife to show what he carried for personal protection. After opening the knife, the employee began to flip it in the air and catch it by its handle. The last of his flips was too strong, and somehow the knife hit the patron in the eye.

At trial, the employer argued that there was no **vicarious liability on the employer's part** because nothing the employee did in stabbing the plaintiff was even close to being in the scope of employment. However, the jury awarded the patron $200,000. On appeal, the New York Court of Appeals concluded that the employee was acting in the scope of employment when he struck the plaintiff in the eye. The court's rationale was that the employee—who only worked part-time in the small bar—was someone who would occasionally work in the kitchen (where knives were), and part of his job involved mingling with customers so that they would stay longer (and order more drinks). Therefore, the jury could have thought the employee was in the scope of employment at the time, and the employer could have anticipated such a type of **malfeasance**.

Source: *Riviello v. Waldron*, 391 N.E.2d 1278 (N.Y. 1979)

Reviewing What You Learned

After studying the chapter, write the answers to each of the following questions:

1. Name the three relationships that need to be distinguished when discussing agency law. _____
   _____
   _____
   _____
   _____

2. When a principal authorizes an agent to enter into a contract, between what parties is the contract?_____
   _____
   _____
   _____
   _____

3. When can an agent be held liable on a contract by a third party?
   _____
   _____
   _____
   _____

4. When an undisclosed principal is involved, whom may a third party hold liable in the event of a suit for breach of contract?
   _____
   _____
   _____
   _____

5. Under what circumstances may employees also be agents?
   _____
   _____
   _____

6. Describe two advantages of hiring independent contractors.
   _____
   _____

   _____
   _____

7. Give an example of a general agent and a special agent._____
   _____
   _____
   _____
   _____
   _____

8. Describe the method of selling goods on consignment._____
   _____
   _____
   _____
   _____

9. Why is apparent authority also called *agency by estoppel?*___
   _____
   _____
   _____
   _____
   _____

10. From whom may injured parties recover damages when employees commit torts within the scope of their employment? _____
    _____
    _____
    _____
    _____
    _____

11. What is a dummy corporation and when might it be used?
    _____
    _____
    _____
    _____

5

Understanding Legal Concepts

Indicate whether each statement is true or false. Then, change the italicized word or phrase of each false statement to make it true.

ANSWERS

_____ 1. When a principal authorizes an agent to enter into a contract on the principal's behalf, the resulting contract is between the *agent* and the third party.

_____ 2. An agent who contracts on behalf of an undisclosed principal *can* be held liable on the contract.

_____ 3. Employees *may also be* agents if they have been authorized to enter into contracts with third parties on behalf of their employers.

_____ 4. People who have independent contractors perform work for them *must* withhold taxes from their pay.

_____ 5. A person hired to manage a business is an example of a *special* agent.

_____ 6. When goods are sold on consignment, title to the goods *does not pass* between the consignor and the consignee.

_____ 7. Agents may be appointed expressly, *either orally or in writing*.

_____ 8. When agents are given express authority to perform certain acts, they have *no* implied authority.

_____ 9. Apparent authority comes about when *an agent* makes it appear that the agent has authority when none exists.

_____ 10. Someone who is injured by an employee's wrongful act may recover damages from *either* the employer or the employee.

Checking Terminology

From the list of legal terms that follows, select the one that matches each definition.

ANSWERS

a. agency
b. agency by estoppel
c. agency by ratification
d. agent
e. apparent authority
f. attorney in fact
g. consignee
h. consignment
i. consignor
j. del credere agent
k. dummy corporation
l. employee
m. employer
n. express authority
o. factor
p. general agent
q. implied authority
r. impute
s. independent contractor
t. malfeasance
u. master
v. misfeasance
w. nonfeasance
x. power of attorney
y. principal
z. respondeat superior
aa. scope of employment
bb. servant
cc. special agent
dd. third party
ee. undisclosed principal
ff. vicarious liability

_____ 1. A rule of law that makes principals and employers responsible for the torts of their agents and servants committed within the scope of their authority or employment.

_____ 2. To charge; to lay the responsibility or blame.

_____ 3. Liability that is imputed to principals and employers because of the wrongdoings of their agents and employees.

_____ 4. A relationship that exists when one person is authorized to act under the control of another person.

_____ 5. A factor who sells consigned goods on credit and who guarantees to the consignor that the buyer will pay for the goods.

_____ 6. A bailee to whom goods are consigned for sale.

_____ 7. One who is authorized to act for another.

_____ 8. One who authorizes another to act on his or her behalf.

_____ 9. One who performs services under the direction and control of another. (Select two answers.)

_____ 10. One who performs services for another, but who is not under the other's control.

_____ 11. An agent who is authorized to conduct all of a principal's activity in connection with a particular business.

_____ 12. An agent who is authorized to carry out a single transaction or to perform a specified act.

_____ 13. Authority that is given explicitly.

_____ 14. A formal writing that authorizes an agent to act for a principal.

_____ 15. Authority of an agent to perform incidental functions that are reasonably and customarily necessary to enable the agent to accomplish the overall purpose of the agency.

_____ 16. Authority that comes about when a principal, through some act, makes it appear that an agent has authority when none actually exists. (Select two answers.)

_____ 17. The failure to do an act that ought to be done.

_____ 18. A relationship that occurs when someone performs an act on behalf of another without authority to do so, but the other person later approves of the act.

_____ 19. The process of delivering goods to a bailee, called a factor, who attempts to sell them and who may return those that are unsold.

_____ 20. One who is not known by a third party to be a principal for an agent.

_____ 21. The doing of an act that ought not to be done at all.

_____ 22. In agency law, one who deals with an agent in making a contract with the agent's principal.

_____ 23. An agent who is authorized to act under a power of attorney.

5

____ 24. One who makes a consignment.

____ 25. That zone in which employees operate.

____ 26. One who employs the services of others in exchange for wages or salaries. (Select two answers.)

____ 27. A lawful corporation created to take title to assets while safeguarding the corporation owner's identity and liability.

____ 28. The improper doing of an act.

____ 29. One to whom a consignment is made.

Sharpening Your Latin Skills

In the space provided, write the definition of the following legal terms, referring to the Glossary when necessary.

caveat _____

caveat emptor _____

caveat venditor _____

nulla bona _____

respondeat superior _____

Using Legal Language

Read the following story and fill in the blank lines with legal terms taken from the list of terms at the beginning of this chapter:

Darlene, who was the general manager and thus a(n) _____ for Johnson Service Co., hired Amos to work as a(n) _____ or _____ under the company's direction and control. The company was the _____ or _____ of Amos. One year later, Amos took a three-week vacation trip to Europe. Because his house was for sale at the time, he appointed Betsy to be his _____ solely for the purpose of selling the house in the event that a buyer might come along while he was away. Because he used a formal written instrument called a(n) _____ to make the appointment, Betsy became known as a(n) _____. Claude learned that the house was for sale and went to look at it. Betsy, meanwhile, was at the house and had just removed the well cover to see how much water was in it when Claude arrived. She introduced herself to him and showed him around, not telling him that she was not the owner. Claude decided to buy the house and signed a contract agreeing to do so. Betsy signed as the seller, not telling Claude

that this was a(n) _____ relationship and that she was a(n) _____ acting on behalf of Amos, the _____, and that Claude was a(n) _____. Amos would be described as a(n) _____, because Claude was not aware of the particular relationship. As he walked from the house, Claude fell into the uncovered well and was injured. Under a doctrine known as _____, Amos would be _____ liable—that is, Betsy's negligent act of leaving the well uncovered would be _____ to him. After recuperating from his injuries, Claude converted part of his new house into a small gift shop where he sold other people's goods on _____, which is an arrangement under which title to the goods did not pass to Claude and he could return those that did not sell. People who left goods in his store for sale were called _____. Claude, who was known as a(n) _____, was also a type of agent called a(n) _____. Whenever

5

he sold goods on credit and guaranteed payment, he was a(n) _____. Claude hired Eva to paint the shop for him. She was a(n) _____, because she was not under Claude's control in doing the work. One day, Claude left the gift shop to go fishing and told Eva to look after business while she painted. Eva had _____ to take care of incidental functions that were reasonably and customarily necessary to accomplish her purpose. Before Claude returned, Eva sold an expensive antique for one-tenth of its value to a knowledgeable customer. Claude attempted to rescind the sale on the ground that Eva had no authority, but he failed in his attempt because Eva had _____; this was a(n) _____, because Claude made it appear that Eva had authority by leaving the store in her care.

PUZZLING OVER WHAT YOU LEARNED

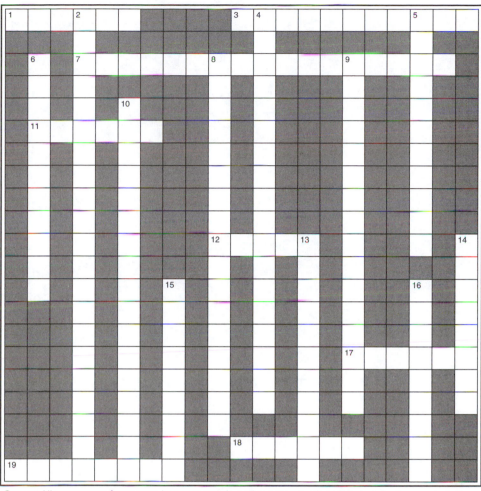

Caveat: Allow squares for spaces between words and punctuation (apostrophes, hyphens, etc.) when filling in crossword.

Across

1. To charge; to lay the responsibility or blame.
3. The doing of an act that ought not to be done at all.
7. A factor who sells consigned goods on credit with a guarantee of payment.
11. A bailee to whom goods are consigned for sale.
12. One who is authorized to act for another.
17. Relationship that exists when one person is authorized to act for another.
18. One who employs the services of others in exchange for wages.
19. One who performs services under the direction and control of another.

Down

2. One who is not known by a third party to be a principal for an agent.
4. Authority caused by a principal making it appear that a non-agent has authority.
5. The failure to do an act that ought to be done.
6. The improper doing of an act.
8. Authority that is given explicitly.
9. An agent who is authorized to act under a power of attorney.
10. A formal writing that authorizes an agent to act for a principal.
13. One who deals with an agent in making a contract with the agent's principal.
14. One who employs the services of others in exchange for wages.
15. One to whom a consignment is made.
16. One who authorizes another to act on his or her behalf.

5

Terms Used in Law of Wills and Estates

The drafting of wills is a customary part of the practice of most law offices because many people realize that a will is an important document and should be drafted professionally. Even law offices that specialize in other areas of law often draft wills as part of their practice. Litigation relating to the settling of estates is also very common in the United States. Chapter 24 explains who may make a will, describes the requirements of drafting and executing a proper will, and examines advance directives. Chapter 25 discusses the methods of revoking a will and explains the failure of legacies and devises, including lapse and ademption. The principal clauses in a will are outlined in Chapter 26; and Chapter 27: spousal protection, dower and curtesy, pretermitted children, distinctive relationships, and the law of intestacy comprise. The types of personal representatives are discussed in Chapter 28, and the procedure for settling an estate is outlined in Chapter 29. The parties to a trust and the various kinds of trusts are explored in Chapter 30.

6

Wills, Testaments, and Advance Directives

ANTE INTERROGATORY

A written expression of a person's wishes to be allowed to die a natural death and not be kept alive by heroic or artificial methods is a (A) medical power of attorney, (B) holographic will, (C) will and testament, (D) living will.

CHAPTER OUTLINE

Parties to a Will

Statutory Requirements
Eighteen Years of Age
Sound Mind
Writing

Signature
Attestation and Subscription
Testator's Presence
Two or More Competent Witnesses

Advance Directives

KEY TERMS

advance directive *(ad·VANS de·REK·tiv)*

agent *(AY·jent)*

attest *(a·TEST)*

attesting witness *(a·TEST·ing WIT·nes)*

beneficiary *(ben·e·FISH·ee·air·ee)*

bequeath *(be·KWEETH)*

bequest *(be·KWEST)*

decedent *(de·SEE·dent)*

devise *(de·VIZE)*

devisee *(dev·i·ZEE)*

devisor *(dev·i·ZOR)*

directive to physicians *(der·EK·tiv to fi·ZI·shens)*

durable power of attorney *(DER·ebel POW·er ov a·TERN·ee)*

estate planning *(es·TATE PLAN·ing)*

euthanasia *(you·the·NAY·zhia)*

exordium clause *(eks·ORD·ee·um)*

health care declaration *(dek·la·RAY·shun)*

health care proxy *(PROK·see)*

holographic will *(hol·o·GRAF·ik)*

intestate share *(in·TESS·tate)*

legacy *(LEG·a·see)*

legatee *(leg·a·TEE)*

legator *(leg·a·TOR)*

living will

medical directive *(MED·i·kel der·EK·tiv)*

medical power of attorney *(MED·i·kel POW·er ov a·TERN·ee)*

nuncupative will *(NUN·kyoo·pay·tiv)*

personal property *(PER·son·al PROP·er·tee)*

6

proponent *(pro·PO·nent)*

real property *(reel PROP·er·tee)*

right-to-die laws

soundness of mind

springing power *(SPRING·ing POW·er)*

subscribe *(sub·SKRIBE)*

surrogate *(SER·o·get)*

testament *(TES·te·ment)*

testamentary capacity *(test·e·MEN·ter·ee ka·PAS·e·tee)*

testamentary disposition *(test·e·MEN·ter·ee dis·po·ZI·shun)*

testate *(TES·tate)*

testator *(tes·tay·TOR)*

testatrix *(tes·tay·TRIX)*

Uniform Probate Code (UPC) *(YOON·i·form PRO·bate kode)*

will

will and testament *(TES·te·ment)*

The branch of the law known as **estate planning** involves arranging a person's assets in a way which fulfills that person's desires about protecting her or his assets during life and passing them on at death. The fields of taxation, insurance, property ownership, trusts, and wills are important facets of estate planning.

The term **will** is an Anglo-Saxon word that originally referred to an instrument that disposed of **real property** (land and anything that is permanently attached to it). Even today, a gift of real property in a will has a special name. It is called a **devise**. The person who makes the gift of real property is called the **devisor**, and the person to whom the gift is made is called the **devisee**.

The term **testament**, which is Latin, referred to an instrument that disposed of **personal property** (things other than real property) under early English law. A gift of personal property in a will today is known as a **bequest** or a **legacy**. The person who makes a gift of personal property in a will is called a **legator**, and the person to whom the gift is made is called a **legatee**.

Under early English law, **will and testament** disposed of both real and personal property. In practice today, the distinction between the two terms is not made. Thus, the terms "will" and "will and testament" are used interchangeably. It is common, however, to see the phrase "I give, devise, and bequeath. . . ." in a will referring to both real and personal property, as the verb **bequeath** means "to give personal property in a will."

PARTIES TO A WILL

The person who makes a will is called a **testator** if a man and a **testatrix** if a woman. A **beneficiary** is someone who receives a gift under a will. The word **testate** refers to the state of a person who has made a will, and the phrase **testamentary disposition** means a gift of property that is not to take effect until the one who makes the gift dies.

STATUTORY REQUIREMENTS

Today in the United States, each state has enacted its own statutes governing the formalities of executing wills. Sixteen states (see Figure 24-1) have adopted the entirety of the **Uniform Probate Code (UPC)**, which is a uniform law, published in 1969, that attempts to standardize and modernize laws relating to the affairs of **decedents** (deceased persons), minors, and certain other people who need protection. In fact, most states have adopted at least some part of the UPC. The UPC has changed the definitions of some commonly used legal terms. For example, in states that have adopted the UPC, the term **devise** refers to a gift under a will of either real or personal property, and the term **devisee** refers to a person who receives a gift of either real or personal property under a will.

6

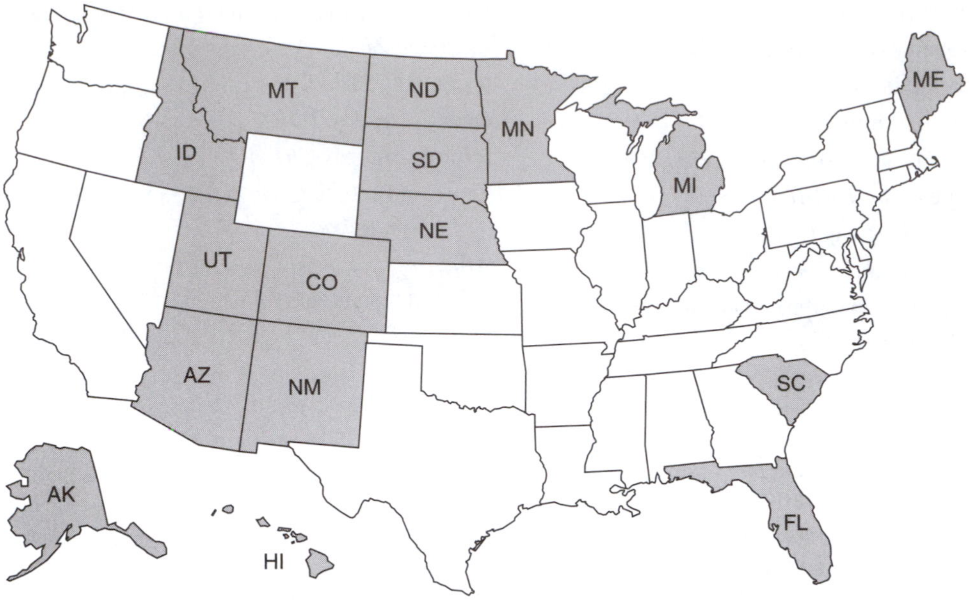

FIGURE 24-1   States that have adopted the Uniform Probate Code.

A typical state statute (non-UPC) reads, in part, as follows:

Every person 18 years of age or older and of sound mind may by his last will in writing, signed by him or by a person in his presence and by his express direction, and attested and subscribed in his presence by two or more competent witnesses, dispose of his property, real and personal.

An analysis of the preceding statute reveals the following requirements for executing a will in that particular state:

1. eighteen years of age
2. sound mind
3. writing
4. signed
5. attested
6. subscribed in the testator's presence
7. two or more competent witnesses

Word Wise
To Write

Both the root "graph" used in "holographic" and the root "scrib" used in "subscribe" mean "to write." Other words with these roots are the following:

Word	Meaning
circumscribe [*circum* (around) + *scribe*]	To draw a line around
manuscript [*manu* (by hand) + *script*]	A document written by hand
telegraph [*tele* (far) + *graph*]	Message sent over a distance
autograph [*auto* (self) + *graph*]	Written with one's own hand

Eighteen Years of Age

Although most state laws set the minimum age for making a will at 18, a few states allow wills to be made at an earlier age for military personnel and married persons. People become 18 years of age on the day before their 18th birthday, because the law considers persons as having lived an entire day if they live any part of that day. Because the day of birth is counted, a child will have lived 365 days on the day before the child's first birthday.

Sound Mind

Soundness of mind, which is also referred to as **testamentary capacity**, may be proved by showing that, at the time of the execution of the will, the testator met all of the following requirements:

1. The testator had the ability to understand and carry in mind, in a general way, the nature and extent of property owned, and his or her relationship to those persons who would naturally have some claim to the estate.
2. The testator was free from delusions that might influence the disposition of his or her property.
3. The testator had the ability to comprehend the nature of the act—that is, knew that he or she was making a will.

Generally, if the question of soundness of mind is raised in a contested will case, only the following people are allowed to testify as to the testator's mental condition: the witnesses to the will, the testator's family physician, and experts of skill and experience in the knowledge and treatment of mental diseases. The **proponent** of the will—that is, the one who presents the will to the court for allowance—has the burden of proving the soundness of mind of the testator.

TERMS IN ACTION

Is it possible that the kinds of **bequests** that a person leaves in his or her **will** can show that he or she lacks **testamentary capacity**? Generally, no. William Shakespeare's will was written in 1616, and after his death later that year it passed on many assets to Shakespeare's family, including his daughters, his sister, and his friends. But to his wife Anne, Shakespeare gave only his "second best bed." Julia H. Egan, a woman from New York City who had once been put in what then was called an "asylum," died with a will that left her husband $5, as retaliation because he had called her crazy. Canadian lawyer and investor Charles Vance Millar died in 1926, leaving a will that has become famous for its **testator's** love of bequests that continued—after death—his love of irony. His will opens by stating that it is "proof of my folly in gathering and retaining more than I required in my lifetime." He gave shares of his stock in a Catholic-run beer company to some Methodist ministers, provided that they participate in management of the company (which included beer tasting). And he gave his Jamaican vacation home to three men known to hate each other. But the bequest that eventually became the subject of the movie "The Great Stork Derby" was the one which gave the bulk of his estate to the Canadian woman who would bear the most children during the decade after his death. More than a few of his distant relatives attempted to have his will set aside, but after a decade of litigation, Millar's will, which had been **attested** to and **subscribed** to by two **attesting witnesses**, was proven to be air-tight. Four women eventually shared the estate prize, each having had nine children during that prosperous decade.

Sources: timemagazine.com; archives.gov.on.ca; william-shakespeare.info; nytimes.com

Writing

The writing that is sufficient for a will may be printed, typewritten, or written entirely in the hand of the testator. A will that is written entirely by the testator and signed by the testator, but has no witnesses, is called a **holographic will**. Because of the lack of witnesses, holographic wills are not recognized as valid in some jurisdictions, but the UPC authorizes the use of holographic wills. It is believed that the shortest valid will on record is one written by a German, Herr Karl Tausch, whose holographic will was two words (but in English, three): "All to wife." A will need not be under seal. With exceptions, only a soldier in the military service or a mariner at sea may make a **nuncupative will** (oral), which is limited to the disposition of personal property.

Signature

According to the statute on wills quoted above, the signature of the testator may be anywhere on the instrument. Thus, in a case in which a testator wrote his name in the **exordium clause** (the first paragraph) of his handwritten will, but failed to sign it at the end, the court allowed the will. Some states require that the testator sign at the end of the will.

The signature need not be in any particular form. It may be made by an "X" or any other mark of the testator so long as it is intended to be the testator's signature. Under this particular statute, another person may sign for the testator if it is done in the testator's presence and by his or her express direction. Also, under this statute, the testator is not required to sign in the presence of the witnesses.

Attestation and Subscription

To **attest** means to bear witness to the testator's signature. To **subscribe** means to write below or underneath. An early English case held that "to attest" and "to subscribe" are different actions. Attestation is the act of the senses; subscription is the act of the hand. The one is mental; the other mechanical. To attest to a will is to know that it was published as a will; to subscribe is only to write on the same paper the names of the witnesses for the sole purpose of identification.

A will was held to be properly executed when the testator acknowledged his or her signature, which he or she had previously placed thereon, by showing the paper to the witness, stating that it was his or her will, and requesting the person to sign it as a witness. In another case, a will was disallowed by the court because the testator intentionally covered up his signature so that the witnesses could not see it. In that case, the court said that a person does not acknowledge a signature to be his when no signature can be seen by the witness. In a contrasting case, however, a will was allowed by the court when the signature of the testator was unintentionally covered up by a fold in the paper.

Attesting witnesses (people who witness the signing of a document and then sign the document as the witnesses) should sign below the testator's signature and after the testator signs the instrument. They may subscribe either by making a mark or by writing their names in full, as long as they do so with the intent of subscribing to the will. In a case in which a witness unintentionally wrote his correct first name, but the middle initial and last name of the person who signed above his name, the court, in allowing the will, said that any form of writing adopted by the witness is sufficient to satisfy the statute.

Testator's Presence

The witnesses must subscribe in the presence of the testator. It has been said that witnesses are not in the presence of the testator unless they are within the testator's sight; however, a person may take note of the presence of another by the other senses, such as hearing or touch. If two blind people, for example, are in the same room talking together, no question exists that they are in each other's presence.

A will was disallowed in a case in which the witnesses watched the testator (who was ill in bed) sign the will and then withdrew to another room to subscribe as witnesses. The court strictly held that the witnesses did not subscribe in the presence of the testator.

Two or More Competent Witnesses

Under the statute set forth earlier, a will must have two witnesses. That particular state statute continues on to read as follows:

> Any person of sufficient understanding shall be deemed to be a competent witness to a will, . . . but a beneficial devise or legacy to a subscribing witness or to the husband or wife of such witness shall be void unless there are two other subscribing witnesses to the will who are not similarly benefited there under.

This statement means that if a beneficiary or a beneficiary's spouse witnesses a will, he or she cannot take the gift that was given under the will unless two extra witnesses receive nothing under the will. Note that no age requirement of a witness exists under this statute. The only requirement is that the witness be "of sufficient understanding." Some states have age requirements for witnesses.

All states but two in the United States require two witnesses to a will. Pennsylvania has no witness requirement unless the testator signs by mark (meaning that the testator is unable to sign his or her name), and Louisiana calls for two witnesses plus a notary public. Vermont used to require three witnesses, but reduced the requirement to two in 2005. Notwithstanding this requirement, holographic wills need not be witnessed in over half of the states. Some states allow witnesses who are named as beneficiaries to inherit under the will. Still others, including California, Indiana, and Texas, allow witnesses who are named as beneficiaries in a will to inherit only an amount that does not exceed their **intestate share** (the amount they would have inherited had the decedent died without a will). In Florida, the entire will is void when any of the witnesses are named as beneficiaries.

ADVANCE DIRECTIVES

Right-to-die laws have become prevalent in recent years. These are laws that allow dying people to refuse extraordinary life-prolonging treatment. In *Cruzan* v. *Director, Missouri Department of Health* (497 U.S. 261 (1990)), the U.S. Supreme Court held that the right to refuse medical treatment is protected by the Fourteenth Amendment of the U.S. Constitution. In the *Cruzan* case, the court encouraged people to make **advance directives**—that is, written statements specifying whether they want life-sustaining medical treatment if they become desperately ill.

Web Wise

- Find out about the U.S. Living Will Registry at www.uslivingwillregistry.com
- Print out your own state's advance directive by going to www.partnershipforcaring.org

---

Individual state laws regulate advance directives. Some states authorize the use of the **living will**, a written expression of a person's wishes to be allowed to die a natural death and not be kept alive by heroic or artificial methods. Other states use a health care proxy for the same purpose. A **health care proxy**, also called a **medical power of attorney**, is a written statement authorizing an **agent** or **surrogate** (person authorized to act for another) to make medical treatment decisions for an individual in the event of that individual's inability to do so. Still other states use a durable power of attorney for this purpose. A **durable power of attorney** is a document authorizing another person to act on one's behalf, with language indicating that the authorization either is to survive one's incapacity or is to become effective when one becomes incapacitated. In the latter instance, the power is called a **springing power**, because it does not become effective until the person making it actually becomes incapacitated. A durable power of attorney is not limited to health care issues in most states. A living will is sometimes called a **directive to physicians,** a **medical directive**, or a **health care declaration**.

6

Many states have *surrogate decision-making laws* that permit a close relative or friend to make health care decisions for patients who have no advance directives.

TERMS IN ACTION

A **living will** is likely the most well known of the **advance directives**, but unlike a **will**, living wills are more recent estate planning devices. Luis Kitner, an attorney from Chicago, is credited with having been the inventor of the living will. It is thought that Kitner was prompted to begin drafting living wills in 1967 after watching the agonizingly slow death of a good friend who had been violently beaten while being robbed. Eventually, all states came to recognize the validity of living wills. Kitner was a brilliant attorney who entered law school at 15, worked while in law school for Clarence Darrow (considered by many to be the greatest criminal defense lawyer in American history), and co-founded the human rights organization Amnesty International.

Sources: nytimes.com

One controversial and confusing issue regarding end-of-life law is whether someone has the legal authority to enlist another person to assist in a suicide attempt. Still today in many jurisdictions attempted suicide is a crime. The procedure commonly called **euthanasia** (an active procedure to hasten the death of one who is terminally ill or in immense suffering) is illegal in America, and in 1997 the Supreme Court unanimously declared, in *Washington v. Glucksberg*, (521 U.S. 702), that there is no constitutional right to an assisted suicide. But, in the 2006 case *Gonzales v. Oregon*, (546 U.S. 243), the Supreme Court decided that the federal government could not intervene by prohibiting doctors in Oregon from over-prescribing drugs to terminally ill patients who would then overdose the drugs to take their own lives. The case was the result of a suit filed after a law known as the "Death with Dignity Act" passed in Oregon. In 2008, Washington State passed its own version of that law.

Reviewing What You Learned

After studying the chapter, write the answers to each of the following questions:

1. What was the difference between a will and a testament under early law?

   _____

   _____

   _____

   _____

2. List the seven requirements for executing a will under a typical state statute.

   _____

   _____

   _____

   _____

3. When do people become 18 years old?

   _____

   _____

   _____

   _____

4. What three facts prove soundness of mind of a testator?

   _____

   _____

   _____

   _____

6

5. Generally, who is considered competent to give an opinion of the testator's mental condition?

_____

_____

_____

6. Generally, who may make an oral will? To what is it limited?

_____

_____

_____

7. What is the difference between "attest" and "subscribe"?

_____

_____

_____

8. Read the two state statutes that are provided in this chapter, and answer the following questions relating to them:

a. Where on the will may the signature of the testator be located?

_____

_____

_____

b. In what form must the signature be?

_____

_____

_____

c. Must the testator sign in the presence of the witnesses?

_____

_____

_____

d. Where on a will must the witnesses sign their names?

_____

_____

_____

e. In whose presence must witnesses attest and subscribe?

_____

_____

_____

f. How many witnesses must a will have?

_____

_____

_____

g. Who may be a witness to a will?

_____

_____

_____

h. What will result if a beneficiary or beneficiary's spouse witnesses a will?

_____

_____

_____

9. Name three advance directives that are in common use.

_____

_____

_____

Understanding Legal Concepts

Indicate whether each statement is true or false. Then, change the italicized word or phrase of each false statement to make it true.

ANSWERS

_____ **1.** Originally, the term _will_ referred to an instrument that disposed of personal property, and the term _testament_ referred to an instrument that disposed of real property.

_____ **2.** A devise is a gift of _personal_ property in a will.

_____ **3.** The word "testate" refers to the state of a person who dies _without_ a will.

_____ **4.** A person becomes 18 years of age on the _day before_ his or her 18th birthday.

_____ **5.** If the question of soundness of mind is raised in a contested will case, the witnesses to the will _may not_ testify.

_____ **6.** A nuncupative will is limited to the disposition of _real_ property.

_____ **7.** A will _may never be_ signed by an "X."

_____ **8.** Attestation is the act of the _senses;_ subscription is the act of the hand.

_____ **9.** In all states, a witness to a will _must be_ 18 years of age.

_____ **10.** Witnesses _must_ subscribe in the presence of the testator.

Checking Terminology

From the list of legal terms that follows, select the one that matches each definition.

ANSWERS

a. advance directive
b. agent
c. attest
d. attesting witnesses
e. beneficiary
f. bequeath
g. bequest
h. decedents
i. devise
j. devisee
k. devisor
l. directive to physicians
m. durable power of attorney
n. estate planning
o. euthanasia
p. exordium clause
q. health care declaration
r. health care proxy
s. holographic will
t. intestate share
u. legacy
v. legatee
w. legator
x. living will
y. medical directive
z. medical power of attorney
aa. nuncupative will
bb. personal property
cc. proponent
dd. real property
ee. right-to-die laws
ff. soundness of mind
gg. springing power
hh. subscribe
ii. surrogate
jj. testament
kk. testamentary capacity
ll. testamentary disposition
mm. testate
nn. testator
oo. testatrix
pp. Uniform Probate Code (UPC)
qq. will
rr. will and testament

_____ 1. Originally, a legal instrument stating a person's wishes as to the disposition of real property at death, but now referring to both real and personal property.
_____ 2. A legal instrument stating a person's wishes as to the disposition of personal property at death.
_____ 3. Someone who actually receives a gift under a will; also, one for whose benefit a trust is created.
_____ 4. A gift of real property in a will.
_____ 5. A woman who makes or has made a testament or will.
_____ 6. An oral will.
_____ 7. A gift of property that is not to take effect until the one who makes the gift dies.
_____ 8. A male who makes or has made a testament or will.
_____ 9. A person to whom real property is given by a will.
_____ 10. Land and anything that is permanently attached to it.
_____ 11. Things other than real property.
_____ 12. A gift of personal property in a will. (Select two answers.)
_____ 13. A person who gives real property by will.
_____ 14. The state of a person who has made a will.
_____ 15. Under early English law, a legal instrument that disposed of both real and personal property at death.
_____ 16. A person who receives a gift of personal property under a will.
_____ 17. Deceased persons.
_____ 18. An amount that is inherited when a decedent dies without a will.
_____ 19. A law attempting to standardize and modernize laws relating to the affairs of decedents, minors, and certain other people who need protection.
_____ 20. Sufficient mental ability to make a will. (Select two answers.)
_____ 21. A will written entirely in the hand of the testator.
_____ 22. To bear witness to.
_____ 23. A person who makes a gift of personal property by will.
_____ 24. To sign below or at the end; to write underneath.
_____ 25. The introductory paragraph of a will.
_____ 26. To give personal property in a will.
_____ 27. Laws allowing dying people to refuse extraordinary treatment intended to prolong life.
_____ 28. A written expression of a person's wishes to be allowed to die a natural death and not be kept alive by heroic or artificial methods. (Select four answers.)
_____ 29. A written statement specifying whether a person wants life-sustaining medical treatment if he or she becomes desperately ill.
_____ 30. A power in a durable power of attorney that does not become effective until the person making it actually becomes incapacitated.
_____ 31. A document authorizing another person to act on one's behalf, with language indicating that it either is to survive one's incapacity or is to become effective when one becomes incapacitated.
_____ 32. A written statement authorizing an agent or surrogate to make medical treatment decisions for another in the event of the other's inability to do so. (Select two answers.)
_____ 33. A person authorized to act for another. (Select two answers.)
_____ 34. People who witness the signing of a document.
_____ 35. Arranging a person's assets in a way that maintains and protects the family most effectively both during and after a person's life.
_____ 36. One who proposes or argues in support of something.
_____ 37. An active procedure to hasten the death of one who is terminally ill or undergoing immense suffering.

6

Using Legal Language

Read the following story and fill in the blank lines with legal terms taken from the list of terms at the beginning of this chapter:

When Jason signed his last _____ and _____, he was not aware that the term "will" originally referred to an instrument that disposed of _____ and that the term "testament" originally referred to an instrument that disposed of _____. He was glad to be _____, however, which refers to the state of a person who has made a will. Jason is called a(n) _____, because he is a man. When his wife Julia signed her will, she was referred to as a(n) _____. These wills were not oral; therefore, they were not _____. They were not entirely in their own handwriting; therefore, they were not _____. The wills were witnessed by two _____. Jason and Julia both _____ (willed) their real estate to their children, which made them _____ and their children _____. They made a special _____ of their automobile to Julia's brother James. This made them _____, and James was a(n) _____ as to this _____. Because they were both of sound mind, they had _____, and the _____ was valid. They were pleased to have accomplished some _____, which is the arranging of their assets in a way that would maintain and protect their family most effectively both while they were alive and after their death.

PUZZLING OVER WHAT YOU LEARNED

Caveat: Allow squares for spaces between words and punctuation (apostrophes, hyphens, etc.) when filling in crossword.

Across

1. Sufficient mental ability to make a will.
4. A person to whom real property is given by will.
5. A gift of real property in a will.
6. Instrument stating person's wishes as to real property at death.
8. Things other than real property.
9. A gift of personal property in a will.
10. A person who makes a gift of personal property by will.
12. A woman who makes or has made a testament or will.
14. Instrument stating person's wishes as to personal property at death.
16. To bear witness to.
17. To give personal property in a will.
18. A will written entirely in the hand of the testator.

Down

2. Deceased person.
3. Land and anything that is permanently attached to it.
4. A person who gives real property by will.
7. A gift of personal property in a will.
11. A person who receives a gift of personal property under a will.
13. The state of a person who has made a will.
15. A male who makes or has made a testament or will.

6

Revocation, Lapses, and Ademption

ANTE INTERROGATORY

A legacy of money is called a (A) demonstrative legacy, (B) pecuniary legacy, (C) specific legacy, (D) lapsed legacy.

CHAPTER OUTLINE

Revocation
Destruction of Will
Execution of New Will
Subsequent Marriage
Divorce or Annulment

Failure of Legacies and Devises
Lapsed Legacies and Devises
Ademption
Simultaneous Deaths and Slayer Statutes

KEY TERMS

adeemed *(a·DEEMD)*

ademption *(a·DEMP·shun)*

advancement *(ad·VANSE·ment)*

antilapse statute *(an·tee·LAPS STAT·shoot)*

codicil *(KOD·i·sil)*

demonstrative legacy *(de·MON·stre·tiv LEG·a·see)*

execute *(EK·se·kyoot)*

extinction *(eks·TINK·shun)*

general legacy *(JEN·e·rel LEG·a·see)*

general pecuniary legacy *(JEN·e·rel pee·KYOO·nee·er·ee LEG·a·see)*

intestate *(in·TESS·tate)*

intestate succession *(in·TESS·tate suk·SESH·en)*

issue *(ISH·oo)*

lapsed devise *(lapsd de·VIZE)*

lapsed legacy *(lapsd LEG·a·see)*

pecuniary gift *(pe·KYOO·nee·er·ee)*

predeceased *(pre·de·SEESD)*

republishing a will *(re·PUB·lish·ing)*

residuary clause *(re·ZID·joo·er·ee)*

revocable *(REV·e·ke·bel)*

revocation *(rev·o·KA·shun)*

revoke *(re·VOKE)*

satisfaction *(sat·is·FAK·shun)*

simultaneous deaths *(sy·mul·TAY·nee·us)*

slayer statute *(SLAY·er STAT·shoot)*

specific legacy *(spe·SIF·ic LEG·a·see)*

6

REVOCATION

The term **revoke** means to cancel or rescind. **Revocable** means capable of being revoked, and **revocation** means the act of revoking. With variations from state to state, a will may be revoked in the following ways:

1. destruction of the will (burning, tearing, cancelling, or obliterating)
2. execution of a new will (To **execute** means to complete, to make, to perform, or to do, such as signing a will.)
3. subsequent marriage
4. divorce or annulment of marriage (but only as to gifts made in a will to a former spouse)

TERMS IN ACTION

Bill Groza of Arkansas died in 2006, leaving no will behind, at least so he thought. But relatives of his wife, who had died a few years before Bill, had a copy of Groza's will, claiming that it made them beneficiaries of his estate. However, Groza had **revoked** his will prior to his death. Among the things he did to show his intent to revoke was that he used liquid paper over the names of certain beneficiaries listed in his will, he wrote "void" on every paragraph, and he even wrote "bastard" and "get nothing" throughout the will. As if that wasn't enough, he put the will through a paper shredder in front of his insurance agents. But his dead wife's relatives, who were the obvious source of his revocation desires, claimed that Groza suffered from insane delusions at the time he attempted to disinherit them, such that he lacked the **testamentary capacity** to revoke his will. The jury disagreed with those relatives, and so did the appellate court. Part of its opinion included the following, wonderful sentence: "The evidence clearly showed that Bill was an irascible, angry, suspicious, controlling, profane, and difficult man for most of his adult life; however, we cannot say that the trial court erred in refusing to find that he labored under insane delusions."

Source: *Goza v. Potts*, 2010 Ark.App. 149 (Ark.App. 2010)

Destruction of Will

When a will is revoked by burning, tearing, canceling, or obliterating it, the act must be done with the intent to revoke the will. Thus, a will destroyed when the testator's house is accidentally burned would not, without the testator's intent, be revoked. In such a case, a copy of the signed will, if available, might be used in court as evidence of the unrevoked will.

The court in one case decided that when an elderly testatrix made marks on her previously executed will, she had no intention of revoking it, and the will was allowed. Other cases, however, have held that lines drawn through a line, paragraph, or portion of a will were effective to revoke those particular parts of the will that were marked out.

In another case, a testatrix left a sizable **pecuniary gift** (gift of money) in her will to a friend. Later, she decided to leave her friend a larger sum of money in the will. Without consulting a lawyer, she drew a line through the first amount and wrote above it the larger amount. When the testatrix died, her friend received nothing. The line drawn through the smaller amount effectively canceled that gift and the larger amount written above had no effect because the will had not been reexecuted by the testator or reattested and resubscribed by the proper number of witnesses after the change was made.

Execution of a New Will

Frequently, testators wish to revoke or make changes in their wills. In fact, it is a good idea to review a will every five years or so to be sure that it still meets one's needs and desires. One way to revoke or change a will is to make a new will. Another way is to make a **codicil**, which is an alteration or addition to an existing will. A codicil must be executed with the same formalities as a will (signed and attested by the testator, and subscribed in the testator's presence by two or more competent witnesses) and must refer specifically to the existing will so as to identify it.

A will and codicil are read together as one instrument. A properly executed codicil has the effect of **republishing a will**, which means that it will reestablish a will that has been formerly revoked or improperly executed.

Subsequent Marriage

In most states, the marriage of a person after that person has executed a will has no effect on the will. However, subsequent marriage (after making a will) revokes the will in the following states: Connecticut, Georgia, Kansas, Kentucky, Massachusetts, Nevada, Oregon, Rhode Island, South Dakota, West Virginia, and Wisconsin. In those states, if it appears within the body of the will that it was made in contemplation of marriage, the will is not revoked. In Maryland and Tennessee, subsequent marriage revokes a will only when a child is born of the marriage, and in the state of Washington, it revokes only those gifts in the will to the surviving spouse.

Divorce or Annulment

In most states, a divorce or annulment revokes a gift in a will made to the former spouse. It does not revoke the entire will. Similarly, a divorce or annulment revokes any nomination of the former spouse as executor, trustee, conservator, or guardian, unless the will expressly provides otherwise.

FAILURE OF LEGACIES AND DEVISES

A gift made in a will may fail in two ways. The first occurs when the person who is to receive the gift (the devisee or legatee) dies before the testator. The second occurs when the gift itself is not owned by the testator at the time of death. These two situations are discussed subsequently.

Lapsed Legacies and Devises

When a legatee or devisee dies before the testator, the bequest or devise in the will to that person is called a **lapsed legacy** or **lapsed devise** and takes no effect. Instead, it falls into the residuary fund of the estate, which is established by the residuary clause of the will. The **residuary clause** is the clause of a will that leaves "all the rest, residue and remainder" of the estate to named beneficiaries after specific gifts, if any, are provided for. If no residuary clause is in a will and the legatees and devisees have **predeceased** (died before) the testator, the lapsed gift passes to the heirs according to the law of **intestate succession**. This law governs the distribution of property of one who dies without a will—that is, **intestate**.

ANTILAPSE STATUTES.   Some states have enacted **antilapse statutes** designed to minimize the effect of lapse. Here is a typical one:

> If a devise or legacy is made to a child or other relation of the testator, who dies before the testator, but leaves issue surviving the testator, such issue shall, unless a different disposition is made or required by the will, take the same estate which the person whose issue they are would have taken if he had survived the testator. The words "child," "issue," and "other relation," as used in this section, shall include adopted children.

Under this statute, a gift that is made in a will to a child or other relative who predeceases the testator does not lapse. Instead, it passes to the issue of the child or other relative of the testator. **Issue** are all people who have descended from a common ancestor such as the decedent's children, grandchildren, great-grandchildren, and so forth.

If the testator does not want the issue of a deceased legatee or devisee to receive a gift under the antilapse statute, a statement to that effect must be made in the will. For example, a clause in a will leaving a gift "To my daughter, Shirley, if she shall survive me," would prevent the antilapse statute from taking effect.

Ademption

If the exact thing that is bequeathed or devised is not in existence or has been disposed of at the time of the testator's death, the legacy or devise is **adeemed** (taken away), and the legatee's or devisee's rights are gone. This is known as **ademption** or **advancement** and occurs in either of two ways: satisfaction or extinction.

SATISFACTION.   A **satisfaction** is defined as "the discharge of a legal obligation by paying a party what is due." Thus, a satisfaction takes place when all or part of the amount of a **general pecuniary legacy** (a gift of money out of the general assets of the estate) is paid to the legatee during the testator's life with the intent that such payment is in lieu of the legacy. In such a case, the legatee will not receive the legacy when the testator dies because the gift is said to have been adeemed. It was given to the legatee while the testator was alive.

Word Wise
Prefixes that Mean "Against"

Prefix	Examples	Meaning
ant-	antonym	A word of opposite meaning
anti-	antilapse	To minimize lapse
contra-	contradict	To say the opposite
contro-	controversy	A dispute
ob-	obstruct	To block
oc- (before *c*)	occupy	To seize
of- (before *f*)	offend	To insult
op- (before *p*)	oppose	To set against
o- (before *m*)	omit	To neglect

Legacies and devises are classified into three types—specific, general, and demonstrative. A **specific legacy** is a gift by will of a particular piece of personal property. For example, if a clause in a will reads, "I leave my 2003 Cadillac to my son, Timothy," the gift is a specific legacy. A **general legacy** is a gift (usually, of money) that comes out of the estate generally. For example, if a clause in a will reads, "I leave $10,000 to my daughter, Jennifer," the gift is a general legacy. A **demonstrative legacy** is a combination of the two. When it is used, the testator intends to make a general gift, but wishes to have it satisfied out of specific property. An example of a demonstrative legacy is a clause in a will that reads, "I bequeath $10,000 to my son, Matthew, and I direct that my shares of Symantic stock be sold and the proceeds applied to the payment of this gift."

EXTINCTION.   An **extinction** occurs by a destruction or disposal of a specific legacy by the testator during his or her lifetime. Thus, in the first example given earlier, if the testator does not own the 2003 Cadillac upon death, the legacy will adeem by extinction. Timothy will not receive the car because it is not part of the decedent's estate.

A general legacy does not adeem by extinction unless the general assets of the estate are not enough to pay it. Similarly, a demonstrative legacy does not adeem. In the third example given earlier, if the testator does not own any shares of Symantic stock at the time of death, Matthew will still receive the $10,000 gift. It will come out of the general assets of the estate.

Simultaneous Deaths and Slayer Statutes

Simultaneous deaths are the deaths of two or more people in such a way that it is impossible to determine who died before whom. All states have adopted some version of the Uniform Simultaneous Death Act. This law comes into effect when the disposition of the decedents' property depends on who died first and this cannot be determined—often, when two or more people die in a common disaster. The act allows the property of each decedent to be distributed as if he or she had survived, unless a will or trust provides otherwise.

People are not allowed to inherit from someone they murder. Instead, state laws called **slayer statutes** regard the murderer as having died before the victim, thus preventing any inheritance from going to the wrongdoer.

TERMS IN ACTION

Slayer statutes prevent killers from inheriting the estates of their victims. Before statutes were enacted to prevent such unjust inheritances, the common law prohibited it. In 1886, the U.S. Supreme Court first ruled that an insurance company did not have to pay life insurance proceeds to the estate of a man who had been hanged for killing a person six weeks after the killer bought a life insurance policy on the victim. Three years later, the New York Court of Appeals ruled, in a case not involving life insurance, that a grandson who murdered his grandfather could not qualify as a beneficiary of the grandfather's estate. The **Uniform Probate Code** created a slayer statute in the 1960s, and many states then followed suit. In 2004, the Maryland Supreme Court was faced with the question of whether the children of a man who murdered his own father could inherit their dead grandfather's estate through **intestate succession**, since the grandfather died without a will. The court ruled against the grandchildren, finding that because their father (the murderer) had no current right to inherit and was still alive, then his children could not have any intestacy rights. But in 2009, the Georgia Supreme Court ruled that two lawyers who represented a woman accused of murdering her husband could keep the $75,000 she paid them from her husband's estate to prepare her defense, which was paid before she pled guilty to murder. At the time she paid them, she wasn't—legally speaking—a murderer.

Sources: *Mutual Life Insurance Co. v. Armstrong*, 117 U.S. 591 (1886); *Riggs v. Palmer*, 22 N.E. 188 (N.Y. 1889); *Cook v. Grierson*, 845 A.2d 1231 (Md. 2004); *Levenson v. Ward*, 686 S.E.2d 236 (Ga. 2009)

Reviewing What You Learned

After studying the chapter, write the answers to each of the following questions:

1. What four ways may a will be revoked, depending on state statute?

   _____

   _____

   _____

2. To revoke a will by burning, tearing, canceling, or obliterating, what must accompany the act? _____

   _____

   _____

   _____

3. How must a codicil be executed? _____

   _____

   _____

   _____

   _____

4. A properly executed codicil republishes a will that is defective in what two ways? _____

   _____

   _____

6

_____

_____

5. In the State of Washington, what effect does a subsequent marriage have on a will made before the marriage? In the state of Massachusetts? _____

_____

_____

_____

_____

6. What effect does a divorce or annulment have on a will made before the divorce or annulment? _____

_____

_____

_____

7. What effect does a divorce have on the appointment of the former spouse as executor, trustee, conservator, or guardian, unless the will expressly provides otherwise? _____

_____

_____

_____

8. In what two ways may a gift in a will fail? _____

_____

_____

_____

_____

9. Who will receive a gift that is made in a will to a legatee who dies before the testator if a residuary clause is in the will? If no residuary clause is in the will? _____

_____

_____

_____

10. Under the antilapse statute, what will happen to a gift made in a will to a child or other relative who predeceases the testator? What language can be used in a will to keep this from happening? _____

_____

_____

_____

_____

11. In what two ways may an ademption occur? _____

_____

_____

_____

_____

12. When may a gift adeem by satisfaction? _____

_____

_____

_____

13. Give an example of a specific legacy, a general legacy, and a demonstrative legacy. _____

_____

_____

_____

_____

14. How may a gift adeem by extinction? _____

_____

_____

_____

_____

6

Understanding Legal Concepts

Indicate whether each statement is true or false. Then, change the italicized word or phrase of each false statement to make it true.

ANSWERS

_____ 1. A _codicil_ must be signed by the testator and attested and subscribed in the testator's presence by two or more competent witnesses.

_____ 2. A properly executed codicil _will reestablish_ a will that has been formerly revoked or improperly executed.

_____ 3. In _every state,_ it is important for a person to make a new will after becoming married if he or she had a will before the marriage.

_____ **4.** In most states, a divorce revokes a *will* that was made before the divorce.

_____ **5.** When a legatee or devisee dies before the testator, the bequest or devise in the will to that person *falls into the residuary fund* of the estate.

_____ **6.** Under an antilapse statute, a gift that is made in a will to a *friend* who predeceases the testator does not lapse.

_____ **7.** A clause in a will leaving a gift "to my daughter, Linda, if she shall survive me," would *cause* the antilapse statute *to take* effect.

_____ **8.** A *satisfaction* occurs when all or part of the amount of a general pecuniary legacy is paid to a legatee during the testator's life with the intent that such payment is in lieu of the legacy.

_____ **9.** If a clause in a will reads, "I leave $10,000 to my daughter, Deborah," the gift is a *specific* legacy.

_____ **10.** An *extinction* occurs by a destruction or disposal of a specific legacy by the testator during his lifetime.

Checking Terminology

From the list of legal terms that follows, select the one that matches each definition:

ANSWERS

a. adeemed
b. ademption
c. advancement
d. antilapse statute
e. codicil
f. demonstrative legacy
g. execute
h. extinction
i. general legacy
j. general pecuniary legacy
k. intestate
l. intestate succession
m. issue
n. lapsed devise
o. lapsed legacy
p. pecuniary gift
q. predeceased
r. republishing a will
s. residuary clause
t. revocable
u. revocation
v. revoke
w. satisfaction
x. simultaneous deaths
y. slayer statutes
z. specific legacy

_____ 1. The act of revoking.
_____ 2. Cancel or rescind.
_____ 3. Capable of being revoked.
_____ 4. To complete, to make, to perform, or to do, such as sign a will.
_____ 5. Gift of money.
_____ 6. An amendment to a will that must be executed with the same formalities as the will itself.
_____ 7. Reestablishing a will that has been formerly revoked or improperly executed.
_____ 8. The clause in a will that disposes of all of the testator's property not otherwise distributed.
_____ 9. A gift of personal property in a will that fails because the legatee predeceased the testator.
_____ 10. The act or process of an heir's becoming beneficially entitled to the property of one who dies without a will.
_____ 11. die before.
_____ 12. Having made no valid will.
_____ 13. All people who have descended from a common ancestor.
_____ 14. A bequest of a certain sum of money with a direction that it be paid out of a particular fund.
_____ 15. Taken away.
_____ 16. The testator's disposing of or giving to a beneficiary, while alive, that which was provided in a will, so as to make it impossible to carry out the will. (Select two answers.)
_____ 17. Laws designed to minimize the effect of lapse.
_____ 18. The discharge of a legal obligation by paying a party what is due.
_____ 19. A gift of money out of the general assets of the estate. (Select two answers.)
_____ 20. A gift by will of a particular article of personal property.
_____ 21. The act of extinguishing or putting to an end.
_____ 22. A gift of real property in a will that fails because the devisee predeceased the testator.
_____ 23. Laws enacted by legislatures stating that murderers cannot inherit from their victims.
_____ 24. The deaths of two or more people in a way that it is impossible to determine who died before whom.

Using Legal Language

Read the following story and fill in the blank lines with legal terms taken from the list of terms at the beginning of this chapter:

Because Jason sold the automobile that he had bequeathed to James before he died, a(n) _____ occurred. The automobile, which was a(n) _____ (kind of gift), _____ by extinction.

The gift of money—that is, the _____, which is also known as a(n) _____ or _____—went to his children, who were his _____. Because they did not

_____ (die before) him, it was not a(n) _____, and the house they inherited was not a(n) _____. The gift of $1,000 to Julie's brother, James, to be taken from the sale of stock, was a(n) _____. Because Jason died with a will, he did not die _____, and the laws of _____ did not apply to him. He had not made a(n) _____—that is, an addition to his will. Because he did not _____ (cancel or rescind) the instrument after he had _____ (signed) it, no _____ of the instrument had occurred. The _____ of the will gave all the rest, residue, and remainder of Jason's estate to his wife, Julie.

6

PUZZLING OVER WHAT YOU LEARNED

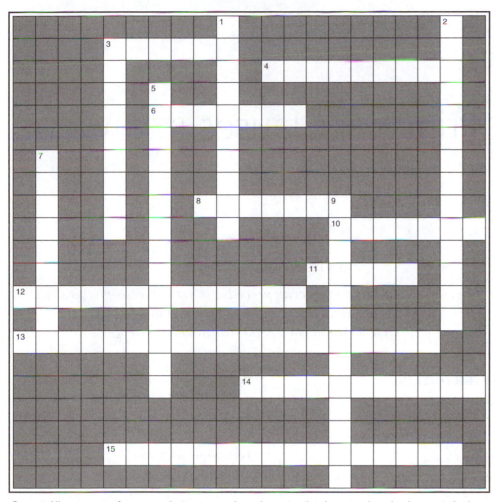

Caveat: Allow squares for spaces between words and punctuation (apostrophes, hyphens, etc.) when filling in crossword.

Across

3. Cancel or rescind.
4. The extinction or satisfaction of a legacy or devise before death.
6. To complete, to make, to perform, or to do, such as sign a will.
8. An amendment to a will that must be executed with the same formalities as a will.
10. Taken away.
11. All people who have descended from a common ancestor.
12. Gift of real property in a will that fails due to prior death of the devisee.
13. Reestablishing a will that has been formerly revoked.
14. Died before.
15. Clause in a will that disposes of all the testator's property not given out.

Down

1. The act of revoking.
2. A gift of money out of the general assets of the estate.
3. Capable of being revoked.
5. Gift of money.
7. Having made no valid will.
9. Gift of personal property in will that fails due to prior death of legatee.

Principal Clauses in a Will

ANTE INTERROGATORY

The clause in a will that directly precedes the testator's signature is called the (A) residuary clause, (B) testimonium clause, (C) attestation clause, (D) exordium clause.

CHAPTER OUTLINE

Exordium Clause

Debts and Funeral Expenses

Dispositive Clauses

Residuary Clause

Personal Representative, Guardian, and
    Trustee

No Surety on Bond

Powers Given to Fiduciaries

Tax Clause

No-Contest Clause

Testimonium Clause

Attestation Clause

Self-proving Affidavit

KEY TERMS

administrator *(ad·MIN·is·tray·tor)*

administratrix *(ad·MIN·is·tray·triks)*

attestation clause *(a·tes·TAY·shun)*

bond

conservator *(kon·SER·ve·tor)*

dispositive clauses *(dis·POS·a·tiv)*

domicile *(DOM·i·sile)*

executor *(eg·ZEK·yoo·tor)*

executrix *(eg·ZEK·yoo·triks)*

exordium clause *(eks·ORD·ee·um)*

fiduciary *(fi·DOO·she·air·ee)*

guardian *(GAR·dee·en)*

guardian ad litem *(GAR·dee·en ad LY·tem)*

incorporation by reference
    (in·kore·per·AY·shen by REF·e·renss)

in terrorem clause *(in ter·RAW·rem)*

no-contest clause *(no·KON·test)*

per capita *(per KAP·i·ta)*

per stirpes *(per STIR·peez)*

publication clause *(pub·li·KAY·shun)*

residuary clause *(re·ZID·joo·er·ee)*

residuary estate *(re·ZID·joo·er·ee es·TATE)*

self-proving affidavit *(a·fi·DAY·vit)*

signature clause *(SIG·na·cher)*

surety *(SHOOR·e·tee)*

testimonium clause *(tes·ti·MOH·nee·um)*

trustee *(trus·TEE)*

6

Beyond having the necessary elements required in the testator's jurisdiction, a will need not follow a singular format. In fact, a properly drawn will is a highly individualized instrument tailored to the particular needs of the testator and the testator's family. A will drafted by a lawyer, however, will contain many of the following clauses:

EXORDIUM CLAUSE

The **exordium clause**, also called the **publication clause**, is the introductory paragraph setting out the full name and **domicile** (principal residence) of the testator and stating that he or she revokes all previous wills and codicils made at an earlier time.

DEBTS AND FUNERAL EXPENSES

A will commonly contains a clause directing that the just debts and funeral expenses be paid out of the residuary estate. The **residuary estate** is the estate—if any—remaining after all individual items have been given by the will.

DISPOSITIVE CLAUSES

The **dispositive clauses** make up the main part of the will. In these clauses, the testator names his or her beneficiaries and states exactly what each is to receive. Often, when the testator leaves the entire estate to one person or in equal shares to several people, the only dispositive clause is the residuary clause discussed later.

A gift made in a will to one's issue then living **per stirpes** (by right of representation) means that the children of any deceased heirs inherit their deceased parent's share. For example, if, at death, the testator has two children and each child has two children, the two children would each get equal portions of the estate and the grandchildren would get nothing. But if one of the children (call her A) had predeceased the testator, then the surviving child would get that same certain portion of the estate and the two grandchildren from A would share their mother's share (so to speak) by getting half of their mother's allotted portion each. In contrast, a gift made to one's issue then living **per capita** (per head) means that heads are counted and all living issue share the amount of the gift equally. Going back to the example, if the testator has two children and four grandchildren alive at the time that the will is probated, each of them would get 1/6 of the estate in a per capital gift. If, however, A is also dead, then B and the four grandchildren would each get 1/5 of the estate.

A will's reference to another document, such as a list of items to be given to someone, makes the other document a part of the will; this inclusion is known as **incorporation by reference**. To be valid, the document that is referred to must be in existence at the time that the will is executed.

RESIDUARY CLAUSE

The **residuary clause** disposes of all of the testator's property not otherwise given out. If the residuary clause is omitted from the will, or if all of the residuary legatees and devisees predecease the testator, the residue usually passes to the heirs according to the law of intestate succession.

PERSONAL REPRESENTATIVE, GUARDIAN, AND TRUSTEE

Separate clauses are used to appoint the personal representative, guardian, and trustee in a will.

Except in states that have adopted the Uniform Probate Code, the **executor** (if a man) or **executrix** (if a woman) is the personal representative of the estate and is responsible for settling the estate. He or she gathers the assets of the estate, pays the debts (including taxes and cost of administration), and distributes the remainder according to the testamentary provisions of the will. This distribution is done under the supervision of the probate court. If a testator fails to appoint an executor or if the executor predeceases the testator or otherwise fails to carry out the responsibility (or declines serving as executor or executrix), a court will appoint someone else to perform the task. The person whom the court appoints to be the personal representative of the estate is called an **administrator** or **administratrix**.

It is common for people to name someone in their will to serve as guardian of their minor children. As well, adults sometimes need the services of a guardian. A **guardian** is one who legally has the responsibility over the care and management of the person, or person and property, of a minor or someone who is incompetent. A **guardian ad litem** (meaning "for the suit") is a guardian appointed by a court to protect a minor who brings or defends a lawsuit. A **conservator**, conversely, is one who legally has the care and management of the property, but not the person, of someone who is incompetent.

A **trustee** is someone who is appointed in a will to hold property for the benefit of another when one or more of the gifts are left in trust. (Trusts will be discussed in more detail in a later chapter.)

NO SURETY ON BOND

A will usually contains a clause stating that the executor (often, the guardian and trustee) is to serve without giving surety on his or her bond. In some states, without this clause in the will, the executor will have to have a **surety** on the bond—that is, either two persons or a surety company that will stand behind the executor's obligation. A **bond** is a promise by the personal representative and the sureties (if any) to pay the amount of the bond to the probate judge if the representative's duties are not faithfully performed.

POWERS GIVEN TO FIDUCIARIES

A clause is often included in the will to give the **fiduciaries** (people in positions of trust who have a duty to act in the best interest of others, such as the executor, guardian, and trustee) specific power and authority to conserve and manage the property under all foreseeable conditions. Without such a clause, the executor would be required to obtain permission (sometimes, a license) from the court each time he or she wished to carry out an extraordinary administrative function such as selling real property belonging to the estate.

TAX CLAUSE

The purpose of the tax clause is to establish the source for the payment of estate taxes, which are sometimes called death taxes. Often, the clause directs that taxes be paid out of the residuary estate.

NO-CONTEST CLAUSE

A **no-contest clause**, also known as an **in terrorem (in terror or warning) clause**, attempts to disinherit any legatee, devisee, or beneficiary who contests the provisions of the will. In states that have adopted the Uniform Probate Code, such a clause is unenforceable if there is probable cause to contest the will. California enforces no-contest clauses, whereas Florida specifically states that "a provision in a will purporting to penalize any interested person for contesting the will or instituting other proceedings relating to the estate is unenforceable." Fla. Stat. §732.517.

TERMS IN ACTION

Texas oilman Alfred C. Glassell, Jr., died in 2008 at the age of 95, leaving behind an estate valued at around $500 million. Over his life, he had executed and revoked 12 wills, but his 13th will, from 2003, was the source of a lawsuit by his 52-year-old daughter Curry, who attempted to set it aside in favor of her father's 1998 will. In the 1998 will, Curry Glassell was slated to receive millions more than the $3 million that she would have received under her father's 2003 will. That will split most of his fortune between the Glassell family foundation and Houston's Museum of Fine Arts. Curry's brother, Alfred, III, opposed his sister's claim that her ailing and weak father had been coerced by his lawyers into changing his will in 2003. If she won at the 2009 trial, it would have meant a $100 million difference in her inheritance. If she lost, she would have received nothing, thanks to her father's **in terrorem clause**. She lost. The jury took 40 minutes to decide against her, including the time it took for lunch.

Sources: chron.com; bloomberg.com

TESTIMONIUM CLAUSE

The clause immediately preceding the testator's signature is called the **testimonium clause** or the **signature clause**. It is a declaration that the testator's signature is attached in testimony of the preceding part of the instrument and begins with the words "IN WITNESS WHEREOF" or "IN TESTIMONY WHEREOF." Often, it contains a statement that the testator has initialed each of the previous pages.

Word Wise
Per

The Latin word *per* means "by," "through," "by way of," or "by means of."

per annum = by the year; annually (*annum* means "year")

per autre vie (also spelled pur autre vie) = for or during another's life; for the period that another person is alive (*autre* means "other"; *vie* means "life")

per capita = by heads; for each person; as individuals (*capita* means "heads")

per centum = (usually shortened to percent) by the hundred (*centum* means "hundred")

per curiam = by the court; an opinion of the whole court rather than an opinion of any one judge (*curiam* means "court")

per diem = by the day; an allowance or amount of so much per day (*diem* means "day")

per formam doni = by the form of a gift; by designation of the giver rather than by the operation of the law (*formam* means "form"; *doni* means "gift")

per fraudem = by fraud (*fraudem* means "fraud")

per infortunium = by misadventure or misfortune (*infortunium* means "misfortune")

per se = by itself, by herself, by himself, in isolation; unconnected to other matters (*se* means "itself," "herself," or "himself")

per stirpes = by (family) roots; by representation (*stirpes* means "stems" or "roots")

ATTESTATION CLAUSE

The **attestation clause** precedes the witnesses' signatures and recites that the will was witnessed at the request of the testator and that it was signed by the witnesses in the presence of the testator and in the presence of each other.

The most desirable arrangement of the signature page of a will is to have at least three lines of the text of the will on the same page with the testimonium clause, the testator's signature, the attestation clause, and the witnesses' signatures.

SELF-PROVING AFFIDAVIT

In some states, the courts will allow a will without the testimony of witnesses if it contains a **self-proving affidavit** and no one objects to its allowance. This clause contains an affidavit by the testator that the testator declared the instrument to be his last will and that he signed it willingly as his free and voluntary act. It also contains affidavits by the witnesses that they signed the will as witnesses and that to the best of their knowledge the testator was 18 years of age or older, of sound mind, and under no constraint or undue influence.

Here is a self-proof clause that is authorized by statute in Massachusetts:

We, the undersigned witnesses, each do hereby declare in the presence of the aforesaid testator that the testator signed and executed this instrument as his last will in the presence of each of us, that he signed it willingly, that each of us hereby signs this will as witness in the presence of the testator, and that to the best of our knowledge the testator is eighteen (18) years of age or over, of sound mind, and under no constraint or undue influence.

_____   _____
(witness)   (address)

_____   _____
(witness)   (address)

COMMONWEALTH OF MASSACHUSETTS COUNTY OF ESSEX
Subscribed, sworn to and acknowledged before me by the said testator and witnesses this _____ day of _____, 20___.

_____
Notary Public
My commission expires:

TERMS IN ACTION

Elizabeth Edwards was the wife of John Edwards, who was a former trial lawyer, U.S. Senator from North Carolina, vice presidential nominee, and Democratic presidential candidate in 2008. At the time of Mrs. Edwards's death from cancer on December 7, 2010, she was estranged from John Edwards due to his infidelity with a former campaign employee with whom he fathered a child—a child whom John Edwards originally denied was his. Mrs. Edwards, who was also a lawyer, executed a **will** six days before her death, and the absence of any mention of her husband on the five-page document was something to be noticed. Mrs. Edwards's will, which was first made publicly available by the television show "Inside Edition," opens with the required **exordium clause** and makes provisions to pay for her debts and funeral expenses. She appointed her daughter Catherine Elizabeth Edwards to be her **executor**. Mrs. Edwards directed in her first **dispositive clause** that all her personal tangible property be distributed to her three children, **per stirpes**, in a manner over which her executor had sole discretion. The **residuary estate** was then directed to be distributed to a trust that Mrs. Edwards had established in 1992. The **attestation clause** included the signature of two witnesses, and the will concluded with a **self-proving affidavit**.

Source: insideedition.com

Reviewing What You Learned

After studying the chapter, write the answers to each of the following questions:

1. What particular form must a will follow? _____

   _____

   _____

   _____

   _____

2. What is the name given to the first clause of a will in which the testator sets forth his or her name and domicile and states that he revokes all previous wills and codicils made by him or her?

   _____

   _____

   _____

   _____

   _____

   _____

3. Why is the clause directing that the just debts and funeral expenses be paid out of the residuary estate often omitted from the will? _____

   _____

   _____

   _____

4. On what occasion is the residuary clause the only dispositive clause in a will? _____

   _____

   _____

   _____

5. What will happen to the residue of an estate if the residuary clause is omitted from a will? _____

   _____

   _____

   _____

6. What are the principal duties of the executor or executrix? __

   _____

   _____

   _____

   _____

7. On what occasions, when a person dies testate, will the court appoint an administrator or administratrix? _____

   _____

   _____

   _____

8. In some states, what will be required if a will does not state that the executor is to serve without giving surety on his or her bond?

   _____

   _____

   _____

   _____

9. If no "powers" clause is in a will, what will the executor be required to do each time he or she wishes to carry out an extraordinary administrative function? _____

   _____

   _____

   _____

   _____

10. What is the purpose of the tax clause in a will? _____

   _____

   _____

   _____

   _____

11. Where, on a will, is the testimonium clause located? What are the first few words of the testimonium clause? _____

   _____

   _____

   _____

   _____

6

12. Where, on a will, is the attestation clause located? _____

_____

_____

13. What is the most desirable arrangement of the signature page of a will?

_____

_____

_____

_____

14. Explain the reason for using a self-proving affidavit in a will.

_____

_____

_____

_____

Understanding Legal Concepts

Indicate whether each statement is true or false. Then, change the italicized word or phrase of each false statement to make it true.

ANSWERS

_____ **1.** Will *must* follow a particular form.

_____ **2.** The exordium clause is the *last* clause in a will.

_____ **3.** The *residuary* estate is the estate remaining after individual items have been given out by the will.

_____ **4.** Often, when the testator leaves the entire estate to one person or in equal shares to several people, the only dispositive clause is the *residuary* clause.

_____ **5.** If the residuary clause is omitted from a will, the residue will usually pass to the heirs according to the law of *intestate succession.*

_____ **6.** In some states, the court will allow a will *without* the testimony of witnesses if it contains a self-proving affidavit and no one objects to its allowance.

_____ **7.** The clause that precedes the witnesses' signatures is called the *testimonium* clause.

_____ **8.** If a testator fails to appoint an executor in a will, the court will appoint a *trustee* to perform the task.

_____ **9.** Unless a will contains a clause stating that the executor is to serve without giving surety on his or her bond, the *executor* will have to have a surety on the bond.

_____ **10.** The clause preceding the testator's signature is called the *attestation* clause.

Checking Terminology

From the list of legal terms that follows, select the one that matches each definition.

ANSWERS

a. administrator
b. administratrix
c. attestation clause
d. bond
e. conservator
f. dispositive clauses
g. domicile
h. executor
i. executrix
j. exordium clause
k. fiduciary
l. guardian
m. guardian ad litem
n. incorporation by reference
o. in terrorem clause
p. no-contest clause
q. per capita
r. per stirpes

_____ **1.** The estate remaining after individual items have been given out by a will.

_____ **2.** A person's principal place of abode; the place to which, whenever a person is absent, he or she has the present intent of returning.

_____ **3.** The introductory paragraph of a will. (Select two answers.)

_____ **4.** A man nominated in a will of a decedent to carry out the terms of the will; a personal representative of an estate.

_____ **5.** A person in a position of trust, such as an executor, administrator, guardian, or trustee.

_____ **6.** A woman nominated in a will of a decedent to carry out the terms of the will; a personal representative of an estate.

_____ **7.** The clause in a will that disposes of all of the testator's property not otherwise given out.

_____ **8.** The clause in a will that states exactly what each beneficiary is to receive.

_____ **9.** A clause in a will containing an affidavit that allows the will to be recognized by the court without the testimony of witnesses.

_____ **10.** A man appointed by the court to administer the estate of an intestate decedent.

_____ **11.** A woman appointed by the court to administer the estate of an intestate decedent.

_____ **12.** One who legally has the care and management of the person, property, or both, of a minor or incompetent.

s. publication clause
t. residuary clause
u. residuary estate
v. self-proving affidavit
w. signature clause
x. surety
y. testimonium clause
z. trustee

_____ 13. A person who holds property in trust for another.

_____ 14. A clause in a will that attempts to disinherit any legatee, devisee, or beneficiary who contests the provisions of the will. (Select two answers.)

_____ 15. One who undertakes to stand behind another—that is, pay money or do any other act—in the event that his or her principal fails to meet an obligation.

_____ 16. The clause in a will that precedes the witnesses' signatures.

_____ 17. A written instrument promising the payment of a sum of money if certain duties are not performed.

_____ 18. The clause in a will that precedes the testator's signature. (Select two answers.)

_____ 19. By right of representation.

_____ 20. One who legally has the care and management of the property, but not the person, of someone who is incompetent.

_____ 21. Per head.

_____ 22. A guardian appointed by a court to protect a minor who brings or defends a lawsuit.

_____ 23. Making a document part of another document by referring to it in the second document and stating the intention of including it.

Using Legal Language

Read the following story and fill in the blank lines with legal terms taken from the list of terms at the beginning of this chapter:

In his will, Jason named his wife, Julie, to be the _____—that is, the personal representative of his estate—and said that she was to serve without giving _____ (naming someone to stand behind) on her official _____. Had he died without a will, Julie probably would have been appointed _____. The _____ in Jason's will set forth his name and _____—that is, his principal residence—and stated that he revoked all previous wills and codicils made by him. The _____ in his will listed the items that each beneficiary was to receive. The _____ gave all the rest, residue, and remainder of Jason's estate, called the _____, to his wife, Julie, who was named _____ to care for their minor daughter, Jennie, and _____ to hold property for Jennie's benefit. These latter positions made her a(n) _____, because she was in a position of trust. A(n) _____, also called a(n) _____, was not needed because Jason expected no beneficiary to contest the will. The will contained a(n) _____ preceding the testator's signature and a(n) _____ preceding the witnesses' signatures. The will ended with a(n) _____ that contained an affidavit by Jason that he declared the instrument to be his last will and that he signed it willingly as a free and voluntary act.

PUZZLING OVER WHAT YOU LEARNED

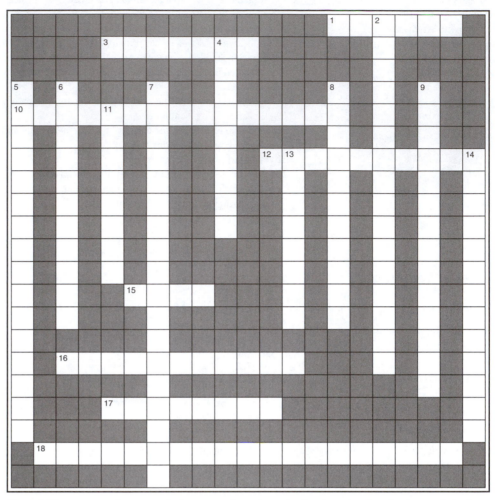

Caveat: Allow squares for spaces between words and punctuation (apostrophes, hyphens, etc.) when filling in crossword.

Across

1. One who undertakes to stand behind another.
3. A person who holds property in trust for another.
10. The introductory paragraph of a will.
12. Per head.
15. An instrument promising the payment of money if duties are not performed.
16. People in positions of trust.
17. One who has the care of the person and property of a minor.
18. Clauses in a will that state exactly what each beneficiary is to receive.

Down

2. Clause in a will that disposes of all property not otherwise given out.
4. A woman nominated in a will to carry out the terms of the will.
5. Estate remaining after individual items have been given out by a will.
6. One who legally has management of the property but not the person of an incompetent.
7. The introductory paragraph of a will.
8. By right of representation.
9. A woman appointed by the court to administer the estate of an intestate.
11. A person's principal place of abode.
13. A man nominated in a will to carry out the terms of the will.
14. A man appointed by the court to administer the estate of an intestate.

6

Disinheritance and Intestacy

ANTE INTERROGATORY

When property reverts to the state, it is said to (A) escheat,
(B) lapse, (C) adeem, (D) vest.

CHAPTER OUTLINE

Spousal Protection
Dower and Curtesy
Pretermitted Children
Homestead Protection

Distinctive Relationships
Intestacy
    Rights of Surviving Spouse
    Rights of Other Heirs

KEY TERMS

adoption *(a·DOP·shun)*

adoptive parents *(a·DOP·tiv)*

affiliation proceedings *(a·fil·ee·AY·shun pro·SEED·ings)*

collateral relatives *(ko·LAT·er·el REL·e·tivs)*

coparceners *(koh·PAR·se·ners)*

coverture *(KUV·er·cher)*

curtesy *(KUR·te·see)*

decedent *(de·SEE·dent)*

degree of kindred *(de·GREE ov KIN·dred)*

descendants *(de·SEN·dents)*

descent *(de·SENT)*

disinheritance *(dis·in·HAIR·uh·tents)*

distribution *(dis·tre·BYOO·shun)*

dower *(DOW·er)*

elective share *(e·LEK·tiv)*

escheat *(es·CHEET)*

forced heir *(forssd air)*

forced share

full age *(ayj)*

half-blood

homestead exemption *(HOME·sted ex·EMP·shun)*

homestead *(HOME·sted)*

illegitimate children *(il·e·JIT·i·met CHIL·dren)*

intestacy *(in·TESS·te·see)*

intestate *(in·TESS·tate)*

intestate succession *(in·TESS·tate suk·SESH·en)*

kindred *(KIN·dred)*

legal fiction *(LEE·gul FIK·shun)*

life estate *(es·TATE)*

lineal ascendants *(LIN·ee·el a·SEN·dents)*

lineal descendants *(LIN·ee·el de·SEN·dents)*

majority *(ma·JAW·ri·tee)*

next friend

6

next of kin

nonmarital children *(non·MAR·i·tel)*

paternity proceeding *(pa·TERN·i·tee pro·SEED·ing)*

pretermitted child *(pre·ter·MIT·ed)*

primogeniture *(pry·mo·JEN·e·cher)*

probated *(PRO·bate·ed)*

vested *(VES·ted)*

waive a spouse's will *(SPOW·sez)*

SPOUSAL PROTECTION

Surviving spouses are protected against being disinherited by their husbands and wives. State laws allow surviving spouses to disclaim the provisions made for them in their deceased spouse's will and instead take a statutorily designated amount, called an **elective share** (also known as a **statutory share** or a **forced share**). A surviving spouse who elects to disclaim the provisions of a deceased spouse's will is sometimes referred to as a **forced heir**.

Some states allow a disinherited spouse to take the amount that he or she would have inherited had the spouse died without a will. Other states use a different formula to determine the amount of a spouse's inheritance. For example, in Massachusetts, the surviving husband or wife who wishes to **waive a spouse's will**—that is, renounce or disclaim it—must file a petition to do so with the court within six months after the spouse's will is **probated** (the court process by which a will is proven to be valid). On waiver of the will, the surviving spouse will be entitled to receive the following from the estate of the deceased spouse:

1. If the deceased spouse is survived by issue, one-third of all of the real property and one-third of all of the personal property, but of that share no more than $25,000 outright and a life estate in the remainder. A **life estate** is an ownership interest whose duration is limited to the life of some person.
2. If the deceased spouse is survived by no issue but **kindred** (blood relatives), $25,000 outright plus a life estate in one-half of the remaining real and one-half of the remaining personal property.
3. If the deceased spouse is survived by no issue or kindred, $25,000 outright plus one-half of the remaining real and personal property absolutely.

Under this particular statute, a will cannot be waived by the surviving spouse if the deceased testator or testatrix obtained a legal separation from the spouse before death.

DOWER AND CURTESY

Centuries ago in England, the rights of dower and curtesy developed as a way to protect the interest of a surviving spouse of one who owned real property. These rights were especially important in those days, when land was the chief form of income from either rents or profits from the land. **Dower** was a right that a widow had to a life estate in one-third of all real property owned by her husband during **coverture** (marriage). **Curtesy** was a right that a widower (a man) had, only if issue of the marriage were born alive, to a life estate in all real property owned by his wife at any time during coverture. Both dower and curtesy were exempt from the claims of the decedent's creditors—an important consideration today.

Many states today have either abolished common law dower and curtesy or amended it to treat men and women equally. They also apply it only to real property that was owned by a spouse upon death rather than during coverture. This change eliminates the need to obtain a release of dower or curtesy of a spouse on a married person's deed.

Usually, a person cannot accept dower and, at the same time, waive the will of a deceased spouse. In states that follow this law, a surviving spouse of a person who dies testate has a choice of (1) accepting the provisions of the will, (2) waiving the will and taking the amount provided for by statute, or (3) taking the right of dower or curtesy. Usually, the last would not be elected unless the decedent's estate were insolvent, because the second choice would normally provide a greater inheritance.

TERMS IN ACTION

When does a surviving spouse lose her or his right to an **elective** or **statutory share**? When that person is, technically, not married, according to her or his state's requirements. Here is a telling case from Florida. Rose Zyontz married Isaac Litzky on May 13th, 1971. The wedding ceremony was performed by an orthodox Rabbi, in conformity to the couple's Orthodox Jewish faith, and the Rabbi issued them a Hebrew marriage certificate, called a Ksuba. On October 1st, 1971, Isaac died, leaving behind no will. Because Isaac died **intestate**, Rose sought her **statutory share** (or **dower** rights), but was denied because the court concluded that she wasn't Mr. Litzky's legal spouse. Even though Rose took Litzky's last name, and even though their apartment mailbox was labeled "Mr. and Mrs. Isaac Litzky," the couple never obtained a marriage license from the State of Florida. Because Florida invalidated common law marriage in 1968, a valid marriage license on file with the state is what determines legal marriage between two people. Another fact that hurt Rose's claim to her dead "husband's" intestate estate was that, while living with Mr. Litzky, Rose was still receiving the Social Security checks sent to her as the widow of a Mr. Nathan Zyontz. Rose even accepted the Social Security checks after Mr. Litzky died. If you're wondering how Social Security checks meant for a Mrs. Zyontz could be mailed to the address of Mrs. Litzky, the apartment's mailbox actually said "Mr. and Mrs. Isaac Litzky and Rose Zyontz."

Source: *In re Litzky's Estate*, 296 So.2d 638 (Fl. App. 1974)

PRETERMITTED CHILDREN

Sometimes, a testator or testatrix will leave a child out of a will. When this occurs, the omitted child, called a **pretermitted child**, will receive nothing from the parent's estate unless the child can prove that the omission was unintentional—that is, done by mistake. Here is a typical statute:

> If a testator omits to provide in his will for any of his children, whether born before or after the testator's death, or for the issue of a deceased child, whether born before or after the testator's death, they shall take the same share of his estate which they would have taken if he had died intestate, unless they have been provided for by the testator in his lifetime or unless it appears that the omission was intentional and not occasioned by accident or mistake.

Notice that the burden is on the omitted child to prove that his or her omission from the will was unintentional. This must be done through another person (called a **next friend**) if the child is still a minor, because a person cannot bring a lawsuit until reaching **majority**, or becoming of **full age**—that is, an adult. To avoid a will contest when a child is **disinherited** (purposely omitted from a will), it is best to mention in the will that the child was omitted intentionally and that it was not done by accident or mistake.

TERMS IN ACTION

Joan Crawford was one of the biggest movie stars of all time. Starting in 1928, she made over 70 movies throughout a six-decade career, was one of the highest-paid women in America, and won an Academy Award for Best Actress in 1945. She was ambitious and driven, so much so that after being declared "box office poison" in 1933, she made an Oscar-winning comeback in the following decade. Joan Crawford adopted four children and was married

6

four times. Her last husband was the CEO of Pepsi, and she sat on its board of directors after his death. But, Crawford is probably most famous for being "Mommie Dearest," which was the title of the book and movie about her, written by her oldest child, Christina. The book and movie were particularly unflattering portraits of a bitter mean-spirited cleanliness-obsessed woman who was a physically and emotionally abusive mother to Christina and her brother Christopher. What might have prompted a daughter to write such a tell-all about her own mother? **Disinheritance**, maybe. Joan Crawford's will was executed on October 28th, 1976, and was opened after her death on May 10th, 1977. It was not written as a will that could be subjected to a claim by a **pretermitted child**. Although Ms. Crawford gave $77,000 bequests to her two younger children, her will's dispositive clauses end with this line: "It is my intention to make no provision herein for my son Christopher or my daughter Christina for reasons which are well known to them."

Sources: imdb.com; answers.com

HOMESTEAD PROTECTION

To allow families to remain in their homes when tragedy strikes, states have **homestead exemptions**, which allow a head of household to designate a house and land as a homestead. A **homestead** is property that is beyond the reach of creditors and claims of others so long as the family uses it as a home. In many states, a homestead allowance up to a certain amount of money continues after the death of the head of household to provide a residence for the surviving spouse and minor children. For example, Minnesota's homestead exemption applies to up to 160 acres of property, and the value is up to $300,000; however, if the property is used for farming, the exemption is $750,000 (MINN. STAT. 510.02).

DISTINCTIVE RELATIONSHIPS

Half-blood relatives have one parent in common, but not both. For example, a half-sister might have the same mother, but not the same father, as her half-brother. Under the laws of many states, half-blood relatives inherit the same as whole-blood relatives. In a few states, half-blood relatives inherit only when there are no whole-blood relatives. In Florida, half-blood kindred receive only half as much as whole-blood kindred unless there is no one of the whole blood.

Adoption is the legal process by which a child's legal rights and duties toward his or her natural parents are replaced by similar rights and duties toward his or her adopting parents. Under most state laws today, adopted children inherit from and through their **adoptive (adopting) parents** and not from their natural parents. The term **descendants** means those who are of the bloodstream (including adopted children) of a common ancestor. This paradox is known as a **legal fiction**—an assumption, for purposes of justice, of a fact that does not exist.

Children born out of wedlock (formerly called bastards but now referred to as **illegitimate children** or **nonmarital children**, inherit from their mother and any maternal ancestors. In addition, they inherit from and through their fathers who have acknowledged paternity, have been adjudicated to be their fathers in paternity proceedings, or have married their mothers. A **paternity proceeding**, also called an **affiliation proceeding**, is a court action to determine whether a person is the father of a child born out of wedlock.

INTESTACY

When people die without a will—that is, **intestate**—their personal property passes to others according to the law of the state where they were domiciled when they died. In contrast, their real property passes according to the law of the state in which the property is located. These laws were called the **laws of descent and distribution** under early English law, which distinguished real property from personal property. Real property descended to the eldest son of the **decedent** (deceased person) under a doctrine known as **primogeniture**. If parents had no sons, all daughters took the property together as a single heir (as **coparceners**, or joint heirs). Personal property of the decedent, in those early days, was distributed by church officials "for the good of the soul of the deceased." Thus, the word **descent** technically refers only to real property, and the word **distribution** refers to personal property.

Today, the law of **intestacy** (the circumstance of dying without having made a valid will) is called the law of **intestate succession**. The early distinction between real and personal property is still followed. Ownership of real property becomes **vested** (fixed or absolute) in the decedent's heirs at the moment of death; ownership of personal property, however, passes to the administrator or administratrix to be distributed by him or her.

Present American statutes of intestate succession are based on the English Statute of 1670 and apply to both real and personal property. Under most state laws, after an amount is allotted to a surviving spouse, if any, the balance passes to the decedent's lineal descendants. **Lineal descendants** are people who are in a direct line of descent (downward) from the decedent—children, grandchildren, and great-grandchildren. When there are no living lineal descendants, the balance passes to the decedent's lineal ascendants. **Lineal ascendants** are people who are in a direct line of ascent (upward) from the decedent—parents, grandparents, and great-grandparents. When there are no living descendants or ascendants, the balance passes to the decedent's **collateral relatives**—those not in a direct line, such as brothers, sisters, nieces, nephews, uncles, aunts, and cousins. Remember: A will is for your loved ones; intestate succession is for your relatives. Although the statutes differ from state to state, a fairly typical one is discussed here.

Word Wise
The Prefix "Co-"

This Latin prefix meaning "together" appears in hundreds of English words. Its four spelling variations (col-, com-, con-, and cor-) make pronunciation easier before various roots. Some examples are as follows:

Word	*Meaning*
collaborate [*col* + *laborare* (to work)]	To work together
companion [*com* + *panis* (bread)]	Someone who accompanies another; originally, someone who shared bread
contact [*con* + *tact* (to touch)]	Touch by meeting
coparceners	Joint heirs
corroborate [*cor* + *roborare* (strength)]	To make certain; confirm

---

Rights of Surviving Spouse

According to a Massachusetts statute, if a person dies intestate, a surviving spouse is entitled to the following:

1. if the deceased is survived by issue, one-half of the estate;
2. if the deceased is survived by kindred, but no issue, $200,000 and one-half of the remainder of the estate;
3. if the deceased is survived by no issue and no kindred, the whole estate.

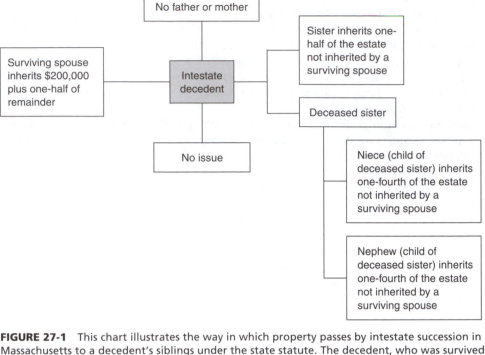

FIGURE 27-1   This chart illustrates the way in which property passes by intestate succession in Massachusetts to a decedent's siblings under the state statute. The decedent, who was survived by no issue, mother, or father, was survived by a spouse, one sister, and two children of a deceased sister.

Rights of Other Heirs

Under this state statute, if a person dies intestate, his or her property will pass, subject to the rights of the surviving spouse (stated earlier), as follows:

1. If the deceased is survived by issue, the property will pass in equal shares to the surviving children. The issue of any deceased children take their parent's share by right of representation.
2. If the deceased is survived by no issue, but by a father or mother, the property will pass in equal shares to the father and mother or the survivor of them.
3. If the deceased is survived by no issue and no mother or father, the property will pass in equal shares to brothers and sisters. The issue of any deceased brothers or sisters take their parent's share by right of representation.
4. If the deceased is survived by no issue, and no mother or father, and no brothers or sisters or their issue (nieces or nephews), the property will pass in equal shares to the **next of kin** (those most nearly related by blood). To determine the closest relatives, each relationship is assigned a number called a **degree of kindred**. The relationship with the lowest number usually inherits to the exclusion of all others. For example, first cousins (fourth-degree kindred) would inherit before second cousins (sixth-degree kindred).
5. If the deceased is survived by no kindred and no surviving spouse, the property will **escheat**—that is, pass to the state.

Reviewing What You Learned

After studying the chapter write the answers to each of the following questions:

1. If a testator fails to provide for a spouse in a will and the surviving spouse waives the will, how much will the surviving spouse be entitled to receive, in a state that follows the statute mentioned in this chapter?

   a. If the deceased was survived by issue? _____

   _____

   _____

   b. If the deceased was survived by no issue, but kindred?

   _____

   _____

   _____

   c. If the deceased was survived by no issue or kindred?

   _____

   _____

   _____

2. On what occasion may a will *not* be waived by the surviving spouse under that particular statute? _____

   _____

   _____

   _____

3. For what reason did the rights of dower and curtesy develop in early England? _____

   _____

   _____

   _____

4. What was the difference between dower and curtesy years ago in England? _____

   _____

   _____

   _____

5. What choices are available to a surviving spouse who does not like the provisions of the will of his or her spouse? _____

   _____

   _____

   _____

6. What must a pretermitted child prove to inherit from a parent's estate? _____

   _____

   _____

   _____

7. What should testators do to avoid a will contest when a child is purposely omitted from a will? _____

   _____

   _____

   _____

   _____

8. Differentiate between the words "descent" and "distribution."

   _____

   _____

   _____

   _____

9. Explain the difference between the vesting of real property and the passing of personal property under today's law. _____

   _____

   _____

   _____

   _____

10. What is the purpose of homestead exemptions? _____

   _____

   _____

   _____

6

11. How do half-blood relatives inherit under the laws of many states?

_____

_____

_____

_____

12. Under most state laws today, from whom do adopted children inherit? _____

_____

_____

_____

13. Under what circumstances do nonmarital children inherit from and through their fathers?_____

_____

_____

_____

_____

14. Who will inherit, and in what amount, under the law of intestate succession, from the estate of a person who dies intestate survived by the following:

    a. a spouse and two children ($120,000 estate)?_____

_____

_____

_____

b. a spouse and a father and mother ($260,000 estate)? _____

_____

_____

_____

c. a spouse and no issue or kindred ($120,000 estate)?_____

_____

_____

_____

d. three children ($120,000 estate)?_____

_____

_____

_____

e. no issue or kindred and no surviving spouse ($120,000 estate)? _____

_____

_____

_____

f. a spouse and a 96-year-old uncle ($400,000 estate)? _____

_____

_____

_____

Understanding Legal Concepts

Indicate whether each statement is true or false. Then, change the italicized word or phrase of each false statement to make it true.

ANSWERS

_____ **1.** Under today's laws, if a surviving spouse is unhappy with the provisions of his or her spouse's will, he or she can _do nothing about_ it.

_____ **2.** Under the state statute referred to earlier, a will _cannot be_ waived by the surviving spouse if the deceased testator or testatrix had obtained a legal separation from his or her spouse before death.

_____ **3.** Years ago in England, _dower_ was a right that a widower had if issue of the marriage were born alive, but not otherwise, to a life estate in all real property owned by his wife at any time during coverture.

_____ **4.** Both dower and curtesy were exempt from the claims of the decedent's _creditors,_ which is an important consideration today.

_____ **5.** A child who is omitted from a parent's will can receive nothing from the parent's estate unless the child can prove that the omission was _unintentional._

_____ **6.** A person can bring a lawsuit by himself or herself at _any age._

_____ **7.** If a person dies without a will and is survived by heirs, the property will pass _to the state._

_____ **8.** Today, real property vests in the decedent's heirs at the moment of death of the owner, whereas _personal property_ passes to the administrator or administratrix to be distributed by him or her.

_____ **9.** Under the state statute referred to in this chapter, if a person dies intestate and is

_____   **a.** survived by _kindred, but no issue,_ a surviving spouse is entitled to one-half of the estate.

_____ **b.** survived by *no issue and no kindred,* a surviving spouse is entitled to the whole estate.

_____ **c.** survived by issue, his or her property will pass, subject to the rights of the surviving spouse, in equal shares, to the surviving *grandchildren.*

_____ **d.** survived by no issue, but a father or mother, his or her property will pass, subject to the rights of

the surviving spouse, to the surviving *father and mother.*

_____ **e.** survived by no issue and no mother or father, the decedent's property will pass, subject to the rights of the surviving spouse, to his or her *next of kin.*

_____ **10.** Under some state statutes, illegitimate children inherit from their *father* and any *paternal* ancestor.

Checking Terminology

From the list of legal terms that follows, select the one that matches each definition:

ANSWERS

a. adoption	_____ 1. Relatives who have one parent in common, but not both.
b. adoptive parents	_____ 2. To die without a will.
c. affiliation proceeding	_____ 3. A statutory sum given to a surviving spouse who disclaims the provisions made for him or her in a deceased spouse's will. (Select two answers.)
d. bastards	
e. collateral relatives	_____ 4. At common law, the right of a widow to a life estate in one-third of all real property owned by her husband during coverture.
f. coparceners	
g. coverture	_____ 5. At common law, the right of a widower, if issue of the marriage were born alive, to a life estate in all real property owned by his wife during coverture.
h. curtesy	
i. decedent	_____ 6. Renounce or disclaim a spouse's will.
j. degree of kindred	_____ 7. Blood relatives.
k. descendants	_____ 8. An ownership interest whose duration is limited to the life of some person.
l. descent	_____ 9. A court action to determine whether a person is the father of a child born out of wedlock. (Select two answers.)
m. disinheritance	
n. distribution	_____ 10. Children born out of wedlock. (Select three answers.)
o. dower	_____ 11. The legal process in which a child's legal rights and duties toward his or her natural parents are replaced by similar rights and duties toward his or her adopting parents.
p. elective share	
q. escheat	_____ 12. One acting for the benefit of an infant in bringing a legal action.
r. forced heir	_____ 13. A child who is omitted by a testator from a will.
s. forced share	_____ 14. Marriage.
t. full age	_____ 15. Adulthood. (Select two answers.)
u. half-blood	_____ 16. The act or process of an heir's becoming beneficially entitled to the property of one who dies without a will.
v. homestead	
w. homestead exemption	_____ 17. Succession to the ownership of real property by inheritance (early English law).
x. illegitimate children	_____ 18. The apportionment and division of the personal property of an intestate among his or her heirs (early English law).
y. intestacy	
z. intestate	_____ 19. The state of being the first born among several children of the same parents (early English law).
aa. intestate succession	
bb. kindred	_____ 20. Persons to whom an estate of inheritance descends jointly; joint heirs (early English law).
cc. legal fiction	_____ 21. The state of dying without having made a valid will.
dd. life estate	_____ 22. A surviving spouse who elects to disclaim the provisions of a deceased spouse's will.
ee. lineal ascendants	_____ 23. Parents who adopt a child.
ff. lineal descendants	_____ 24. Those most nearly related by blood.
gg. majority	_____ 25. The reversion of property to the state if the property owner dies without heirs.
hh. next friend	_____ 26. Fixed or absolute; not contingent.
ii. next of kin	_____ 27. A deceased person.
jj. nonmarital children	_____ 28. Proved and allowed by the court.
kk. paternity proceeding	_____ 29. Property that is beyond the reach of creditors' and others' claims as long as the family uses the property as a home.
ll. pretermitted child	
mm. primogeniture	_____ 30. The relationship between a decedent and his or her relatives to determine who are most nearly related by blood.
nn. probated	
oo. vested	_____ 31. Relatives not in a direct line, such as brothers, sisters, nieces, nephews, uncles, aunts, and cousins.
pp. waive a spouse's will	
	_____ 32. Those who are of the bloodstream (including adopted children) of a common ancestor.

6

_____   33. An assumption, for purposes of justice, of a fact that does not exist.

_____   34. People who are in a direct line of ascent (upward) from the decedent—parents, grand-parents, and great-grandparents.

_____   35. People who are in a direct line of descent (downward) from the decedent—children, grandchildren, and great-grandchildren.

_____   36. Purposely omitted from a will.

_____   37. **The provision that** allows a head of a household to designate a house and land as a homestead.

Using Legal Language

Read the following story and fill in the blank lines with legal terms taken from the list of terms at the beginning of this chapter:

When Jason, the _____, died testate, his wife, Julie, who was of _____— that is, an adult—could choose to accept the provisions of the will, _____ (renounce or disclaim) the will, or take her right of _____, which at common law was the right to a(n) _____ in one-third of all real property owned by Jason during _____. Had she been a man, this right would be called _____. Jason's real property passed under the will by _____ to his devisee, and _____ at the moment of death. His personal property passed by _____ through his personal representative to his legatees. The will had to be _____ —that is, proved and allowed by the court. Jason did not fail to provide for any of his children; therefore, no _____ would, if he or she had not reached _____, have to bring suit by a _____. He had no _____—that is, children born out of wedlock—and none of his children were of the _____—that is, had one parent in common, but not both. Had Jason died without a will, on death, his personal property would have passed to his heirs according to the law of _____ in the state where he died domiciled. His _____—that is, those most nearly related by blood and sometimes referred to as _____—would have inherited from his estate along with his surviving spouse.

6

PUZZLING OVER WHAT YOU LEARNED

Caveat: Allow squares for spaces between words and punctuation (apostrophes, hyphens, etc.) when filling in crossword.

Across

7. Another name for a forced share.
10. Right of a widow to a life estate in one-third of real property owned by a husband.
12. Surviving spouse who elects to disclaim the provisions of a spouse's will.
14. To die without a will.
16. The state of dying without having made a valid will.
17. Fixed or absolute.
18. Blood relatives.
19. Adulthood.

Down

1. Renounce or disclaim a spouse's will.
2. Succession to the ownership of real property by inheritance.
3. A statutory sum given to a surviving spouse who disclaims will's provisions.
4. A child who is omitted by a testator from a will.
5. One acting for the benefit of an infant in bringing a legal action.
6. Right of a widower to a life estate in real property owned by his wife.
8. An ownership interest whose duration is limited to someone's life.
9. Marriage.
11. Proved and allowed by the court.
13. A deceased person.
15. The reversion of property to the state if the owner dies without heirs.

Personal Representative of the Estate

ANTE INTERROGATORY

*An official who administers the estate of a person who dies intestate
and no relative, heir, or other person appears who is entitled to act
as administrator is called a(n) (A) public administrator, (B) special
administrator, (C) ancillary administrator, (D) voluntary administrator.*

CHAPTER OUTLINE

Estate Settlement

Titles of Personal Representatives

Successor Personal Representatives

Particular-Purpose Administrators

KEY TERMS

administrator (*ad·MIN·is·tray·tor*)

administrator ad litem (*ad LY·tem*)

administrator c.t.a.

administrator cum testamento annexo *(kum
tes·ta·MENT·o an·EKS·o)*

administrator d.b.n.

administrator d.b.n.c.t.a.

administrator de bonis non *(de BO·nis non)*

administrator de bonis non cum testamento
annexo

administrator pendente lite *(pen·DEN·tay
LIE·tay)*

administrator with the will annexed
(an·EKSD)

administrator w.w.a.

administratrix *(ad·MIN·is·tray·triks)*

ancillary administrator *(AN·sil·a·ree
ad·MIN·is·tray·tor)*

Court of Ordinary *(OR·di·ner·ee)*

executor *(eg·ZEK·yoo·tor)*

executor de son tort *(eg·ZEK·yoo·tor day
sown tort)*

executrix *(eg·ZEK·yoo·triks)*

fiduciary capacity *(fi·DOO·she·air·ee
ka·PASS·e·tee)*

Orphan's Court

personal representative *(PER·son·al
rep·re·ZEN·ta·tiv)*

Prerogative Court *(pre·ROG·a·tiv)*

Probate and Family Court *(PRO·bate)*

public administrator *(PUB·lik
ad·MIN·is·tray·tor)*

special administrator *(SPESH·el
ad·MIN·is·tray·tor)*

successor personal representatives
*(suk·SESS·or PER·son·al
rep·re·ZEN·ta·tiv)*

6

summary administration *(SUM·e·ree
ad·min·is·TRAY·shun)*
Surrogate's Court *(SER·o·gets)*

voluntary administrator *(VOL·en·ter·ee
ad·MIN·is·tray·tor)*
will contest

ESTATE SETTLEMENT

When a person dies, solely owning property of any kind, the estate must be settled. This task is undertaken by the court, which acts through an executor or administrator (called the **personal representative**), who is appointed for that purpose and who acts in a **fiduciary capacity**—that is, a position of trust. The court that exercises this function is called by different names in different states. For example, in New York it is called the **Surrogate's Court**, in Pennsylvania the **Orphan's Court**, in New Jersey the **Prerogative Court**, in Massachusetts the **Probate and Family Court**, and in Georgia the **Court of Ordinary**. In California, the Superior Court has jurisdiction over probate proceedings.

TITLES OF PERSONAL REPRESENTATIVES

In states that have adopted the Uniform Probate Code (see Chapter 24), a personal representative is referred to as the same, a **personal representative** In other states, personal representatives are given different titles, depending on the method by which they gained their position or the particular task that they are to perform. An **executor** (if a man) or **executrix** (if a woman) is a person nominated in the will of a decedent to carry out the terms of the will. An **administrator** (if a man) or **administratrix** (if a woman) is a person appointed by the court to administer the estate of an intestate decedent.

TERMS IN ACTION

When Doris Duke's father died in 1925, she inherited a $100 million fortune at the age of 13. Her tobacco tycoon father, James Buchannan Duke, was so rich that a certain university in North Carolina to which he had given so much of his fortune took his last name in 1924. Doris's life of hyper-wealth was fraught with sadness, oddness, and tragedy. She gave birth to a daughter in 1940 who only lived for a day, and in 1957, Doris accidentally ran over and killed a friend while he was opening the gates to a mansion so that she could enter the driveway. By the time of her death in 1993, she was a secluded, gravely ill, highly medicated 80-year-old woman whose constant companion was her Irish butler, Bernard Lafferty. Because her will made that butler the **executor** of her billion-dollar estate, many disgruntled beneficiaries filed lawsuits against Lafferty, alleging that the barely literate man had applied undue influence on the mentally incompetent Duke to get her to put her estate under his control. After three years of litigation, Lafferty agreed in April 1996 to a settlement, giving up control of Doris Duke's estate in exchange for $4.5 million and an annual payment of $500,000 for as long as he lived. He lived seven months longer.

Sources: nytimes.com; trutv.com

Successor Personal Representatives

An **administrator de bonis non** (administrator of goods not administered), also known as **administrator d.b.n.**, is appointed by the court to complete the settlement of an estate in which a previously appointed administrator has died, has resigned, or has been removed. An **administrator cum testamento annexo** (**administrator with the will annexed**), also known as **administrator c.t.a.** or **administrator w.w.a.**, is appointed by the court to administer a testate estate in which no executor is nominated, or in which the person named to be executor, before being appointed, either has died or has been adjudged incompetent, or refuses or neglects to perform the task. An **administrator de bonis non cum testamento annexo** (administrator of goods not administered with the will annexed), also known as **administrator d.b.n.c.t.a.**, is appointed by the court to take the place of a previously appointed executor or administrator cum testamento annexo who has died, has resigned, or has been removed. In Uniform Probate Code states, all of these people are referred to as **successor personal representatives**. They are appointed to succeed previously appointed personal representatives.

Particular-Purpose Administrators

A **special administrator** is one who is appointed by the court to handle the affairs of an estate for a limited time only, such as when a delay occurs in the allowance of a will or dispute over the appointment of an executor. The special administrator takes care of affairs that are in need of immediate attention.

A **public administrator** is an official who administers the estate of a person who dies intestate and no relative, heir, or other person appears who is entitled to act as administrator.

A **voluntary administrator** is a person who undertakes the informal administration of a small estate. Some states allow this provision as an easy method of settling small estates. For example, in Massachusetts, if an estate consists entirely of personal property the total value of which does not exceed an $15,000, not counting an automobile, then a surviving spouse (or a child, parent, or sibling of the decedent) may, after the expiration of 30 days from the date of death, file certain information and become a voluntary administrator. The powers of a voluntary administrator cease if a regular administrator or executor is appointed to settle the estate. In California, a similar procedure, known as **summary administration**, is used to settle estates that do not exceed $30,000.

Word Wise
The Prefix "Ad-"

The Latin prefix "ad" means "to" or "toward." Its spelling variations facilitate different pronunciations before different roots.

Prefix	Example
ad-	administrator
a- (before *sc, sp, st*)	ascend, aspect, astride
ac- (before *c* or *q*)	accept, acquit
af- (before *f*)	affect
ag- (before *g*)	aggravated
an- (before *n*)	annulment
ap- (before *p*)	approve
ar- (before *r*)	arraignment
as- (before *s*)	assault
at- (before *t*)	attempt

An **ancillary administrator** is one who is appointed by the court to handle the affairs of a decedent in a foreign state. For example, if a decedent domiciled in New York dies owning real property in Connecticut, ancillary administration will have to be taken out in Connecticut, in addition to there being a New York executor or administrator, to settle the Connecticut real property. It is also necessary to take out ancillary administration if one is to bring suit or collect debts of a nonresident decedent.

An **administrator pendente lite** (pending suit) is a temporary administrator appointed by the court to protect estate assets when there is a **will contest** (a suit over the allowance or disallowance of a will). In contrast, an **administrator ad litem** (for the suit) is appointed by the court to supply a necessary party to a suit in which the estate has an interest, as when the estate is a party to a lawsuit.

An **executor de son tort** is the name given to a person who performs the duties of an executor without authority to do so. Notice that the word "tort" is in the name. Such a person is said to be an intermeddler and is held responsible for his or her acts.

TERMS IN ACTION

When Herman Rockefeller, of Melbourne Australia, failed to return home three days after a business trip that ended on January 21, 2010, his wife Victoria made a public plea for help. Unfortunately, Mrs. Rockefeller subsequently had to endure both the news that her husband had been killed, as well as the circumstances surrounding his death and dismemberment. The 52-year-old businessman was worth $400 million, but he wasn't killed for his money. Unbeknownst to his wife and two children, Rockefeller frequented swingers' parties and attended one on the night he returned from his business trip. At that party, Rockefeller angered a couple whom he had already known from a prior party. They expected Rockefeller to bring a woman with him, as he had earlier promised them while at a prior party. That argument escalated until the couple beat him to death at the party. Once the couple realized whom they had just killed, they moved his body to a secluded location, and then dismembered and burned it. Despite his immense wealth, Rockefeller died **intestate**; so, after his death his wife went to court in July 2010 to seek the appointment as **administrator** of her husband's estate. She was made the administrator in February 2011. Then Mrs. Rockefeller learned that her husband allegedly also had a long-time mistress, who was claiming rights to the estate as well.

Source: heraldsun.com.au

Reviewing What You Learned

After studying the chapter, write the answers to each of the following questions:

1. Name the title of the personal representative who is nominated in a will. _____

   _____

   _____

   _____

2. Name the title of the personal representative of an intestate estate.

   _____

   _____

   _____

   _____

3. If the original personal representative of an intestate estate dies before completing the task, what is the title given to the person who is appointed to take his or her place? _____

   _____

   _____

4. If the personal representative who is nominated in the will dies before the testator, and then the testator dies, what is the title given to the person who is appointed to settle the estate? _____

   _____

   _____

   _____

   _____

5. If the personal representative who is nominated in the will begins, but does not complete, the task, what is the title given to the person who is appointed to settle the estate? _____

   _____

   _____

   _____

   _____

6. What kind of affairs does the special administrator usually handle? _____

   _____

   _____

   _____

   _____

7. Under what circumstances does a public administrator administer an estate? _____

   _____

   _____

   _____

   _____

8. Under what ccss would an ancillary administrator be appointed in one state for a person who dies while domiciled in another state?

   _____

   _____

   _____

   _____

9. What is the difference between an administrator pendente lite and an administrator ad litem? _____

   _____

   _____

   _____

   _____

10. Why would you think that an executor de son tort is said to be an intermeddler? _____

    _____

    _____

    _____

    _____

Understanding Legal Concepts

Indicate whether each statement is true or false. Then, change the italicized word or phrase of each false statement to make it true.

ANSWERS

_____ 1. Another name for an executor or administrator is *personal representative*.

_____ 2. In California, the court that undertakes the settlement of estates is called the *Surrogate's Court*.

_____ 3. An *executor* is a male appointed by the court to administer the estate of an intestate decedent.

_____ 4. An *administratrix* is a woman nominated in a will to carry out the terms of the will.

_____ 5. An *administrator de bonis non* is appointed by the court to complete the settlement of an estate in which a previously appointed administrator has died, has resigned, or has been removed.

_____ 6. An administrator cum testamento annexo is also called an *administrator with the will annexed*.

_____ 7. An administrator de bonis non cum testamento annexo is appointed by the court to take the place of a previously appointed *executor* who has died, has resigned, or has been removed.

_____ 8. A *public* administrator is a person who undertakes the informal administration of a small estate.

_____ 9. The powers of a voluntary administrator *cease* if a regular administrator or executor is appointed to settle the estate.

_____ 10. A *voluntary* administrator is one who is appointed by the court to handle the affairs of a decedent in a foreign state.

6

Checking Terminology

From the list of legal terms that follows, select the one that matches each definition.

ANSWERS

a. administrator
b. administrator ad litem
c. administrator cum testamento annexo (c.t.a.)
d. administrator d.b.n.
e. administrator d.b.n.c.t.a.
f. administrator de bonis non
g. administrator de bonis non cum testamento annexo
h. administrator pendente lite
i. administrator with the will annexed (w.w.a.)
j. administratrix
k. ancillary administrator
l. Court of Ordinary
m. executor
n. executor de son tort
o. executrix
p. fiduciary capacity
q. Orphan's Court
r. personal representative
s. Prerogative Court
t. Probate and Family Court
u. public administrator
v. special administrator
w. successor personal representatives
x. summary administration
y. Surrogate's Court
z. voluntary administrator
aa. will contest

_____ 1. A man nominated in a will of a decedent to carry out the terms of the will; a personal representative of an estate.
_____ 2. A woman appointed by the court to administer the estate of an intestate decedent.
_____ 3. A person appointed by the court to complete the settlement of an estate in which a previously appointed administrator has died, has resigned, or has been removed. (Select two answers.)
_____ 4. A person who undertakes the informal administration of a small estate.
_____ 5. A woman nominated in a will of a decedent to carry out the terms of the will; a personal representative of an estate.
_____ 6. A person appointed by the court to administer a testate estate in which no executor is nominated or in which the executor has died or for some other reason does not settle the estate. (Select two answers.)
_____ 7. A person who performs the duties of an executor without authority to do so.
_____ 8. A temporary administrator appointed by the court to protect estate assets when there is a will contest.
_____ 9. A position of trust.
_____ 10. People appointed to succeed previously appointed personal representatives.
_____ 11. An administrator appointed by the court to supply a necessary party to a suit in which the estate has an interest.
_____ 12. A suit over the allowance or disallowance of a will.
_____ 13. A male appointed by the court to administer the estate of an intestate decedent.
_____ 14. A person appointed by the court to replace a previously appointed executor who has died, has resigned, or has been removed. (Select two answers.)
_____ 15. A person appointed by the court to handle the affairs of an estate, for a limited time only, to take care of urgent affairs.
_____ 16. An official who administers the estate of a person who dies intestate when no relative, heir, or other person appears who is entitled to act as administrator.
_____ 17. A person appointed by the court to handle the affairs of a decedent in a foreign state.
_____ 18. The executor or administrator of a deceased person.
_____ 19. The name given to the court that exercises the function of settling a decedent's estates. (Select five answers.)
_____ 20. An informal procedure used in California to settle estates that do not exceed $30,000.

Using Legal Language

Read the following story and fill in the blank lines with legal terms taken from the list of terms at the beginning of this chapter:

In his will, Kevin named Katherine to be the person who would settle his estate when he died. She was called a(n) _____, which is the name given to a female _____ of an estate. In her will, Katherine named Kevin to be the _____. Kevin was killed in an automobile accident. His huge vegetable garden, from which he made a living, was just about to be harvested when Kevin died and needed immediate attention; thus, the court appointed a(n) _____ to take care of the garden at once. Because he was domiciled in Georgia when he died, Katherine was given her fiduciary appointment by the Court of _____, which is called the _____ in New York, the _____ in Pennsylvania, the _____ in New Jersey, and the _____ in Massachusetts. Six months later, while giving birth to a child, Katherine died. Because she had not completed the settlement of Kevin's estate, her brother-in-law, Keith, was appointed _____ to finish the job. Keith was also appointed the fiduciary to settle Katherine's estate. In that position, he was known as a(n) _____ because the person Katherine had named to complete the task had predeceased her. Katherine's newborn child, Kelley, who had inherited a sizable estate from her mother, lived only for six days and then died. Because Kelley died without a will, Katherine's sister, Karen, was appointed _____ by the court to settle Kelley's estate. Had Karen been a man instead of a woman, she would have been called a(n) _____. Before completing her task, Karen became mentally ill and could not complete the job. Her friend, Kaleb, was appointed a(n) _____ by the court to finish the task. No need existed to appoint a(n) _____, because relatives could settle all of the estates involved here. A(n) _____ was not needed, because no out-of-state property was involved. None of these estates was small; therefore, none met the requirements for the appointment of a(n) _____.

PUZZLING OVER WHAT YOU LEARNED

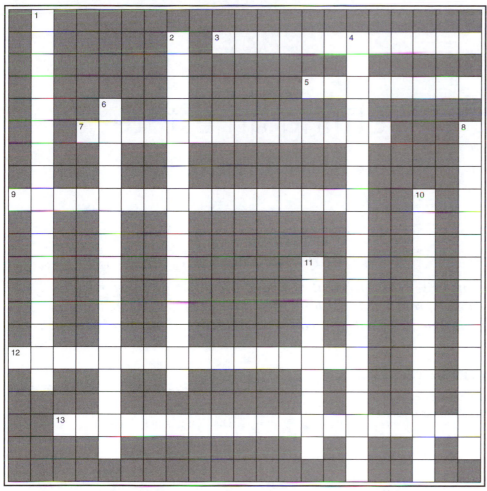

Caveat: Do **not** allow squares for spaces between words and punctuation (apostrophes, hyphens, etc.) when filling in crossword.

Across

3. The name given to the court that exercises the function of settling decedent's estates.
5. A man nominated in a will to carry out the terms of the will.
7. A woman appointed by the court to administer the estate of an intestate decedent.
9. A person appointed by the court to administer a testate estate in which no executor is nominated or in which the executor has died or for some reason does not settle the estate.
12. The name given to the court that exercises the function of settling decedent's estates.
13. An official who administers the estate of a person who dies intestate when no relative, heir, or other person appears who is entitled to act as administrator.

Down

1. A person who performs the duties of an executor without authority to do so.
2. A person appointed by the court to administer a testate estate in which no executor is nominated or in which the executor has died or for some reason does not settle the estate.
4. A person appointed by the court to handle the affairs of an estate for a limited time only to take care of urgent affairs.
6. A person appointed by the court to complete the settlement of an estate in which a previously appointed administrator has died.
8. The name given to the court that exercises the function of settling decedent's estates.
10. A male appointed by the court to administer the estate of an intestate decedent.
11. A woman nominated in a will to carry out the terms of the will.

6

Settling an Estate

ANTE INTERROGATORY

A promise by the personal representative to pay an amount of money to the probate judge if the representative's duties are not faithfully performed is called a (A) covenant, (B) surety, (C) decree, (D) bond.

CHAPTER OUTLINE

Steps in Estate Settlement
Petitioning the Court
Fiduciary's Bond
Letters
Inventory

Federal Estate Tax
Federal Gift Tax
State Death Taxes
Distribution and Accounting
Contesting a Will

KEY TERMS

bond
burden of proof *(BER·den)*
decree *(de·KREE)*
estate tax *(es·TATE)*
fiduciary *(fi·DOO·she·air·ee)*
first and final account *(a·KOWNT)*
gifts causa mortis *(KAWS·ah MORE·tes)*
gifts made in contemplation of death
     (kon·tem·PLAY·shun)
gift tax
gross estate *(es·TATE)*
heir *(air)*

heirs at law *(airs)*
inheritance tax *(in·HER·i·tense)*
inter vivos *(IN·ter VY·vose)*
inventory *(IN·ven·tor·ee)*
judgment *(JUJ·ment)*
letters of administration
     (ad·min·is·TRAY·shun)
letters testamentary *(test·e·MEN·ter·ee)*
marital deduction *(MAR·i·tal de·DUK·shun)*
proponent *(pro·PO·nent)*
sponge tax *(spunj taks)*
sureties *(SHOOR·e·tees)*
tax credit

6

STEPS IN ESTATE SETTLEMENT

Several steps are involved in the settling of an estate. These include petitioning the court for appointment, filing a bond, filing an inventory, making out tax returns, paying debts and expenses of administration, making distribution of the assets of the estate, and filing an account with the court.

Petitioning the Court

If the decedent died testate, the executor named in the will or some other interested person petitions the court for the allowance of the will and for appointment as executor or administrator cum testamento annexo of the will. If the decedent died intestate, one or more of the heirs, next of kin, or creditors petition the court for appointment as administrator of the estate. An **heir**, in the broadest usage of the term, is a person who inherits property from a decedent's estate.

Notice of a hearing on the petition is given to all interested parties, including heirs at law, by service of process, mail, or newspaper publication, depending on the particular state statute. **Heirs at law** are people who would have inherited had the decedent died intestate. After a waiting period (usually, three weeks), a hearing is held to decide on the petition, and the court issues a **decree** (decision of a court of equity) or **judgment** (decision of a court of law) that either allows or disallows the will, if one exists, and appoints the executor of the will or the administrator of the estate.

Word Wise

Variations of "Heir": Related Terms and Spellings

heir [the *h* is silent; pronounced "air"]

heirdom *(AIR·dum)*

heirloom *(AIR·loom)*

The *i* disappears and the *h* is pronounced in these words:

heredity *(her·ED·i·tee)*

hereditament *(herr·e·DIT·a·ment)*

hereditary *(her·ED·i·terr·ee)*

A prefix is added in these words:

inherit *(in·HER·it)*

inheritance *(in·HER·i·tense)*

inheritor *(in·HER·i·tor)*

Fiduciary's Bond

Before being appointed, the executor or administrator (called a **fiduciary**, meaning a person who holds a position of trust) must file a bond with the court. A **bond** is a promise by the personal representative and the sureties (if any) to pay the amount of the bond to the probate judge if the representative's duties are not faithfully performed. **Sureties** are people who stand behind the personal representative in the event that he or she fails to do the job. The amount of the bond is usually twice the value of the personal property of the estate. Sureties on the bond are often required unless the will otherwise provides or unless all interested parties consent to a bond without sureties.

Letters

When a satisfactory bond with sufficient sureties has been filed, the court issues a certificate of appointment to the personal representative. The certificate is known as **letters testamentary** in a testate estate and **letters of administration** in an intestate estate. In California, the judge signs an "order for probate" and the personal representative is given a form explaining the duties and liabilities of the position.

Inventory

After his or her appointment, one of the first duties of the personal representative is to file an inventory with the court. The **inventory** is a document that lists the assets of the estate together with their appraised value.

A waiting period (from nine months to a year) then elapses to give time for creditors to present their claims. After this period runs out, creditors are barred from bringing claims, and the debts of the estate may be paid.

Federal Estate Tax

An **estate tax** is a tax imposed on the estate of a deceased person. A federal estate tax return (form 706) must be filed within nine months after the date of death in cases in which the gross estate exceeds an amount that is exempt from the tax. The amount up to and including $2 million was exempt in 2007 and 2008. That amount increased to $3.5 million in 2009. The federal estate tax disappeared altogether in 2010, but was scheduled to resurface in 2011. Congress then passed a late-term bill in December 2010, which exempted the first $5 million of an estate from taxation, and anything over that amount is subject to a 35 percent tax. The **gross estate** for tax purposes includes all property that the decedent owned at death, including individually owned real or personal property, jointly owned real or personal property, life insurance, **inter vivos** (between the living) trusts, and **gifts made in contemplation of death**. Gifts made within three years of the date of death are presumed to be made in contemplation of death unless shown to the contrary. They are sometimes referred to as **gifts causa mortis**.

The following are deductible from the gross estate: debts of the decedent, funeral expenses, administration expenses, amounts given by will to charity, amounts inherited by a surviving spouse (called the **marital deduction**), and other miscellaneous items.

TERMS IN ACTION

Whereas there is never a good time to die, there is a better time to die: it is better to die when there are no **estate taxes**. As far back as 700 B.C., estate taxes existed. The ancient Egyptians levied a 10 percent tax on property transferred at the owner's death. The first inheritance tax in America was the 1797 Stamp Act, although it was repealed in 1802. Estate taxes seemed to be permanent by the 1920s—that is, until Congress passed a law in 2001 that effectively lowered the estate tax every year until it disappeared in 2010 (but only in 2010). In 2011, the federal estate tax reappeared. So, when Dan Duncan, of Houston, Texas, died on March 28th, 2010, he became the first billionaire to completely escape the estate tax. Born in 1933 and raised by his grandmother, the once-poor Duncan started his oil services business 1968 with $10,000 and a truck. At his death, he was the 74th richest person in the world, with an estimated **gross estate** of $9.8 billion. Had he died in 2009, or even worse, in 2011, his family members would have lost up to $4 billion of their inheritance.

Sources: heritage.org; forbes.com; thetrustadvisor.com

Federal Gift Tax

With exceptions, a federal **gift tax** is imposed on gifts made during one's lifetime that total more than $5 million. That means that the donor would owe no gift taxes unless the total amount of gifts made during the donor's life exceeds a $5 million **tax credit** (which is a sum of money that is used to offset what is owed in taxes). However, anyone can make gifts of up to $13,000 per donee per year without incurring gift tax calculations. Married persons may give $26,000 per donee per year. Any gift tax due is collected from the donor's estate, if the estate is large enough to be taxable, when the donor dies.

State Death Taxes

In addition to the federal estate tax, many states impose their own death taxes. They are called either **estate** or **inheritance taxes**, depending on whether the tax is imposed on the estate or on the people receiving the inheritance. An inheritance tax is a tax imposed on a person who inherits from a decedent's estate. California and many other states impose an estate tax equal to the credit allowed for state death taxes on the federal estate tax return if it is required to be filed. It is called a **sponge tax** because it soaks up money for the state that the estate is being given credit for in any event.

Distribution and Accounting

After the taxes and debts have been paid and the time has expired for creditors to submit claims, the remaining assets for the estate are distributed according to the terms of the will or the laws of intestate succession. Finally, an accounting, called the **first and final account** if it is the only one, is prepared. This report details the amounts received and distributed by the personal representative of the estate. When the final account is allowed by the court, the estate is settled.

CONTESTING A WILL

A will may be contested only on one of the following grounds: (a) the will was improperly executed; (b) the testator was of unsound mind; or (c) the will's execution was obtained through the use of undue influence or fraud. If a will is contested on either of the first two grounds, the **proponent** of the will—that is, the person offering it for probate—has the **burden of proof** (the duty of proving a fact) either that the will was properly executed or that the testator was of sound mind. In contrast, if a will is contested on the ground of undue influence or fraud, the person claiming those acts must prove that they took place. A will may be contested only by someone who has an interest in opposing it, such as an heir at law or a devisee or legatee of an earlier-made will.

TERMS IN ACTION

At his death in 1877, Cornelius Vanderbilt was the richest man on the planet. He was so rich that his estate of around $100 million would, in today's dollars, be worth well over $140 billion dollars. Known as "The Commodore," Vanderbilt started out ferrying passengers between New York and New Jersey on the Hudson River, and his fortune was built on shipping and railroads. Although he fathered 13 children (to one wife, who died before he did), at his death he had 10 living children. He gave 95 percent of his estate to his oldest son, William, and the rest to his eight daughters and his other son, named Cornelius Jeremiah Vanderbilt, a disfavored son who suffered from epilepsy. A few of the disgruntled daughters and Cornelius contested their father's will on the grounds that he lacked the testamentary capacity when his will was drafted and executed in 1875, and was at that time under the undue influence of a spiritualist. The tawdry and scandalous lawsuit, known as "The Great Will Contest," lasted well over a year. At its conclusion in 1789, the judge ruled in favor of William Vanderbilt, the will's **proponent**. William then paid the legal fees of his losing siblings and also enlarged their bequests. Three years later, Cornelius shot himself in a hotel room and died a few hours later, with his older brother at his bedside.

Sources: americanheritage.com; nytimes.com

Reviewing What You Learned

After studying the chapter, write the answers to each of the following questions:

1. What is the first step in administering an estate if the decedent dies testate? _____

   _____

   _____

   _____

   _____

2. How is notice of a hearing given to all interested parties?____

   _____

   _____

   _____

   _____

3. What is the significance of the decree or judgment that is issued after the court hearing? _____

   _____

   _____

   _____

   _____

4. Under what circumstances are sureties required on a personal representative's bond? _____

   _____

   _____

   _____

   _____

5. What is the usual amount of the bond? _____

   _____

   _____

   _____

   _____

6. On what grounds may a will be contested? _____

   _____

   _____

   _____

   _____

7. If a will is contested on the ground that the testator was not of sound mind, who has the burden of proof? _____

   _____

   _____

   _____

   _____

8. After being appointed, what is one of the first duties of the personal representative of an estate? _____

   _____

   _____

   _____

   _____

9. What is the length of time that creditors have to make claims against a decedent's estate? _____

   _____

   _____

   _____

   _____

10. In general, when must a federal estate tax return be filed? ___

    _____

    _____

    _____

    _____

11. What does the gross estate include?_____

    _____

    _____

    _____

    _____

12. What is the final report that is prepared to close an estate?___

    _____

    _____

    _____

    _____

Understanding Legal Concepts

Indicate whether each statement is true or false. Then, change the italicized word or phrase of each false statement to make it true.

ANSWERS

_____ 1. If the decedent died *intestate,* the executor named in the will or some other interested person petitions the court for the allowance of the will and appointment as executor.

_____ 2. Notice of a hearing on the petition is given to *all interested parties* by service of process, mail, or newspaper publication.

_____ 3. Before being appointed, the executor or administrator must file a *bond* with the court.

_____ 4. The amount of the bond is usually *three times* the value of the personal property of the estate.

_____ 5. Sureties on the fiduciary's bond are *never* required.

_____ 6. A certificate of appointment of the personal representative in a *testate* estate is known as letters of administration.

_____ 7. After being appointed, one of the first duties of the personal representative is to file an *inventory* with the court.

_____ 8. A waiting period from nine months to *a year* elapses to give creditors time to present their claims.

_____ 9. The gross estate, for tax purposes, *does not* include jointly owned property.

_____ 10. When the *final account* is allowed by the court, the estate is settled.

Checking Terminology

From the list of legal terms that follows, select the one that matches each definition.

ANSWERS

a. bond
b. burden of proof
c. decree
d. estate tax
e. fiduciary
f. first and final account
g. gifts causa mortis
h. gifts made in contemplation of death
i. gift tax
j. gross estate
k. heir
l. heirs at law
m. inheritance tax
n. inter vivos
o. inventory
p. judgment
q. letters of administration
r. letters testamentary
s. marital deduction
t. proponent
u. sponge tax
v. sureties
w. tax credit

_____ 1. A person who inherits property.
_____ 2. The decision of a court of law.
_____ 3. People who undertake to pay money or to do any other act in the event that their principal fails to meet an obligation.
_____ 4. A certificate of appointment as executor of a will.
_____ 5. A detailed list of articles of property in an estate, made by the executor or administrator thereof.
_____ 6. A promise made by the personal representative to pay an amount of money to the probate judge if the representative's duties are not faithfully performed.
_____ 7. A person in a position of trust, such as an executor, administrator, guardian, or trustee.
_____ 8. People who would have inherited had a decedent died intestate.
_____ 9. A person offering a will for probate.
_____ 10. The decision of a court of equity.
_____ 11. A certificate of appointment as administrator of an estate.
_____ 12. Gifts made within three years of the date of death and subject to the federal estate tax. (Select two answers.)
_____ 13. Amounts inherited from the estate of one's spouse, not subject to the federal estate tax.
_____ 14. All property that the decedent owned at death, including individually and jointly owned property, life insurance, living trusts, and gifts made in contemplation of death.
_____ 15. Between the living.
_____ 16. A tax imposed on the estate of a deceased person.
_____ 17. An accounting, if it is the only one, presented to the court in final settlement of a decedent's estate.
_____ 18. A tax imposed on a person who inherits from a decedent's estate.
_____ 19. A tax that soaks up money for the state that the estate is being given credit for in any event.
_____ 20. The duty of proving a fact.
_____ 21. A federal tax that is imposed (with exceptions) on gifts totaling more than $5 million made during one's lifetime.
_____ 22. A sum of money used to offset an amount owed in taxes.

Using Legal Language

Read the following story and fill in the blank lines with legal terms taken from the list of terms at the beginning of this chapter:

Soon after Kevin died, Karen filed a petition for the probate of the will and for the allowance of her _____, which is her promise to pay an amount of money to the probate judge if her duties are not faithfully performed. She was not required to have _____— that is, people who would stand behind her in the event that she failed to do her job. She then notified Kevin's next of kin and all of his _____—that is, the people who inherited from his estate. After a waiting period, a hearing was held, and the court issued its decision, called a(n) _____ or _____, allowing the will. The court then issued Karen a certificate of her appointment, called _____, because this was a testate case, rather than _____, which would have been issued had Kevin died intestate. She could

now be called a(n) _____—that is, a person who holds a position of trust. Karen's first job was to file a(n) _____ listing the assets of the estate. Her next task was to file a federal estate tax return listing the _____, which includes the value of all property Kevin owned at his death, both in his own name and jointly with others, as well as life insurance, _____ (between the living) trusts, and gifts made within three years of death, called _____ or _____. Anything left to Kevin's surviving spouse, which is known as the _____, was not taxable. Many states now have a(n) _____, which is a tax equal to the credit allowed for state death taxes on the federal estate tax return.

PUZZLING OVER WHAT YOU LEARNED

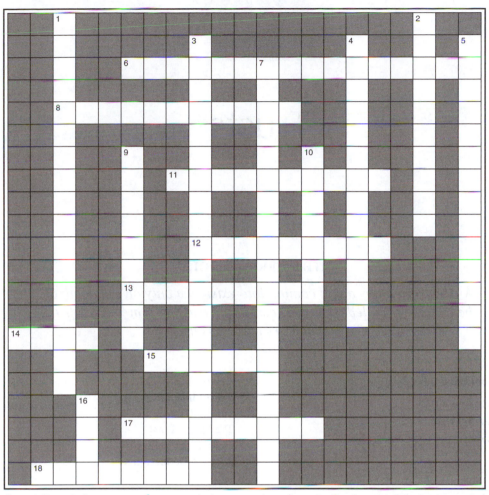

Caveat: Do **not** allow squares for spaces between words and punctuation (apostrophes, hyphens, etc.) when filling in crossword.

Across

6. Amounts inherited from the estate of one's spouse.
8. All property that the decedent owned at death, including individually and jointly owned property, life insurance, living trusts, and gifts made in contemplation of death.
11. Between the living.
12. A detailed list of articles of property in an estate.
13. A tax imposed on the estate of a deceased person.
14. A person who inherits property.
15. The decision of a court of equity.
17. A person in a position of trust.
18. The decision of a court of law.

Down

1. A tax that soaks up money for the state that the estate is being given credit for in any event.
2. People who would have inherited had a decedent died intestate.
3. An accounting, if it is the only one, presented to the court in final settlement of a decedent's estate.
4. The duty of proving a fact.
5. A tax imposed on a person who inherits from a decedent's estate.
7. A certificate of appointment as executor of a will.
9. A person offering a will for probate.
10. A federal tax imposed on gifts totaling more than $1 million made during one's lifetime.
16. A promise by the personal representative to pay an amount of money to the probate judge if the representative's duties are not faithfully performed.

6

Trusts

ANTE INTERROGATORY

A trust created by a will coming into existence only on the death of the testator is called a (an) (A) cestui que trust, (B) inter vivos trust, (C) testamentary trust, (D) trust res

CHAPTER OUTLINE

Parties to a Trust

Kinds of Trusts

Testamentary Trust

Living Trust

Spendthrift Trust

Charitable Trust

Sprinkling Trust

Implied Trust

Precatory Trust

Pour-Over Trust

Marital Deduction Trust

KEY TERMS

A–B trust

beneficial title *(ben·e·FISH·el TY·tel)*

beneficiary *(ben·e·FISH·ee·air·ee)*

bypass trust *(BY·pass)*

cestui que trust *(SES·twee kay)*

charitable remainder annuity trust (CRAT) *(CHAR·i·ta·bel re·MANE·der a·NYOO·i·tee)*

charitable remainder trust *(CHAR·i·ta·bel re·MANE·der)*

charitable remainder unitrust (CRUT) *(CHAR·i·ta·bel re·MANE·der YOO·nee·trust)*

charitable trust *(CHAR·i·ta·bel)*

constructive trust *(kon·STRUK·tiv)*

conveyance in trust *(kon·VAY·enss)*

corpus *(KOR·pus)*

credit-shelter trust *(Kred·et·SHEL·ter)*

Crummey powers *(KRUM·ee)*

cy pres doctrine *(sy pray DOK·trin)*

declaration of trust *(dek·la·RAY·shun)*

discretionary trust *(dis·KRE·shun·air·ee)*

donor *(doh·NOR)*

equitable title *(EK·wit·a·bel TY·tel)*

exemption equivalent trust *(eg·ZEMP·shun)*

grantor *(gran·TOR)*

implied trust *(im·PLIDE)*

inter vivos trust *(IN·ter VY·vose)*

irrevocable living trust *(ir·REV·e·ke·bel)*

legal title *(LEE·gul TY·tel)*

living trust

marital deduction *(MAR·i·tal de·DUK·shun)*

marital deduction trust

pay on death (POD) account *(pay on death uh·COWNT)*

pour-over trust *(pore·O·ver)*

precatory trust *(PREK·a·tore·ee)*

public trust *(PUB·lik)*

qualified terminable interest property (QTIP) trust *(KWAH·li·fide TERM·in·a·bel IN·trest PROP·er·tee)*

resulting trust *(re·ZULT·ing)*

revocable living trust *(REV·e·ke·bel)*

rule against perpetuities *(per·pe·TYOO·i·teez)*

settlor *(SET·ler)*

spendthrift *(SPEND·thrift)*

spendthrift trust

spray trust

sprinkling trust *(SPRINK·ling)*

testamentary trust *(test·e·MEN·ter·ee)*

Totten trust *(TOT·en)*

trust

trust deed

trustee *(trus·TEE)*

trust fund

trust indenture *(in·DEN·cher)*

trustor *(trus·TOR)*

trust principal *(PRIN·se·pel)*

trust property *(PROP·er·tee)*

trust res *(reyz)*

vest

PARTIES TO A TRUST

A **trust** is a form of property ownership in which someone controls and manages the property, but does so for the benefit of another. When a trust is established, the **legal title** (full, absolute ownership) in a particular item of property is separated from the **equitable** or **beneficial title** (the right to beneficial enjoyment) in the same property. The person who establishes the trust is called the **settlor** (or the **trustor**, the **grantor**, or the **donor**). The person who holds the legal title to the property for the other's benefit is called the **trustee**. The person who holds the equitable or beneficial title is known as the **beneficiary**. The beneficiary, also known as the **cestui que trust**, is the one for whom the trust is created and who receives the benefits from it. The property that is held in trust is called the **corpus** (or the **trust res**, the **trust fund**, the **trust property**, or the **trust principal**).

Generally, there are no limitations on who can be a trustee, assuming that the person has the legal capacity to own and transfer property. Trustees do not have to be human persons; corporations can serve as trustees. In fact, banks offer trust services through their trust departments.

An example that is typical of how a married couple could use a trust is as follows: The husband gives property to a trustee—either during his lifetime or by will when he dies—to be held in trust with instructions to pay the income from the property to his wife for as long as she lives and, on her death, to divide what remains among his children.

KINDS OF TRUSTS

Trusts go back to the Middle Ages, and, many different kinds of trusts exist. The most common ones are described briefly in this chapter.

Testamentary Trust

A **testamentary trust** is a trust that is created by a will. It comes into existence only on the death of the testator. The terms of the trust, together with the names of the trustee and the beneficiaries, are set out in the body of the will itself. Here is the beginning of a typical trust clause in a will:

> I direct that each share of my residuary estate payable to an individual under the age of 25 shall be held in trust for that individual under Article III. (Article III of the will contains the provisions of the trust.)

Living Trust

A **living trust**, also called an **inter vivos trust**, is created by the settlor while he or she is alive and is established by either a conveyance in trust or a declaration of trust. The instrument creating the trust is called a **trust deed** or a **trust indenture**. In a **conveyance in trust**, the settlor conveys away the legal title to a trustee to hold for the benefit of either the settlor or another as beneficiary. In a **declaration of trust**, the settlor declares in writing that he or she is holding the legal title to the property as trustee for the benefit of some other person (the beneficiary) to whom he or she now conveys the equitable (beneficial) title.

Word Wise

Cestui Que Trust (Ses·twee kay trust) ("trust beneficiary")

Cestui is a French term meaning "to him" or "to her." Here are some other "cestui" phrases:
  cestui que use = someone for whose use and benefit land, tenements, etc., are held by another. The *cestui que use* may receive profits and benefits of the estate, but the legal title and possession rest with the other.
  cestui que vie = the person whose life determines the duration of the trust, gift, estate, or insurance contract. The *cestui que vie* is the person on whose life the insurance is written.

A living trust may be either irrevocable or revocable. If it is an **irrevocable living trust**, the settlor loses complete control over the trust corpus during his or her lifetime and cannot change the trust. The advantage of an irrevocable trust is that the income from the trust is not taxable to the settlor. The trust itself or the beneficiaries pay the taxes on the trust's income. Such a trust has a disadvantage, however, in that it may never be changed. The settlor can never get back that which he or she put in trust, regardless of the circumstances.

TERMS IN ACTION

One of the more interesting forms of **trusts** that have been gaining popularity is what is known as a gun trust. Certain kinds of weapons are classified as Title II weapons, under federal law, and the purchase of those weapons (a machine gun, for instance) is more difficult than for the purchase of traditional weapons. So, rather than buying such a weapon, a person becomes a **settlor** and forms an **irrevocable trust**, which takes title to the gun. Such a form of ownership avoids some of the red tape associated with buying Title II firearms, including fingerprinting. It also allows the trust-owned weapons to be possessed by heirs of the settlor without any parties' having to actually take title (or risk losing title). A gun trust, formally known as a National Firearms Act Trust, was the creation in 2007 of Jack Goldman, an attorney from Jacksonville, Florida. He has since copyrighted his gun trust and licensed its use to other attorneys in 20 states.

Sources: abajournal.com; guntrustlawyer.com

A **revocable living trust** may be rescinded or changed by the settlor at any time during his or her lifetime. It has neither estate tax nor income tax benefits. Such a trust, however, can serve the purpose of relieving the cares of management of money or property, as well as other purposes, including protecting the assets in the trust from loss due to the beneficiary's negligence.

6

Spendthrift Trust

A **spendthrift** is one who spends money very unwisely and without any self-control. A **spendthrift trust** is designed to provide a fund for the maintenance of a beneficiary and, simultaneously, to secure it against the beneficiary's improvidence or incapacity. In some states, all trusts are considered such. In other states, such as Massachusetts, to create a spendthrift trust requires that a clause be placed in the trust instrument to the effect that the beneficiary cannot assign either the income or the principal of the trust, and that neither the income nor the principal of the trust can be reached by the beneficiary's creditors. Still other states do not permit spendthrift trusts to be established.

Charitable Trust

A **charitable** or **public trust** is one established for charitable purposes such as the advancement of education; relief to the aged, ill, and poor; and promotion of religion. For a charitable trust to be valid, the person to be benefited must be uncertain. A **charitable remainder trust** is a trust in which the donor, or a beneficiary, retains the income from the trust for life or other period, after which the trust corpus is given to a charity. Under a **charitable remainder annuity trust**, a fixed *amount* of income is given annually to a beneficiary, and the remainder is given to a charity. Under a **charitable remainder unitrust**, a fixed *percentage* of income (at least 5 percent of the trust corpus) is given annually to a beneficiary, with the remainder going to a charity.

A charitable trust can be written to last indefinitely; it is not affected by the rule against perpetuities. The **rule against perpetuities** is one of the most difficult common law rules to understand. It provides that every interest in property is void unless it must **vest**, if at all, not later than 21 years after some life in being, plus the period of gestation, at the time of the creation of the interest. To "vest" means that a future right or benefit becomes presently owned. By way of example, the right to vote is contingent when you're not yet 18. But at 18, the right to vote is vested, even if the next election is months away. Going back to the rule against perpetuities, a trust established for "my grandchildren who shall reach the age of 21" would be void because other children yet may be born to the settlor and they would not be "lives in being" when the trust was created. Some states have rewritten the rule to provide that property interests must vest either no later than 21 years after some life in being at the time of the creation of the interest or within 90 years of such creation.

When the original purpose of a charitable trust can no longer be fulfilled, instead of causing the trust to end the court may apply the **cy pres doctrine**, a doctrine meaning "as near as possible." Under this doctrine, the court allows the trust fund to be held for another purpose that meets as nearly as possible the intent of the settlor.

Web Wise

These sites are good starting points for looking up information about trusts and other legal subjects:

- *http://www.yahoo.com/law*
- *http://www.catalaw.com*
- *http://www.law.cornell.edu*
- *http://www.lawcrawler.com*

Sprinkling Trust

A **sprinkling** or **spray trust** allows the trustee to use discretion to decide how much will be given to each beneficiary. Such a trust is also called a **discretionary trust**. The advantage of this type of trust is that the trustee can determine the tax brackets of the beneficiaries and pay a lesser tax amount by giving more money to those beneficiaries in the lowest tax brackets. It also has built-in spendthrift provisions. The chief objection is that it gives the trustee too much control over the distribution of the trust property.

TERMS IN ACTION

Leona Helmsley was one of the more notable characters of New York Society in the 1970s and 1980s. After becoming a real estate broker in Manhattan, she met and eventually married real estate developer Harry Helmsley. Leona Helmsley became known as the "Queen of Mean." She was exceptionally unkind to her employees, and in 1992 she went to prison for 19 months for tax evasion, her conviction based in part on the testimony of her maid, who reported that Helmsley said about the rich, "We don't pay taxes, only the little people pay taxes." She died in 2007, leaving behind an estate valued at around $8 billion. While giving next to nothing in her will to her relatives, Mrs. Helmsley left $12 million in a **testamentary trust** for her dog, a Maltese poodle named Trouble. Helmsley left the remainder of her estate to a **charitable trust** named after her and her husband, for the care and welfare of stray dogs. That would make the Helmsley trust larger than the combined assets of all of the 7,000-plus animal-related nonprofit groups in America. At the request of the **trustees**, a judge in 2008 reduced the $12 million trust for Helmsley's dog to $2 million. And in 2009, a judge ruled that Helmsley's charitable trust wasn't limited to caring for stray dogs, but that the trustees could distribute the money in any charitable manner that they saw fit. This was due to the phrasing in the trust documents and mission statement that were vague enough to allow for the care of people, as well as animals, making a **sprinkling trust** for dogs into a fully **discretionary trust**.

Sources: wsj.com; nytimes.com; abajournal.com

Implied Trust

A trust that arises by implication of law from the conduct of the parties is known as an **implied trust**. Two examples of implied trusts are resulting trusts and constructive trusts.

A **resulting trust** arises when a transfer of property is made to one person, but the purchase price for the property is paid by another person. In such a case, a trust results in favor of the person who furnished the consideration. This allows the person who actually paid for the property to obtain title to it (under the theory of a resulting trust) if he or she wishes to do so.

A **constructive trust** is imposed by a court to avoid the unjust enrichment of one party at the expense of the other when the legal title to the property was obtained by fraud. For example, if someone embezzles money from his employer and then uses the money to buy a luxury beach house, the employer could ask a court to declare a constructive trust, which would transfer the property from the embezzler to his employer. Notice that in a constructive trust, the trust is a fiction created to prevent the fraudulent one from continuing to wrongfully own property.

Totten Trusts and Crummey Powers

Two legal terms used in the law of trusts are derived from the names of cases. A **Totten trust** is a bank account in the name of the depositor as trustee for another person. While alive, the depositor can deposit and withdraw from the account. Upon the depositor's death, the account belongs to the named beneficiary. The name of the trust comes from a 1906 New York case, *In re Totten*, 71 N.E. 748. Also known as a **pay on death (POD) account**, this kind of trust is sometimes referred to as a "poor man's trust" because a Totten trust costs next to nothing to create and administer. Those who do call it a poor man's trust might need a history lesson, because the Totten trust was created by a woman—who wasn't poor.

Crummey powers give trust beneficiaries the right to withdraw each year the money that is contributed to the trust during that year. This term comes from the case of *Crummey* v. *Commissioner*, 397 F.2d 82 (1968).

Precatory Trust

A **precatory trust** is an express trust that sometimes arises from the use of polite language by a testator in a will, which is not worded strongly enough to be a trust, on its face. For example, a testatrix wrote the following in her will: "I give and bequeath unto my husband . . . the use, income, and improvement of all the estate . . . for and during the term of his natural life, in the full confidence that upon my decease he will, as he has heretofore done, continue to give and afford my children [enumerating them] such protection, comfort and support as they or either of them may stand in need of." The court held this to be a trust for the benefit of the children. This type of trust, like a constructive trust, is not a trust by design.

Pour-Over Trust

A **pour-over trust** is a misnomer. It is actually a provision in a will leaving a bequest or devise to the trustee of an existing living trust. When the testator dies, the will pours the particular gift into the trust—thus the name "pour-over trust."

Marital Deduction Trust

A **marital deduction trust** is a trust which is arranged to make maximum use of the marital deduction that is found in the federal estate tax law. The **marital deduction** is the amount that passes from a decedent to a surviving spouse and is not taxable under the federal estate tax law.

One type of marital deduction trust, called a **credit-shelter trust**, an **A–B trust**, a **bypass trust**, or an **exemption equivalent trust,** reduces the taxation of the second spouse to die by limiting the amount in that person's estate to a sum that is not taxable. With this type of trust, the property of the first spouse to die passes to a two-part trust rather than to the surviving spouse. Trust A is an irrevocable trust that provides only income to the surviving spouse for life, with the principal passing to someone else (such as children) upon the surviving spouse's death, tax free. Trust B, for an amount that is tax exempt (see Chapter 29), is for the benefit of the surviving spouse. When the surviving spouse dies, that estate is not large enough to be taxable.

Another marital deduction trust, called a **qualified terminable interest property (QTIP) trust,** gives all trust income to a surviving spouse for life, payable at least annually, with the principal passing to someone else upon the spouse's death. This type of trust was the example used near the start of the chapter, and it provides for the surviving spouse for life, yet leaves the principal untouched for someone else when the surviving spouse dies.

Reviewing What You Learned

After studying the chapter, write the answers to each of the following questions:

1. When a trust is created, how is title to the property separated?

   _____

   _____

   _____

   _____

2. List four names that are used to describe a person who establishes a trust._____

   _____

   _____

   _____

   _____

3. List five names that are used to describe the property that is held in trust. _____

   _____

   _____

   _____

   _____

6

4. How is a testamentary trust created? Under what circumstances does it come into existence?_____

_____

_____

_____

5. What is another name for a living trust? _____

_____

_____

_____

6. Describe what occurs when a conveyance of trust is created.

_____

_____

_____

7. Describe what occurs when a declaration of trust arises.

_____

_____

_____

8. What are the advantages and disadvantages of an irrevocable living trust?_____

_____

_____

_____

_____

_____

9. What is necessary for a charitable or public trust to be valid?

_____

_____

_____

_____

10. What is the advantage of a sprinkling or spray trust? _____

_____

_____

_____

11. What is the difference between a resulting trust and a constructive trust? _____

_____

_____

_____

_____

12. Why is the term **pour-over trust** a misnomer? _____

_____

_____

_____

_____

Understanding Legal Concepts

Indicate whether each statement is true or false. Then, change the italicized word or phrase of each false statement to make it true.

ANSWERS

_____ 1. When a trust is established, the *legal title* in a particular item of property is separated from the equitable or beneficial title in the same property.

_____ 2. A *testamentary* trust comes into existence only on the death of the testator.

_____ 3. An *inter vivos* trust is a trust that is created by a will.

_____ 4. In a *declaration of* trust, the settlor conveys away the legal title to a trustee to hold for the benefit of either the settlor or the beneficiary.

_____ 5. The advantage of a *revocable* living trust is that the income from the trust is not taxable to the settlor.

_____ 6. A *spendthrift* trust is designed to provide a fund for the maintenance of a beneficiary and, simultaneously, to secure it against his or her improvidence or incapacity.

_____ 7. For a *charitable* trust to be valid, the person to be benefited must be uncertain.

_____ 8. The chief objection to a sprinkling or spray trust is that it gives the *trustee* too much control over the distribution of the trust property.

_____ 9. A *resulting* trust is imposed by law to avoid the unjust enrichment of one party at the expense of the other when the legal title to the property was obtained by fraud.

_____ 10. A precatory trust is an *implied* trust that sometimes arises from the use of polite language by a testator in a will.

Checking Terminology (Part A)

From the list of legal terms that follows, select the one that matches each definition.

ANSWERS

a. A–B trust
b. beneficial title
c. beneficiary
d. bypass trust
e. cestui que trust
f. charitable remainder annuity trust (CRAT)
g. charitable remainder trust
h. charitable remainder unitrust (CRUT)
i. charitable trust
j. constructive trust
k. conveyance in trust
l. credit-shelter trust
m. Crummey powers
n. cy pres doctrine
o. declaration of trust
p. equitable title
q. exemption equivalent trust
r. implied trust
s. inter vivos trust
t. irrevocable living trust
u. legal title
v. living trust
w. marital deduction
x. marital deduction trust
y. pay on death account
z. pour-over trust
aa. precatory trust
ab. vest

_____ 1. A trust that is created by the settlor when he or she is alive. (Select two answers.)

_____ 2. A trust established for charitable purposes. (Select two answers.)

_____ 3. A bank account in the name of the depositor for the benefit of another person. Upon death, the account belongs to the named beneficiary and avoids estate taxes.

_____ 4. An express trust that arises from the use of polite, noncommanding language by a testator in a will.

_____ 5. The amount that passes from a decedent to a surviving spouse and is not taxable under the federal estate tax law.

_____ 6. A trust in which a fixed amount of income is given annually to a beneficiary and the remainder is given to a charity.

_____ 7. A written declaration by a settlor that he or she is holding legal title to property as trustee for the benefit of another person.

_____ 8. The right to beneficial enjoyment. (Select two answers.)

_____ 9. Authority that gives trust beneficiaries the right to withdraw each year the money that is contributed to the trust during that year.

_____ 10. An implied trust that arises in favor of one who is defrauded when title to property is obtained by fraud.

_____ 11. A future right or benefit becomes presently owned.

_____ 12. A type of marital deduction trust that reduces the taxation of the second spouse to die by limiting the amount in that person's estate to a sum that is not taxable. (Select four answers.)

_____ 13. A trust which is arranged to make maximum use of the marital deduction that is found in the federal estate tax law.

_____ 14. A trust in which a fixed percentage of income (at least 5 percent of the trust corpus) is given annually to a beneficiary and the remainder is given to a charity.

_____ 15. A provision in a will leaving a bequest or devise to the trustee of an existing living trust.

_____ 16. A trust that may not be rescinded or changed by the settlor at any time during his or her lifetime.

_____ 17. A trust that arises by implication of law from the conduct of the parties.

_____ 18. A trust in which the donor, or a beneficiary, retains the income from the trust for life or other period, after which the trust corpus is given to a charity.

_____ 19. A transfer of legal title to property by the settlor to a trustee to hold for the benefit of a beneficiary.

_____ 20. One for whose benefit a trust is created. (Select two answers.)

_____ 21. Full, absolute ownership.

_____ 22. As nearly as possible.

Checking Terminology (Part B)

From the list of legal terms that follows, select the one that matches each definition.

ANSWERS

a. corpus
b. discretionary trust
c. donor
d. grantor
e. qualified terminable interest property (QTIP) trust
f. resulting trust
g. revocable living trust

_____ 1. A trust that may be rescinded or changed by the settlor at any time during his or her lifetime.

_____ 2. A person who establishes a trust. (Select four answers.)

_____ 3. A person who holds legal title to property in trust for another.

_____ 4. A trust designed to provide a fund for the maintenance of a beneficiary and, at the same time, to secure it against the beneficiary's improvidence or incapacity.

_____ 5. The principle that no interest in property is good unless it must vest, if at all, not later than 21 years after some life in being, plus the period of gestation, at the creation of the interest.

6

h. rule against perpetuities
i. settlor
j. spendthrift
k. spendthrift trust
l. spray trust
m. sprinkling trust
n. testamentary trust
o. Totten trust
p. trust
q. trust deed
r. trustee
s. trust fund
t. trust indenture
u. trustor
v. trust principal
w. trust property
x. trust res

____ 6. A bank account in the name of the depositor as trustee for another person.
____ 7. A marital deduction trust that gives all trust income to a surviving spouse for life, payable at least annually, with the principal passing to someone else upon the spouse's death.
____ 8. The body, principal sum, or capital of a trust. (Select five answers.)
____ 9. A trust that is created by will and that comes into existence only on the death of the testator.
____ 10. An instrument that creates a living trust. (Select two answers.)
____ 11. An implied trust that arises in favor of the payor when property is transferred to one person after being paid for by another person.
____ 12. A right of ownership to property held by one person for the benefit of another.
____ 13. A trust that allows the trustee to decide how much will be given to each beneficiary at the trustee's discretion. (Select three answers.)
____ 14. One who spends money profusely and improvidently.

Sharpening Your Latin Skills

In the space provided, write the definition of each of the following legal terms, referring to the glossary when necessary.

ad litem _____

corpus _____

cum testamento annexo _____

de bonis non _____

pendent elite _____

per capita _____

per stirpes _____

Using Legal Language

Read the following story and fill in the blank lines with legal terms taken from the list of terms at the beginning of this chapter:

Leon decided to put $10,000 in _____ _____. Because he established it, Leon could be referred to as the _____, the _____, the _____, or the _____. Lois was known as the _____. Leon's wife, Laura, was given legal title to the money; therefore, she was called the _____. The money itself could be termed the _____, the _____, the _____, the _____ _____, or the _____. Called a(n) _____, the instrument was designed to provide a fund for Lois and, at the same time,

for the benefit of his daughter, Lois. He created a(n) _____, which is also known as a(n) _____, while he was alive, by the use of an instrument called either a(n) _____ or a(n) _____. It was not called a(n) _____, because it was not created by a will. Because Leon transferred legal title to the money to another, the transaction was known as a(n) _____ rather than a(n) _____, which it would have been called had he retained legal title to the money. Leon could rescind this trust whenever he wished; therefore, it was known as a(n) _____ rather than a(n) _____ to protect against her improvidence because she was a(n) _____—that is, one who spends money profusely. It was not a(n) _____ or _____, because it was not for charitable purposes; thus, the rule known as the _____ was applicable. Leon did not give Laura discretion in the trust to decide how much would be given to different beneficiaries. For that reason, this was not a(n) _____ or a(n)

_____. Because the trust did not arise by implication of law from the conduct of the parties, it was not either one of the _____— that is, a(n) _____ or a(n) _____. In addition, because it did not arise from the use of polite language in a will, it was not a(n) _____.

6

PUZZLING OVER WHAT YOU LEARNED

Caveat: Allow squares for spaces between words and punctuation (apostrophes, hyphens, etc.) when filling in crossword.

Across

1. Full, absolute ownership.
6. Person who establishes a trust.
7. The right to beneficial enjoyment.
9. One for whose benefit a trust is created.
10. Person who holds legal title to property in trust for another.
12. The body, principal sum, or capital of a trust.
13. A person who establishes a trust.
14. One for whose benefit a trust is created.
15. The body, principal sum, or capital of a trust.
16. The body, principal sum, or capital of a trust.

Down

2. The right to beneficial enjoyment.
3. Right of ownership to property held by one person for another.
4. A trust that allows the trustee to decide how much to give each beneficiary.
5. A trust that is created by will.
8. A person who establishes a trust.
11. A person who establishes a trust.
14. The body, principal sum, or capital of a trust.

6

Terms Used in Law of Real Property

S ome law firms specialize in the field of real property law, other firms work in the field as part of a general practice, and still others work in the field only occasionally or not at all. Knowledge of real property law, in any event, is important to all of us because we all must reside somewhere, whether we own the property, rent it, or live there with someone else who does. Chapter 31 explains the various estates in real property that are available to property owners. Co-ownership of real property is discussed in Chapter 32, and the methods of acquiring title to real property are outlined in Chapter 33. The requirements of a valid deed and the different types of deeds are examined in Chapter 34, followed by a discussion of mortgages in Chapter 35. Finally, Chapter 36 provides an overview of landlord and tenant law.

Estates in Real Property

ANTE INTERROGATORY

The estate that restricts ownership of real property to a particular family bloodline is (A) fee simple estate, (B) estate pur autre vie, (C) life estate, (D) fee tail estate.

CHAPTER OUTLINE

Freehold Estates
    Fee Simple Estate
    Fee Tail Estate

Determinable Fee Estate
Life Estate
Leasehold Estates

KEY TERMS

apt words

condition subsequent *(kon·DISH·en SUB·se·kwent)*

defeasible estate *(de·FEEZ·i·bel es·TATE)*

determinable fee *(de·TER·min·e·bel)*

determine *(de·TER·min)*

esquire *(ES·kwyr)*

estate *(es·TATE)*

estate pur autre vie *(per OH·tra vee)*

estate tail male

estate tail special *(SPESH·el)*

fee

fee simple absolute *(SIM·pel ab·so·LOOT)*

fee simple determinable *(de·TER·min·e·bel)*

fee simple estate *(es·TATE)*

fee tail estate *(es·TATE)*

fixture *(fix·chur)*

freehold estate *(FREE·hold es·TATE)*

leasehold estate *(LEESS·hold es·TATE)*

life estate *(es·TATE)*

life tenant *(TEN·ent)*

possibility of reverter *(pos·i·BIL·i·tee ov re·VERT·er)*

real property *(PROP·er·tee)*

remainder interest *(re·MANE·der IN·trest)*

reversionary interest *(re·VER·zhen·e·ree IN·trest)*

revert *(re·VERT)*

waste

Ownership of interests in **real property**—that is, the ground and anything permanently attached to it—in the United States follows the estate concept that developed under the English feudal system. **Estates** (ownership interests) in real property are divided into two groups: freehold estates and leasehold estates. Personal property that is permanently attached to real property becomes part of the real property and is known as a **fixture**. Something as slight as a bathroom towel rack, or as heavy as a marble countertop, changes its status by its placement in a home (or on the property; e.g., a shed). Fixtures, generally, stay with or on the property when real estate is sold or otherwise transferred.

FREEHOLD ESTATES

A **freehold estate** is an estate in which the holder owns the land for life or forever. At common law, only freehold estates were considered to be real property. There are four types of freehold estates:

1. fee simple
2. fee tail
3. determinable fee
4. life

Fee Simple Estate

The **fee simple estate** (sometimes called **fee** or **fee simple absolute**) is the largest estate that one can own in land, giving the holder absolute ownership that descends to the owner's heirs on his or her death. In addition, it can be sold or granted out by the owner at will during the owner's lifetime. In early conveyances, a fee simple estate was created by a deed containing the words "To (a person) and his heirs." If the words "and his heirs," called the **apt words** (the suitable words), were omitted from the deed, the grantee received only a life estate. Today, real estate statutes declare that the words "and his heirs" are no longer required to be in a deed to create a fee simple estate.

Fee Tail Estate

A **fee tail estate** restricts ownership of real property to a particular family bloodline. It was created by statute in England in 1285 (when land was the basis for the family fortune) as a way to keep real property in the family forever. Under the statute, the property could not be alienated. If the bloodline became extinct, the property reverted to the original owner's line.

Origin of Real Property Law

THE FEUDAL SYSTEM

Under the feudal system in England, which began in the year 1066 when William the Conqueror of Normandy took over England after the Battle of Hastings, the king was the personal owner of all land in the kingdom. In exchange for services, the king granted land in large tracts to his tenants-in-chief (barons) who, in turn, granted land to lesser lords. These lesser lords granted land to still lesser noblemen. In exchange for use of the land, continuous services were required. Thus was created a pyramid with the king at the top and the people who worked the land at the bottom. Rights in the land moved down the pyramid (each step down being a lesser right), while a constant flow of services moved up.

In its early stage, feudalism was a military system designed to protect the king. Since the king was short of money, he used land to purchase military services. Thus, the highest type of ownership of land was a military tenure called knight's service. The vassal swore allegiance to the king and also agreed to give him the services of a number of knights and squires (depending on the amount of land received) for 40 days in the year. The services were perpetual. The land reverted to the king if the knights were not productive.

(Continued)

Today in the United States, the term **esquire** is used as a title (abbreviated Esq.) following the name of an attorney, in place of the prefixes Mr., Mrs., Miss, or Ms. In English nobility, esquire (abbreviated squire) was a social rank higher than a gentleman, but lower than a knight.

Oath of Fealty

In return for land, each tenant down the line swore *fealty* (allegiance) and agreed to do *homage* (a particular service) to his landlord in a ceremony called *feoffment*. The landlord was called the *feoffor* and the tenant was called the *feoffee*. The feoffee made the following oath of fealty:

> I become your man from this day forward of life and limb and of earthly worship, and unto you shall be true and faithful, and bear to you faith for the tenements that I claim to hold of you, saving the faith that I owe unto our sovereign lord the king.

Tenant's Service

The tenant's service to his lord varied greatly. *Cornage* required the tenant to blow a horn to warn the country on the approach of the king's enemies. *Villeinage* required the tenant to plow the lord's land and make his hedges. A *tenant in sergeanty* was a servant such as a chamberlain, an armoror, a cook, or an esquire. Churches held land in *frank-almoign* (free alms) in exchange for services such as the saying of masses for the donor. *Socage* tenure required the oath of faithfulness, but only nominal services for the land such as the giving of one red rose at midsummer, or the delivery of one peppercorn annually. This was often done when a father parceled out land to his children. The word *nominal* means "in name only; not real or substantial."

Life Estate

In the early feudal period, the greatest estate that one could own was a life estate, and that could not be transferred by a tenant without his lord's assent. When the tenant died, the lord was under no obligation to accept the tenant's heir as successor; however, he customarily did so in exchange for a payment called *relief*. This payment was the forerunner of our present estate tax. When a tenant died leaving an infant heir, the child became the ward of the lord, who kept the child's income and profit from the land, during minority, in exchange for support, education, and protection. The lord also had the power to choose the minor's spouse. Wardships and marriages were bought and sold by the lord, and upon his death, they passed by will or intestate succession to the lord's heirs.

Fee Simple Estate

As time went on, a lord could accept, if he wished, the tenant's heir in advance by granting land "to him and his heir." The heir at that time would usually be the tenant's eldest son. If the grant was "to him and his heirs," it was a grant to the tenant, then the tenant's heir, then the heir's heir, and on down the line. These words eventually became the term that created a *fee simple estate* (absolute ownership of property). When a tenant died without heirs, his property *escheated*, that is, reverted to the lord. None of this law applied to women who, in those days, had few legal rights.

Gradually, statutes were passed in England allowing tenants to transfer their property rights to others without permission of the lord and also to pass their interest in the land to their heirs. The feudal system was finally abolished in England in 1660 by King Charles II.

At common law, an estate tail was created by the apt words in a deed "to (the grantee) and the heirs of his body" and was often given by a parent to a child as part of a marriage settlement. The word "tail" comes from the French word *tailler*, meaning "to carve." The idea was that the grantor was carving an estate to his liking. Variations included the **estate tail special**, in which land was given to both the husband and wife and the heirs of their two bodies, and the **estate tail male**, which restricted ownership to men in the family line.

As time went on in England, methods were devised that allowed property in an estate tail to be alienated from the family line. Today, the estate tail has been either abolished or made ineffective by state statutes.

TERMS IN ACTION

The **fee tail estate** was eradicated in most jurisdictions because it can create a perpetual restriction on real estate. The statutes that abolish the fee tail estate tend to use language that is similar in construction. Pennsylvania's statute abolishing the fee tail states, "Whenever by any conveyance an estate in fee tail would be created according to the common law of the Commonwealth, it shall pass an estate in **fee simple**, and as such shall be inheritable and freely alienable." Michigan's abolishment of the fee tail includes the effective date and says, "All estates tail are abolished, and every estate which would be adjudged a fee tail, according to the law of the territory of Michigan, as it existed before the second day of March, 1821, shall for all purposes be adjudged a fee simple; and if no valid remainder be limited thereon, shall be a fee simple absolute."

Sources: Pa. Cons. Stat. § 6116Mich. Comp. Laws Section 554.3

Determinable Fee Estate

A **determinable fee**, also called a **fee simple determinable**, is an estate in real property that is capable of coming to an end automatically because of the happening of some event, If the event occurs, the estate will **determine**—that is, will come to an end. If the event never occurs, the estate will be absolute. To illustrate, if a person conveys real property to a particular church "so long as the premises shall be used for church purposes," the church has a fee simple determinable. The property will **revert** (go back) to the grantor or his or her heirs if it is not used for church purposes. The grantor has a **possibility of reverter** interest in the property because it is always possible that the event will occur.

A similar type of **defeasible estate**—that is, one that can be lost or defeated—is called a *fee simple subject to a* **condition subsequent** (a qualification that comes later). This exists when a condition is placed in a deed, making it possible to have the ownership terminated at a future time. For example, if a deed contains the language "subject to the condition that the premises never be used for the sale of alcohol" and the property is later used for the sale of alcohol, the former owner (or his or her heirs) could bring legal action to take back the property. The estate does not automatically come to an end, as in the case of a determinable fee; rather, legal action must be taken to end it.

Word Wise
The "Vert" in Revert

The Latin root "vert" and its variation "vers" mean "turn." For example, the term "revert" [re (back) + *vert* (turn)] means "to go back" or "to return."

"Vert" may mean "turn" in the physical or literal sense, as in the word "invert" [in + *vert* = to turn in], which could include turning inside out or upside down or reversing the order.

"Vert" may also be used in a nonphysical sense, as in the word "advertise," meaning that consumer attention is hopefully "turned" toward a product or service.

Consider how the root functions in these words: adversary, vertigo, perverse, diversion.

Life Estate

A **life estate** is an estate limited in duration to either the life of the owner or the life of another person. It may be created by deed, will, or operation of law.

If A either deeds or wills real property "to B for life and on B's death to C," B will own an estate for life, and C will own a **remainder interest** (an interest that takes effect after another estate is ended) in fee simple. Life tenants may convey their interest to others; however, they can convey only that which they own, nothing greater. Thus, if B conveys his or her interest (a life estate) to D, D will own a life estate for the duration of B's life, after which the property will belong to C, the holder of the fee. It is known as an **estate pur autre vie** when one holds property for the duration of the life of another person.

When a person grants a life estate, either by will or by deed, to another and retains the fee, he or she is said to have a **reversionary interest** (a right to the future enjoyment of property that one originally owned). On the death of the life tenant, the estate reverts to the owner or the owner's heirs.

Legal life estates are created by the operation of some law. For example, the rights of dower and curtesy and the right of a surviving spouse to waive the will of a deceased spouse sometimes create life estates, depending on state statutes.

Owners of life estates, known as **life tenants**, own legal title to the property during their lifetime. They must pay the taxes, but are entitled to possession of the property and to any income that comes from it. Life tenants are responsible to the owners of the fee for the commission of **waste**, which is the destruction, alteration, or deterioration of the premises, other than from natural causes or from normal usage.

▎TERMS IN ACTION

Dr. Kirk Deibert and his wife Lillian owned a 70-acre property in **fee simple absolute** in Florence, Alabama. They bought the property in 1952 and turned it into a beautiful horse farm called Rolling Acres. Having no children and desiring that more parks be created in their town, decades later the Deibert granted to themselves **life estates** in the property and gave the city a **remainder interest**, with the condition that the city turn their property into a public park. Another **condition subsequent** on the transfer of their property to the city was that the property never be used for commercial development. Dr. Deibert passed away in 1993, and eventually Mrs. Deibert decided to give up her life estate so that before she passed away the city could begin its work on what was now the city's property in **fee simple determinable**, Mrs. Deibert continued to live at her home on the property, watching her gift to the public become reality, until February 9, 2009, when she died at the age of 94. She was buried in the park, which has a playground, ponds, pavilions, paved walking trails, and a children's museum.

Source: timesdaily.com

LEASEHOLD ESTATES

A **leasehold estate** is an estate that is less than a freehold estate, in that it provides a temporary right to property. At common law, and in most states today, leasehold estates are treated as personal property rather than real property. There are four types of leasehold estates:

1. *Tenancy for years*—an estate for a definite or fixed period of time, such as "for two years," or "for nine months," or even, "until the crops have been harvested."
2. *Periodic tenancy*—an estate that continues for successive periods until one of the parties terminates it by giving notice to the other party. The phrase "month-to-month tenancy" or "week-to-week tenancy" is an alternative term to "periodic tenancy" and, unlike the tenancy for years, there is no stated ending date, even though there is a specified term.
3. *Tenancy at will*—an estate for an indefinite period. A tenant at will might rent for years, but what distinguishes the tenancy at will from the aforementioned tenancies is that there is no fixed or set period established at the start of the tenancy.
4. *Tenancy at sufferance*—an estate held wrongfully, held over after termination of a rightful tenancy, consisting of illegal possession only. A tenant at sufferance is not breaking the law until the landlord has asked the tenant to vacate the premises, and such a tenant will be liable for the past rent, and bound by the terms of the prior lease.

Landlord and tenant law are discussed in detail in Chapter 36.

Reviewing What You Learned

After studying the chapter, write the answers to each of the following questions:

1. Estates in real property are divided into what two groups?

   _____

   _____

   _____

2. List four types of freehold estates. _____

   _____

   _____

   _____

3. What will happen to an estate owned solely by an individual in fee simple when the owner dies? Under what circumstances may the owner sell or grant out the property? _____

   _____

   _____

   _____

4. What was the original purpose of the estate in fee tail? What was an estate tail male? _____

   _____

   _____

   _____

5. Give an example of a conveyance that is a determinable fee.

   _____

   _____

   _____

6. In what three ways may a life estate be created? _____

   _____

   _____

   _____

   _____

7. What is the difference between a remainder interest and a reversionary interest? _____

   _____

   _____

   _____

   _____

8. If A conveys her interest in real property to B for B's life, and upon B's death to C, and B thereafter conveys her interest to D, who will own the property when B dies? _____

   _____

   _____

   _____

9. Give an example of a law that will create a life estate.

   _____

   _____

   _____

   _____

10. What is the difference between a freehold estate and a leasehold estate? _____

    _____

    _____

    _____

    _____

11. List four types of leasehold estates. _____

    _____

    _____

    _____

Understanding Legal Concepts

Indicate whether each statement is true or false. Then, change the italicized word or phrase of each false statement to make it true.

ANSWERS

_____ 1. Ownership of interests in land in the United States follows the estate concept that developed under the *English feudal system.*

_____ 2. A freehold estate is an estate in which the holder owns the land *only for life.*

_____ 3. A fee simple estate *cannot* be sold during the owner's lifetime.

_____ 4. Today, by statute, the words "and his heirs" are *no longer required* to be in a deed to create a fee simple estate.

_____ 5. Today, the *estate tail* has been either abolished or made ineffective by state statutes.

_____ 6. A determinable fee is an estate in real property that *never comes to an end.*

_____ 7. Legal action *must be* taken to end an estate in fee simple subject to a condition subsequent if the condition occurs.

_____ 8. A life estate may *not be* created by will.

_____ 9. When a person grants a life estate to another and retains the fee, he or she is said to have a *remainder* interest.

_____ 10. Life tenants are responsible to the owners of the fee for the commission of *waste.*

Checking Terminology

From the list of legal terms that follows, elect the one that matches each definition.

ANSWERS

a. apt words
b. condition subsequent
c. defeasible estate
d. determinable fee
e. determine
f. esquire
g. estate
h. estate pur autre vie
i. estate tail male
j. estate tail special
k. fee
l. fee simple absolute
m. fee simple determinable
n. fee simple estate
o. fee tail estate
p. fixture
q. freehold estate
r. leasehold estate
s. life estate
t. life tenant
u. possibility of reverter
v. real property
w. remainder interest
x. reversionary interest
y. revert
z. waste

_____ 1. Ownership interest.

_____ 2. The largest estate that one can own in land, giving the holder the absolute ownership and power of disposition during life and descending to the owner's heirs at death. (Select three answers.)

_____ 3. A freehold estate that restricts ownership of real property to a particular family blood line.

_____ 4. A freehold estate restricting ownership to men in the family line.

_____ 5. Come to an end.

_____ 6. An estate that can be lost or defeated.

_____ 7. An estate limited in duration to either the life of the owner or the life of another person.

_____ 8. A right to the future enjoyment of property that one originally owned.

_____ 9. Destruction, alteration, or deterioration of a premises other than from natural causes or normal use.

_____ 10. An estate in which the holder owns the land for life or forever.

_____ 11. Suitable words.

_____ 12. A freehold estate restricting ownership to a husband and wife and the heirs of their two bodies.

_____ 13. An estate in real property that is capable of coming to an end automatically because of the happening of some event. (Select two answers.)

_____ 14. Go back.

_____ 15. A qualification that comes later.

_____ 16. An interest that takes effect after another estate is ended.

_____ 17. Personal property that is permanently attached to real property.

_____ 18. An estate that is less than a freehold estate.

_____ 19. An interest in property due to the possibility that an event will occur that causes the property to revert to the grantor.

_____ 20. The ground and anything permanently attached to it.

_____ 21. An estate that a person holds for the duration of the life of another person.

_____ 22. A title following the name of an attorney in place of the prefixes Mr., Mrs., Miss, or Ms.

_____ 23. The owner of a life estate.

Using Legal Language

Read the following story and fill in the blank lines with legal terms taken from the list of terms at the beginning of this chapter:

Harvey owned a(n) _____ in real property, which was limited to the duration of his life. It is not a(n) _____—that is, an estate that a person holds for the duration of the life of another. He was known as a(n) _____ and was responsible to others for the commission of _____, which is the destruction or deterioration of the premises.

On Harvey's death, the _____—that is, the ownership interest—went to Harriet, a new owner who had a(n) _____, which took effect after Harvey's estate ended. It was not a(n) _____, because title did not _____— that is, go back—to an earlier owner. Similarly, it was not a(n) _____ designed to restrict ownership of real property to a particular family blood line, with its variations of _____ _____ and _____. The deed conveying title to Harriet contained the _____—that is, the suitable words—to give her the largest estate that one can own in land. This estate has various names, including _____,_____ and just plain _____. The estate was not a(n) _____—that is, an estate

in real property that is capable of coming to an end—nor was it _____, meaning one that can be lost or defeated. It was not a fee simple subject to a(n) _____, because no conditions were in the deed. In addition, it was not a(n) _____, because it was not less than a(n) _____, which is an estate in which the holder owns the land for life or forever.

PUZZLING OVER WHAT YOU LEARNED

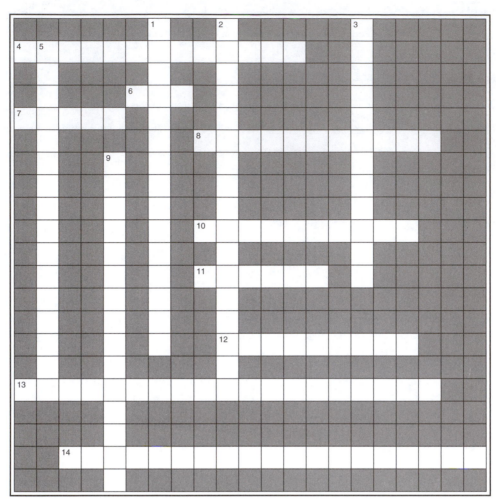

Caveat: Allow squares for spaces between words and punctuation (apostrophes, hyphens, etc.) when filling in crossword.

Across

4. The ground and anything permanently attached to it.
6. The largest estate that one can own in land.
7. Destruction, alteration, or deterioration of a premises.
8. Estate limited in duration to the life of the owner or another person.
10. Comes to an end.
11. Go back.
12. Suitable words.
13. The largest estate that one can own in land.
14. A freehold estate restricting ownership to a husband, wife, and bodily heirs.

Down

1. An estate in which the holder owns land for life or forever.
2. The largest estate that one can own in land.
3. Owners of a life estate.
5. A freehold estate restricting ownership to men in the family line.
9. A freehold estate that restricts ownership of real property to a family bloodline.

32

Multiple Ownership of Real Property

ANTE INTERROGATORY

When two or more persons own real property as joint tenants, it is known as (A) joint tenancy, (B) community property, (C) tenants in common, (D) unity of interest.

CHAPTER OUTLINE

Co-Ownership of Real Property
  Tenants in Common
  Joint Tenants
  Community Property
  Tenants by the Entirety

  Tenants in Partnership
Multi-Ownership of Real Property
  Condominiums
  Cooperatives
  Timesharing

KEY TERMS

common areas *(KOM·on AIR·ee·uz)*

community property
  (kom·YOON·i·tee PROP·er·tee)

concurrent ownership
  (kon·KER·ent OH·ner·ship)

condominium *(kon·de·MIN·ee·um)*

condominium association
  (kon·de·MIN·ee·um a·so·see·AY·shun)

cooperative apartment
  (koh·OP·er·a·tive a·PART·ment)

co-ownership *(koh·OH·ner·ship)*

co-tenants *(koh·TEN·entz)*

covenants, conditions, and restrictions
  (CC&R) *(KOV·e·nentz kon·DI·shuns and
  re·STRIK·shuns)*

creditors *(KRED·et·ers)*

homeowners association (HOA) *(home
  oh·ners uh·so·she·A·shun)*

interval ownership *(IN·ter·vel OH·ner·ship)*

joint tenancy *(TEN·en·see)*

joint tenancy with the right of survivorship
  (ser·VIVE·or·ship)

joint tenants *(TEN·entz)*

levy on execution *(LEV·ee on
  ek·se·KYOO·shen)*

master deed *(MAS·ter deed)*

moiety *(MOY·e·tee)*

partition *(par·TI·shun)*

proprietary lease *(pro·PRY·e·ter·ee)*

several *(SEV·er·el)*

tenancy by the entirety
   (TEN·en·see by the en·TY·re·tee)
tenancy in partnership
   (TEN·en·see in PART·ner·ship)
tenants in common *(TEN·entz in KOM·on)*
timesharing
unit deed *(YOON·it)*

units *(YOON·its)*
unity of interest *(YOON·i·tee ov IN·trest)*
unity of possession
   (YOON·i·tee ov po·SESH·en)
unity of time *(YOON·i·tee)*
unity of title *(YOON·i·tee ov TY·tel)*

CO-OWNERSHIP OF REAL PROPERTY

When real property is owned separately by one person, it is referred to as being owned **severally**. In contrast, when real property is owned by more than one person, this is known as **concurrent ownership** or **co-ownership**, and the owners are known as **co-tenants**. Notice that "tenant" can have more than one meaning; it does not just apply to renters. It used to be said that co-owners of property own by moieties. **Moiety** means a part, portion, or fraction. The most common co-tenant relationships are tenants in common, joint tenants, tenants by the entirety, and tenants in partnership.

Tenants in Common

When two or more persons own real property as **tenants in common**, each person owns an un-divided share, and on one owner's death that person's share passes to his or her heirs. Tenants in common have **unity of possession**, which means that each owner is entitled to possession of the entire premises. This tenancy may be created by deed or by will, but more commonly it comes about by operation of law, such as when a person dies intestate, leaving real property to two or more heirs. Such heirs will take the property as tenants in common.

Any of the tenants in common may sell or grant out their interests to others without permission of the other co-tenants, and any new owners become tenants in common with the remaining owners. To say that each tenant in common has an undivided share does not automatically mean that each co-tenant has an equal share. For example, a will might make a child and two cousins tenants in common, and the child owns a one-half interest in the property and the two cousins each own a one-quarter interest. As tenants in common, they own a unified right to be on the property, but they individually own a financial stake (based on their given share), which they can sell (or give) to someone else, not comprehended by the grantor of the tenancy in common. From the preceding example, one of the cousins could sell his or her one-quarter share to a neighbor, without the other co-tenants being able to prevent the sale.

Tenants in common may separate their interests in the property by petitioning the court for a partition of the premises. When a **partition** occurs, the court either divides the property into separate parcels so that each co-tenant will own a particular part outright, or orders the property sold and divides the proceeds of the sale among the co-tenants. **Creditors** (people who are owed money) may reach the interest of a tenant in common and have the interest sold or hold it with the remaining tenants in common.

Joint Tenants

When two or more persons own real property as joint tenants, the estate created is a single estate with multiple ownership. This is known as **joint tenancy** or **joint tenancy with the right of survivorship**. **Joint tenants** are two or more persons holding one and the same interest, accruing by one and the same conveyance, commencing at one and the same time, and held by one and the same undivided possession. Each tenant owns the entire estate, subject to the equal rights of the other joint tenants. All joint tenants' interests are equal (**unity of interest**), and all have the right to possession of the entire estate (**unity of possession**). All owners must take title at the same time (**unity of time**), and each must receive title from the same instrument or conveyance, such as a will or a deed (**unity of title**). A joint tenant may not transfer his or her own ownership to someone else, including by using a will, and at the death of any joint tenant, the surviving tenant(s) owns the property in its entirety.

A joint tenant may petition the court for a partition of the estate, which would end the joint tenancy. Creditors may levy on the interests of a joint tenant on execution and take over the joint tenant's interest as a tenant in common with the remaining joint tenants. To **levy on execution** means "to collect a sum of money by putting into effect the judgment of a court."

TERMS IN ACTION

Joint tenancy with the right of survivorship isn't dependent on which of the joint tenants paid how much for the property. In a 1997 case from Pennsylvania, two people bought real estate and titled it as joint tenants with rights of survivorship. Later, one of the joint tenants went to court to have the property partitioned. The joint tenant seeking **partition** argued that it was warranted because he had paid more than five times the amount of money that his joint tenant had paid. But the court ruled that unless there is evidence of fraud, disproportionate contributions toward buying the property don't warrant partition of such a joint tenancy.

Source: *D'Arcy v. Buckley*, 71 Bucks Co. L. Rep. 167 (1997)

Word Wise
The "Cur" in Concurrent

The Latin root "cur," or "cour," means "to run." Other words with this root are as follows:

Word	Meaning
concur (verb) [*con* (together) + *currere* (to run)]	to run or happen together
concurrent (adjective) [*concur* + *ent* (that has, shows, or does)]	occurring at the same time
cursory (adjective) [*currere* (to run) + *ory* (relating to)]	hastily, superficially
incur (verb) [*in* (toward) + *currere* (to run)]	to run into
precursor (noun) [*pre* (before) + *currere* (to run) + *or* (person or thing that)]	person or thing that goes before
recur (verb) [*re* (again) + *currere* (to run)]	to occur again
recurrent (adjective) [*recur* + *ent* (that has, shows, or does)]	occurring again

Community Property

Spain originated a form of property ownership for husbands and wives, called community property. It has been adopted as the default from of marital property ownership in the nine states indicated on the map in Figure 32-1. Alaska is thought of as an opt-in community property state, which allows spouses to create a community property agreement. **Community property** is property (other than a gift or inheritance) acquired by a husband or wife during marriage that belongs to both spouses equally. Under this system, property acquired by the efforts of either spouse during marriage belongs to both spouses equally—that is, each spouse owns an undivided one-half interest in the whole premises.

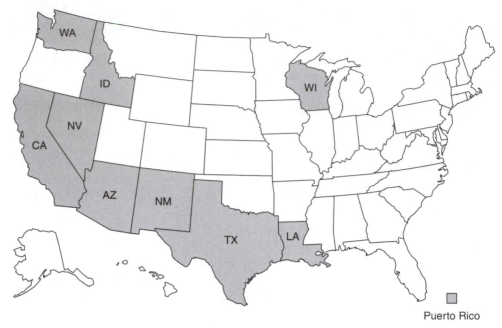

FIGURE 32-1   Community property jurisdictions

Tenants by the Entirety

A **tenancy by the entirety** may be held only by a husband and wife and is based on the common law doctrine that a husband and wife are regarded, in law, as one person. Under common law theory, each spouse owns the entire estate, which neither can destroy by any separate act. The husband, however, has the entire control over the estate, including the exclusive right to possession and the right to all rents and profits. On the death of either spouse, the survivor owns the entire estate outright.

In recent years, because of the unequal rights of spouses in the tenancy by the entirety, some states no longer use it as a form of co-ownership of real property. Other states have modified the common law version to give equal rights to the spouses, while at the same time retaining the feature of protection against attachment by creditors. Here is an example of a modern state statute:

> A husband and wife shall be equally entitled to the rents, products, income or profits and to the control, management and possession of property held by them as tenants by the entirety. The interest of a debtor spouse in property held as tenants by the entirety shall not be subject to seizure or execution by a creditor of such debtor spouse so long as such property is the principal residence of the nondebtor spouse; provided, however, both spouses shall be liable jointly or severally for debts incurred on account of necessaries furnished by either spouse or to a member of their family.

A divorce, by operation of law, automatically converts a tenancy by the entirety owned by the former spouses into a tenancy in common.

Tenants in Partnership

Tenancy in partnership is a form of ownership of real property that is available to business partners if they choose to use it. It is governed by the Uniform Partnership Act (UPA) in those states that have adopted it. Under the act, individual partners cannot transfer their interests in the property to others unless all of them do so, and individual partners' interests in the property are not subject to attachment or execution except on a claim against the partnership.

On the death of a partner, the decedent's rights in specific partnership property become vested in the surviving partners, who may possess such property only for partnership purposes. Death causes a dissolution of a partnership, however, and the surviving partners must account to the estate of the decedent and pay over to the estate the value of the deceased partner's equity in the partnership.

MULTI-OWNERSHIP OF REAL PROPERTY

Separate ownership of property by different people is accomplished by way of condominiums, cooperatives, and time-sharing arrangements. Because of the challenges associated with coordinated ownership arrangements, developers create **covenants, conditions, and restrictions (CC&R)** that are made part of the deeds to the individual properties. CC&R's are used to regulate the appearance and use of the property in ways that are stricter than local ordinances or zoning laws, but are thought necessary to maintain the value of the common properties. For instance, CC&R's might limit the number of cars parked on the street next to a homeowner's property, or regulate the color of paint on a property, or prohibit certain kinds of trees or shrubs from being grown. Developers often incorporate **homeowners associations** as nonprofit corporations, for the purposes of marketing and managing the housing developments. When a buyer purchases a property that is part of a multi-ownership development, the buyer becomes a member of the homeowners association and then is subject to its covenants, conditions, and restrictions.

Condominiums

A **condominium** is a parcel of real property, portions of which, called **units**, are owned separately in fee simple by individual owners, and the remainder of which, called the **common areas**, is owned as tenants in common by all of the unit owners. Common areas include entrances, hallways, sidewalks, swimming pools, yards, roofs, and outside walls, and are maintained and managed by a **condominium association** consisting of unit members. Unit owners pay monthly maintenance fees in addition to real property taxes. An ownership interest in a condominium is considered to be real property. A **master deed**, describing the entire property that is owned by the condominium association, is recorded at the registry of deeds, together with restrictions that are placed on the use of the property. The transfer of ownership of each unit is accomplished by the use of a **unit deed**, which is a deed to the individual unit being transferred.

Cooperatives

A **cooperative apartment** is a dwelling unit in which the occupants lease individual units and, at the same time, own shares of stock in the corporation that owns the building. The corporation owns the complex, which is occupied by the tenants who are the stockholders of the nonprofit corporation. The lease is known as a **proprietary lease** because it is a lease to an owner of the property. Tenants pay rent to the corporation, and the corporation maintains the property and pays the real property taxes. An ownership interest in a cooperative is personal property rather than real property, and a transfer of ownership is accomplished by sale of stock in the controlling corporation.

TERMS IN ACTION

Smoking is quite expensive, especially in New York, where the price of a pack of cigarettes is around $15. But for Harry Lysons, the cost of smoking in his apartment in a Manhattan **cooperative apartment** building became nearly priceless. He enjoyed smoking cigars in his apartment, but some of his neighbors—Amanda and Russell Poses, who have two small children—did not enjoy inhaling his secondhand smoke. The tensions persisted for over a year, and then the Poses sued Lysons in 2011 for $2 million, claiming that they were being harmed in their apartment, which shared a common wall with his, by the invasion of his "foul and noxious odors." Lysons settled with the Poses quickly, agreeing to pay them $2,000 dollars every time he lit up a cigar in his apartment. According to the court-approved agreement, if the Poses suspect that Lysons has been smoking in his apartment, they may request to come over and conduct a smell test. Lysons's lawyer claims that no payments will need to be made, because Lysons will find somewhere else to smoke.

Source: nypost.com

Timesharing

Timesharing, also called **interval ownership**, is a fee simple ownership of a unit of real property in which the owner can exercise the right of possession for only an interval, such as a week or two, each year. Other people possess the property at other intervals of the year. Like condominium owners, interval owners have the right to use the common areas of the property. An ownership interest in a time-share is considered to be real property, unless it is established by a lease, and the transfer of ownership is accomplished with the use of a deed to the individual unit being transferred. Timesharing is popular in vacation and resort areas of the country.

Reviewing What You Learned

After studying the chapter, write the answers to each of the following questions:

1. List the four most common co-tenant relationships. _____
   _____
   _____
   _____
   _____

2. Each tenant in common is entitled to possession of what part of the premises? _____
   _____
   _____
   _____

3. What happens to the interest in real property of a tenant in common at death? _____
   _____
   _____
   _____
   _____

4. May tenants in common grant out their interests in real property without permission to do so from the other co-tenants? May joint tenants do so? May tenants by the entirety do so?
   _____
   _____
   _____
   _____

5. How may tenants in common separate their interests in the property from other tenants in common? _____
   _____
   _____
   _____

6. Name the four unities in a joint tenancy. _____
   _____
   _____
   _____
   _____

7. What happens to a joint tenant's interest in real property at death? _____
   _____
   _____
   _____

8. Who may own real property as tenants by the entirety? _____
   _____
   _____
   _____

9. Describe ownership rights of a husband and a wife under the community property system. _____
   _____
   _____
   _____

10. What jurisdictions follow the community property system?
   _____
   _____
   _____
   _____

11. What rights does the husband have that the wife does not have under the common law theory of tenants by the entirety?

_____

_____

_____

12. Why is a tenancy by the entirety a popular method of owner-ship by a husband and wife? _____

_____

_____

_____

_____

13. In what way have some states modified the common law version of the tenancy by the entirety? _____

_____

_____

_____

_____

14. Under a tenancy in partnership, when is a partner's interest subject to attachment? _____

_____

_____

_____

_____

_____

15. When a partner dies, who owns the property under tenancy in partnership? _____

_____

_____

_____

_____

_____

16. Explain the difference between covenants, conditions, & re-strictions and a homeowners association (HOA).

_____

_____

_____

_____

_____

Understanding Legal Concepts

Indicate whether each statement is true or false. Then, change the italicized word or phrase of each false statement to make it true.

ANSWERS

_____ 1. Real property may be owned severally—that is, by *two or more persons.*

_____ 2. When two or more people own real property as tenants in common, each owner is entitled to the possession of *his or her part of the premises only.*

_____ 3. Any of the tenants in common *may* grant out their in-terests to others without permission of the other co-tenants.

_____ 4. All joint tenants' interests *are* equal.

_____ 5. If a joint tenant grants out his or her interest to a new owner, the new owner becomes a *joint tenant* with the remaining joint tenants.

_____ 6. Under common law, the husband, in a tenancy by the entirety, had the *exclusive* right to possession of the premises.

_____ 7. Under common law, a wife *can* transfer her interest in a tenancy by the entirety to someone else without her husband's consent.

_____ 8. The court *has no power* to partition a tenancy by the entirety.

_____ 9. A divorce, by operation of law, automatically converts a tenancy by the entirety into a *joint tenancy.*

_____ 10. In a *tenancy in partnership,* individual partners cannot transfer their interests in the property to others unless all of them do so.

Checking Terminology

From the list of legal terms that follows, select the one that matches each definition:

ANSWERS

a. common areas
b. community property

_____ 1. Property (other than a gift or inheritance) acquired by a husband or wife during mar-riage that belongs to both spouses equally.

c. concurrent ownership
d. condominium
e. condominium association
f. cooperative apartment
g. co-ownership
h. co-tenants
i. covenants, conditions, & restrictions (CC&R)
j. creditors homeowners association
k. interval ownership
l. joint tenancy
m. joint tenancy with the right of survivorship
n. joint tenants
o. levy on execution
p. master deed
q. moiety
r. partition
s. proprietary lease
t. several
u. tenancy by the entirety
v. tenancy in partnership
w. tenants in common
x. timesharing
y. unit deed
z. units
aa. unity of interest
bb. unity of possession
cc. unity of time
dd. unity of title

_____ 2. Two or more owners of real property.
_____ 3. The individual portions of a condominium that are owned separately in fee simple by individual owners.
_____ 4. Equal interest in property by all owners.
_____ 5. A dwelling unit in which the occupants lease individual units and, at the same time, own shares of stock in the corporation that owns the building.
_____ 6. Separate, individual, and independent.
_____ 7. The division of land held by joint tenants or tenants in common into distinct portions so that they may hold them separately.
_____ 8. The part of a condominium or cooperative apartment building that is owned as tenants in common by all of the unit owners.
_____ 9. Two or more persons holding one and the same interest, accruing by one and the same conveyance, commencing at one and the same time, and held by one and the same undivided possession.
_____ 10. Ownership in which each person has an interest in partnership property and is a co-owner of such property.
_____ 11. A lease to an owner of the property.
_____ 12. Ownership by more than one person. (Select two answers.)
_____ 13. All owners of property taking title at the same time.
_____ 14. The estate owned by joint tenants. (Select two answers.)
_____ 15. People who are owed money.
_____ 16. A type of joint tenancy held by a husband and wife that offers protection against attachment and that cannot be terminated by one spouse alone.
_____ 17. A group of condominium unit owners that manages and maintains a condominium.
_____ 18. Equal rights to possession of the entire property by all owners.
_____ 19. Two or more persons holding an undivided interest in property, with each owner's interests going to his or her heirs on death rather than to the surviving co-owners.
_____ 20. A fee simple ownership of a unit of real property in which the owner can exercise the right of possession for only an interval, such as a week or two, each year. (Select two answers.)
_____ 21. A deed to the individual unit being transferred.
_____ 22. A parcel of real property, portions of which are owned separately in fee simple by individual owners, and the remainder of which is owned as tenants in common by all of the unit owners.
_____ 23. All owners of property receiving title from the same instrument.
_____ 24. To collect a sum of money by putting into effect the judgment of a court.
_____ 25. Regulates the appearance and use of property in ways that are stricter than local ordinance and zoning laws.
_____ 26. A deed to a condominium that describes the entire property that is owned by the condominium association.
_____ 27. A part, portion or fraction.
_____ 28. Markets and manages housing developments.

Using Legal Language

Read the following story and fill in the blank lines with legal terms taken from the list of terms at the beginning of this chapter:

James and Kathleen, who were business partners, took title to a parcel of real property as _____ to protect their interests from being attached except on a claim against the partnership. When the partnership was dissolved, Kathleen bought out James's interest and owned the property _____—that is, separately. She sold the property to Larry, Mary, and Nancy, who took title as _____, which means that on the death of one of them, the entire ownership would remain in the surviving owners. They were called _____, because of the _____ ownership, and they had the following unities: _____, _____, _____, and _____. Mary decided to sell her interest in the property, but couldn't find a buyer. To avoid having the court _____ the property—that is, divide it into separate parcels—Larry and Nancy bought Mary's share. They decided to take title as _____ so that if one of them died, his or her share would go to his or her heirs. Later, however, when Larry and Nancy got married, they had their attorney change the way in which they owned the property to _____ so that they would have protection against attaching _____ (people who are owed money), who could _____

to collect money owed them by putting into effect a court judgment. They did not live in a(n) _____ jurisdiction in which all property (other than a gift or inheritance) acquired by either of them during marriage would belong to both equally. Eventually, Larry and Nancy sold the property and bought a _____, which is a parcel of real property, portions of which, called _____, are owned separately in fee simple by individual owners, and the remainder of which, called the _____, is owned as tenants in common by all the owners.

PUZZLING OVER WHAT YOU LEARNED

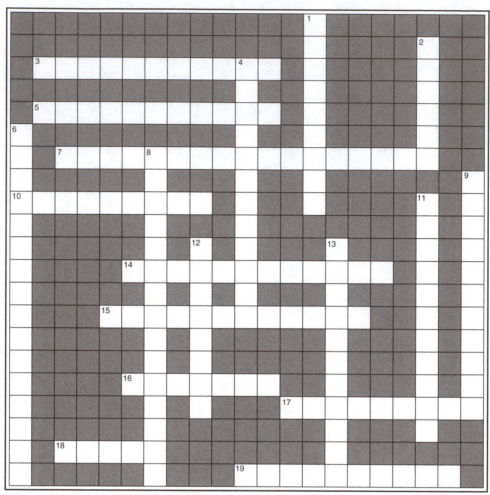

Caveat: Do not allow squares for spaces between words and punctuation (apostrophes, hyphens, etc.) when filling in crossword.

Across

3. A parcel of real property, portions of which are owned separately in fee simple by individual owners, and the remainder of which is owned as tenants in common by all the unit owners.
5. Owned by more than one person.
7. Property (other than a gift or inheritance) acquired by a husband or wife during marriage that belongs to both spouses equally.
10. The division of land held by tenants in common into distinct portions so that they may hold them separately.
14. The estate owned by joint tenants.
15. Two or more persons holding one and the same interest, accruing by one and the same conveyance, commencing at one and the same time, and held by one and the same undivided possession.
16. Separate, individual, and independent.
17. Two or more owners of real property.
18. The individual portions of a condominium that are owned separately in fee simple by individual owners.
19. A deed to a condominium that describes the entire property owned by the condominium association.

Down

1. People to whom money is owed.
2. A part, portion, or fraction.
4. All owners of a property receiving title from the same instrument.
6. A lease to an owner of the property.
8. Equal interest in a property by all owners.
9. The part of a condominium or apartment that is owned as tenants in common by all unit owners.
11. A fee simple owner of a unit of real property in which the owner can exercise the right of possession for only an interval each year.
12. A deed to an individual condominium unit.
13. All owners of a property taking title at the same time.

7

Acquiring Title to Real Property

ANTE INTERROGATORY

A formal written instrument used to transfer title from one person to another is a (A) convey, (B) deed, (C) reliction, (D) seisin

CHAPTER OUTLINE

Original Grant

Deed

Inheritance

Sale on Execution

Mortgagee's Foreclosure Sale

Tax Title

Adverse Possession

Slow Action of Water

KEY TERMS

accretion *(a·KREE·shun)*

adverse possession *(AD·verse po·SESH·en)*

alluvion *(a·LOO·vee·en)*

attachment *(a·TACH·ment)*

convey *(kon·VAY)*

conveyance *(kon·VAY·enss)*

deed

disseised *(di·SEEZD)*

divested *(dy·VEST·ed)*

erosion *(e·RO·shen)*

foreclose *(for·KLOZE)*

Homestead Act

infancy *(IN·fen·see)*

mortgagee *(more·gej·EE)*

mortgagee's foreclosure sale *(more·gej·EES for·KLOH·zher)*

mortgagor *(more·gej·OR)*

record owner *(REK·erd)*

reliction *(re·LIK·shun)*

right of redemption *(re·DEMP·shun)*

seal

seisin *(SEE·zin)*

sheriff's sale *(SHERR·ifs)*

tacking

vendee *(ven·DEE)*

vendor *(ven·DOR)*

Title to real property may be acquired in the following ways:

1. original grant
2. deed

3. inheritance
4. sale on execution
5. mortgagee's foreclosure sale
6. tax title
7. adverse possession
8. slow action of water

ORIGINAL GRANT

Originally, land in America was owned by the various foreign governments that had settled here, such as England, France, Spain, and Mexico. Individuals obtained title to the land by grants from the crowns of those countries. After the American Revolution, any land that was not owned by individuals became the property of either the state or the federal government, which **conveyed** (transferred) much of it out by public grant to homesteaders or settlers under laws enacted by Congress. Perhaps the most famous of these land grants was the 1862 **Homestead Act**, signed into law by President Lincoln. It allowed anyone who was at least 21 years old and who had never taken up arms against the United States to get up to 160 acres of public, undeveloped land. An application first had to be filed, and then the applicant had to demonstrate improvements on the land for a five-year period. Finally, the applicant could seek a deed. Success wasn't guaranteed, however; over half of the homesteaders failed. A shorter alternative to getting the property allowed homesteaders to buy their property from the government for $1.25 per acre after six months of living on the land. By the turn of the nineteenth century, over 80 million acres moved from public to private ownership.

DEED

The most common method of acquiring title to real property is by the use of a deed signed by the grantor and delivered to the grantee. A **deed** is a formal written instrument used to transfer title from one person to another. It is also known as a **conveyance**. The transfer can be as a result of a sale, a gift, or an inheritance. A person who transfers property or goods by sale is a **vendor**. A purchaser or buyer of property or goods is a **vendee**. Traditionally, a deed was required to be under seal to be effective; however, many states statutorily have done away with that requirement. A **seal** is a mark or impression (originally made with wax) placed next to the party's signature. Some states require that a deed be witnessed; others have no such requirement. The deed is discussed in detail in Chapter 32.

INHERITANCE

When people die owning real property either separately or with others as tenants in common, title to the property vests in their heirs or devisees at the moment of death. No deed is necessary for them to receive title, because title passes to them by operation of law. Such vesting of title, however, is subject to being **divested** (taken away) by the executor or administrator of the estate if it is necessary to obtain money from the sale of the property to pay estate taxes, administrative expenses, and other claims against the estate.

When someone dies owning real property with others as joint tenants, the surviving joint tenants own the entire property outright at the moment of death of the decedent. In this case, it is not necessary to probate the estate to obtain title because title passes automatically to the surviving joint tenants. It is usually necessary to obtain estate tax releases for the surviving joint tenants to have clear title to the property, however.

SALE ON EXECUTION

At the beginning of a lawsuit, the plaintiff will often attach the defendant's real property. An **attachment** has the effect of bringing the property under the jurisdiction of the court as security for the debt. If the defendant loses the case and does not pay the amount of the judgment to the plaintiff, the sheriff may levy and sell on execution the real property that was attached. This is often referred to as a **sheriff's sale** and is done by public auction after notice and a prescribed amount of time, set by state statute, is given to the property owner.

MORTGAGEE'S FORECLOSURE SALE

A **mortgagee's foreclosure sale** occurs when the holder of a mortgage on real property (known as the **mortgagee** and usually a bank or lender to the homeowner) is not paid and decides to sell the property to obtain the amount owed by the homeowner (the **mortgagor**). The mortgagee's foreclosure sale is the last stage of **foreclosure**, which is the legally established judicial process for obtaining title to property that is the collateral for an unpaid loan or is available to satisfy an outstanding judgment against the property owner. The sale is by auction and occurs under the jurisdiction of the court. The proceeds of the sale are applied to the payment of the mortgage debt, with any surplus going to the mortgagor. Some states have a statutory power of sale provision for mortgages that regulates the foreclosure sale and must be strictly followed when a foreclosure sale occurs. Foreclosure sales under a deed of trust (see Chapter 35) typically are not subject to court supervision.

TERMS IN ACTION

A record 2.9 million homes were foreclosed in 2010, which was approximately a 3 percent higher number than in 2009. About half of all **foreclosures** took place in five states: California, Florida, Michigan, Arizona, and Illinois. Five years earlier, there were 885,000 foreclosures in America, roughly one-third of the 2010 amount. Most foreclosures involve one person or family losing one home, but this is not necessarily so with celebrities. Between 2009 and 2010, Nicholas Cage was foreclosed upon four times. The Academy Award-winning actor and star of such films as "The Rock" and "National Treasure" was hard hit by the international financial meltdown of 2008 and became beset by unpaid taxes and mortgage payments. In 2009, he sued his manager for swindling him out of millions of assets. That case settled. In November 2009, Cage lost to **mortgagee's foreclosure sale** the two homes he owned in New Orleans, one of which was located in the famous French Quarter. Both homes brought a total of $5.7 million, although their appraisals totaled $6.8 million. In January 2010, Cage's Las Vegas home sold for $4.95 million, nearly half the price of the $8.5 million that Cage had paid in 2006 for the 14,000-sqare-foot home, which has an elevator and an underground 16-car garage. And then in November 2010, Cage's Bel Air, California, mansion was sold in foreclosure for $10.5 million. The 12,000-square-foot home was originally listed for sale at $34 million and had once been owned by Dean Martin.

Sources: zillow.com; realtytrac.com; tampabay.com; money.cnn.com; latimesblogs.latimes.com

---

TAX TITLE

Municipalities have the power to take real property for unpaid taxes. Usually, a city or town must first make a demand for payment on the record owner of the property. The **record owner** is the person who appears to be the owner of the property according to the records at the registry of deeds. If the tax is not paid within a certain number of days after demand, the tax collector may take the property for the city or town, or sell it at a public auction. In some states, this is done by a foreclosure suit brought by the taxing authority.

A purchaser of real property at a tax sale, however, takes the property subject to the former owner's **right of redemption** (right to take the property back). The latter can get the property back upon payment to the city or town of the back taxes, interest, and expenses incurred in the tax title sale. The purchaser of tax title property, to obtain clear title, must petition the court to

7

foreclose (terminate) the right of redemption. Only when the court does this does title become absolute in the owner who purchased it at the tax sale.

ADVERSE POSSESSION

Title to real property may be obtained by taking actual possession of the property, under the following required conditions: 1) openly; 2) notoriously; 3) exclusively; 4) under a claim of right; and 5) continuously for the statutory period, which is 20 years in many states. This method of obtaining title to real property, called **adverse possession**, developed at common law under the theory that two persons (unless they are co-owners) could not have **seisin** (possession of a freehold) of the same land at the same time. If one person took possession of land under a claim of right, the real owner was said to be **disseised** (dispossessed) and would have to bring an action to regain possession within 20 years or be forever barred from doing so.

In calculating the 20-year or other statutory period, any uninterrupted continuous use by previous nonowner occupiers may be added to the time. Such an accumulation of possession by different occupiers who are not record owners is called **tacking**.

Certain disabilities on the part of the true owner (including **infancy**—that is, under the age of majority—insanity, imprisonment, and absence from the United States), if they occur at the beginning of the adverse possession, will give the true owner a longer time to regain possession of the premises.

In some states, clear record title by adverse possession may be had by simply filing an affidavit with the proper office. Other states require a court proceeding to obtain clear title.

▌TERMS IN ACTION

Adverse possession has a long history in America. It was based on the idea that allowing a trespasser to take title to someone else's property, after enough time, was beneficial because the trespasser has made the property more useful. But an adverse possession case from Boulder, Colorado, shows that times have changed. In 2006, Richard McLean, retired judge and former Boulder mayor, and his wife Edith Stevens, an attorney, sought title by adverse possession to one third of the 4,750-square-foot lot of Don and Susie Kirlin, who had purchased the undeveloped property in 1980, planning eventually to build their dream home. McLean and Stevens sued in 2006, claiming that that their use of the property entitled them to ownership. Their evidence of "use" was the claim that they had trespassed on the property sufficiently to create a path on the undeveloped lot, had hosted political events around the area of the path, and had been using the property as if it were their own for the statutorily required uninterrupted 18-year time frame. The Kirlins countered that the politically connected neighbors were trying to steal what was valued to be an $800,000 lot. After a few years and $400,000 in legal fees, the Kirlins finally settled the case, agreeing to transfer ownership of 12 percent of what was once their land. The outcry over what happened to the Kirlins resulted in the Colorado legislature's passing a stricter adverse possession law in 2008, which, among other things, requires those claiming adverse possession to have a "good faith belief" that the land is theirs. It also increases the burden of proof in an adverse possession case to "clear and convincing evidence."

Sources: denverpost.com; fwlaw.com; landgrabber.org

▌Word Wise
Seise or Seize?

The legal term "seisin" means "possession"; the term "disseised" means "dispossessed." "Seise" is the legal variation of the word "seize," which has the broader meaning of "grasping something suddenly and forcibly." Both words have the same pronunciation.

SLOW ACTION OF WATER

Any addition to the soil made by nature, such as the gradual accumulation of soil on land next to a stream caused by the action of water, is called **accretion**. Another term used to describe this addition to the soil is **alluvion**. Such addition to the soil belongs to the owner of the soil to which it is added. In contrast, when one side of a stream gains soil by the slow action of water, the opposite side of the stream often loses soil. This process is known as **erosion**, which is defined as "the gradual eating away of the soil by the operation of currents or tides."

Real property owners sometimes gain additional land when adjoining water permanently recedes. This gradual recession of water, leaving land permanently uncovered, is referred to as **reliction**.

7

Reviewing What You Learned

After studying the chapter, write the answers to each of the following questions:

1. List the ways that title may be acquired to real property._____

_____

_____

_____

_____

2. From whom did individuals originally obtain title to land in America?_____

_____

_____

_____

3. What happened, after the American Revolution, to land that was not owned by individuals?_____

_____

_____

_____

4. What were the particular conditions of the Homestead Act of 1862?_____

_____

_____

_____

_____

5. What is the most common method of acquiring title to real property, and what are the requirements of this method?_____

_____

_____

6. When an individual owner of real property dies, who becomes the immediate owner of the property? To what is this ownership subject?_____

_____

_____

_____

7. Briefly describe a sale on execution._____

_____

_____

_____

_____

8. When does a mortgagee's foreclosure sale occur?_____

_____

_____

_____

9. Why does the purchaser of real property at a tax sale take a risk?_____

_____

_____

_____

_____

7

10. How long must one possess real property to own it by adverse possession?_____

_____

_____

_____

_____

11. Who becomes the owner of soil that is gradually added to land adjoining a stream as a result of the action of water?_____

_____

_____

_____

_____

Understanding Legal Concepts

Indicate whether each statement is true or false. Then, change the italicized word or phrase of each false statement to make it true.

ANSWERS

_____ 1. Originally, land in America was owned by the various *foreign governments* that had settled here.

_____ 2. Traditionally, a deed was required to be under seal to be effective; however, many states *have* done away with that requirement.

_____ 3. *Some* states have no requirement that a deed be witnessed.

_____ 4. When people die owning real estate separately, *a deed* is necessary to pass title to their heirs.

_____ 5. For title to pass to a surviving joint tenant, it *is necessary* to probate the estate of a deceased joint tenant.

_____ 6. An attachment has the effect of bringing property under the jurisdiction of *the court* as security for a debt.

_____ 7. A mortgagee's foreclosure sale is a *private sale* that occurs under the jurisdiction of the court.

_____ 8. A purchaser of real property at a tax sale takes the property subject to the former owner's right to *take the property back.*

_____ 9. In calculating the period required to obtain title by adverse possession, any uninterrupted use by previous nonowner occupiers *may not be* added to the time period.

_____ 10. Any addition to the soil made by nature, such as the *very rapid* accumulation of soil on land next to a stream, is called accretion.

Checking Terminology

From the list of legal terms that follows, select the one that matches each definition.

ANSWERS

a. accretion
b. adverse possession
c. alluvion
d. attachment
e. convey
f. conveyance
g. deed
h. disseised
i. divested
j. erosion
k. foreclose
l. Homestead Act
m. infancy
n. mortgagee
o. mortgagee's foreclosure sale
p. mortgagor
q. record owner
r. reliction
s. right of redemption
t. seal
u. seisin
v. sheriff's sale
w. tacking

_____ 1. A formal, written instrument used to transfer title to real property from one person to another. (Select two answers.)

_____ 2. A mark or impression, originally made with wax, placed next to a party's signature.

_____ 3. The act of taking or seizing property by the use of a writ, summons, or other judicial order and bringing it into the custody of the court.

_____ 4. One who borrows money and gives a mortgage—that is, pledges property—to the lender as security for the loan.

_____ 5. A sale of property at public auction conducted by a sheriff.

_____ 6. Right to take property back.

_____ 7. Title to real property obtained by taking actual possession of it openly, notoriously, exclusively, under a claim of right, and continuously for a period set by statute.

_____ 8. Dispossessed.

_____ 9. Any gradual addition to the soil made by nature, such as the gradual accumulation of soil on land next to a stream caused by the action of water. (Select two answers.)

_____ 10. To transfer.

_____ 11. Taken away.

_____ 12. One who lends money and takes back a mortgage as security for the loan.

_____ 13. One who appears to be the owner of real property according to the records at the registry of deeds.

_____ 14. A sale of real property that terminates all rights of the mortgagor in the property covered by the mortgage.

_____ 15. A federal land grant that encouraged people to improve the land over five years in order to gain a deed to the property.

x. vendee

y. vendor

_____ 16. Possession of a freehold.

_____ 17. The addition of previous occupants' possession to one's own possession to meet the statutory period for adverse possession.

_____ 18. The gradual eating away of the soil by the operation of currents or tides.

_____ 19. The gradual recession of water, leaving land permanently uncovered.

_____ 20. Under the age of majority.

_____ 21. A purchaser or buyer of property or goods.

_____ 22. Terminate.

7

Using Legal Language

Read the following story and fill in the blank lines with legal terms taken from the list of terms at the beginning of this chapter:

Arlene inherited some real property that adjoined a river. Title to the property vested in Arlene at the moment of death of the decedent, but was subject to being _____ to pay claims against the estate. Arlene was the _____, because she was the person who appeared to be the owner according to the records at the Registry of Deeds. She received a notice in the mail from her bank saying that a(n) _____ was about to occur, because she was behind in her mortgage payments. She was the _____; the bank was the _____. Arlene took the money that she had saved to pay property taxes and other creditors and used it to pay the money owed on the mortgage. One of her creditors brought suit against her and placed a(n) _____ on her property, which had the effect of bringing it under the jurisdiction of the court as security for the debt. To prevent a(n) _____—that is, a sale on execution of the property—Arlene paid the amount that was owed to the creditor. She then had the property lines surveyed and discovered that the garage belonging to her next-door neighbor, Ben, extended four feet onto her land. Although Ben had owned the property for 10 years, the garage had been placed there by Carl, the previous owner, 22 years earlier. Ben can add his 10 years of ownership to that of Carl's under a method called _____. Ben obtained title to the land under the garage by _____, a method which had developed at common law under the theory that two persons could not have _____ of the same land at the same time. If one person took possession of land under a claim of right, the real owner was said to be _____—that is, dispossessed—of the property. Because Arlene had failed to pay the property tax, the local tax collector took the property and sold it at a public auction to Darlene. The _____—that is, the transfer to Darlene—was made by the use of a(n) _____, which is a formal written instrument used to transfer title from one person to another. The instrument was under _____, which is a mark or impression next to the party's signature. Darlene bought the property subject to Arlene's _____ that is, the right to take the property back—unless Darlene is successful in petitioning the court to _____ (terminate) that right. By then, a considerable amount of land had been added to the property by _____, which is also called _____, caused by the slow action of the adjoining river.

PUZZLING OVER WHAT YOU LEARNED

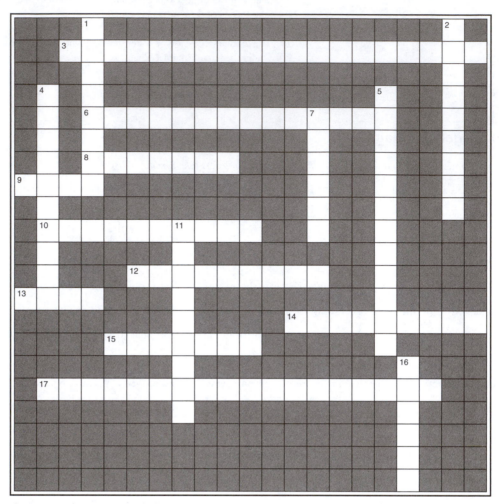

Caveat: Allow squares for spaces between words and punctuation (apostrophes, hyphens, etc.) when filling in crossword.

Across

3. Right to take property back.
6. A sale of property at public auction conducted by a sheriff.
8. Gradual eating away of the soil by the operation of currents or tides.
9. A written instrument used to transfer title of real property.
10. Act of taking property and bringing it into the custody of the court.
12. One who borrows money and gives a mortgage to the lender as security.
13. A mark or impression.
14. Dispossessed.
15. Under the age of majority.
17. Title to real property obtained by taking actual possession of it.

Down

1. Taken away.
2. Terminate.
4. A written instrument used to transfer title of real property.
5. One who appears to be the owner of real property according to the records.
7. Possession of a freehold.
11. One who lends money and takes back a mortgage as security for a loan.
16. To transfer.

Deeds

ANTE INTERROGATORY

The most desirable form of a deed, which gives assurances that title is good, is a (A) bargain and sale deed, (B) quitclaim deed, (C) special warranty deed, (D) general warranty deed.

CHAPTER OUTLINE

Sealed Instrument

Requirements of a Modern Deed

Describing Real Property

Types of Deeds

    General Warranty Deed

    Special Warranty Deed

    Quitclaim Deed

    Bargain and Sale Deed

KEY TERMS

acknowledgment *(ak·NAWL·ej·ment)*

bargain and sale deed *(BAR·gen)*

base lines

bounds

conveyancing *(kon·VAY·ens·ing)*

covenant *(KOV·e·nent)*

deed

deed without covenants *(KOV·e·nents)*

encumbrance *(en·KUM·brens)*

fiduciary deed *(fi·D00·she·air·ee)*

full covenant and warranty deed
    (KOV·e·nent and WAR·en·tee)

general warranty deed
    (JEN·e·rel WAR·en·tee)

government survey system
    (GUV·ern·ment SUR·vey SYS·tem)

grantee *(gran·TEE)*

grantor *(gran·TOR)*

habendum clause *(ha·BEN·dum)*

heirlooms *(AIR·looms)*

hereditaments *(herr·e·DIT·a·ments)*

limited warranty deed *(LIM·i·ted WAR·en·tee)*

locus *(LOH·kus)*

locus sigilli *(LOH·kus se·JIL·i)*

meridians *(mer·ID·ee·ens)*

metes *(meets)*

metes and bounds

monuments *(MON·yoo·ments)*

notary public *(NO·tar·ee PUB·lick)*

plat

plat book

plat map

plot

quitclaim deed *(KWIT·klame)*

range *(rainj)*

rectangular survey system (*rek·TANG·yoo·ler SUR·vey SYS·tem*)

section (*SEK·shun*)

special warranty deed (*SPESH·el WAR·en·tee*)

tenements (*TEN·e·mentz*)

township (*TOUN·ship*)

tract of land (*trakt*)

warrant (*WAR·ent*)

Centuries ago in England, before the use of the deed, real property was transferred from one person to another in a public ceremony known as *livery of seisin*. The one transferring the property would hand the other a clod of dirt or a twig from a tree, symbolizing the transfer. The ceremony was called *livery in deed* when it took place on the property itself, and *livery in law* when it was done in sight of the property, but not actually on it.

SEALED INSTRUMENT

As time went on and more people learned to read and write, the written deed replaced the formal ceremony of transferring real property. In those days, a person's seal was of foremost importance. One reason is that the seal was more difficult to forge than a handwritten signature. Any contract that was under seal and contained **covenants** (promises) was called a **deed**.

Later, but still under the common law, a deed became defined as "a writing under seal by which lands, tenements, or hereditaments are conveyed for an estate not less than freehold." **Tenements** were defined as "everything of a permanent nature which may be holden, and in a more restrictive sense, houses or dwellings." **Hereditaments** were "things capable of being inherited, including not only lands and everything thereon, but also **heirlooms**" (valued possessions with sentimental value passed down through generations within a family).

Originally, a seal was an impression on wax, paper, wafer, or some other firm substance upon which an impression could be made. Eventually, the impression was replaced by a round, red, paper seal pasted on the instrument, or the word "seal," or a phrase such as "Witness my hand and seal," or the letters "L.S." (the abbreviation for **locus sigilli**—the place of the seal) written beside a party's signature. Whatever method is used to put a deed under seal is not the same as a **notary public's** seal used by a notary (a person authorized by his or her state to serve as an official, impartial witness to those acts requiring a witness's signature; also known as a public notary) to acknowledge an instrument. These two types of seals are separate and distinct, one having nothing to do with the other.

Today, a **deed** may be defined as a formal, written instrument by which title to real property is transferred from one person to another. The deed is the most common method of **conveyancing** (transferring title to real property from one person to another). By statute, in many states, a deed is no longer required to be under seal.

The person who transfers title is known as the **grantor**, and the person to whom title is transferred is known as the **grantee**.

REQUIREMENTS OF A MODERN DEED

A deed must convey a present ownership interest to the grantee, even though the grantee's right to possess the premises may be delayed until a later time. For a conveyance to be valid, a deed must meet the following requirements:

1. be in writing
2. identify the grantor
3. be signed by the grantor
4. identify the grantee
5. contain words of conveyance, such as "grant," "convey," or "transfer"
6. describe the **locus** (exact parcel) being conveyed

7. be delivered to the grantee
8. be accepted by the grantee

To be effective as to third parties, a deed must also be recorded. To be recorded, a deed must be acknowledged. An **acknowledgment** is a formal declaration before an authorized official, by a person who executes an instrument, that it is his or her free act and deed. A certificate of acknowledgment, signed and sealed by the official (usually, a notary public), is placed at the bottom of the deed following the signature of the grantor.

DESCRIBING REAL PROPERTY

There are three principal systems in use today by which to describe real property in a deed: (1) the metes and bounds system, (2) the rectangular survey system, and (3) by reference to a plat or survey.

Metes and bounds is a system of describing real property by its outer boundaries, with reference to courses, distances, and **monuments** (visible marks indicating boundaries). **Metes** are the distances between points, and **bounds** are the directions of the boundaries that enclose a parcel of land. This system came from England and is used in the eastern part of the United States, where the original 13 colonies were located. Here is an example:

> Beginning at the Southwesterly corner of the wall, by Haverhill Road, (Main Street) and land now owned by Raymond Pearl (formerly owned by B. Ford Parsons) and thence running
>
> | | |
> |---|---|
> | Easterly | by said wall and fence and by land of said Pearl about four hundred thirty-four (434) feet to a corner of the fence by land now of Charles M. Moulton; thence running |
> | Northerly | by the wall, and by land of said Moulton, one hundred sixty-seven feet (167) to land now or formerly of Charles F. Austin; thence running |
> | Westerly | by said land about four hundred and forty-four feet (444) to said Haverhill Road (Main Street); thence running |
> | Southerly | by said Haverhill Road (Main Street) one hundred eighty-eight feet (188) to the point begun at. |

Following the Revolutionary War, the United States Congress ordered a survey of the vast area of land west of the original 13 colonies. The **rectangular survey system**, also known as the **government survey system**, was established at that time. It is a method of describing real property according to the property's relationship to intersecting lines called **base lines** (running east and west) and *principal* or *prime* **meridians** (lines running north and south). The intersections of the lines create 24-mile squares, which are further divided into 6-mile squares called **townships**. Each township is divided into 26 equal squares called sections. A **section** is a square mile of land, containing 640 acres. A row of townships running north and south is called a **range**.

A third method of describing real property is by reference to a recorded survey that is made when a **tract of land** (a large piece of land) is subdivided. A map of the subdivision, called a **plat**, **plat map**, or **plot**, is drawn. The size and shape of each lot is designated, and the plat is given a name or number so that it can be identified. When it is recorded, the plat is entered into a **plat book** at the registry of deeds.

TYPES OF DEEDS

There are four types of deeds in general use today:

1. general warranty deed
2. special warranty deed
3. quitclaim deed
4. bargain and sale deed

The first two deeds contain warranties. The latter two do not.

General Warranty Deed

A **general warranty deed**, sometimes known as a **full covenant and warranty deed**, is the most desirable form of deed, from the viewpoint of the grantee, because it **warrants** (gives assurances) that the title is good. The typical general warranty deed contains the following four covenants made by the grantor to the grantee:

1. The grantor has good title.
2. No **encumbrances** (liens or claims by others) exist.
3. The grantor has good right to sell and convey the property.
4. The grantor will warrant and defend the title against the claims of all persons.

Because of its lengthy covenants, the warranty deed is extremely long and wordy. To illustrate, the clause called the **habendum clause**, which defines the extent of ownership, reads as follows in a long-form warranty deed:

TO HAVE AND TO HOLD THE GRANTED PREMISES, with all the privileges and appurtenances thereto belonging, to the said (grantee), and his [or her] heirs and assigns, to their own use and behoof forever.

Similarly, the clause containing the covenants in a long-form general warranty deed reads as follows:

And I hereby, for myself and my heirs, executors, and administrators, COVENANT with the grantee and his [or her] heirs and assigns that I am lawfully seized in fee simple of the granted premises; that they are free from all encumbrances; that I have good right to sell and convey the same as aforesaid; and that I will, and my heirs, executors, and administrators shall, WARRANT AND DEFEND the same to the grantee and his [or her] heirs and assigns forever against the lawful claims and demands of all persons.

To avoid the use of such lengthy and complicated language, many states have created short forms of deeds, which give the same warranties as the long forms, but use fewer words. For example, the words "convey and warrant" create a general warranty deed in Alaska, Illinois, Kansas, Michigan, Minnesota, and Wisconsin. The words "warrant generally" mean the same in Pennsylvania, Vermont, Virginia, and West Virginia deeds. The words "grant, bargain, and sell" create a general warranty deed in Arkansas, Florida, Idaho, Missouri, and Nevada. Finally, the words "with warranty covenants" mean the same in Massachusetts deeds.

TERMS IN ACTION

Seven thousand properties in Taos County, New Mexico, were put in real estate limbo in 2011 after someone filed **warranty deeds** to all of the properties in the county. The claimant filing the deeds asserted that he was the heir of the 42,000 acres in question, citing title documents going as far back as the 1848 Treaty of Guadalupe Hidalgo, which ended the Mexican–American war and made New Mexico an American territory. But the treaty also honored land grants that had been made to individuals by the Spanish King and Mexican government. Because of the filings, title companies were stymied; real estate brokers didn't know what to do; sellers and buyers couldn't close on their transactions. Then it came to light that the party asserting the title claim was Robert O. Gonzales, a trustee of one of the land grants and an heir of one of the original **grantees** from that 1848 treaty. Gonzales's stated reason for filing the deeds was his annoyance that no one ever attended the trustees' meetings, and so he wanted to stir up interest in them.

Sources: abqjournal.com; taosnews.com

Word Wise
More Words Ending in "or" and "ee"

grantor (*gran·TOR*)	One who transfers real property to another.
grantee (*gran·TEE*)	One to whom real property is transferred.
mortgagor (*more·gej·OR*)	One who borrows money and gives a mortgage as security.
mortgagee (*more·gej·EE*)	One who lends money and takes a mortgage as security.
obligor (*ob·li·GOR*)	One bound by contract to perform an obligation.
obligee (*ob·li·GEE*)	One to whom an obligation is owed under a contract.
pledgor (*plej·OR*)	One who gives property to another as security for a loan.
pledgee (*plej·EE*)	One to whom property is given as security for a loan.
promisor (*prom·i·SOHR*)	One who makes a promise.
promisee (*prom·i·SEE*)	One to whom a promise is made.

Special Warranty Deed

A **special warranty deed**, sometimes called a **limited warranty deed**, warrants that no defects arose in the title during the time that the grantor owned the property, but no warranty is made as to defects that may have arisen before the grantor owned the property. In a special warranty deed, the grantor warrants the following:

1. The premises are free from all encumbrances made by the grantor.
2. The grantor will warrant and defend the title only against claims through him or her.

As in the case of the general warranty deed, many states have created short forms of special warranty deeds. For example, the words "warrant specially" create a special warranty deed in Mississippi, Pennsylvania, Vermont, Virginia, and West Virginia. The word "grant" means the same in California, Idaho, and North Dakota deeds. The words "with quitclaim covenants" are used to create a special warranty deed in Massachusetts.

Quitclaim Deed

A **quitclaim deed** (called a **deed without covenants** or a **fiduciary deed** in some states) conveys only the grantor's interest, if any, in the real property and contains no warranties. It is commonly used when a deed is necessary to cure a defect in the chain of title or when the grantor is not sure whether his or her title is good or bad. Executors, administrators, and other fiduciaries often use this form of deed when conveying real property.

TERMS IN ACTION

The **quitclaim deed** lacks the guarantees of the traditional **warranty deed**, but one would think that the quitclaim deed would, at least, guarantee that the signatures were authentic. That isn't always the case. In 2005, a Minnesotan named Marc Smyth sought to refinance the home that he and his wife owned in an exclusive beach-front community on Alabama's Ono Island. But Smyth and his wife were divorcing at the time, and she didn't know that he had applied for a $496,000 refinance loan on that property. She also didn't know that her ex-husband-to-be found a female friend in Alabama who used Mrs. Smyth's driver's license and then forged Mrs. Smyth's signature on a quitclaim deed that purported to give Mr. Smyth sole ownership of the property, providing him the qualification to apply for the refinance loan by himself. He then used the loan to pay off the mortgage on the home and to buy a $225,000 boat. Mr. Smyth was caught and indicted for fraud and identity theft in 2010. His by-then ex-wife and the mortgage company sued him for fraud, for which they won an $800,000 default judgment, and in 2011, he pled guilty to the criminal charges.

Source: www.blog.al.com

Bargain and Sale Deed

A **bargain and sale deed** conveys the land itself rather than merely the interest that the grantor has in the property, as is done in a quitclaim deed. The form is the same as a warranty deed except that the covenants (warranties) are omitted. Consideration is required in a bargain and sale deed, which means that a bargain and sale deed may not be used to transfer land by way of a gift.

Reviewing What You Learned

After studying the chapter, write the answers to each of the following questions:

1. What was considered to be a deed under the early days of common law?_____

_____

_____

_____

2. List the requirements of a valid deed._____

_____

_____

_____

_____

3. What are the four types of deeds that are in general use today?

_____

_____

_____

_____

4. Why is a general warranty deed the most desirable form of deed, from the viewpoint of the grantee? How many covenants are made in a general warranty deed?_____

_____

_____

_____

_____

5. What have many states done to avoid the use of long and complicated language in a deed?_____

_____

_____

_____

_____

6. Describe the two warranties made in a special warranty deed.

_____

_____

_____

_____

7. Under what circumstances is a quitclaim deed commonly used?_____

_____

_____

_____

_____

8. Describe the form of a bargain and sale deed._____

_____

_____

_____

_____

Understanding Legal Concepts

Indicate whether each statement is true or false. Then, change the italicized word or phrase of each false statement to make it true.

ANSWERS

_____ 1. In the early days of common law, a deed and a sealed instrument were *practically synonymous.*

_____ 2. For a conveyance to be valid, a deed must be *delivered* to the grantee.

_____ 3. A general warranty deed *is not* the most desirable form of deed, from the viewpoint of the grantee.

_____ 4. A general warranty deed *does not* contain a warranty that the grantor has good title.

_____ 5. To avoid use of lengthy and complicated language, many states have created *short forms* of deeds.

_____ **6.** The *habendum clause* begins with the words "TO HAVE AND TO HOLD."

_____ **7.** A special warranty deed protects against defects that arose *before* the grantor owned the property.

_____ **8.** A quitclaim deed contains *a warranty that title is good.*

_____ **9.** A *quitclaim* deed is commonly used when a deed is necessary to cure a defect in the chain of title.

_____ **10.** Consideration *is not* required in a bargain and sale deed.

Checking Terminology

From the list of legal terms that follows, select the one that matches each definition.

ANSWERS

a. acknowledgment
b. bargain and sale deed
c. base lines
d. bounds
e. conveyancing
f. covenant
g. deed
h. deed without covenants
i. encumbrance
j. fiduciary deed
k. full covenant and warranty deed
l. general warranty deed
m. government survey system
n. grantee
o. grantor
p. habendum clause
q. heirlooms
r. hereditaments
s. limited warranty deed
t. locus
u. locus sigilli
v. notary public
w. meridians
x. metes
y. metes and bounds
z. monuments
aa. plat
bb. plat book
cc. plat map
dd. plot
ee. quitclaim deed
ff. range
gg. rectangular survey system
hh. section
ii. special warranty deed
jj. tenements
kk. township
ll. tract of land
mm. warrant

_____ 1. Valued possessions with sentimental value passed down through generations within a family.
_____ 2. A place.
_____ 3. A map designating the size and shape of a specific land area. (Select three answers.)
_____ 4. To give assurance.
_____ 5. A claim, lien, charge, or liability attached to and binding real property.
_____ 6. A square mile of land, containing 640 acres, in the United States government survey.
_____ 7. A system of describing real property by its outer boundaries, with reference to courses, distances, and monuments.
_____ 8. A deed that conveys land itself, rather than people's interests therein, and requires consideration.
_____ 9. The portion of a deed beginning with the words "To have and to hold," which defines the extent of the ownership of the property granted.
_____ 10. A person to whom real property is transferred.
_____ 11. Visible marks indicating boundaries.
_____ 12. A row of townships running north and south in the United States government survey.
_____ 13. A promise or assurance.
_____ 14. A six-square-mile portion of land in the United States government survey.
_____ 15. Horizontal lines running east and west in the United States government survey.
_____ 16. Vertical lines running north and south in the United States government survey.
_____ 17. A deed containing warranties under which the grantor guarantees the property to be free from all encumbrances made during the time that he or she owned the property and to defend the title only against claims through him or her. (Select two answers.)
_____ 18. A method of describing real property according to the property's relationship to intersecting lines running east and west and lines running north and south. (Select two answers.)
_____ 19. Transferring title to real property.
_____ 20. A formal written instrument by which title to real property is transferred from one person to another.
_____ 21. A person who transfers real property to another.
_____ 22. A large piece of land.
_____ 23. A deed containing warranties under which the grantor guarantees the property to be free from all encumbrances and to defend the title against the claims of all persons. (Select two answers.)
_____ 24. Everything of a permanent nature that may be possessed and, in a more restrictive sense, houses or dwellings.
_____ 25. Directions of the boundaries that enclose a parcel of land.
_____ 26. A book that is recorded at the registry of deeds, containing plat maps.
_____ 27. Things capable of being inherited, including not only lands and everything thereon, but also heirlooms.
_____ 28. A deed to real property in which the grantor transfers only his or her interest, if any, in the property and gives no warranties of title. (Select three answers.)
_____ 29. Distances between points.
_____ 30. Place of the seal.
_____ 31. A formal declaration before an authorized official, by a person who executes an instrument, that it is his or her free act and deed.
_____ 32. A person authorized as an official witness to acts requiring a witness's signature.

Using Legal Language

Read the following story and fill in the blank lines with legal terms taken from the list of terms at the beginning of this chapter:

Clifford purchased a parcel of real property from Diane, who was the executrix of an estate. In the _____, which was the formal written instrument by which title was transferred, Diane was the _____ and Clifford was the _____. The instrument, which conveyed only the grantor's interest and contained no warranties, is called a(n) _____ in some states, a(n) _____ in others, and a(n) _____ in still others. The _____ system is used to describe the property by its outer boundaries, with reference to courses, distances, and _____ (visible marks indicating boundaries). _____ are the distances between points, and _____ are the directions of the boundaries that enclose a parcel of land. Later, Clifford sold the property to Emily, who was schooled in the subject of _____—that is, trans-

ferring title to real property—and wanted the kind of deed that _____ (gives assurances) that title is good. Emily insisted that Clifford give her a deed containing four promises, or guarantees, called _____. This type of deed is known as a(n) _____ in some states and a(n) _____ in others. The _____ in this deed begins with the words "To have and to hold." The day after receiving title, Emily transferred the exact parcel—that is, the _____ to Frank by giving him a(n) _____, which is called a(n) _____ _____ in some states and warrants that the premises are free from all _____ made by the grantor. In her state, the _____, which conveys the land itself and requires consideration, is not used.

PUZZLING OVER WHAT YOU LEARNED

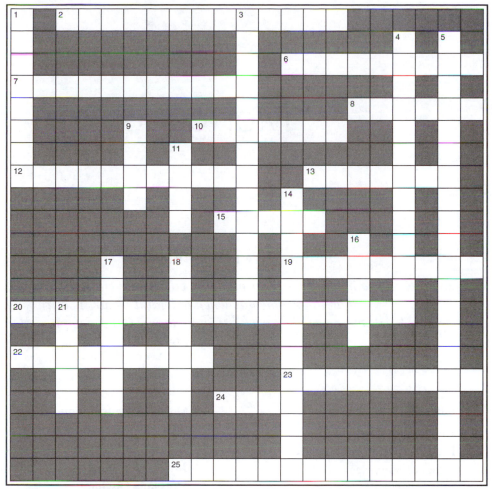

Caveat: Do **not** allow squares for spaces between words and punctuation (apostrophes, hyphens, etc.) when filling in crossword.

Across

2. Things capable of being inherited, including not only lands and everything thereon but also heirlooms.
6. Horizontal lines running east and west in the United States government survey.
7. A claim, lien, charge, or liability attached to and binding real property.
8. Directions of the boundaries that enclose a parcel of land.
10. A person who transfers real property to another.
12. A large piece of land.
13. To give assurance.
15. A place.
19. Everything of a permanent nature that may be possessed and, in a more restrictive sense, houses or dwellings.
20. A deed that conveys land itself, rather than people's interest therein, and requires consideration.
22. Visible marks indicating boundaries.
23. Lines running north and south in the United States government survey.
24. A formal written instrument by which title to real property is transferred from one person to another.
25. The portion of a deed beginning with the words *to have and to hold,* which defines the extent of the ownership of the property granted.

Down

1. A promise or assurance.
3. A system of describing real property by its outer boundaries, with reference to courses, distances, and monuments.
4. Another name for *quitclaim deed.*
5. Another name for *quitclaim deed.*
9. A map designating the size and shape of a specific land area.
11. Another name for *plot.*
14. A deed to real property in which the grantor transfers only his or her interests, if any, in the property and gives no warranties of title.
16. Distances between points.
17. Another name for *plot.*
18. A person to whom real property is transferred.
21. A row of townships running north and south in the United States government survey.

7

Mortgages

ANTE INTERROGATORY

A clause in a mortgage or note that causes the entire balance of the loan to become due when a default occurs is a(n) (A) acceleration clause, (B) default clause, (C) redemption clause, (D) power of sale clause.

CHAPTER OUTLINE

Historical Background

Prevailing Mortgage Theories

Types of Mortgages
Deed of Trust

Mortgage Redemption

Mortgage Foreclosure

Transfer of Mortgaged Premises

Junior Mortgages

Mortgage Discharge

KEY TERMS

acceleration clause *(ak·sel·er·AY·shun)*

adjustable rate mortgage *(a-JUS-ti-bul rate MOR-guj)*

amortization *(a-mor-ti-ZAY-shun)*

balloon mortgage *(ba·LOON MORE·gej)*

collateral *(ko-LA-ter-al)*

common law theory of mortgages *(KOM·on law THEE·ree ov MORE·ge·jes)*

court of equity *(EK·wi·tee)*

deed of release *(re·LEESS)*

deed of trust

default *(de·FAWLT)*

defeasance clause *(de·FEE·senz)*

deficiency judgment *(de·FISH·en·see JUJ·ment)*

equitable theory of mortgages *(EK·wit·a·bel THEE·ree ov MORE·ge·jes)*

equity of redemption *(EK·wi·tee ov re·DEMP·shun)*

fixed-rate mortgage *(fiksd-rate MORE·gej)*

flexible-rate mortgage *(FLEKS·i·bel-rate MORE·gej)*

foreclose *(for·KLOZE)*

graduated-payment mortgage *(GRAD·yoo·ay·ted PAY·ment MORE·gej)*

junior mortgage *(JOO·nyer MORE·gej)*

lien (leen)

lien theory of mortgages *(leen THEE·ree ov MORE·ge·jes)*

mortgage *(MORE·gej)*

mortgage assignment *(MORE·gej a·SINE·ment)*

mortgage assumption *(MORE·gej a·SUMP·shun)*

mortgage deed

mortgage discharge *(MORE·gej DIS·charj)*

mortgagee *(more·gej·EE)*

mortgage take-over

mortgagor *(more·gej·OR)*

partial release *(PAR·shell re·LEESS)*

power of sale clause *(POW·er)*

promissory note *(PROM·i·sore·ee)*

redeem *(re·DEEM)*

refinance *(ree·FI·nanse)*

reverse mortgage *(ree·VERS MORE·gej)*

right of redemption *(rite ov re·DEMP·shun)*

second mortgage *(SEK·end MORE·gej)*

security *(se·KYOOR·i·tee)*

short sale

title theory of mortgages *(TY·tel THEE·ree ov MORE·ge·jes)*

variable-rate mortgage *(VAR·ee·a·bel·rate MORE·gej)*

7

Most people who buy real property do not have enough money to pay for the property outright. They must borrow it. Lenders, however, wish to have some **security** for their loan—that is, something they can sell to get their money back in case of default. A security interest is also known as **collateral**, and collateral is either possessory (meaning that the lender takes physical possession of the collateral or security interest until the loan is repaid) or non-possessory. A **mortgage**, sometimes called a **mortgage deed**, meets the lender's need for a security interest, because a mortgage is a conveyance of real property for the purpose of securing a debt. The one who borrows money and gives a mortgage to the lender as security for the loan is the **mortgagor**. The one who lends money and takes back a mortgage as security for the loan is the **mortgagee**. In addition to signing a mortgage deed when the loan is made, the mortgagor signs a **promissory note**, which is a written promise by the borrower to pay a sum of money to the lender.

▐ TERMS IN ACTION

Dorothy Rhue Allen purchased a home in Deptford, New Jersey, in 1976, signing a **promissory note** and obtaining a 30-year **mortgage** for the $40,000 she borrowed from LaSalle Bank. She never missed any of the 359 payments, but on her 360th payment—the final payment—the 85-year-old Dorothy was in the hospital and the $490 wasn't sent to the bank. So, LaSalle Bank began **foreclosure** proceedings against her in 2006. When she tried to cure the **default**, the bank's law firm told her that she needed to pay $5,700. Dorothy's attorney then helped her to file a class =-action lawsuit against LaSalle Bank and its law firm, alleging that they violated the Fair Debt Collections Practices Act by overcharging her various fees, including title recording fees and the bank's attorney fees.

Sources: courthousenews.com

HISTORICAL BACKGROUND

Mort means "dead" and *gage* means "pledge." In early times, a mortgage was a "dead pledge." The mortgagor pledged the property to the mortgagee and gave up possession of the property, as well as all income from it, until the debt was paid. In addition, the mortgagor lost all title to the property if the debt was not paid precisely when it was due. As time went on, the **court of equity**, which is a court designed to do that which is just and fair, allowed the mortgagor additional time after a default to **redeem** (buy back) the property. Current legal theories governing mortgages follow.

7

PREVAILING MORTGAGE THEORIES

Two principal legal theories relating to mortgages are followed in the United States. They are the common law theory and the lien theory.

Under the **common law theory** (called the **title theory** in some states), a mortgage is a conveyance of title by the mortgagor to the mortgagee. A clause in the mortgage, known as the **defeasance clause** provides that the mortgage deed shall be void on payment of the obligation. The mortgagor has the right to possession of the premises and the right to all rents and profits from the property. The mortgagee has no right to enter the premises unless a **default** (the failure to perform a legal duty) by the mortgagor occurs, but he or she does have the right to prevent waste through court action.

Under the **lien theory** (called the **equitable theory** in some states), a mortgage is not regarded as a conveyance of title to the mortgagee, but merely a lien against the property. A **lien** is a claim or charge on the property for the payment of a debt. Under this mortgage theory, the mortgagor retains legal title to the premises. A lien theory state makes foreclosure more difficult to complete, because the title remains with the borrower rather than being transferred to the lender, as is the case in title theory states.

Word Wise
The Prefix "Equi-" in Equity

The Latin prefix *equi* means "equal" and is used in many English words. Here are some examples:

Words	Meaning
equiangular	equal angles
equidistant	equally distant
equilateral	equal sides
equinox	equal nights
equity	equal treatment

Some states follow a modified form of the title theory of mortgages. For example, in Missouri, the mortgagee has a lien before a default of the mortgage, but obtains legal title to the property after a default.

TYPES OF MORTGAGES

There are a variety of mortgages in use today. A **fixed-rate mortgage** is a mortgage with an interest rate that does not change during the life of the mortgage. A **variable-rate mortgage**, also called a **flexible-rate mortgage** or **adjustable rate mortgage (ARM)**, is a mortgage with an interest rate that fluctuates according to changes in an index to which it is connected. A **graduated-payment mortgage** is a mortgage under which payments increase gradually over the life of the loan. A **balloon mortgage** is a mortgage with low, fixed payments during the life of the loan, ending with one large final payment. A **reverse mortgage** is one in which a bank pays a homeowner the equity in his or her home in exchange for taking title to the home. Rather than borrowing to buy a home, the borrower—who must be at least 62, according to federal law—is, in effect, borrowing to stay in a home. But, rather than being required to pay back the "loan," in monthly installments or otherwise, the homeowner has no obligation to repay until the homeowner moves from the home or dies. In the latter instance, the bank (or other lender) takes title to the property.

Deed of Trust

In some states, a **deed of trust** is used instead of a mortgage. This instrument conveys title to a third party (often, a title insurance company), called a **trustee** who holds it as security for the

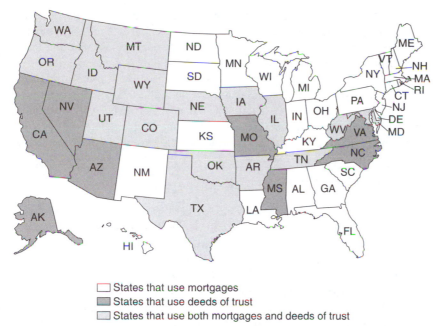

FIGURE 35-1 States that use mortgages, states that use deeds of trust, and states that use both mortgages and deeds of trust.

debt. When the debt is paid, title is returned to the borrower. If the borrower defaults, however, the trustee can sell the property, without going to court, in order to pay the amount of the debt to the lender.

MORTGAGE REDEMPTION

Under modern laws, the mortgagor has the **equity of redemption**, which is the right to redeem the property any time before the completion of a foreclosure proceeding by paying the amount of the debt, interest, and costs. In addition, in some states, the mortgagor has the **right of redemption**, which is a statutory right to redeem the property even after a foreclosure sale. In states that recognize this latter right, a buyer at a mortgage foreclosure sale does not receive good title to the premises until the time for the mortgagor's right of redemption elapses, which ranges from six months to two years after the foreclosure sale, depending on the state.

MORTGAGE FORECLOSURE

Foreclose means to "shut out," "bar," or "terminate." Thus, a foreclosure proceeding terminates the mortgagor's equity of redemption in the property. The mortgagee has a right to foreclose when the mortgagor defaults in the payment of the debt or fails to follow a condition (requirement) of the mortgage. An **acceleration clause** in the mortgage or note causes the entire balance of the loan to become due when a default occurs.

The most common method of foreclosure is by judicial sale, which is a sale at public auction under the jurisdiction of the court. Another method of foreclosure is by "power of sale" under the terms of a **power of sale clause** found in the mortgage instrument. This clause allows the mortgagee to hold the foreclosure sale alone, without involving the court. Still another method of foreclosure found in some states allows the mortgagee to enter and possess the premises for a specific period. This method may be used only when the entry and possession can be made peaceably.

Sometimes, a foreclosure sale does not bring enough money to pay off the amount owed to the mortgagee. When this occurs, the court may issue a deficiency judgment against the mortgagor. A **deficiency judgment** is a judgment for the amount remaining due on the mortgage after a foreclosure sale.

Because of the severity of the downturn in the real estate market, which began in 2007, many homeowners who could not afford their mortgages, but wanted to avoid foreclosure, sought to sell their homes, even though the sales prices would be less than the loan balances. This type of sale is known as a **short sale** and can be done only if the lender allows it. A lender might allow it, however, because it avoids the costs associated with foreclosure. Lenders who allow homeowners to short sell their homes can still require the sellers to be liable for the difference between the sale price and the remaining loan balance. Borrowers who are the beneficiaries of loan forgiveness need to pay income taxes on the amount forgiven, but Congress passed a law, the Mortgage Foreclosure Relief Act of 2007, which provided relief to those taxpayers.

TERMS IN ACTION

Of the many tragedies associated with America's recent mortgage crisis, one of them seems almost unthinkable: homeowners with **reverse mortgages** being **foreclosed** upon. A reverse mortgage allows persons who are at least 62 years old to be paid the equity in their homes without having to move from the home, unlike the way a seller would take possession in a traditional sale. With a reverse mortgage, the homeowner borrows the equity from a bank, who takes title to the property in exchange for providing cash to the borrower. As of 2011, approximately 30,000 homeowners in America were in **default** on their reverse mortgages, with Florida having just under 20 percent of the total number of those in default. According to the researchers who discovered this sad fact, many elderly homeowners take their equity payments in one lump sum and spend the money, not realizing that they will need some of that cash to continue to pay the insurance and real estate taxes on their homes. The Federal Housing Administration has responded by proposing new rules that would minimize the chance of reverse mortgage default.

Sources: orlandosentinel.com; usnews.com

TRANSFER OF MORTGAGED PREMISES

Usually, when mortgagors sell real property, they convey it free and clear of the mortgage by paying it off out of the proceeds of the sale. Sometimes, however, a buyer will agree to buy property with the mortgage still on it—that is, "subject to the mortgage." This agreement means that the new buyer takes the property subject to the mortgagee's rights. Only the equity of redemption is sold. The original mortgagor must still pay the mortgagee, and the mortgagee can foreclose against the new buyer if a default of the mortgage payments by the new mortgagor occurs.

Web Wise

Mortgage information abounds on the Web. Here are a few reliable choices:

Bank Rate (a website with information related to all things involving in borrowing money)

www.bankrate.com/brm

Homefair.com (a comprehensive website on everything from looking for homes to investigating the school systems in locations where one might be buying a home)

www.homefair.com

Homepath (a property foreclosure listing service from Fannie Mae, which is formally known as the Federal National Mortgage Association, a government-sponsored company)

www.homepath.com

Interest.com (a thorough website providing interest rate information, interest rate calculators, and articles on buying and selling homes)

www.interest.com

Sometimes, a mortgagor will sell the premises "subject to the mortgage that the grantee assumes and agrees to pay." This is commonly referred to as a **mortgage take-over** or a **mortgage assumption**. In this situation, the new buyer not only takes the property subject to the mortgagee's rights, but also agrees to pay the balance of the mortgage payments to the mortgagee as they fall due. Generally, such a mortgage transfer is subject to the approval of the lender. The original mortgagor is still liable on the debt, however, and becomes a surety on the loan. Unless released from liability by the lender, he or she must pay the mortgage if the new buyer, who took it over, fails to do so.

It is common for banks who are mortgagees to put "due on sale" clauses in their mortgages which state that if title to the property vests in someone other than the mortgagor, the mortgage is immediately due and payable. This language prevents the assumption of a mortgage by another person without the bank's permission.

Mortgagees often transfer their interests in mortgages to other parties. This transfer is done by the use of an instrument known as a **mortgage assignment**. When this occurs, the original mortgagor makes the mortgage payments to the new mortgagee to whom the mortgage has been assigned.

JUNIOR MORTGAGES

A **junior mortgage**, also called a **second (or third) mortgage**, is a mortgage on the equity of redemption, or a mortgage subject to a prior mortgage. A junior mortgagee may foreclose only on the mortgagors' equity of redemption, and because a junior mortgage is subordinate to a first mortgage, such a foreclosure is subject to the rights of the first mortgagee. If a first mortgagee forecloses, the second mortgagee's recourse is to pay the mortgagor's debt and then foreclose also. As a practical matter, however, both mortgages are foreclosed in the same proceeding; the proceeds of the sale are paid to the first mortgagee, and any balance remaining is paid to junior mortgagees. As interest rates drop, especially as they did between 2007 and 2010, homeowners often **refinance** their mortgages. Refinancing involves extinguishing a debt obligation and replacing it with a new debt that has different terms, such as a different interest rate or **amortization** schedule. "Amortization" is a Middle English word that originally meant to kill, but today means to reduce or decrease over time. In lending, amortization shows how the loan balance is reduced until it is paid off.

MORTGAGE DISCHARGE

When a mortgage debt is paid, the mortgagor signs a **mortgage discharge**, a document stating that the mortgage debt is satisfied. The mortgage discharge is recorded at the registry of deeds. A **deed of release** (a deed releasing property from an encumbrance) is sometimes used for this purpose, especially by a trustee of a deed of trust, to divest the trustee of legal title and revest title in the original owner. A **partial release** is used to show that specified parcels are released from the encumbrance.

Reviewing What You Learned

After studying the chapter, write the answers to each of the following questions:

1. What need does the mortgage meet? _____
   _____
   _____
   _____

2. In addition to signing a mortgage deed when a loan is made, what else does a mortgagor sign? _____
   _____
   _____
   _____

7

3. What was a mortgage in early times? _____

_____

_____

_____

4. Describe the difference between the mortgagor and the mortgagee.

_____

_____

_____

5. Who holds the legal title to the property under the common law mortgage theory? Under the lien theory? _____

_____

_____

_____

6. Who has the right to possession under the common law mortgage theory? _____

_____

_____

_____

7. Name six types of mortgages and give a short definition of each.

_____

_____

_____

_____

8. What is the difference between the equity of redemption and the right of redemption? _____

_____

_____

_____

9. Name three methods of foreclosure. _____

_____

_____

_____

10. If a new buyer takes the property subject to a mortgage, what can the mortgagee do if a default of the mortgage payments by the new mortgagor occurs? _____

_____

_____

_____

11. If a first mortgagee forecloses on the mortgage, what is the second mortgagee's recourse? _____

_____

_____

_____

12. Describe the way that a deed of trust is used to provide security for a debt. _____

_____

_____

_____

13. What does "refinancing" mean? _____

_____

_____

_____

Understanding Legal Concepts

Indicate whether each statement is true or false. Then, change the italicized word or phrase of each false statement to make it true.

ANSWERS

_____ 1. The mortgagor is the *lender*.

_____ 2. In early times, a mortgage was a *dead pledge* because the property owner gave up possession of the property until the debt was paid.

_____ 3. As time went on, the court of equity allowed the *mortgagor* additional time after a default to redeem the property.

_____ 4. Under the lien theory of mortgages, a mortgage is a conveyance of title by the mortgagor to the mortgagee.

_____ 5. Under the common law theory of mortgages, the mortgagee has the right to possession of the premises.

_____ 6. The right of redemption is the right to redeem the property any time before the completion of a foreclosure proceeding.

_____ 7. The most common method of foreclosure is by entry and possession of the premises.

_____ 8. When property is sold "subject to the mortgage," the original mortgagor must still pay the mortgagee.

_____ 9. When a mortgagee transfers an interest in a mortgage to another, it is known as a mortgage assignment.

_____ 10. A junior mortgagee's foreclosure is subject to the rights of the first mortgagee.

Checking Terminology

From the list of legal terms that follows, select the one that matches each definition.

ANSWERS

a. acceleration clause
b. adjustable rate mortgage
c. amortization
d. balloon mortgage
e. collateral
f. common law theory of mortgages
g. court of equity
h. deed of release
i. deed of trust
j. default
k. defeasance clause
l. deficiency judgment
m. equitable theory of mortgages
n. equity of redemption
o. fixed-rate mortgage
p. flexible-rate mortgage
q. foreclose
r. graduated-payment mortgage
s. junior mortgage
t. lien
u. lien theory of mortgages
v. mortgage
w. mortgage assignment
x. mortgage assumption
y. mortgage deed
z. mortgage discharge
aa. mortgagee
bb. mortgage take-over
cc. mortgagor
dd. partial release
ee. power of sale clause
ff. promissory note
gg. redeem
hh. refinance
ii. reverse mortgage
jj. right of redemption
kk. second mortgage
ll. security
mm. short sale
nn. title theory of mortgages
oo. variable-rate mortgage

_____ 1. Assurance (usually in the form of a pledge or deposit) given by a debtor to a creditor to make sure that a debt is paid.
_____ 2. One who lends money and takes back a mortgage as security for the loan.
_____ 3. Buy back.
_____ 4. The right of a mortgagor to redeem the property any time before the completion of a foreclosure proceeding by paying the amount of the debt, interest, and costs.
_____ 5. A clause in a mortgage providing that the mortgage deed shall be void on payment of the obligation.
_____ 6. A claim or charge on the property for the payment of a debt.
_____ 7. A statutory right to redeem the property even after a foreclosure sale.
_____ 8. An agreement by a new owner of real property to pay the former owner's mortgage. (Select two answers.)
_____ 9. A mortgage with an interest rate that fluctuates according to changes in an index to which it is connected. (Select two answers.)
_____ 10. A clause in a mortgage or note that causes the entire balance of the loan to become due when a default occurs.
_____ 11. A mortgage with an interest rate that does not change during the life of the mortgage.
_____ 12. A mortgage subject to a prior mortgage. (Select two answers.)
_____ 13. A conveyance of real property for the purpose of securing a debt. (Select two answers.)
_____ 14. One who borrows money and gives a mortgage to the lender as security for the loan.
_____ 15. A court designed to do that which is just and fair.
_____ 16. A failure to perform a legal duty.
_____ 17. To shut out, bar, or terminate.
_____ 18. The transfer of a mortgagee's interest in a mortgage to another person.
_____ 19. A mortgage with low, fixed payments during the life of the loan, ending with one large, final payment.
_____ 20. A written promise by a borrower to pay a sum of money to a lender.
_____ 21. A mortgage under which payments increase gradually over the life of the loan.
_____ 22. An instrument used in some states that replaces a mortgage, by which the legal title to real property is placed in a trustee to secure the repayment of a debt.
_____ 23. A judgment for the amount remaining due on the mortgage after a foreclosure sale.
_____ 24. A deed releasing property from an encumbrance.
_____ 25. A document stating that a mortgage debt is satisfied.
_____ 26. The legal theory that a mortgage is a conveyance of title, which becomes void on payment of the obligation. (Select two answers.)
_____ 27. The legal theory that a mortgage is not a conveyance of title, but merely a lien against the property. (Select two answers.)
_____ 28. A clause in a mortgage allowing the mortgagee to hold a foreclosure sale without involving the court when a default in payment of the mortgage occurs.
_____ 29. A document stating that specified parcels of property are released from an encumbrance.
_____ 30. To reduce or decrease over time.
_____ 31. A bank pays a homeowner the equity in his or her home in exchange for taking title to the home.
_____ 32. Security interest for a loan, such as a mortgage deed.
_____ 33. Extinguishing one debt obligation and replacing it with a new debt with different terms.
_____ 34. With permission of the lender, selling a home for a sale price lower than the loan balance.
_____ 35. A mortgage with an interest rate that fluctuates according to changes in an index to which the mortgage is connected. (Select three answers.)

Using Legal Language

Read the following story and fill in the blank lines with legal terms taken from the list of terms at the beginning of this chapter:

When Steve and Linda bought their house, they gave a(n) _____—that is, a conveyance of real property for the purpose of securing a debt—to the bank as _____ for the loan. They were called the _____; the bank was the _____. The instrument contained a(n) _____ providing that the mortgage deed would be void on payment of the obligation. It also contained a(n) _____, which allows the mortgagee to hold a foreclosure sale without involving the court when a default in payment of the mortgage occurs. Steve and Linda hold the _____, which is the right to _____ (buy back) the property any time before the completion of a foreclosure proceeding. The state where they live does not recognize the _____, which is the right to redeem the property even after a foreclosure sale. Similarly, their state does not use the _____

in place of a mortgage, which involves conveying title to a third party to hold as security for the debt. Steve and Linda gave a(n) _____, also known as a(n) _____, which is a mortgage subject to a prior mortgage, to Elliott, who sold them their house. Soon thereafter, Elliott made a(n) _____—that is, a transfer of his mortgage interest—to an out-of-town lending institution. The instrument represented a(n) _____, which is a claim or charge on the property for the payment of a debt. Possibly, when Steve and Linda sell their house, a(n) _____ or a(n) _____ will occur, wherein the new owner agrees to pay their existing mortgage. They were very careful not to _____—that is, fail to perform their legal duty—on either of their obligations, because they did not want anyone to _____ (shut out, bar, or terminate) their equity of redemption.

PUZZLING OVER WHAT YOU LEARNED

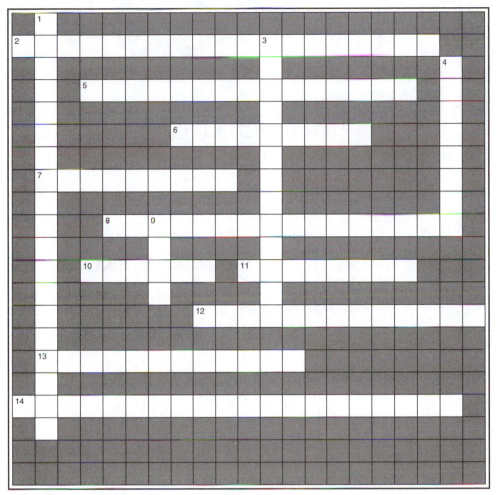

Caveat: Allow squares for spaces between words and punctuation (apostrophes, hyphens, etc.) when filling in crossword.

Across

2. A mortgage with an interest rate that does not change.
5. A written promise by a borrower to pay a sum of money to a lender.
6. One who lends money and takes back a mortgage as security for the loan.
7. To shut out, bar, or terminate.
8. Mortgage with low fixed payments during its life, ending with one large payment.
10. Buy back.
11. Assurance, usually in pledge form, given to make sure a debt is paid.
12. Instrument by which legal title to real property is placed in trust as security.
13. Legal theory that a mortgage is a conveyance of title.
14. Clause in a mortgage allowing the mortgagee to hold a foreclosure sale.

Down

1. Statutory right to redeem property even after a foreclosure sale.
3. A conveyance of real property for the purpose of securing a debt.
4. Another name for a mortgage deed.
9. A claim or charge on the property for the payment of a debt.

Landlord and Tenant

ANTE INTERROGATORY

*A tenancy that continues for successive periods until one of the parties
terminates is a tenancy (A) at will, (B) at sufferance,
(C) for years, (D) from year to year.*

CHAPTER OUTLINE

Leasehold Estates
    Tenancy for Years
    Periodic Tenancy
    Tenancy at Will
    Tenancy at Sufferance

License
The Lease
Tenants' Rights
Eviction
Tort Liability

KEY TERMS

constructive eviction *(kon·STRUK·tiv
    e·VIK·shun)*
deed-poll *(deed-pole)*
demise *(de·MIZE)*
dispossessory warrant proceedings
    *(dis·po·SESS·o·ree WAR·ent
    pro·SEED·ings)*
ejectment *(e·JEKT·ment)*
eviction *(e·VIK·shun)*
forcible entry and detainer *(FORSS·i·bel
    EN·tree and de·TAYN·er)*
holdover tenant *(HOLD·o·ver TEN·ent)*
indenture *(in·DEN·cher)*
landlord

lease *(leess)*
leasehold estate *(LEESS·hold es·TATE)*
lessee *(less·EE)*
lessor *(less·OR)*
license *(Ly·sense)*
licensee *(ly·sen·SEE)*
periodic tenancy *(peer·ee·ODD·ik
    TEN·en·see)*
quiet enjoyment *(KWY·et en·JOY·ment)*
retaliatory eviction *(re·TAL·ee·a·tore·ee
    e·VIK·shun)*
sublet
sublease *(SUB·leess)*
summary ejectment *(SUM·eree e·JEKT·ment)*

summary process *(SUM·e·ree PROSS·ess)*

tenancy at will *(TEN·en·see)*

tenancy for years *(TEN·en·see)*

tenancy from year to year *(TEN·en·see)*

tenant *(TEN·ent)*

tenant at sufferance *(TEN·ent at SUF·er·ense)*

underlease *(UN·der·leess)*

unlawful detainer *(de·TAYN·er)*

warranty of habitability *(WAR·en·tee ov hab·i·ta·BIL·i·tee)*

A lease is a contract granting the use of certain real property by its owner (called the **lessor** or **landlord**) to another (called the **lessee** or **tenant**) for a specified period in return for the payment of rent. In their strictest meaning, the terms *lessor* and *lessee* refer only to the parties to a lease. In contrast, the terms *landlord* and *tenant* are broad terms that refer to the parties under a tenancy at will as well as the parties under a lease.

LEASEHOLD ESTATES

The interest that is conveyed by a lease is called a **leasehold estate** and was treated as personal property at common law. The following are leasehold estates:

1. tenancy for years
2. periodic tenancy
3. tenancy at will
4. tenancy at sufferance

Tenancy for Years

A **tenancy for years** is an estate for a definite or fixed period, no matter how long or how short. Such a tenancy can be for 1 month, 6 months, 1 year, 5 years, 99 years, or any period, so long as it is ascertained. By statute in some states, a tenancy for 100 years or more creates a fee simple estate. This rule of law prompted the use of 99-year leases.

Word Wise
Compound Words

Compound words are made by joining two or more words already in usage to create a new word with a new meaning. Some compound words found in this chapter are the following:

Word	Meaning
holdover	To hold over from a previous period
landlord	A lord (person with authority or power) over land
leasehold	To hold by lease
sublease	A lease that is "sub" (less than) the full period
underlease	A lease that is under (less than) the full period

Some states require that a tenancy for years be in writing to be enforceable; others require a writing only if the period exceeds one-year. Indiana requires three-year or longer leases to be in writing, to satisfy the statute of frauds. In some states, leases for long periods must be recorded to be effective as to third parties. For example, a lease for seven years or more (or a notice thereof) must be recorded at the registry of deeds, under Massachusetts law, to be valid as to persons other than the lessor. Under this statute, if the owner of a building rents the building to a lessee for 10 years and the lease is not recorded, the owner can sell the building to someone else and the new owner will not be bound by the lease.

Periodic Tenancy

A **periodic tenancy**, which is also called a **tenancy from year to year** (or from month to month, or from week to week), is a tenancy that continues for successive periods until one of the parties terminates it by giving notice to the other party. It is created when a lease agreement has no specified ending date. The notice requirement differs from state to state, but is typically the period between rent payment due dates. This tenancy may be created by implication if the landlord accepts rent payment from a tenant whose lease has run out or who is wrongfully in possession of the premises. Some states that do not recognize periodic tenancies treat the latter situation as a tenancy at sufferance (to be explained shortly).

Tenancy at Will

A **tenancy at will** is an estate in real property for an indefinite period. No writing is required to create this tenancy, and it may be terminated at the will of either party by issuance of the proper statutory notice. A landlord may seek to increase the rent in a tenancy at will by providing notice one payment period in advance. That does not mean, however, that the rent may be raised unilaterally, because the tenant may refuse the increase. But the refusal will result in the landlord's either seeking to terminate the tenancy or keeping the rent the same.

Tenancy at Sufferance

A tenant who wrongfully remains in possession of the premises after the tenancy has expired is called a **holdover tenant** or a **tenant at sufferance**. Such a tenant has no estate or title, but holds possession wrongfully. He or she is not entitled to notice to vacate and is liable to pay rent for the period of occupancy.

LICENSE

A lease conveys an interest in land and transfers possession, whereas a **license** to real estate conveys no property right or interest to the land, but merely allows the licensee to do certain acts that would otherwise be a trespass. Lodgers who occupy rooms and advertisers who place signs on buildings are examples of **licensees** (people who have permission to do certain acts).

THE LEASE

A lease is an express contract between the parties in which real property is **demised** (leased) by the lessor to the lessee. The lease is usually executed in duplicate and signed by both parties (called an **indenture**, which simply means an official document executed in two or more identical copies), although a lease signed by the lessor only (a **deed-poll**) will be binding if accepted by the lessee. No particular form is necessary so long as the instrument identifies the parties, describes the demised premises, sets out the terms of the lease, provides for possession by the lessee, and contains consideration.

An *assignment* of a lease occurs when the lessee conveys the interest in the demised premises to another person for the balance of the term of the lease. It is called a **sublease** (or **underlease**) if the transfer is for a part of the term, but not for the remainder of it. The word **sublet** is sometimes used instead of "sublease." A tenant's ability to sublet the property is subject to the landlord's approval of it (as provided in the lease), including approving the subtenant.

TENANTS' RIGHTS

Tenants have the right to **quiet enjoyment** of the leased premises, which means that they have the right to possess the property and to be undisturbed in that possession. Thus, if the landlord locks out the tenant or interferes with the tenant's possession in any way, it is a breach of the tenant's right to quiet enjoyment.

When real property is rented for residential purposes, an implied warranty exists by the landlord that the premises are fit for human habitation, which is known as the implied **warranty of habitability**. In general, to be habitable, the property must meet the sanitary code of the local community. Legislation in some states allows the tenant to pay the rent to the court, instead of to the landlord, when the property is not fit for human habitation and violates the sanitary code. This action places the court in a position to prevent tenants from being evicted for complaining that the property which they rent is uninhabitable. In other states, the tenant, after giving notice to the landlord, can correct a sanitary code defect at the tenant's own expense and withhold rent up to the cost of having the defect corrected.

TERMS IN ACTION

Does a landlord's implied **warranty of habitability** extend to a tenant's automobile? In Montpelier, Vermont, heavy snow isn't a surprise, but surprise is just one of the emotions Karen Weiler felt in February 2008 when a heavy pile of snow and ice slid off the roof of the apartment she rented, landing on her van and destroying it as it sat in the parking space that came with her apartment lease. So, the single mother of six sued her landlord, Richard Hooshiari, alleging that the warranty of habitability extended to a landlord-provided parking space. She won at trial, but lost in the Vermont Supreme Court. In concluding that the warranty of habitability applies only to human habitation in the livable space, the Supreme Court wrote as follows: "[Weiler] maintains that a conventional lifestyle involving children and employment requires ready transportation, meaning that a secure parking place is a critical component of human habitation. While it may be exceptionally inconvenient not to have access to a parking space and therefore access to a car, the absence of a parking space is not an equivalent threat to health and safety as that posed by clogged toilets, raw sewage, and poisoned water."

Source: *Weiler v. Hooshiari*, ___ A.3rd. ___ (Vt. 2011)

EVICTION

An **eviction** is the act of depriving a person of the possession of real property, either by reentry or by legal process. A landlord may not use force to evict a tenant. Instead, the landlord must give the tenant whatever notice is required by state law and use legal process (described later) to evict a tenant.

Retaliatory eviction is the eviction of a tenant for reporting to the authorities sanitary-code or building-code violations in the rented property. This type of eviction is illegal in most states today.

A **constructive eviction** occurs when the landlord does some act that deprives the tenant of the beneficial enjoyment of the premises. Examples are depriving the tenant of heat, light, power, or some other service that was called for under the lease. When a constructive or other illegal eviction occurs, the tenant has the right to leave the premises without being in breach of the lease. The tenant may also withhold rent for the length of the eviction.

The legal action used by landlords to evict tenants was called **ejectment** at common law. Today, the name given to the action varies from state to state and includes **summary process**, **summary ejectment**, **forcible entry and detainer**, **dispossessory warrant proceedings**, and **unlawful detainer**.

The landlord is required to give the proper statutory notice to the tenant before commencing such action, and the court, in its discretion, may allow time for the tenant to find another place to live.

7

TERMS IN ACTION

In what may seem like a story from the fake news website "The Onion," Donald Trump was sued by the Trump Plaza in 2009, when its cooperative board sought to **evict** him from one of its apartments. Built in 1984, the Trump Plaza is one of Donald Trump's buildings, but his company, Trump Corporation, also rents apartment units from it. According to the eviction lawsuit, Trump Corporation missed rent payments on its units, totaling $87,000, in April and May of 2009. According to the complaint, the **lease** terminated on May 6, five days after Trump Corporation missed its May rent deadline. Notice of default had been sent on April 10th, after April's rent had gone unpaid. Whereas those may seem like harsh termination terms, the lease contract was created by Trump's attorneys, and, according to Andrew Perel, President of the Trump Plaza Owners, Inc. co-op, "If you don't pay the rent when Donald Trump is your landlord, he comes down on you like a hammer. Well, lo and behold, he signed a lease that was his own lease and he's the tenant. And he missed April and May." Perel is a lawyer, so it likely came as no shock to him that a few days after the co-op sued Trump, Trump sued the co-op—for $18.1 million in damages for what seemed very much like a **constructive eviction** allegation. Part of the allegations Trump leveled against his own building's co-op was shoddy repairs and water damage to the units that his company occupies, going back as far as 2007.

Source: amlawdaily.typepad.com

TORT LIABILITY

When a person is injured on rented or leased property, the one who is in control of that part of the premises where the injury occurs is generally responsible if the injury was caused by negligence. For example, the landlord may be responsible for injury to others caused by a defect in the common areas over which he or she has control, such as hallways, stairways, and so forth. Likewise, the tenant may be responsible for injury to persons caused by defects in the portion of the premises over which he or she has control.

Legislation in some states has changed this common law rule of liability by allowing the tenant to give notice to the landlord of any unsafe conditions in that part of the premises under the tenant's control and making the landlord responsible thereafter for injury caused by the unsafe condition if the landlord fails to correct the condition.

Reviewing What you Learned

After studying the chapter, write the answers to each of the following questions:

1. What are the differences between the terms *landlord* and *tenant* and the terms *lessor* and *lessee*? _____

   _____

   _____

   _____

   _____

2. A leasehold estate was what kind of property at common law?

   _____

   _____

   _____

   _____

3. List the four types of leasehold estate. _____

   _____

   _____

   _____

   _____

4. For what length of time may a tenancy for years last?

   _____

   _____

   _____

   _____

5. What does a tenancy for 100 years create in some states?_____

_____

_____

_____

6. How may a periodic tenancy be created by implication?_____

_____

_____

_____

7. Describe a tenancy at will, including the method for its termination. _____

_____

_____

_____

8. What is another name for a tenant at sufferance? How much notice must be given to evict such a tenant? _____

_____

_____

_____

_____

9. Compare a lease with a license. _____

_____

_____

_____

10. Who usually signs a lease?_____

_____

_____

_____

_____

11. Differentiate between an assignment of a lease and a sublease.

_____

_____

_____

12. Recent legislation in some states provides for what remedy to a tenant if the premises are not fit for human habitation?_____

_____

_____

_____

13. What is the difference between a retaliatory eviction and a constructive eviction?_____

_____

_____

_____

_____

14. List five names, given by different states, for the eviction action.

_____

_____

_____

_____

15. Who is responsible for a negligently caused injury that takes place

a. in the common areas of an apartment building?

_____

_____

_____

_____

b. in an area of the building that is controlled by a tenant?

_____

_____

_____

_____

Understanding Legal Concepts

Indicate whether each statement is true or false. Then, change the italicized word or phrase of each false *statement to make it true.*

ANSWERS

_____ **1.** The terms *lessor* and *lessee* are broad terms that refer to the parties under a tenancy at will as well as the parties under a lease.

_____ **2.** A *tenancy for years* can be for any period so long as it is ascertained.

_____ **3.** A periodic tenancy continues for *successive periods* until one of the parties terminates it by giving notice to the other party.

_____ **4.** A writing *is necessary* to create a tenancy at will.

_____ **5.** A tenant at sufferance *is not* entitled to notice to vacate.

_____ **6.** A lease differs from a license in that a *license* conveys an interest in land and transfers possession.

_____ **7.** An *assignment* occurs when the lessee conveys part of the term of a lease, but not the remainder of it, to another person.

_____ **8.** *Quiet enjoyment* means that a tenant has the right to possess the property and to be undisturbed in that possession.

_____ **9.** A *retaliatory* eviction occurs when the landlord deprives the tenant of heat, light, power, or some other service called for under the lease.

_____ **10.** When a person is injured on leased property, the one in control of that part of the premises where the injury occurs *is generally responsible* if the injury was caused by negligence.

Checking Terminology

From the list of legal terms that follows, select the one that matches each definition.

ANSWERS

a. constructive eviction
b. deed-poll
c. demise
d. dispossessory warrant proceedings
e. ejectment
f. eviction
g. forcible entry and detainer
h. holdover tenant
i. indenture
j. landlord
k. lease
l. leasehold estate
m. lessee
n. lessor
o. license
p. licensee
q. periodic tenancy
r. quiet enjoyment
s. retaliatory eviction
t. sublease/sublet
u. summary ejectment
v. summary process
w. tenancy at will
x. tenancy for years
y. tenancy from year to year
z. tenant
aa. tenant at sufferance
bb. underlease
cc. unlawful detainer
dd. warranty of habitability

_____ 1. A contract granting the use of certain real property by its owner to another for a specified period in return for the payment of rent.

_____ 2. A person who owns real property and who rents it to another under a lease. (Select two answers.)

_____ 3. A person who has temporary possession of, and an interest in, real property of another under a lease. (Select two answers.)

_____ 4. The interest that is conveyed by a lease.

_____ 5. An estate in real property for a definite or fixed period of time no matter how long or how short.

_____ 6. An estate in real property that continues for successive periods until one of the parties terminates it by giving notice to the other party. (Select two answers.)

_____ 7. A lease given by a lessee to a third person conveying the same interest for a shorter term than the period for which the lessee holds it. (Select two answers.)

_____ 8. The right of a tenant to possess the rented property and to be undisturbed in that possession.

_____ 9. A legal action used by landlords to evict tenants. (Select six answers.)

_____ 10. An estate in real property for an indefinite period.

_____ 11. A tenant who wrongfully remains in possession of the premises after a tenancy has expired. (Select two answers.)

_____ 12. A person who has permission to do certain acts.

_____ 13. A grant or permission to do a particular thing.

_____ 14. To lease.

_____ 15. A deed or lease to which two or more persons are parties.

_____ 16. A deed or lease in which only the party making the instrument executes it.

_____ 17. Dispossession caused by an act of the landlord that deprives the tenant of the beneficial enjoyment of the demised premises.

_____ 18. The act of depriving a person of the possession of real property either by reentry or by legal process.

_____ 19. The eviction of a tenant for reporting to the authorities sanitary code or building code violations of the leased property.

_____ 20. An implied warranty by a landlord that the premises are fit for human habitation.

Sharpening Your Latin Skills

In the space provided, write the definition of each of the following legal terms, referring to the glossary when necessary.

et al. _____

et seq _____

et ux _____

fructus industriales _____

fructus naturalis _____

habendum _____

lis pendens _____

locus _____

locus sigilli _____

pendente lite _____

Using Legal Language

Read the following story and fill in the blank lines with legal terms taken from the list of terms at the beginning of this chapter:

Priscilla rented an apartment to Peter under a one-year _____ (contract). Priscilla was the _____ or _____, and Peter was the _____ or _____ of the _____ that is, the interest that was conveyed by the lease. Both parties signed the contract; therefore, it was a(n) _____ rather than a(n) _____, which is signed only by one party. Because the arrangement was for a definite period, it was called a(n) _____ rather than a(n) _____ (or _____), which continues for successive periods until one party terminates it by giving notice to the other party. A month later, Peter transferred his interest in the tenancy to Paul for a three-month period by the use of a(n) _____, which is also called a(n) _____. It was not a(n) _____, because Peter was to return to finish the remainder of the lease. Priscilla did not deprive Paul of heat, light, power, or other services called for under the lease; therefore, no _____ occurred. Paul did not pay the rent, however, which caused Priscilla to seek a(n) _____, which is the act of depriving him of the possession of the property. Paul continued to stay on even after being evicted, thus becoming a(n) _____, which is also called a(n) _____. After Paul left, Priscilla _____ (leased) the premises to Prudence for an indefinite period, creating a(n) _____. Prudence allowed Pauline to live with her as a lodger, the latter being a(n) _____, because she had no property right or interest in the premises.

PUZZLING OVER WHAT YOU LEARNED

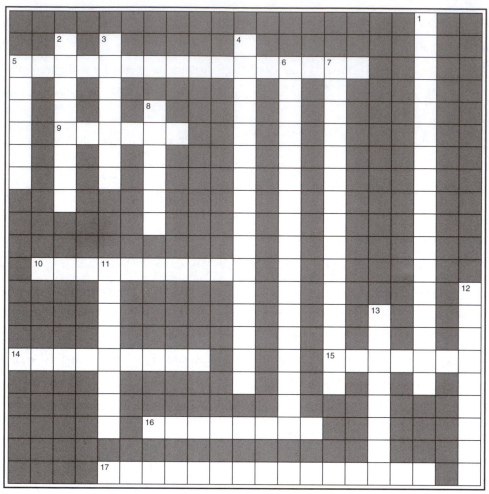

Caveat: Allow squares for spaces between words and punctuation (apostrophes, hyphens, etc.) when filling in crossword.

Across

5. The interest that is conveyed by a lease.
9. Person who has temporary possession of real property under a lease.
10. Lease given by a lessee to a third person for a shorter term.
14. Legal action used by landlords to evict tenants at common law.
15. A grant or permission to do a particular thing.
16. Lease given by a lessee to a third person for a shorter term.
17. Right of a tenant to the undisturbed possession of the rented property.

Down

1. Legal action used by landlords to evict tenants.
2. Person who owns real property and who rents it to another.
3. Leased
4. Estate that continues for successive periods until notice is given.
5. Person who owns real property and who rents it to another under a lease.
6. Estate in real property for a definite or fixed period of time.
7. Estate in real property for an indefinite period of time.
8. Person who has temporary possession of real property under a lease.
11. Act of depriving a person of the possession of real property.
12. A deed or lease to which two or more persons are parties.
13. Person who has permission to do certain acts.

PART EIGHT

Terms Used in Family Law

CHAPTER 37
Marriage, Divorce, and
Dissolution of Marriage

CHAPTER 38
Divorce Procedure

8

Although many unmarried couples today live together, the institution of marriage remains firmly embedded in our culture. Divorce and dissolution of marriage also continue to occur at towering rates, and divorce courts and lawyers specializing in family law are heavily occupied. After a discussion of prenuptial agreements and marriage formalities, Chapter 37 compares annulment with marriage dissolution. It then examines the principal grounds for divorce. Chapter 38 discusses domicile and residence, foreign divorce, defenses to divorce actions, alimony, and support and custody of children.

Marriage, Divorce, and Dissolution of Marriage

ANTE INTERROGATORY

*Common grounds for a no-fault divorce are
(A) irretrievable breakdown, (B) reconciliation, (C) criminal
conversation, (D) marriage banns.*

CHAPTER OUTLINE

Prenuptial Agreements
Marriage Formalities
Same-Sex Marriage and Civil Unions
Annulment of Marriage
Separation of Spouses
Divorce or Dissolution of Marriage
　No-fault Divorce

Fraud or Duress
Adultery
Cruelty
Desertion
Alcohol or Drug Addiction
Impotency
Nonsupport
Conviction of a Felony

KEY TERMS

adultery *(a·DUL·ter·ee)*

age of consent *(aje ov kon·SENT)*

alienation of affections *(ale·ee·a·NA·shun ov
　a·FEK·shuns)*

alleged *(a·LEJD)*

annulment *(a·NUL·ment)*

antenuptial agreement *(an·tee·NUP·shel
　a·GREE·ment)*

banns of matrimony *(MAT·ri·mone·ee)*

breach of promise to marry *(PROM·iss)*

civil union *(SIV·el YOON·yun)*

cohabit *(koh·HAB·it)*

common law marriage *(KOM·on law MAR·ej)*

community property *(kom·YOON·i·tee
　PROP·er·tee)*

conjugal *(KON·je·gel)*

consortium *(kon·SORE·shum)*

copulate *(KOP·yoo·late)*

co-respondent *(KOH·re·spond·ent)*

covenant marriage *(KOV·e·nent MAR·ej)*

crime of moral turpitude *(MOR·el
　TER·pi·tyood)*

criminal conversation *(KRIM·i·nel
　kon·ver·SAY·shun)*

cruelty *(KROO·el·tee)*

desertion *(des·ER·shun)*

discretion *(dis·KRE·shun)*

dissolution of marriage *(dis·o·LU·shun ov
　MAR·ej)*

divorce *(de·VORSE)*

divorce from bed and board

gay marriage

heart balm statutes *(hart bahm STAT·shoots)*

impotency *(IM·pe·ten·see)*

incompatibility *(in·kom·pat·e·BIL·i·tee)*

irreconcilable differences *(ir·rek·en·SY·le·bel DIF·ren·sez)*

irretrievable breakdown *(ir·ree·TREE·ve·bel BRAKE·down)*

limited divorce *(LIM·i·ted de·VORSE)*

marriage *(MAR·ej)*

marriage banns

no-fault divorce

polygamy·*(LIG·e·mee)*

premarital agreement *(pre·MAR·i·tel KON·trakt)*

prenuptial (pre-nup) agreement *(pre·NUP·shel (PREE·nup) a·GREE·ment)*

proxy marriage *(PROK·see MAHR·ej)*

reconciliation *(rek·on·sil·ee·AY·shun)*

same-sex marriage

separation of spouses *(sep·a·RAY·shun ov SPOW·sez)*

solemnized *(SAW·lem·nized)*

PRENUPTIAL AGREEMENTS

A **prenuptial agreement**, also called a **premarital** or **antenuptial agreement**, is a written contract made in contemplation of marriage between prospective spouses, setting forth, among other points, the rights each spouse will have to property brought into the marriage. A prenuptial agreement (commonly called a pre-nup) takes effect on marriage. To be upheld by the court, the contract must be fair and reasonable, and the parties must fully disclose their assets to each other. In many states, when an attorney drafts a prenuptial contract, each party must be represented by a separate attorney. One attorney cannot represent both parties, because a prenuptial agreement is a contract, and a lawyer representing both sides to the same contract has a severe conflict-of-interest problem. For instance, suppose that the wife-to-be (the wealthier side of the relationship) hires her lawyer to represent her and her fiancé in drafting a prenuptial agreement. How would that lawyer protect the interests of the husband-to-be, while also protecting the interests of the one paying the legal bill?

TERMS IN ACTION

Bill Murray, the star of such films as *Caddy Shack*, *Stripes*, and *Lost in Translation*, was sued for **divorce** in May 2008 by his wife of 10 years, Jennifer. In the filing, she accused him of infidelity, abusive behavior, marijuana abuse, and abandonment. But their divorce was finalized a month later, most likely as the result of the **prenuptial agreement** that they entered into in July 1997. The 23-page agreement stated that both parties waived the right to have any review of each other's separate assets or financial documents, and waived the right to alimony or any marital property distribution, in the event of divorce. As consideration for signing the agreement, Bill promised to buy a $1-million home in South Carolina for Jennifer that was to be titled only in her name. The prenuptial agreement states that in the event of a divorce, Jennifer Murray would receive a $7 million payment within 60 days after the divorce decree. Each party waived the right to the other's retirement accounts. The prenuptial agreement stated that each spouse had independent legal representation. Ironically, even though the divorce got off to a very public and ugly start, the prenuptial agreement's opening paragraph states that "this Agreement will enhance and encourage a harmonious marital relationship between them and will enable them to avoid any conflict or controversy in the future arising out of any dissolution of the marriage."

Sources: www.slate.com; thesmokinggun.com

MARRIAGE FORMALITIES

The term **marriage** is defined by the federal government and most states as "the union of one man and one woman." (The topic of gay marriage is discussed later in the chapter.) Despite the continual evolution of the law, men and women who live together without being married have few, if any, rights beyond those given to single persons. In contrast, people who are married have legal rights beyond the **conjugal rights** (the mutual rights and privileges of co-habitation, sexual relations, and companionship) that are deeply embedded in the law. These rights include protection of property, provisions for maintenance and support, and the right of inheritance.

Most states require marriages to be **solemnized**—that is, performed in a ceremonial fashion with witnesses present. Although no particular form of ceremony is required, state laws determine who is authorized to perform a marriage ceremony. In a unique ceremony in 2007, an American soldier in Iraq married his fiancée in Minnesota by the use of video teleconferencing and the help of a chaplain.

A **common law marriage** is a marriage without a formal ceremony. It is currently allowed in only 10 states and the District of Columbia*, and five other states** permit certain common law marriages if they were valid before statutes prohibiting common law marriage were enacted in those states. Where allowed, common law marriage has the same legal effect as a ceremonial marriage. To enter into a common law marriage, the couple must (1) agree by words to each other in the present tense that they are married, (2) **cohabit** (live together), and (3) hold themselves out to the community as husband and wife. In order to qualify as common law married, the couple has to continuously live together as common law spouses for a required period, usually 7 or 10 years.

Word Wise
Prefix Review

Key Term	Prefix	Prefix Meaning
prenuptial (*pre·NUP·shel*)	pre-	before
antenuptial (*an·tee·NUP·shel*)	ante-	before
cohabit (*koh·HAB·it*)	co-	together
incompatibility (*in·kom·pat·e·BIL·i·tee*)	in-	not
irretrievable (*ir·ree·TREE·ve·bel*)	ir-	not
impotency (*IM·pe·ten·see*)	im-	not
reconciliation (*rek·on·sil·ee·AY·shun*)	re-	again

The Uniform Marriage and Divorce Act, which has been adopted in some states, allows a marriage by proxy when a party to the marriage cannot be present. A **proxy marriage** is a ceremonial marriage in which one of the parties is absent, but represented by an agent who stands in his or her place.

The **covenant marriage** has been adopted in Arizona, Arkansas, and Louisiana in an attempt to decrease the divorce rate and to safeguard children from traumatic experiences. It is a form of marriage whose roots are religious in nature. Whereas it is not the only form of marriage in those states, couples who choose a covenant marriage agree to go through counseling before the marriage and also during the marriage to resolve conflicts. With exceptions, they can divorce only after a two-year separation, and causes for divorce are limited to domestic violence, adultery, or a felony with incarceration.

---

*Alabama, Colorado, the District of Columbia, Iowa, Kansas, Montana, Oklahoma, Rhode Island, South Carolina, Texas, Utah.

**Georgia, Idaho, New Hampshire, Ohio, and Pennsylvania.

Some religions require public notice of a marriage contract, called **banns of matrimony**, or **marriage banns**, for a certain number of weeks before the wedding date. This Middle English term, which means "proclamation," provides anyone the time and opportunity to object to the marriage if there is just cause to do so. In addition, many state laws require a waiting period ranging from one to five days after the wedding license is issued before the wedding can occur. Also, many states require the couple to have blood tests to determine the presence of rubella (German measles), venereal disease, sickle cell anemia, and/or AIDS.

SAME-SEX MARRIAGE AND CIVIL UNIONS

Historically, marriage has been exclusively recognized only between one man and woman. In fact, **polygamy** (marriage between more than two spouses) is illegal in America, even if considered to be allowed in one's religion. Until recently, the same could be said for **same-sex marriage**, also called **gay marriage**, which was prohibited in all jurisdictions until Hawaii became the first state to recognize same-sex marriage. The U.S. Congress passed a law, signed by President Clinton in 1996, called the Defense of Marriage Act, which defines marriage as between one man and one woman and declares that if a given state recognizes gay marriage, no other state would have to recognize it as valid marriage. As of the beginning of 2010, statutes in 36 states prohibit gay marriage, and many states also have constitutional amendments defining marriage as heterosexual.

But by the latter part of the 2000s, some state and federal courts began to recognize gay marriage, despite the laws or voter referendums in those states that called to prohibit it. Massachusetts's highest court held that its marriage law violated the Massachusetts constitution, leading to the recognized validity of same-sex marriages in that state. And, whereas California voters passed a direct referendum and change in the California constitution in 2008 (known as Proposition 8), which declared marriage to be only between a man and a woman, federal courts in California (including the 9th Circuit Court of Appeals) concluded that Proposition 8 violated the constitutional rights of homosexuals. It is likely that the U.S. Supreme Court will take a case dealing with the legal debate over same-sex marriage or the Defense of Marriage Act, which has also been declared unconstitutional by the 9th Circuit Court of Appeals.

Going in the opposite direction of the majority of states that have prohibited same-sex marriage, the states of Vermont, Connecticut, and New Jersey have passed laws making civil unions legal. A **civil union** is a relationship in which same-sex couples have the same rights and duties as married couples. California's domestic partners law is a variation of the laws regarding civil union.

ANNULMENT OF MARRIAGE

Marriages may be dissolved either by divorce or by annulment. An **annulment** is a judicial declaration that no valid marriage ever existed.

The principal grounds for annulment, which vary from state to state, are underage marriage, lack of marital intent, duress, fraud, pregnancy by someone other than the husband, incurable venereal disease, mental illness at the time of marriage, and physical incapacity.

At common law, the marriage of a girl under 12 or a boy under 14 was voidable. The marriage could be annulled by the court. Today, a marriage of a person below the age allowed by state law (called the **age of consent**) can be annulled at the court's **discretion**. The power of discretion is one that judges have to make decisions based on their own judgment and conscience.

With some exceptions, the courts have held that a marriage entered into as a joke without any intent that the marriage be binding may be annulled as long as the parties to the marriage do not cohabit. For example, the Connecticut court annulled the marriage of a boy and girl who were married as a result of a "dare" by a group of teenagers out on a joy ride one evening. Neither party intended at the time to enter into the marital status, and they returned to their respective homes without cohabiting.

Some courts have annulled marriages in cases in which the wife, at the time of the marriage, was pregnant by someone other than the husband. Conversely, a woman who is incapable of bearing a child by her husband at the time of the marriage is thought, according to judicial opinions, unable to perform an important part of the marriage contract. Most courts allow an annulment of a marriage when an undissolved, prior marriage of one of the parties exists.

TERMS IN ACTION

An **annulment** is a legal fiction; if a person has entered into a lawful marriage, concluding later that it never existed is a curious thing. But where divorce is against one's religion, annulment is a possible option. King Henry VIII created the Church of England because the pope wouldn't grant Henry an annulment to Catherine of Aragon so that he could marry Anne Boleyn. Catherine had been married to Henry's brother Arthur for a few months before Arthur's death. Because of that, Henry needed a special dispensation to marry Catherine in the first place, since marrying your brother's wife was considered incest at the time. The first claim for annulment was that Catherine never consummated her marriage to Arthur. So, when the Catholic Church refused to grant Henry his annulment—this time, for the reason that Catherine had lied about not consummating her prior marriage with Arthur—Henry was convinced that he could grant himself an annulment if he were the head of his own church. Henry split from Catholicism, and in 1530 Parliament declared the king head of the Church of England. When the very-Catholic Sir Thomas More (the king's Lord Chancellor) refused to support the annulment, Henry had him beheaded. After Anne Boleyn failed to give birth to a male heir, which was Catherine's marital blemish, Henry had her accused of incest and treason and she was beheaded. Centuries later, Brittney Spears got a much less-violent annulment. She was actually once married to someone before she married and divorced Kevin Federline. In January 2004, Spears married a high-school classmate named Jason Alexander, at the Little White Wedding Chapel in Las Vegas, at 5:00 a.m. Fifty-five hours later she got the marriage annulled. Her stated reason for being deserving of an annulment—as opposed to a divorce—was that "she lacked the understanding of her actions to the extent that she was incapable of agreeing to the marriage." That may be legalese for "I was too drunk at the time to know what I was doing."

Sources: wsu.edu; forbes.com

SEPARATION OF SPOUSES

Instead of issuing a divorce decree, a court may order a **separation of spouses** also called a **limited divorce**, or, in some places, a **divorce from bed and board** (an arcane term), which is the discontinuance of cohabitation by the spouses. A legal separation formalizes the cessation of marital cohabitation, without going as far as a divorce—which is the formal disintegration of the legal union. If minor children are involved, a separation order will include temporary measures for support and custody. A separation for a statutory period, whether by agreement or judicial decree, is required in many states before a no-fault divorce action can be initiated.

DIVORCE OR DISSOLUTION OF MARRIAGE

A **divorce** (called **dissolution of marriage** in California) is the action by a court of terminating a valid marriage. A divorce requires a valid marriage to begin with, whereas an annulment does not. The principal grounds for divorce follow:

> no-fault
>
> fraud or duress
>
> adultery

cruelty

desertion

alcohol or drug addiction

impotency

nonsupport

conviction of a felony

No-Fault Divorce

All states have now enacted statutes that provide for the dissolution of marriage without regard to fault, known as **no-fault divorce**. For example, Nevada has for many years allowed a divorce on the ground of **incompatibility**. In that state, instead of requiring a showing of fault, it is necessary to show only that the couple has a personality conflict so deep that no chance for a **reconciliation** (the renewal of amicable relations) exists. Common grounds for a no-fault divorce are **irretrievable breakdown** of the marriage and **irreconcilable differences**.

In some states, a choice exists between two procedures that may be followed to obtain a no-fault divorce. One procedure is used if both parties agree to the divorce; the other procedure is followed if the parties do not agree to it. The procedures differ from state to state.

In California, couples who, among other requirements, have no children, have been married less than five years, and own less than $25,000 worth of community property may divorce without going to court, under a *summary dissolution* procedure. **Community property** is property other than a gift or inheritance, acquired by a husband or wife during marriage, that belongs to both spouses equally without regard to who "earned" the property.

Fraud or Duress

Although most states allow an annulment rather than a divorce on the grounds of fraud and duress, a few states allow a divorce on both of these grounds.

Adultery

Adultery is voluntary sexual intercourse by a married person with someone other than a spouse or by an unmarried person with a married person. In addition to being a ground for divorce, it is a crime in some states. (Remember the Terms in Action in Chapter 14 that discussed the New York woman charged with adultery in 2010.)

Because of its private nature, adultery is most commonly proved by circumstantial evidence. In a divorce action, it is ordinarily enough to show that the **alleged** (claimed) adulterer had the opportunity together with the inclination or disposition to commit the act. For example, in a case in which a husband alleged adultery between his wife and a roomer who lived in the same house, the Illinois court held that adultery could be inferred because the marriage relationship between the husband and wife had not existed for years and the wife often visited bars and went on dates with other men. The court said that both the opportunity and the inclination existed.

To protect the character and reputation of innocent third persons, the name of the **correspondent** (the person charged with committing adultery with the defendant) may not be used in the pleadings until a judge finds probable cause in a closed hearing.

In years past, a tort action called **criminal conversation** could be brought by a husband or wife against a third party who committed adultery with the husband's or wife's spouse. Damages for loss of **consortium** (the fellowship between a husband and wife) were often sought in such cases. But courts began to be less inclined to hear such awkwardly intimate disputes, and **heart balm statutes**, as they are known, have been passed in most states abolishing this cause of action along with actions for **breach of promise to marry** (breaking off the engagement) and **alienation of affections** (willful and malicious interference with the marriage relation by a third party without justification or excuse).

> **Web Wise**
>
> - Refer to a divorce law dictionary at **www.divorcenet.com/dictionary.html**.
> - A divorce helpline is available at **inbox@divorcehelp.com**.
> - Look for divorce forms at **www.divorce-forms.com**.
> - Much information on divorce law, including jurisdiction-specific resources, can be found at **http://topics.law.cornell.edu/wex/Divorce**.
> - Every state's grounds for at-fault divorce can be accessed at **http://www.themodernwomansdivorceguide.com/articles/grounds-for-divorce.php**

Cruelty

Cruelty is a common ground for divorce. It is called by different names, including the following, in different states:

> cruel and abusive treatment
>
> cruel and barbarous treatment
>
> cruel and inhuman treatment
>
> cruelty of treatment
>
> extreme and repeated cruelty
>
> extreme cruelty
>
> intolerable cruelty

Regardless of the name given to it, the requirements for proving cruelty are quite similar throughout the country. In general, plaintiffs must prove actual personal violence that endangers their life, limb, or health or that creates a reasonable apprehension of such danger and renders cohabitation unsafe or unbearable.

Usually, more than a single act of violence must occur to obtain a divorce on this ground. For example, a court held that a single act by a husband of slapping his wife on the back—which was not severe, left no mark, and was the only act of violence in 25 years of marriage—was not a ground for divorce. In a contrasting case, however, the same court said that one single incident of violence was enough to grant a divorce when a husband, while drunk, struck, knocked down, and beat his wife in an argument, resulting in bruises on the wife's back, throat, arms, and legs.

Arguments alone, nagging, or the denial of sexual intercourse is not enough by itself to obtain a divorce on the grounds of cruelty. Mental suffering can be held to be cruelty if it impairs the health of the spouse. For example, a husband was allowed a divorce on the ground of cruelty when his wife persisted in seeing another man over his objections, because such conduct resulted in the deterioration of the husband's health.

Desertion

Desertion is defined as the voluntary separation of one spouse from the other, for the statutory period, without justification and with the intent of not returning. The abandoned spouse must not consent to the spouse's absence and must not have committed acts that justified the other's leaving. The time period for desertion varies from state to state.

Alcohol or Drug Addiction

Habitual drunkenness, by either alcohol or drugs, is a ground for divorce in most states. The habit must be confirmed (well established), persistent, voluntary, and excessive.

Impotency

Impotency is the incapacity of either party to consummate the marriage by sexual intercourse because of some physical infirmity or disarrangement. The test is the ability to **copulate**, which means to engage in sexual intercourse. It is not related to sterility, which is the inability to beget or bear a child.

Nonsupport

In many states, nonsupport is available only to the wife and not to the husband as a ground for divorce. In those states that have made the equal rights of men and women part of their state law, however, it is available to both spouses if the state recognizes it as a ground for divorce. The spouse against whom the divorce is sought must have sufficient ability to provide support and must willfully fail to do so.

Conviction of a Felony

Most states allow a divorce if either party is convicted of a felony, an infamous crime, or a **crime of moral turpitude** (a crime that is base, vile, and depraved). Pennsylvania, for example, allows a spouse to divorce on the ground that the other spouse has been convicted of a crime and sentenced to at least two years in prison. In some jurisdictions, life imprisonment automatically dissolves the marriage without further legal process; most states, however, require a divorce proceeding.

Reviewing What You Learned

After studying the chapter, write the answers to each of the following questions:

1. What is required for a prenuptial contract to be upheld by the court?_____

_____

_____

_____

2. The legal rights given to people who are married include what?

_____

_____

_____

_____

3. What are the requirements for entering into a common law marriage? _____

_____

_____

_____

_____

4. List the principal grounds for an annulment. _____

_____

_____

_____

_____

5. At common law, the marriage of people under what age was voidable? _____

_____

_____

_____

_____

6. Today, a marriage of a person below what age can be annulled?

_____

_____

_____

_____

7. List the principal grounds for a divorce. _____

_____

_____

_____

_____

8. On what ground has Nevada allowed a divorce for many years? What must be shown to obtain such a divorce? _____

_____

_____

_____

_____

9. What are two common grounds for a no-fault divorce?_____

_____

_____

_____

10. In a divorce action for adultery, it is ordinarily enough to show what two elements on the part of the alleged adulterer?_____

_____

_____

_____

_____

11. What is done to protect the character and reputation of innocent third persons in divorce actions for adultery?_____

_____

_____

_____

_____

12. What is generally required to obtain a divorce for cruelty?____

_____

_____

_____

_____

13. Name three activities that, by themselves, are not enough to establish cruelty. _____

_____

_____

_____

14. To establish desertion, the abandoned spouse must not consent to what? _____

_____

_____

_____

15. What four words describe the habit necessary to establish habitual drunkenness? _____

_____

_____

_____

16. Explain the difference between impotency and sterility._____

_____

_____

_____

17. What is required of the spouse against whom a divorce is sought on the ground of nonsupport? _____

_____

_____

_____

_____

Understanding Legal Concepts

Indicate whether each statement is true or false. Then, change the italicized word or phrase of each false statement to make it true.

ANSWERS

_____ **1.** To be upheld by the court, a prenuptial agreement must be fair and reasonable and the parties *must* fully disclose their assets to each other.

_____ **2.** Men and women who live together without being married have *many* rights beyond those given to single persons.

_____ **3.** Common law marriages are allowed in *all* jurisdictions in the United States.

_____ **4.** At common law, the marriage of a girl under *12* or a boy under 14 was voidable.

_____ **5.** An *annulment* requires a valid marriage to begin with.

_____ **6.** To prove adultery in a divorce action, it is ordinarily enough to show that the alleged adulterer had the *opportunity* together with the inclination, to commit the act.

_____ **7.** The name of the co-respondent in a divorce action involving adultery may *not be* used in the pleadings until a judge finds probable cause in a closed hearing.

_____ **8.** Arguments or nagging is usually *enough* to obtain a divorce on the grounds of cruelty.

_____ **9.** To obtain a divorce for desertion, the abandoned spouse *must not* consent to the spouse's absence.

_____ **10.** The test to determine impotency is the ability to *beget or bear a child.*

Checking Terminology

From the list of legal terms that follows, select the one that matches each definition.

ANSWERS

a. adultery
b. age of consent
c. alienation of affections
d. alleged
e. annulment
f. antenuptial agreement
g. banns of matrimony
h. breach of promise to marry
i. civil union
j. cohabit
k. common law marriage
l. community property
m. conjugal
n. consortium
o. copulate
p. co-respondent
q. covenant marriage
r. crime of moral turpitude
s. criminal conversation
t. cruelty
u. desertion
v. discretion
w. dissolution of marriage
x. divorce
y. divorce from bed and board
z. gay marriage
aa. heart balm statutes
bb. impotency
cc. incompatibility
dd. irreconcilable differences
ee. irretrievable breakdown
ff. limited divorce
gg. marriage
hh. marriage banns
ii. no-fault divorce
jj. polygamy
kk. premarital agreement
ll. prenuptial agreement
mm. proxy marriage
nn. reconciliation
oo. same-sex marriage
pp. separation of spouses
qq. solemnized

_____ 1. The action by a court of terminating a valid marriage. (Select two answers.)

_____ 2. A judicial declaration that no valid marriage ever existed.

_____ 3. The power that a judge has to make a decision based on his or her own judgment and conscience.

_____ 4. A dissolution of marriage without regard to fault.

_____ 5. The renewal of amicable relations.

_____ 6. Voluntary sexual intercourse by a married person with someone other than a spouse or by any unmarried person with a married person.

_____ 7. The age at which one may be married under state law.

_____ 8. Conflicts in personalities and dispositions that are so deep as to be irreconcilable and irremediable and that render it impossible for married parties to continue to live together in a normal marital relationship. (Select three answers.)

_____ 9. The person charged with committing adultery with the defendant in a divorce action.

_____ 10. In a divorce action, personal violence by one spouse that endangers the life, limb, or health of the other spouse.

_____ 11. The voluntary separation of one spouse from the other, for the statutory period, without justification and with the intent of not returning.

_____ 12. The incapacity of either party to consummate a marriage by sexual intercourse because of some physical infirmity or disarrangement.

_____ 13. Live together.

_____ 14. Claimed, asserted, or charged.

_____ 15. Public notice of a marriage contract for a certain number of weeks before the wedding date. (Select two answers.)

_____ 16. A ceremonial marriage in which one of the parties is absent, but represented by an agent who stands in his or her place.

_____ 17. Engage in sexual intercourse.

_____ 18. An agreement made in contemplation of marriage between prospective spouses setting forth, among other points, the rights each spouse will have to property brought into the marriage. (Select three answers.)

_____ 19. Performed in a ceremonial fashion with witnesses present.

_____ 20. A marriage without a formal ceremony.

_____ 21. Property (other than a gift or inheritance) acquired by a husband or wife during marriage that belongs to both spouses equally.

_____ 22. A crime that is base, vile, and depraved.

_____ 23. The willful and malicious interference with the marriage relation by a third party without justification or excuse.

_____ 24. The fellowship between a husband and wife.

_____ 25. A tort action brought by a husband or wife against a third party who committed adultery with the husband's or wife's spouse.

_____ 26. The discontinuance of cohabitation by the spouses. (Select three answers.)

_____ 27. Laws passed in most states abolishing actions for loss of consortium, breach of promise to marry, and alienation of affections.

_____ 28. The destruction of fellowship between a husband and wife.

_____ 29. Breaking off an engagement to marry.

_____ 30. A marriage in which the parties agree to go through counseling before the marriage and also during the marriage in order to resolve conflicts.

_____ 31. Pertaining to the marriage relationship.

_____ 32. Marriage between two men or two women. (Select two answers.)

_____ 33. Marriage between more than two spouses.

Using Legal Language

Read the following story and fill in the blank lines with legal terms taken from the list of terms at the beginning of this chapter:

Although she looked older, Sonia was only 14 when she married Seth. This was below the _____, which is the age at which persons were allowed by the law of her state to marry; however, the couple did _____ —that is, live together. Whether or not she could obtain a(n) _____, which is a judicial declaration that no valid marriage ever existed, was in the court's _____. She decided to seek a(n) _____, which is the act of terminating a marriage. Evidence existed that Seth had the opportunity together with the inclination to commit _____, which is a crime in many states in addition to being a ground for divorce. It was _____ (claimed) that he had gone to Sarah's apartment on several occasions. If Sarah were to be charged as being a(n) _____, her name could not be used in the pleadings unless probable cause were found by a judge in a closed hearing. Seth had not committed _____, which is personal violence endangering a spouse's life, limb, or health. He had the ability to _____—that is, engage in sexual intercourse—ruling out Sonia's obtaining a divorce on the ground of _____. A divorce could not be obtained on the ground of _____, either, because no voluntary separation of one spouse from the other had occurred. After thinking it over, Sonia decided to seek a(n) _____, which provides for the _____ without regard to fault. She considered getting a divorce in Nevada on the ground of _____, which required a showing that the couple had a personality conflict so deep that no chance for a(n) _____ existed. In some states, this ground for divorce is called _____, and in others, it is known as _____.

PUZZLING OVER WHAT YOU LEARNED

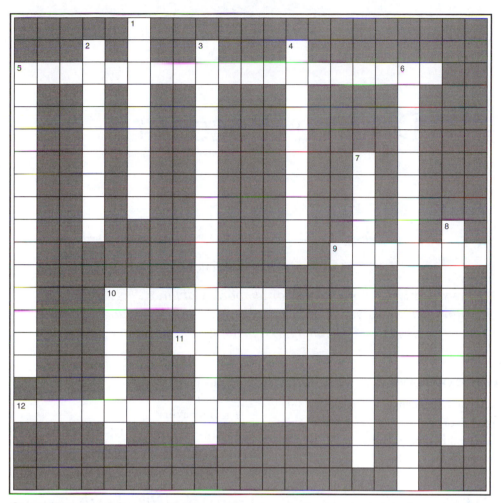

Caveat: Allow squares for spaces between words and punctuation (apostrophes, hyphens, etc.) when filling in crossword.

Across

5. A contract made in contemplation of marriage.
9. Live together.
10. Sexual intercourse by a married person with someone other than the spouse.
11. Act of terminating a valid marriage by a court.
12. Person charged with committing adultery with the defendant in a divorce action.

Down

1. Inability to have sexual intercourse.
2. Judicial declaration that no valid marriage ever existed.
3. Public notice of a marriage contract before the marriage.
4. Performed in a ceremonial fashion with witnesses present.
5. Ceremonial marriage in which one party is represented by an agent.
6. A marriage without a formal ceremony.
7. The age at which one may be married under state law.
8. Power that a judge has to make a decision based on his or her own conscience.
10. Claimed, asserted, or charged.

8

Divorce Procedure

ANTE INTERROGATORY

Some states issue a provisional or temporary divorce decision until a statutory period is over. This is called (A) response, (B) judgment nisi, (C) comity, (D) pendent lite.

CHAPTER OUTLINE

Domicile and Residence
Foreign Divorce
Defenses to Divorce Actions
    Condonation
    Connivance
    Collusion
    Recrimination
Alimony and Property Distribution
Support and Custody of Children

KEY TERMS

alimony *(AL·i·mohn·ee)*
appearance *(a·PEER·ens)*
bilateral foreign divorce *(by·LAT·er·el FOR·en de·VORSE)*
child support *(su·PORT)*
collusion *(ke·LOO·shen)*
comity *(KOM·i·tee)*
condonation *(kon·do·NAY·shun)*
connivance *(ke·NY·vens)*
custody of children *(KUS·te·dee)*
decree *(de·KREE)*
divided custody *(de·VIE·ded KUS·te·dee)*
domicile *(DOM·i·sile)*
emancipated *(e·MAN·si·pay·ted)*
equitable distribution laws *(EK·wit·a·bel dis·tre·BYOO·shun)*
ex parte foreign divorce *(eks PAR·tay FOR·en de·VORSE)*

foreign divorce *(FOR·en de·VORSE)*
foreign jurisdiction *(FOR·en joo·res·DIK·shen)*
forum *(FOR·em)*
full faith and credit clause *(KRED·et)*
interlocutory decree *(in·ter·LOK·ye·tore·ee de·KREE)*
joint custody *(joynt KUS·te·dee)*
judgment nisi *(JUJ·ment NIE·sie)*
libel *(LIE·bel)*
libelant *(lie·bel·AHNT)*
libelee *(lie·bel·EE)*
maintenance *(MAIN·ten·ens)*
pendente lite *(pen·DEN·tay LIE·tay)*
petition *(pe·TI·shun)*
petitioner *(pe·TI·shun·er)*
physical custody *(FIZ·i·cal KUS·te·dee)*
proceeding *(pro·SEED·ing)*
recrimination *(re·krim·i·NAY·shun)*

residence (*RES·e·dens*)
respondent (*re·SPON·dent*)
response (*re·SPONS*)

spousal support (*SPOWS·el su·PORT*)
temporary custody (*TEM·po·rare·ee KUS·te·dee*)

As divorce law has changed throughout the past decades, many of the terms have also changed. Formerly, the person bringing a divorce action was called the **libelant** and the person against whom the divorce was sought was called the **libelee**. The pleading beginning the action was called a **libel**. Although some states still use those terms, in others, *plaintiff* and *defendant* describe the parties to a divorce action. The initial pleading is called a *complaint*. The divorce court's decision, formerly called a **decree** (a decision of a court of equity), is now called a judgment in states that have changed their terminology.

But, in many other states, including California, the procedure for obtaining a dissolution of marriage is called a **proceeding** and the process is begun by the filing of a **petition** (a written application for a court order) with the court. The parties to the proceeding are the **petitioner** (one who presents a petition to a court) and the **respondent** (one who is called on to answer a petition). The written answer filed by a respondent is a **response**.

Instead of issuing a final decision immediately, the courts of some states issue a provisional or temporary decision, called a **judgment nisi** in some states and an **interlocutory decree** in others. The provisional decision becomes final at the end of a statutory period unless a valid reason is shown for not issuing it.

DOMICILE AND RESIDENCE

In a divorce action or dissolution petition, jurisdiction is based on **domicile**, which is a person's permanent place of abode. Notwithstanding that people move or live in different states throughout the year, one's domicile is the place to which, whenever a person is absent, he or she has the present intent of returning. It cannot be abandoned or surrendered until another is acquired. It differs from a **residence** in that where one is currently living on a long-term basis (as opposed to a vacation) is one's residence. But one's current residence may not be that person's domicile. People may have several residences, but they can have only one domicile at a particular time. For example, students may reside in a college dormitory in one state, spend their summer working at a resort in another state, yet be domiciled at their home in a third state.

The plaintiff or petitioner in a divorce action must be domiciled within the jurisdiction of the court. Whether or not a legal domicile has been established is determined by the law of the **forum**, which is the place of litigation. The states are free to determine that a specific duration of residency is the equivalent of domicile.

All states except Alaska, South Dakota, and Washington require the plaintiff in a divorce action to reside in their state for a minimum time before filing for divorce. The period ranges from six weeks in a few states to one year in others.

TERMS IN ACTION

The most expensive **divorce** ever is thought to be that between Rupert and Anna Murdoch. Mr. and Mrs. Murdoch were divorced in 1999, after 32 years of marriage. Rupert Murdoch is the Australian-born billionaire who founded News Corp., the media company that owns the Fox Broadcast Network, Fox News Network, and other media outlets including the *New York Post* and the *Wall Street Journal*. Anna Murdoch filed the divorce **petition** in California, which was the couple's **domicile** at the time, although their **residence** was New York City. Their divorce settlement was valued at $1.7 billion. Seventeen days after the divorce, Rupert Murdoch married a woman 38 years younger than himself.

Source: cnbc.com; nymag.com

FOREIGN DIVORCE

Before so many states allowed no-fault divorces, people would sometimes go to a **foreign jurisdiction** (another state or country) to obtain a **foreign divorce**. They did this because they did not have grounds for a divorce in their own state or because they wanted an immediate divorce without a waiting period. Nevada was attractive because domicile could be established in six weeks and a divorce could be obtained on the ground of incompatibility. Mexico allowed quick, easy divorces (including those by mail order) at one time, but its laws have been amended, ending such practice.

Haiti and the Dominican Republic were once popular places to obtain overnight divorces. Jurisdiction was established by the fact that both parties submitted themselves to the jurisdiction of the court—the plaintiff in person and the defendant, in most cases, by filing an **appearance**. This voluntary submission to the court's jurisdiction, either in person or by an agent, was often accomplished by the filing of a power of attorney with the court, without the filer being personally present.

Word Wise
Opposite Parties

appellant *(a·PEL·ent)*	a party bringing an appeal
appellee *(a·pel·EE)*	a party against whom an appeal is brought
defendant *(de·FEN·dent)*	a person against whom a legal action is brought
libelant *(lie·bel·AHNT)*	the plaintiff in a divorce action
libelee *(lie·bel·EE)*	the defendant in a divorce action
petitioner *(pe·TI·shun·er)*	one who presents a petition to a court
plaintiff *(PLAIN·tif)*	a person who brings a legal action against another
respondent *(re·SPON·dent)*	one who is called on to answer a petition

---

A **bilateral foreign divorce** occurs when both parties file an appearance, as mentioned earlier, in a foreign state or country. A divorce obtained in a state other than the parties' state of domicile is recognized as valid by all of the United States under the **full faith and credit clause** of the U.S. Constitution. This clause requires that full faith and credit be given by each state to the judicial proceedings of every other state. The doctrine of **comity** applies a similar rule to judicial proceedings of foreign countries. This doctrine states that the courts of one jurisdiction will give effect to the laws and judicial decisions of another jurisdiction, not as a matter of obligation, but out of deference and respect.

An **ex parte foreign divorce** occurs when one spouse appears in the foreign jurisdiction, and the other spouse does not appear and fails to respond to the notice of divorce or service of process. This type of divorce may be attacked by the spouse who did not appear and declared void on the ground of lack of jurisdiction of the court granting the divorce. Such an attack may come when a spouse brings suit for separate support or when a spouse dies and the other spouse claims an inheritance.

DEFENSES TO DIVORCE ACTIONS

When one seeks a divorce on the grounds allowed for divorce, the other spouse has the opportunity to raise various defenses (described next), in an attempt to prevent the divorce from being granted. But with the adoption of no-fault divorce laws, some states have eliminated the traditional defenses to divorce actions that had been available.

Condonation

Condonation is the forgiveness of a matrimonial offense. It is a defense to a divorce action that applies as long as the offense is not repeated and the wrongdoer remains faithful thereafter. The voluntary continuance of cohabitation or the resumption of sexual intercourse with knowledge of a marital offense usually amounts to condonation.

Connivance

The plaintiff's secret cooperation in the commission of a marital wrong committed by the defendant, called **connivance**, is a defense to a divorce action. A spouse who procures the commission of adultery, for example, or facilitates such an act is guilty of connivance. One cannot legally "smooth the path to the adulterous bed."

Collusion

An agreement between a husband and wife that one of them will commit a marital offense so that the other may obtain a divorce, an agreement not to defend a divorce action, and an agreement to withhold evidence in such an action are examples of **collusion**, which is a defense to a divorce action, other than no-fault.

Recrimination

The common law doctrine of **recrimination** held that neither party could obtain a divorce when both were guilty of a marital wrong. Before no-fault divorce laws, this defense was widely used in the United States. Conduct on the part of the plaintiff that constituted a ground for divorce was a defense to a divorce action. The offense by the plaintiff did not have to be the same offense alleged in the complaint for divorce; however, it did have to be a ground for divorce in that particular state.

ALIMONY AND PROPERTY DISTRIBUTION

Alimony (called **spousal support** in California) is an allowance made to a divorced spouse by a former spouse for support and maintenance. Its concept stems from the common law right of a wife to be supported by a husband during marriage. Today, however, many states award alimony or spousal support payments to either the ex-husband or the ex-wife. The power of the court to award alimony and spousal support is strictly statutory and comes solely from the statutes of the particular state making the award. In general, the court having jurisdiction to award a divorce also has the power to award alimony.

Alimony **pendente lite**, meaning litigation pending, is temporary alimony that may be granted to a spouse during the pendency of a divorce or separate support action. Temporary alimony rests largely in the discretion of the court and need not be awarded when the parties have entered into an agreement in that regard or when one spouse is voluntarily providing for the other spouse's support.

No set formula exists for determining the amount of alimony or spousal support that may be awarded. The determination rests in the sound discretion of the court. Such items as income and earning capacity, financial resources, future prospects, current obligations, dependents, and number of former and subsequent spouses are considered. Also considered are the spouse's situation in life, earning capacity, separate property, contribution to a spouse's property, age, health, obligations, and number of dependents.

Some jurisdictions will not award alimony or spousal support to a spouse who has a sufficient estate to provide for himself or herself. Similarly, a spouse who was at fault during the marriage will not be awarded alimony when the divorce was obtained for that reason.

The remarriage of a person who is receiving alimony or spousal support does not necessarily end a former spouse's obligation to pay it; however, that fact is usually a persuasive reason for a court to modify its judgment. The death of either party usually terminates the obligation to pay alimony or spousal support, although some state statutes authorize the continuance of alimony payments from the estate of the deceased spouse.

Courts, in most instances, will reserve the right to modify an alimony or spousal support award. Under some state laws, if the court does not reserve the right to do so in its judgment, the judgment cannot be changed after the expiration of the appeal period. Some states allow an alimony or spousal support award to be modified by agreement of the parties.

Many states have **equitable distribution laws** that give courts the power to distribute property equitably between the parties upon divorce. Both parties are usually required to disclose their financial situation and provide paycheck stubs and income tax returns. Although the spouses are considered to jointly own the marital estate, the court is given authority to determine how to divide the property in a way that is thought to be fair and just. State statutes often provide criteria to be followed by the court in making the distribution.

SUPPORT AND CUSTODY OF CHILDREN

The legal obligations of parents to contribute to the economic maintenance and education of their children is known as **child support** or **maintenance**. Parents are required to support their minor children who are not **emancipated**—that is, freed from parental control. In a divorce proceeding, the parties may set the amount of child support by agreement, subject to approval of the court, or the court may determine the amount. Under the Uniform Reciprocal Enforcement of Support Act, which has been adopted by every state in the United States, a support order of one state can be enforced in every state.

The welfare or best interest of the child is the most important factor in determining the **custody of children**—that is, their care, control, and maintenance. In deciding who shall have **physical custody** of a child (which is the day-to-day care the child, including the place of his or her residence), the court considers such points as the stability of the person seeking custody; the physical safety of the child; and the emotional, social, spiritual, and economic needs of the child. The child's wishes are also considered in determining who shall have custody.

Temporary custody of children is often awarded to a parent, pending the outcome of a divorce or separation action. When the court orders **divided custody** of a child, it means that the child will live with each parent part of the year, the other parent usually having visitation rights. The parent with whom the child is living has complete control over the child during that period. In contrast, when the court orders **joint custody** of a child, both parents share the responsibility and authority of child rearing regardless of where the child resides at a given time.

▌ TERMS IN ACTION

Frequently, a **custody** battle will be part of a divorce. The spouse who wins physical custody of the couple's child or children will also receive the child support payments that have to be made by the other spouse. **Child support** payments are based on a formula that includes as a variable the paying spouse's income. Some celebrities' child support obligations make it into the news, at least the entertainment section. In the Brittney Spears–Kevin Federline divorce (mentioned in Chapter 37), Federline won custody of the couple's two sons, and the court ordered Spears to pay $20,000 a month in child support. The mother of one of the children of rapper Sean "P. Diddy" Combs won an increase of her child support payments in 2004, when a magistrate ordered Combs to up his $5,000 monthly payments to $35,000. Entertainment mogul Russell Simmons, who was married to model and reality TV performer Kimora Lee Simmons, agreed in his divorce settlement to pay $40,000 a month in child support for the care of the couple's two daughters, until each is 19½ years old. Additionally, Mr. Simmons agreed that every three years he would provide a new car worth at least $60,000 for his daughters' use.

Sources: usatoday.com; cnbc.com; eonline.com

Reviewing What You Learned

After studying the chapter, write the answers to each of the following questions:

1. In former years, what terms described the plaintiff, the defendant, and the initial pleading in a divorce action? _____ _____ _____ _____

2. What factors determine jurisdiction in a divorce action or dissolution petition? _____ _____ _____ _____ _____

3. What is the difference between a residence and a domicile? _____ _____ _____ _____

4. How many domiciles can a person have at any given time? _____ _____ _____ _____

5. What law determines whether or not a legal domicile has been established? _____ _____ _____ _____

6. What doctrine applies the full faith and credit rule to judicial proceedings of foreign countries? _____ _____ _____ _____

7. In an ex parte foreign divorce, do one, both, or neither of the parties appear in the foreign jurisdiction? _____ _____ _____

_____ _____

8. On what ground may an ex parte foreign divorce be attacked, and under what circumstances may it successfully occur? _____ _____ _____ _____

9. On what theory were the traditional defenses to divorce actions based? _____ _____ _____ _____

10. What is the difference between connivance and collusion? _____ _____ _____ _____

11. From what common law right does the concept of alimony and spousal support stem? _____ _____ _____ _____ _____

12. What points are considered in determining the amount of alimony and spousal support that may be awarded? _____ _____ _____

13. What is the most important factor in determining the custody of children? _____ _____ _____ _____

Understanding Legal Concepts

Indicate whether each statement is true or false. Then, change the italicized word or phrase of each false statement to make it true.

ANSWERS

_____ 1. In many states, the person bringing a divorce action used to be called the *libelee*.

_____ 2. In a divorce action, jurisdiction is based on the *residence* of the plaintiff.

_____ 3. All states except *Alaska, South Dakota, and Washington* require the plaintiff in a divorce action to reside in their state a minimum time before filing for a divorce.

_____ 4. The doctrine of *comity* applies to the acceptance of judicial proceedings of foreign countries.

_____ 5. A bilateral foreign divorce may be attacked by the spouse who did not appear and declared void on the ground of *lack of jurisdiction* of the court granting the divorce.

_____ 6. The *traditional defenses* to divorce actions were based on the theory that a divorce is granted because one party was at fault and the other was not.

_____ 7. The common law doctrine of *connivance* held that neither party could obtain a divorce when both were guilty of a marital wrong.

_____ 8. Today, *many* states award alimony or spousal support payments to either the ex-husband or the ex-wife.

_____ 9. A set formula *exists* for determining the amount of alimony that may be awarded.

_____ 10. A child's wishes *are not* considered in determining who shall have custody of the child.

Checking Terminology

From the list of legal terms that follows, select the one that matches each definition.

ANSWERS

a. alimony
b. appearance
c. bilateral foreign divorce
d. child support
e. collusion
f. comity
g. condonation
h. connivance
i. custody of children
j. decree
k. divided custody
l. domicile
m. emancipated
n. equitable distribution laws
o. ex parte foreign divorce
p. foreign divorce
q. foreign jurisdiction
r. forum
s. full faith and credit clause
t. interlocutory decree
u. joint custody
v. judgment nisi
w. libel
x. libelant
y. libelee
z. maintenance
aa. pendente lite
bb. petition
cc. petitioner
dd. physical custody
ee. proceeding
ff. recrimination

_____ 1. The plaintiff in a divorce action (no longer used by some states).

_____ 2. A person's principal place of abode; the place to which, whenever one is absent, he or she has the present intent of returning.

_____ 3. The place of litigation.

_____ 4. The voluntary submission to the court's jurisdiction, either in person or by an agent.

_____ 5. The initial pleading in a divorce action (no longer used by some states).

_____ 6. A rule of law requiring that full faith and credit be given by each state to the judicial proceedings of every other state.

_____ 7. A divorce that occurs when both parties make an appearance in a foreign state or country.

_____ 8. A divorce that occurs when one spouse appears in a foreign jurisdiction and the other spouse does not appear and fails to respond to the notice of divorce or service of process.

_____ 9. The forgiveness of a matrimonial offense.

_____ 10. An agreement between a husband and wife that one of them will commit a marital offense so that the other may obtain a divorce.

_____ 11. An allowance made to a divorced spouse by a former spouse for support and maintenance. (Select two answers.)

_____ 12. The defendant in a divorce action (no longer used by some states).

_____ 13. A decision of a court of equity.

_____ 14. A provisional or temporary decision of a court. (Select two answers.)

_____ 15. Another state or country.

_____ 16. A place where a person actually lives.

_____ 17. A doctrine stating that the courts of one jurisdiction will give effect to the laws and judicial decisions of another jurisdiction, not as a matter of obligation, but out of deference and respect.

_____ 18. The plaintiff's secret cooperation in the commission of a marital wrong by the defendant, which is a common law defense to an action for divorce.

_____ 19. Conduct on the part of the plaintiff that constitutes a ground for divorce, which is a common law defense to an action for divorce.

_____ 20. Litigation pending.

_____ 21. The procedure in California for obtaining a dissolution of marriage.

_____ 22. A written application for a court order.

_____ 23. One who presents a petition to a court.

gg. residence
hh. respondent
ii. response
jj. spousal support
kk. temporary custody

_____ 24. One who is called on to answer a petition.
_____ 25. The written answer to a petition filed by a respondent.
_____ 26. Freed from parental control.
_____ 27. The legal obligations of parents to contribute to the economic maintenance and education of their children. (Select two answers.)
_____ 28. The care, control, and maintenance of children.
_____ 29. Custody in which the child will live with each parent part of the year, the other parent usually having visitation rights, but not control of the child during that period.
_____ 30. A divorce in a state or country other than that in which the party lives.
_____ 31. Custody in which both parents share the responsibility and authority of childrearing.
_____ 32. Custody of a child awarded to a parent on a temporary basis, pending the outcome of a divorce or separation action.
_____ 33. The day-to-day custody of a child, including residence.

Using Legal Language

Read the following story and fill in the blank lines with legal terms taken from the list of terms at the beginning of this chapter:

Some years ago, before no-fault divorce was readily available, Rodney brought a divorce action against Heather on the ground of adultery. He was the _____, she was the _____, and the initial pleading was called a(n) _____. The _____—that is, the place of litigation—where Rodney brought the action was located in his principal place of abode, known as his _____. Because it was the place where he actually, presently lived, it was also his _____. Before the action, Heather had agreed with Rodney to commit adultery so that he could divorce her, setting up the defense of _____ if Heather wanted to use it. In addition, Rodney secretly arranged to have his friend Rudolph spend the weekend with Heather while he was out of town, making available to her the defense of _____. In addition, Rodney deserted Heather, leaving her without means for support. Because this conduct was on the part of the plaintiff, which constituted a ground for divorce, it was also a defense called _____. Before the case went to trial, the parties forgave each other for their indiscretions, and the two resumed cohabitation, which created the defense of _____. Their reunion did not work out, however, and Heather decided to go to Haiti, a _____, to obtain an overnight divorce. Rodney refused to voluntarily submit to that court's jurisdiction by filing a(n) _____, which meant that this was a(n) _____ action rather than a(n) _____ action. As a result, the doctrine of _____, stating that the courts of one jurisdiction will give effect to the laws and judicial decisions of another jurisdiction, did not apply. Heather did not ask for _____—that is, an allowance for support and maintenance—as part of the court's _____ (decision).

PUZZLING OVER WHAT YOU LEARNED

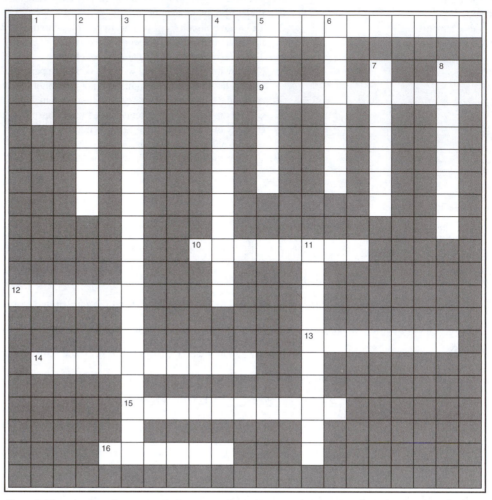

Caveat: Allow squares for spaces between words and punctuation (apostrophes, hyphens, etc.) when filling in crossword.

Across

1. Another state or country.
9. One who presents a petition to a court.
10. The plaintiff in a divorce action.
12. Courts of one jurisdiction will give effect to the laws of another.
13. Allowance made to a divorced spouse by a former spouse for support.
14. The procedure in California for obtaining a dissolution of marriage.
15. One who is called on to answer a petition.
16. A decision of a court of equity.

Down

1. The place of litigation.
2. Place where a person actually lives.
3. Provisional or temporary decision of a court.
4. A provisional judgment.
5. Written answer to a petition filed by a respondent.
6. Principal place of abode.
7. The defendant in a divorce action.
8. A written application for a court order.
11. Voluntary submission to the court's jurisdiction.

PART NINE

Terms Used in Business Organizations and Bankruptcy

9

Before opening a business, persons must give thought to the type of business organization best suited for that particular enterprise. Similarly, when a business fails or an individual suffers financial loss, consideration must be given to the desirability of filing for bankruptcy. Chapter 39 discusses the principal kinds of business organizations, including the sole proprietorship, the partnership, the corporation, the limited liability company, the joint venture, and the franchise. Chapter 40 explains bankruptcy proceedings generally, including pointing out some of the sweeping changes made by the U.S. Congress in 2005. This is followed by a discussion of exemptions provided by the law of bankruptcy and an examination of the different types of bankruptcy proceedings.

39

Business Organizations

ANTE INTERROGATORY

A relationship in which two or more people combine their labor or property for a single business undertaking is called a (A) co-venture, (B) limited liability company, (C) ostensible partners, (D) de facto corporation.

CHAPTER OUTLINE

Sole Proprietorship
Partnership
Corporation

Limited Liability Company
Joint Venture
Franchise

KEY TERMS

articles of organization (*AR·ti·kels ov or·ge·ni·ZAY·shun*)

articles of incorporation (*AR·ti·kels ov in·kor·por·AY·shun*)

blue-sky laws

C corporation (*kor·por·AY·shun*)

certificate of incorporation (*ser·TIF·i·ket ov in·kor·por·AY·shun*)

charter (*CHAR·ter*)

close corporation (*klose kor·por·AY·shun*)

common stock (*KOM·on stok*)

co-partnership (*koh-PART·ner·ship*)

corporation (*kor·por·AY·shun*)

co-venture (*KOH-ven·cher*)

de facto corporation (*de FAK·toh kor·por·AY·shun*)

de jure corporation (*de ZHOOR·ee kor·por·AY·shun*)

derivative action (*de·RIV·a·tiv AK·shun*)

directors (*de·REK·ters*)

dissolution (*DIS·o·lew·shun*)

dividends (*DIV·i·denz*)

domestic corporation (*do·MES·tik kor·por·AY·shun*)

dormant partner (*DOR·ment PART·ner*)

double taxation (*DUB·el taks·AY·shun*)

eleemosynary corporation (*el·ee·MOS·en·er·ee kor·por·AY·shun*)

foreign corporation (*FOR·en kor·por·AY·shun*)

franchise (*FRAN·chize*)

franchisee (*fran·chize·EE*)

franchiser (*FRAN·chize·er*)

general partner *(JEN·e·rel PART·ner)*

general partnership *(JEN·e·rel PART·ner·ship)*

incorporators *(in·KOR·por·ay·tors)*

joint enterprise *(joynt EN·ter·prize)*

joint venture *(joynt VEN·cher)*

limited liability company (LLC) *(LIM·i·ted ly·a·BIL·i·tee KUM·pe·nee)*

limited liability limited partnership *(LLLP) (LIM·i·ted ly·a·BIL·i·tee LIM·i·ted PART·ner·ship)*

limited liability partnership *(LLP) (LIM·i·ted ly·a·BIL·i·tee PART·ner·ship)*

limited partner *(LIM·i·ted PART·ner)*

limited partnership *(LIM·i·ted PART·ner·ship)*

liquidate *(LIK·wi·date)*

managers *(MAN·a·jers)*

members *(MEM·bers)*

nominal partner *(NOM·i·nel PART·ner)*

not-for-profit corporation

operating agreement *(OP·er·ate·ing a·GREE·ment)*

ostensible partner *(os·TEN·si·bel PART·ner)*

partnership *(PART·ner·ship)*

preferred stock *(pre·FERD)*

promoters *(pro·MO·ters)*

S corporation *(kor·por·AY·shun)*

secret partner *(SEE·kret PART·ner)*

shareholders *(SHARE·hold·ers)*

silent partners *(SY·lent PART·ners)*

sole proprietorship *(pro·PRY·e·tor·ship)*

stock certificate *(ser·TIF·i·ket)*

stockholders *(STOK·hold·ers)*

syndicate *(SIN·de·ket)*

ultra vires act *(UL·tra VY·res)*

unlimited liability *(un·LIM·i·ted ly·a·BIL·i·tee)*

winding-up period *(WINE·ding-up PEER·ee·ed)*

9

T he principal kinds of business organizations are the sole proprietorship, partnership, corporation, and limited liability company. Joint ventures and franchises are also commonly used.

SOLE PROPRIETORSHIP

A **sole proprietorship** is a form of business that is owned and controlled by one person. Because a corporation can be owned by one shareholder, it is important to think of a sole proprietorship as a one-owner unincorporated business. It is the least formal type of business organization, having few requirements for its establishment and being subject to less government regulation than more elaborate forms of business ownership. Everything from a lemonade stand in the front yard to a lawyer practicing law without any other law partners can qualify as a sole proprietorship.

The sole proprietor owns and controls the business, although a sole proprietor can hire employees and outside business consultants. Unlike a partnership (to be discussed later), the employees are not owners. A sole proprietor receives all profits and incurs all losses, and is taxed personally on business profits. Single taxation is one of the historical advantages of an unincorporated business such as a sole proprietorship. In contrast, corporations are subject to double taxation: corporate taxes for the corporate income, and if the net income is then paid to the shareholders as dividends, the shareholders must pay personal income taxes on that income. Double taxation is discussed later in this chapter in the section on corporations. The biggest disadvantage of a sole proprietorship is that the proprietor has **unlimited liability** for all debts and liabilities incurred from its operation, which means that the proprietor is personally liable for every debt and judgment against the business, no matter how large. Unlimited liability is liability without bounds. A sole proprietorship comes to an end at the owner's death, but the business assets can pass to the proprietor's heirs.

PARTNERSHIPS

A **partnership**, sometimes called a **co-partnership**, is an association of two or more persons for the purpose of carrying on as co-owners in a business for profit. It may be created by an oral or written agreement of the parties, by an informal arrangement between them, or by their

9

conduct. Simply doing business together with another person is enough to create a partnership whether or not the parties intend such a result. Partnership law is based on either the Uniform Partnership Act (UPA), which was adopted by every state except Louisiana, or the Revised Uniform Partnership Act (RUPA), which has been enacted in approximately 35 states. The significance of the existence of these laws is that a state's version of the UPA or RUPA will control what happens in partnership matters (between the partners), unless the partners have a written partnership agreement that covers those issues.

A **general partnership** is one in which the parties carry on a business for the joint benefit and profit of all partners. In this type of partnership, every partner is an agent of the partnership for business purposes, which means that every general partner has equal management authority. Similarly, every partner is personally liable for the debts and wrongdoings caused by every other partner while transacting partnership business. This is known as unlimited liability, and is the principal disadvantage of a partnership. For instance, if a partner is out of town when the other partner commits negligence while working on partnership business, both partners are personally liable.

A **limited partnership** is a partnership formed by two or more persons and having as members one or more general partners and one or more limited partners. **General partners** manage the business and are personally liable for its debts and obligations. **Limited partners** invest money or other property in the business, but are not liable for the debts or obligations of the partnership. Their liability is limited to the extent of their financial investments. They may not participate in the operation of the business (or else they risk losing their limited liability status), and the surname of a limited partner may not be used in the partnership name unless it is also the name of a general partner.

Word Wise
Hyphenated Words

A hyphen is often used to join two words to form a compound word. Some words join together to describe a noun, as in "well-known actress," "winding-up period," "English-speaking people," and "blue-sky laws."

A hyphen usually separates a prefix from a capital letter, as in "un-American" or "non-European." Some prefixes, such as "self-," "all-," and "ex-," always require hyphens, as in "self-control," "all-inclusive," and "ex-parte foreign divorce."

A hyphen facilitates reading when the same vowels appear together, as in "de-emphasize" (rather than "deemphasize") and helps to clarify meaning when a prefix causes confusion, as in the homonymous "recreation" (a pleasurable activity) and "re-creation" (a new creation).

There is a type of partnership that removes the aspect of unlimited liability—the chief disadvantage of a general partnership. This is the **limited liability partnership (LLP)**, sometimes called a *registered limited liability partnership (RLLP),* a general partnership in which only the partnership as a whole, and not the individual partners, is liable for the *tort* liabilities of the partnership. In some states, only the partnership as a whole, and not the individual partners, is liable for the *contractual* liabilities of the partnership as well. The limited liability partnership is established by filing a simple registration form and paying a filing fee to the appropriate state office. The combination of a limited partnership and a limited liability partnership is called a **limited liability limited partnership (LLLP)**.

Nominal partners, also called **ostensible partners**, are partners in name only. Their names appear in some way in connection with the business in order to make it appear that they are partners, but they have no real interest in the partnership. **Silent partners** are ones who may be known to the public as partners, but who take no active part in the business. **Dormant partners** are not known to the public as partners and take no active part in the business. **Secret partners** take an active part in the business, but are not known to the public as partners.

Partnerships do not last forever and begin to end when **dissolution** occurs. Dissolution is an act or occurrence that requires the partnership to eventually terminate. For example, the UPA states that when any partner dies, the partnership goes into dissolution. When a partnership is dissolved, a **winding-up period** first occurs. During this time, the partnership assets are **liquidated** (turned into cash), debts are paid, an accounting is made, and any remaining assets are distributed among the partners or the heirs of deceased partners according to the terms of the partnership agreement. At the conclusion of the winding-up period, the partnership is said to be terminated.

Partners cannot transfer their interest in the partnership to other people without the consent of all other partners. In addition, any partner may end a partnership at any time by withdrawing from it. Under the Revised Uniform Partnership Act, the withdrawal of a partner (called a *dissociation*) often results in a buyout of the withdrawing partner's interest rather than a winding up of the entire business.

TERMS IN ACTION

Some of the biggest publicly traded **corporations** in America began as **partnerships**. The movie studio Warner Bros. was formed by four brothers, Sam, Jack, Albert, and Harry Warner, who were Polish Jews. They revolutionized the film industry when they released "The Jazz Singer" in 1927, the first movie with live talking (called a "talkie"). Computer giant Hewlett-Packard is the offspring of the partnership of Bill Hewlett and David Packard, who began working part-time out of a rented garage, making sound equipment. They eventually formed a partnership in 1939, flipping a coin to determine whose name would be first. But later they transformed their partnership into a corporation, which was first listed on the New York Stock Exchange in 1961. Before Ray Krok bought the entire McDonald's business for $2.7 million in 1961, it was a fast-food **franchise** created by Richard and Maurice McDonald in 1948. Ice cream favorite Ben & Jerry's is now owned by Unilever. But it began when Ben Cohen and Jerry Greenfield, who met in the seventh grade, opened their first ice cream shop in Vermont in 1978. That venture cost them $12,000, and their ice cream shop was a former gasoline station. Although Bill Gates is whom one naturally thinks of when it comes to Microsoft, he co-founded that original partnership with Paul Allen, who first met Gates in 1968 at the private school in Seattle they both attended. Fittingly, Apple wasn't started just by Steve Jobs. His partner was Steve Wozniak, whom Jobs met in the early 1970s through Wozniak's employment—at Hewlett-Packard.

Source: images.businessweek.com

CORPORATIONS

A **corporation** is a legal entity, created under state law, with the power to conduct its affairs as though it were a person. It comes into existence when the state government issues a **certificate of incorporation** (sometimes called **articles of incorporation** or **charter**), which is applied for by one or more persons known as **incorporators**. **Promoters** are people who are used sometimes to begin a corporation by obtaining investors and taking control up to the time of the corporation's existence.

When a corporation is established in strict compliance with the law, it is called a **de jure corporation**. In contrast, if a technical defect in its establishment occurs, it is called a **de facto corporation**. It exists in fact, although not by right, and it must be recognized as a valid corporation unless set aside by the state. Any corporate act done outside of the corporation's authority as set forth in its charter is called an **ultra vires act** and can be challenged by a stockholder or other affected party. For example, if a corporation's bylaws state that the chief executive officer (CEO) may not be paid more than 15 times the salary or wages of the lowest-paid employee, then the corporation would be engaged in an ultra vires act if it hired a new CEO and paid him or her a salary 20 times that of the lowest-paid employee. A corporation that is created for charitable and benevolent purposes is known as an **eleemosynary corporation**, or, more commonly, a **not-for-profit corporation**. A **domestic corporation** is organized in the state in which it is operating. In contrast, a **foreign corporation** is organized in a state other than that in which it is operating.

A corporation is owned by **stockholders** (also called **shareholders**). They are not personally responsible for the debts and liabilities of the corporation and can lose only their investment in the company's shares, in a worst-case scenario of the corporation ending in bankruptcy. This rule of law is a principal advantage of the corporate form of business organization. When stockholders die, their shares of stock pass to their heirs and the corporation continues in existence. Shares of stock may be sold or given away to other people by stockholders at any time unless the corporation is a **close corporation**, which has restrictions on the transfer of shares. In a close corporation, a stockholder who wishes to sell stock to someone else must first offer to sell it to the corporation. In this way, the ownership of the corporation can be kept within a limited group of people.

Because the income that a corporation earns is taxed directly by the federal government, and because dividends earned by stockholders are also taxed, corporate income is taxed twice, a process referred to as **double taxation**. A corporation that is taxed in this manner is called a **C corporation**, a corporation governed by Subchapter C of the Internal Revenue Code. To avoid double taxation, small corporations can elect to be treated as S corporations. An **S corporation** is governed by Subchapter S of the Internal Revenue Code, which stipulates that the income of the corporation will be taxed directly to the shareholders rather than to the corporation itself.

Each stockholder is issued a **stock certificate**, which evidences ownership of stock in the corporation. **Common stock** is voting stock with no preferences. Common stockholders have the right to vote, the right to receive profits (called **dividends**) if they are declared by the board of directors, and the right to receive a proportionate share of capital when the corporation is dissolved. **Preferred stock** is stock that has a superior right to dividends and to capital when the corporation is dissolved. Preferred stockholders usually have no voting rights.

Members of the Board of Directors are elected by the shareholders at their annual meeting. **Directors** are given legal responsibility to manage the corporation in the best interests of the shareholders. Officers, including a president, clerk, and treasurer, are appointed by the board of directors and are responsible for the daily operation of the corporate business.

When directors refuse to bring a lawsuit, on behalf of the corporation against a third party, to which it is entitled, a stockholder can bring a derivative action to enforce the right of the corporation. A **derivative action** is a suit by a stockholder to enforce a corporate cause of action. If a shareholder wins the derivative action, the damages are paid back to the corporation, not to the shareholders personally.

The sale of stock of corporations over a certain size is regulated by both state and federal laws. State laws designed to protect the public from the sale of worthless stocks are known as **blue-sky laws**.

▌ TERMS IN ACTION

Shareholders of the Disney Corporation sued the Disney **Board of Directors** in 2004, seeking $260 million in a **derivative action**. At the heart of the lawsuit was the allegation that the board members were negligent in their duty to the shareholders when, in 1995, the board approved of a $140 million-dollar severance payment to President Michael Ovitz, who had been fired by CEO Michael Eisner, after just 14 months of working for Eisner. When he hired Ovitz, Eisner referred to him as "my best friend," but a little over a year later, Eisner concluded that Ovitz had to go. Ovitz's contract called for that gigantic payment to be made if he was fired, and the shareholders claimed that by failing to carefully inspect Ovitz's employment contract before approving it, the board was liable for this error and should have to pay that money back to the corporation (rather than to the shareholders, personally), which is the purposes of a derivative action. The suit was filed in the Delaware Court of Chancery in 1997, and in 2005 the judge dismissed it. He concluded that the directors (which included Michael Eisner, who was the Chairman of the Disney Board) didn't violate their fiduciary duty to the shareholder and were protected by a doctrine known as the business judgment rule. But the judge didn't exactly praise the board for its actions, either, writing that the board's conduct "fell significantly short of the best practices of ideal corporate governance."

Sources: cfo.com; *In re Walt Disney Co. Derivative Action*, 907 A.2d 693 (Del.Ch. 2005)

LIMITED LIABILITY COMPANY

A relatively new type of business organization has developed in recent years that is neither a partnership nor a corporation, but that combines some aspects of both. A **limited liability company (LLC)** is a nonpartnership form of business organization that has the tax benefits of a partnership and the limited liability benefits of a corporation. Owners of a limited liability company are called **members**. Rather than having articles of incorporation, an LLC has **articles of organization**, and rather than having bylaws, a limited liability company has an **operating agreement**, which sets forth the rights and obligations of the members and establishes the rules of operation. In place of officers to run the company, the LLC is managed either by its members or by **managers**, people designated by the members to manage the LLC. Like stockholders of a corporation, members of an LLC are not liable for the contractual or tort liabilities of the business. A limited liability company is established by filing articles of organization with the Secretary of State's office and paying a filing fee.

JOINT VENTURE

A **joint venture**, also called a **joint enterprise**, **co-venture**, or **syndicate**, is an enterprise relationship in which two or more people combine their labor or property for a single business undertaking. It differs from a partnership in that it involves only one undertaking and comes to an end at the completion of the undertaking. Like partners, joint venturers have unlimited liability. Each is responsible for the others' wrongdoings conducted within the scope of the joint venture.

FRANCHISE

A **franchise** is an arrangement in which the owner of a trademark, trade name, or copyright licenses others, under special conditions or limitations, to use the trademark, trade name, or copyright in purveying goods and/or services. Many fast-food chains use the franchise method of conducting business. The **franchiser** (person who gives a franchise to another) and the **franchisee** (person to whom a franchise is given) are considered to be independent contractors, and their respective rights and duties are governed by the contract between them as regulated by state and federal laws.

Reviewing What You Learned

After studying the chapter, write the answers to each of the following questions:

1. Describe what happens to a sole proprietorship when the owner dies.

2. In what ways may a partnership be created?

3. What is the principal disadvantage of a partnership?

4. What is the difference between a general partner and a limited partner?

5. In what ways do silent partners, dormant partners, and secret partners differ?_____

_____

_____

_____

6. Describe the procedure that occurs when a partnership is dissolved. _____

_____

_____

_____

7. Under what conditions does a corporation come into existence?

_____

_____

_____

_____

8. What is a principal advantage of the corporate form of business organization? _____

_____

_____

_____

_____

9. Compare what happens to a corporation when a stockholder dies with what happens to a partnership when a partner dies.__

_____

_____

_____

10. In a close corporation, what must a stockholder do before selling stock to someone else?_____

_____

_____

_____

11. What is the difference between common stock and preferred stock? _____

_____

_____

_____

_____

_____

12. Compare the duties of the directors of a corporation with the duties of the officers of a corporation._____

_____

_____

_____

_____

13. How does a joint venture differ from a partnership?_____

_____

_____

_____

_____

Understanding Legal Concepts

Indicate whether each statement is true or false. Then, change the italicized word or phrase of each false *statement to make it true.*

ANSWERS

_____ 1. A sole proprietorship is the *most* formal type of business organization.

_____ 2. A partnership *may only be* created by a written agreement.

_____ 3. In a general partnership, *every partner* is an agent of the partnership for business purposes.

_____ 4. Limited partners *are liable* for the debts or obligations of the partnership.

_____ 6. Dormant partners take *an active* part in the business and are not known to the public as partners.

_____ 6. When a corporation is established in strict compliance with the law, it is called a *de facto* corporation.

_____ 7. Stockholders of a corporation *are not* personally responsible for the debts and liabilities of the corporation and can lose only the amount they paid for the stock.

_____ 8. *Preferred* stockholders usually have no voting rights.

_____ 9. A joint venture differs from a *partnership* in that it involves only one undertaking and comes to an end at the completion of the undertaking.

_____ 10. Franchisers and franchisees are considered to be *independent contractors.*

Checking Terminology (Part A)

From the list of legal terms that follows, select the one that matches each definition.

ANSWERS

a. articles of organization
b. article of incorporation
c. blue-sky laws
d. C corporation
e. certificate of incorporation
f. charter
g. close corporation
h. common stock co-partnership
i. corporation
j. co-venture
k. de facto corporation
l. de jure corporation
m. derivative action
n. directors
o. dividends
p. domestic corporation
q. dormant partner
r. double taxation
s. eleemosynary corporation
t. foreign corporation
u. franchise
v. franchisee
w. franchiser
x. general partner
y. general partnership
z. incorporators
aa. joint enterprise
bb. joint venture
cc. not-for-profit corporation
dd. syndicate

_____ 1. Profits distributed to the stockholders of a corporation.
_____ 2. An arrangement in which the owner of a trademark, trade name, or copyright licenses others, under special conditions or limitations, to use the trademark, trade name, or copyright in purveying goods or services.
_____ 3. A legal entity created under state law with the power to conduct its affairs as though it were a natural person.
_____ 4. A person who gives a franchise to another.
_____ 5. A document that gives authority to an organization to do business as a corporation. (Select three answers.)
_____ 6. Taxes on a corporation's income and on the dividends earned by the corporation's stockholders.
_____ 7. People who are elected by stockholders to manage a corporation.
_____ 8. A corporation organized in a state other than the one in which it is operating.
_____ 9. People who organize a corporation by filing articles of organization with the state government.
_____ 10. State laws designed to protect the public from the sale of worthless stocks.
_____ 11. A partner who manages the business and is personally liable for its debts and obligations.
_____ 12. A partner who is not known to the public as a partner and who takes no active part in the business.
_____ 13. A corporation that is established in strict compliance with the law.
_____ 14. An enterprise relationship in which two or more people combine their labor or property for a single business undertaking. (Select four answers.)
_____ 15. A corporation that is governed by Subchapter C of the Internal Revenue Code and that pays corporate taxes on its income.
_____ 16. A partnership in which the parties carry on a business for the joint benefit and profit of all partners.
_____ 17. A corporation that is created for charitable and benevolent purposes. (Select two answers.)
_____ 18. A corporation that has a defect in its establishment, but that must be recognized as a valid corporation unless set aside by the state.
_____ 19. A corporation that has restrictions on the transfer of shares.
_____ 20. A corporation that was organized in the state in which it is operating.
_____ 21. Stock that has no preferences, but that gives the owner the right to vote.
_____ 22. A suit by a stockholder to enforce a corporate cause of action.

Checking Terminology (Part B)

From the list of legal terms that follows, select the one that matches each definition.

ANSWERS

a. co-partnership
b. dissolution
c. limited liability company (LLC)
d. limited liability limited partnership (LLLP)
e. limited liability partnership (LLP)
f. limited partner
g. limited partnership
h. liquidate

_____ 1. Stock that has a superior right to dividends and capital when the corporation is dissolved.
_____ 2. A partner in name only, who has no real interest in the partnership. (Select two answers.)
_____ 3. A form of business that is owned and operated by one person.
_____ 4. A general partnership in which only the partnership, and not the individual partners, is liable for the tort liabilities of the partnership.
_____ 5. People who are designated by its members to manage a limited liability company.
_____ 6. A partner who takes an active part in the business, but is not known to the public as a partner.
_____ 7. A partner who invests money or other property in the business, but who is not liable for the debts or obligations of the partnership.

i. managers
j. members
k. nominal partner
l. operating agreement
m. ostensible partner
n. partnership
o. preferred stock
p. promoters
q. S corporation
r. secret partner
s. shareholders
t. silent partner
u. sole proprietorship
v. stock certificate
w. stockholders
x. ultra vires act
y. unlimited liability
z. winding-up period

_____ 8. Liability that has no bounds.

_____ 9. A document that evidences ownership of stock in a corporation.

_____ 10. An association of two or more persons to carry on as co-owners a business for profit. (Select two answers.)

_____ 11. Partners who may be known to the public as partners, but who take no active part in the business.

_____ 12. A corporation governed by Subchapter S of the Internal Revenue Code and in which the income of the corporation is taxed directly to the shareholders rather than to the corporation itself.

_____ 13. Turn into cash.

_____ 14. A partnership formed by two or more persons, and having as members one or more general partners and one or more limited partners.

_____ 15. Owners of a limited liability company.

_____ 16. A period during which partnership assets are liquidated, debts are paid, an accounting is made, and any remaining assets are distributed among the partners.

_____ 17. People who own shares in a corporation. (Select two answers.)

_____ 18. A nonpartnership form of business organization that has the tax benefits of a partnership and the limited liability benefits of a corporation.

_____ 19. A corporate act committed outside of the corporation's authority.

_____ 20. An agreement that sets forth the rights and obligations of the members and establishes the rules for operating a limited liability company.

_____ 21. People who begin a corporation by obtaining investors and taking charge up to the time of the corporation's existence.

_____ 22. An act or occurrence that requires the partnership to eventually terminate.

Sharpening Your Latin Skills

In the space provided, write the definition of each of the following legal terms, referring to the glossary when necessary:

de facto_____

de jure_____

ex parte_____

pendente lite_____

ultra vires_____

Using Legal Language

Read the following story and fill in the blank lines with legal terms taken from the list of terms at the beginning of this chapter:

Julio and Juan became good friends while working for the Señor Tacos restaurant chain. The chain used a(n) _____ method of operation, because its owner licensed others to use its trade name in making and selling tacos. Julio and Juan worked under the direction of Carmen, the _____, who had the license to operate the business, given to her by Señor Tacos, the _____. Every evening after work, Julio and Juan spent their time together inventing a greaseless taco fryer. Because this relationship involved two people com-

bining their labor and property for a single business undertaking, it was known as a(n) _____, which is also called a(n) _____, a(n) _____, or a(n) _____. When the fryer was completed, Juan left his job with Carmen and opened a taco shop of his own. It was a(n) _____, because Juan owned and operated it himself. The business thrived, and although he had no further money to invest, Juan felt it necessary to expand. His friend Julio offered to invest money in the business, but did not want to be liable for its debts or obligations. The two formed a(n) _____, making Juan a(n) _____ partner and Julio a(n) _____ partner. Because she was well-known in the trade, Carmen lent her name to the business, but because she had no real interest in it, she was a(n) _____ or _____ partner. Soon it became necessary to expand again, and Juan and Julio decided to establish a(n) _____, which is a legal entity created under state law with the power to conduct its affairs as though it were a natural person. Juan and Julio were the _____, because they applied for the _____,

which is also called _____ or _____. The organization was established in strict compliance with the law; therefore, it was a(n) _____. Miguel, a friend of Juan and Julio, invested in the business, and all three became _____, which are also known as _____. Because restrictions were placed on the transfer of shares, the business was a(n) _____. Miguel, Juan, and Julio received _____ as evidence of their ownership in the business. The stock they received was _____, which had no preferences and gave each owner the right to vote. All three were elected as _____ to manage the business.

PUZZLING OVER WHAT YOU LEARNED

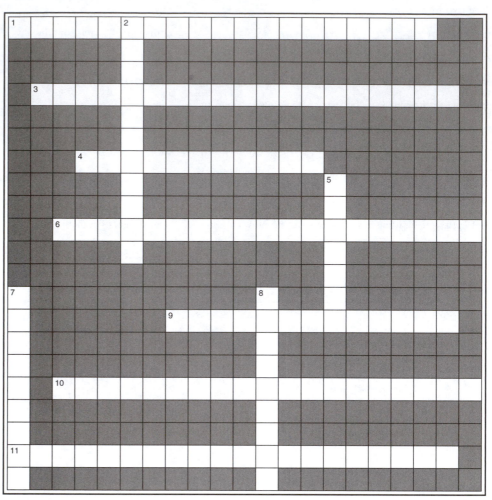

Caveat: Allow squares for spaces between words and punctuation (apostrophes, hyphens, etc.) when filling in crossword.

Across

1. A form of business that is owned and operated by one person.
3. Partnership with one or more general partners and one or more limited partners.
4. Legal entity created under state law with powers of a natural person.
6. Liability that has no bounds.
9. People who organize a corporation.
10. Corporation that is established in compliance with the law.
11. Corporation with a defect in its establishment but recognized as valid.

Down

2. Association of two or more persons to carry on a business.
5. Document that gives authority to a corporation to do business.
7. Profits distributed to the stockholders of a corporation.
8. People who begin a corporation by obtaining investors.

CHAPTER

40

The Law of Bankruptcy

ANTE INTERROGATORY

Chapter 7 bankruptcy is also called (A) involuntary bankruptcy, (B) reorganization, (C) liquidation, (D) homestead exemption.

9

CHAPTER OUTLINE

Goals of Bankruptcy Code
Types of Bankruptcy Proceedings

Chapter 7 Bankruptcy
Chapter 11 Bankruptcy
Chapter 12 Bankruptcy
Chapter 13 Bankruptcy

KEY TERMS

assets *(ASS·ets)*

automatic stay *(aw·toh·MAT·ic)*

automatic suspension *(aw·toh·MAT·ic sus·PEN·shun)*

bankrupt *(BANK·rupt)*

bankruptcy *(BANK·rupt·see)*

Bankruptcy Abuse Prevention and Consumer Protection Act of 2005 (BAPCA)

Chapter 7 bankruptcy *(BANK·rupt·see)*

Chapter 11 bankruptcy *(BANK·rupt·see)*

Chapter 12 bankruptcy *(BANK·rupt·see)*

Chapter 13 bankruptcy *(BANK·rupt·see)*

claim

creditors *(KRED·et·ers)*

debtor *(DET·er)*

debtor-in-possession *(DET·er in po·SESH·en)*

discharge in bankruptcy *(DIS·charj in BANK·rupt·see)*

exemptions *(eg·ZEMP·shuns)*

homestead exemption *(HOME·sted eg·ZEMP·shun)*

involuntary bankruptcy *(in·VOL·en·ter·ee BANK·rupt·see)*

liquidate *(LIK·wi·date)*

liquidation *(lik·wi·DAY·shun)*

means testing

order for relief *(re·LEEF)*

preferences *(PREF·er·en·ses)*

proof of claim

prorated *(PRO·rate·ed)*

reorganization *(re·or·ge·ni·ZAY·shun)*

secured creditors *(se·KYOORD KRED·et·ers)*

straight bankruptcy *(strayt BANK·rupt·see)*

trustee in bankruptcy *(trus·TEE in BANK·rupt·see)*

voluntary bankruptcy *(VOL·en·ter·ee BANK·rupt·see)*

wage earner's plan *(wayj ER·ners)*

One of the express powers that Article I of the U.S. Constitution grants to Congress is the power to make bankruptcy laws. Although bankruptcy has been a societal problem for centuries, the United States Bankruptcy Code attempts to give debtors a fresh start (as opposed to a term in debtor's prison) by providing debt relief, while giving creditors an opportunity to collect some portion of the debts owed to them by bankrupt debtors. Bankruptcy is administered by U.S. Bankruptcy Courts, which have exclusive jurisdiction over bankruptcy cases. Bankruptcy courts are attached to district courts within the federal court system. Each state and territory in the United States has at least one federal district court within its boundaries.

In 2005, the U.S. Congress made sweeping changes to the Bankruptcy Code, with the passage of the **Bankruptcy Abuse Prevention and Consumer Protection Act** (BAPCA). Among its many attributes, BAPCA makes it more difficult for people to declare bankruptcy and extends the time between repeat bankruptcy filings. The discussion that follows highlights some of the changes brought by the 2005 bankruptcy code amendments.

GOALS OF THE BANKRUPTCY CODE

The goals of the Bankruptcy Code are twofold: (1) to convert the debtor's property into cash and distribute it among **creditors** (people to whom money is owed), and (2) to give the debtor a fresh start by leaving some of his or her **assets** (property) untouched. **Bankruptcy** is the legal process by which the assets of a debtor are sold to pay off creditors so that the debtor can make a fresh start financially. **Bankrupt** means the state of a person (including a business) who is unable to pay debts as they become due. The state of being bankrupt is not about having more debts than assets on a balance sheet; it is about having insufficient cash flow to pay off one's debts. The term **debtor** (one who owes a debt to another) is used in place of the term *bankrupt* in the Bankruptcy Code.

TYPES OF BANKRUPTCY PROCEEDINGS

There are five principal types of bankruptcy proceedings, and they are named after the respective chapter in the Federal Bankruptcy Code in which they are found: Chapter 7 (liquidation), Chapter 9 (municipalities), Chapter 11 (business reorganization), Chapter 12 (family farmers), and Chapter 13 (adjustment of debts of individuals).

Chapter 7 Bankruptcy

Chapter 7 bankruptcy, also called **liquidation** or **straight bankruptcy**, is a proceeding designed to **liquidate** (convert to cash) a debtor's property, pay off creditors, and discharge the debtor from most debts. A Chapter 7 bankruptcy may be either voluntary or involuntary. Businesses may "file Chapter 7" when they go out of business, but the emphasis in this section will focus on nonbusiness debtors in Chapter 7 bankruptcy.

> **Word Wise**
> *"Bankrupt" Replaced by "Debtor"*
>
> A person who files for bankruptcy under today's law is called a "debtor." This is a change from earlier law, under which a person who filed for bankruptcy was referred to as "the bankrupt." In 1978, Congress passed the Bankruptcy Reform Act with the aim of giving debtors who are overwhelmed with debt a fresh start. Congress also wanted to reduce the stigma connected with the term "bankrupt" and did so by eliminating the term from the law and replacing it with the word "debtor."

VOLUNTARY BANKRUPTCY.   **Voluntary bankruptcy** is a bankruptcy proceeding that is initiated by the debtor. To be eligible to file for this type of bankruptcy, debtors must

1. satisfy the *means test;* which is explained below.
2. meet with an approved nonprofit credit counselor before filing for bankruptcy;

3. furnish a federal income tax return for the most recent tax year; and
4. take a course in financial management after filing for bankruptcy.

When a debtor files a voluntary bankruptcy petition with the court, an **order for relief** (the acceptance of the case by the bankruptcy court) automatically takes place. At that time, an automatic stay goes into effect. An **automatic stay** (also called an **automatic suspension**) is a self-operating postponement of collection proceedings against the debtor. Creditors must stop all efforts to collect debts except for debts caused by fraud, amounts owed for back taxes, family support, and student loans that do not impose a hardship on the debtor. Creditors, such as credit card companies and lenders of unsecured revolving loans, cannot bring suit for what is owed them. Debit cards can no longer be used, because any money in the debtor's bank belongs automatically to the bankruptcy trustee.

INVOLUNTARY BANKRUPTCY.   **Involuntary bankruptcy** is a bankruptcy proceeding that is initiated by one or more creditors. When there are less than 12 creditors, a single creditor who is owed more than $13,475 may file an involuntary bankruptcy petition. However, when there are 12 or more creditors, at least 3 of them must join in the bankruptcy petition, and the total debt must exceed $13,475. The debtor has 20 days to file an objection in an involuntary case, and if this is done, a hearing is held to determine whether an order for relief will be issued.

MEANS TESTING.   Perhaps the most significant change in the bankruptcy code is that a debtor must meet the eligibility requirements to be in Chapter 7. That involves the debtor's taking an average of his or her income six months prior to filing and multiplying that times 12 (for an estimated annual income). If two spouses file a joint petition, their combined incomes are used. For means testing purposes, income is broader than taxable income. Then, the debtor compares that number with the median annual income of the debtor's state (according to the U.S. Census Bureau), and factors in family size.

If the debtor's average is above the state median, then a second **means test** must be performed. This is a more detailed comparison between the debtor's aggregate current monthly income over a five-year period (less certain statutorily allowed deductions) to a threshold amount. If the debtor's disposable income is above that threshold, the debtor is presumed to be ineligible for Chapter 7. (This ineligibility is known as a presumption of abuse.) Unless the debtor can overcome that presumption by showing special circumstances that make the initial calculations unreliable, the debtor will need to file a Chapter 13 bankruptcy.

TERMS IN ACTION

Means testing is the most significant change in the 2005 amendments to the Bankruptcy Code. Whether a debtor can be in Chapter 7's liquidation bankruptcy or, instead, has to be in Chapter 13's reorganization bankruptcy is largely determined by means testing. The correct forms can be found on the Department of Justice's website, and many bankruptcy-related websites offer means testing calculators. Chapter 13 also uses a similar means test, to determine how much disposable income the petitioner has available to pay back a portion of his or her debts to the **creditors**. In 2011, the U.S. Supreme Court issued a ruling on Chapter 13's means testing, concluding that debtors who own their cars outright may not claim an "ownership deduction" for the cost of maintaining and fixing their cars (for means testing purposes), whereas those who still are making loan or lease payments on their cars may take the deduction for those payments.

Sources: justice.gov; *Ransom v. MBNA*, 562 U.S. ___ (2011)

EXEMPTIONS.   As part of the "fresh start" policy of the Bankruptcy Code, some items of property, referred to as **exemptions**, are excepted from bankruptcy proceedings and may be retained by the debtor. Each state has its own list of exemptions. The Federal Bankruptcy Code also has a list of exemptions. The Bankruptcy Code allows states to decide whether their debtors will use the federal exemptions or, instead, the state-granted exemptions. Many states require that their state exemptions be taken rather than the federal exemptions. In other states, however, debtors may choose to take either the state or the federal exemptions. The 2005 Bankruptcy Code, nevertheless, requires that a debtor be domiciled in a state for two years for that state's exemption rules to apply.

The **homestead exemption** is the exemption from bankruptcy of one's residence up to a certain amount depending on state or federal law. Except for family farmers, the 2005 Bankruptcy Code limits a state homestead exemption to $125,000 if the property was acquired within the previous 40 months from the bankruptcy filing. For example, if a debtor files bankruptcy in a state that allows its filers a homestead exemption of up to $150,000, and the debtor's home is worth $175,000, the debtor may use only the $125,000 exemption, because of the federal cap on state homestead exemptions.

State bankruptcy exemptions are too varied to list here, but a sampling of the federal exemptions include the following:

- the homestead exemption to the extent of $21,625 (unless the state exemption applies, as described previously)
- a motor vehicle: $3,450
- household furnishings and personal apparel: $475 per item and $11,525 total
- jewelry: $1,450
- tools of the trade: $2,175
- unmatured life insurance policies: $11,525
- personal injury lawsuit awards: $21,625
- Individual Retirement Account (IRA): $1,171,650.

According to recent amendments to the Bankruptcy Code, these exemptions are adjusted for inflation every three years, and the exemptions outlined here were effective to bankruptcies filed on or after April 1, 2010.

TRUSTEE IN BANKRUPTCY.   When bankruptcy proceedings begin, the court appoints a person, called a **trustee in bankruptcy**, to hold the debtor's nonexempt assets in trust for the benefit of creditors. The trustee's duties are to collect the debtor's property and, with the exception of items that the law allows the debtor to keep, convert it to cash and pay the creditors according to certain priorities established by law. Among other things, the trustee has the power to invalidate **preferences**—that is, transfers made by the debtor to creditors before the bankruptcy proceeding—enabling them to receive a greater percentage of their claim than they would have otherwise received.

Among the papers filed by the debtor in a bankruptcy proceeding are a list of assets, as well as a list of creditors and the amount owed to each. The court notifies the creditors of the time and place of the first meeting of creditors. At this meeting, which usually takes place approximately a month after the petition is filed, the creditors are given an opportunity to question the debtor under oath. The court also notifies creditors that they must file, within 90 days after the first meeting, a **proof of claim**, which is a written, signed statement setting forth a creditor's claim together with the basis for it. A **claim** is a right to payment or other equitable right, such as the right to receive specific performance of a contract.

Once the debtor's property is collected by the trustee and liquidated, the proceeds are distributed to creditors with allowable claims. **Secured creditors** (those who hold mortgages and other liens) receive payment to the exclusion of other creditors. After they are paid, the remaining nonexempt assets are used to pay administrative expenses and unsecured creditors according to a priority list established by the Bankruptcy Code. Normally, there is not enough to pay unsecured creditors in full, so their shares are **prorated**—that is, divided proportionately. A **discharge in bankruptcy** releases the debtor from all debts that were proved in the bankruptcy proceeding.

Debtors who file under Chapter 7 must wait at least eight years before filing for bankruptcy again. Before the 2005 BAPCA, there was a six-year waiting period between Chapter 7 filings. The filing fee for a Chapter 7 bankruptcy petition is $299.

Chapter 11 Bankruptcy

Chapter 11 bankruptcy, also called **reorganization**, provides a method for businesses to reorganize their financial affairs, keep their assets, and remain in business—although Chapter 11 is not limited exclusively to businesses. Because the business continues to operate, the debtor in a Chapter 11 bankruptcy case is referred to as a **debtor-in-possession**. Performing the function of a trustee, the debtor develops a reorganization plan, setting forth a method of repaying debts and separating creditors into various classes. To be acceptable by the court, the plan must be feasible and must be approved by over half of the creditors in each class. Like Chapter 7, a Chapter 11 bankruptcy may be either voluntary or involuntary. The filing fee for a Chapter 11 bankruptcy petition is $1,039.

TERMS IN ACTION

For millions of Americans, **bankruptcy** is the result of job loss, unforeseen medical bills, or business failure. But for millions of others, it is the consequence of poor money management and overspending. Even the brilliant third President of the United States, Thomas Jefferson, filed bankruptcy. Also included in that group are more than a few celebrities who, while earning millions of dollars, had a similar financial blind spot. Oscar-award-winning actress Kim Basinger filed **Chapter 11 bankruptcy** in 1993, not long after her career hit some bumpy spots, and after she and other investors bought the town of Braselton, Georgia, for $20 million. *Sports Illustrated* reported in 2009 that 78 percent of all NFL players are bankrupt within two years after retiring, and that 60 percent of all NBA players are broke within five years after retiring. Hall of Fame NBA player Scottie Pippen, who won six championships with Michael Jordan, is reported to have spent most of the $127 million that he made. Former baseball slugger Jack Clark filed **Chapter 7 bankruptcy** in 1992, while in the second year of a three-year $8.7-million contract with the Boston Red Sox. He spent much of his fortune on luxury homes and cars, and at one time had 18 cars and 17 car payments. The king of all sports bankruptcies is Mike Tyson. Despite earning over $400 million from boxing, he filed Chapter 11 bankruptcy in 2003. **Chapter 13 bankruptcy** wasn't an option for Tyson or the other celebrities listed here, because their debts exceeded what is allowed in Chapter 13. At the time of his filing, Tyson listed $27 million in debts. Among other debts, he owed the IRS over $13 million in back taxes, he owed $52,000 in back child support obligations, and he owed a limousine company over $300,000. Tyson was and is an avid lover of pigeons, and those birds cost him a lot of money to maintain, but not as much as the $140,000 that he spent on two Bengal tigers. Pigeons can make a person dirty, which might explain the $2 million bathtub Tyson bought for his first wife.

Sources: variety.com; legalzoom.com; sportsillustrated.cnn.com; nytimes.com; thesmokinggun.com; washingtonpost.com

Web Wise

Congress can change the federal bankruptcy law at any time. Look for information about the latest bankruptcy law at the following sites:

- *www.bankruptcyaction.com*
- *www.moranlaw.net*
- *www.uscourts.gov/FederalCourts/Bankruptcy/BankruptcyResources.aspx*

Chapter 12 Bankruptcy

Chapter 12 bankruptcy provides a method for family farmers and family fishing businesses to adjust their financial affairs while continuing to operate. To qualify, they must receive more than 50 percent of their total income from farming or fishing. Also, if a family farmer, at least 50 percent, and if a family fishing business, at least 80 percent of debt must relate to farming or fishing operations. Total debts may not exceed $3,792,650 for farming or $1,757,475 for fishing. The debtor must develop a reorganization plan, as is required in Chapter 11 bankruptcies, and serve as a debtor-in-possession, performing the functions of a trustee. The filing fee for a Chapter 12 bankruptcy petition is $239.

Chapter 13 Bankruptcy

Chapter 13 bankruptcy provides a method for an individual with regular income to pay debts from future income over an extended period without being hassled by creditors. Debtors who do not qualify for Chapter 7 bankruptcy (discussed earlier) may file for Chapter 13 Bankruptcy. To be eligible, debtors must first meet with an approved nonprofit credit counselor. Their unsecured debts may not exceed $360,475 and their secured debts may not exceed $1,081,400. Debtors must make a good-faith effort to repay their debts. They must submit a plan, sometimes referred to as a **wage earner's plan**, for the installment payments of outstanding debts, including the eventual payment in full of all claims within three to five years. Chapter 13 Bankruptcy is voluntary. Unlike Chapter 7, there is no waiting period before filing for bankruptcy again. The filing fee for a Chapter 13 bankruptcy petition is $274.

Reviewing What You Learned

After studying the chapter, write the answers to each of the following questions:

9

1. What are the goals of the Bankruptcy Code?_____

   _____

   _____

   _____

   _____

2. Under what conditions do bankruptcy proceedings begin?

   _____

   _____

   _____

   _____

3. Under what circumstances may a single creditor file an involuntary bankruptcy petition? _____

   _____

   _____

   _____

   _____

4. Describe the duties of a trustee in bankruptcy. _____

   _____

   _____

   _____

   _____

5. Name some papers filed by a debtor in a bankruptcy proceeding.

   _____

   _____

   _____

   _____

6. How are the proceeds from the sale of a debtor's property distributed?_____

   _____

   _____

   _____

   _____

7. List five exemptions under the Federal Bankruptcy Code.

   _____

   _____

   _____

   _____

8. How does a Chapter 7 bankruptcy differ from a Chapter 11 bankruptcy? _____

   _____

   _____

   _____

9. How does a Chapter 13 bankruptcy differ from a Chapter 11 bankruptcy? _____

_____

_____

_____

10. What is the purpose of a Chapter 12 bankruptcy? _____

_____

_____

_____

Understanding Legal Concepts

Indicate whether each statement is true or false. Then, change the italicized word or phrase of each false statement to make it true.

ANSWERS

_____ 1. Bankruptcy proceedings *end* with the filing of a petition with the federal court.

_____ 2. An order for relief automatically takes place when an *involuntary* bankruptcy petition is filed.

_____ 3. When there are less than 12 creditors, a single creditor who is owed more than *$3,000* may file an involuntary bankruptcy petition.

_____ 4. An *order for relief* brings into play an automatic suspension, preventing further efforts by creditors to collect their debts.

_____ 5. A trustee in bankruptcy has the power, among other things, to *invalidate* preferences.

_____ 6. The court notifies creditors that they must file, within 90 days after the first meeting, a proof of claim.

_____ 7. As part of the *nonstop* policy of the Bankruptcy Code, some items of property are exempt from bankruptcy proceedings.

_____ 8. The federal homestead exemption is one's residence to the extent of *$15,500.*

_____ 9. *Chapter 7* bankruptcy provides a method for businesses to reorganize their financial affairs, keep their assets, and remain in business.

_____ 10. *Chapter 13* bankruptcy provides a method by which an individual with regular income can pay his or her debts from future income over an extended period.

Checking Terminology

From the list of legal terms that follows, select the one that matches each definition.

ANSWERS

a. assets
b. automatic stay
c. automatic suspension
d. bankrupt
e. bankruptcy
f. BAPCA
g. Chapter 7 bankruptcy
h. Chapter 11 bankruptcy
i. Chapter 12 bankruptcy
j. Chapter 13 bankruptcy
k. claim
l. creditors
m. debtor
n. debtor-in-possession
o. discharge in bankruptcy
p. exemptions
q. homestead exemption
r. involuntary bankruptcy
s. liquidate
t. liquidation
u. means testing
v. order for relief

_____ 1. People to whom money is owed.

_____ 2. A right to payment.

_____ 3. The legal process by which the assets of a debtor are sold to pay off creditors so that the debtor can make a fresh start financially.

_____ 4. Items of property that are excepted from bankruptcy proceedings and may be retained by the debtor.

_____ 5. Creditors who hold mortgages and other liens.

_____ 6. A self-operating postponement of collection proceedings against a debtor. (Select two answers.)

_____ 7. A bankruptcy proceeding that is initiated by the debtor.

_____ 8. The state of a person (or a business) of being unable to pay debts as they become due.

_____ 9. A proceeding designed to liquidate a debtor's property, pay off creditors, and discharge the debtor from most debts. (Select three answers.)

_____ 10. Divided proportionately.

_____ 11. A person appointed by a bankruptcy court to hold the debtor's assets in trust for the benefit of creditors.

_____ 12. Convert to cash.

_____ 13. A method for businesses to reorganize their financial affairs, keep their assets, and remain in business. (Select two answers.)

_____ 14. A method for family farmers to adjust their financial affairs while continuing to operate their farms.

_____ 15. Property.

w. preferences
x. proof of claim
y. prorated
z. reorganization
aa. secured creditors
bb. straight bankruptcy
cc. trustee in bankruptcy
dd. voluntary bankruptcy
ee. wage earner's plan

____ 16. A bankruptcy proceeding that is initiated by one or more creditors.

____ 17. One who owes a debt to another.

____ 18. Another name for a debtor in Chapters 11 and 13 cases.

____ 19. Transfers made by a debtor to creditors, before a bankruptcy proceeding, enabling them to receive a greater percentage of their claim than they would have otherwise received.

____ 20. A method by which an individual with regular income can pay his or her debts from future income over an extended period.

____ 21. A plan for the installment payments of outstanding debts under a Chapter 13 bankruptcy.

____ 22. In bankruptcy, the exemption of one's residence to the extent of $16,150.

____ 23. The acceptance of a case by a bankruptcy court.

____ 24. A signed, written statement setting forth a creditor's claim together with the basis for it.

____ 25. A release of a debtor from all debts that were proved in a bankruptcy proceeding.

____ 26. A 2005 change in the Bankruptcy Code, making it more difficult for people to declare bankruptcy and extending the time between repeat bankruptcy filings.

____ 27. A comparison to determine whether a debtor meets the eligibility requirements to be in Chapter 7 or 13.

Using Legal Language

Read the following story and fill in the blank lines with legal terms taken from the list of terms at the beginning of this chapter:

Valerie worked in a law office that specialized in _____—that is, the legal process by which the assets of a(n) _____ (one who owes a debt to another) are sold to pay off _____ (people to whom money is owed) so that a fresh start can be made financially. Mr. Rodham, a client, had just left, and Attorney Jones had instructed Valerie to prepare the papers for a(n) _____ bankruptcy, which is also called _____ or _____, and is designed to _____(covert to cash) Mr. Rodham's property, pay off his debts, and discharge him from most debts. Since the petition will be filed by Mr. Rodham, this will be a(n) _____ case, and a(n) _____ will automatically take place. When the petition is filed, a(n) _____, also called a(n) _____ _____, occurs, which is a self-operating post-ponement of collection proceedings against the debtor. A(n) _____ will hold Mr. Rodham's assets in trust for the benefit of creditors, some of whom may receive a(n) _____share—one that is divided proportionately. Creditors will be required to file a(n) _____ within 90 days after their first meeting. The holder of the mortgage on Mr. Rodham's house is known as a(n) _____ and will receive payment to the exclusion of other creditors. Any _____ (earlier transfers resulting in greater percentages to some creditors) that may have occurred will be invalidated. Because of the so-called _____, Mr. Rodham may be able to retain an interest in his residence to the extent of $16,150. When the case is finalized, Mr. Rodham will receive a(n) _____—that is, a release from all debts that were proved in the proceeding.

PUZZLING OVER WHAT YOU LEARNED

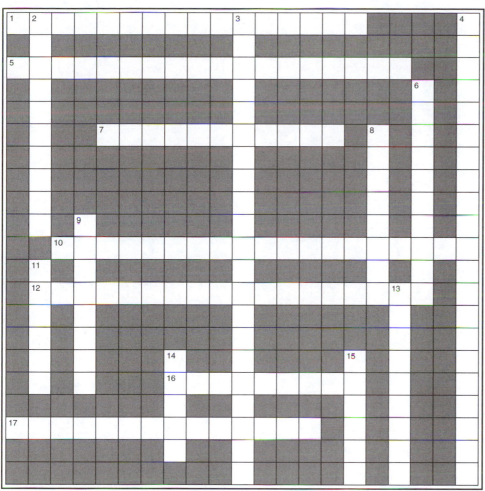

Caveat: Do **not** allow squares for spaces between words and punctuation (apostrophes, hyphens, etc.) when filling in crossword.

Across

1. Creditors who hold mortgages and other liens.
5. Another name for a debtor in Chapters 11, 12, and 13 cases.
7. A proceeding designed to liquidate a debtor's property, pay off creditors, and discharge the debtor from most debts.
10. A person appointed by a bankruptcy court to hold the debtor's assets in trust for the benefit of creditors.
12. A proceeding designed to liquidate a debtor's property, pay of creditors, and discharge the debtor from most debts.
16. Convert to cash.
17. A method for businesses to reorganize their financial affairs, keep their assets, and remain in business.

Down

2. Items of property that are excepted from bankruptcy proceedings and may be retained by the debtor.
3. A release of a debtor from all debts that were proved in a bankruptcy proceeding.
4. A bankruptcy proceeding that is initiated by one or more creditors.
6. The legal process by which the assets of a debtor are sold to pay off creditors so that the debtor can make a fresh start financially.
8. The state of a person who is unable to pay debts as they become due.
9. Divided proportionately.
11. Property.
13. People to whom money is owed.
14. A right to payment.
15. One who owes a debt to another.

GLOSSARY OF LEGAL TERMS

abortion (*a·BOR·shun*) The act of stopping a pregnancy.

absolute liability (*ab·so·LOOT ly·a·BIL·i·tee*) Liability for an act that causes harm without regard to fault or negligence. Also called *strict liability*.

A–B trust A type of marital deduction trust that reduces the taxation of the second spouse to die by limiting the amount in that person's estate to a sum that is not taxable. Also called *bypass trust, credit-shelter trust,* and *exemption equivalent trust.*

acceleration clause (*ak·sel·er·AY·shun*) A clause in a mortgage or note that causes the entire balance of the loan to become due when a default occurs.

accessory after the fact (*ak·SESS·o·ree*) One who receives, relieves, comforts, or assists another with knowledge that the other has committed a felony.

accessory before the fact (*ak·SESS·o·ree*) One who procures, counsels, or commands another to commit a felony, but who is not present when the felony is committed.

accomplice (*a·COM·pliss*) Anyone who takes part with another in the commission of a crime.

accord and satisfaction (*a·KORD and sat·is·FAK·shun*) An agreement to perform in a different manner than originally called for, and the completion of that agreed-upon performance.

accretion (*a·KREE·shun*) Any gradual addition to the soil made by nature, such as the gradual accumulation of soil on land next to a stream, caused by the action of water. Also called *alluvion.*

acknowledgment (*ak·NAWL·ej·ment*) A formal declaration before an authorized official, by a person who executes an instrument, that an act or deed is his or her free act or deed.

acquitted (*a·KWIT·ed*) Discharged from accusation.

action (*AK·shun*) Lawsuit or court proceeding.

actionable (*AK·shun·a·bel*) Furnishing legal ground for a lawsuit.

actus reus (*AK·tus REE·us*) A voluntary act.

ad damnum (*ad DAM·num*) The clause in the complaint stating the damages claimed by the plaintiff.

adeemed (*a·DEEMD*) Taken away.

ademption (*a·DEMP·shun*) The discharge of a legal obligation by paying a party what is due.

adhesion contract (*ad·HEE·shen KON·trakt*) A contract that is drawn by one party to that party's benefit and whose terms must be accepted, as is, on a take-it-or-leave-it basis, if a contract is to result.

adjudicating (*a·JOO·di·kay·ting*) Determining finally by a court.

adjudication (*a·joo·di·KAY·shun*) A court judgment.

adjustment of debts of individuals (*a·JUST·ment ov dets ov in·de·VID·joo·els*) A method by which an individual with regular income can pay his or her debts from future income over an extended period. Also called and *Chapter 13 bankruptcy.*

administrator (*ad·MIN·is·tray·tor*) A male appointed by the court to administer the estate of an intestate decedent.

administrator ad litem (*ad LY·tem*) An administrator appointed by the court to represent the interests of an estate in an action.

administrator c.t.a. A person appointed by the court to administer a testate estate in which no executor is nominated or in which the executor has died or for some reason does not settle the estate. (c.t.a. is an abbreviation for cum testamento annexo.) Also called *administrator with the will annexed* and *administrator w.w.a.*

administrator cum testamento annexo (*kum tes·ta·MENT·o an·EKS·o*) A person appointed by the court to administer a testate estate in which no executor is nominated or in which the executor has died or for some reason does not settle the estate. Also called *administrator c.t.a., administrator with the will annexed,* and *administrator w.w.a.*

administrator d.b.n. A person appointed by the court to complete the settlement of an estate in which a previously appointed administrator has died, resigned, or been removed. (d.b.n. is an abbreviation for de bonis non.)

administrator d.b.n.c.t.a. A person appointed by the court to take the place of a previously appointed executor who has died, resigned, or been removed. (d.b.n.c.t.a. is an abbreviation for de bonis non cum testamento annexo.)

administrator de bonis non (*de BO·niss non*) A person appointed by the court to complete the settlement of an estate in which a previously appointed administrator has died, resigned, or been removed. Also called *administrator d.b.n.*

administrator de bonis non cum testamento annexo A person appointed by the court to take the place of a previously appointed executor who has died, resigned, or been removed. Also called *administrator d.b.n.c.t.a.*

administrator pendente lite (*pen·DEN·tay LIE·tay*) A temporary administrator appointed by the court to protect estate assets when there is a will contest.

administrator with the will annexed (*AN·eksd*) A person appointed by the court to administer a testate estate in which no executor is nominated or in which the executor has died or for some reason does not settle the estate. Also called *administrator c.t.a., administrator cum testamento annexo,* and *administrator w.w.a.*

administrator w.w.a. A person appointed by the court to administer a testate estate in which no executor is nominated or in which the executor has died or for some reason does not settle the estate. (w.w.a. is an abbreviation for with the will annexed.) Also called *administrator c.t.a.* and *administrator cum testamento annex.*

administratrix (*ad·MIN·is·tray·triks*) A female appointed by the court to administer the estate of an intestate decedent.

admiralty (*AD·mer·ul·tee*) Pertaining to the sea.

admissible evidence (*ad·MISS·e·bel EV·i·dens*) Evidence that is pertinent and proper to be considered in reaching a decision following specific rules.

adoption (*a·DOP·shun*) The legal process in which a child's legal rights and duties toward his or her natural parents are replaced by similar rights and duties toward his or her adopting parents.

adoptive parents (*a·DOP·tiv*) Parents who adopt a child.

adultery (*a·DUL·ter·ee*) Voluntary sexual intercourse by a married person with someone other than that person's spouse, or by an unmarried person with a married person.

advance directive *(ad·VANS de·REKT·iv)* A written statement specifying whether a person wants life-sustaining medical treatment if he or she becomes desperately ill.

advancement *(ad·VANSE·ment)* The testator's disposing of or giving to a beneficiary, while alive, that which was provided in a will, so as to make it impossible to carry out the will. Also called *satisfaction.*

adverse possession *(AD·verse po·SESH·en)* Title to real property obtained by taking actual possession of it openly, notoriously, exclusively, under a claim of right, and continuously for a period set by statute.

affiant *(a·FY·ent)* A person who signs an affidavit. Also called *deponent.*

affidavit *(a·fi·DAY·vit)* A written statement sworn to under oath before a notary public as being true to the affiant's own knowledge, information, and belief.

affiliation proceeding *(a·fil·ee·AY·shun pro·SEED·ing)* A court action to determine whether a person is the father of a child born out of wedlock. Also called *paternity proceeding.*

affinity *(a·FIN·i·tee)* The relationship that one spouse has to the blood relatives of the other.

affirm *(a·FERM)* Approve.

affirmative defense *(a·FERM·a·tiv de·FENSE)* A defense that admits the plaintiff's allegations, but introduces another factor that avoids liability. Also called *confession and avoidance.*

agency *(AY·jen·see)* A relationship that exists when one person is authorized to act under the control of another person.

agency by estoppel *(AY·jen·see by es·TOP·el)* Authority that comes about when a principal, through some act, makes it appear that an agent has authority when none actually exists. Also called *apparent authority.*

agency by ratification *(AY·jen·see by rat·i·fi·KAY·shun)* A relationship that occurs when someone performs an act on behalf of another without authority to do so, but the other person later approves of the act.

agent *(AY·jent)* A person authorized to act on behalf of another and subject to the other's control. Also called *surrogate.*

age of consent *(aje ov con·SENT)* The age at which one may be married under state law.

aggravated assault *(AG·ra·va·ted a·SAWLT)* An assault committed with the intention of committing some additional crime.

aiding and abetting *(a·BET·ing)* Participating in a crime by giving assistance or encouragement.

adjustable rate mortgage def *(a·JUSS·ta·bl rate MORE·gej)* A mortgage with an interest rate that fluctuates according to changes in an index to which it is connected.

alderpeople *(AL·der·pee·pel)* People elected to serve as members of the legislative body of a city.

alibi *(AL·i·by)* A defense that places the defendant in a different place than the crime scene so that it would have been impossible for him or her to commit the crime.

alienation of affections *(ale·ee·e·NA·shun ov a·FEK·shuns)* The willful and malicious interference with the marriage relation by a third party without justification or excuse.

alimony *(AL·i·mohn·ee)* An allowance made to a divorced spouse by a former spouse for support and maintenance. Also called *spousal support.*

allegation *(al·e·GAY·shun)* A statement or claim that the party making it expects to prove.

allege *(a·LEJ)* To make an allegation; to assert positively.

alleged *(a·LEJD)* Claimed, asserted, or charged.

alluvion *(a·LOO·vee·en)* Any gradual addition to the soil made by nature, such as the gradual accumulation of soil on land next to a stream caused by the action of water. Also called *accretion.*

alternate jurors *(AHL·ter·net JOOR·ors)* Additional jurors impaneled in case of sickness or removal of any of the regular jurors who are deliberating.

alternative dispute resolutions *(al·TERN·a·tiv dis·PYOOT res·o·LOO·shuns)* Procedures for settling disputes by means other than litigation.

amortization *(a·MORE·ti·ZAY·shun)* Reducing or decreasing over time. In a loan, it shows how the loan balance is reduced until it is paid off.

American Bar Association (ABA) *(uh·MARE·ih·kan bar uh·so·she·A·shun)* The largest voluntary bar association in the United States; it sets academic standards for law schools and formulates a model of ethical codes related to the legal profession.

ancillary administrator *(AN·sil·a·ree ad·MIN· is·tray·tor)* A person appointed by the court to handle the affairs of a decedent in a foreign state.

animus furandi *(AN·i·mus fer·AN·day)* An intent to steal.

annulment *(a·NUL·ment)* A judicial declaration that no valid marriage ever existed.

answer *(AN·ser)* The main pleading filed by the defendant in a lawsuit in response to the plaintiff's complaint.

antenuptial agreement *(an·tee·NUP·shel a·GREE·ment)* A contract made in contemplation of marriage between prospective spouses setting forth, among other points, the right each spouse will have to property brought into the marriage. Also called *premarital agreement* and *prenuptial agreement.*

anticipatory breach *(an·TISS·i·pa·tore·ee)* The announcement, before the time for performance, by a party to a contract that he or she is not going to perform.

antilapse statutes *(an·tee·LAPS STAT·shoots)* Laws designed to minimize the effect of lapse.

apparent authority *(a·PAR·ent aw·THAW·ri·tee)* Authority that comes about when a principal, through some act, makes it appear that an agent has authority when none actually exists. Also called *agency by estoppel.*

appeal *(a·PEEL)* A request to a higher court to review the decision of a lower court.

appeal bond A bond often required as security to guarantee the cost of an appeal, especially in civil cases.

appearance *(a·PEER·ens)* The voluntary submission to the court's jurisdiction, either in person or by an agent.

appellant *(a·PEL·ent)* A party bringing an appeal.

appellate courts *(a·PEL·et)* Courts that review the decisions of lower courts. Also called *courts of appeal.*

appellate jurisdiction (*a·PEL·et joo·res·DIK·shen*) The power to hear a case when it is appealed.

appellee (*a·pel·EE*) A party against whom an appeal is brought. Also called *defendant in error* and *respondent*.

apt words Suitable words.

arbitration (*ar·be·TRAY·shun*) A method of settling disputes in which a neutral third party makes a decision after hearing the arguments on both sides.

arbitrator (*ar·be·TRAY·tor*) A neutral third party in an arbitration session who listens to both sides and makes a decision with regard to the dispute.

arbitrator's award (*ar·be·TRAY·torz uh·wohrd*) An arbitrator's final written decision in binding arbitration.

arraignment (*a·RAIN·ment*) The act of calling a prisoner before the court to answer an indictment or information.

array (*a·RAY*) The large group of people from which a jury is selected for a trial. Also called *jury panel, jury pool,* and *venire*.

arrest (*a·REST*) To deprive a person of his or her liberty.

arrest warrant (*a·REST WAR·ent*) A written order of the court commanding law enforcement officers to arrest a person and bring him or her before the court.

arson (*AR·sen*) The willful and malicious burning of the dwelling house of another.

articles of incorporation (*ARE·ti·clz ov in·core·pore·AY·shun*) The basic charter of a corporation, which states the name, basic purpose, incorporators, amount and types of stock that may be issued, and special characteristics such as being a not-for-profit corporation.

articles of organization (*AR·ti·kels ov or·ge·ni·ZAY·shun*) A document that gives authority to an organization to do business as a corporation. Also called *certificate of incorporation* and *charter*.

asportation (*as·por·TAY·shun*) The carrying away of goods.

assault (*a·SAWLT*) The intentional creation of a reasonable apprehension of an imminent battery. An attempt to commit a battery.

assets (*ASS·ets*) Property.

assignee (*ass·en·EE*) One to whom a right is transferred by assignment.

assignment (*a·SINE·ment*) The transfer of a right from one person to another.

assignor (*ass·en·OR*) One who transfers a right by assignment.

assumption of the risk (*a·SUMP·shun*) The condition that exists when the plaintiff assumes the consequences of injury and/or when an employee agrees that dangers of injury shall be at his or her own risk.

attachment (*a·TACH·ment*) The act of taking or seizing property by the use of a writ, summons, or other judicial order and bringing it into the custody of the court so that it may be applied toward the defendant's debt if the plaintiff wins the case.

attempted arson (*a·TEMT·ed AR·sen*) An attempt to commit the crime of arson, but falling short of its commission.

attempted larceny (*a·TEMPT·ed LAR·sen·ee*) An attempt to commit larceny, but falling short of its commission.

attest (*a·TEST*) To bear witness to.

attestation clause (*a·tes·TAY·shun*) The clause in a will that immediately precedes the witnesses' signatures.

attesting witnesses (*a·TEST·ing WIT·ness*) People who witness the signing of a document.

Attorney–client privilege (*a·turn·ee KLY·ent PRIV·lej*) The privilege related to the duty of confidentiality that an attorney has with a client, but coming from evidence law; protects a lawyer from having to testify against his or her client even when issued a subpoena.

attorney-in-fact (*a·TERN·ee*) An agent who is authorized to act under a power of attorney.

attractive nuisance doctrine (*a·TRAK·tiv NOO·sens DOK·trin*) A doctrine establishing property owners' duty to use ordinary care toward trespassing children who might reasonably be attracted to their property.

auction sale (*AWK·shun*) A sale of property to the highest bidder.

auction without reserve An auction in which the auctioneer must sell the goods to the highest bidder.

auction with reserve (*ree·ZERV*) An auction in which the auctioneer may withdraw the goods without accepting the highest bid.

automatic stay (*aw·toh·MAT·ic*) A self-operating postponement of collection proceedings against a debtor. Also called *automatic suspension*.

automatic suspension (*aw·toh·MAT·ic sus·PEN·shun*) A self-operating postponement of collection proceedings against a debtor. Also called *automatic stay*.

aver (*a·VER*) To make an allegation; to assert positively.

averments (*a·VER·ments*) Claims that the party making them expects to prove.

avoid (*a·VOID*) To annul, cancel, or make void. To get out of a voidable contract; repudiate. Also called *disaffirm*.

bail Money or property left with the court to assure that the person will return to stand trial; nonrefundable if the person "skips" bail.

bailee (*bay·LEE*) One to whom personal property is given under a bailment contract.

bailment (*BAYL·ment*) The relationship that exists when possession (but not ownership) of personal property is transferred to another for a specific purpose.

bailment for the sole benefit of the bailee (*bay·LEE*) A gratuitous bailment benefiting only the bailor.

bailment for the sole benefit of the bailor (*bay·LOR*) A gratuitous bailment benefiting only the bailor.

bailor (*bay·LOR*) The owner of personal property that has been temporarily transferred to a bailee under a contract of bailment.

balloon mortgage (*ba·LOON MORE·gej*) A mortgage with low fixed payments during the life of the loan, ending with one large final payment.

bankrupt (*BANK·rupt*) The state of a person (including a business) who is unable to pay debts as they become due.

bankruptcy (*BANK·rupt·see*) A legal process that aims to give debtors who are overwhelmed with debt a "fresh start" and to provide a fair way of distributing a debtor's assets among all creditors.

Bankruptcy Abuse and Prevention Consumer Protection Act (BAPCA) *(BANK·rupt·see uh·BEWS and pree·VEN·shun kon·SUE·mer pro·TECT·shun act)* A 2005 change in bankruptcy code that makes it more difficult for people to declare bankruptcy and that extends the time allowed between repeat bankruptcy filings.

banns of matrimony *(MAT·ri·mone·ee)* Public notice of a marriage contract for a certain number of weeks before the wedding date. Also called *marriage banns.*

Bar exam *(bar ex·AM)* The exam that lawyers have to pass in order to get licensed to practice law.

bare licensee *(ly·sen·SEE)* A person allowed on another's premises by operation of law, such as a fire-fighter or police officer.

bargain *(BAR·gen)* Agreement.

bargain and sale deed *(BAR·gen)* A deed that conveys land itself, rather than people's interests therein, and requires consideration.

base lines Horizontal lines running east and west in the United States government survey.

bastards *(BAS·terds)* Children born out of wedlock. Also called *illegitimate children* and *nonmarital children.*

battery *(BAT·er·ee)* Intentional contact with another person without that person's permission and without justification; the unlawful application of force to another person.

beastiality *(beest·ee·AL·i·tee)* Sexual intercourse by a man or woman with an animal.

bench trial *(tryl)* A trial without a jury. Also called *jury waived trial.*

beneficial title *(ben·e·FISH·el TY·tel)* The right to beneficial enjoyment. Also called *equitable title.*

beneficiary *(ben·e·FISH·ee·air·ee)* Someone who actually receives a gift under a will; also, one for whose benefit a trust is created. Also called *cestui que trust.*

bequeath *(be·KWEETH)* To give personal property in a will.

bequest *(be·KWEST)* A gift of personal property in a will.

beyond a reasonable doubt *(REE·zen·e·bel)* The condition that exists when the fact finder is fully persuaded that the accused has committed the crime.

bidder *(BID·er)* Offeror.

bifurcated trial *(BY·fer·kay·ted tryl)* A trial that is divided into two parts, providing separate hearings for different issues in the same lawsuit.

bigamy *(BIG·a·mee)* The state of a man who has two wives, or of a woman who has two husbands, living at the same time.

bilateral contract *(by·LAT·er·el KON·trakt)* A contract containing two promises, one made by each party.

bilateral foreign divorce *(by·LAT·er·el FOR·en de·VORSS)* A divorce that occurs when both parties make an appearance in a foreign state or country.

bilateral mistake *(by·LAT·er·el mis·TAKE)* The situation that exists when both parties are mistaken about an important aspect of an agreement. Also called *mutual mistake.*

bill of particulars *(par·TIK·yoo·lars)* A written statement of the particulars of a complaint, showing the details of the amount owed.

bill of sale A signed writing evidencing the transfer of personal property from one person to another.

binding arbitration *(BINE·ding ar·be·TRAY·shun)* Arbitration in which the decision of the arbitrator will prevail and must be followed.

blue-sky laws State laws designed to protect the public from the sale of worthless stocks.

boilerplate *(BOY·ler·plate)* Standard language used commonly in documents of the same type.

bond A written instrument promising the payment of a sum of money if certain duties are not performed.

bounds Directions of the boundaries that enclose a parcel of land.

breach of contract *(KON·trakt)* The failure of a party to a contract to carry out the terms of the agreement.

breach of promise to marry *(PROM·iss)* Breaking off an engagement to marry.

breaking *(BRAKE·ing)* The first part of "breaking and entering," which traditionally has meant using some method to wrongfully gain entrance into a house or other occupiable structure by force, including breaking a window or picking a lock.

bribery *(BRY·be·ree)* The giving or receiving of a reward to influence any official act.

bulk transfer *(TRANS·fer)* A transfer, not in the ordinary course of business, in bulk, of a major part of the materials, supplies, merchandise, or other inventory of an enterprise.

burden of proof *(BER·den)* The duty of proving a fact.

burglary *(BUR·gler·ee)* At common law, the breaking and entering of a dwelling house of another, in the nighttime, with intent to commit a felony.

business invitee *(BIZ·ness in·vy·TEE)* One invited on the premises for a business or commercial purpose.

bypass trust *(BY·pass)* A type of marital deduction trust that reduces the taxation of the second spouse to die by limiting the amount in that person's estate to a sum that is not taxable. Also called *A–B trust, credit-shelter trust,* and *exemption equivalent trust.*

Canons of Professional Ethics *(KAN·onz ov pro·FEH·shun·al EH·thicks)* The first set of ethics rules created by the American Bar Association in 1908.

capacity *(ka·PASS·e·tee)* Legal competency.

capital crime *(KAP·i·tel krym)* A crime that is punishable by death.

capital criminal case *(KAP·i·tel KRIM·i·nel kase)* A case in which the death penalty may be inflicted.

carnal knowledge *(KAR·nel NOL·ej)* Sexual intercourse; the slightest penetration of the sexual organ of the woman by the sexual organ of the man.

case in chief *(cheef)* The introduction of evidence to prove the allegations that were made in the pleadings and in the opening statement.

castle doctrine *(KAS·el DOK·trin)* A doctrine that allows people to use all necessary force, without first retreating, to defend themselves when they are in their homes.

caucus (*KAW·kuss*) A private session with a mediator in which the mediator learns what the interests are behind each side's demands.

causation (*kaw·ZAY·zhun*) The direct and proximate cause of someone's injuries.

cause of action (*cawz ov AK·shun*) The ground on which a suit is maintained.

C corporation (*kor·por·AY·shun*) A corporation governed by Subchapter C of the Internal Revenue Code, that pays corporate taxes on its income.

cert. den. (*ser·sho·RARE·ee dee·NIDE*) Abbreviation meaning certiorari denied.

certificate of incorporation (*ser·TIF·i·ket ov in·kore·per·AY·shen*) A document that gives authority to an organization to do business as a corporation. Also called *articles of organization* and *charter*.

cestui que trust (*SES·twee kay*) One for whose benefit a trust is created. Also called *beneficiary*.

challenge (*CHAL·enj*) To call or put in question.

challenge for cause (*CHAL·enj for kaws*) A challenge of a juror made when it is believed that the juror does not stand indifferent.

challenge to the array (*CHAL·enj to the a·RAY*) A challenge to the entire jury because of some irregularity in the selection of the jury. Also called *motion to quash the array*.

Chapter 7 bankruptcy (*BANK·rupt·see*) A proceeding designed to liquidate a debtor's property, pay off creditors, and discharge the debtor from most debts. Also called *liquidation* and *straight bankruptcy*.

Chapter 11 bankruptcy (*BANK·rupt·see*) A method for businesses to reorganize their financial affairs, keep their assets, and remain in business. Also called *reorganization*.

Chapter 12 bankruptcy (*BANK·rupt·see*) A method for family farmers to adjust their financial affairs while continuing to operate their farms. Also called *family farmer debt adjustment*.

Chapter 13 bankruptcy (*BANK·rupt·see*) A method by which an individual with regular income can pay his or her debts from future income over an extended period. Also called *adjustment of debts of individuals*.

charitable remainder annuity trust (*CHAR·i·ta·bel re·MANE·der a·NYOO·i·tee*) A trust in which a fixed amount of income is given annually to a beneficiary and the remainder is given to a charity.

charitable remainder trust (*CHAR·i·ta·bel re·MANE·der*) A trust in which the donor, or a beneficiary, retains the income from the trust for life or other period, after which the trust corpus is given to a charity.

charitable remainder unitrust (*CHAR·i·ta·bel re·MANE·der YOO·nee·trust*) A trust in which a fixed percentage of income (at least 5 percent of the trust corpus) is given annually to a beneficiary and the remainder is given to a charity.

charitable trust (*CHAR·i·ta·bel*) A trust established for charitable purposes. Also called a *public trust*.

charter (*CHAR·ter*) A document that gives authority to an organization to do business as a corporation. Also called *articles of organization* and *certificate of incorporation*.

chattels (*CHAT·els*) Anything that is the subject of ownership other than real property. Also called *personal property* and *personalty*.

check A draft that is drawn on a bank and payable on demand.

child support (*su·PORT*) The legal obligations of parents to contribute to the economic maintenance and education of their children. Also called *maintenance*.

chose in action (*shohz in AK·shun*) Evidence of a right to property, but not the property itself.

circuits (*SER·kits*) Name given to division of U.S. district courts.

circumstantial evidence (*ser·kum·STAN·shel EV·i·dens*) Evidence that relates to some fact other than the fact in issue; indirect evidence.

citation (*sy·TAY·shun*) A written order by a judge (or a police officer) commanding a person to appear in court for a particular purpose.

civil action (*SIV·el AK·shun*) A noncriminal lawsuit.

civil union (*SIV·el YOON·yun*) A relationship in which same-sex couples have the same rights and duties as married couples.

claim A right to payment.

class action (*klas AK·shun*) A lawsuit brought, with the court's permission, by one or more persons on behalf of a very large group of people who have the same interest in the matter.

click-wrap agreement (*clik-rap a·GREE·ment*) An advertising contract online in which the offeree enters into a contract by clicking on a dialog box on an Internet website.

close corporation (*klose kor·por·AY·shun*) A corporation that has restrictions on the transfer of shares.

closing argument (*AR·gyoo·ment*) Final statement by an attorney summarizing the evidence that has been introduced. Also called *summation*.

code (*KOHD*) A systematic collection of statutes, administrative regulations, and other laws.

codicil (*KOD·i·sil*) An amendment to a will that must be executed with the same formalities as the will itself.

coercion (*ko·ER·zhen*) Compelling someone to do something by threat or force.

cohabit (*koh·HAB·it*) To live together.

collateral (*co·LA·ter·al*) Something lenders can sell to get their money back in case of default; security interest for a loan.

collateral relatives (*ko·LAT·er·el REL·e·tivs*) Relatives not in a direct line, such as brothers, sisters, nieces, nephews, uncles, aunts, and cousins.

collusion (*ke·LOO·zhen*) An agreement between a husband and wife that one of them will commit a marital offense so that the other may obtain a divorce.

comity (*KOM·i·tee*) A doctrine stating that the courts of one jurisdiction will give effect to the laws and judicial decisions of another jurisdiction, not as a matter of obligation, but out of deference and respect.

Comments (*KAW·ments*) Remarks that help a reader understand the focus of the Rules in the American Bar Association Model of Rules.

commerce clause (*KOM·erss*) A clause in the U.S. Constitution giving Congress the power to regulate commerce with foreign nations and among the different states.

common areas *(KOM·on AIR·ee·uz)* The part of a condominium or apartment building that is owned, as tenants in common, by all the unit owners.

common law *(KOM·on)* The case law used in England and the American Colonies before the American Revolution.

common law marriage *(KOM·on law MAR·ej)* A marriage without a formal ceremony or issuance of a legal license.

common law theory of mortgages *(KOM·on law THEE·ree ov MORE·ge·jes)* The legal theory that a mortgage is a conveyance of title, which becomes void on payment of the obligation. Also called *title theory of mortgages.*

common stock *(KOM·on stok)* Stock that has no preferences, but that gives the owner the right to vote.

community property *(kom·YOON·i·tee PROP·er·tee)* Property (other than a gift or inheritance), acquired by a husband or wife during marriage, that belongs to both spouses equally.

commutation of sentence *(kom·yoo·TAY·shun ov SEN·tense)* The changing of a sentence to one that is less severe.

comparative fault *(kom·PAR·e·tiv fawlt)* Another term for comparative negligence.

comparative negligence *(kom·PAR·e·tiv NEG·li·jens)* The proportionate sharing between the plaintiff and the defendant of compensation for injuries, the division based on the relative negligence of the two.

compensatory damages *(kom·PEN·sa·tor·ee DAM·e·jez)* Damages that compensate the plaintiff for actual losses resulting from the breach.

competent *(KOM·peh·tent)* The capability to adequately represent the client by possessing the underlying substantive and procedural legal expertise that is needed for the matter.

complaint *(kom·PLAYNT)* A formal document containing a short and plain statement of the claim, indicating that the plaintiff is entitled to relief and containing a demand for the relief sought.

compulsory arbitration *(kom·PUL·so·ree ar·be· TRAY·shun)* Arbitration that is required by agreement or by law. Also called *mandatory arbitration.*

computer fraud *(frawd)* Use of a computer to obtain money, property, or services by false pretenses.

conciliation *(kon·sil·ee·AY·shun)* An informal process in which a neutral third person listens to both sides and makes suggestions for reaching a solution. Also called *mediation.*

conciliator *(kon·SIL·ee·ay·tor)* A neutral third person in a conciliation session who listens to both sides and makes suggestions for reaching a solution. Also called a *mediator.*

concurrent jurisdiction *(kon·KER·ent joo·res·DIK·shen)* The power of two or more courts to decide a particular case.

concurrent ownership *(kon·KER·ent OH·ner·ship)* Ownership by more than one person. Also called *co-ownership.*

concurrent sentences *(kon·KER·ent SEN·ten·sez)* Two or more sentences imposed on a defendant, to be served at the same time.

condition precedent *(kon·DISH·en pree·SEE·dent)* An event that must first occur before an agreement (or deed or will) becomes effective.

condition subsequent *(kon·DISH·en SUB·se·kwent)* A qualification that comes later.

condominium *(kon·de·MIN·ee·um)* A parcel of real property, portions of which are owned separately in fee simple by individual owners and the remainder of which is owned as tenants in common by all the unit owners.

condominium association *(kon·de·MIN·ee·um a·so·see·AY·shun)* A group of people consisting of condominium unit owners that manages and maintains a condominium.

condonation *(kon·do·NAY·shun)* The forgiveness of a matrimonial offense.

confession and avoidance *(kon·FESH·en and a·VOY·denss)* A defense that admits the plaintiff's allegations, but introduces another factor that avoids liability. Also called *affirmative defense.*

confidentiality agreement *(kon·fe·den·shee·AL·i·tee a·GREE·ment)* An agreement to refrain from disclosing trade secrets to others. Also called *nondisclosure agreement.*

confidential communication *(kon·fi·DEN·shul kom·yoo·ni·KAY·shun)* a conversation or writing that expresses personal or private information.

conforming goods *(kon·FORM·ing)* Goods that are in accordance with the obligations under the contract.

conjugal *(KON·je·gel)* Pertaining to the marriage relationship.

connivance *(ke·NY·venss)* The plaintiff's secret cooperation in the commission of a marital wrong—that is a common law defense to an action for divorce—committed by the defendant.

consanguinity *(kon·san·GWIN·i·tee)* Related by blood.

consecutive sentences *(kon·SEK·yoo·tiv SEN· ten·sez)* Two or more sentences imposed on a defendant to be served one after the other. Also called *cumulative sentences.*

consent decree *(kon· SENT de ·KREE)* A decree that is entered by consent of the parties, usually without admission of guilt or wrongdoing.

consequential damages *(kon·se·KWEN·shel DAM·e·jez)* Losses that flow not directly from a breach of contract, but from the consequences of it.

conservator *(kon·SER·ve·tor)* One who legally has the care and management of the property, but not the person, of someone who is incompetent.

consideration *(kon·sid·er·AY·shun)* An exchange of benefits and detriments by the parties to an agreement.

consignee *(kon·sine·EE)* One to whom a consignment is made.

consignment *(kon·SINE·ment)* The process of delivering goods to a bailee, called a factor, who attempts to sell them.

consignor *(kon·sine·OR)* One who makes a consignment.

consortium *(kon·SORE·shum)* The fellowship between a husband and wife.

conspiracy *(kon·SPIR·a·see)* The getting together of two or more people to accomplish some criminal or unlawful act.

constructive eviction *(kon·STRUK·tiv e·VIK·shun)* Dispossession caused by the landlord's doing some act that deprives the tenant of the beneficial enjoyment of the demised premises.

constructively *(kon·STRUK·tiv·lee)* Made so by legal interpretation.

constructive possession *(kon·STRUK·tiv po·SESH·en)* Possession not actual, but assumed to exist.

constructive service *(kon·STRUK·tiv SER·viss)* A type of service in which the summons and complaint are left at the defendant's last and usual place of abode.

constructive trust *(kon·STRUK·tiv)* An implied trust that arises in favor of one who is defrauded when title to property is obtained by fraud.

contract *(KON·trakt)* Any agreement that is enforceable in a court of law.

contract implied in fact *(KON·trakt im·PLIDE)* A contract that arises from the conduct of the parties rather than from their express statements.

contract implied in law *(KON·trakt im·PLIDE)* A contract imposed by law to prevent unjust enrichment. Also called *quasi contract.*

contract to sell *(KON·trakt)* A contract under which title to goods is to pass at a future time.

contractual capacity *(kon·TRAK·chew·el ka·PA·si·tee)* The legal ability to be able to enter into a contract.

contributory negligence *(kon·TRIB·u·tor·ee NEG·li·jens)* Negligence on the part of the plaintiff that contributed to his or her injuries and is a proximate cause of them.

controlled substance *(kon·TROLED SUB·stanss)* A drug that is included in any of the five schedules established by the Federal Controlled Substances Act.

conversion *(kon·VER·zhun)* The wrongful exercise of dominion and control over the personal property in another's possession.

convey *(kon·VAY)* To transfer.

conveyance *(kon·VAY·enss)* A formal, written instrument by which title to real property is transferred from one person to another. Also called a *deed.*

conveyance in trust *(kon·VAY·enss)* A transfer of legal title to property by the settlor to a trustee to hold for the benefit of a beneficiary.

conveyancing *(kon·VAY·enss·ing)* Transferring title to real property.

convict *(KON·vict)* A person who is found guilty of a crime.

convicted *(kon·VICT·ed)* Found guilty of a crime.

cooperative apartment *(koh·OP·er·a·tiv a·PART·ment)* A dwelling unit in which the occupants lease individual units and, at the same time, own shares of stock in the corporation that owns the building.

co-ownership *(koh-OH·ner·ship)* Ownership by more than one person. Also called *concurrent ownership.*

coparceners *(koh·PAR·se·ners)* Persons to whom an estate of inheritance descends jointly and by whom it is held as an entire estate (early English law).

co-partnership *(koh-PART·ner·ship)* An association of two or more persons to carry on as co-owners of a business for profit. Also called *partnership.*

copulate *(KOP·yoo·late)* to engage in sexual intercourse.

copulation *(kop·yoo·LA·shun)* Sexual intercourse.

copyright *(KOP·ee·rite)* The exclusive right given to an author, composer, artist, or photographer to publish and sell exclusively a work for the life of the author plus 70 years.

copyright infringement *(KOP·ee·rite in·FRINJ·ment)* The unauthorized use of copyrighted material.

co-respondent *(KOH-re·spond·ent)* The person charged with committing adultery with the defendant in a divorce action.

corporation *(kor·por·AY·shun)* A legal entity created under state law with the power to conduct its affairs as though it were a natural person.

corpus *(KOR·pus)* The body, principal sum, or capital of a trust. Also called *trust fund, trust principal, trust property,* and *trust res.*

corpus delicti *(KOR·pus de·LIK·tie)* A body on which a crime has been committed.

co-tenants *(koh-TEN·ents)* Two or more owners of real property.

counterclaim *(KOWN·ter·klame)* A claim that the defendant has against the plaintiff.

counteroffer *(KOWN·ter·off·er)* A response to an offer in which the terms of the original offer are changed.

court *(KORT)* A body of government organized to administer justice.

court of equity *(EK·wi·tee)* A court that administers justice according to the system of equity.

Court of Ordinary *(OR·di·ner·ee)* A name given, in some states, to the court that exercises the function of settling decedents' estates.

court of appeal *(a·PEEL)* A court that reviews the decisions of a lower court. Also called an *appellate court.*

covenant *(KOV·e·nent)* A promise or assurance.

covenant, conditions and restrictions *(CC&R)* Part of a deed used to regulate the appearance and use of a property that is part of a condominium or cooperative that are stricter that local ordinances or zoning laws.

covenant marriage *(KOV·e·nent MAR·ej)* A marriage in which the parties agree to go through counseling before the marriage and also during the marriage to resolve conflicts.

co-venture *(KOH-ven·cher)* A relationship in which two or more people combine their labor or property for a single business undertaking. Also called *joint enterprise, joint venture,* and *syndicate.*

cover *(KUV·er)* The right of a buyer, after breach by a seller, to purchase similar goods from someone else.

coverture *(KUV·er·cher)* Marriage.

creditors *(KRED·et·ers)* People to whom money is owed.

credit-shelter trust *(KRED·et-SHEL·ter)* A type of marital deduction trust that reduces the taxation of the second spouse to die by limiting the amount in that person's estate to a sum that is not taxable. Also called *A–B trust, bypass trust,* and *exemption equivalent trust.*

crime *(krym)* A wrong against society.

crime of moral turpitude *(MOR·el TER·pi·tood)* A crime that is base, vile, and depraved.

criminal complaint *(KRIM·i·nel kom·PLAYNT)* A written statement of the essential facts making up an offense charged in a criminal action.

criminal conversation *(KRIM·i·nel kon·ver·SAY·shun)* A tort action brought by a husband or wife against a third party who committed adultery with the husband's or wife's spouse.

criminal fraud (*KRIM·i·nel frawd*) Knowingly and deliberately obtaining the property of another by false pretenses with intent to defraud. Also called *larceny by false pretenses.*

cross claim (*kross klame*) A claim brought by one defendant against another defendant in the same suit.

cross complaint (*kross kom·PLAYNT*) A pleading used in California by a defendant to file a claim against another defendant, a third party, and the plaintiff in the same action.

cross-examination (*kross-eg·zam·in·AY·shun*) The examination of an opposing witness.

cross questions (*kross KWES·chens*) Questions asked by a deponent in response to questions asked at a deposition.

cruelty (*KROO·el·tee*) In a divorce action, personal violence by one spouse that endangers the life, limb, or health of the other spouse.

Crummey powers (*KRUM·ee*) Authority that gives trust beneficiaries the right to withdraw each year the money that is contributed to the trust that year.

culpable negligence (*KUL·pe·bel NEG·li·jens*) The intentional commission of an act that a reasonable person knows would cause injury to another. Also called willful, wanton, and reckless conduct.

cumulative sentences (*KYOOM·yoo·la·tiv SEN· tensses*) Two or more sentences imposed on a defendant to be served one after the other. Also called *consecutive sentences.*

cure (*kyoor*) To correct.

curtesy (*KUR·te·see*) At common law, the right of a widower, if issue of the marriage were born alive, to a life estate in all real property owned by his wife during coverture.

curtilage (*KUR·til·ej*) The enclosed space of ground and buildings immediately surrounding a dwelling house.

custody (*KUSS·te·dee*) The care and keeping of anything.

custody of children (*KUSS·te·dee*) The care, control, and maintenance of children.

cybercrime (*SY·ber krym*) Criminal activity associated with a computer.

cyberlaw (*SY·ber law*) The area of law that involves computers and their related problems.

cyber stalking Using a computer to communicate willful, malicious and repeated harassment and threats to a person with violence intended to place the person in fear or serious bodily injury. Some state interchange laws on cyber bullying and cyber harassment, which are related.

cybertort (*SY·ber·tort*) A tort associated with a computer.

cy pres doctrine (*sy pray DOK·trin*) As near as possible.

damages (*DAM·e·jez*) The monetary loss suffered by a party as a result of a wrong.

dangerous instrumentalities (*DAYN·jer·ess in· stroo·men· TAL· i·tees*) Hazardous items such as explosives and wild animals.

dangerous weapon (*DAYN·jer·ess WEP·en*) An item that is, from the way it is used, capable of causing death or serious bodily injury. Also called *deadly weapon.*

deadly weapon (*DED·lee WEP·en*) An item that is, from the way it is used, capable of causing death or serious bodily injury. Also called *dangerous weapon.*

debtor (*DET·er*) One who owes a debt to another.

debtor-in-possession (*DET·er-in-po·SESH·en*) Another name for a debtor in Chapter 11, 12, and 13 bankruptcy cases.

decedent (*de·SEE·dent*) A deceased person.

deceit (*dee·SEET*) A misrepresentation of a material, existing fact, knowingly made, that causes someone reasonably relying on it to suffer damages. Also called *fraud.*

declaration (*dek·la·RAY·shun*) At common law, a formal document containing a short and plain statement of the claim, indicating that the plaintiff is entitled to relief and containing a demand for the relief sought.

declaration of trust (*dek·la·RAY·shun*) A written declaration by a settlor that he or she is holding legal title to property as trustee for the benefit of another person.

decree (*de·KREE*) The decision of a court of equity.

deed A formal, written instrument by which title to real property is transferred from one person to another. Also called *conveyance.*

deed of release (*re·LEESS*) A deed releasing property from an encumbrance.

deed of trust An instrument used in some states that replaces a mortgage, by which the legal title to real property is placed in a trustee to secure the repayment of a debt.

deed-poll (*deed-pole*) A deed or lease in which only the party making the instrument executes it.

deed without covenants (*KOV·e·nents*) A deed to real property in which the grantor transfers only his or her interest, if any, in the property and gives no warranties of title. Also called *fiduciary deed* and *quitclaim deed.*

de facto corporation (*de FAK·toh kor·por·AY·shun*) A corporation that has a defect in its establishment, but that must be recognized as a valid corporation unless set aside by the state.

defamation (*de·fa·MAY·shun*) The wrongful act of damaging another's character or reputation by the use of false statements.

default (*de·FAWLT*) A failure to perform a legal duty.

default judgment (*de·FAWLT JUJ·ment*) A court decision entered against a party who has failed to plead or defend a lawsuit.

defeasance clause (*de·FEE·zenss*) A clause in a mortgage providing that the mortgage deed shall be void on payment of the obligation.

defeasible estate (*de·FEEZ·i·bel es·TATE*) An estate that can be lost or defeated.

defendant (*de·FEN·dent*) A person against whom a legal action is brought.

defendant in error (*de·FEN·dent in ERR·er*) A party against whom an appeal is brought. Also called *appellee* and *respondent.*

defense (*de·FENSS*) Evidence offered by a defendant to defeat a criminal charge or civil lawsuit.

deficiency judgment (*de·FISH·en·see JUJ·ment*) A judgment for the amount remaining due to the mortgagee after a foreclosure sale.

degree of kindred (*de·GREE ov KIN·dred*) The determination of the respective relationships between a decedent and his or her relatives, undertaken to measure who are most nearly related by blood.

de jure corporation *(de JOOR·ee kor·por·AY·shun)* A corporation that is established in strict compliance with the law.

del credere agent *(del KREH·de·ray AY·jent)* A factor who sells consigned goods on credit and who guarantees to the consignor that the buyer will pay for the goods.

delegation *(del·e·GA·shun)* The transfer of a duty by one person to another.

deliberate *(dee·LIB·e·rate)* To consider slowly and carefully.

demand for bill of particulars *(de·MAND for bill of par·TIK·yoo·lars)* A pleading calling for details of a claim or the separate items of an account.

demise *(de·MIZE)* To lease.

demonstrative legacy *(de·MON·stre·tiv LEG·a·see)* A bequest of a certain sum of money with a direction that it be paid out of a particular fund.

demurrer *(de·MER·er)* A pleading used by the defendant to attack the plaintiff's complaint by raising a point of law, such as the failure of the complaint to state a cause of action.

deponent *(de·PONE·ent)* One who gives testimony under oath. A person who signs an affidavit. Also called *affiant.*

deposition *(dep·e·ZISH·en)* The testimony of a witness, given under oath, but not in open court, and later reduced to writing.

deposition on oral examination *(eg·zam·in·AY·shun)* A deposition in which lawyers orally examine and cross-examine a witness.

deposition on written questions *(KWES·chens)* A deposition in which lawyers examine and cross-examine a witness who has received, in advance, written questions to be answered.

derivative action *(de·RIV·a·tiv AK·shun)* A suit by a stockholder to enforce a corporate cause of action.

descendants *(de·SEN·dents)* Those who are of the bloodstream (including adopted children) of a common ancestor.

descent *(de·SENT)* Succession to the ownership of real property by inheritance (early English law).

desertion *(des·ER·shun)* The voluntary separation of one spouse from the other, for the statutory period, without justification and with the intent of not returning.

design defect *(dee·ZINE DEE·fekt)* The theory that a product was negligently designed or could have been designed more safely.

destination contract *(des·te·NAY·shun KON·trakt)* A contract that requires the seller to deliver goods to a destination.

determinable fee *(de·TER·min·e·bel)* An estate in real property that is capable of coming to an end automatically because of the happening of some event. Also called *fee simple determinable.*

determine *(de·TER·min)* Coming to an end.

detriment *(DET·ri·ment)* The giving up of a legal right.

devise *(de·VIZE)* A gift of real property in a will.

devisee *(dev·iy·ZEE)* A person to whom real property is given by will.

devisor *(dev·iy·ZOR)* A person who gives real property by will.

direct evidence *(de·REKT EV·i·dens)* Evidence that directly relates to the fact in issue.

direct examination *(de·REKT eg·zam·in·AY·shun)* The examination of one's own witness.

directive to physicians *(de·REKT·iv to fi·ZI·shens)* A written expression of a person's wishes to be allowed to die a natural death and not be kept alive by heroic or artificial methods. Also called *health care declaration, living will,* and *medical directive.*

directors *(de·REK·ters)* People who are elected by stockholders to manage a corporation.

disaffirm *(diss·a·FERM)* To get out of a voidable contract; repudiate. Also called *avoid.*

discharge in bankruptcy *(DIS·charj in BANK·rupt·see)* A release of a debtor from all debts that were proved in a bankruptcy proceeding.

discovery *(diss·KUV·e·ree)* Methods that allow each party to obtain information from the other party and from witnesses about a case before going to court.

discovery sanction *(diss·KOV·er·ee SANK·shun)* Court-ordered penalties for failing to produce evidence.

discretion *(diss·KRE·shun)* The power that a judge has to make a decision based on his or her own judgment and conscience.

discretionary trust *(dis·KRE·shun·air·ee)* A trust that allows the trustee to decide, in the trustee's discretion, how much will be given to each beneficiary. Also called *spray trust* and *sprinkling trust.*

dismissal *(diss·MISS·el)* An order disposing of an action without a trial of the issues.

dismissal without prejudice A dismissal in which the plaintiff is allowed to correct the error and bring another action on the same claim.

dismissal with prejudice *(PREJ·e·diss)* A dismissal in which the plaintiff is barred from bringing another action on the same claim.

dispositive clauses *(diss·POS·a·tiv)* The clauses in a will that state exactly what each beneficiary is to receive.

dispossessory warrant proceedings *(diss·po·SESS·o·ree WAR·ent pro·SEED·ings)* The legal action used by landlords to evict tenants. Also called *forcible entry and detainer, summary ejectment, summary process,* and *unlawful detainer.*

disseised *(di·SEEZD)* Dispossessed.

dissolution *(diss·uh·LOO·zhun)* An act or occurrence that requires the partnership to eventually terminate.

dissolution of marriage *(diss·o·LU·shun ov MAR·ej)* The act, by a court, of terminating a valid marriage. Also called *divorce.*

distribution *(diss·tre·BYOO·shun)* The apportionment and division of the personal property of an intestate among his or her heirs (early English law).

divested *(dy·VEST·ed)* Taken away.

diversity of citizenship *(dy·VER·sit·ee ov SIT·e·sen·ship)* A phrase used in connection with the jurisdiction of the federal courts.

divided custody *(de·VIE·ded KUS·te·dee)* Custody in which the child lives with each parent part of the year, the other parent usually having visitation rights, but not control of the child, during that period.

dividends *(DIV·i·denz)* Profits distributed to the stockholders of a corporation.

divorce *(de·VORSS)* The act, by a court, of terminating a valid marriage. Also called *dissolution of marriage*.

divorce from bed and board The discontinuance of cohabitation by the spouses. Also called *limited divorce* and *separation of spouses*.

DNA Abbreviation for deoxyribonucleic acid. The double strand of molecules that carries a cell's unique genetic code.

DNA sample Biological evidence of any nature that is utilized to conduct DNA analysis.

docket *(DOK·et)* A record of cases that are filed with the court.

docket number *(DOK·et NUM·ber)* A number assigned to each case by the clerk of the court.

doctrine of charitable immunity *(DOK·trin ov CHAR·i·ta·bel im·YOO·ni·tee)* A legal doctrine under which charitable institutions are immune from tort liability.

doctrine of respondeat superior *(res·PON·dee·at soo·PEER·e·or)* A legal doctrine under which a master is responsible for the torts of his or her servants, that are committed within the scope of employment.

doctrine of sovereign immunity *(SOV·er·in im·YOO·ni·tee)* A legal doctrine under which governmental bodies are immune from tort liability.

documentary evidence *(dok·u·MENT·ta·ree EV·i·denss)* Evidence consisting of such documents as written contracts, business records, correspondence, wills, and deeds.

Doe defendants *(de·FEN·dents)* The device used to refer to defendants whose names are unknown.

domestic corporation *(do·MES·tik kor·por·A·shun)* A corporation organized in the state in which it is operating.

domestic violence *(do·MES·tik VY·o·lenss)* The abuse of a closely related person such as a present or former spouse or cohabitant.

domicile *(DOM·i·sile)* A person's principal place of abode; the place to which, whenever one is absent from it, one has the present intent of returning.

donee *(doh·NEE)* A person who receives a gift.

donor *(doh·NOR)* A person who gives a gift. A person who establishes a trust. Also called *grantor, settlor,* and *trustor*.

dormant partner *(DOR·ment PART·ner)* A partner who is not known to the public as a partner and who takes no active part in the business.

double jeopardy *(DUB·el JEP·er·dee)* The situation in which a defendant is tried twice for the same offense.

double taxation *(DUB·el taks·AY·shun)* Taxes on a corporation's income and on the dividends earned by the corporation's stockholders.

dower *(DOW·er)* At common law, the right of a widow to a life estate in one-third of all real property owned by her husband during coverture.

drugs Chemical substances that have an effect on the body or mind.

drug trafficking *(TRAF·ik·ing)* The unauthorized manufacture or distribution of any controlled substance, or the possession of such a substance with the intention of manufacturing or distributing it illegally.

due process clause *(dew PRO·sess)* A clause in the U.S. Constitution requiring that no person shall be deprived of life, liberty, or property without fairness and justice.

dummy corporation *(DUM·mee kor·por·AY·shun)* A lawful corporation created to take title assets while safeguarding the corporation owner's identity and liability.

durable power of attorney *(DYOOR·e·bel POW·er ov a·TERN·ee)* A document authorizing another person to act on one's behalf, with language indicating that the authorization either is to survive one's incapacity or is to become effective when one becomes incapacitated.

duress *(dyoor·ESS)* The overcoming of a person's free will by the use of threat or physical harm.

duty of care *(DYOO·tee ov kare)* A legal obligation of carefulness or prudence toward those likely to be injured by one's conduct.

dwelling house *(DWEL·ing)* A house in which the occupier and family usually reside, including all outbuildings within the curtilage.

easement appurtenant *(EEZ·ment a·PER·ten·ent)* An easement that benefits a particular tract of land.

e-commerce *(ee-KOM·erss)* Abbreviation for electronic commerce. The buying and selling of goods and services, or the transfer of money, over the Internet.

e-contracts *(ee KON·traks)* Contracts entered into over the Internet, including licenses to use software.

e-discovery *(ee diss·KOV·er·ee)* Obtaining electronic communications or other information stored electronically for the purposes of trial preparation.

efficacy *(EF·i·ka·see)* Effectiveness.

ejectment *(e·JEKT·ment)* At common law, the legal action used by landlords to evict tenants.

elective share *(e·LEK·tiv)* A statutory sum given to a surviving spouse who disclaims the provisions made for him or her in a deceased spouse's will. Also called *forced share*.

Electronically stored information (ESI) *(ee·lek·TRON·i·kel·lee stord in·fore·MAY·shun)* Information created, manipulated, communicated, and stored by computer.

eleemosynary corporation *(el·ee·MOS·en·er·ee kor·por·AY·shun)* A corporation that is created for charitable and benevolent purposes.

emancipated *(e·MAN·si·pay·ted)* Freed from parental control.

embezzlement *(em·BEZ·ul·ment)* The fraudulent appropriation of property by a person to whom it has been entrusted.

emotional distress *(e·MO·shun·el dis·TRESS)* Emotional suffering caused by the infliction of extreme and outrageous intentional conduct by another.

employee *(em·PLOY·ee)* One who performs services under the direction and control of another.

employer *(em·PLOY·er)* One who employs the services of others in exchange for wages or salaries.

encumbrance *(en·KUM·brenss)* A claim that one has against the property of another. A lien, charge, or liability attached to and binding on real property.

enjoin *(en·JOYN)* To require a person to perform, or to abstain from performing, some act.

entrapment *(en·TRAP·ment)* A defense that may be used when a police officer induces a person to commit a crime that the person would not have otherwise committed.

equal protection clause *(EE·kwell pro·TEK·shen)* A clause in the U.S. Constitution requiring similarly situated persons to receive similar treatment under the law.

equitable distribution laws *(EK·wit·a·bel dis·tre·BYOO·shun)* Laws that give courts the power to distribute property equitably between the parties upon divorce.

equitable theory of mortgages *(EK·wit·a·bel THEE·ree ov MORE·gejes)* The legal theory that a mortgage is not a conveyance of title, but merely a lien against the property. Also called *lien theory of mortgages.*

equitable title *(EK·wit·a·bel TY·tel)* The right to beneficial enjoyment. Also called *beneficial title.*

equity *(EK·wi·tee)* That which is just and fair.

equity of redemption *(EK·wi·tee ov re·DEMP·shun)* The right of a mortgagor to redeem the property at any time before the completion of a foreclosure proceeding by paying the amount of the debt, interest, and costs.

erosion *(e·RO·zhen)* The gradual eating away of the soil by the operation of currents or tides.

escheat *(es·CHEET)* The reversion of property to the state if the property owner dies without heirs.

e-signature *(ee·SIG·na·choor)* Abbreviation for electronic signature, a method of signing an electronic message that identifies the sender and signifies his or her approval of the message's content.

Esquire *(ES·kwyr)* A title following the name of an attorney, in place of the prefixes Mr., Mrs., Miss, or Ms. (abbreviated Esq.)

establishment clause *(es·TAB·lish·ment)* A clause in the U.S. Constitution that prohibits the government from establishing a state religion.

estate *(es·TATE)* Ownership interest.

estate planning *(es·TATE PLAN·ing)* Arranging a person's assets in a way that maintains and protects the family most effectively both during the person's life and after the person's death.

estate pur autre vie *(per OH·tra vee)* An estate that a person holds during the life of another person.

estate tail male A freehold estate restricting ownership to men in the family line.

estate tail special *(SPESH·el)* A freehold estate restricting ownership to a husband and wife and the heirs of their two bodies.

estate tax *(es·TATE)* A tax imposed upon the estate of a deceased person.

euthanasia *(yooth·e·NAY·zha)* An active procedure to hasten the death of one who is terminally ill or in immense suffering.

eviction *(e·VIK·shun)* The act of depriving a person of the possession of real property either by reentry or by legal process.

exclusionary rule *(eks·KLOO·shun·a·ree)* Evidence obtained by an unconstitutional search or seizure, that cannot be used at the trial of a defendant.

exclusive jurisdiction *(eks·KLOO·siv joo·res·DIK·shen)* The power of one court only to hear a particular case, to the exclusion of all other courts.

exculpatory clause *(eks·KUL·pa·toh·ree)* A clause that is used in a contract to escape legal responsibility.

excusable homicide *(eks·KYOO·se·bel HOM·i·side)* The taking of a human life when an excuse exists.

execute *(EK·se·kyoot)* To complete, to make, to perform, or to do, such as sign a will.

executed *(EK·se·kyoo·ted)* Carried out or performed.

executor *(eg·ZEK·yoo·tor)* A male nominated in a will of a decedent to carry out the terms of the will; a personal representative of an estate.

executor de son tort *(eg·ZEK·yoo·tor day sown tort)* A person who performs the duties of an executor without authority to do so.

executory *(eg·ZEK·yoo·tor·ee)* That which is yet to be executed or performed.

executrix *(eg·ZEK·yoo·triks)* A female nominated in a will of a decedent to carry out the terms of the will; a personal representative of an estate.

exemplary damages *(eg·ZEMP·le·ree DAM·e·jez)* Damages as a measure of punishment for the defendant's wrongful acts. Also called *punitive damages.*

exemption equivalent trust *(eg·ZEMP·shun)* A type of marital deduction trust that reduces the taxation of the second spouse to die by limiting the amount in that person's estate to a sum that is not taxable. Also called *A–B trust, bypass trust,* and *credit-shelter trust.*

exemptions *(eg·ZEMP·shuns)* Items of property that are excepted from bankruptcy proceedings and may be retained by the debtor.

exhibits *(eg·ZIB·its)* Tangible items that are introduced in evidence.

exordium clause *(eks·ORD·ee·um)* The introductory paragraph of a will. Also called *publication clause.*

ex parte *(eks PAR·tay)* On one side only.

ex parte foreign divorce *(eks·PAR·tay FOR·en de·VORSS)* A divorce that occurs when one spouse appears in a foreign jurisdiction, and the other spouse does not appear and fails to respond to the notice of divorce or service of process.

ex post facto *(eks post FAC·toh)* After the fact.

express authority *(eks·PRESS aw·THAW·ri·tee)* Authority that is given explicitly.

express contract *(eks·PRESS KON·trakt)* A contract in which the terms are stated or expressed by the parties.

express warranty *(eks·PRESS WAR·en·tee)* A statement of fact or promise that goods have certain qualities.

extinction *(eks·TINK·shun)* The act of extinguishing or putting to an end.

extortion *(eks·TOR·shun)* The corrupt demanding or receiving by a person in office of a fee for services that should be performed gratuitously.

extradition *(ex·tre·DI·shun)* A process that permits the return of fugitives, to the state in which they are accused of having committed a crime, by the governor of the state to which they have fled.

fact finder *(fakt FINE·der)* The jury in a jury trial or the judge in a nonjury trial.

factor *(FAK·ter)* A bailee to whom goods are consigned for sale.

failure of consideration *(FAYL·yer ov kon·sid· er·AY·shun)* A defense available when the consideration provided for in an agreement is not in fact given to the party being sued.

failure to warn *(FALE·yer to warn)* The theory that dangerous products were inadequately labeled or the danger inadequately communicated to the consumer or user.

fair-use doctrine *(DOK·trin)* A rule stating that the fair use of a copyrighted work for purposes such as criticism, comment, news reporting, teaching, scholarship, or research is not a copyright infringement.

false arrest *(a·REST)* The intentional confinement of a person without legal justification. Also called *false imprisonment.*

false imprisonment *(im·PRIS·on·ment)* The intentional confinement of a person without legal justification. Also called *false arrest.*

family farmer debt adjustment *(a·JUST·ment)* A method for family farmers to adjust their financial affairs while continuing to operate their farms. Also called *Chapter 12 bankruptcy.*

federal district courts *(FED·er·el DISS·trikt korts)* Also known as U.S. District Courts. The Courts that hear most federal cases before an appeal. Each state, territory, and the District of Columbia has at least one.

federal question *(FED·er·ul KWES·chen)* A matter that involves the U.S. Constitution, acts of Congress, or treason.

fee The largest estate that one can own in land, giving the holder the absolute ownership and power of disposition during life, and descending to the owner's heirs at death. Also called *fee simple absolute* and *fee simple estate.*

fee simple absolute *(SIM·pel ab·so·LOOT)* The largest estate that one can own in land, giving the holder the absolute ownership and power of disposition during life, and descending to the owner's heirs at death. Also called *fee* and *fee simple estate.*

fee simple determinable *(de·TER·min·e·bel)* An estate in real property that is capable of coming to an end automatically because of the happening of some event. Also called *determinable fee.*

fee simple estate *(es·TATE)* The largest estate that one can own in land, giving the holder the absolute ownership and power of disposition during life, and descending to the owner's heirs at death. Also called *fee* and *fee simple absolute.*

fee tail estate *(es·TATE)* A freehold estate that restricts ownership of real property to a particular family blood line.

felon *(FEL·en)* A person who has committed a felony.

felonious homicide *(fe·LONE·ee·es HOM·i·side)* Homicide done with the intent to commit a felony.

felony *(FEL·en·ee)* A major crime, punishable by imprisonment in a state prison.

felony murder *(FEL·en·ee MER·der)* Murder committed while in the commission or attempted commission of a crime punishable with death or imprisonment for life.

feticide *(FET·e·side)* The killing of a fetus in the womb; abortion.

fiduciary *(fi·DOO·shee·air·ee)* A person in a position of trust, such as an executor, administrator, guardian, or trustee.

fiduciary capacity *(fi·DOO·shee·air·ee ka·PASS·e·tee)* A position of trust.

fiduciary deed *(fi·DOO·shee·air·ee)* A deed to real property in which the grantor transfers only his or her interest, if any, in the property and gives no warranties of title. Also called *deed without covenants* and *quitclaim deed.*

firm offer *(OFF·er)* A merchant's written promise to hold open an offer for the sale of goods.

first and final account *(a·KOWNT)* An accounting, if it is the only one, presented to the court in final settlement of a decedent's estate.

first-degree murder *(de·GREE MER·der)* Murder committed with deliberately premeditated malice aforethought, or with extreme atrocity or cruelty, or while in the commission of a crime punishable by life in prison.

fixed-rate mortgage *(fiksd-rate MORE·gej)* A mortgage with an interest rate that does not change during the life of the mortgage.

fixture *(FIKS·cher)* Personal property that is physically attached to real property and becomes part of the real property.

flexible-rate mortgage *(FLEKS·i·bel-rate MORE·gej)* A mortgage with an interest rate that fluctuates according to changes in an index to which it is connected. Also called *variable-rate mortgage.*

f.o.b. the place of destination *(des·te·NAY·shun)* Free on board (no delivery charges) to the place of destination.

f.o.b. the place of shipment *(SHIP·ment)* Free on board (no delivery charges) to the place of shipment.

forbearance *(for·BARE·enss)* Refraining from taking action.

forced heir *(forssd air)* A surviving spouse who elects to disclaim the provisions of a deceased spouse's will.

forced share A statutory sum given to a surviving spouse who disclaims the provisions made for him or her in a deceased spouse's will. Also called *elective share.*

forcible entry and detainer *(FORSS·i·bel EN·tree and de·TAYN·er)* The legal action used by landlords to evict tenants. Also called *dispossessory warrant proceedings, summary ejectment, summary process,* and *unlawful detainer.*

foreclose *(for·KLOZE)* To shut out, bar, or terminate.

foreign corporation *(FOR·en kor·por·AY·shun)* A corporation that is organized in a state other than that in which it is operating.

foreign divorce *(FOR·en de·VORSS)* A divorce in a state or country other than the one in which the party lives.

foreign jurisdiction *(FOR·en joo·res·DIK·shen)* A jurisdiction, such as another state or country, other than that in which a current litigation is taking place.

foreperson *(FORE·per·son)* The presiding member of a jury who speaks for the group.

foreseeable *(fore·SEE·e·bel)* Known in advance; anticipated.

forgery *(FOR·jer·ee)* The fraudulent making or altering of a writing whereby the rights of another might be prejudiced.

fornication *(for·ni·KAY·shun)* Sexual intercourse between two unmarried persons.

forum *(FOR·em)* The place of litigation.

forum non conveniens *(FOR·em non kon·VEEN·yenz)* The right of a court to refuse to hear a case if it believes that justice would be better served if the trial were held in a different court.

franchise *(FRAN·chize)* An arrangement in which the owner of a trademark, trade name, or copyright licenses others, under special conditions or limitations, to use the trademark, trade name, or copyright in purveying goods or services.

franchisee *(fran·chize·EE)* A person to whom a franchise is given.

franchiser *(FRAN·chize·er)* A person who gives a franchise to another.

fratricide *(FRAT·re·side)* The killing of one's brother.

fraud *(frawd)* A misrepresentation of a material, existing fact, knowingly made, that causes someone reasonably relying on it to suffer damages. Also called *deceit*.

fraud in esse contractus *(ESS·ay kon·TRAKT·es)* Fraud as to the essential nature of the transaction.

fraud in the execution *(frawd in the ex·e·KEW·shun)* Fraud as to the essential nature of the transaction. Also called fraud in esse contractus.

fraud in the inducement *(in·DEWSS·ment)* Fraud that induces another to enter into a contract.

freedom of assembly *(FREE·dum ov a·SEM·blee)* A clause in the U.S. Constitution that guarantees to all persons the right to peaceably associate and assemble with others.

freedom of speech *(FREE·dum)* A clause in the U.S. Constitution that guarantees to all persons the right to speak, both orally and in writing.

freedom of the press *(FREE·dum)* A clause in the U.S. Constitution that guarantees to all persons the right to publish and circulate their ideas, without governmental interference.

free exercise clause *(EKS·er·size)* A clause in the U.S. Constitution that guarantees to all persons the right to freely practice their religion.

freehold estate *(FREE·hold es·TATE)* An estate in which the holder owns the land for life or forever.

fruit of the poisonous tree doctrine *(DOK·trin)* Evidence generated or derived from an illegal search or seizure, that cannot be used at the trial of a defendant.

full age *(ayj)* Adulthood.

full covenant and warranty deed *(KOV·e·nent and WAR·en·tee)* A deed containing warranties under which the grantor guarantees the property to be free from all encumbrances and to defend the title against the claims of all persons. Also called *general warranty deed*.

full faith and credit clause *(KRED·et)* A clause in the U.S. Constitution requiring each state to recognize the laws and court decisions of every other state.

full warranty *(WAR·en·tee)* An express warranty given for consumer goods under which the seller must repair or replace, without cost to the buyer, defective goods or else refund the purchase price.

fungible goods *(FUN·ji·bel)* Goods such as grain or oil, of which any unit is the same as any like unit.

future goods *(FEW·cher)* Goods that are not yet in existence or under anyone's control.

garnishee *(gar·nish·EE)* A third party who holds money or property of a debtor that is subject to a garnishment action.

garnishment *(GAR·nish·ment)* A procedure for attaching a defendant's property that is in the hands of a third person.

gay marriage *(gay MA·rij)* The union of two same-sex partners; also called same-sex marriage.

general agent *(JEN·e·rel AY·jent)* An agent who is authorized to conduct all of a principal's activity in connection with a particular business.

general damages *(JEN·er·el DAM·e·jez)* Money meant to compensate the plaintiff for pain and suffering (physical discomfort and emotional trauma).

general legacy *(JEN·e·rel LEG·a·see)* A gift of money out of the general assets of the estate. Also called *general pecuniary legacy*.

general partner *(JEN·e·rel PART·ner)* A partner who manages the business and is personally liable for its debts and obligations.

general partnership *(JEN·e·rel PART·ner·ship)* A partnership in which the parties carry on a business for the joint benefit and profit of all partners.

general pecuniary legacy *(JEN·e·rel pee·KYOO·nee·er·ee LEG·a·see)* A gift of money out of the general assets of the estate. Also called *general legacy*.

general warranty deed *(JEN·e·rel WAR·en·tee)* A deed containing warranties under which the grantor guarantees the property to be free from all encumbrances and to defend the title against the claims of all persons. Also called *full covenant and warranty deed*.

generic term *(jen·ER·ik)* A term that means relating to or characteristic of a whole group.

genocide *(JEN·o·side)* The killing of a racial or political group.

gifts causa mortis *(KAWS·ah MORE·tes)* Gifts made within three years of the date of death; subject to the federal estate tax. Also called *gifts made in contemplation of death*.

gifts made in contemplation of death *(kon·tem·PLAY·shun)* Gifts made within three years of the date of death; subject to the federal estate tax. Also called *gifts causa mortis*.

gift tax A federal tax that is imposed (with exceptions) on gifts totaling more than $1 million during one's lifetime.

good faith exception to the exclusionary rule *(ek·SEP·shun)* Evidence that is discovered by officers acting in good faith, but under the mistaken belief that a search was valid, and that can be used at the trial of a defendant.

goods Things that are movable.

Good Samaritan statutes *(sem·EHR·i·ten STAT·shoots)* Laws providing that physicians, nurses, and certain other medical personnel will not be liable for negligent acts that occur when they voluntarily, without a fee, render emergency care or treatment outside of the ordinary course of their practice.

government survey system *(GUV·ern·ment SER·vay SIS·tem)* A method of describing real property according to the property's relationship to intersecting lines running east and west (base lines) and lines running north and south (principal, or prime, meridians). Also called *rectangular survey system.*

graduated-payment mortgage (GRAD·yoo·ay·ted-PAY·ment MORE·gej) A mortgage under which payments increase gradually over the life of the loan.

grand jury (JOOR·ee) A jury consisting of not more than 23 people who listen to evidence and decide whether or not to charge someone with the commission of a crime.

grand larceny (LAR·sen·ee) Larceny that is a felony.

grantee (gran·TEE) A person to whom real property is transferred.

grantor (gran·TOR) A person who transfers real property to another. A person who establishes a trust. Also called *donor, settlor,* and *trustor.*

gratuitous bailment (gra·TYOO·i·tes BAYL·ment) A bailment for the sole benefit of either the bailor or the bailee, in which no consideration is given by one of the parties in exchange for the benefits bestowed by the other.

gratuitous guest (gra·TYOO·i·tes) One invited on the premises for nonbusiness purposes.

gravamen (GRAH·ve·men) The essential basis or gist of a complaint field in a lawsuit.

gross estate (es·TATE) All property that the decedent owned at death, including individually and jointly owned property, life insurance, living trusts, and gifts made in contemplation of death.

gross negligence (NEG·li·jenss) Extreme negligence.

guardian (GAR·dee·en) One who legally has the care and management of the person, property, or both of a minor or incompetent.

guardian ad litem (GAR·dee·en ad LY·tem) Guardian for the suit. A guardian appointed by a court to protect a minor who brings or defends a lawsuit.

guilty (GILL·tee) The state of having committed a crime.

habendum clause (ha·BEN·dum) The portion of a deed beginning with the words "To have and to hold," which defines the extent of the ownership of the property granted.

half-blood A relatives who has one parent in common with another relative, but not both.

health care declaration (dek·la·RAY·shun) A written expression of a person's wishes to be allowed to die a natural death and not be kept alive by heroic or artificial methods. Also called *directive to physicians, living will,* and *medical directive.*

health care proxy (PROK·see) A written statement authorizing an agent or surrogate to make medical treatment decisions for another in the event of the other's inability to do so.

heart balm statutes (hart bahm STAT·shoots) Laws passed in most states abolishing actions for loss of consortium, breach of promise to marry, and alienation of affections.

heir (air) A person who inherits property.

heirlooms (AIR·looms) Valued possessions with sentimental value passed down through generations within a family.

heirs at law (airs) People who would have inherited had a decedent died intestate.

hereditaments (her·e·DIT·a·ments) Things capable of being inherited, including not only lands and everything thereon, but also heirlooms.

high treason (hy TREE·zun) Acts against the king (under the English common law).

holdover tenant (HOLD·o·ver TEN·ent) A tenant who wrongfully remains in possession of the premises after a tenancy has expired. Also called *tenant at sufferance.*

holographic will (hol·o·GRAF·ik) A will written entirely in the hand of the testator.

homestead (HOME·sted) Property that is beyond the reach of creditors' and others' claims as long as the family uses the property as a home.

Home Owner's Association (HOA) A non-profit organization for the purpose of marketing and managing a housing development.

homestead exemption (HOME·sted eg·ZEMP·shun) In bankruptcy, the exemption of one's residence up to a specific amount.

homestead exemption laws (HOME·sted eg·ZEMP·shun lawz) a bankruptcy law that grants the debtor a credit up to a certain amount in the value in their home.

homicide (HOM·i·side) The killing of a human being by a human being.

hot pursuit doctrine (pur·SYOOT DOK·trin) The principle that a search warrant is not needed when police pursue a fleeing suspect into a private area.

humanitarian doctrine (hew·man·i·TAYR·ee·en DOK·trin) The doctrine which holds that a defendant who had the last clear chance to avoid injuring the plaintiff is liable even though the plaintiff was contributorily negligent. Also called the *last clear chance doctrine.*

hung jury (JOOR·ee) A deadlocked jury; one that cannot agree.

identified goods (eye·DENT·i·fyd) Goods that have been selected as the subject matter of a contract.

illegal profiling (ill·EE·gul PRO·fyl·ing) A law enforcement action, such as a detention or arrest, based solely on race, religion, national origin, ethnicity, gender, or sexual orientation.

illegitimate children (il·e·JIT·i·met CHIL·dren) Children born out of wedlock. Also called *bastards* and *nonmarital children.*

imminent danger (IM·i·nent DANE·jer) The situation that exists when an unlawful attack is about to happen.

immune (im·YOON) Exempt.

impaneled (im·PAN·eld) Listed as members of the jury.

impeach (im·PEECH) Call into question.

impediment (im·PED·i·ment) Disability or hindrance to the making of a contract.

implied authority (im·PLIDE aw·THAW·ri·tee) The power granted to an agent to perform incidental functions that are reasonably and customarily necessary to accomplish the overall purpose of the agency.

implied contract (im·PLIDE KON·trakt) A contract in which the terms are not stated or expressed by the parties.

implied trust (im·PLIDE) A trust that arises, by implication of law, from the conduct of the parties.

implied warranty (im·PLIDE WAR·en·tee) A warranty that is imposed by law rather than given voluntarily.

impossibility (im·pos·i·BIL·i·tee) A method of discharging a contract that is impossible to perform, not merely difficult or costly.

impotency (*IM·pe·ten·see*) The incapacity of either party to consummate a marriage by sexual intercourse because of some physical infirmity or disarrangement.

impute (*im·PEWT*) To charge; to lay the responsibility or blame.

imputed liability (*im·PEW·ted ly·a·BIL·i·tee*) Vicarious responsibility for the torts committed by another person.

inadmissible (*in·ad·MISS·i·bel*) Cannot be received.

incarceration (*in·kar·ser·AY·shun*) Confinement.

incest (*IN·sest*) Sexual intercourse between people who are related, by consanguinity or affinity, in such a way that they cannot legally marry.

incidental beneficiary (*in·si·DEN·tal ben·uh·FISH·air·ee*) One who is indirectly benefited by a contract.

incidental damages (*in·si·DEN·tel DAM·e·jez*) Reasonable expenses that indirectly result from a breach of contract.

incompatibility (*in·kom·pat·e·BIL·i·tee*) Conflicts in personalities and dispositions that are so deep as to be irreconcilable and irremediable and that render it impossible for the parties to continue to live together in a normal marital relationship. Also called *irreconcilable differences* and *irretrievable breakdown*.

incorporation by reference (*in·kore·per·AY·shen by REF·e·renss*) Making a second document part of first document by referring to it in the first document and stating the intention of including it.

incorporators (*in·KOR·por·ay·tors*) People who organize a corporation by filing articles of organization with the state government.

indenture (*in·DEN·cher*) A deed or lease to which two or more persons are parties.

independent contractor (*in·de·PEN·dent KON·trak·ter*) One who performs services for others, but who is not under the others' control.

indictment (*in·DITE·ment*) A formal, written charge of a crime made by a grand jury.

indifferent (*in·DIF·rent*) Impartial, unbiased, and disinterested.

infancy (*IN·fen·see*) Under the age of majority.

infant (*IN·fent*) The legal name for a minor.

infanticide (*in·FANT·e·side*) The killing of an infant soon after birth.

information (*in·for·MA·shun*) A formal written charge of a crime made by a public official rather than by a grand jury.

inheritance tax (*in·HER·i·tenss*) A tax imposed on a person who inherits from a decedent's estate.

injunction (*in·JUNK·shun*) An order of a court of equity to do or refrain from doing a particular act.

in pari delicto (*in PAH·ree de·LIK·toh*) In equal fault.

in personam action (*in per·SOH·nem AK·shun*) A lawsuit in which the court has jurisdiction over the person.

personam jurisdiction (*per·SOH·nem joo·res·DIK·shen*) Jurisdiction over the person.

in rem action (*in rem AK·shun*) A lawsuit that is directed against property rather than against a particular person.

insanity (*in·SAN·i·tee*) A defense available to mentally ill defendants who can prove that they did not know the nature and quality of their actions or did not appreciate the criminality of their conduct.

intangible personal property (*in·TAN·je·bel PER·son·al PROP·er·tee*) Property that is not perceptible to the senses and that cannot be touched.

intellectual property (*in·te·LEK·choo·el PROP·er·tee*) An original work fixed in a tangible medium of expression.

intended beneficiary (*in·TEN·ded ben·e·FISH·air·ee*) The third party of a contract made with the purpose of benefiting that party.

intentional infliction of emotional distress (IIED) (*in·TEN·shun·el in·FLIK·shun ov ee·MO·shun·el diss·TRESS*) A type of tort whereby the intentional conduct of a person results in extreme emotional suffering.

intentional torts (*in·TEN·shun·el*) Torts that are committed intentionally. Also called *willful torts*.

interlocutory decree (*in·ter·LOK·ye·tore·ee de·KREE*) A provisional or temporary decision of a court.

interrogatories (*in·te·RAW·ga·tore·rees*) A form of discovery in a civil action in which parties are given a series of written questions to be answered under oath.

in terrorem clause (*in ter·RAW·rem*) A clause in a will that attempts to disinherit any legatee, devisee, or beneficiary who contests the provisions of the will. Also called *no-contest clause*.

interval ownership (*IN·ter·vel OH·ner·ship*) A fee simple ownership of a unit of real property in which the owner can exercise the right of possession for only an interval, such as a week or two, each year. Also called *time-sharing*.

inter vivos (*IN·ter VY·vose*) A legal term referring to a transfer or gift made during one's lifetime as opposed to a gift that takes effect at death.

inter vivos trust (*IN·ter VY·vose*) A trust that is created by the settlor when he or she is alive. Also called a *living trust*.

intestacy (*in·TESS·te·see*) The state of having died without having made a valid will.

intestate (*in·TESS·tate*) The state of having made no valid will.

intestate share (*in·TESS·tate*) An amount that is inherited when a decedent has died without a will.

intestate succession (*in·TESS·tate suk·SESH·en*) The act or process of an heir's becoming beneficially entitled to the property of one who has died without a will.

intoxication (*in·tox·i·KAY·shun*) A state in which a person is under the influence of drugs or alcohol—a defense that rarely works.

invasion of privacy (*in·VA·zhun ov PRY·ve·see*) A violation of the right of privacy.

inventory (*IN·ven·tor·ee*) A detailed list of articles of property in an estate, made by the executor or administrator thereof.

invitation to deal (*in·vi·TA·shun*) A request to an individual or to the public to make an offer. Also called *invitation to negotiate*.

invitation to negotiate (*ne·GO·shee·ate*) A request to an individual or to the public to make an offer. Also called *invitation to deal*.

involuntary bankruptcy (*in·VOL·en·ter·ee BANK·rupt·see*) A bankruptcy proceeding that is initiated by one or more creditors.

involuntary manslaughter (*in·VOL·en·ter·ee MAN·slaw·ter*) The unintentional killing of another while in the commission of an unlawful act or while in the commission of a reckless act.

irreconcilable differences *(ir·rek·en·SY·le·bel DIF·ren·sez)* Conflicts in personalities and dispositions that are so deep as to be irreconcilable and irremediable and that render it impossible for the parties to continue to live together in a normal marital relationship. Also called *incompatibility* and *irretrievable breakdown.*

irretrievable breakdown *(ir·ree·TREE·ve·bel BRAKE·down)* Conflicts in personalities and dispositions that are so deep as to be irreconcilable and irremediable and that render it impossible for the parties to continue to live together in a normal marital relationship. Also called *incompatibility* and *irreconcilable differences.*

irrevocable living trust *(ir·REV·e·ke·bel)* A trust that may not be rescinded or changed by the settlor at any time during his or her lifetime.

issue *(ISH·oo)* All people who have descended from a common ancestor.

joint custody *(joynt KUSS·te·dee)* Custody in which both parents share the responsibility and authority of child rearing.

joint enterprise *(joynt EN·ter·prize)* A relationship in which two or more people combine their labor or property for a single business undertaking. Also called *co-venture, joint venture,* and *syndicate.*

joint liability *(joynt ly·a·BIL·i·tee)* Liability under which all joint tortfeasors must be named as defendants in a lawsuit.

joint tenancy *(TEN·en·see)* The estate owned by joint tenants. Also called *joint tenancy with the right of survivorship.*

joint tenancy with the right of survivorship *(ser·VIVE·er·ship)* The estate owned by joint tenants. Also called *joint tenancy.*

joint tenants *(TEN·entz)* Two or more persons holding one and the same interest, accruing by one and the same conveyance, commencing at one and the same time, and held by one and the same undivided possession.

joint tortfeasors *(tort·FEE·zors)* Two or more people who participate in the commission of a tort.

joint venture *(joynt VEN·cher)* A relationship in which two or more people combine their labor or property for a single business undertaking. Also called *co-venture, joint enterprise,* and *syndicate.*

judgment *(JUJ·ment)* The decision of a court of law.

judgment nisi *(JUJ·ment NY·sie)* A provisional judgment that becomes final at the end of a stated period unless a valid reason is shown for not issuing it.

judgment notwithstanding the verdict *(VER·dikt)* A judgment rendered in favor of one party notwithstanding a verdict in favor of the other party. Also called *judgment n.o.v.*

judgment n.o.v. A judgment rendered in favor of one party notwithstanding a verdict in favor of the other party (n.o.v. is the abbreviation for non obstante verdicto, which means notwithstanding a verdict).

judgment on the merits *(MER·its)* A court decision based on the evidence and facts introduced.

judgment on the pleadings *(PLEED·ings)* A judgment rendered without hearing evidence when the court determines that it is clear from the pleadings that one party is entitled to win the case.

junior mortgage *(JOO·nyer MORE·gej)* A mortgage subject to a prior mortgage.

jurisdiction *(joo·res·DIK·shen)* The power or authority that a court has to hear a case.

jurors *(JOOR·ors)* Members of a jury.

jury *(JOOR·ee)* A group of people selected according to law and sworn to determine the facts in a case.

jury charge *(JOOR·ee charj)* Instructions to a jury on matters of law.

jury panel *(JOOR·ee PAN·el)* The large group of people from which a jury is selected for a trial. Also called *array, jury pool,* and *venire.*

jury pool *(JOOR·ee pool)* The large group of people from which a jury is selected for a trial. Also called *array, jury panel,* and *venire.*

jury waived trial *(JOOR·ee waved tryl)* A trial without a jury. Also called *bench trial.*

justice *(JUSS·tis)* The title of an appellate court judge.

justiciable *(jus·TISH·e·bel)* Appropriate for court assessment.

justifiable homicide *(jus·ti·FY·a·bel HOM·i·side)* The taking of a human life when an excuse exists.

kindred *(KIN·dred)* Blood relatives.

lack of consideration *(kon·sid·er·AY·shun)* A defense available to a party being sued when no consideration is contained in the agreement that is the subject of the suit.

landlord A person who owns real property and who rents it to another under a lease. Also called *lessor.*

lapsed devise *(lapsd de·VIZE)* A gift of real property in a will that fails because the devisee predeceased the testator.

lapsed legacy *(lapsd LEG·a·see)* A gift of personal property in a will that fails because the legatee predeceased the testator.

larceny *(LAR·sen·ee)* At common law, the wrongful taking and carrying away of personal property of another with the intent to steal.

larceny by false pretenses *(PRE·ten·sez)* Knowingly and deliberately obtaining the property of another by false pretenses with the intent to defraud. Also called *criminal fraud.*

last clear chance doctrine *(DOK·trin)* The doctrine which holds that a defendant who had the last clear chance to avoid injuring the plaintiff is liable even though the plaintiff was contributorily negligent. Also called *humanitarian doctrine.*

leading questions *(LEE·ding)* Questions that suggest to the witness the desired answer.

lease *(leess)* A contract granting the use of certain real property by its owner to another for a specified period in return for the payment of rent.

leasehold estate *(LEESS·hold es·TATE)* An estate that is less than a freehold estate. The interest that is conveyed by a lease.

legacy *(LEG·a·see)* A gift of personal property in a will.

legal fiction *(LEE·gul FIK·shun)* An assumption, for purposes of justice, of a fact that does not exist.

legal issues *(LEE·gul ISH·oos)* Questions of law to be decided by the court in a lawsuit.

legal tender *(LEE·gul TEN·der)* Coin, paper, or other currency that is sufficient under law for the payment of debts.

legal title *(LEE·gul TY·tel)* Full, absolute ownership.

legatee (*leg·a·TEE*) A person who receives a gift of personal property under a will.

legator (*leg·a·TOR*) A person who makes a gift of personal property by a will.

lessee (*less·EE*) A person who has temporary possession of and an interest in real property of another under a lease. Also called *tenant*.

lesser included offense (*o·FENSS*) A crime that contains some, but not all, elements of a greater offense, making it impossible to commit the greater offense without also committing the lesser offense.

lessor (*less·OR*) A person who owns real property and who rents it to another under a lease. Also called *landlord*.

letters of administration (*ad·min·iss·TRAY·shun*) A certificate of appointment as administrator of an estate.

letters testamentary (*test·e·MEN·ter·ee*) A certificate of appointment as executor of a will.

levy on execution (*LEV·ee on ek·se·KYOO·shen*) To collect a sum of money by putting into effect the judgment of a court.

liability (*ly·a·BIL·i·tee*) Legal responsibility, obligation, or duty.

libel (*LIE·bel*) Defamation communicated by a writing, drawing, photograph, television program, or other means that is directed toward the sense of sight. The initial pleading in a divorce action.

libelant (*lie·bel·AHNT*) The plaintiff in a divorce action.

libelee (*lie·bel·EE*) The defendant in a divorce action.

license (*LY·sense*) A grant or permission to do a particular thing.

licensee (*ly·sen·SEE*) A person who has permission to do certain acts.

lien (*leen*) A claim or charge on property for the payment of a debt.

lien theory of mortgages (*leen THEE·ree ov MORE·ge·jes*) The legal theory that a mortgage is not a conveyance of title, but merely a lien against the property. Also called *equitable theory of mortgages*.

life estate (*es·TATE*) An estate limited in duration to either the life of the owner or the life of another person.

life tenant (*TEN·ent*) The owner of a life estate.

limited divorce (*LIM·i·ted de·VORSS*) The discontinuance of cohabitation by the spouses. Also called *divorce from bed and board* and *separation of spouses*.

limited liability company (**LLC**) (*LIM·i·ted ly·a·BIL·i·tee KUM·pe·nee*) A nonpartnership form of business organization that has the tax benefits of a partnership and the limited liability benefits of a corporation.

limited liability limited partnership (**LLLP**) The combination of a limited partnership and a limited liability partnership.

limited liability partnership (**LLP**) (*LIM·i·ted ly·a·BIL·i·tee PART·ner·ship*) A general partnership in which only the partnership, and not the individual partners, is liable for the tort liabilities of the partnership. Also called *registered limited liability partnership (RLLP)* and *registered partnership having limited liability (RPLL)*.

limited partner (*LIM·i·ted PART·ner*) A partner who invests money or other property in the business, but who is not liable for the debts or obligations of the partnership.

limited partnership (*LIM·i·ted PART·ner·ship*) A partnership formed by two or more persons having as members one or more general partners and one or more limited partners.

limited warranty (*LIM·i·ted WAR·en·tee*) An express warranty given for consumer goods that is less than a full warranty.

limited warranty deed (*LIM·i·ted WAR·en·tee*) A deed containing warranties under which the grantor guarantees that the property is free from all encumbrances made during the time that he or she owned the property and agrees to defend the title only against claims through him or her. Also called *special warranty deed*.

lineal ascendants (*LIN·ee·el e·SEN·dents*) People who are in a direct line of ascent (upward) from the decedent—parents, grandparents, and great grandparents.

lineal descendants (*LIN·ee·el de·SEN·dents*) People who are in a direct line of descent (downward) from the decedent—children, grandchildren, and great grandchildren.

liquidate (*LIK·wi·date*) Turn into cash.

liquidated damages (*LIK·wi·day·ted DAM·e·jez*) Damages that are agreed on by the parties at the time of the execution of a contract in the event of a subsequent breach.

liquidation (*lik·wi·DAY·shun*) A proceeding designed to liquidate a debtor's property, pay off creditors, and discharge the debtor from most debts. Also called *Chapter 7 bankruptcy* and *straight bankruptcy*.

litigants (*LIT·i·gants*) Parties to a lawsuit.

litigation (*lit·i·GAY·shun*) A suit at law.

living trust A trust that is created by the settlor when he or she is alive. Also called *inter vivos trust*.

living will A written expression of a person's wishes to be allowed to die a natural death and not be kept alive by heroic or artificial methods. Also called *directive to physicians, health care declaration,* and *medical directive*.

local action (*LO·kel AK·shun*) A lawsuit that can occur only in one place.

locus (*LOH·kus*) Place; locality.

locus sigilli (*LOH·kus se·JIL·i*) Place of the seal.

long-arm statutes (*STAT·shoots*) Statutes that allow one state to reach out and obtain personal jurisdiction over a person in another state.

loss of consortium (*kon·SORE·shum*) The destruction of fellowship between a husband and wife.

mail fraud (*frawd*) Using mail to obtain money, property, or services by false pretenses.

maim (*maym*) To cripple or mutilate in any way.

maintenance (*MAIN·ten·ens*) The legal obligations of parents to contribute to the economic maintenance and education of their children. Also called *child support*.

majority (*ma·JAW·ri·tee*) Full age; adulthood.

mala in se (*MAL·ah in say*) Wrong in and of itself.

mala prohibita (*MAL·ah pro·HIB·i·ta*) Prohibited wrong.

malefactor (*mal·e·FAK·ter*) A person found guilty of a crime.

malfeasance (*mal·FEE·zenss*) The doing of an act that ought not to be done at all.

malice aforethought (*MAL·iss e·FOR·thawt*) Evil intent; that state of mind which is reckless of law and of the legal rights of others.

malicious prosecution *(ma·LISH·us pros·e·KYOO·shun)* Prosecution begun in malice without probable cause.

malpractice *(mal·PRAK·tiss)* Professional misconduct; negligence of a professional.

managers *(MAN·a·jers)* People who are designated by the members of a limited liability company to manage the company.

mandatory arbitration *(MAN·da·tor·ee ar·be·TRAY·shun)* Arbitration that is required by agreement or by law. Also called *compulsory arbitration.*

mandatory sentence *(MAN·da·tor·ee SEN·tenss)* A fixed sentence that must be imposed with no room for discretion.

manslaughter *(MAN·slaw·ter)* The unlawful killing of one human being by another without malice aforethought.

manufacturing defect *(man·yew·FAK·chur·ing DEE·fekt)* The theory that a product was negligently built or built with substandard materials.

marital deduction *(MAR·i·tal de·DUK·shun)* The amount that passes from a decedent to a surviving spouse and is not taxable under the federal estate tax law.

maritime *(MER·i·tym)* Pertaining to the sea.

marriage *(MAR·ej)* Under the laws of the federal government and most states, the union of one man and one woman.

marital deduction trust *(MAR·i·tal de·DUK·shun)* A trust that is arranged to make maximum use of the marital deduction that is found in the federal estate tax law.

marriage banns *(MAR·ej)* Public notice of a marriage contract for a certain number of weeks before the wedding date. Also called *banns of matrimony.*

master *(MAS·ter)* An employer. A lawyer appointed by the court to hear testimony in a case and report back to the court as to his or her findings or conclusions.

master deed *(MAS·ter deed)* A deed to a condominium that describes the entire property that is owned by the condominium association.

matricide *(MAT·ri·side)* Killing one's mother.

mayhem *(MAY·hem)* At common law, violently depriving others of the use of such members as may render them less able in fighting.

means testing *(meenz TEST·ing)* A comparison to determine whether a debtor meets eligibility requirements to be in Chapter 7 or Chapter 13 bankruptcy.

mediation *(mee·dee·AY·shun)* An informal process in which a neutral, third person listens to both sides and makes suggestions for reaching a solution. Also called conciliation.

mediator *(MEE·dee·ay·tor)* A neutral, third person in a mediation session who listens to both sides and makes suggestions for reaching a solution. Also called a *conciliator.*

medical directive *(MED·i·kel de·REKT·iv)* A written expression of a person's wishes to be allowed to die a natural death and not be kept alive by heroic or artificial methods. Also called *directive to physicians, health care declaration,* and *living will.*

medical power of attorney *(MED·i·kel POW·er ov e·TERN·ee)* A written statement authorizing an agent or surrogate to make medical treatment decisions for another in the event of the other's inability to do so.

members *(MEM·bers)* Owners of a limited liability company.

memorandum *(mem·o·RAN·dum)* The writing that is necessary to satisfy the statute of frauds.

mens rea *(menz RAY·eh)* Criminal intent.

merchant *(MER·chent)* A person who sells goods of the kind sold in the ordinary course of business or who has knowledge or skills peculiar to those goods.

meridians *(mer·ID·ee·ens)* Lines running north and south in the United States government survey. Also called *prime meridians* and *principal meridians.*

metadata *(ME·te·da·te)* Computer information that is akin to an electronic fingerprint.

metes *(meets)* Distances between points.

metes and bounds A system of describing real property by its outer boundaries, with reference to courses, distances, and monuments.

minimum sentence *(MIN·i·mum SEN·tenss)* The smallest amount of time that a prisoner must serve before being released or placed on parole.

mini-trials *(tryls)* Informal trials run by private organizations established for the purpose of settling disputes out of court.

minor *(MY·ner)* A person under the age of majority; usually under 18.

Miranda warnings *(mer·AN·de)* The constitutional right given to people who are arrested to be told before being questioned that they have the right to remain silent, that any statements made by them may be used against them, that they have a right to have a lawyer present, and that a lawyer will be provided without cost if they cannot afford one.

miscegenation *(mis·sej·e·NA·shun)* Marriage between people of different races.

misdemeanor *(mis·de·MEEN·er)* A minor crime; not a felony.

misfeasance *(mis·FEE·zenss)* The improper doing of an act.

misnomer *(mis·NO·mer)* Mistake in name.

misrepresentation *(mis·rep·rez·en·TAY·shun)* A false or deceptive statement or act.

mistrial *(MIS·tryl)* An invalid trial of no consequence.

mitigate *(MIT·i·gate)* Lessen; keep as low as possible.

moiety *(MOY·e·tee)* A part, portion, or fraction.

money laundering *(MUN·ee LAWN·der·ing)* A metaphor used to describe how money acquired through criminal activities is "washed" so that it can appear to have been earned legitimately.

monuments *(MON·yoo·ments)* Visible marks indicating boundaries.

mortgage *(MORE·gej)* A conveyance of real property for the purpose of securing a debt. Also called *mortgage deed.*

mortgage assignment *(MORE·gej e·SINE·ment)* The transfer of a mortgagee's interest in a mortgage to another person.

mortgage assumption *(MORE·gej e·SUMP·shun)* An agreement by a new owner of real property to pay the former owner's mortgage. Also called *mortgage take-over.*

mortgage deed (*MORE·gej*) A conveyance of real property for the purpose of securing a debt. Also called *mortgage*.

mortgage discharge (*MORE·gej DIS·charj*) A document stating that a mortgage debt is satisfied.

mortgagee (*more·gej·EE*) One who lends money and takes back a mortgage as security for the loan.

mortgagee's foreclosure sale (*more·gej·EEZ for·KLOH·zher*) A sale of real property that terminates all rights of the mortgagor in the property covered by the mortgage.

mortgage take-over (*MORE·gej*) An agreement by a new owner of real property to pay the former owner's mortgage. Also called *mortgage assumption*.

mortgagor (*more·gej·OR*) One who borrows money and gives a mortgage—that is, pledges property to the lender as security for the loan.

motion (*MOH·shun*) A written or oral request made to a court for certain action to be taken.

motion for a directed verdict (*de·REK·ted VER·dikt*) In a jury trial, a motion asking the court to find in favor of the moving party as a matter of law, without having the case go to the jury.

motion for a more definite statement (*DEF·e·net STATE·ment*) A motion by a party, when a pleading is vague, asking the court to order the other party to make a more definite statement.

motion for judgment on the pleadings (*JUJ·ment on the PLEED·ings*) A motion by either party for a judgment in that party's favor based solely on information contained in the pleadings.

motion for order compelling discovery (*com·PEL·ing diss·KUV·e·ree*) A motion asking the court to order the other party to produce certain writings, photographs, or other requested items.

motion for recusal (*re·KYOO·zel*) A request that a judge disqualify himself or herself from a case because of bias or prejudice.

motion for summary judgment (*MOH·shun for SUM·er·ee JUJ·ment*) A motion that may be made when all of the papers filed in a case show that there is no genuine issue of fact and that the party making the motion will win the case as a matter of law.

motion in limine (*MOH·shun in LIM·e·nee*) A pretrial motion asking the court to prohibit the introduction of prejudicial evidence by the other party.

motion to dismiss (*dis·MISS*) A motion made by the defendant asking the court to dismiss the case.

motion to quash the array (*MOH·shun to kwawsh the e·RAY*) A challenge to the entire jury because of some irregularity in the selection of the jury. Also called *challenge to the array*.

motion to strike A motion asking the court to order the other party to remove from a pleading any insufficient defense or any redundant, immaterial, impertinent, or scandalous matter.

murder (*MER·der*) The unlawful killing of a human being by another with malice aforethought.

mutual benefit bailment (*MYOO·choo·el BEN·e·fit BAYL·ment*) A bailment in which both the bailor and the bailee receive some benefit.

mutual mistake (*MYOO·choo·el mis·TAKE*) The situation that exists when both parties are mistaken about an important aspect of an agreement. Also called *bilateral mistake*.

mutuum (*MYOO·choo·um*) A loan of goods, on the agreement that the borrower may consume them, returning to the lender an equivalent in kind and quantity.

necessaries (*NESS·e·seh·reez*) Food, clothing, shelter, and medical care that are needed by an infant, but not supplied by a parent or guardian.

negligence (*NEG·li·jenss*) The failure to use that amount of care and skill that a reasonably prudent person would have used under the same circumstances and conditions.

negotiable instrument (*ne·GOH·shee·e·bel IN·stre·ment*) A written, unconditional order or promise to pay money, which can be transferred by the original receiver to others.

negotiation (*ne·go·shee·AY·shun*) A two-party process in which each side attempts to conclude a dispute by bargaining with the other until one side agrees to the other side's offer or settlement.

next friend One acting for the benefit of an infant in bringing a legal action.

next of kin Those most nearly related by blood.

nighttime The time between one hour after sunset on one day and one hour before sunrise on the next day.

no-contest clause (*no-KON·test*) A clause in a will that attempts to disinherit any legatee, devisee, or beneficiary who contests the provisions of the will. Also called *in terrorem clause*.

no-fault divorce (*de·VORSE*) A dissolution of marriage without regard to fault.

nolo contendere (*NO·lo kon·TEN·de·ray*) A plea in which the defendant neither admits nor denies the charges.

nominal damages (*NOM·i·nel DAM·e·jez*) Damages in name only.

nominal partner (*NOM·i·nel PART·ner*) A partner in name only, who has no real interest in the partnership. Also called *ostensible partner*.

nonbinding arbitration (*non·BIND·ing ar·be·TRAY·shun*) Arbitration in which the arbitrator's decision is simply a recommendation and need not be complied with.

nonconforming goods (*non·ken·FORM·ing*) Goods that are not the same as those called for under the contract.

nondisclosure agreement (*non·diss·KLOH·zher e·GREE·ment*) An agreement to refrain from disclosing trade secrets to others. Also called *confidentiality agreement*.

nonfeasance (*non·FEE·zenss*) The failure to do an act that ought to be done.

nonmarital children (*non·MAR·i·tel*) Children born out of wedlock. Also called *bastards* and *illegitimate children*.

non obstante veredicto (*non ob·STAN·tee ver·DIK·toh*) Abbreviated n.o.v. Notwithstanding a verdict.

nonsuit (*NON·soot*) The termination of an action that did not adjudicate issues on the merits.

notary public (*NOH·te·ree PUB·lik*) A person authorized to administer oaths, attest to and certify documents, take acknowledgments, and perform other official acts.

not-for-profit corporation (*not fore PRO·fit*) A corporation created for charitable and benevolent purposes.

novation *(noh·VAY·shun)* An agreement whereby an original party to a contract is replaced by a new party.

nudum pactum *(NOO·dum PAK·tum)* Barren promise with no consideration.

nuisance *(NYOO·senss)* The use of one's property in a way that causes annoyance, inconvenience, or discomfort to another.

nullity *(NUL·i·tee)* Nothing; as though it had not occurred.

nuncupative will *(NUN·kyoo·pay·tiv)* An oral will.

obscenity *(ob·SEN·i·tee)* Material or conduct that shows or describes some kind of sexual activity and is designed to sexually arouse people.

offer *(OFF·er)* A proposal made by an offeror.

offeree *(off·er·EE)* One to whom an offer is made.

offeror *(off·er·OR)* One who makes an offer.

one day–one trial jury system *(JOOR·ee SYS·tem)* A system designed to provide the courts with juries consisting of fair cross sections of the community and to reduce the burden of jury duty on certain classes of citizens.

opening statement *(OH·pen·ing STATE·ment)* An attorney's outline, to the jury, of anticipated proof.

operating agreement *(OP·er·ate·ing e·GREE· ment)* An agreement that sets forth the rights and obligations of the members and establishes the rules for operating a limited liability company.

option contract *(OP·shen KON·trakt)* A binding promise to hold an offer open.

order for relief *(re·LEEF)* The acceptance of a case by a bankruptcy court.

ordinary negligence *(OR·di·ner·ee NEG·li·jens)* The want of ordinary care.

original jurisdiction *(o·RIJ·i·nel joo·res·DIK·shen)* The power to hear a case when it first goes to court.

Orphan's Court A name given, in some states, to the court that exercises the function of settling decedents' estates.

ostensible partner *(os·TEN·si·bel PART·ner)* A partner in name only, who has no real interest in the partnership. Also called *nominal partner.*

output contract *(OWT·put KON·trakt)* A contract to sell "all the goods a company manufactures" or "all the crops a farmer grows."

overrule *(o·ver·ROOL)* To annul, make void, or refuse to sustain.

pain and suffering *(SUF·er·ing)* Physical discomfort and emotional trauma.

pardon *(PAR·den)* A setting aside of punishment altogether by a government official.

parole *(pa·ROLE)* A conditional release from prison; allows the person to serve the remainder of a sentence outside of prison under specific terms.

parole board A group of people authorized to grant parole. Also called *parole commission.*

parole commission *(ke·MISH·en)* A group of people authorized to grant parole. Also called *parole board.*

parolee *(pa·role·EE)* A person placed on parole.

parol evidence rule *(pa·ROLE EV·i·denss)* The rule that oral evidence of prior or contemporaneous negotiations between the par-

ties is not admissible in court to alter, vary, or contradict the terms of a written agreement.

partial release *(PAR·shell re·LEESS)* A document stating that specified parcels of property are released from an encumbrance.

partition *(par·TI·shun)* The division of land, held by joint tenants or tenants in common, into distinct portions so that they may hold them separately.

partnership *(PART·ner·ship)* An association of two or more persons to carry on as co-owners of a business for profit. Also called *co-partnership.*

party to a suit *(PAR·tee)* A person or organization participating or having a direct interest in a legal proceeding.

patent *(PAT·ent)* A grant by the U.S. Government of the exclusive right to make, use, and sell an invention for 20 years.

patent infringement *(PAT·ent in·FRINJ·ment)* The unauthorized making, using, or selling of a patented invention during the term of the patent.

paternity proceeding *(pa·TERN·i·tee pro·SSEED·ing)* A court action to determine whether a person is the father of a child born out of wedlock. Also called *affiliation proceeding.*

patricide *(PAT·ri·side)* The killing of one's father.

pecuniary gift *(pee·KYOO·nee·er·ee)* Gift of money.

penal laws *(PEE·nel)* Laws that impose a penalty or punishment for a wrong against society.

pendente lite *(pen·DEN·tay LIE·tay)* Litigation pending.

per capita *(per KAP·i·ta)* Per head.

peremptory challenge *(per·EMP·ter·ee CHAL·enj)* The challenge of a juror, for which no reason need be given.

performance *(per·FORM·enss)* The discharging of a contract by doing that which one agreed to do under the terms of the contract.

periodic tenancy *(peer·ee·ODD·ik TEN·en·see)* An estate in real property that continues for successive periods until one of the parties terminates it by giving notice to the other party. Also called *tenancy from year to year.*

perjury *(PER·jer·ee)* The giving of false testimony under oath.

per se *(per say)* In and of itself; taken alone.

personal property *(PER·son·al PROP·er·tee)* Anything that is the subject of ownership other than real property. Also called *chattels* and *personalty.*

personal recognizance *(PER·son·al re·KOG·ni· zense)* A personal obligation by a person to return to stand trial.

personal representative *(PER·son·al rep·re· ZEN·ta·tiv)* The executor or administrator of a deceased person.

personal service *(PER·son·al SER·viss)* The personal delivery of a copy of the summons and complaint to the defendant.

personalty *(PER·sen·el·tee)* Anything that is the subject of ownership other than real property. Also called *chattels* and *personal property.*

per stirpes *(per STIR·peez)* By right of representation.

petition *(pe·TI·shun)* A written application for a court order.

petitioner *(pe·TI·shun·er)* One who presents a petition to a court.

petit jury *(PET·ee JOOR·ee)* The ordinary jury of 6 or 12 people; used for the trial of a civil or criminal action.

petit larceny (*PET·ee LAR·sen·ee*) Larceny that is a misdemeanor rather than a felony. Also called *petty larceny*.

petit treason (*PET·ee TREE·zan*) Acts against one's master or lord (under the English common law).

petty larceny (*PET·ee LAR·sen·ee*) Larceny that is a misdemeanor rather than a felony. Also called *petit larceny*.

physical custody (*FIZ·i·cul CUSS·te·dee*) The day-to-day care of a child, including his or her residence.

plaintiff (*PLAIN·tif*) A person who brings a legal action against another.

plain view doctrine (*DOK·trin*) The principle which asserts that search warrant is not needed for a police officer to seize items that are in plain view of a lawfully positioned police officer.

plat A map designating the size and shape of a specific land area. Also called *plat map* and *plot*.

plat book A book that is recorded at the registry of deeds, containing plat maps.

plat map A map designating the size and shape of a specific land area. Also called *plat* and *plot*.

plea bargaining (*plee BAR·gen·ing*) The working out of a mutually satisfactory disposition of a case by the prosecution and the defense.

pleadings (*PLEED·ings*) The written statements of claims and defenses used by the parties in a lawsuit.

plenary jurisdiction (*PLEN·e·ree joo·res·DIK·shen*) Complete jurisdiction over both the parties and the subject matter of a lawsuit.

plot A map designating the size and shape of a specific land area. Also called *plat* and *plat map*.

polling the jury (*POLE·ing*) A procedure in which each individual juror is asked whether he or she agrees with the verdict given by the jury foreperson.

polygamy (*po·LIG·e·mee*) The state of having several wives or husbands at the same time.

pornography (*por·NAW·graf·ee*) Material or conduct that shows or describes some kind of sexual activity and is designed sexually arouse people.

possession (*po·SESH·en*) The detention and control of anything.

possibility of reverter (*pos·i·BIL·i·tee ov re·VERT·er*) An interest in property due to the possibility that an event will occur that will cause the property to revert to the grantor.

pour-over trust (*pore-OH·ver*) A provision in a will leaving a bequest or devise to the trustee of an existing living trust.

power of attorney (*POW·er ov a·TERN·ee*) A formal writing that authorizes an agent to act for a principal.

power of sale clause (*POW·er*) A clause in a mortgage allowing the mortgagee to hold a foreclosure sale without involving the court when a default in payment of the mortgage occurs.

precatory trust (*PREK·a·tore·ee*) An express trust that arises from the use of polite, noncommanding language by a testator in a will.

predecease (*pree·de·SEEZ*) To die before.

preferences (*PREF·er·en·sez*) Transfers made by a debtor to creditors before a bankruptcy proceeding, enabling the creditors to receive a greater percentage of their claim than they would have otherwise received.

preferred stock (*pre·FERD*) Stock that has a superior right to dividends and to capital when the corporation is dissolved.

preliminary hearing (*pre·LIM·i·ner·ee HEER·ing*) A hearing before a judge to determine whether there is sufficient evidence to believe that the person has committed a crime. Also called *probable cause hearing*.

preliminary injunction (*pre·LIM·i·ner·ee in·JUNK·shun*) An injunction issued by a court before hearing the merits of a case.

premarital agreement (*pre·MAR·i·tel a·GREE·ment*) A contract made in contemplation of marriage between prospective spouses setting forth, among other points, the right that each spouse will have to property brought into the marriage. Also called *antenuptial agreement* and *prenuptial agreement*.

premeditated malice aforethought (*pre·MED·i·tay·ted MAL·iss a·FORE·thawt*) Thinking over, deliberating on, or weighing in the mind beforehand.

prenuptial agreement (*pre·NUP·shel a·GREE·ment*) A contract made in contemplation of marriage between prospective spouses setting forth, among other points, the right that each spouse will have to property brought into the marriage. Also called *antenuptial agreement* and *premarital agreement*.

preponderance of evidence (*pre·PON·der·enss ov EV·i·denss*) Evidence having the greater weight.

Prerogative Court (*pre·ROG·e·tiv*) A name given in some states to the court that exercises the function of settling decedents' estates.

pretermitted child (*pre·ter·MIT·ed*) A child who is omitted by a testator from a will.

pretrial hearing (*PREE·tryl HEER·ing*) A hearing before the judge prior to a trial, attended by the attorneys, for the purpose of speeding up the trial.

prima facie case (*PRY·mah FAY·shee*) Legally sufficient for proof unless rebutted or contradicted by other evidence.

prime meridians (*mer·ID·ee·ens*) Lines running north and south in the United States government survey. Also called *meridians* and *principal meridians*.

primogeniture (*pry·mo·JEN·e·cher*) The state of being the first born among several children of the same parents (early English law).

principal (*PRIN·se·pel*) One who authorizes another to act on one's behalf.

principal in the first degree (*de·GREE*) One who actually commits a felony.

principal in the second degree One who did not commit the crime, but was present, aiding and abetting another in the commission of a felony.

principal meridians (*PRIN·se·pel mer·ID·ee·ens*) Lines running north and south in the United States government survey. Also called *meridians* and *prime meridians*.

private nuisance (*PRY·vet NYOO·sens*) A nuisance that disturbs one neighbor only.

privileges and immunities clause (*PRIV·i·leg·ez and im·YOO·ni·teez*) A clause in the U.S. Constitution requiring states to give out-of-state citizens the same rights as it gives its own citizens.

privity of contract *(PRIV·i·tee ov KON·trakt)* The relationship that exists between contracting parties.

probable cause *(PROB·a·bel kawz)* Reasonable grounds for belief that an offense has been committed.

probable cause hearing *(PROB·a·bel kawz HEER·ing)* A hearing before a judge to determine whether there is sufficient evidence to believe that the person has committed a crime. Also called *preliminary hearing*.

probate *(PROH·bate)* To prove and have allowed by the court; usually, of a will.

Probate and Family Court A name given in some states to the court that exercises the function of settling decedents' estates.

proceeding *(pro·SEED·ing)* The name given in California for the procedure for obtaining a dissolution of marriage.

process *(PROSS·ess)* The means of compelling the defendant in an action to appear in court.

process server *(PROSS·ess SERV·er)* A person who carries out service of process.

pro-choice *(pro-choyss)* Favoring legislation that allows abortion.

product liability *(PROD·ukt ly·a·BIL·i·tee)* Liability of manufacturers and sellers to compensate people for injuries suffered because of defects in the manufacturers' and sellers' products.

pro-life *(pro-life)* Favoring legislation that disallows abortion.

promisee *(prom·i·SEE)* One to whom a promise is made.

promisor *(prom·i·SOHR)* One who makes a promise.

promissory estoppel *(PROM·i·sore·ee ess·TOP·el)* A doctrine under which no consideration is necessary when someone makes a promise that induces another's action or forbearance, and injustice can be avoided only by enforcing the promise.

promoters *(pro·MOH·terz)* People who begin a corporation by obtaining investors and taking charge up to the time of the corporation's existence.

proof of claim A signed, written statement setting forth a creditor's claim together with the basis for it.

proponent *(pro·POH·nent)* One who proposes or argues in support of something, such as the allowance of a will.

proprietary lease *(pro·PRY·e·ter·ee)* A lease to an owner of the property.

prorated *(PROH·ray·ted)* Divided proportionately.

prosecute *(PROSS·e·kyoot)* To proceed against a person criminally.

prosecution *(pross·e·KYOO·shun)* A criminal action. The party by whom criminal proceedings are started or conducted; the state.

prosecutor *(PROSS·e·kew·ter)* The person representing the jurisdiction in which the crime occurred, who brings charges against those the police have arrested.

proximate cause *(PROK·si·met kaws)* The dominant or moving cause.

proxy marriage *(PROK·see MAR·ej)* A ceremonial marriage in which one of the parties is absent, but is represented by an agent who stands in his or her place.

prudent *(PROO·dent)* Cautious.

prurient interest *(PROO·ree·ent IN·trest)* A shameful or morbid interest in sex.

public administrator *(PUB·lik ad·MIN·iss·tray·tor)* An official who administers the estate of a person who dies intestate when no relative, heir, or other person appears who is entitled to act as administrator.

publication clause *(pub·li·KAY·shun)* The introductory paragraph of a will. Also called *exordium clause*.

public domain *(PUB·lik doh·MAYN)* Owned by the public.

public nuisance *(PUB·lik NYOO·sens)* A nuisance that affects the community at large.

public policy *(PUB·lik POL·i·see)* Underlying, foundational principles that bind various peoples into a close-knit society.

public trust *(PUB·lik)* A trust established for charitable purposes. Also called *charitable trust*.

puffing *(PUF·ing)* Statements made by sellers that are opinions and attempts to put their goods in the best light possible; not warranties.

punitive damages *(PYOON·i·tiv)* Damages as a measure of punishment for the defendant's wrongful acts. Also called *exemplary damages*.

qualified indorsement *(KWAH·li·fide in·DORSS·ment)* An indorsement that limits the liability of the indorser.

qualified terminable interest property (QTIP) trust *(KWAH·li·fide TERM·in·a·bel IN·trest PROP·er·tee)* A marital deduction trust that gives all trust income to a surviving spouse for life, payable at least annually, with the principal passing to someone else upon the spouse's death.

quasi *(KWAY·zy)* As if; almost as it were.

quasi contract *(KWAY·zy KON·trakt)* A contract imposed by law to prevent unjust enrichment. Also called *contract implied in law*.

quasi in rem action *(KWAY·zi in rem AK·shun)* A lawsuit in which the court has jurisdiction over the defendant's property, but not over the defendant's person.

questions of fact *(KWES·chens)* Questions about the activities that took place between the parties which caused them to go to court.

questions of law Questions relating to the application or interpretation of law

quid pro quo *(kwid proh kwoh)* Something for something; one thing in return for another.

quiet enjoyment *(KWY·et en·JOY·ment)* The right of a tenant to possess the rented property and to be undisturbed in that possession.

quitclaim deed *(KWIT·klame)* A deed to real property in which the grantor transfers only his or her interest, if any, in the property and gives no warranties of title. Also called *deed without covenants* and *fiduciary deed*.

racketeering *(rak·e·TEER·ing)* Activities of organized criminals who extort money from legitimate businesses.

range *(rainj)* A row of townships running north and south in the United States government survey.

rape At common law, the unlawful, forcible carnal knowledge by a man of a woman against her will or without her consent.

rape shield laws *(sheeld)* Laws passed to help prevent rape victims from being victimized.

ratify *(RAT·i·fy)* Approve; confirm.

real evidence *(reel EV·i·denss)* Actual objects that have a bearing on the case, such as an item of clothing, a weapon found at the scene of the crime, a photograph, a chart, or a model.

real property *(reel PROP·er·tee)* The ground and anything permanently attached to it, including land, buildings, and growing trees; and the airspace above the ground.

reasonable care *(REE·zen·e·bel)* The degree of care that a reasonable person would have used under the circumstances then known.

reasonable doubt *(REE·zen·e·bel dowt)* Doubt based on reason.

reasonable time *(REE·zen·e·bel)* A time, left to the discretion of the judge, that may be fairly allowed depending on the circumstances.

rebuttal *(re·BUT·el)* The introduction of evidence that will destroy the effect of the evidence introduced by the other side.

receiving stolen goods *(re·SEEV·ing STOH·len)* The buying, receiving, or aiding in the concealment of stolen or embezzled property, knowing it to have been stolen.

reconciliation *(rek·on·sil·ee·AY·shun)* The renewal of amicable relations.

recrimination *(re·krim·i·NAY·shun)* Conduct on the part of the plaintiff that constitutes a ground for divorce, which is a common law defense to an action for divorce.

recross questions *(RE·kross KWES·chens)* Further questions asked by a deponent in response to redirect questions.

rectangular survey system *(rek·TANG·yoo·ler SER·vey SIS·tem)* A method of describing real property according to the property's relationship to intersecting lines running east and west (base lines) and lines running north and south (principal, or prime, meridians). Also called *government survey system.**

recuse *(re·KYOOZ)* Disqualify.

redeem *(re·DEEM)* Buy back.

redirect questions *(re·de·REKT KWESS·chenz)* Further questions asked by an examiner at a deposition in response to cross questions.

refinance *(ree·FY·nanss)* To extinguish a debt obligation and replace it with new debt that has different terms, such as a different interest rate or amortization schedule.

registered limited liability partnership (RLLP) *(REJ·is·terd)* A general partnership in which only the partnership, and not the individual partners, is liable for the tort liabilities of the partnership. Also called *limited liability partnership (LLP)* and *registered partnership having limited liability (RPLL).*

registered partnership having limited liability (RPLL) A general partnership in which only the partnership, and not the individual partners, is liable for the tort liabilities of the partnership. Also called *limited liability partnership (LLP)* and *registered limited liability partnership (RLLP).*

rejection *(re·JEK·shun)* The refusal by an offeree of an offer.

relevant evidence *(REL·e·vent EV·i·denss)* Evidence tending to prove or disprove an alleged fact.

reliction *(re·LIK·shun)* The gradual recession of water, leaving land permanently uncovered.

remainder interest *(re·MANE·der IN·trest)* An interest that takes effect after another estate is ended.

remand *(re·MAND)* To send back.

rendition *(ren·DI·shun)* The return of fugitives to the state in which they are accused of having committed a crime by the governor of the state to which they have fled.

reorganization *(ree·or·ge·ni·ZAY·shun)* A method for businesses to reorganize their financial affairs, keep their assets, and remain in business. Also called *Chapter 11 bankruptcy.*

reply *(re·PLY)* The plaintiff's answer to the defendant's counterclaim.

republishing a will *(re·PUB·lish·ing)* Reestablishing a will that has been formerly revoked or improperly executed.

requirements contract *(re·KWIRE·ments KON·trakt)* A contract to buy "all the fuel (or other goods) needed for one year."

res *(rayz)* The property; the thing.

rescind *(ree·SIND)* To cancel.

rescission *(ree·SIZH·en)* Cancellation.

reservation *(rez·er·VAY·shun)* The act of keeping back.

residence *(REZ·e·denss)* A place where a person actually lives.

residuary clause *(re·ZID·joo·er·ee)* The clause in a will that disposes of all of the testator's property not otherwise distributed.

residuary estate *(re·ZID·joo·e·ree es·TATE)* The estate remaining after individual items have been given out by a will.

res ipsa loquitur *(rayz IP·sa LO·kwe·ter)* The thing speaks for itself.

respondeat superior *(res·PON·dee·at ssoo·PEER·ee·or)* A rule of law that makes principals and employers responsible for the torts of their agents and servants committed within the scope of their authority or employment.

respondent *(re·SPON·dent)* One who is called on to answer a petition. A party against whom an appeal is brought. Also called *appellee* and *defendant in error.*

response *(re·SPONSS)* The written answer to a petition filed by a respondent.

restitution *(ress·ti·TEW·shun)* Restoration made to an injured person to his or her original position prior to a loss.

restraining order *(re·STRANE·ing)* An order forbidding a person from doing a particular act.

resulting trust *(re·ZULT·ing)* An implied trust that arises in favor of the payor when property is transferred to one person after having been paid for by another person.

retaliatory eviction *(re·TAL·ee·a·tore·ee e·VIK·shun)* The eviction of a tenant for reporting sanitary or building code violations to the authorities.

reverse *(re·VERSS)* Make void. Also called *set aside.*

reversionary interest *(re·VER·zhen·e·ree IN·trest)* A right to the future enjoyment of property that one originally owned.

revert *(re·VERT)* To go back.

reverse mortgage *(re·VERSS MORE·gej)* A mortgage in which a bank pays a homeowner the equity in the home in exchange for taking title to the home.

revocable (*REV·e·ke·bel*) Capable of being revoked.

revocable living trust (*REV·e·ke·bel*) A trust that may be rescinded or changed by the settlor at any time during his or her lifetime.

revocation (*rev·o·KAY·shun*) The act of revoking; the taking back of an offer by an offeror before it has been accepted.

revoke (*re·VOKE*) To cancel or rescind.

RICO (*REE·coh*) Acronym for Racketeer Influenced and Corrupt Organizations Act, a federal statute designed to stop organized criminal activity from invading legitimate businesses.

right of contribution (*kon·tri·BYOO·shun*) The right to share a loss among joint tortfeasors or other codefendants.

right of privacy (*PRY·ve·see*) The right to be left alone, the right to be free from uncalled-for publicity, and the right to live without unreasonable interference by the public in private matters.

right of redemption (*re·DEMP·shun*) The right to take property back. A statutory right to redeem the property even after a foreclosure sale.

right-to-die laws Laws allowing dying people to refuse extraordinary treatment to prolong life.

ripe for judgment (*JUJ·ment*) The stage of a trial at which everything has been completed except the court's decision.

ripeness doctrine (*RIPE·ness DOK·trin*) A principle under which the court will not hear a case unless there is an actual, present controversy for the court to decide.

risk of loss Responsibility in case of damage or destruction.

robbery (*ROB·e·ree*) The wrongful taking and carrying away of the personal property of another, from the other's person or personal custody, against his or her will, by force and violence.

rule against perpetuities (*per·pe·TYOO·i·teez*) The principle that no interest in property is good unless it must vest, if at all, not later than 21 years after some life in being, plus the gestation period, at the creation of the interest.

rules of civil procedure (*SIV·el pre·SEED·jer*) Regulations that govern the proceedings in civil cases.

rules of criminal procedure (*KRIM·i·nel pre·SSEED·jer*) Regulations that govern the proceedings in criminal cases.

Safe harbor provision (*safe HAR·ber pre·VI·zhun*) Protection of a party from discovery sanctions when the party cannot produce electronically stored information (ESI) because it was lost through the routine good-faith operation of an electronic information system.

sale The passing of title from the seller to the buyer, for a price.

sale on approval (*e·PROOV·el*) The sale of goods that are for the buyer's use rather than for resale, and that may be returned even though they conform to the contract.

sale or return (*re·TURN*) The sale of goods that are primarily for resale and that may be returned even though they conform to the contract.

same-sex marriage (*same sex MAR·ej*) The union of two same-sex partners; also called gay marriage.

satisfaction (*sat·iss·FAK·shun*) The testator's disposing of or giving to a beneficiary, while alive, that which was provided in a will, so as to make it impossible to carry out the will. Also called *advancement*.

scienter (*si·EN·ter*) Knowingly.

scope of employment (*skope ov em·PLOY·ment*) The zone in which employees operate, which is acknowledged to be broader than the employee's stated job description.

S corporation (*kor·por·AY·shun*) A corporation governed by Subchapter S of the Internal Revenue Code, in which the income of the corporation is taxed directly to the shareholders rather than to the corporation itself.

seal A mark, impression, the word "seal," or the letters L.S. placed on a written contract next to a party's signature.

search warrant (*WAHR·ent*) A written order of the court authorizing law enforcement officers to search and seize certain property.

second-degree murder (*SEK·end-de·GREE MER·der*) Murder that is not found to be in the first degree.

second mortgage (*SEK·end MORE·gej*) A mortgage subject to a prior mortgage. Also called *junior mortgage*.

secret partner (*SEE·kret PART·ner*) A partner who takes an active part in the business, but is not known to the public as a partner.

section (*SEK·shun*) A square mile of land, containing 640 acres, in the United States government survey.

secured creditors (*se·KYOORD KRED·et·ers*) Creditors who hold mortgages and other liens.

security (*se·KYOOR·i·tee*) Assurance (usually in the form of a pledge or deposit) given by a debtor to a creditor to make sure that a debt is paid.

seisin (*SEE·zin*) Possession of a freehold.

seizure (*SEE·zhoor*) The action of the police taking evidence of criminality from a person or from his or her property.

selectpeople (*sel·EKT·pee·pel*) People elected to serve as the chief administrative authority of a town.

self-defense (*de·FENSS*) A valid excuse for the use of force in resisting attack, especially for killing an assailant.

self-proving affidavit (*a·fi·DAY·vit*) A clause in a will containing an affidavit that allows the will to be allowed by the court without the testimony of witnesses.

sentence (*SEN·tenss*) The judgment of the court imposing punishment when the defendant is found guilty in a criminal case.

separation of spouses (*sep·a·RAY·shun ov SPOW·sez*) The discontinuance of cohabitation by the spouses. Also called *divorce from bed and board* and *limited divorce*.

sequester (*see·KWEST·er*) To set apart; isolate.

servant (*SER·vent*) One who performs services under the direction and control of another; an employee.

servicemark (*SER·viss·mark*) A term used to describe trademark protection for services.

service of process (*SER·viss ov PROSS·ess*) The delivering of summonses or other legal documents to the people who are required to receive them.

set aside (*a·SYD*) Make void. Also called *reverse*.

settlor (*SET·lor*) A person who establishes a trust. Also called *donor, grantor,* and *trustor*.

several (*SEV·er·el*) Separate, individual, and independent.

several liability (*SEV·er·el ly·a·BIL·i·tee*) Liability under which joint tortfeasors may be sued separately in a lawsuit.

severance of actions *(SEV·er·ense ov AK·shuns)* The separation of lawsuits or prosecutions involving multiple parties into separate, independent cases, resulting in separate, final judgments.

sexual assault *(SEKSS·yoo·el e·SALT)* Any unwanted sexual contact.

shareholders *(SHARE·hold·ers)* People who own shares in a corporation. Also called *stockholders*.

sheriff's sale *(SHER·ifss)* A sale of property at public auction conducted by a sheriff.

shipment contract *(SHIP·ment KON·trakt)* A contract under which the seller turns the goods over to a carrier for delivery to a buyer.

short sale *(short sale)* The sale of a home for a price lower than the loan balance; occurs only if the lender allows it.

signature clause *(SIG·na·cher)* The clause in a will that precedes the testator's signature. Also called *testimonium clause*.

silent partners *(SY·lent PART·nerz)* Partners who may be known to the public as partners, but who take no active part in the business.

simultaneous death *(sy·mul·TAY·nee·us)* The death of two or more people in such a way that it is impossible to determine who died before whom.

slander *(SLAN·der)* Defamation that is communicated by the spoken word.

slayer statutes *(SLAY·er STAT·shoots)* Laws enacted by legislatures, stating that murderers cannot inherit from their victims.

sodomy *(SOD·e·mee)* Oral or anal copulation. The act that state statutes often describe as an "abominable and detestable crime against nature."

solemnized *(SAW·lem·nized)* Performed in a ceremonial fashion with witnesses present.

sole proprietorship *(pro·PRY·e·ter·ship)* A form of business that is owned and operated by one person.

sororicide *(so·ROR·i·side)* The killing of one's sister.

soundness of mind Sufficient mental ability to make a will.

special administrator *(SPESH·el ad·MIN· iss·tray·tor)* A person appointed by the court to handle the affairs of an estate for a limited time only to take care of urgent affairs.

special agent *(SPESH·el AY·jent)* An agent authorized to carry out a single transaction or to perform a specified act.

special damages *(SPE·shel DAM·e·jez)* Measurable amounts of losses, including the cost of hospital and medical treatment and any loss of wages.

special warranty deed *(SPESH·el WAR·en·tee)* A deed containing warranties under which the grantor guarantees that the property is free from all encumbrances made during the time that he or she owned the property and agrees to defend the title only against claims through him or her. Also called *limited warranty deed*.

specific legacy *(spe·SIF·ic LEG·a·see)* A gift by will of a particular article of personal property.

specific performance *(spe·SIF·ic per·FORM·enss)* An order by the court commanding a breaching party to do that which he or she agreed to do under the terms of the contract.

spendthrift *(SPEND·thrift)* One who spends money profusely and improvidently.

spendthrift trust A trust designed to provide a fund for the maintenance of a beneficiary and at the same time to secure it against the beneficiary's improvidence or incapacity.

sponge tax *(spunj taks)* A tax that soaks up money for the state that the estate is being given credit for in any event.

spousal support *(SPOWZ·el su·PORT)* An allowance made to a divorced spouse by a former spouse for support and maintenance. Also called *alimony*.

spray trust A trust that allows the trustee to decide, in the trustee's discretion, how much will be given to each beneficiary. Also called *discretionary trust* and *sprinkling trust*.

springing power *(SPRING·ing POW·er)* A power in a durable power of attorney that does not become effective until the person making it actually becomes incapacitated.

sprinkling trust *(SPRINK·ling)* A trust that allows the trustee to decide, in the trustee's discretion, how much will be given to each beneficiary. Also called *discretionary trust* and *spray trust*.

stalking *(STAW·king)* The willful, malicious, and repeated following, harassing, and threatening of another person, intended to place the person in fear of death or serious bodily injury.

standing to sue *(STAND·ing to SOO)* The condition that exists when a party has a tangible, legally protected interest at stake in a lawsuit.

statute *(STAT·shoot)* A law passed by a legislature.

statute of frauds *(STAT·shoot of frawdz)* The law that deems that certain contracts must be in writing to be enforceable.

statute of limitations *(STAT·shoot ov lim·i·TAY·shunz)* A time limit, set by statute, within which suit must be commenced after the cause of action accrues.

statute of repose *(STAT·shoot ov re·POSE)* An absolute time limit for bringing a cause of action regardless of when the cause of action accrues.

statutory arson *(STAT·shoo·tore·ee AR·sen)* The burning of a building other than a dwelling house or the burning of one's own house to collect insurance.

statutory burglary *(STAT·shoo·tore·ee BUR·gler·ee)* Burglary that does not contain all of the elements of common law burglary.

statutory rape *(STAT·shoo·tore·ee)* Sexual intercourse with a child under the age set by state statute regardless of whether the child consented or not. Also called *unlawful sexual intercourse*.

stipulate *(STIP·yoo·late)* Agree.

stipulation *(stip·yoo·LA·shun)* An agreement between the parties to an action regulating any matter relative to the proceedings.

stock certificate *(ser·TIF·i·ket)* A document that evidences ownership of stock in a corporation.

stockholders *(STAWK·hold·erz)* People who own shares in a corporation. Also called *shareholders*.

stop and frisk rule A rule that allows police officers who believe that a person is acting suspiciously and could be armed to stop and frisk that person for weapons, without a search warrant.

straight bankruptcy *(strayt BANK·rupt·see)* A proceeding designed to liquidate a debtor's property, pay off creditors, and discharge the debtor from most debts. Also called *Chapter 7 bankruptcy* and *liquidation*.

strict liability (*strikt ly·a·BIL·i·tee*) Liability for an act that causes harm, without regard to fault or negligence. Also called *absolute liability.*

sublease (*SUB·leess*) (**to sublet, v.**) A lease given by a lessee to a third person conveying the same interest for a shorter term than the period for which the lessee holds it. Also called *underlease.*

subpoena (*suh·PEEN·uh*) An order commanding a person to appear and testify in a legal action. Also called *subpoena ad testificandum.*

subpoena ad testificandum (*suh·PEEN·a ad tes·te·fe·KAN·dem*) An order commanding a person to appear and testify in a legal action. Also called *subpoena.*

subpoena duces tecum (*suh·PEEN·a DOO·sess TEK·um*) An order commanding a person to appear and bring certain papers or other materials that are pertinent to a legal action.

subscribe (*sub·SKRIBE*) To sign below or at the end; to write underneath.

substantial performance (*sub·STAN·shel per·FORM·enss*) A doctrine allowing a contracting party to sue the other party for breach, even though slight omissions or deviations were made in the first party's own performance of the contract.

substituted service (*SUB·sti·tew·ted SER·viss*) A type of service in which the summons and complaint are delivered to the defendant's agent, mailed, or published in a newspaper.

successor personal representative (*suk·SESS·or PER·son·al rep·re·ZEN·ta·tiv*) A person appointed to succeed a previously appointed personal representative.

suicide (*SOO·i·side*) Deliberate, lethal self-destruction.

summarily (*sum·EHR·i·lee*) Quickly.

summary administration (*SUM·e·ree ad·min·iss·TRAY·shun*) An informal method used to settle estates that do not exceed $75,000.

summary ejectment (*SUM·e·ree e·JEKT·ment*) The legal action used by landlords to evict tenants. Also called *dispossessory warrant proceedings, forcible entry and detainer, summary process,* and *unlawful detainer.*

summary judgment (*SUM·er·ee JUJ·ment*) An immediate decision by the court, without going to trial, based on the papers filed by the parties.

summary proceeding (*SUM·e·ree pre·SEED·ing*) A short and simple trial.

summary process (*SUM·e·ree PROSS·ess*) The legal action used by landlords to evict tenants. Also called *dispossessory warrant proceedings, forcible entry and detainer, summary ejectment,* and *unlawful detainer.*

summation (*sum·AY·shun*) Final statement by an attorney summarizing the evidence that has been introduced. Also called *closing argument.*

summons (*SUM·enz*) A formal notice to the defendant that a lawsuit has begun and that the defendant must file an answer within the number of days set by state law or else lose the case by default.

supervening cause (*soo·per·VEEN·ing*) A new occurrence that became the proximate cause of the injury.

Supremacy Clause (*soo·PREM·i·see*) A clause in the U.S. Constitution making the U.S. Constitution and federal laws the supreme law of the land.

surety (*SHOOR·e·tee*) One who undertakes to stand behind another—that is, to pay money or do any other act in the event that his or her principal fails to meet an obligation.

surrogate (*SER·o·get*) A person authorized to act on behalf of another and subject to the other's control. Also called *agent.*

Surrogate's Court (*SER·o·gets*) A name given in some states to the court that exercises the function of settling decedents' estates.

suspended sentence (*suss·PEN·ded SEN·tenss*) A sentence that is given formally, but not actually served.

sustain (*sus·TANE*) To support.

syndicate (*SIN·de·ket*) A relationship in which two or more people combine their labor or property for a single business undertaking. Also called *co-venture, joint enterprise,* and *joint venture.*

tacking The addition of a previous occupants' possession to one's own possession in order to meet the statutory period for adverse possession.

talesmen and taleswomen (*TAYLZ·men and taylz·WO·men*) Bystanders or people from the county at large chosen by the court to act as jurors when there are not enough people left on the venire.

tangible personal property (*TAN·je·bel PER·son·al PROP·er·tee*) Property that has substance and that can be touched.

tax credit (*tax CREH·dit*) Prepaid income tax (such as that deducted from dividend payment) that can be offset against the total income tax payable by an entity.

temporary custody (*TEM·po·rare·ee KUSS·te·dee*) Custody of a child awarded to a parent on a temporary basis, pending the outcome of a divorce or separation action.

tenancy at will (*TEN·en·see*) An estate in real property for an indefinite period.

tenancy by the entirety (*TEN·en·see by the en·TY·re·tee*) A type of joint tenancy held by a husband and wife that offers protection against attachment and that cannot be terminated by one spouse alone.

tenancy for years (*TEN·en·see*) An estate in real property for a definite, or fixed, period no matter how long or how short.

tenancy from year to year (*TEN·en·see*) An estate in real property that continues for successive periods until one of the parties terminates it by giving notice to the other party. Also called *periodic tenancy.*

tenancy in partnership (*TEN·en·see in PART·ner·ship*) Ownership in which each person has an interest in partnership property and is a co-owner of such property.

tenant (*TEN·ent*) A person who has temporary possession of and an interest in real property of another under a lease. Also called *lessee.*

tenant at sufferance (*TEN·ent at SUF·er·enss*) A tenant who wrongfully remains in possession of the premises after a tenancy has expired. Also called *holdover tenant.*

tenants in common (*TEN·entz in KOM·on*) Two or more persons holding an undivided interest in property, with each owner's interests going to his or her heirs on death rather than to the surviving co-owners.

tender of payment *(TEN·der)* To offer to the other party the money owed under a contract.

tender of performance *(per·FORM·ens)* To offer to do that which one has agreed to do under the terms of a contract.

tenements *(TEN·e·mentz)* Everything of a permanent nature that may be possessed and, in a more restrictive sense, houses or dwellings.

testament *(TESS·te·ment)* A legal instrument stating a person's wishes as to the disposition of personal property at death.

testamentary capacity *(test·e·MEN·ter·ee ca·PASS·i·tee)* Sufficient mental ability to make a will.

testamentary disposition *(test·e·MEN·ter·ee diss·pe·ZI·shun)* A gift of property that is not to take effect until the one who makes the gift dies.

testamentary trust *(test·e·MEN·ter·ee)* A trust that is created by will and that comes into existence only on the death of the testator.

testate *(TES·tate)* The condition of a person's having made a will.

testator *(TES·tay·tor)* A man who makes or has made a testament or will.

testatrix *(TES·tay·trix)* A woman who makes or has made a testament or will.

testimonial evidence *(tes·ti·MOH·nee·el EV·i·denss)* Oral testimony of witnesses made under oath in open court.

testimonium clause *(tess·ti·MOH·nee·um)* The clause in a will that immediately precedes the testator's signature. Also called *signature clause.*

third party *(PAR·tee)* In agency law, one who deals with an agent in making a contract with the agent's principal.

third-party beneficiary *(ben·e·FISH·ee·air·ee)* Someone for whose benefit a promise is made, but who is not a party to the contract.

threat of force *(thret ov forss)* Intimidation designed to put someone in fear that he or she will be the victim of violence; equivalent to force.

time is of the essence *(ESS·ens)* Time is critical.

time-sharing A fee simple ownership of a unit of real property in which the owner can exercise the right of possession for only an interval, such as a week or two, each year. Also called *interval ownership.*

title *(TY·tel)* Ownership.

title theory of mortgages *(TY·tel THEE·ree ov MORE·ge·jes)* The legal theory that a mortgage is a conveyance of title, which becomes void on payment of the obligation. Also called *common law theory of mortgages.*

toll *(tohl)* To bar, defeat, or take away.

tort A wrong against an individual.

tortfeasor *(tort·FEE·zor)* One who commits a tort.

tortious *(TOR·shus)* Wrongful; implying or involving tort.

tortious bailee *(TOR·shus bay·LEE)* A person who is wrongfully in possession of another's personal property.

Totten trust *(TOT·en)* A bank account in the name of the depositor as trustee for another person.

township *(TOUN·ship)* A six-square-mile portion of land in the United States government survey.

tract of land *(trakt)* A large piece of land.

trade fixture *(FIKS·cher)* Personal property, necessary to carry on a trade or business, that is physically attached to real property, but does not become part of the real property.

trademark *(TRADE·mark)* Any word, name, symbol, or device used by a business to identify goods and distinguish them from those manufactured or sold by others.

trade secret *(SEE·kret)* A plan, process, or device that is used in business and is known only to employees who need to know the secret to accomplish their work.

transitory action *(TRAN·zi·tore·ee AK·shun)* A lawsuit that may be brought in more than one place as long as the court in which it is heard has proper jurisdiction.

treason *(TREE·zun)* Levying war against the United States or giving aid and comfort to its enemies.

trespass *(TRESS·pass)* The intentional and unauthorized entry by a person onto the land of another.

trespass de bonis asportatis *(de BO·nis as·por·TAH·tis)* An action brought to recover damages from a person who has taken goods or property from its rightful owner.

trial docket *(tryl DOK·et)* The calendar of cases that are ready for trial. Also called *trial list.*

trial list *(tryl list)* The calendar of cases that are ready for trial. Also called *trial docket.*

trust A right of ownership to property held by one person for the benefit of another.

trust deed An instrument that creates a living trust. Also called *trust indenture.*

trustee *(trus·TEE)* A person who holds legal title to property in trust for another.

trustee in bankruptcy *(trus·TEE in BANK·rupt·see)* A person appointed by a bankruptcy court to hold the debtor's assets in trust for the benefit of creditors.

trustee process *(trus·TEE PROSS·ess)* A procedure for attaching the defendant's property that is in the hands of a third person.

trust fund The body, principal sum, or capital of a trust. Also called *corpus, trust property,* and *trust res.*

trust indenture *(in·DEN·cher)* An instrument that creates a living trust. Also called *trust deed.*

trustor *(trus·TOR)* A person who establishes a trust. Also called *donor, grantor,* and *settlor.*

trust principal *(PRIN·se·pel)* The body, principal sum, or capital of a trust. Also called *corpus, trust fund, trust property,* and *trust res.*

trust property *(PROP·er·tee)* The body, principal sum, or capital of a trust. Also called *corpus, trust fund, trust principal,* and *trust res.*

trust res *(reyz)* The body, principal sum, or capital of a trust. Also called *corpus, trust fund, trust principal,* and *trust property.*

ultra vires act *(UL·tra VY·rees)* A corporate act committed outside of the corporation's authority.

unconscionable *(un·KON·shun·e·bel)* So harshly one-sided and unfair that the court's conscience is shocked.

underlease *(UN·der·leess)* A lease given by a lessee to a third person, conveying the same interest for a shorter term than the period for which the lessee holds it. Also called *sublease*.

undisclosed principal *(un·dis·KLOZED PRIN·se·pel)* A person or company on whose behalf an agent acts, but who is not revealed to the third party..

undue influence *(un·DEW IN·flew·enss)* The overcoming of a person's free will by misusing a position of trust and taking advantage of the other person who is relying on the trust relationship.

unenforceable contract *(un·en·FORSS·e·bel KON·trakt)* A contract that cannot be enforced for some legal reason.

Uniform Commercial Code *(UCC) (YOON·i·form ke·MERSH·el kode)* A uniform law, adopted in every state, that governs various commercial transactions.

Uniform Probate Code *(UPC) (YOON·i·form PROH·bate kode)* A law attempting to standardize and modernize laws relating to the affairs of decedents, minors, and certain other people who need protection.

unilateral contract *(yoon·i·LAT·er·el KON·trakt)* A contract containing one promise in exchange for an act.

unilateral mistake *(yoon·i·LAT·er·el miss·TAKE)* A mistake made by only one party to a contract.

unintentional torts *(un·in·TEN·shun·al)* Torts that are committed accidentally.

unit deed *(YOON·it)* A deed to an individual condominium unit being transferred.

units *(YOON·its)* The individual portions of a condominium that are owned separately in fee simple by individual owners.

unity of interest *(YOON·i·tee ov IN·trest)* Equal interest in a property by all owners.

unity of possession *(YOON·i·tee ov po·SESH·en)* Equal rights to possession of the entire property by all owners.

unity of time *(YOON·i·tee)* The condition that exists when all owners of a property take title at the same time.

unity of title *(YOON·i·tee ov TY·tle)* The condition that exists when all owners of a property receive title from the same instrument.

unjust enrichment *(un·JUST en·RICH·ment)* The situation that occurs when one person retains money, property, or other benefit that in equity and justice belongs to another.

unlawful detainer *(de·TAYN·er)* The legal action used by landlords to evict tenants. Also called *dispossessory warrant proceedings, forcible entry and detainer, summary ejectment,* and *summary process.*

unlawful sexual intercourse *(un·LAW·ful SEKS·yoo·el IN·ter·korss)* Sexual intercourse with a child under the age set by state statute regardless of whether the child consented or not. Also called *statutory rape.*

unlimited liability *(un·LIM·i·ted ly·a·BIL·i·tee)* Liability that has no bounds.

usury *(YOO·zer·ee)* The charging of a greater amount of interest than is allowed by law.

uttering *(UT·er·ing)* Offering a forged, negotiable instrument to another person, knowing it to be forged and intending to defraud.

uxoricide *(uks·OR·i·side)* The killing of one's wife.

vacate *(VAY·kate)* To annul.

valid *(VAL·id)* Good; having legal effect.

variable-rate mortgage *(VAR·ee·a·bel-rate MORE·gej)* A mortgage with an interest rate that fluctuates according to changes in an index to which it is connected. Also called *flexible-rate mortgage.*

variance *(VAYR·ee·enss)* An exception to the zoning regulation.

vendor *(VEN·der)* A person who transfers property or goods by sale.

vendee *(ven·DEE)* A purchaser or buyer of property or goods.

venire *(ven·EYE·ree)* The large group of people from whom a jury is selected for a trial. Also called *array, jury panel,* and *jury pool.*

venue *(VEN·yoo)* The place where the trial is held.

verbatim *(ver·BATE·im)* Word for word.

verdict *(VER·dikt)* The decision of a jury.

verdict contrary to law *(KON·trare·ee)* A verdict that is incorrect as a matter of law.

verification *(ver·i·fi·KAY·shun)* A written statement under oath confirming the correctness, truth, or authenticity of a pleading.

vested *(VES·ted)* Fixed or absolute; not contingent.

viable *(VY·e·bel)* Having the appearance of being able to live.

vicarious liability *(vy·KEHR·ee·us)* Liability that is imputed to principals and employers because of the wrongdoings of their agents and employees.

victim's impact statement *(VIK·temz IM·pakt)* A statement to the court, at the time of sentencing, relative to the impact that the crime had on the victim or the victim's family.

void Not good; having no legal effect.

voidable *(VOID·e·bel)* Capable of being disaffirmed or voided.

voir dire *(vwar deer)* To speak the truth. The examination of jurors by the court to see that they stand indifferent.

voluntary administrator *(VOL·en·ter·ee ad·MIN·is·tray·tor)* A person who undertakes the informal administration of a small estate.

voluntary bankruptcy *(VOL·en·ter·ee BANK·rupt·see)* A bankruptcy proceeding that is initiated by the debtor.

voluntary manslaughter *(VOL·en·ter·ee MAN·slaw·ter)* The unlawful killing of another, without malice, when an intention to kill exists, but through the violence of sudden passion.

wage earner's plan *(wayj ER·ners)* A plan for the installment payments of outstanding debts under a Chapter 13 bankruptcy.

waive a spouse's will *(SPOW·sez)* To renounce or disclaim a spouse's will.

warrant *(WAHR·ent)* To give assurance.

warranty of fitness for a particular purpose *(WAHR·en·tee ov FIT·ness)* An implied warranty, given when a buyer relies on any seller's skill and judgment in selecting goods, that the goods will be fit for a particular purpose.

warranty of habitability (*WAR·en·tee ov hab·i· ta·BIL·i·tee*) An implied warranty by a landlord that the premises are fit for human habitation.

warranty of merchantability (*WAR·en·tee ov mer·chent· a·BIL·e·tee*) An implied warranty, given by merchants in all sales unless excluded, that goods are fit for the ordinary purpose for which such goods are used.

warranty of title (*WAR·en·tee ov TY·tel*) A guarantee that title is good, that the transfer is rightful, and that no unknown liens on the goods exist.

waste The abuse or destructive use of property that is in one's rightful possession.

white collar crime (*hwite KOL·er krime*) Types of crimes such as racketeering, mail fraud, wire fraud, and computer fraud. The term was coined in 1939 to refer to crimes committed by those with high social status and respect in the course of their employment.

will Originally, a legal instrument stating a person's wishes as to the disposition of real property at death, but now referring to both real and personal property.

will and testament (*TES·te·ment*) Under early English law, a legal instrument that disposed of both real and personal property at death.

will contest A suit over the allowance or disallowance of a will.

willful torts (*WIL·ful*) Torts that are committed intentionally. Also called *intentional torts*.

willful, wanton, and reckless conduct (*WIL·ful WON·ten REK·less KON·dukt*) The intentional commission of an act that a reasonable person knows would cause injury to another. Also called *culpable negligence*.

winding-up period (*WINE·ding-up PEER·ee·ed*) A period during which partnership assets are liquidated, debts are paid, an accounting is made, and any remaining assets are distributed among the partners.

wire fraud (*frawd*) Using the wires to obtain money, property, or services by false pretenses.

writ A written order of a court, returnable to the same, commanding the performance or nonperformance of an act.

writ of attachment (*a·TACH·ment*) A written order to the sheriff, commanding the sheriff to attach the real or personal property of the defendant.

writ of certiorari (*ser·sho·RARE·ee*) An order from a higher court to a lower court to deliver its records to the higher court for review.

writ of execution (*ek·se·KYOO·shen*) A written order to the sheriff, commanding the sheriff to enforce a judgment of the court.

writ of garnishment (*GAR·nish·ment*) A written order of a court ordering a garnishee not to give out money or property held for another, but to appear and answer the plaintiff's suit.

writ of venire facias (*ven·EYE·ree FAY·shes*) A written order to cities and towns to provide a designated number of jurors for the next sitting of the court.

wrongful death action (*RONG·ful deth AK·shun*) A suit brought by a decedent's personal representative for the benefit of the decedent's heirs, claiming that death was caused by the defendant's negligent act.

wrongful death statutes (*RONG·ful deth STAT·shoots*) Legislative enactments that govern wrongful death actions.

year-and-a-day rule The rule stating that DDDeath must have occurred within a year and a day after the blow occurred in order for a defendant to be convicted of homicide.

GLOSSARY OF LATIN TERMS AND PHRASES

a fortiori. with stronger reason; much more — ah for·she·OR·i

a posteriori. from the effect to the cause; from what comes after — ah po·steer·ee·OR·i

a prendre. to take; to seize. — ah PRAWN·dre

a priori. from the cause to the effect; from what comes before — ah pri·OR·i

ab initio. from the beginning — ab in·ish·ee·oh

actio criminalis. a criminal action — AK·shee·oh kri·mi·NAH·lis

actio damni injuria. an action for damages — AK·shee·oh DAM·ni in·JUR·ee·ah

actio ex delicto. an action arising out of fault — AK·shee·oh eks da·lik·toh

ad damnum. to the damage; money loss claimed by the plaintiff — ad DAHM·num

ad hoc. for one special purpose — ad HOK

ad infinitum. indefinitely; forever — ad in·fin·ITE·em

ad litem. for the suit — ad LY·tem

ad respondendum. to make answer — ad ree·spon·DEN·dem

additur. addition by a judge to the amount of damages awarded by a jury — AH·di·toor

amicus curiae. friend of the court — a·MEE·kes KYOOR·ee

animus furandi. intent to steal — AN·i·mus fer·AN·di

animus testandi. intent to make a will — AN·i·mus tes·TAN·di

anno Domini. (A.D.) in the year of our Lord — AN·oh DOM·eh·ni

ante. before — AN·tee

arguendo. in arguing — ar·gyoo·EN·doh

assumpsit. he promised — a·SUMP·sit

bona fide. in good faith — BONE·ah FIDE

caveat. beware — KA·vee·at

caveat emptor. let the buyer beware — KA·vee·at EMP·tor

caveat venditor. let the seller beware — KA·vee·at VEN·de·tor

certiorari. to be informed of; to be assured — ser·sho·RARE·ee

cestui que trust. beneficiary of a trust — SES·twee KAY

compos mentis. sound of mind — KOM·pes MEN·tis

consortium. fellowship of husband and wife — kon·SORE·shum

contra. against — KON·trah

coram. before; in the presence of — KOR·em

corpus delicti. body of the crime — KORE·pus de·LIK·tie

corpus juris. body of law — KORE·pus JOOR·ess

cum testamento annexo. with the will annexed — kum tes·ta·MENT·o an·EKS·o

damnum absque injuria. loss without injury in the legal sense — DAM·num AHB·skwee in·JOO·ree·ah

de facto. in fact; actually — dee FAK·toh

de jure. according to law; rightfully — dee JUR·ee

de minimus. of little importance — dee MIN·e·mes

de novo. anew, afresh, a second time — dee NOH·voh

dictum. unessential statement or remark in a court decision — DIK·tum

doli capaz. capable of criminal intent; able to distinguish between right and wrong — DO·li KAY·paks

duces tecum. bring with you — DOO·sess TEK·um

ergo. therefore; hence — EHR·go

et al. abbreviation for et alii; and others — et AHL

et seq. abbreviation for et sequentia; and the following — et SEK

et ux. abbreviation for et uxor; and wife — et UKS

et vir. and husband — et VEER

ex contractu. out of a contract — eks kon·TRAK·too

ex delicto. out of a tort or wrong — eks de·LIK·toh

ex officio. by virtue of an office — eks oh·FISH·ee·oh

ex parte. apart from; one side only — eks·PAR·tay

ex post facto. after the fact — eks post FAK·toh

forum non conveniens. inconvenient court — for·em non kon·VEEN·yenz

gratis. without reward or consideration — GRAT·is

habeas corpus. you have the body — HAY·bee·ess KORE·pus

habendum. to have thus; clause in a deed that defines extent of ownership — ha·BEN·dum

ibid. abbreviation for ibedim; in the same place — IBid

id. abbreviation for idem; the same — id

in camera. in chambers; in private — in KAM·er·ah

in curia. in court — in KYOOR·ee·ah

in flagrante delicto. in glaring fault; a crime in full light — in flay·GRAN·tee de·LIK·toh

in initio. at the beginning — in i·NISH·ee·o

in litem. during the suit — in LY·tem

in loco. in the place of — in LOH·ko

in loco parentis. in the place of a parent — in LOH·ko pa·REN·tis

in pari delicto. in equal fault — in pah·ree de·LIK·toh

in personam. against or with reference to a person — in per·SOH·nem

in re. in the matter of; concerning — in RAY

in rem. against the thing — in REM

in toto. in the whole; in total — in TOH·toh

infra. below, beneath — IN·frah

injuria absque damno. wrong without damage — in·JUR·ee·ya abs·kwee DAM·no

inter alia. among other things — IN·ter AY·lee·ah

inter vivos. between the living — IN·ter VY·vose.

ipse dixit. he himself says it — IP·see DIK·sit

ipso facto. by the fact itself — IP·soh FAK·toh

428

juris. of right; of law — JOOR·is

jus habendi. right to have something — jes he·BEN·di

jus tertii. right of a third party — jes ter·SHEE·yi

lis pendens. pending suit — liss PEN·denz

locus sigilli. place of the seal — LOH·kus se·JIL·i

malum in se. wrong in itself — MAL·um in SEH

malum prohibita. wrong because it is prohibited — MAL·um pro·HIB·i·ta

mandamus. we command; order by a court commanding a public official to perform a duty — man·DAY·mus

mens rea. guilty mind — menz RAY·ah

modus operandi. manner of operation — MOH·dus op·er·AN·di

mortis causa. by reason of death — MORE·tis KAW·sa

n.b. abbreviation of nota bene; note well; observe

nil. contraction of nihil; nothing — nil

nisi. unless — NIE·sie

nolle prosequi. prosection not pursued — NO·lee PROSS·e·kwi

nolo contendere. I will not contest the action — NO·lo kon·TEN·de·ree

non assumpsit. not undertaken or promised — non a·SUMP·sit

non compos mentis. not of sound mind; insane — non KOM·pes MEN·tiss

non obstante verdicto. notwithstanding the verdict — non ob·STAN·tay ver·DIK·toh

non sequitur. it does not follow — non SEK·wi·ter

nudum pactum. naked promise; bare agreement without consideration — NOO·dum PAK·tum

nul tort. no wrong has been done — nul TORT

nulla bona. no goods — null·a·BONE·ah

nunc pro tunc. now for then — nunk pro tunk

obiter dictum. words of a prior decision unnecessary for the decision of the case — OH·bih·ter DIK·tum

onus probandi. burden of proof — OH·nus pro·BAN·di

pendente lite. pending suit — pen·DEN·tay lie·tay

per annum. by the year — per AN·num

per capita. by the head — per KA·pi·tah

per curiam. by the court — KYOO·ree·am

per diem. by the day — per DEE·em

per quod. whereby — per KWOD

per se. by itself; taken alone — per SAY

per stirpes. by representation — per STER·peez

post mortem. after death — post MOR·tem

prima facie. at first sight; on the face of it — PRY·muh FAY·shee

pro bono publico. for the public good — pro BO·no POOB·lek·oh

pro forma. as a matter of form — pro FORM·ah

pro rata. proportionately — pro RAY·ta

pro se. for himself or herself — pro say

pro tanto. for as far as it goes — pro TAHN·tah

pro tempore (pro tem.). temporary; for the time being — pro TEM·po·re

quantum meruit. as much as he or she deserves — KWAN·tum MEHR·oo·it

quasi. as if; almost as it were — KWAY·zie

quasi in rem. as if against the thing — KWAY·zie in REM

quid pro quo. something for something; one thing for another — kwid proh KWOH

res. thing, object — reyz

res gestae. things that have been done — reyz JESS·tee

res ipsa loquitur. thing speaks for itself — res IP·sa LO·kwe·ter

res judicata. thing decided or judged (also res adjudicata) — res joo·di·KAY·ta

respondeat superior. let the superior answer — re·SPOND·ee·yat se·PEER·ee·or

retraxit. he or she has withdrawn — re·TRAK·sit

scienter. knowingly — si·EN·ter

scilicet. to wit; namely; that is to say — SIL·e·set

scintilla. spark — sin·TIL·ah

secundum. according to — se·KUN·dem

seriatim. separately; one by one — see·ree·AH·tem

sic. thus; in such a manner — sik

sigillum. seal — se·JIL·um

simplex obligato. single obligation — SIM·pleks ob·le·GAT·oh

sine qua non. without which, the thing cannot be — SI·nee kway NON

stare decisis. to stand by the decision — STAHR·ee de·SY·sis

sua sponte. of its own motion — SOO·ah SPON·tay

sub curia. under law — sub KURE·ee·ah

sub judice. under judicial consideration — sub JOO·de·say

sub silentio. under silence — sub se·LEN·shee·oh

subpoena. under penalty; a process to cause a witness to appear and give testimony — suh·PEEN·a

subpoena duces tecum. bring with you; a subpoena ordering a witness to produce a paper — suh·PEEN·a DOO·sess TEK·um

sui generis. one of a kind; unique — SOO·ee JEN·e·ris

sue juris. of one's own right; not under guardianship — SOO·ee JOOR·is

supersedeas. writ commanding a stay in the proceedings — soo·per·SEE·dee·es

supra. above; earlier — SOO·prah

ultra vires. beyond the powers — UL·tra VY·res

venire facias. order to the sheriff to bring people to court to serve as jurors — ven·EYE·ree FAY·she·as

versus. against — VER·ses

viz. abbreviation for videlicit; to make more specific that which has been previously stated — viz

volenti non fit injuria. volunteer suffers no wrong — voh·LEN·tie non fit in·JOOR·ee·ah

INDEX